500 Brickwall Solutions

Solutions

To Genealogy Problems

500 Brickwall Solutions
To Genealogy Problems

To Genealogy Problems

Published by Moorshead Magazines Ltd.
www.familychronicle.com

Thank you to: Jodi Avery, Ronnie MacCarl, Victoria Moorshead, Suzanne Rent, Rosanne Van Vierzen, Ron Wild, Ed Zapletal and all Brickwall Solutions submitters

First published in May 2003

Portions of this book have previously appeared in Family Chronicle Magazine © 2000, 2001, 2002, 2003

Published by Family Chronicle Magazine
500-505 Consumers Road
Toronto ON M2J 4V8
416-491-3699, 1-800-326-2476
www.familychronicle.com

ISBN 0-9731303-1-8

National Library of Canada Cataloguing in Publication

500 brickwall solutions to genealogy problems.

Includes index.
ISBN 0-9731303-1-8

1. Genealogy. I. Title: Five hundred brickwall solutions.

CS16.F53 2003   929'.1'072   C2003-902298-6

Printed and bound in Canada by Transcontinental Printing Inc.

Table of Contents

Introduction

This book is the culmination of many people's work.

A pattern does emerge about how genealogical brickwall problems have been solved. Most of the solutions have been reached by heeding the following advice:

- use others as sounding boards and network;
- revisit the information you already have;
- maintain an open mind;
- pay attention to the smallest piece of information;
- be prepared to spend money;
- take classes and get involved in the social side of genealogy;
- make educated guesses;
- stay abreast of the latest technology;
- remember that the original documents might contain clues that are missed or mistranscribed;
- visit the places your ancestors lived in;
- do on-site research;
- study the collateral lines;
- above all, never give up.

Each story's solution is a credit to inspiration and hard work, and the research techniques demonstrate the application of experience and insight. The stories, whether set in the Azores or in Wyoming, are applicable for most countries and for most research periods.

The spectrum of subjects covered ranges from searching for ancestors' arrival dates and birth records to places of burial. The solutions have been found in such places as websites, people's memories or even in the notes already gathered.

All submissions were edited for length, style and consistency; however, we tried to retain the original wording and personality of each submitter. The illustrations came from numerous sources and as such their quality is not consistent. Illustrations were selected for relevance to the story, not quality.

To save on unnecessary repetition, several abbreviations have been used throughout the text, but a glossary can be found at the end of the book. Please note that great-great-grandparents are identified as second-great-grandparents, great-great-great-grandparents are identified as third-great-grandparents and other generations in the same manner to avoid any misunderstandings in the text.

Please note that each submitter was given the choice of credit and contact information. *Family Chronicle* cannot provide any more information than is published here and we will not forward any reader requests for information onto Brickwall submitters. *Family Chronicle* would also like to make it clear that the Brickwall submitters are under no obligation to respond to any inquiries from readers.

We hope this book will inspire you.

It's All Relative

My fascination with my Wenner ancestry began as a child because of my grandmother's family tales and the mystery of her father's disappearance. Unfortunately, I only listened and failed to ask questions concerning Louis Wenner, my great-grandfather.

My grandmother, Lena Wenner, was the eldest of four children born to Louis Wenner and Jennie Pauline McCall of Darlington, SC. Lena was about 12 years old when her father disappeared on a trip north. Lena never said anything else about her father or his family, or their place of origin, except that the family's name was von Wenner and the von was eventually dropped. From family records it appears that Louis married Jennie in Florida. Their first three children were born in Palmetto, FL. By 1905 the family was in Gulfport, MS.

Louis established the newspaper *The Tribune* with his brother-in-law, John P. McCall. The first page of *The Gulfport Journal*, another newspaper, lists Louis as the editor and publisher in February 1909. Family lore has it that Louis disappeared while Jennie was pregnant with their fourth child. Although I can't locate a birth certificate for this child, it is believed he was born in May 1910.

When I began this journey I contacted the sole living relative of Lena's generation, Thelma, whom I had only seen a few times. Lena's sister-in-law Thelma invited me to her home where I learned what little Thelma knew of her husband's father Louis. Some 50 years ago Thelma had somehow met her father-in-law's brother, Ted Wenner, who sent her a letter providing some information on the Wenner family. Amazingly, Thelma saved this letter, written in 1948, for almost 50 years.

Ted named his siblings. From this I learned the eldest son was George, married to Josephine. Next was Fredrika (Ricker) married to George Pousson; their children were George, Elizabeth and Elsie, who married Jack Glasser, parents of Dorothy. Louis, my great-grandfather, was the third child. Ben was married to Annie and Charles to Ida. All had been born in New York City. The letter states that their father was Louis who lived to the age of 85 and that Charles had named his daughter Madeline after their mother. Thelma even had a photo of the father, Louis, the immigrant. In her possession was a death notice for Ted Wenner who died in Detroit, MI. I eventually located, met and remain in contact with George Wenner's grandson, Roger.

I found a gold mine and had solved my brickwall by contacting who I first felt was an unlikely source of information. — Ann Boudreaux, LA, genbuff01@aol.com

A letter saved for 50 years turned out to be a goldmine for Ann Boudreaux.

*   *   *

Don't Believe Everything Your Family Tells You

For many years my father, his siblings and their children, all said that my grandfather, Nels Wahlquist, was from Malmö, Sweden and that no one knew who his parents were, what his birth date was or exactly when he came to the US. Nels died in 1918 and never became a citizen of the US. We joked that he must have been on the run from the law or maybe jumped ship, because his origin was such a mystery.

I have a cousin who has been trying to find out about Nels for years, just as I have. He had been to the cemetery where our grandparents were buried, but there was no headstone for Nels. I had looked on the Internet for ships' passenger lists for the years between 1886 and 1890 as his immigration year was listed as 1888 on the 1910 census. No luck.

I went to Salt Lake City and spent two days looking in the FHL's extensive Swedish records for Nels Wahlquists from Malmö who might be my grandfather. But nothing proved out.

Then my husband, my cousin and I drove to the town where Nels and his family lived. It's a tiny town in Iowa and the newspaper office is about the size of my living room. But they have their archives right there in a back room and they looked up the next weekly issue that came out after our grandfather died and there was an obituary that gave his exact birth date (four years later than we thought) and his birthplace — Ystad, Sweden, not Malmö! It was true that Ystad is in Malmöhus county, but we had the wrong town. It turned out that he came to the US in 1883, not 1888, so looking for ships passenger lists for 1886-90 had been a mistake. Census records are often wrong, because the person who gave the information to the census taker was misinformed or just guessing.

Then we went to the County Recorder's office in the county seat and asked to see the marriage license records for the date our grandparents were married. There were his parents' names! Now I can start re-examining Swedish records for more information about his family and perhaps trace our ancestry back even further. All this was found out in a matter of hours on one day. (Although I went in person to look for the information on my grandfather, very often you can do it by mail or e-mail.)

Obituary

On Saturday, Dec. 14, the mortal remains of Nels Wahlquest were laid at rest in the Inwood cemetery where for some years past he has labored and toiled to keep the grounds neat and attractive. It is the experience of all that some day sooner or later what we have done for others will in some form have to be performed for us. For many years past Nels Wahlquest has been a very familiar and well known person in Inwood. He has always been both honest and industrious working many times when he was not able and beyond his strength. He with the aid of his good wife has provided a comfortable home for his family and given them thus far the advantages of an education. He has been in precarious health since he was stricken at the cemetery a year ago and has had some bad spells since that time. He was up and about prior to his death as usual and the stroke came upon him suddenly and with little warning and he very soon passed away.

Obituary of Nels Wahlquist from the Inwood, Iowa Register dated 18 December 1918, giving his actual birthday and birthplace.

So even though family lore can yield clues to looking for your ancestors, don't limit yourself to what everybody in the family knows. This is doubly true for me. — Charnee Smit, CA

Mortuary Records Can Hold Keys To The Past

All we had for my husband's grandfather and grandmother were dates of birth, marriage and death. We just couldn't seem to find anything else.

When my father died, the mortuary requested his parents' names and places of birth. That clicked on a light bulb. We went to the mortuary that had handled grandfather's funeral and asked for the records (from 1921) and they still had them. On the record was my great-grandfather's name and state of birth. I would previously never have thought of that source.

We haven't been able to verify that information yet, but it gave us some hope and something to work on. — Laveda J. Fleming, CA

No Harm In Trying

When I was a child, I would hang around when family members started talking about other relatives. I learned quite a bit about the family but one member in particular was a big question and no one had the answers.

Stories circulated about my great-grandmother, but they were just stories and possibly whoever told them knew what they were talking about. One great-aunt was supposed to be the family member who knew about her mother. This great-aunt told my mother that her mother, my great-grandmother was born on the ship they were immigrating on to come to the US. However, her parents became sick and died on the ship. A family on board cared for the baby and raised her as their own. I thought I would never learn about my second-great-grandparents and their ancestors in that particular lineage.

I located my great-grandmother's obituary as well as a wedding anniversary article as she and my great-grandfather were married 60 years.

I was also able to locate her death certificate, my grandfather's birth certificate and my grandfather's death certificate. Between all these documents, the problem wasn't solved, it was compounded. My grandfather's birth certificate had his mother's name shown as Amelia Johnson; on her death certificate as Anna Johnson and on my grandfather's death certificate as Anna Harms. What is her name? It said that she was seven years old when with her mother and stepfather Mrs. and Mr. Harm Johnson immigrated to the US. So what happened to the boat birth? At least I knew where the Johnson surname came from, but what about her first name or her birth surname?

My great-grandparents were primarily associated with only one church and I decided to search the church records. I hit a gold mine after all these years and stories all from one source, my great-aunt who was the daughter of this woman. The confirmation records gave her father's full name. It was John Oken Harms. It also gave her name as Anna A., which I believe to be Anna Amelia.

Family stories are great to hear but that's about it until you can prove them to be true or false when it comes to genealogy. — Debbi Geer, MO

Military Medals

We knew our great-grandfather had served in the British Army in the mid 1800s, but we did not know the unit he served in or where. We had a medal of his that had been handed down in the family from his eldest son. We also had hit a brickwall in locating his town of birth in England. We recalled that we had read in the past that the British Army engraved the recipient's name, rank and unit on the edge of the medal. On checking we found "Pte. R. Ringham Q.O.R.". With this information we contacted the National Archives of Canada and received copies of his enlistment, unit (The Queen's Own Rifles), where he served and where he was discharged. Also copies of documents applying for a Veterans Patented Land Grant were found. If you have old British Army medals examine the medal's edge. — LR

Typos

Since the early 1980s I had been researching the history of my ancestor, James Atkey, who came to Canada in 1853 as a missionary to the Ojibwa. One of my earliest sources was the United Church Archives of Canada, which included his published missionary reports from both the Methodist and Congregational Missionary Societies. His last report for the Canada Indian Missionary Society (Congregationalist) stated that his salary had been contributed by the Society for the Propagation of the Gospel, Boston.

Painting of James Atkey.

So far as I could determine, the latter referred to the missionary arm of the Church of England, who had no missionaries in the Bruce Peninsula/ Georgian Bay area. For years, I let this stand, until about two years ago when I began to turn my research into a book called *When We Both Got To Heaven*. I was nagged by the question, "Why was the Church of England supporting a Congregationalist mission?" I found that the then-Bishop of Huron, Benjamin Cronyn, was friendly with non-conformists and even

attended the ordination of a leading Methodist. I also learned Cronyn had received requests for support from settlers on the Bruce Peninsula. I thought I had settled the mystery, but then the archives of the Anglican Church of Canada destroyed my theory: the Society for the Propagation of the Gospel could not have had an office in Boston, as their American operations ceased after the War of Independence.

Then a librarian at Rhodes Library at Oxford University told me that there was another organization, The Society For Propagating the Gospel Among the Indians and Others in North America, which was Congregationalist. Had I really been misled by a typesetting error?

I found the archives of the latter organization were located at the Peabody Essex Museum in Saloom, MA. When I wrote to them, they enthusiastically replied that they had, in their files, more than 50 pages of correspondence regarding James Atkey. — Mel Atkey, London, UK

Where There's A Will, There's A Way

Wills played an important role in the discovery of my second-great-grandmother Sarah Scott's whereabouts in Pleasant Unity, PA. The first will was of Thomas Scott, who died in July 1842 at age 34. He named his wife, Sarah (Lose) and five children, William, George, Mary Elizabeth, Amanda and Sarah. A crumbling old page from a family Bible recorded Sarah's birth as 22 February 1842 and, armed with a previous hunch that Thomas and Sarah were Sarah's parents, I felt I had found my family.

However, when I looked for the widow Sarah Scott and her children in the 1850 census, they were not to be found. Upon learning Thomas' debts had exceeded his assets and his farm had been sold, I thought perhaps the family was living with relatives. Unfortunately, I could not find them.

The second will was that of Sarah's brother, William, who died in 1858. He named as his heirs his brother, two sisters and his mother, Sarah McMaster. His sister Sarah was not mentioned and I feared perhaps she died and I had the wrong family after all. But now I knew that Sarah Scott had remarried and that was a valuable clue. I then looked up McMaster in the 1850 census and found the widow Sarah Scott had married William McMaster. Living with them were children from his previous marriage and two Scott daughters, Mary Elizabeth and Amanda. I assumed the boys had left home by then, but again, little Sarah was missing.

I still felt I was on the right track because McMaster rang a bell with me. When Sarah grew up, she married William C. Gardner and one of their sons was named William McMaster Gardner, so I felt she must have lived with William McMaster at some point. The quirky Gardners, however, had a penchant for naming their children after the neighbors. So it was to the neighbors I next turned, heeding the advice of a genealogist who once told our class, "Remember to look at the neighbors." In 1850, William C. Gardner was 14 years old and living in Pleasant Unity with his parents, Abraham and Elizabeth, and his siblings. I didn't have far to go to strike gold. On the previous page from the Gardners were John Latta, 60, his wife Elizabeth, 51, Elizabeth Chambers, 17 (Elizabeth Latta's niece)

and Sarah Scott, age eight. There she was — living practically next door to her future husband! And she was still there 10 years later.

This page from a family Bible provided a starting point for Kathleen Borne in her search for her second-great-grandmother.

Any doubt that this was my ancestor was removed by the third will, that of John Latta. It never occurred to me to send away for his 1872 will since I learned from the Latta website that this couple was childless and therefore not Sarah's grandparents, but it was sent to me by a sharp researcher at the Westmoreland County Historical Society to whom I had turned for help. Part nine of the will stated simply, "I give and bequeath to Sarah Gardner two hundred dollars." Sarah and William Gardner's first child was named Elizabeth Latta Gardner. They also had a son named John.

Later, I found in an entry for Thomas Scott on RootsWeb.com's WorldConnect that Sarah's sister Mary Elizabeth had married a widower named Boyd and one of her stepsons was Dempsey Boyd. Another bell chimed, as I knew Sarah's daughter May Gardner married a D.B. Boyd. So I clicked on Dempsey Boyd and there was May!

I still don't know why Sarah wasn't living with her mother and siblings and may never know, but I'm just happy I found her. — Kathleen Borne, OH, kathyborne@aol.com

Death Notice

The wife of a friend of mine, who has an interest in genealogy, said that when her father died she listed notice of his death in the *London Telegraph* as the family was London-oriented.

Soon after, she had an inquiry about the death notice. It was from a man who was raised as an orphan. His parents hadn't married and his father disappeared soon after learning he was to be a father. The mother had no means to support her son so he was placed in an orphanage and was adopted. The man read the notice and recognized the name. He contacted my friend and she was able to make a connection to him. She talked to older family members and remembered some family stories that were able to give the man some closure to this part of his life.

By placing the death notice in an area the family had been distantly a part of, my friend was able to make some family connections. — Parke Brown, Jr., MD, plb.ksb@erols.com

Use Several Sources

A few years back it seemed as though I would never learn the maiden name of one of my second-great-grandmothers, Ardelia Garretson. She and her husband, John Garretson, were raising their family in Mercer county, WV, in 1880. But I had no information about their family after that and no leads.

While searching census records at the NARA, I noticed there was an Ardelia Garretson living in Calhoun county, WV, in 1900 and 1910. Her age was consistent with that of my second-great-grandmother. In 1900, she was living with a son, George, and in 1910, with another son, Abraham.

These were the names of two of my second-great-grandmother's sons. This raised the possibility that the family moved from Mercer to Calhoun county sometime between 1880 and 1900, but due to the destroyed 1890 census, I was faced with a brickwall.

Thinking that perhaps some living Garretson descendants might still be in that area of Calhoun, I wrote letters to a handful of them. (I found their names and addresses on the Internet.) One of the letters found its way to someone who answered many of my questions. It seems that my ancestors did indeed move to Calhoun and are buried there. John Garretson died in 1892, which explains why I didn't find his name in the 1900 census. However, his wife, Ardelia, lived with her sons until her death in 1911. The contact was my distant Garretson cousin. He was able to tell me that Ardelia's maiden name was Blankenship and that he had a photograph of her. He said he would show the photograph to me if I were ever in his area for a visit. I thanked him and made a mental note to try and visit as soon as possible.

It turns out that I didn't have to wait long. Recently I was corresponding with a researcher in Calhoun. When I mentioned my ancestor, she said that she had a surprise for me. Shortly thereafter I received an electronic version of the very same photograph I had discussed with my relative. It turned out the researcher collects photographs from families in the area and had contacted my Garretson relative a few years back. The photo was just as he described it and I could see the clear family resemblance.

This shows how sometimes only following leads from several sources can break a brickwall. — Steve Bonner, MD

*   *   *

Adding Branches To Your Family Tree

My third-great-grandfather was Charles Harris. He married Dicey Davis in 1811 in Wayne county, KY. I suspected Charles' father was a John Harris that had been the bondsman at his wedding, but I could never quite prove it. I had found a will probated in January 1815 for a John Harris in that county, but it mentioned only the oldest daughter and two youngest sons — not Charles. I finally decided to search all the surname message boards for Harris at GenForum.com, GenConnect.com and Family-History.com and the mailing list archives at RootsWeb.com for that surname. I also searched the Wayne county, KY lists on those sites as well as the mailing list archives for the County as well as the Cumberland River Region.

```
CNIDR Isearch-cgi 1.20.06 (File: 109)
========================================
Date: Thu, 25 Feb 1999 22:30:09 -0600
From: "Linda G. Murtaugh" <L.Murtaugh@m.cc.utah.edu>
To: CUMBERLAND-RIVER@rootsweb.com
Message-ID: <36D6234C.3B7C@m.cc.utah.edu>
Subject: #22 Wayne County, KY misc. Court Orders Vol A - 1814
Content-Type: text/plain; charset=us-ascii
Content-Transfer-Encoding: 7bit

December Court 1814 continued
p. 262
Micah Taul late Clerk of this Court acknowledged himself indebted to
this County in the Sum of L36.18.4 fine money & the amount of the
purchase money for lot purchased by John S Moore from the Court

Ordered that the Sheriff Collect of each Titheable in this cty the Sum
of Seventy five cents and accounts for the Same according Law

Nicholas Loyd Esq comes into Court and acknowledges himself indebted to
this County in the Sum of $4.00 being the amount of fine moneys
Certified to be in the hands of John Willis Constable for the year 1814
to be charged against him a Collector of the Cty levy for the present
year and the Said Willis is discharged

Present Wm Scott  John Stephenson & Evan Jones Esqr  Absent the others

An Instrument of writing purporting to be the noncupative will of John
Harris decd was produced in Court and it is ordered that a Summon Issue
against Catharine Nicholas Charles Sally Susanna Darky John & Thomas
Harris to appear here at the next Court to Show cause if any they have
why the Said will may not be established

George McWhorter    Appellant
vs                  upon an appeal from the Judgement of
Joshua Dean         Appellee Roger Oatts Esquire
The Appellee having failed to enter his appearance into Court according
to a rule of this Court is ordered that the Judgement of the Justice in
the Case be reversed and that the appellant recover against
p. 263
the Appellee his costs by him in this behalf expended

John Huffaker       Appellant
vs                  upon an appeal from the Judgement of Roger Oatts Esquire
James Ally          Appellee
This day Came the parties aforesaid by their attornies And after hearing
the evidence and arguments of Counsel &c it is the opinion of the Court
& it is accordingly ordered that the Judgement jof the Justice be
confirmed & that the Appellee recover against the appellant his costs by
him in this behalf expended

Ordered that Court be adjourned till Court in Course
                                           John Stephenson

This is the last bit I have from the 1814 Court.  Subsequent pages begin
with the August 1815 Court.
```

Transcription of court record for December 1814 for John Harris.

That's when I found success. Some kind soul had been transcribing minutes of the court for Wayne county on that regional list a couple of years before. I found a court order from December 1814, which listed all John's children and Charles was among them.

To make things even better, in reviewing my notes on Harrises in Wayne county, I noted that John had given consent for his daughter Sally's marriage on 26 September 1814, so it seems likely that he died in either October or November of that year. — Lori Thornton, TN

A Sense Of Heritage

My paternal grandparents divorced when my father was four years old. My father never saw his father after 1934 and no one mentioned his name at home. Upon his father's death in 1966, an attorney notified my father of where and when his father died. That was the only information we had, aside from the fact that his parents had been divorced in Allegheny Co., PA in the early 1930s.

I knew how difficult it could be to locate records from after the turn of the century. I began by searching the SSDI and located my grandfather's name. I sent away for the SS-5. I received back a copy of his handwritten application for a Social Security card. The application listed his birthplace, date and parents' names, along with his mother's maiden name. I found out that a Social Security Application is a great source for women's maiden names!

With this information I searched the 1900 census and located records for my great-grandparents. I found information about their marriage and that they had both emigrated from England at different times in the late 1880s. I also obtained the 1881 British census, which listed my second-great-grandparents with my great-grandfather living at home. The census also listed a sister-in-law, so I was able to learn my second-great-grandmother's maiden name. With this information I searched the FreeBMD online and located a marriage record and birth record for her.

I am now back five generations all because I was able to locate that Social Security Application record. Before this, my father had no information regarding his father or that side of his family. With this research, he now feels he has a sense of heritage for the first time. — Ella Ann Hatfield, DC

You Might As Well Check

When I began researching my husband's family, we only had six clues to their origin: a printed silk ribbon from a Civil War unit reunion from his great-grandfather, James, that says "6th Indiana Cavalry, 71st Regiment, Terre Haute", two old letters to James from his sister Cassandra, James' obituary, James' second marriage certificate and the family's tombstones. We knew that James' parents were Joseph and Elizabeth. They are buried in Effingham county, IL.

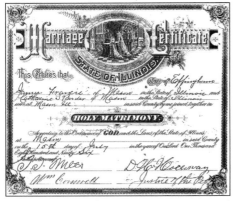

Marriage certificate of James Francis and Catherine Barder.

From the silk ribbon we figured James lived near Terre Haute, IN. In the State Adjutant's book we discovered James enlisted in Bowling Green, IN, so he could have lived in Clay county. Our first step was to write the Vigo County Indiana Library. The librarian there sent us a newspaper article about the soldiers' reunion. He also found Joseph and Elizabeth in 1860 in nearby Owen county, with five children, including Cassandra. The letters confirmed that we had the right family. James was two households away. According to his obituary, he was one of 12 children. In 1860, his parents were old enough they could have six older children. They were all in Owen again in 1870. Cassandra married and moved to Clay county.

Joseph was my brickwall. The obituary says James was born in Jennings county, IN and his mother was a Haines, but I couldn't find Joseph and Elizabeth in Indiana before 1860. Though I checked various records for five years, Joseph just did not want to be found. I decided to side step him and started working on Cassandra. She lived in Clay county her entire life, except going to Effingham county, IL to have two of her children. One of her letters mentions pictures of their parents. Eventually, through a query, I received a GEDCOM from one of her descendants. I was able to e-mail him and asked about the photographs. Unfortunately, an older aunt had pitched them because no one knew who they were. Though I gained more information on Cassandra and James, her trail had led me no closer to Joseph.

Tracing their other siblings hadn't got very far. All this time, I still searched for any information on Joseph. There were no Indiana land patents for him. To make things more complicated, another Joseph and Elizabeth Francis lived in Indiana at the same time. Then I attended the 1999 St. Louis National Genealogical Society Conference.

Wandering among the vendors I passed a table and a thin, hand-bound book caught my eye. It was *Early*

Jennings County, Indiana Marriages. I thought I might as well look, even though I've had no luck in Jennings county. When I casually opened to Francis, there it was — Joseph's marriage to Elizabeth Haines, 1831, eight years before James was born! I was so excited my hands began to shake violently. Of course, I bought the book!

Funeral card of James Francis, son of Joseph Francis.

I have since found a marriage for one of James' sisters in next-door Ripley county, IN but cannot place Joseph in 1840 or 1850. So Joseph remains my brickwall, but that brickwall has moved forward about 10 steps. — Dawn Francis, MO

The British Census And National Index

Even though I had the marriage certificate of my second-great-grandfather Thomas Wild to Maria Conroy, a search of the 1881 British census on film had been very disappointing. All I found was a widow, Maria Wild with a daughter Ann, but no mention of Thomas and his son Samuel, my grandfather. Over the ensuing years I looked many times but without result.

When the 1881 British Census and National Index arrived on CD it was hardly out of its package before I had it in the computer. Same result, but because the index was easy to search I brought up all the Thomas Wild names and looked at every one again without result. I even looked at Wilde without success since this was how my grandfather was shown on his marriage record. There were many Thomas Wilde listings so I just kept going past the end of them and came across some Thomas Wilds, with an S. One was shown living in Bradford, Yorkshire, my home town.

So I brought up the full enumeration and there was Thomas, Maria, Samuel and Ann all listed as Wilds. What a relief it was to find them and to realize again how important it is to check name variations even for a simple name like Wild. — Ron Wild, ON

The Back-Door Approach

For about 50 years my grandfather searched for his great-grandfather, William H. Cone Sr. My grandfather had found William's parents and we had William's 1850 census record in Marion county, OH with his second wife, Rosanna Free Cone and William's 1860 census entry. But he then disappeared from the records. All his descendants knew was that "he went west."

For many, years my grandpa tried to trace him. Grandpa died in 1978 and when my children were grown I started to look for members of my family tree. I was successful in many branches, but not this one. Finally, I tried to trace his children, with no success. I could not find even one of them for sure. This went on for 10 years. I mulled this over for a few years, after having gone to genealogy libraries, etc. One day I was checking over his records when I checked his brother-in-law, who had been his next-door neighbor in Ohio. Lo and behold he was missing from Ohio also!

William's next-door neighbor was Truman Gaylord Briggs. There seemed to be many William Cones in many places, but not Truman Gaylord Briggs. I did an Internet search for the name of Truman Gaylord Briggs and found one in Iowa. I did not know if he was the one though. I then wrote to the RootsWeb.com connection for his county, Ringgold county, IA. I received an e-mail that although the person answering did not know anything about Truman Briggs, she recognized the name from the county history. She did, however, know someone in the community that descended from Truman and contacted her with my query. I received an e-mail the next day from the Truman Briggs descendant, saying she did not know anything about Truman other than when he lived in Iowa and did not know anything about his wife, Phebe Cone. She said she was not into genealogy but was interested in anything I knew about her ancestor, Truman Briggs. She also said that she had heard in her youth that the family was related to the Cones in some way, now unknown. She wished me well and we had several further contacts. I now had a connection to the place.

I placed another query, asking if someone would be so kind to see if there was a William and Rosanna Cone in the 1870 census in Ringgold county. I got another reply and a few days later, I did get a connection. They were in the index! So I got into the car and headed for Fort Wayne, IN to the genealogy library to check the 1870 census. There they were. I had

solved my grandpa's mystery, which would have been impossible without the Internet and the help of a few kind people. I was later able to find William's death date, though not Rosanna's. He is either buried in an unmarked grave, or in a neighboring county; I haven't yet found that out. I believe that the family did keep in contact for a few years after they moved to Iowa, as we had the names of his children.

However, William had a first wife and two children from that marriage. It was from one of these children, William Cone Jr., who died in the US Civil War, from whom I descend. At the point that William Cone Jr.'s father "went west" there was no one left directly descended from him, but for a small child, his grandchild, Benjamin Franklin Cone, my great-grandfather, now living with his mother and a stepfather. I speculate William lost too much in the war and had moved on to greener pastures.

Sometimes, when you hit that brickwall, go back through all you know about the family connections and start the search there. The back door is often the only way into the information you want to find. — Margaret Motter, OH

County Poorhouses

My father always referred to his Grandmother as Grace Guettner. She died before I took any interest in my lineage. I could not find an obituary for her under her married name of Ruhl nor could I find any information on her birth name. I checked every possible spelling of Guettner because the name obviously lent itself to many variations. A friend lent me a log of our county "poorhouse" for research on another project. Suddenly, there she was in this log. The family had placed her there because she needed constant care and the hospital would not keep terminally ill patients. Her name was Mary Gidtner Ruhl. The only clue being her date of death, which my father was sure of and the names of the family members, including her husband, my grandfather who came to claim the body. Sometimes you find the most useful information when you are looking for something else entirely! — Kathie Ruhl Rothrock, PA, budnot@velocity.net

Unexpected Locations

I had been unable to locate my Lantz family in censuses for 1870. The oral information that was passed down to me said that the family moved from Ohio to Illinois. I had checked census indexes for both states and scanned the censuses for the counties where I had expected them to be. Through historical research I had discovered that a group of people from that area had indeed moved to Illinois about the time I suspected and had decided that they had moved with the group but had not been counted in the census for some reason.

The Lantz family.

One day a friend who was using the Kokomo-Howard county (Indiana) Library website and knew I was researching Lantzes e-mailed me to say she'd seen some Lantzes in some of the cemetery information on the site. I really didn't expect to find anything but I went to the site and was amazed to discover that my second-great-grandmother was buried in that cemetery. (*The Lantz Family Record* by Jacob Lantz published in 1930 had stated that she died in 1887 and was buried in Kansas.) I found her daughter in that cemetery, as well as a grandchild. I went on to explore other things on the site and discovered the 1870 mortality schedule for Howard county was posted that listed her cause of death. I was living in Cincinnati at the time and went to the public library there and checked the 1870 census for the county and found the rest of the family.

Because of that serendipitous e-mail, I discovered that my family had lived in an unexpected location. — Lori Thornton, TN

Letters To Little Towns

In 1991, after four years of research on my Miller line, using all the old familiar sources, I still needed that something to make my family history records special. After pouring over the data I had collected, it became apparent that I had to tap the personal side of this family and move beyond the proverbial brickwall.

I did not have the funds or the time to travel to Hardin county, KY. I decided to make a friend that was native to the area. I chose the little town of White Mills to send my letter to.

I addressed an envelope to the White Mills Chamber of Commerce and enclosed a self-addressed envelope, along with a short note. It asked the reader to please forward this to any grade school in the district and ask a teacher to assign my request to one of the students. That request was a brief history of Hardin county and a description of the area as it is today. As I lived in a small town while growing up, I knew two things: there was no Chamber of Commerce in White Mills and no letter ever left a little town without getting read.

A few weeks passed before receiving a reply. It came from a 75-year-old resident of the area that was considered the expert on Hardin county genealogy. A member of the volunteer fire department had knocked on his door and explained that they received it from the Post Office. The first letter I received had a picture of an old mill with a brief summary of the history of the County and an offer to be of any further service. That friendship continues to this day.

I guarantee if you send one inquiry a week for three months, you will not be able to keep up with the research you generate. Just figure it like this: Each letter is one brick out of that wall. — Larry Schleutker, IL, l3532@aol.com

Don't Lock Your Thinking

The only information on my great-grandparents, August and Christine Steeb, was August's obituary. This provided quite a bit of information for him, but very little for Christine. A diligent probate clerk obtained their marriage record, even though both of their surnames were listed incorrectly.

In August's Civil War Pension Records, he referred to her as Christine Koenig and that she died seven years after they were married, leaving behind three children. I obtained a copy of her record of death that showed "Woodland Ave." in the margin. This turned out to be the cemetery in which she was buried. The Western Reserve Historical Society in Cleveland, OH told me this cemetery was no longer functioning, but their records had been transferred to the Highland Park Cemetery. I wrote there many times over a period of a year, without response. The

Western Reserve Historical Society verified the information and even made some telephone calls on my behalf, obtaining promises, but no results. This was my brickwall.

The marker for Christine Koenig's grave.

Months went by and an unexpected letter arrived from the City of Cleveland Department of Parks, Recreation and Properties. Although I did not receive a copy of an original document, the letter included a great deal of information. I now had the cemetery, name, age, address, native country, cause of death, date of death, date of burial, lot, tier and grave for Christine and seven other people buried in the same family plot. It turns out that Christine was the only one in the plot listed as being born as a Koenig. One other person in the plot was born in Germany, all others were born in Holland. All others went by the surname King. Since that time, I have found census records that link some of these people into family groups and even more Kings I never knew existed.

Don't lock your thinking into one name, one cemetery, one country, one source or you'll become one sorry genealogist. — Robert Gilmour, CT, rgilmour@rcn.com

A Brickwall In Sweden

My father's family is all from Sweden. I had lots of death certificates, obituaries and census records which stated that they were from Smoland or Vastergotland or Sweden. These place names are virtually useless because researching records from Sweden requires the parish name and the farm name. Even looking for emigration from Sweden is difficult. You can imagine how many Andersons and Johnsons left Sweden in 1881 or 1882. To make it worse my Swedes had a habit of changing their names, not only last names but also their first names. I really needed to get into the records at the FHL; they have microfilmed the parish records in Sweden. However, it was impossible for me to get there at that time.

The brickwall solution was a visit to the Swenson Swedish Immigration Research Center at the Augustana College in Rock Island, IL. We went there to use their cd-rom on emigration records from Sweden. In conversation with workers there, I discovered that they have the microfilmed records from many Swedish Lutheran Churches in the US. Looking through their list, there it was — Hebron Lutheran Church of Burdick, KS. I looked at the microfilm and there they were. All my ancestors' names were in the Church Register. It had their real names, the ones they were born with in Sweden. It also had a

great deal of other information such as the dates of birth, dates of baptism, where they were born (with parish and county name) and when they arrived in the US. I could have cried I was so excited.

Church record from Hebron Lutheran Church of Burdick, KS.

I have since been to the FHL. I now have a minimum of two, and in one case five, generations more of my family. — Connie Ohlman Bradish, TX, bradish@escapees.com

A Double Life

The ancestor who has proved the most difficult for me to trace was my second-great-grandfather, Samuel Etherington. He fathered nine children in Sydney, Australia between 1857 and 1877, but none of the births were registered, despite this being compulsory from 1856. The children's marriage and death certificates did at least list their parents' names, Samuel Henry Etherington and Sarah (Everitt). However, I could find no evidence of Samuel either being born in or immigrating to the colony, nor of him marrying Sarah nor indeed any evidence of his burial.

By dates on tombstones and talking to other descendants, I pieced together dates of birth for the children. I found the immigration record for Sarah arriving as a child in the colony with her family, but I could find nothing to indicate where Samuel was born or died. I checked the records for other states of Australia, but found no evidence of him there either.

The Sands Directory allowed me to trace where the family lived and learn that Samuel's occupation was a carpenter and a builder. Except, that is, on the marriage certificate of one daughter, in 1883, where his occupation was listed as baker. By following him in the electoral roll I found that while he was still registered to vote in 1883, he was not in 1884 and when Sarah died in 1885, she was described as a widow. However, Sarah shared her grave with a granddaughter, not Samuel.

For many years I hunted for others descended from the Etherington family. I started collecting every instance of the name in Australia and then researched the families of those immigrants. One was a Thomas Etherington who came to Australia in 1857, who had a brother Samuel born back in England. When I learned the names of Thomas' parents, Joseph and Henrietta, these were reflected in the names of the children of my Samuel, even though I could find no other evidence connecting them, at least I had a theory.

I checked books, magazines and the Internet for contact with others researching the name and advertised my interest in the name lists of all these places. I advertised in the Etherington section of GenForum.com "looking for a Samuel Etherington who started having children in Sydney in 1857 and who might or might not be the son of Joseph and Henrietta Etherington of Bermondsey in London." This led to contact with a descendant of Thomas' sister Anna, who gave me the clue that led through my particular brickwall.

There was an old letter, dating from 1903, where Henry Samuel Holmes tried to make contact with the Etherington family in London. In the letter Henry said he was the son of their son Samuel, who had died recently, after living in Australia as a baker under the surname Holmes!

Everything then fell into place. I found that Samuel had migrated to Sydney as Samuel Holmes in 1837, listing dual occupations of "baker and joiner". He and Hester Holmes had a number of children in Sydney (surnamed Holmes), with their father listed as Samuel Holmes, baker. The oldest of these children was Henry, the one who tried to contact the Etherington family in 1903. After about 18 years with Hester, Samuel went back to England where he gave his sister Anna Etherington a prayer book, inscribed "commemorating my return to London after an absence of 20 years", signed Samuel Etherington. Anna's descendant still has that prayer book.

Then Samuel returned to Sydney, where he partnered my second-great-grandmother Sarah, having nine children with her, under the surname Etherington. I do not yet know whether he continued contact with his first family, but certainly he was still listed in the Sands Register as "Samuel Holmes, baker" at the same time as "Samuel Etherington, carpenter". The areas where the two families lived were never far apart.

Something must have happened in 1883, because when one of the Etherington daughters married that year, her father's occupation was listed as baker rather than carpenter. It must have been around that time that Samuel left Sydney and went to live in Bombala, with his oldest son, using the surname Holmes again and that is where he eventually died and was buried.

I had checked every source I could find for evidence of Samuel Etherington's origins. Along the way I learned a lot about where he lived and what his life was like. But it was researching the origins of other immigrants of the same surname that led me to a theory that my Samuel might be the brother of that Thomas and then advertising my theory in enough places, that eventually located the key to my puzzle. — Kerry Farmer, New South Wales, Australia, farmer@compuserve.com

*   *   *

Remember Ezekiel

I have been researching my family history for nearly nine years now and I have experienced some wonderful successes. However, I was discouraged with the abrupt ending of one branch of my family tree. This was because of the family name; Smith.

I was determined to find the parents of my great-grandfather, Ezekiel W. Smith. I knew Ezekiel Smith died in Potter Valley, located in Mendocino county, CA, in 1906. From the 1873 *California Great Register for Mendocino County*, I learned his middle name was either William or Williams. The Great Registers are a list of voters (males over 18) compiled every two years from 1866-90. Many are still in existence and some are available on microfilm from the FHL.

Armed with a full name for Ezekiel Smith and 1906 as an approximate date of death, I ordered his death certificate. I anticipated Ezekiel's death certificate for several months. It finally arrived, only to have the dreaded "Unknown" for his father and mother's names and places of birth. The death certificate did give his birth date of 14 April 1849 and corroborated that his place of birth was Missouri, which I knew from census records. His death certificate also revealed that Ezekiel Smith had been in California for approximately 45 years, since the early 1860s.

After much pondering and searching for ideas, the only solution seemed to be searching all the Smiths in the 1850 federal census for Missouri looking for Ezekiel as a one year old. This was a huge task. The Smiths on the 1850 census index in Missouri take up six pages. Over the next three or four years I worked on this census but became discouraged. My niece had found Ezekiel later in life in California on the 1880 census, which showed his parents were born in Tennessee, another clue. Then in 1996, my niece, my husband and I

went to Mendocino county, CA to research the Brower side of our family. Ezekiel Smith married Mary Emilia Brower in 1876.

We were excited to find Ezekiel Smith's tombstone at the Potter Valley Cemetery. Next to him was a tombstone that read "Sarah Smith (1809-1874) wife of E.W. Smith" and another tombstone that read "Elanora Smith (1846-1863)". Sarah was the right age to be his mother and Elanora the right age to be a sister. Now, we had something to go on! I went to work on all the name variations in 1850 Missouri, keeping in mind a possible wife Sarah (both born in Tennessee) and a daughter Elanora and one-year-old Ezekiel. I found nothing. I was discouraged again. So, I put him away for three years but did not put him completely out of my mind.

The 1850 federal census for Missouri showing the information for one-year-old Ezekiel W. Smith.

In 1999, I brushed Ezekiel off again, with renewed determination to extend the branches of my family tree. I went through all my notes looking for something I might have missed but still came back to finishing up the Smiths in the 1850 census; a daunting task.

One day I was using my husband as a sounding board. He said, "What about looking for Sarah? Maybe E.W. is dead." Well, you guessed it; he found Sarah Smith on the first film he looked at which was Andrew Co.,

MO. There was Sarah Smith, born in Tennessee, Elanora and one-year-old Ezekiel. There were also several other brothers and sisters I knew nothing of, 10 children in all.

I will pay attention from now on when something I ordinarily would ignore is suggested. During the next two weeks we found Sarah Smith and family on the 1860 census in California; found an abstract of the Andrew county will for Ezekiel's father E.W., (who turned out to be Ezekiel also); and learned Ezekiel Smith Sr. died in 1849, probably the time his son Ezekiel was born.

Our family now has a battle cry for our difficult research projects; instead of "Remember the Alamo," we say "Remember Ezekiel". — Barbara Leimback, WA, bleimback@earthlink.net

Nun Sense

I had been searching for my second-great-grandfather, Octave Guay, and had been unable to come up with when and where he was born, or who his parents were.

I came across a photograph that my grandmother had given me before she died. It was a formal photograph of a nun. On the back of the picture, was the name of a studio in Victoria, BC. The only thing written on the back was "Octave Guay's sister, a nun".

My curiosity got the better of me and I wrote to the British Columbia Archives and

Philomene Guay, later to be known as Sister Marie-Virginie of the Sisters of St. Anne. She spent her years at the convent in British Columbia and was in charge of an orphanage.

Records Service in Victoria and sent them a photocopy of my picture. I asked if they could help me identify my nun, or if they knew who might be able to help me. They wrote back and told me that the nun's habit was certainly of the type worn by the Sisters of St. Anne, who had a convent in Victoria. They gave me the name of the convent.

I wrote to the Sisters of St. Anne and was thrilled when they sent me a lovely letter, along with the copy of an obituary of my nun, who I learned was known as Sister Marie-Virginie. Her given name was Philomene Guay. They also told me to write to their motherhouse in Lachine, PQ, for information on her birth and baptism. I did so and they sent me information leading to St. Cyprien's Catholic Church in Napierville, PQ. Not only did I receive the birth and baptismal information on Sister Marie-Virginie, but on all her brothers and sisters, including my second-great-grandfather, Octave Guay. St. Cyprien's also put me in touch with another person in Napierville, who had done extensive research on the Guay family. Before I knew it, I had information on all my Guays, dating back to the 1630s in France.

Never discount the smallest piece of information, or photograph of an unknown person, particularly if there is anything stamped on the back. You never know where it might lead. — Myrna Schosser, TX

Just One Book

All I knew about the family I was researching was that the couple had been married in Iowa. I stood in the front of the Iowa section at the Library of the Genealogical Forum of Oregon. The only marriage book at that time was from Marion county. Luckily, this book had the Bennett line I was looking for. I wrote down what little information was in the book.

Next, I wrote to the county courthouse for a copy of the marriage record. They in turn gave my request to a member of the local genealogical society, who wrote me back. This wonderful man not only provided all the written information, obituaries and newspaper articles, but he went to the cemetery and took pictures of the tombstones and the entrance of the cemetery. He even ordered a Revolutionary War Pension record for me. The man's charge was minimal for all the work he did — less then $20. This was 15 years ago but I remember just how finding one book of marriages breached this family brickwall. — Marcia L. Staunton, OR, mls94@attbi.com

General Register Office

I was unable to find the birth registration for William James Tapper, first born of my great-grandparents, William Allen Tapper and Eliza Platt. The birth date, 1 March 1851, and the place, Sheepcote Lane, Battersea, were given to me by his daughter. His marriage and death certificates also confirmed his age, but his birth certificate eluded me.

I decided to try another tactic and look for his parents' marriage. I found the General Register Office reference numbers for his mother, Eliza Platt's marriage in 1850 but there was no corresponding information for his father, William Allen Tapper or variants.

Not wanting to waste money, I decided against ordering. After much searching and further frustration, I relented and requested a marriage certificate, mentioning only Eliza Platt. Well, the mystery was solved! Eliza Platt married William Allen Tapper Watson. Watson being the maiden name of his grandmother. This made it easy to find their son, William James Tapper Watson's birth in the indices. The certificate did indeed identify his father's surname as Watson. The reported date was correct but he was born on Lillington Street in Westminster. This discovery allowed me to find the family in the census up to 1891.

Subsequently, I found that my second-great-grandfather, William Henry Tapper, born 1804 in Galmpton (near Dartmouth) Devon, whose mother was Anney Watson, had started calling himself Watson after moving to London, around the 1820s.

Taking a chance and buying a likely certificate solved two brickwalls. — Ab Tapper, ON, abtapper@pathcom.com

Serendipity And Hard Work

Both serendipity and diligent hard work yield answers to the brickwalls in our family history pursuit.

Always follow up with queries, both those you place and those published ones you spot. Julia Knudsen did that. Seeing a query she contacted me on our Goss family. She even flew to Washington to meet me and she received 50 pages of information from me.

Be alert to chance meetings. Standing in line at the 2001 National Genealogical Society conference in Portland, OR, Judy Dye heard somebody say, "Paris, Texas". Excitedly, Judy tapped the woman and found she lived in that itty-bitty Texas town and that she was the distant cousin with whom Judy had been corresponding for 10 years but had never met.

Be prepared by personal genealogical study and education. Seeing the light go on in genealogy-beginner Frances White's eyes when in class I explained to her "find each ancestor on every census year of his or her life" was exciting to both of us.

Develop your networking skills. Chat with Person #1 about your ancestors or genealogy brickwalls leads to Persons #2-3-4-5 and then Person #6 gets back to you with an answer or suggestion — this does work. — Donna Potter Phillips, WA

Everything Seemed To Fit

I have had great success in carrying my maternal line back to the *Mayflower* and a few hundred years beyond. My paternal half has always ended in a brickwall with my grandfather's father.

Gramps was Frank William Bouley Sr., a dancing master in Spokane, WA for 40 years. Grandpa told me stories about my great-grandfather when I was a child, but never mentioned the name of his mother or stepmother.

When I became interested in genealogy, I tried to trace him. I checked all the census files from 1840 to 1900 in Missouri, West Virginia, and Kentucky. I came up blank. My eyes were sore from reading all that microfilm. I checked the IGI and found nothing. I tried to find military records for Samuel Bouley/Boulet — again I drew a blank.

Grandpa had said that he had made a minor change in the spelling of his name because it sounded more professional. I checked the 1910 census for Spokane and had no trouble finding him. He listed his father as being born in Kentucky and gave his own birthplace as Wheeling, WV. I wrote to Wheeling for a birth certificate but again came up empty.

Years went by, one day I decided to take another look at the 1850 census for Missouri. As before, I found no Bouley/Boulet but I did find a listing for Samuel Boley who was 16 years old. His age at the time made it possible for this man to be my great-grandfather. Boley was not that different to Bouley.

Back to the census and IGI lists. Suddenly it started clicking. I found Samuel Franklin Boley and his entire family listing. It wasn't perfect but there were so many matches. Samuel's third son, Fielding, was born in 1867 in Wheeling, MO, the same year as Grandpa. I went to the atlas and sure enough found a Wheeling only a few miles from where the Boley family lived.

The 1870 census showing the family of Samuel and Elizabeth Boley, including three-year-old Fielding Boley, Frank Bouley's grandfather.

Everything seemed to fit. With this new knowledge, I wrote for the NARA to see if any pension award had been granted to Charlotte, Samuel's second wife. I received a huge report. In any case, Charlotte got her pension. Granted, I have not proved beyond a doubt that Samuel Boley is my great-grandfather but the coincidences would lead me to believe so. — Frank Bouley, NJ, fbouley@prodigy.net

Open Your Mind

One day while searching for an ancestor's marriage record, I found a likely record with very similar first names and the ages were very close. However, the surnames were not a match and I was faced with a brickwall. Looking at the handwriting, I thought to myself, what would the surname sound like to a non German-speaking clerk or look like to a transcriber not familiar with German letters?

With this in mind I found the proof that Anna Erdwins married Fred Williams, the record read "Anje Ecrtheens m. Frederick Wilhelms", not matches, but close enough for me to prove that this was my ancestors' marriage record. In addition to this the name was indexed under Wilckens. — Buddy Samuels, MO

Website As A Brickwall Solution

I started wanting to do my family genealogy when I visited relatives in West Virginia. We were sitting around and looking at pictures and family notes. I ask why there weren't a lot and that's what got me started looking for my information.

When I came home to Ohio I started contacting family members asking questions about what they remember about their grandparents. I then started looking on the Internet for people that had my names. I bought a genealogy computer program called Family Tree to see if there was anyone in it with some of my names — there were a few but not many. I then went back to West Virginia to talk to my aunt and she was able to give me more names. I then went to the family graveyards and looked at headstones. I was able to start connecting things together more. I talked to the people that took care of the graveyard and found out they were related and have a family reunion every year.

When I came home I started a web page with the information I had collected. I couldn't believe the people that had contacted me looking for the same names. It took me about four years to really get all the information I wanted on my names. My father-in-

law had some of his genealogy of his family done and I was able to through the Internet to go even farther than what he had.

Starting a family history web page is a great way to attract others who are looking for information on their families. Doors can be opened and brickwalls can be overcome.

If it wasn't for the Internet and having my web page I know I wouldn't have got as far as I am. — Darlene (Arbogast) Eastin, OH

Review Your Research Carefully

I tracked my great-grandmother, Julia Ann (Fenwick) Willett, from Union county, KY, to Illinois, to Missouri, to Indian Territory (present-day Oklahoma) to Rogers, AR. She seemed to stay in Arkansas for about 15 years, so I thought that was where I would find her death certificate and grave site.

The state of Arkansas then offered searches of death records for any 10-year period for a fee of $8, whether or not any record was found. I requested a search of Arkansas death records from 1914 to 1924 when she would have been 85, figuring that she probably would have died during that 10-year period. However, no record was found.

We went to Rogers, AR, and checked libraries, church records, funeral homes and half a dozen old cemeteries in the area with no success.

I found her in a city directory in 1919 living with her daughters and a son-in-law, but no further clues. I ordered an Oklahoma death certificate for the same period, again with no success.

Receipt of burial for Julia Ann Willett.

Several months later as I reviewed my research, it dawned on me that she could have lived longer than 85 years, although that seemed quite old to me at the time. Reluctantly, I ordered another Arkansas death record search covering the next 10 years and found what I was looking for. Her death certificate indicated that she had lived to be 87 years old and had died in Rogers, AR on 27 January 1927. The document itself contained some other surprising information. Although she lived many years in Rogers, AR, and died there, she was buried in Chickasha, OK.

By contacting the city clerk, who kept the cemetery records for Chickasha, I was able to identify her exact burial plot and also learn the name of the funeral home that per-formed the services. Even though that business had long since changed owners, they had retained most of the old records and were able to furnish me with additional details of her funeral and burial. I was able to obtain a copy of a 1927 invoice showing that it cost a total of $42 to ship dear Julia Ann from Rogers, AR, nearly 300 miles by rail and bury her in Chickasha, OK.

I have yet to solve the mystery of why Julia Ann was buried in Chickasha, a place where she had no family and no likely connection, instead of in Arkansas where she died and had some family members nearby. — Genevieve Willett Slade, OK, genv@swbell.net

Funeral Sign-In Books

I have been working with my father's cousin Gary Decker and his wife Nancy researching the Magoon side of the family. They decided to hold a small family reunion of sorts at our local library where everyone brought their resources and files. One of the individuals who attended was Jenny Magoon whose husband is my third cousin once-removed.

I mentioned my mother's family and discovered Jenny's great-grand-mother, Margaret Spangler Sopher Harvey, was my second-great-grand-mother. We were unsure of how close a relationship my great-grandfather had to her grandmother. We figured we would never know.

Then I mentioned that when I went through my great-grandfather Decker's funeral sign-in book, I was able to find first names of several husbands and wives that were previously unknown. We were also to find my great-grandfather's correct wedding date.

Jenny remembered she had her grandmother's funeral book. It was signed by my great-grandfather and his wife! We were also able to locate other members of the family. I know I will be looking at my other grandfather's funeral book because his contains not only names, but many addresses as well. — Penny Spacht, PA

Was My Ancestor Hatched?

Even with the aid of the Internet, I became stumped at the same brickwall at which my mother dead-ended 12 years ago in the search for my father's Cook family. It was as if my second-great-grandfather, James Monroe Cook, born in November 1853, had been hatched from an egg!

I could find all sorts of information about his life after he married. He lived in Lowndesville, Abbeville county, SC and raised a family there, but before that there was nothing. More curious than ever, I began to prod family members a bit harder. They were adamant that the family was from South Carolina.

A few weeks later my grandmother casually asked if I had seen the family Bible. Seen it? I didn't know she had it! My aunt retrieved from a plastic bag a Bible, printed in 1851 and inscribed in September 1865 by J.W. Cook, with the names and birth dates of James Monroe Cook's siblings. Unfortunately, most of the names were in initial

Back row: Parents Thomas and wife Jane Elizabeth Taylor Cook, Samuel Dean Cook. Front row: Mary Elizabeth, Minnie Bell, Jess Newton and Thomas Alexander Jr. Taken in Polk county, AR.

form, but I did gain some useful starting places.

I scoured census records for 1860 in a four-district area looking for a Cook family with children matching the ages and initials that were in the Bible. Nothing. Then I jumped into 1870 and began to search for adults matching the initials to see if that would lend a clue. J.W. Cook had inscribed the Bible. I felt sure that his birth date, if any, would be correct. I found a J. Wesley Cook in the 1870 federal census in Anderson county with a first-born son named John. Anderson was the next county over from Abbeville, so I thought I would give this name a shot. I doubtfully typed in the name "John Wesley Cook" into the search bar at Ancestry.com. The search netted 50 matches. I scrolled through looking for one with the right birth date and wife. Not only was there one, but three trees!

I downloaded the three family trees. James Monroe Cook's siblings were all there. But where was James Monroe? James Monroe had been lost to the family. It seems clear now that his father, Thomas Cook, died when he was four months old. Before the 1860 census his mother remarried a Tucker. No wonder I couldn't find him in 1860! The siblings scattered westward, leaving behind their baby brother and the family Bible. — Amanda Cook, GA

*　　*　　*

Wagons Don't Always Go West

All I knew about the parents of my second-great-grandmother, Sarah Cady Fairfield, came from three sources. Her death certificate listed only "Helen Lyons" for her mother's name. Censuses reported her father's birthplace as Connecticut and her mother's as Massachusetts. In an interview the local newspaper did with Sarah shortly before her death in 1932 she said her father was August Cady and the family had traveled by ox-drawn covered wagon. She also said she was born in Southbridge, MA on 22 March 1836. I could not find any August Cady or Helen Lyons in Massachusetts during this time period.

A researcher sent me a birth and death record for an infant born in Southbridge in June 1835 to William A. Cady and Melita Vinton, suggesting August might stand for William Augustus. This seemed to strike out on three counts because the baby was born approximately nine months before Sarah, the mother's name was incorrect and the father's name not quite right. I searched both western Massachusetts and New York for the elusive Cady parents to no avail.

One day, a second cousin told me about a mutual descendant of Sarah's who lived next door to the old Fairfield farmstead here in Michigan. I called him. He couldn't help me with Sarah's parentage but he did give me the telephone number of Sarah's granddaughter, a lady whom I knew when I was young but had lost track of over the years. I called her but she couldn't help me with the names. She did say that she helped her grandmother write letters to cousins in Connecticut. I began to wonder if August Cady moved from Massachusetts back to his birthplace of Connecticut.

There were a couple of possibilities, Augustus Cadys living in Windham county, CT on the border with Southbridge. However, their ages were wrong. There was also a William A. I looked up this man in the 1850 census and he was my guy: William A. Cady, living in Woodstock, CT with wife Melita and daughter Sarah. Sarah was the right age and Woodstock was the right town. Working then with the name Melita Vinton instead of Helen Lyons I discovered *The Vinton Memorial*, a genealogy compiled in 1858. Sure enough, there was Melita, husband William Augustus Cady of Brooklyn, CT, a town near Woodstock and daughter Sarah. *The Vinton Memorial* told me Helen Lyons was Sarah's cousin.

And what of the birth record for the infant born in June 1835? It was still close, but perhaps the baby had been premature. Sarah herself may have been premature but survived. While *The Vinton Memorial* gave me the line of Melita, I am still tangled up with the many Cady families in Windham county. However, thanks to a little creativity with a name and the realization that wagons didn't always go west, I have identified Sarah's elusive parents. — Suzanne Wesbrook Frantz, MI

Over The Brickwall And Down The Lane

I began my research for my maternal grandmother's mother with the 1881 British Census and National Index on CD. Most of the official information that existed for Emma Reeves, or "Great-grandma-in-hospital" as I knew her, was gathered from her death notice which gave her full married name, age and date of death.

I began my search in the early evening and after scrolling through a long list of Reeves, the description of an "Emma Reeves" appeared on the screen. This Emma Reeves was a tailoress, rented to boarders and had two daughters, Emma and Henrietta. The description of Emma Reeves fit my memories of Great-grandma-in-hospital perfectly and Em and Hetty were the names of two of my great-aunts. The entry also gave the surname of Girling as my Great-grandma-in-hospital's maiden name and that surname was somewhere in my memories of childhood. I had found my Great-grandma-in-hospital and my great-grandfather who I had never met.

Not wanting to begin another search on the census that evening, I decided instead to explore the surrounding neighborhood, which one can do with this census on CD and learn the professions of the neighbors. I wanted to get a feel for the type of neighborhood and society that they had lived in. I scrolled up the street, from Emma living at number eight to the end of the street, which happened to be very short. The street name changed and I idly decided to follow on.

A few doors down the second street, I came across an Emma Girling. The chances of there being another Emma Girling who was not related in such a short distance was inconceivable. My mother's family had always lived near one another and my own parents had bought the house next door to my grandmother from an aunt. Great-grandma-in-hospital had lived on a street of six houses, three of which were owned and occupied by

Emma Reeves (1864-1954).

her married daughters. The widowed Emma Girling fit the description of my second-great-grandmother and she still had two sons at home whose names were familiar, the grandsons of which had lived, and still do, three doors away from my childhood home. I had found my second-great-grandmother.

My second-great-grandmother was listed as a widow and although I have never found second-great-grandfather Girling, I know from relatives that he was hunchbacked, deeply religious, drank too much and owned a traveling merry-go-round business, so he sounds very interesting. But I am still looking for him. With more luck, you might read about him in Brickwall Solutions II! — MPWM

A New Brown Family Legacy

Ellen Matilda Mitchell, our mother's grandmother, was born in 1838 to George Mitchell and Susanna Paap (or Mary Pope) in New Jersey and grew up in Brooklyn, NY.

Ellen met her future husband Alexander Brown when her family was visiting Illinois. His family had recently migrated from Kentucky to take advantage of the fertile farmland. After Ellen returned home, their courtship continued by correspondence. A family story written by Mother's second cousin, Jessie, says that Alexander's mother did not think

Ellen would be a suitable wife for a farmer. It tells that Ellen's father owned a hardware store and that Ellen and her sisters went to finishing school, enjoyed music, the arts and fine needlework. After her father died, his wife's second husband squandered the family fortune.

Alexander and Ellen were married on 5 January 1860 in Illinois. Their son George Brooks Brown, my grandfather, was born 30 October 1860. In the summer of 1863, they traveled with their growing family and with members of Alex's family along the Oregon Trail and the California Trail to northern California where they established a sheep and horse ranch. During the following years, Ellen and Alex had nine children in total.

In 1982, Jessie wrote *The Brown Family Legacy* as she had heard it from her mother, who was a younger sister of George. The story told of the Brown family living on a Kentucky plantation, freeing their slaves and moving to Illinois, of the romance between Alexander and Ellen Michell, of the Oregon Trail and other details. Mother had not heard some of these stories before and some contradicted what her own father had told her.

After my mother died my sisters and I decided to continue the family research. We started with old family letters, Jessie's story, family pictures and memories of what our mother had told us. We wrote letters to all the living Brown descendants that could be contacted. We sent for birth, marriage and death certificates, searched the IGI, the census, county and state histories, family genealogies and land records, you name it, using alternate spellings and every method we knew. We received a wealth of information on other ancestors, discovered several new cousins, but could not get any more information on Ellen's parents. We proved and disproved some of the information in *The Brown Family Legacy* and other family lore. (For example: there is no record of slave holding by the Browns in census or inventories.)

Ellen Brown's death certificate, indicating her parents' names. The informant, Miss Effie Brown, M.D., was Ellen's daughter. Howard F. Rand who was Ellen's attending physician was her son-in-law married to daughter Nellie.

The marriage license, the marriage certificate and the county marriage register for Alexander and Ellen spelled the surname three different ways: Michel, Michell and Mitchell. I tired every technique I knew and, after 10 years of searching, I still could not let this one rest.

One night, on a whim, I searched RootsWeb.com's WorldConnect for George Michell. Imagine my shock to find a George Michell, married to a Susan Pape who had a daughter Ellen who married an Alex Brown and who had a son named George! I immediately contacted the submitter. Trish was as surprised as I was and thrilled to receive information on Ellen's family and descendants. She descends from Susan Pape's sister and not only has information that takes George and Susan back to England, with baptismal and marriage records, etc., but also has quite extensive information on Ellen's family that remained in Brooklyn.

A bonus in breaking through this brickwall was that Trish and I discovered that we are also fifth cousins in our shared Bigelow lines. It pays to leave no stone unturned! — Winona K. Aastrup, MA

A Toll By Any Other Name...

The Toll family brickwall in my genealogy research baffled me for years. The line seemed to stop with a second-great-grandfather. I had many of his descendants (he married three times and had large families with each wife), but I could not find parents or siblings for this second-great-grandfather.

As it turned out, the solution to this puzzle was so basic that it is one of the first things that beginner researchers are told: You should always consider that the spelling of your ancestor's name might have variations. I knew this rule, but had just been so convinced that my grandmother would have known that some of her ancestors had spelled the name Tolle. — JL

The Mysterious Case Of The Pennsylvania Dutchmen

I grew up in my grandmother's home. Each spring we would journey to the cemetery to tend the graves of my grandfather's family. I would ask her where they were born and she would answer that they were Pennsylvania Dutchmen.

Years later I began looking for my Pennsylvania Dutchmen. Since this moniker was the only clue I had, I began to search the Pennsylvania records. My brickwall came when I tried to follow this family westward. After the birth of my great-grandfather Alfred Wilt Bongey in 1832, I could no longer find them in any Pennsylvania records. He was miss-

ing from records for the next 30 or so years of his life.

In my grandmother's attic I found a deed book sketch of a farm in Michigan. This allowed me to pick up the trail. Alfred married there and in 1861 my grandfather was born. I also had found a wonderful 1854 letter written to my second-great-grandfather Jacob from a daughter. It revealed Jacob and Alfred were coopers making barrels for Ong's mill.

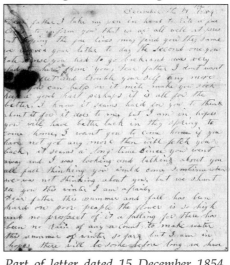

Part of letter dated 15 December 1854, sent to Jacob from his daughter Mary Clemmons.

Because of Grandma's attic the trail became rich and I followed them to Iowa in 1871 and on to Wisconsin in 1886. While doing research in the courthouse in Madison, WI, I located my great-grandfather's death certificate. His youngest daughter provided the information on the certificate. In place of birth she had written Ohio. This puzzled me because I knew Alfred was born in Pennsylvania. It was then my brickwall began to crumble. I realized that while Alfred was born in Pennsylvania he must have lived in Ohio during those first 30 years. In a search of the 1850 federal census for Ohio I found my family and the miller Ong.

Sometimes a piece of misinformation can be the clue that solves a problem. — Elaine Bongey Wendt, WI, bewendt@newnorth.net

Family Bibles And Photographs

In the spring of 1995 while attending a niece's wedding, we visited the lighthouse museum at Pointe Aux Barques, MI. Here I discovered that my great-grandfather, Andrew Jackson Mathewson, was the chief lighthouse keeper from 1895 until 1904. The genealogy search was on! The family tree was traced quickly to about the early 1800s.

However, the Williams line hit a brickwall. My father died in 1965 and his only brother died in 1967. Their father and my grandfather, Cecil Mathewson, was killed in 1912 and his wife Anne Marie Williams Mathewson, died in 1922. After that, the two boys stayed in Bay City, MI, with Uncle Milfred and Aunt Emma Williams. Milfred is my grandmother's brother.

During his life, my dad had little contact or discussion about his family life and relatives. After my mother died in 1993, some old photographs, letters and notes surfaced, but there was little about the Williams side of the family. Visiting my cousin we reviewed some of her family photos and letters. She mentioned our father had a very much younger cousin, George Williams, who lived in Bay City, MI. George's father was Milfred Williams, the maternal uncle who cared for my father and his brother. My cousin said George died in 1994, but thought his widow still was living in the Bay City area.

So we returned to Bay City to do some more research. Checking the Bay City telephone book, several George Williamses and one Mrs. George Williams were listed. No one answered at the Mrs. Williams number, but I noted the home address.

Returning to Oklahoma, I wrote her a letter of introduction; who I was, my family interests, etc., sending the letter with a SASE to the address. Just before Thanksgiving 1999, a letter arrived from her. Her son forwarded my letter to her in Florida where she lived in the winter months. The letter contained valuable information about my grandmother's family and she invited us to visit her.

Recently, we spent two days with Mrs. Williams, the widow of my dad's youngest cousin. She had numerous photographs, letters and historical information about my great-grandparents, Aaron and Martha Williams; plus great-aunts and great-uncles and their children. There were even photos of my dad and his brother, my uncle.

Family events recorded in the Bible of Aaron Williams. The lower sign points to the birth date of Richard J. Mathewson, written in his father's hand.

Of the greatest interest and value was the family Bible of Aaron Williams signed by him. Beginning in 1836, the Bible contained the entire Williams' family marriages, births and deaths. To my surprise my own birthday was recorded in my dad's handwriting. What an experience!

Locating Mrs. Williams and the family information she shared with me, has opened doors to trace the Williams immigration through Canada to Michigan. — Richard J. Mathewson, OK

Searching Family Mysteries

The subject of my husband's paternal grandfather had always intrigued me. My husband knew he was a colorful character, but as my husband's parents were deceased there was no one to substantiate the family rumors. When I began doing genealogy, the intrigue and mystery soon turned into a brickwall.

From an elderly family friend I obtained a copy of my husband's grandfather's obituary. It was tucked in a Bible and nearly forgotten. However, other than a birth and death date and place, I still knew little about him. Because I didn't have the luxury of traveling to Michigan where he had died, I knew that my research would have to be done via mail, Internet and phone.

My Internet research turned up nothing. I joined mailing lists and posted to numerous message boards with no results. I couldn't believe that with all the information available nothing matched. My husband's grandfather's surname was slightly unusual. My husband's father was adopted by his stepfather and so the surname I was researching was different from our own. I began using the Internet to see how many people still living in Michigan had that same surname. I found about 80 matches. In desperation I mailed letters to 50 of the people with the same surname. I included a letter explaining who I was and why I was inquiring, a printout of my family history file and a copy of the obituary. I included my e-mail address in the letter and my website.

What a breakthrough! I got an e-mail from a relative my husband never knew he had. The man who contacted me was the great-grandson of our ancestor's brother. He had a plethora of information on the family, including pictures, newspaper clippings and a magazine article.

It seemed that because of my husband's grandfather's colorfulness a lot of family members had distanced themselves from him. They didn't even know we existed. Through this one contact I have learned so much about the family that has given me leads to follow in many directions. — Jennifer F. Davis, VA

Passenger Lists

I searched for many years for the passenger ship list for my grandparents, Anton and Rose Meier. In the beginning of my genealogy search, I had been looking at passenger lists of ships arriving in Canada. This was because my mother and other family members said my grandparents had put ashore in Canada. So I spent hours looking through microfilms of passenger ship lists of Canadian ports on the east coast. I was looking for their arrival in 1901, as this was the information they gave for the 1910 census. Then at a genealogy workshop I learned that if someone had applied for naturalization, they had to write on their application papers when they came to the US, where they came from and the ship that they were on. So I started my quest to see if my grandfather had applied for naturalization. No such luck!

Next I started to research if any of his sons had applied for naturalization. From the research of my three uncles' naturalization application papers, I received three different years of when they came to the US. The application papers of two of my uncles stated they did not remember the name of the ship they came on. My third uncle's papers said the name of the ship was the *Santa Maria*. All papers said they arrived in the port of Boston and had traveled from Liverpool, England. Since all papers named Boston as the port of entry, I now had a specific port to look at passenger ship lists. All the searching through Canadian passenger lists had been for naught.

The NARA has some indexes of names of people arriving in various ports. I first looked at a microfilm of an index for the time period covering December 1899 to June 1900 for Boston. This was to see if the December 1899 date was correct. I had no luck. Next I sent to the NARA asking them to look at the index for 5 July 1900 to 28 December 1900 for the port of Boston. They could not find it.

There are no indexes for the year 1901. So next I had to look methodically and meticulously through sets of microfilms covering the years 1899, 1900 and 1901. I was looking through the months of November and December for these years.

Anyone who has ever looked at microfilms knows this involves slowly looking through several microfilms one name at a time on each and every ship that arrived in Boston during those three years. Finally I found them, it was indeed in 1900 that they came.

The data that was on the passenger ship list showed the name of the ship was not *Santa Maria* but was the *S.S. Ivernia*. It sailed from Liverpool on 4 December 1900. The arrival date of this ship in Boston was not documented on this list. This proves one cannot rely on the memories of our ancestors when they provide information to various government agencies where they applied for naturalization papers. Their final destination was listed as Winnipeg, MB which probably explains why I have heard through the years from my mother that they came to Canada. — Mary Frances Jacobson, WA, francie@clarkston.com

*   *   *

Town Websites

I began my genealogy research with a search for my paternal grandfather, Ferencz Lovasz. After discussions with my father we found his father's letter of intent to become a citizen at the Akron, OH courthouse records department. It listed his birthplace as Doroszlo, Hungary, which is present-day Doroslovo in Serbia and Montenegro, the new name for Yugoslavia.

Clockwise from upper left: Franciscus Lovas, daughter Lila, wife Eelon Lvasz, sons Michael and Frank. Taken c. 1919 in Malverin, OH.

I rented the microfilmed records for births, marriages and deaths from the FHC. I searched for my grandfather using his arrival date, but could find nothing on the microfilm. A hurried check of years before and after produced nothing. Since I had the films, I documented all Lovasz names, addresses, birth dates and compiled many families with the name Lovasz, but not my grandfather's.

As I had no contact with anyone in Hungary or Yugoslavia and I did not know if any of my family was still in Europe, I decided to try the Internet. I searched every site with a suffix of .hu and .yu (the suffixes for Hungarian and Yugoslavian websites). I flooded these sites with e-mails appealing for help in locating family members and signed every Internet guest book I could find. I received an e-mail telling me to check the site for the town of Doroszlo. The website was written in Hungarian, which I cannot read or speak, but the phone book was posted, complete with addresses and an e-mail guest book. I e-mailed the Lovaszes listed there and received one response, a birth certificate for Ferenc Lovasz born in Sombor. So close, but not a match.

I decided to e-mail everyone on the Doroszlo website guest book and received a reply from a teacher at the high school in Doroszlo. He said he knew the Lovasz family and would talk to them at church about my search. He sent a message telling me that my grandfather was not born in Doroszlo but in Szonta, a village five miles away. I couldn't get to the FHC fast enough to order these films.

After five agonizing weeks' wait, I reviewed the Szonta films and there was grandfather. Along with my grandfather, I found four brothers and sisters. Now that I had a baptismal certificate, which identified his parents, I reviewed my list of Lovasz names from Doroszlo. All along I had

Mihaly Lovasz, brother of Franciscus, and wife Julianna Szuces. Copies of this photograph are held by Dennis F. Lovas' aunt and their distant relation, Eszter.

all the other siblings but just couldn't put together the family tree until now.

Two months later, I received a letter from Eszter Lovasz, daughter of Ferenc Lovasz. She sent family pictures and confirmed our relationship. One photo was identical to one my aunt had; she could not identify the man in it, but Eszter said it was my grandfather's brother.

Now the major parts of the family tree are together. None of this would have been possible without the help and guidance of strangers.

After making contact with cousins in Doroszlo, my wife and I visited them in 2001. — Dennis F. Lovas, OH

The Unusual Path To My Great-Grandparents' Marriage Record

For several years I searched for the marriage record of my great-grand-parents. My only real clue was a torn page in an old hymnal with the hand-written name of the Pastor who had married them. I estimated their marriage took place between 1870 and 1874 in an area of Brooklyn known as New Lots. I searched old maps and city directories to find the names and addresses of all the churches in that area in the 1870s. I then wrote to every church I could find in the hope this man preached at one of them. I contacted all the major archives just in case I missed a church, but was unsuccessful. Since these two branches of my family had attended several different denominations I was not sure in which one they might have married. So I sent my letters to each one, with a self-addressed stamped envelope and the offer to reimburse them for their time and expenses. But every response was negative.

Then one day I was reading the Brooklyn Information Page on the Internet. Under that was a subheading called Brooklyn Street History and Beginnings. Then I went further to another subheading of New Lots' History and Street Names and began to read each section under the street names listed. Under the street heading New Jersey Avenue, it mentioned a church was once there and named some early ministers including C.R. Blauvelt, which was the name of the pastor who married my great-grandparents. Finally, a possibility existed. The article stated the church was torn down in 1921. Once again I contacted the main archive to see if these records still existed and where I might write for copies of them but still no luck. No one knew the whereabouts or even if these records had survived.

Several months later I received a copy of a newsletter from the Greater Ridgewood Historical Society of which I am a member. I read that they had recently received a new addition to their library. It was a copy of the Blauvelt family history. So I called and was told that the library was under renovation and that they might not be able to help me for a few months. But I was given the name of another gentleman to contact, who is now in charge of the society. So I wrote to him. Within a couple of weeks, I received a letter with copies of information about a Rev. C.R. Blauvelt from this family history. It stated that he was a minister in the New Lots/East New York area of Brooklyn in the 1870s at the Reformed Dutch Church of East New York. This gentleman also told me that he thought

he knew where the old records were kept and had already forwarded a copy of my letter to that church.

Shortly after I received a letter from the secretary of the Forest Park Reformed Church in Woodhaven, Queens county, NY. The secretary looked up the names of my ancestors and their approximate date of marriage and sent me the full information about my great-grandparents. — Judy Place Maggiore, AZ

Clues In Newspapers

I was having trouble finding out what happened when some family members departed Truro, NS. When the family arrived in Saint John, NB, six months later, some of the members were missing. When I checked census records, death records and other information on all areas between Truro and Saint John, I discovered that some had died en route and were buried in Hopewell, NB, but it is not easy to find out how these people died.

When I check through my home town newspaper, I always look under the feature section "100 years ago today", "50 years ago today", etc. One day, while looking under "71 years ago today", I found a relative that I was looking for who had died from being thrown from his wagon and a wheel passed over his neck, breaking it. — Mary Rosevear, NB

Finding A Birthplace

We knew my husband's second-great-grandfather, Frank Muhrlein, fought in the US Civil War and came from Germany. We had no idea in what area he was born. We read the Civil War Pension records at the NARA for him and had learned the identity of his brothers, the names of his children, when he married and many places of residence, but could not figure out where he was born.

My husband, while on a business trip to Washington, DC, copied the entire pension file including service records. Careful reading of the entire folder finally provided the clue we needed to locate his birthplace. One of the pages in the file was a copy of the Volunteer Enlistment Form completed by Frank when he re-enlisted in 1864. He was born in a place called Waldhausen in Germany.

Frank Muhrlein in a formal Civil War-era photograph.

We still did not know which of the several villages called Waldhausen was the correct one. The pension folder had baptismal records for four of the children from St. Mary's Catholic Church in Iowa City and the 1880 US census records listed Frank's birthplace as a location beginning with the letter B, which we decided was Bayern, the German name for Bavaria. So with this information we narrowed the search to the state of Bavaria and the Catholic parishes serving the three Waldhausen villages there. We wrote three letters seeking confirmation and including some of the identifying clues that we found and funds for return postage.

You can't imagine our delight when the answer to the third letter arrived several weeks later confirming we had located Frank's birthplace and providing even more family information than we already had. Since that time I have utilized the same Volunteer Enlistment Form from the Civil War records to locate the birthplace of a French Canadian ancestor of mine. — Harriet Muhrlein, WA

She Came To Her Census

When I first began my research, I was told my second-great-grandmother's name was Melvina Pruitt. My grandmother vaguely remembered an Uncle Tom Bradshaw. I decided Melvina had to be a Bradshaw otherwise the relationship wouldn't be there. I talked to Grandma again and she told me Grandma Pruitt was a Bradshaw. So I went looking.

I found the marriage license in Jersey county, IL, which proved the Bradshaw maiden name. I also found that Uncle Tom and his wife were buried very near my great-grandparents who were Melvina's son and his third wife. So I knew the Bradshaw family had been in Jersey county. as well. I went through the 1850 federal census of Jersey county and found all the Bradshaw families I could. Only one, but no Melvina was mentioned. I continued looking for years.

Finally I decided to look at that census record again. It finally hit me. Melvina was there but was referred to her by her middle name for years. She was named after her mother. Her parents were Jonas and Nancy Bradshaw. Their first child was named Nancy Melvina Bradshaw who later married George W. Pruitt. — Debbi Geer, MO

Pursue The Unusual

In my genealogy search, I am blessed in one of my husband's lines by having an unusual surname to research, Sofge. This made it easier to search library catalogs and databases that otherwise might prove intimidating. My brickwall is a man who was purported to be brilliant, a virtuoso violinist who, it is claimed, played for European royalty, spoke seven languages, was a 32nd-degree Mason and a well-respected professor of music. For all his accomplishments, though, Ferdinand M. Sofge must have tread rather lightly on the earth, leaving little in the way of footprints for the aspiring family historian.

Ferdinand M. Sofge was born in Hamburg, Germany in 1823. He immigrated to the US in 1838 with his father and one brother. The rest of the family came later. He appeared in the 1840 federal census in Cincinnati as living with his parents and siblings. That is the last we knew of him until he married his second wife in 1868 in Indiana. During that missing 28 years, Ferdinand is believed to have married. He fathered Henry Ferdinand Sofge and perhaps a daughter. An entire branch of the family is related through Henry Ferdinand, so we would really like to pin this one down. One family story about Ferdinand suggested that he lived in Georgia before the US Civil War and fled the area because of disputes over the issue of slavery. He was not listed in the US federal census index for Georgia in 1850 or 1860 or for any other state that we have been able to determine. Family tradition suggested he lived in Rome, GA but checks of land records and tax rolls turned up nothing. Trying to trace his Masonic membership back from his lodge in LaFayette, IN proved fruitless, as he apparently did not indicate the lodge from which he transferred membership when he joined.

A break came through the *Hamilton County Genealogical Society Quarterly, The Tracer* Vol. 22, No. 1. On their computer interest group page, sites were listed, including the Ohio Public Library Information Network genealogy link. This was new to me, so I searched relevant databases for the keyword Sofge, expecting to find information on some of my Cincinnati Sofges. An article from *Scientific American* came up, from 1859, containing a summary of US patents granted in January 1859. Among them was a patent for a modification of horsepower, granted to Ferdinand M. Sofge of Columbus, GA who was not related to my Cincinnati Sofges at all. I had finally placed my brickwall Ferdinand, not only in the US, but in Georgia, during at least some of those missing 28 years.

Above: Christine W. Sofge found a mention of her husband's ancestor as a patent holder in an edition of Scientific American *(shaded area at bottom). Below: an enlargement of the notice.*

> HORSE-POWER—Ferdinand M. Sofge, of Columbus, Ga.: I claim the combination of the cogged wheel, A, having the supporting flange, No. 1, and the wheel, B, with corresponding cogs and bearing, revolving upon the supporting ring, I; the whole constructed and operating substantially, as and for the purpose set forth.

A closer check of the 1850 and 1860 federal census indexes for Columbus still revealed no Sofges. Land records in Muscogee county also turned up nothing. Mountain Press published a book listing Masonic memberships in Georgia in 1854 with a surname index online. Sofge was listed in the index, so I ordered the book and found that

F.M. Sofge was indeed a member, but in Lexington, GA (not Columbus). Further checking of patent records also showed a second patent awarded to Ferdinand M. Sofge in November of 1859. His residence is listed as Macon, GA. Three records, three locations in Georgia and still no traditional records, such as census, land or tax records have been found.

Perhaps our Ferdinand just never let the dust settle on his feet. — Christine Whittaker Sofge, North Yorkshire, UK, sofge@yahoo.com

Starting With Almost Nothing

I knew almost nothing of my father's Wallace ancestry when I started genealogy. I knew my grandfather's family came from Smith's Ferry, PA. I found him with my great-grandfather Harvey and the family on the 1900 federal census for Beaver county, PA. Now I had to find a family with Harvey's siblings and parents.

After many brickwalls, I finally found my great-grandfather Harvey in the 1870 federal census for Pennsylvania. Searching for my great-grandfather's siblings, I found a cousin who did the research and gave me copies of her information, which included the obituary of Harvey's father, James and mentioned all the children. James was a volunteer in the 98th Ohio Volunteer Infantry during the Civil War so I sent for his complete military file from the NARA. It contained his pension records in which he named his children and the date and place of their mother's death in addition to information on his second wife. By then I had found his marriage record to his first wife, Mary Eckle, and her family in Carroll county, OH. My hardest task at hand was next to find James' parents. Since James and Mary married in 1849, the 1850 census was of little help. I did find an 1850 census entry that looked

like a possibility with three children and a wife married after the birth of the oldest child. But how could I prove I was looking at the right family? I found the daughter had later married a Dewell/Duell and that Mary's sister had also married a Duell. This seemed to further tie the families together, but still no proof.

Then another cousin descended from James found a will of John Wallace where he gave James $10 and other bequests to the two children and wife of the second marriage. This almost wrapped up the proof I needed, but was my second great-grandfather the right son James in the will?

My cousin then came up with land transfers where John's widow and children signed their property over to James. Later James and his wife Mary signed the consolidated property back over to his half-brother. The search was over. — Robert E. Wallace, IL, bwal123@aol.com

Alas, An Alias

My grandfather, who I never knew, died in the Chillicothe Veterans Hospital in Ohio in 1960. According to his death certificate he was at the same hospital from 1926 until his death more than 30 years later. Also on the death certificate the years of military service were recorded. So I asked NARA's National Personnel Records Center's Military Personnel Records for a complete copy of his military records. They told me I needed a Social Security number or military number to access records.

My brickwall was that there was no social security number recorded on the death certificate or any number listed in the SSDI. By 1936 he had been in the hospital for 10 years and there was no one to file for social security for him, or no need for one. For the military number, I wrote the Chillicothe Veterans' Hospital with my dilemma. They destroyed any records from before 1963 and no longer had his records to even find a military number for him. They searched their computer and found nothing but a medical number but felt it pertained to their in-house system and would not help obtain a military number. I sent to the National Military Archives copies of my first request, death certificate (highlighting his death date in Veterans' Hospital, military service dates and no social security number) along with a copy of the hospital's response. He had to be in the military service to have spent his life in a veteran's hospital. They told me no records were found. I requested military pension records but nothing was found.

Out of desperation, with copies of my requests, documents and responses in chronological order, I politely wrote the Governor of Ohio's Office. I received a nice reply from the Governor's Office of Veterans' stating my dilemma was being researched but the period of time my grandfather served was considered peacetime and more difficult.

After a few months, I received a 65-page complete copy of his Amry military records from Special Dept. Manager of the National Military Archives. He served two hitches in the Amry, 1914-18 and 1923-24 under an alias! The military file contained signatures of family members' signatures proving his true identity. — Helen A. Batko, OH

First Time Lucky

I had the church record for the birth of my second-great-grandfather. This gave me the names of his parents. I then began a search for the marriage record and found it. But it showed my second-great-grandfather married a widow, Katherine. The record gave details of the parents of the groom. The bride's information was a terse "widow of Johan Knapp." Not much to go on.

After many months the wall crumbled. I had the idea to look up her first marriage. In the 1790s a woman did not stay unmarried for long, especially if she had kids. I found a Katherine married to a Johan Knapp, then found his death date. He had died a few months before she remarried. Her first marriage gave information on her parents and date of birth. It is so obvious now. — J.W. Rettig, OH

Family Photographs

I was stuck on, and really didn't want to work on, Thomas Smith. From his daughter's death certificate, I had a clue to search around Brazil, IN. It wasn't until I inherited the family photographs of several generations that I discovered a picture of Hester A. Smith.

Hettie A. Smith, mother of Thomas Smith, taken shortly before her death in 1892.

On the reverse of a cabinet mount photograph, Hester had inscribed, "Your mother, Hettie A. Smith, age 75 years". The cardboard mount gave the name and location of the photographer in Brazil, IN.

I researched when cabinet mounted photographs were available and made an educated guess for an approximate date based on her clothing. Armed with that information, I went to the Indiana census information and found a Hettie Ann Smith, living in Clay county, IN of the right age. A letter to the Clay County Genealogical Society gave me enough information to determine this was, indeed, Tom Smith's mother. Clay county land records had a partition that named all of Hester's heirs, including Tom Smith. I've since searched a couple more generations past Hester and her husband, Andrew Jackson Smith.

Reverse of photograph of Hettie Smith. Written at the top "Your mother, Hettie A. Smith, age 75 years".

Family photographs, especially the identified ones, are a gold mine.
— Mary Clement Douglass, CGRS, KS

The Ancestry Of William Meacham

It cannot be said too often: consult the originals. My breakthrough came when I was seeking a reference wrongly indexed, about an entry wrongly summarized in a respected publication.

Recently, a distant cousin sent me what he believed was our ancestry all the way back to 1541 in England. Unfortunately, I found later that much of the information claimed for the 16th, 17th and some of the 18th centuries was erroneous and my line could be established only back to William Meacham Sr. who died in 1808 in Chatham county, NC. This would emerge as my major brickwall, as there is no documentary evidence for William Sr.'s date or place of birth or his parents. The main work on Meacham genealogy, Clarence Mitcham's self-published 1971 book *Meacham, Mitcham, Mitchum — Families Of The South*, deals with descendants of the eight children of William Sr. and his wife Elizabeth. It is an enormously valuable resource, but disappointing in the way it treats the founding ancestors William and Elizabeth. Clarence begins with a statement that William's parents were Henry Meacum and Frances Banks and his date of birth is estimated as 1720-25. Both statements proved on examination to be mere guesswork. Another Meacham researcher, in a widely circulated genealogy, put William Sr. under a different set of parents, James and Mary Meacham of Middlesex county, VA, and his birth date as 12 July 1718, but alas this also proved to be speculation. Nonetheless, these two competing versions gained wide distribution and are still encountered today in many articles and websites.

The most likely ancestry of William came to me in a flash, after staring the evidence in the face for more than a year. The clue was in William's wife Elizabeth, namely who she was, and more importantly, who she was not. Clarence Mitcham and everyone since labeled her as Elizabeth Crutchfield, but that was questionable. He wrote: "It is quite possible that Elizabeth Meacham's maiden name was Crutchfield, since William Meacham's will is signed by Thomas Crutchfield and Anderson Crutchfield. Two professional genealogists have told me that a will or deed was almost always witnessed by a relative."

Other evidence is that John Crutchfield sold William a tract of land in North Carolina in 1790. This certainly indicates a strong relationship between William Sr. and the Crutchfields. The problem lay in trying to identify his wife with any known Elizabeth Crutchfield. A lengthy correspondence with a Crutchfield researcher convinced me that the Crutchfield family trees are fairly well documented and there is no Elizabeth who fits the profile of William's wife.

Then there was the curious fact of a Joseph Meacham who married an Elizabeth Crutchfield, as recorded in Middlesex county on 9 January 1728. This fact bothered me; multiple marriages between clans are common, but to find two Elizabeth Crutchfields both marrying Meachams at around the same time seemed highly improbable.

There was a Joseph Mitcham/ Meacham in Caroline county, VA from the 1740s. He is mentioned occasionally in county court records, often in association with Crutchfields. And the executor of his will was wife Elizabeth. So there was a Crutchfield connection through the wife of Joseph. There are references to William Sr. in Caroline county from 1761 to 1775, when he moved to Chatham county, NC. The close links with the Crutchfields, some of whom also had moved to the same county,

carried on, with the sale of the land and the witnessing of his will. The more I considered Clarence's statement — "professional genealogists have told me that a will or deed was almost always witnessed by a relative" — the more perplexing the situation seemed.

Then eureka! William's first son was named Joseph. William's father was Joseph. This would explain the close bond to the Crutchfields, his mother being Elizabeth Crutchfield. If this lineage is true, it could also explain the naming of William's first daughter Jane, as Joseph's mother was a Jane. Several sources give the date of Joseph's death as 1765. I found the following item in T.E. Campbell's book *Colonial Caroline — A History Of Caroline County, Virginia*: in 1765 Joseph Meacham is listed as deceased and the executors of his estate are Joseph and Elizabeth Meacham. I then attempted to locate the original source for this data. Assuming it must have been the Caroline county court records, I found an index that gave two relevant references for 1765: Elizabeth Mitchum 8 September 1765 and 9 December 1765. Neither of these had any mention of Joseph. I then resolved, in order to find the reference to Joseph's will, to read all the original text of the court order books for 1765. This was a daunting task, for the pages are often faded, the script faint and the handwriting difficult to decipher. After several hours, I found it. The first sentence set my heart racing.

"The last will and testament of Joseph Meacham Deceased was brought into Court by Elizabeth Meacham Executrix and William Meacham Executor therein named..." The practice was that a man's widow and/or his eldest son would be named the executors of his estate. It was not an ironclad rule and it is not proven beyond doubt that William was not his cousin. But combined with the other information, the evidence is compelling that William was the son of Joseph and Elizabeth, born after the family moved to Caroline county. Having broken through this barrier, several generations were added to my Meacham line, thanks to the surviving register of Christ Church parish in Middlesex county. — William F. Meacham Jr., TN

The Birthday Surprise

My mother was a Croy. Her father died when she was four months old, leaving her mother with two small children in East St. Louis, IL. Unfortunately, my maternal grandfather, Calvin Croy also lost a parent at a very young age. His mother, Mattie, had died when his younger brother was born in Tennessee in the late 1890s. To complicate matters, Calvin's father, William B. Croy remarried when Calvin was young and wandered a lot, reportedly back to Ohio where he had kin. We didn't even know when or where he died.

Jerri E. Sudderth's mother, Gerealdine Croy Eoff, c. 1945.

By this time all the central characters in this tale had died, save my mother. She had no memories of her father and only scant memories of cousins in Tennessee. Whenever I told her about some new genealogical discovery, she would ask about the Croys. I couldn't find William B. Croy anywhere. I checked with every online research site to find clues and went wherever they led. Every time I found a Croy I asked about William B. but there were no responses that helped.

After years of looking, my daughter called to say she had received a message on her answering machine from a man named William B. Croy in Tennessee. He left a phone number. I tried all day to reach him. Finally, early in the evening, he answered. I identified myself and he responded, "You were looking in the wrong place. Your great-grandfather was my grandfather. And I was named after him." The only remaining first cousin of my mother was, like me, interested in genealogy. He spotted one of my messages and traced me. He called my daughter's house by mistake... but left the right message! We talked for half an hour. He knew of my mother, her deceased brother and mother, and had even met my father.

Finally, he asked if my mother was still living. He asked permission to call her, which he did as a surprise for her birthday! — Jerri E. Sudderth, MN

Send For The Will

I always assumed my husband's third-great grandfather had only one son, John Jr. I could not find any information on John Sr. except in the 1850 and 1860 censuses. I knew even less information about John Jr., except his marriage date that a relative provided me with. John Sr.'s wife's name was Anna and that is all I could find about her. It was a huge brickwall.

Then I found out they were buried at Ivy Hill Cemetery in Philadelphia. Here I learned Anna Sibel had been removed from another cemetery in Philadelphia. So we don't even known when she died — only when she was removed and buried at Ivy Hill.

I sent for his death certificate. All it said was that he died on November 1889; it didn't give me any other information, not even his wife's name. His naturalization papers had the name John Sibal, but his death certificate said Sibel. The tombstone I found spelt his last name Seibel.

So I was then back where I started. Recently there was a death in the family and the will was contested. I then decided to send for John Sr.'s will. When it came back he not only had John Jr., but seven other children. I had seven other families to look for! I eventually found Anna's maiden name on another son's death certificate.

You should send for the will because the person you are looking for has actually written it, not someone else like the birth or death certificate, plus the spouse's name is usually on the will too. — Mary Jo Sibel, PA

Write To The Chamber Of Commerce

My mother had told me her grandparents, John and Mary Gannon, lived near Peterborough, ON and that there was a swinging bridge over water to get to their house.

All normal inquiries came up negative. When I found a notation that said my grandmother, Margaret Gannon, went to school in Lindsay, ON, I found the town in the atlas but

nothing else of any help. I decided to write to the Chamber of Commerce in Lindsay with my problem. I wasn't even sure there was a Chamber of Commerce but I was stumped! Within two weeks I was sent a map, highlighted with the place, Gannon Village, Ennismore, where my grandmother was born. I had names and addresses of churches in the area and pictures of the school my grandmother attended and a letter stating there had been a swinging bridge.

Homestead of the Gannons. Annie, Mary and Michael Gannon are seated on the house's porch.

I wrote to the Catholic Church in Ennismore and was told there were no Gannons on the registry but that the secretary had found the name, first initial only, of a Gannon in a nursing home in Peterborough that might be the family in question. I wrote a letter to the individual, who showed my letter to her niece. The niece wrote me and she turned out to be my second cousin! I now have the family from the great-grandparents down to the present day. — Kathleen Maher, CA

Follow The Females

Tracing female ancestors can be so difficult that a number of how-to books have been written on the subject. In our case, researching the male children failed to reveal their father's name and it was through the widow and female children that we broke through our brickwall for the Se(a)ver(s) family.

In October of 1821, a Henry Seaver died intestate and unmarried, leaving his brothers and sisters as heirs. A Wythe county, VA court case, Chapman vs. Seaver, dealing with the disposition of Henry Seaver's estate names his full siblings as Joseph, John, William C., Jeremiah and Susanna Seaver and states their parents are deceased; also named are Henry's half-sisters: Betsey, Matilda and Nancy Seaver. In the court case, John Seaver, a co-defendant, clearly states his brother died intestate without wife or child and that their parents are deceased. Additionally John states that he, Joseph, William C. and Jeremiah are all brothers of Henry, that Susanna Seaver is a sister of Henry, and Betsey, Matilda and Nancy are sisters of the half blood, but that all are heirs of Henry. We knew Betsey, Matilda and Nancy were children of a second wife because of their ages.

It seemed that with the names of eight children, the names of the parents would be readily available. Such was not the case. Three Bibles given to the Smyth county Historical and Museum Society of Marion, VA by a descendant of John Seaver, provided the dates of birth and death of several of the siblings, but did not include the names of the parents.

We learned that first Joseph and later Jeremiah Seaver moved to Hawkins county, TN, where they raised their families. William C. and John Seaver remained in Wythe county, where John died in 1835 and William C. died in 1869. Records indicate Susanna was living in Indiana during the settlement of Henry Seaver's estate between 1822 and 1825; to date no more is known of her.

The widow and half-sisters were conspicuous by their absence from Wythe county records after the court actions dealing with Henry Seaver's estate. Looking at other counties in

southwestern Virginia, in the 1830 federal census for Scott county, VA, a Peggy Seavers appears as head of household with three female children, who could have been Betsey, Matilda and Nancy. Scott county, VA borders on Hawkins county, TN where at least two of the Seaver siblings moved. A search of Scott county marriage records revealed the marriage of Elizabeth Seavers to James Cleek in 1833. The 1850 federal census for Scott county, VA included a Margaret Seavers, age 75, living with a Nancy, age 37. Living nearby was the family of James and Elizabeth Cleek, age 42. Knowing Peggy was a nickname for Margaret, having the marriage record of Elizabeth Seavers to James Cleek and seeing the match of the half-sisters' names made us believe that we had located the stepmother and two of the half-sisters.

The brickwall came tumbling down when we saw the 1859 death record of Margaret Cleek Seavers naming William Severs as her husband. The informant was listed as James Cleek, her son-in-law. Additional information on the death certificate indicated Margaret was born in Hawkins county, TN and her parents were Michael and Margaret Cleek.

We learned one must search all records for clues and sometimes one must follow the females to find the answer. — Patricia Seaver, TN, Angie Georgeoff, OH and Jane S. Fairburn, SC

How I Solved A Brickwall For A Distant Cousin

In the summer of 1980 my great-aunt passed away. Her husband, my grandfather's brother, was alone as they didn't have any children. In a discussion before the funeral he told me to stop by and we would discuss the family. However, within a few months he became ill and died. My father was in charge of the estate. Going through papers at the house, my father found some family notes and gave them to me. At the time I really didn't think too much about them, but five years later I got them out. I started reading them. A woman from Indiana with the same surname had written to my great-uncle in 1975. My maiden name is not a very common name so when you see it, you wonder if there's some relation. This lady was searching for her great-grandfather and second-great-grandfather. All she knew was that at one time they were in Indiana. After reading the papers very carefully and knowing what I had on the family at that time, I finally saw a connection. She and I share the same second-great-grandfather, she by the first wife and me by the second. My great-uncle didn't know anything about his grandparents since they both died before he was born. I took a chance by calling telephone information to find this woman.

She was still at the same number. We talked and I told her what happened after her second-great-grandparents were divorced. Our second-great-grandfather moved to Jersey county, IL from Tippecanoe county, IN. When he moved he took his eldest son with him. At some point the boy returned to Indiana where he married. He died while his children were still young. However, his great-granddaughter, the woman from Indiana, could never find a burial site for him. I visited the cemetery where her grandparents are buried and just happen to locate the caretaker. He showed us the records and it turned out her great-grandfather is buried in his in-laws' plot in an unmarked grave. I knew our second-great-grandfather moved from Jersey county to Madison county. I obtained records from one cemetery by accident and when reviewing them found

my second-great-grandparents buried there. So now my third cousin and I know where our second-great-grandfather is buried. — Debbi Geer, MO

Travel To Your Ancestors' Birthplaces

I had the obituary for my second-great-grandfather, Thomas William Ryan. He was murdered along with one of his daughters and granddaughters. I had read this story when I was young but now as an adult and addicted to genealogy, I decided to find him.

I had some pedigree charts and family charts on the Ryan family given to me by a distant cousin who was now deceased. I decided I would continue the work. I knew the family was from County Tipperary. My husband and I were going to Ireland the following year.

Killenaule parish church where Margaret Cleary was baptized and later married Thomas Ryan.

The first half of the year I collected records of the Ryan family after they had come to the US sometime before 1850. They were a family of six. I was lucky as Thomas settled and stayed in Chester, IL. I had census, marriage, naturalization, death and cemetery records. I did not have a passenger ship record. The NARA could not find him in the time frame I had. I sent $150 to three Heritage Centers in

County Tipperary asking for their records. Two of the three replied without finding this family.

I felt I might have some success in contacting the other branches of Thomas' family. There were originally four daughters. One was my great-grandmother; one had died with Thomas. Two daughters were left that had descendants that might be able to help me.

I first tried to contact my Burdorff cousins who were the same branch as myself; my letter came back unopened. On the Internet White Pages directory I found 10 more Burdorffs. I wrote to every one. Through phone calls and e-mails we discovered they had the same information as myself, no more. The other two branches were Kennedy and Monahgan. I had already placed messages all over the Internet under both surnames to no avail.

I could not believe I would go to Ireland without the information I needed. I sat on the floor and went through my Ryan file. I went through every single piece of paper looking for something I had missed. I found a handwritten piece of paper with a list of Thomas William Ryan's family; daughters, who they married and their children and sometimes grandchildren and who they married. I found two more surnames for contact; Prost and Tackleberry.

I returned to the White Pages directory and typed Prost and Tackleberry. I picked five of each surname that had e-mails, choosing states close to where the Ryans had lived. A day later I received a reply from someone who lived in Germany! He was the host of a Prost message center and gladly posted my e-mail to his 40 subscribers. From there came a reply from a distant cousin. I did not have any positive results from the Tackleberrys.

The Prost cousin said he was indeed related but didn't know anything but would talk to his mother.

Finally this cousin's mother kindly e-mailed me but she didn't know anything either but she would ask her sister. Three days before we were to leave for Ireland another kind cousin e-mailed me with the information that the Ryan family came from Coleraine, Duella, and County Tipperary.

Cemetery at Dually called Kilhillsberry, County Tipperary.

From there, with the help of IreAtlas Townland Database online and the host, we were able to go directly to Duella, County Tipperary. It was only through his help that we were able to decipher the townland and parish as the spelling had been changed through time. He had Catholic Church directories, which included the priests' names. He explained Duella was not a Civil Parish but an Ecclesiastic Parish. In the mid-1800s the daughters would have given their church parish as part of their birthplace. It is common today to use the Civil Parish in a birthplace.

The Bishop of the Diocese has the copyrights for the records in this parish and all the parishes in this specific Diocese in County Tipperary. Genealogical organizations and even the Government of Ireland cannot copy them. You will not find them at the FHL or at the National Library in Dublin. They can only be accessed through Heritage Centers for a fee. The one heritage center that didn't get back to me had these records. With a name like Thomas Ryan and their records collectively combined with all parishes in the Diocese on the computer, finding my one and only Ryan would have been questionable.

It was only by visiting the parish priest that we obtained the information on Thomas' family. We found two more children for Thomas, the marriage record for Thomas and his wife's baptism, which included her birth date and the names of her parents in a nearby parish. Each parish we visited had a local historian who gave us records and histories for their entire parish. In some cases, records that had never been published but were kept in a church basement. I never would have found my family if I had not gone to Ireland in person. — Patricia Ellis Fenn, MT, pfenn@digisys.net

Figuring Out The Math

For 20 years I was unsuccessful in tracing my Barrett ancestors beyond Richard Barrett and his wife, Martha Redman. They both reported their birthplace as Montgomery county, MD. A trip to the Montgomery County Historical Society in Rockville, MD produced various records on other Barretts and Redmans, but not Richard and Martha.

Several years ago I got an idea. Richard and Martha were born in 1818 and married in Montgomery county in October 1840. Thus, they should be categorized in the Montgomery county censuses as children less than 10 years old in 1820 and as being between 20 and 30 years old in 1840. Examining the 1820 federal census for Montgomery county, I found only two Redman families, that of Jesse K. Redman and Josiah Redman. Both families included a female less than 10 years old. A search of the 1840 census for Montgomery county revealed two Redman families, Joseph W. Redman and Josiah W. Redman, but only the Josiah W. Redman family included a female age 20 to 30. Thus only the Josiah Redman family met the search criteria for both the 1820 and 1840 censuses. Further research on the Josiah Redman family revealed that his wife was Anne Orme and his mother was Cloe Wynn. As Richard and Martha named their first child Imogene Orme and their second daughter Chloe, it seems convincing that I have found the ancestry of Martha Redman. Using this information I was able to trace several lines of Martha's family.

Trying the same approach on Richard was not as successful. No Barrett family reported a boy less than 10 years old in the 1820 census and a male age 20 to 30 in the 1840 census. This was expected, as it is likely that a son age 22 might not be living with his parents. — Richard E. Barrett, OH, rebarrett@compuserve.com

Microfilm Mistakes

I ran into one of my brickwalls while I was searching for the funeral notice of my second-great-uncle Michael J. Lynch, who died in Cohoes, NY on 23 February 1923. Under the circumstances I should have given up but I persisted. Eventually I found the notice, which was on microfilm at the New York State Library in Albany, but only after using a most illogical method.

I was doing research on my second-great-uncle primarily to find more information on his brother and my great-grandfather, Samuel James Lynch. The obituary of Michael J. Lynch which appeared in the city's only newspaper at the time, *The Cohoes American*, revealed to my surprise that he was my great-grandfather's half-brother. Therefore finding the funeral notice became important in the hopes that the names of one of the pallbearers or family members in attendance might shed light on the half-brother discovery.

OBITUARY

Funeral of Michael J. Lynch
The funeral of Michael J. Lynch was held this morning from the residence of his daughter, Mrs. James Croteau, 28 Factory street, at 9 o'clock and at 9:30 from St. Bernard's church where a high mass of requiem was sung by Rev. John F. McDonald, assistant pastor. There was a large attendance. At the offertory, Mrs. Catherine Heffern-Cooley sang "Pie Jesu" and at the conclusion of the mass "Lead, Kindly Light." The bearers were James Maloney, James Ryan, John Ryan, sr., Michael Reilly, Thomas Purner and James Killian. The body was placed temporarily in the vault in Calvary cemetery.

The hard-to-find funeral notice for Michael J. Lynch.

According to the 24 February 1923 issue of *The Cohoes American*, the funeral for Michael J. Lynch was to be held on 27 February. However, I checked all the issues for this daily paper up to 7 March of that year and found nothing. In between every other issue appeared a note that there were mutilated issues. Therefore it seemed that either the funeral notice was not published or it had been in one of these missing pages and not microfilmed. Out of desperation or stubbornness I rewound the reel scanning even the issues prior to my uncle's death. As the reel contained daily issues from 2 January through 30 April 1923, I was not about to search the entire reel but did continue my search to the beginning of February hoping that perhaps mutilated issues might have also meant misplaced issues as well.

Then, after the front page of 2 February, I was surprised to find the entire issue of 27 February. On page eight (which in spite of everything else was mislabeled 26 February 1923) I found what I was looking for!

Near the top of the page under Obituary was the funeral notice of my second-great-uncle. Although nothing in the notice explained the half-brother issue it did reinforce for me that when doing genealogical research anything is possible and that one must be very determined and creative during one's searches. — Edward John Dudek, Jr., NY

A Single Generation May Be Just As Hard

We have had a terrible time locating any concrete information about my grandparents, we didn't even know where to look, when exactly they were born or even what their parents' names were. You'd think that with just a single generation between us, it would be easy.

The problem was that things happened that people didn't talk about back then. My grandfather left my grandmother, there was rumor of a divorce, etc., so much information was lost to tight lips. There was also a fire in the oldest son's home that destroyed what written documents were around. My sister unwittingly solved all our problems when she wrote to the Veterans Administration and was able to obtain a complete copy of the grandfather's file. It had his death certificate, medical file, mother's name and maiden name (which was different than what we had been told), birth date and all the detailed nurses' notes preceding his death. The file is incredibly detailed, even the checklist regarding his regulation placement in the coffin was included.

It told us what line of work he had been in and that he had a child from a second marriage. The woman who thought she was his widow and filed for his death benefits was quite surprised to find he had left a wife and three kids on the east coast, before marrying her on the west coast. All ensuing paperwork is included, about three inches worth; there are handwritten letters from our grandmother to the Veterans Administration which gave us a window into what her life had been like raising three kids on her own in the 1940s. We also found a form in which she had to fill out her birth date and place, which we had never found before.

She also told exactly when and where they were married and even the street address of the church where they were married in 1919. This has been the best thing that we've come across so far. — MB

Will The Real James Barnwell Mills Step Up?

A family legend, told often during my growing-up years in New Orleans, identified my great-grandfather, James Barnwell Mills, M.D., of Alabama, as the son of Robert Mills, architect of the Washington Monument and other magnificent structures. When I became interested in family history, I found that Robert Mills and Eliza Barnwell Smith had only four daughters to reach maturity. Under these constraints, the Mills name could not have been passed along to a descendant.

Author Helen M. Gallagher writes that Robert Mills befriended a widow by choosing "a man child from her flock of girls and boys to become his adopted son. Later this adopted son became known as Dr. James Mills, and, as another genealogical record shows, he was also known as Robert Mills. But any further knowledge of him is missing in the annals of the family" (*Robert Mills, Architect Of The Washington Monument*). Dr. Mills may not be in the annals of Robert Mills' family, but he is in my annals as my great-grandfather.

Augusta Barsha (Norfleet) Mills, at about age 47 with son Ernest LeGarde Mills and second husband Robert A. Dimitry.

Blanche Marsh in her book, *Robert Mills, Architect In South Carolina*, says that around 1820 Robert Mills and Eliza Barnwell Smith were returning to South Carolina and there were five children in their family: Sarah Jane, Jacqueline Smith, Mary Powell, Anne and James. She also mentions that the boy was named James Finegan, but this could not have been my great-grandfather, who was not born until c. 1836. I found in the Dimitry Papers in Tulane University Library, New Orleans, a note that suggests James Barnwell Mills may have been born James Finegan, who was adopted by Robert Mills.

James Barnwell Mills and Augusta Barsha Norfleet were married on 12 May 1869. In the 1880 federal census, James, age 45, and Augusta, age 32, were living in Greene county, AL. Three daughters and a son named Robert Dimitry Mills were listed with them. In addition, "nephew" Robert Dimitry, age 32, born in Louisiana, was living with them. This Robert Andrea Dimitry was the son of Alexander Dimitry and Mary Powell Mills, a daughter of Robert Mills and Eliza Barnwell Smith.

For the 1900 federal census in Jackson county, MS, Augusta B.

Dimitry, age 52, is living at Round Island Light Station, Pascagoula, Jackson county, with Robert A. Dimitry, age 51. She has been married to Robert for six years. In her child-bearing years she has had eight children, six of whom were living in 1900.

I have worked my way through several brickwalls in this search, but there always seems to be a brickwall to follow. In this case, the new brickwall prevents me from knowing who James Barnwell Mills really was, but I know who he isn't and I'm working on it. — Ralph Tabor Williams, HI

Finding The Missing Parents

For years I was searching for the parents of my third-great-grandfather, William Snowdon of Sunderland, Durham, England. I had two sets of parents for him and proving which set belonged to my William became quite the challenge. From the baptismal register for Bishopwearmouth, Sunderland, I found the following William Snowdon, born on 17 December 1809, son of William Snowdon, native of Hartlepool and Elizabeth, his wife, late Robinson, native of Bishopwearmouth. However, from the IGI I found a William Snowdon christened on 2 August 1812 to William Snowdon and Ann Wilkinson, which meant his birth was any time before then.

My second-great-grandfather Michael Snowdon, son of William, moved to Hartlepool, Durham, around the early 1870s. There were only two instances of the forename Michael being connected to the Snowdon surname in Durham. They could be found in Hartlepool and Ryton. I started to believe William's parents were William Snowdon and Elizabeth Robinson because there was a connection to Hartlepool, even though the dates didn't fit that well.

Along with the baptismal records I obtained the following information for my William from the Trafalgar Square Records 1839-56, which are records from retirement homes for seamen and/or dependents giving subsistence allowance and seaman service: "April 1847, William Swondon, age 35, 3 children, abode Sunderland. Master of the Glider, on voyage to Limerick in March 1846 caught severe cold. Certified by Thos Parker, suffering from a disease of the heart causing asthma. Is not probable that he will be able to resume his duties for a long time."

William's death certificate stated he died 4 November 1847 at the age of 36. So then I took his age in April 1847 of 35 years and his age in November 1847 of 36. This ruled out William and Elizabeth Robinson because their William was born 17 December 1809. This left William and Ann Wilkinson as the only set of parents that could possibly be the parents of my William Snowdon. — Jayne McHugh, ON, spiregen@webcomcreations.com

Ring Around The Family

Back in the 1930s a genealogist had tried to find the Hillier family in Wiltshire, UK. I thought I was lucky to have this genealogist's work and tried to build on it. Like her I hit a brickwall.

Finally I made myself forget all that the previous genealogist had done and made a fresh start.

The last accurate record of the Hilliers was in Marshfield, Gloucestershire, UK in the late 1830s showing the baptisms of some of their children. I realized I needed to look at the 1841 census for Marshfield and this would not have been done previously as the other genealogist was doing her research before the 1841 census was available. In no time I had the family. However, the family was not in Marshfield in the 1851 census.

One day I was reading a history book and it mentioned a drought in the central and western part of England in the late 1840s. My family were shepherds so no doubt my third-great-grandfather lost his job due to the drought and had to move away.

I drew a circle around Marshfield, Gloucestershire and started the laborious task of looking at every parish in an ever-increasing circle around Marshfield for my family. My patience and endurance was rewarded when I found them in Kingston, Wiltshire and the 1851 census gives the place of birth for the parents.

Now I know the Hilliers came from Bishops Cannings, Wiltshire and I have found the family back to the 1600s. — Pamela Voss, BC

Don't Overlook Anything

About 11 years ago I became interested in genealogy. I started slowly by researching only the direct lines of my parents. I began with an oral history of our family. Our local library located in Anniston, AL has an excellent genealogy research facility. I found my mother's family had already been researched and was well documented. While researching my father's family, however, I encountered my brickwall.

My grandfather, John Winston Gabriel, knew his grandparents' names but didn't have any further information about his family. His grandfather, Elijah Gabriel, died as a POW at Camp Douglas near Chicago, IL during the US Civil War and his wife, Mary Henson Gabriel, died in childbirth before the war ended. Their four children went to live with an aunt and uncle so not much family history was passed down.

My research started with the census records from Alabama, Georgia and South Carolina, but I didn't find any additional family information. I checked the Civil War records for Alabama units and found that Elijah Gabriel had several spelling variations of his surname. After learning this I checked the census records again. This time I found Elijah and his siblings living with their mother Rutha Gable.

Rutha Gable was listed as the head of the household in the 1840 federal census for Heard county, GA and the 1850 federal census for Randolph county, AL. This information did not provide me with her husband's name so I had to do some detective work. Rutha was probably a widow, and based on her children's ages her husband would have died between 1832 and 1840. She was first listed as head of household living in Heard county, GA and several of her children were born in Georgia. Many families named their eldest son for the father or grandfather and I knew Jacob was the name of Rutha's oldest son. I kept this information in the back of my mind when I checked county histories, marriage records, tax lists, deeds and other records. I just couldn't find any further information on my family.

Georgia Journal
LEGAL NOTICES

Georgia, Carroll County: **Smith Drinkard** applies for letters of administration on the estate of **Jacob Gable**, late of said county, deceased. (Signed) **William L. Parr**, C.C.O.

Thursday, October 10, 1839

This small legal notice helped Deborah Gabriel overcome her brickwall connecting her family with the Gable line that they descended from.

Years went by but I never gave up. One day I was doing research at the library using the Georgia section of reference books, when I was drawn to three volumes of books. The three volumes were *Genealogical Abstracts From The Georgia Journal (Milledgeville) Newspaper, 1809-1840*. My heart raced because I had a feeling I would find my family information in one of the three books. These abstracts provided information on deaths, marriages, divorces, sheriff's sales, administrator's sales and other legal notices.

While scanning through the books, I found a legal notice from Smith Drinkard, Sheriff of Carroll county, GA applying for letters of administration on the estate of Jacob Gable in 1839. Georgia's Carroll and Heard counties border each other and I knew this information fit with my previous research on Rutha Gable and her family.

After finding this information, I was determined to prove Jacob Gable was Rutha's husband and father of Elijah. I used the Internet and found Carl Gable's work *The Gable Family Of The South* on Family Tree Maker. In his information I found Jacob Gable had been married twice and his second wife's name was Rutha Eth(e)ridge. Jacob had passed away around 1839 in Carroll county, GA and was buried in the Sweetwater Cemetery. There were no children or any additional information listed for Jacob and Rutha, but I had proof that they had at least five children.

I contacted Carl Gable and submitted the information I had compiled on my family. I found that I had numerous new cousins and this family had been traced back to Germany.

Now I never overlook any resource no matter how insignificant it may appear to be. — Deborah Gabriel, AL

Those Pesky Vowels

I found my second-great-grandparents, Richard and Lucy Allen, in the 1841 British census in Birmingham, Warwickshire. From the parish register of St. Martin's Church, Birmingham, I knew their first child, John, was born on 19 June 1825 and baptized in 1830. I needed to find the marriage of Richard and Lucy, without knowing Lucy's maiden name. Following the good practice of family

history research, I always searched indexes for all the variant spellings of Allen I could think of — Al(l)en Al(l)in, Al(l)an, Al(l)eyn, Al(l)eyne and so on. I searched the IGI without success, not only for Warwickshire, but also neighboring counties. I also covered a range of dates, in case there was a child before John, or Richard and Lucy had not married until later. I then had searches made of the marriage indexes of these neighboring counties, where they existed, but again without success.

The 1841 British census record for 8 House, 2 Court, Dartmouth Street, Aston, Birmingham.

Finally, I turned to London, where some of the couple's sons had married in the late 1850s, but again could not find the marriage. I had run out of ideas and decided Richard and Lucy had possibly never married. Then I read an article that said surnames beginning with a vowel are often misspelled in records by being given a preceding consonant and that a very common consonant in this situation is H. I went straight back to the Warwickshire IGI and found the marriage immediately: Richard Hallen married Lucy Egginton on 21 February 1825, at Aston, near Birmingham. When Richard gave his name, it must have sounded to the vicar like Hallen. — Rosemary Jenkins, North Yorkshire, UK

Jim Rockford Would Be Proud

With the theme from *The Rockford Files* in my mind, I decided to tackle the brickwall on an 80-plus-year-old mystery.

How did I expect to find an ancestor when others had tried for 20 years or more? The missing ancestor grew up and married young in a large town in Oklahoma. He was divorced by his first wife, married a second time and moved to Houston, TX and changed his name. Those were my only clues.

The 1920 Oklahoma census Soundex was used to locate my subject. Only now he had a new wife, with two daughters who could not be his children due to their ages. I obtained the couple's marriage record and learned the wife's previous married name. I checked the city directories. They were not listed in the 1924 city directory. Was this the year they moved to Houston?

The family was not listed in the Houston city directories before or after 1924. Was the family history correct? Was this the year the name was changed? The brickwall was growing in front of my eyes.

I checked the SSDI. No one by that name and age was there. But while I was in the SSDI, I decided to check on his wife. She did not appear either. Remembering the marriage record, I then inserted the wife's previous married name. There she was!

I went back to the Houston city directories and found them listed under the wife's previous married name, adding new children as they were born.

Using the death date of the wife, I hoped to find an obituary in a Houston newspaper. A generous look-up volunteer provided me with one. No husband was mentioned but many children were listed. A funeral home was listed and with a nervous finger, I dialed the number to ask if this lady's husband was also buried there. The answer was yes. I anxiously noted the information from the funeral home files. The same kind volunteer was able to find an obituary on him, all with their newly assumed name.

Not only did we find our brickwall, we were fortunate to locate the sole surviving child from this second marriage and called him in Houston. We exchanged family information and pictures. A delightful ending to a long and curious search.

It takes many avenues to ferret out a missing relative, many more when they change their names. Census records; marriage records; city directories; newspapers; obituaries; funeral homes; cemeteries; SSDI – all must be checked. And we cannot forget to thank the many kind volunteers who provide us clues and documentation.
— Arlis Renfro, WA

Take A Chance On ".de"

I'd been trying to find the small German town from which an ancestor came from. I just knew it was Baden from a census. I had no contacts in Germany, nor was anyone alive back that far to talk with me. A distant cousin, who is a genealogist, was also stumped on the same ancestor.

I took a chance on the Internet and pulled up a website using Baden.de (.de is the designation for German websites). A screen popped up, which was a tourist/travel advertisement for Baden. Searching this screen, I found an e-mail address. I wrote, begging their pardon that it did not pertain to travel, but that I was searching for my ancestor from Baden. I gave them the name and the details I had. Some kind person put it in the hands of a professional researcher in Germany, who found the ancestor in his files and asked me if I would be willing to pay his fee. Of course, I was!

I received several good newspaper articles on the ancestor, nicely translated — with my ancestor's description, date and town of birth, his wife's and his parents' names. What a find!
— AO

*   *   *

Desperately Seeking Edith

Many genealogists know the challenge of finding women. Edith proved to be my 30-year challenge.

Edith Beal was the wife of a cousin of my father-in-law, Priestly Revitt. Priestly's brother William Dyson Revitt immigrated to Canada from England in 1910 and worked on a farm at Wapella, SK. A cousin, Frank Beal, died in 1918 and William moved to help his widow Edith Beal manage their farm in Laura, SK. The farm prospered and my father-in-law and his wife were invited to come to Canada from England. They arrived in May 1921. The following year, land at Eyre, SK, was advertised for rent. The two Revitt brothers were fortunate to get the half section. Edith sold her quarter section and everyone moved to Eyre. In 1923, Edith left the family in hopes of getting a housekeeping job. The Revitts never heard from her again.

Working from the known to the unknown I requested Frank's burial record by writing to the town clerk at Laura. The reply informed me that Frank had died on 30 May 1918 and was buried in Laura Cemetery. There was no record of Edith's burial. The town clerk kindly forwarded my letter to Mr. Robins who was farming the Beal quarter. Mr. Robins remembered Frank's death and the Revitt brothers farming with Edith, but had no further knowledge of Edith.

Hoping Frank's death registration would help, I filled in the required death form and sent it to Vital Statistics. In receiving the registration I found all to be proven correct. But he had only lived four-and-a-half years at his residence when the time of death occurred, 11 years in the province and 14 years in Canada. Where did he live the other six-and-a-half years?

Time lapsed and new search possi-bilities arose. Through the Saskatchewan Archives Board, I wrote for homestead documents. Photo-copied documents showed that Frank did not homestead land in the Laura District. A married and childless Frank took out a homestead in 1907 at Swanson, SK, and had built a house. More about Frank but still nothing to help me find Edith!

While visiting friends, I was browsing through their Community History Book. The Swanson section had a story about my Beals. I wrote to the author inquiring about Edith. The Beals had been the author's neighbors in Swanson. She knew that they had come from Carman, MB, and that Frank had worked on the railway section. She remembered the Beals moving to Laura and because she had moved to Laura to work, she knew that Frank had passed away and Edith had moved. She knew no more about Edith.

Marriage certificate of Edith Beal and Gilbert Holmes.

In 1986, I put a query into the *Western Producer* magazine. Someone replied. The woman told me she remembered Frank and Edith Beal when she was very young and lived in Swanson. After Frank died, the woman knew Edith had a housekeeping job in Saskatoon. Edith later answered a housekeeping advertisement for a widower Gilbert Holmes who lived in Sovereign, SK. She also remembered Edith marrying Gilbert.

I found another possibility for Edith. Sovereign and District had printed a history book, in the cemetery section, which listed an Edith and

Gilbert Holmes. A history for Gilbert was written listing his children and their whereabouts, but no mention of Edith. I wrote to the daughter in Saskatoon asking about Edith.

A week later I was richly rewarded. Gilbert's daughter sent me Frank and Edith's marriage registration, Frank's death registration, Edith and Gilbert's marriage registration, Edith's death registration, a photo of Edith and a photo of Edith and Gilbert. All were found in Edith's effects after she had passed away. My search for Edith was over. — Dorothy Revitt, SK, dorothyrevitt@sk.sympatico.ca

Don't Beat Your Head Against That Brickwall

My advice to those hitting that brickwall: Don't beat your head against it, just walk away and ignore it for a bit. Come back after you have pursued other leads and try another approach. Go back to your early days of researching and re-read all those bits and pieces of information you gathered but didn't know how to handle.

Very early on, when I revived my interest in my roots (it started as a social studies project in 9th grade), I wrote to my mother's cousin asking for his memories. He was very specific about their shared grandmother who was "a native of Taritara, County Armagh". Good news, I thought, until I discovered that there was no Taritara in County Armagh. I put the letter into the file as I began to chase other Irish ancestors.

A few years later at a seminar hosted by a gentleman from the Ulster Historical Foundation, I asked again about the town and he told me the same, there is no such place. However, he suggested that it just might be a corruption of the proper name since it was passed down orally.

He offered to do a bit of research for me.

Some months later when I had again forgotten about the whole thing, a letter came saying that the best he could do was a town Tataragan in County Armagh, which might or might not be the right one. Off went another letter. A short while later there was Grandmother's marriage record including her maiden name and the names of the couple that stood for them. This whole process took about 20 years, but it was worth it! — Janet R. Enzmann, WA

What Made Him Tick

Aged 51, I decided it was time I learned something of my family background. Having no living grandparents, very little extended family and only a widowed mother, every discovery was like finding a pot of gold.

Marriage certificate for Eric Harle's first marriage.

One day my younger sister knocked me sideways (metaphorically) when she asked me had I ever given any thought to the whereabouts of our half sister and brother; our father's children from his first marriage. I was aware of the marriage from my parents' marriage certificate, but she said our siblings' details were on her birth certificate and she just assumed that I knew what she knew. I did not have a full birth certificate and was totally unaware of any details, let alone names or ages.

Armed with this knowledge I went to the local genealogical library and quickly found the registrations of their births. Once again I was knocked sideways, as they were not registered in the surname of Harle, but of Harle-Cowan, as was my father's first marriage. Apparently, he had a different name then. At that point I applied for my father's birth certificate, his first marriage certificate and the birth certificates of his first two children. The wait for their arrival was nail biting.

Our father had been born Eric Harle to an unwed actress, Sarah Georgina Harle. He was born in Herne Bay, Kent, but her address was in London, in the theatre district. By the time of my father's first marriage he was going by the name of Eric Phroydon Harle-Cowan and he named his father as Edward Harle-Cowan, solicitor, deceased. He was still known by the same name when he registered the birth of his first child. In 1937, when he was divorced, he still had the same name, but by the time of his second marriage in Melbourne, Australia his name had become Eric John Arnold Phroydon Harle and his father was named as Edward Eric Harle, solicitor and his mother Georgina Harle-Cowan.

We were thoroughly confused. My sister was seriously worried about what we would find next and wanted

Eric Harle.

me to stop then and there. I continued with the productive threads along my mother's line, but at the back of my mind there was always this quandary about my father.

Prior to the birth of my first son, Dad had asked me to name him Edward, after his own father. From that we deduced that his father was a solicitor named Edward, but the mother bit was puzzling.

One day, full of resolution, I went to the Postal Museum in Melbourne and perused all the available UK phone books for the name Harle-Cowan. Sure enough, in all of about 40 books, there was only one Harle-Cowan entry. It had to be a relation.

I became sick with apprehension, but my daughter stepped in and rang the number. We were looking for relations or descendants of Eric William Harle-Cowan and the woman who answered was my half-brother's widow. She was amazed and almost speechless. She suggested we ring back in an hour with questions for her and answers to her questions as well.

Among many things she told us was that I had a half-sister in the US, whose address she didn't have.

I kept my sister informed all along the way and could have rested with this discovery for many months, so imagine my surprise when at 6:30 the next morning I received a phone call. A voice said,

"My maiden name was Harle-Cowan. My sister-in-law has rung to say that you are claiming to be my half sister. That could not be correct. My father died in 1938."

Eventually I convinced her that my story was true, but I had to go to work. I finished work at lunchtime and went to my sister's house, where we had a four-way conversation with my half-sister, her husband and the two of us. It was so enlightening and all rather like a fairy tale.

Six months later my husband and I went to Seattle to meet a half sister, 16 years my senior. Six months after that my sister and her husband did the same. They said that it helped them understand their brother, husband and father so much more and it certainly helped me know my father, who in life had been difficult to say the least. Now I feel that I understand a little more what made him tick.

Through my newly found relations, records and books I found so much about my father, his parentage, his upbringing, his running away to join the Navy and his first marriage. Since then, particularly through Internet facilities, I have found ancestors dating back to the 17th century, met many friends and relatives and will have a time-consuming interest for the rest of my life. — Heather Brain, Victoria, Australia.

The Many Wives Of Cassidy

Calvary Cemetery in Queens, NY was a big help learning about Joseph Cassidy's first two families. Speaking on the phone with the sexton I was informed that Joseph Cassidy was buried at Calvary on 16 June 1928. Bridget Cassidy was buried in the same grave on 17 June 1933. Joseph Cassidy purchased the grave on 1 January 1883 for $15. There were six burials in the following years: 1883 (two), 1889 (two), 1928 and 1933. The dates seemed to support the family tradition that there were two previous wives that had died in childbirth. Clearly, the 1928 burial was Joseph and the 1933 burial was Bridget. I did not have the names of the earlier wives or the children. Assuming the children were stillborn, I did not know if they would have names.

The sexton told me that I would have to have a name and a date to learn more about the burials in the plot. Figuring that Joseph would probably not have purchased a grave without needing one, I gave the following information. "I would like burial details for Mrs. Joseph Cassidy and the infant Cassidy buried on 1 January 1883". He checked and found that Margaret Cassidy was buried in the grave on 1 January 1883. He could not find anything on the baby. He could not check the other two without names and dates of death. This puzzled me but led me to check other sources with the limited information I had. Clearly, Margaret Cassidy died at the end of 1882. Getting her death certificate might answer the puzzle.

The first two wives of Joseph Cassidy and their children have been the most interesting people to search in the death records. Knowing from the cemetery that Margaret Cassidy died in late 1882 I checked for her death certificate. Margaret Cassidy died on 29 December 1882 from peritonitis after parturition. My wife, a doctor, suggested that she might have had a Caesarean section, especially in light of the family tradition that she died in childbirth. The doctor cared for her from 22 December to 29 December 1882. Parturition indicated that she had given birth, my wife said.

I wondered then where was the baby? If she had delivered on 22 December then the grave would have been purchased in 1882 to bury the stillborn baby. If she had delivered on the 29th then the baby should have been buried on the same day as Margaret if it had died.

I decided to check the 1883 death index for Cassidy children who would have been born in December 1882. Luckily, there was only one that was a possibility. Mary Cassidy was six months old when she died in late June 1883. Her parents were listed as Joseph and Margaret Cassidy. The address was different than where Margaret died but within a few blocks. I assume she was nursed by a wet nurse and died at her home. Knowing that a doctor had assisted in the delivery I checked the 1882 birth index and found Mary Cassidy was born on 22 December 1882 to Joseph and Margaret (McKeon) Cassidy. This certificate gave quite a bit of information.

Calvary Cemetery certificate.

The death records helped clear away the mystery as to why both burials took place in 1883 but the cemetery could not find baby Cassidy's burial. They were buried six months apart.

The second Mrs. Joseph Cassidy and baby were more of a challenge. I did not know the wife's first name or when she and her baby died. I decided to use the FHL and order the New York City Death Index for 1889. I was nervous that if this woman had died in late December like Margaret Cassidy, then I would have to check the 1888 deaths as well. I was looking through all the female Cassidys who died in 1889 of child-bearing age. Fortunately, only one woman fit this parameter; Ellen Cassidy, age 34. I wrote to the Municipal Archives and

received her death certificate. It said she was the wife of Joseph Cassidy. She had been under the doctor's care for nine months. The 1889 Death Index also had an entry for Ann Cassidy, age 11 months, which proved to be Joseph and Ellen's daughter.

Ultimately I would learn that neither wife nor their daughters had died in childbirth. Margaret Cassidy did die a week later but her daughter Mary lived to be six months old. Ellen Cassidy died nine months after her delivery and her daughter Ann died at 11 months. Both girls were baptized and the names of their godparents proved helpful in my research. — Kevin Cassidy, NE, kmct@earthlink.net

Letters Of Inquiry

After my first year of non-responsive letters of inquiry I began including with my letters two copies of my family tree from my genealogy software. One for them to keep and one asking that they make corrections and additions on the tree and return to me.

With a stamped return envelope the family tree increased my responses dramatically. It makes it easier for them to respond by writing directly on one copy of the tree and helps them visualize how we are related. I always highlight which branch I come from and which is theirs and add any questions I have about various people. I also ask if they do not have their family's genealogy information, if they know of someone else in the family who might have it or has an interest and if I may contact them.

It always surprises me how many people don't think to tell me about someone else in their family doing research until I ask.

I also include a family photo tree which gets attention and generates excitement, especially when they recognize an ancestor or have a photo to add to the gallery. Again, I always ask if they don't have older photos, if there is someone in their family who does.

The last item, which has been helpful, is a return stamped postcard addressed to myself. A pre-printed message says, "I received your inquiry and have reviewed your family tree. Unfortunately we do not appear to be related." My cover letter asks them to drop this postcard in the mail. Knowing someone is not related is as important as knowing who is. — Ann McClary, WA

Great Revelations With Orphans' Court Records

My aunt had, for many years, on the wall of her sitting room, an old sampler with the name "Harriet Darrah" stitched into it and the date "1838". When asked who Harriet was, she would say, "Oh, someone in your grandfather's family." Of course, by the time I became interested, she was the only possible link remaining to those bygone days.

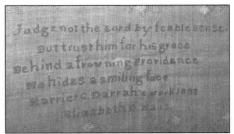

Detail of the sampler that Woodlief Thomas' aunt had on her wall with the name "Harriet Darrah" stitched into it and the date "1838".

In all my research into my Darrah family direct line, including aunts, uncles and cousins, I never came across a Harriet, until 1996. In the Spruance Library of the Bucks County Historical Society in Doylestown, PA, I found a reference to a death notice for a Miss Harriet Darrah who died 1 December 1859 in Doylestown and was interred in Doylestown Cemetery.

The next appearance of Harriet came in late 1997, at the Bucks County Court House, in the "Settlement of the Estate of Thomas Darrah, late of Bedminster Township, dec'd" as a line item: "Harriet Darrah acct. 30.00". Thomas Darrah is my third-great-grandfather, thus finally suggesting a family link, but what type of link was not at all clear.

A few years later, I was again in the Spruance Library in Doylestown, PA, where I found a new book, published recently: *Bucks County, Pennsylvania, Orphans' Court Records 1685-1852* by Thomas G. Meyers. I located from the index all the references to Darrah and found: "File #6054, Feb 1, 1847, Thomas Darrah, Bedminster Twp. Widow Susanna and eight children: Mark, James, Joel, Thomas, Nancy, Harriet, Martha and Andrew Jackson, last two minors." Now I had it. Harriet was a daughter of my third-great-grandfather, a step-sister (as it turns out) of my second-great-grandfather, James — a maiden third-great-aunt!

Until this discovery, I was not aware of the power of the records of the Orphans' Courts. Great revelations can be obtained there about the composition of families: wives' names (unfortunately not usually maiden names), marriages of daughters and their husbands' names and inferences as to the ages of children in that the court had to appoint guardians for minor children and sometimes remove guardians when the children came of age. — Woodlief Thomas, Jr. NY

Persistence Has Its Rewards

According to oral family history, my grandfather, James Hartigan, was born in Circleville, Pickaway county, OH, in 1861 to Martin and Johanna (Hayes/Hays) Hartigan. James had three sisters, Mary A., Catherine J.

and Elizabeth A., all younger, but also born in Pickaway county.

Although there was a Martin and Johanna listed in the 1860 federal census in Pickaway county, OH and the listing included two sons, Patrick, eight, and a six-month-old named James. The Irish names were so repetitious that I couldn't be sure this was my family.

I then checked the 1870 federal census index for Ohio and did not find a listing for Martin Hartigan in Pickaway county. I thought a two-hour trip to Circleville would easily clear some of my confusion. I spent two days searching in the public library as well as the area's separate genealogy library. The volunteer in the genealogy library was so very helpful. She immediately pulled a book from a shelf of a list of Circleville residents in 1859, but there wasn't a Martin Hartigan family listed. She continued to search other sources including an old newspaper clipping collection and she kept handing me material to scan. All to no avail.

The volunteer then asked if the family might have been Catholic and I said, "I thought so." She encouraged me to telephone the Catholic Church and ask if someone could check the baptismal records. The librarian looked up the telephone number for me and offered the use of their phone. I placed the call and explained my problem. I gave the lady at the Church the information that she needed in order to check their records and she asked that I call her again the next day.

Upon calling the Catholic Church the following day, the news was disappointing. The lady had found one Hartigan baptism for the requested time period and it was for a Mary Ellen and the father's name was James. Not quite what I had hoped for.

I decided to borrow the 1870 Pickaway county census microfilm

and using the reader here at home, search line by line for my Hartigan. I discovered the family! The surname as well as Johanna's name were misspelled. The listing read as Martin and Josephine Harticium with James, Mary and Catherine and all ages matching my rough record.

Since I exhausted my available research hours in libraries, while in Circleville the first time, my husband and I decided to return and scour the Pickaway County Court House for Hartigan records. We checked for all possible types of records including naturalizations, but we found not a trace of our Hartigan family.

Above: Baptismal record from 1861.
Below: Baptismal record from 1864.

We then visited the genealogy library again. The volunteer there that day was even more interested in our dilemma than before and was extremely helpful. We once again examined all possible sources in their collection and drew a blank. The volunteer, once again, questioned the religion of the Hartigan family and without hesitation strongly urged us to pay a visit to the Catholic Church, pointing out one of the windows to the Church. We decided to call the Church and make an appointment for the next morning.

The secretary in the Church Office received us warmly. She had the baptismal record books, which covered the 1860s ready for us to view. The basement office was a busy place and the space was cramped and the light rather dim. An ironing board was used as a portable table. If someone wanted to use the copier, we and the ironing board had to move. The first baptismal record book was handed to us and we placed it on the ironing board and started to carefully scan its pages. Can you imagine our exhilaration, when we saw Martin and Johanna Hartigan, in unmistakable handwriting, in the parents' column?

Before leaving the Church, we had found the record of three family baptisms. Two were for Mary Anne and Catherine, the third was recorded in Latin and we are unsure of translation. In the process we received the unexpected bonus of learning that Edward Hays, believed to be Johanna's father, was listed as a sponsor for one of the baptisms.

Although we did not find James' baptism, just seeing Martin and Johanna's names written in the Church's records was so very thrilling and satisfying. I was most grateful to the Church for preserving those old records and graciously making them available to us. Persistence has its rewards. — Joy Ann Wilcox, OH, joyroger@y-city.net

The Advantage Of An Unusual Name

After discovering my second-great-grandparents, Washington and Mary Bazdell (Magee) Moore, I eagerly began the search for his parents. The 1850 federal census for Lewis county, MO revealed that both Washington and Mary were born in Kentucky. This narrowed my search, but I did not know which counties.

As I scanned the index of each federal census for Kentucky, a name in the 1830 census drew my attention. Grizzella Moore was listed as head of a household in Harrison county, KY. Washington and Mary had a daughter named Grizzella. Could she have been named for her grandmother?

Harrison County Courthouse records included a number of deeds in Grizzella's name which concerned the settling of the estate of her late husband, Moses Moore. One of them named their children and spouses, including Washington Moore and his wife, Mary, of Lewis county, MO.

Following my hunch led to identifying Washington's mother, father and his siblings. Fortunately for me, Grizzella lived to be counted in a census after she became a widow. The census in the early years recorded only heads of household by name. — Marilee Moore Helton, OK, marilee@kskc.net

An Ocean Apart

Growing up in Canada, I heard that my paternal grandfather, Thomas Cherryholme, had family in England, particularly a brother John William and a sister Eleanor. It was thought Eleanor had married someone named Britt. My father and twin uncles often spoke of their "Uncle John Willie" with great sadness — They longed to know the family they had never met.

In the late 1980s, I started compiling family tree information to attempt to provide my daughter with a sense of her roots. Genealogy has since become a passion and by the late 1990s, I was pursuing the search for my grandfather's family with vigor.

My Uncle Victor (one of the twins) had traveled to England on at least three occasions, returning each time without having found any trace of his father's family. My parents went to England in the early 1970s and also came back not having found any trace of relatives. They weren't looking in the right place though, insisting that Thomas had been from Sheffield.

On the 1881 British census, every instance of the family name Cherryholme occurs in Barnsley, Yorkshire. There are still several Cherryholme families living in Barnsley and Liversedge — the actual area from which Thomas truly hailed. It is now known that John William had already died by the time Victor made his first trip to England.

Initial research ascertained that Thomas had come to Canada as a Home Child in 1912, a ward of the Dewsbury Union Workhouse following his mother's death at the Workhouse in 1908. I received a copy of my grandfather's emigration record from England and his military record from the National Archives of Canada. Both records helped to provide a lot of previously unknown details about Thomas.

With the arrival of the Internet, some research has become much easier than it had been in earlier times. International telephone directories can now be consulted from home. The Internet provided the link that closed the ocean between the families of John William and Thomas Cherryholme.

In early 1997, letters outlining what little I knew were sent to selected Cherryholme entries in Yorkshire. Those letters were able by then to include the surname Tolan as Thomas' mother's maiden name and that the family had been from Heckmondwike. No replies were received.

Recording every Cherryholme entry in the St. Catherine's birth/marriage/death index back to 1837 and tracking families through census returns allowed me to compile detailed family unit records of my grandfather's ancestry.

In early 1999, I again wrote to Cherryholme entries in Yorkshire — but this time sent a letter to every entry shown and enclosed copies of family group records. In July 1999, a letter arrived from Tom Cherryholme of Cleckheaton:

"My father was called John William... I was called Tom after Dad's brother who went to Canada... This brother had three sons, two of them were twins. Dad said he worked for the Government in Canada. Dad had a sister Eleanor. She was married to a man called Pat Brett... Dad had

some cousins who lived in Batley name of Tolan."

Eighty-seven years after they were separated, and 40 years after their deaths, their descendants made contact. By naming his youngest son in his memory, John William had ensured that his youngest brother would not be forgotten. My grandfather had become a hero to the nephew who was named in his memory — a nephew he never knew he had.

John William Cherryholme's birth certificate.

John William's son, Tom, and I, Thomas' granddaughter, shared a couple of telephone conversations and have exchanged photos, letters and cards. The ocean between the two families now seems much narrower indeed. Sadly, Tom died in Cleckheaton in June 2001, not quite two years after I found him. — Bonnie Fowler, ON

A Gray Mystery

My quest was to obtain the birth registration for Godfray Thomas Roland Gray. We had been told that he was born on 14 May 1894 at Streatham, England. He had two sisters, Gladys Eva and Daisy Eleocadie who were born in England also. Godfray's parents, Arthur and Maud Emily (Sharpe) Gray, along with their three children immigrated to Manitoba in early 1900. The only impediment to my search was a vague rumor that the surname had been changed after they immigrated.

I contacted the Lambeth Archives

Department and applied for the desired certificate. The Superintendent Registrar explained that all entries are referenced by surname and in alphabetical order and divided into quarters. Each quarter at Lambeth in 1894 would contain about 5,000 names. Unfortunately, the records were stored in a similar fashion at St. Catherine's House, but he suggested that I could try the General Register Office located in Southport.

There I was told that, at that time, the cost to search two years each side of a year would cost £9, whether the search was successful or not, plus £12 for each certificate.

Without knowing the correct surname the search could be very long and costly, if not impossible. Soon I became aware that the name change rumor was fact. It was not going to be the easy task I had thought it would be to obtain the birth certificate.

Upon reading my notes again I realized that Maud Emily's maiden name was known — all was not lost. Hopefully that had not been changed. If the registrations are stored alphabetically by name, surely Maude Emily's name should appear in the marriage registrations index.

Could I locate her marriage registration without knowing her spouse's name? Maud and Emily were quite common names and Sharpe was not uncommon.

I went to the British civil registry index for marriages. The eldest daughter, Gladys Eva, was 90 when she died in 1979 making her year of birth circa 1888-89. The marriage would have probably taken place about that time. I started the search and located several Maud Sharps and Maud Sharpes, but just one Maud Emily Sharpe emerged in all three years.

I tried to match registration numbers to determine the name of her spouse but that proved futile. I telephoned a friend in England to share my find. My friend telephoned the record office

*Above: Maude Emily (Sharpe) Gray.
Below: Arthur Gray.*

and called me back to report that this Maud Emily Sharpe had married Walter John Rowland Soper. Could this be Arthur Gray?

I consulted the British civil registration of births index to look for the births of Gladys Eva, Daisy Esme and Godfray Thomas Roland under the Soper surname. With little difficulty all three Soper children were located in the index. I requested the appropriate registration certificates that, when received, provided more family information. The children's names in the records reflected the names of their antecedents. The brickwall had been breached!

We also applied for the birth certificate of Walter John Rowland Soper, also known as Arthur Gray. When we received the birth certificate, we uncovered another mystery. Among the personal effects of Arthur was a picture of a Captain Jean Joseph Rousseau and Mrs. Rousseau, and a letter from Duchess of Berry Marie-Caroline de Bourbon-Sicile, a French noblewoman who led an abortive attempt to get her son on the French throne in the 1830s. In this letter, the Duchess extolled the virtues of Captain Rousseau.

The grandchildren knew that there was a family connection to the illustrious Captain, but could never explore it until the mystery of the name change was solved. Obtaining Arthur's birth was impossible, but the birth certificate for Walter John Rowland Soper stated that his mother was Elescadie Olive Rachel Rousseau. This explained why Eleocadie became part of Daisy's name. — A.J. Tucker, MB

Great-Grandpa Dave's Brickwall

My grandfather, John Pfalser, never talked much about his family, not even to his own children. He passed away while I was relatively young.

When I started asking questions about the family history my grandmother knew her family's history well but little about my grandfather's. She did, however, keep in contact with his younger half-brother's daughter. My correspondence with my first cousin once-removed quickly showed that neither she or my grandmother knew anything about my grandfather's family.

One of my uncles was able to piece together the following information: Grandpa was apparently born on 25 December 1859, the day they arrived from Germany. He had two sisters, Gerty and Phene, and his father's name was Dave Pfalzer, a smith, who died when John was four years old. The family lived in Louisville, KY. His mother's name was Mary who later married a Jacob Rouch, a farmer in southern Indiana.

As John grew older he did not get along with his stepfather so his grandmother, a strict Catholic, raised him. As a young man John worked for the Louisville Bridge and Iron Company. His Uncle John also worked there and to help keep company records straight between the two John Pfalzers my grandfather changed the spelling of his name to Pfalser. In the late 1880s John moved to Kansas and took up farming where he met and married my grandmother.

After I retired, my wife and I made a trip to Louisville to try to trace Great-grandpa Dave. Our first stop was the public library, which was most helpful. Searching though the old city directories we found a number of Pfalzers; John, Jacob, James, Theobold, but no Dave or David.

We then visited the Catholic League offices, which was very helpful in providing church and cemetery information. We visited the original Catholic Church where we were instructed to leave information on who, what, when and where, along with an appropriate donation and when they had time they would see what they could find. This turned into a dead end.

We went to the second oldest Catholic Church were they said their records were open to the public and were most helpful. Although their records showed some Pfalzers, there was no Dave. At the Filson Club tax records also came up short. On the Indiana side of the Ohio River we found no Pfalzers but did find my grandfather and his two sisters under the Rouch name.

After returning home, by luck, I happened upon a microfiche index of immigrants through the Port of New Orleans. There was a Pfalzer in 1859. Further research showed it was Theobold Pfalzer, his wife Mary and daughter Gertrude arriving in late November. Was Dave Pfalzer actually Theobold Pfalzer?

I think so. Conjecture indicates this is my grandpa's family. The circumstances and the timing are about right for Grandpa to be born in Louisville on the family's arrival. — Ivan L. Pfalser, KS

Always Sign The Guest Book

The value of the Internet was brought to the forefront with me in my research into one branch of the family. I was searching for the parents and siblings of my great-grandfather, Alvah Snow. I knew he was from the Gardiner area in Maine. The library in Gardiner was gracious enough to send me copies of entries in the city directory and newspaper clips from the area on Alvah. I also found his marriage on the Internet. But I did not know his parents' names.

One day while researching on the Internet, I decided to look at pages of the various libraries in Maine. I tried one or two just to see what they had. I stumbled into the Milo, Maine library site. The first thing that grabbed me was the music. I had to listen to the

Alvah Snow.

tune to the end and then again before I changed to the next page of that site. I did not find anything in regards to my search so I was ready to leave and go elsewhere. I noted a familiar "Sign our Guest Book" at the bottom of the page. I have never done that before. But the music was so nice and the pages are so impressive, I decided to leave a note. "I enjoyed your site very much. Your music was really neat and I had trouble leaving a page until the tune was done. Thank you. Oh, by the way, I am researching the Snow family. Alvah Snow and I think he was from your area. That was one reason for my visiting your page. Thank you."

I went on about my business and research. The next morning, an e-mail came from the Milo librarian. It turns out she is related to the Snow family.

She is a cousin of mine and had all sorts of information on my ancestors and their families. She even let me know that my great-grandfather's grandfather Philip was one of the scouts and guides for Benedict Arnold in his expedition to Quebec in the Revolutionary War.

Signing the guest book at a website probably isn't a sure-fire method of research in genealogy, but when you have a brickwall, who knows what may help? — Dutch Meyer, MT

Friendly Ladies And Lots Of Walking

We were at a loss on our second-great-grandparents (John and Anne Myers). We had somewhat given up when we received a box from my sister with what she called junk for the family historian. In the box there was a funeral card of my second-great-grandmother. This started that old urge to be a detective again.

We spent hours calling and writing people who we thought might know where they lived. On a whim, I called an old acquaintance of the family from years ago. She indicated she did not know much about them but thought the family traveled to Belle Plaines, IA to see someone.

We visited all the sources in that area with no luck and still had an entire afternoon to spend. We decided to travel to the first town south; Marengo, IA. Coincidence would have it that that very day the Iowa County Genealogical Society was having a meeting. Four great ladies there were just full of energy to dig anything up on my family. Unfortunately I did not find much.

One week later came a letter from one of the ladies. She had census and burial information on our third-great-grandfather (Samuel Ernsberger) who at that time lived with his daughter

according to the census.

I quickly arranged time to go see the cemetery where they were. No one had heard of the Athey Cemetery there. In the library was an old book where Pauline Lilly had spent her time documenting facts about Athey Cemetery. With her directions in hand, I went to that location — no cemetery. I spent the next two-and-a-half hours speaking to farmers in the area and walking up large hills to the old small cemeteries on top.

The view from the cemetery where Howard Pohlman's ancestors, John Myers and his wife Anna, are buried.

I hit pay dirt, literally, on the fourth one. There at the back were 12 plots with stones. The stone on the right end being my second-great-grandparents, to the left was a daughter I didn't know about and a son.

I got pictures for my family book but more than that a great feeling of comfort. I sat on probably the highest point on the west side of the Iowa River and pondered what type of life my ancestors lived back in the 1850s. Looking down the hill towards the fields they homesteaded and worked hard to make ends meet I thought of the family activities that went on. I could almost see them with their horse-drawn wagons bringing crops in together.

Friendly ladies and cemetery walks were my great brickwall crushers. — Howard Pohlman, IA

*   *   *

The Search Finally Ended

The search had begun as my sister and I went through dresser drawers at our home place shortly before our mother's death in 1992. Yellowed newspaper clippings were carefully placed in a plastic bag to be sorted later. Many newspaper obituaries had already been put into a shoebox knowing there would be much information to be gathered from them for the family history I had begun compiling several years before.

However, one clipping caught my eye. It had a woman standing by a portrait of a blind man sitting on a stool strumming a banjo. The man looked familiar — a face from my childhood. I quickly perused the accompanying article. The subject of the picture's names was not given. It must be someone my parents knew or she wouldn't have clipped it, I thought.

I began to think about the banjo. Six or seven years previous Daddy had given me a banjo for my children. He said, "Take good care of this. It belonged to Uncle Roy." Now my memory began a quick flashback to the beginning of my grade school years in the 1940s.

Mother and I were coming out of O.J. Morrison's store on Capitol Street in downtown Charleston, WV, one August afternoon. A man sat playing something and singing a familiar hymn. We stood and listened. When he finished *Rock Of Ages, Cleft For Me* some passersby dropped some coins in the tin cup by his feet. Mother went closer and talked with him. "And is Barbara with you today, Catherine?" he asked.

Looking at the picture again, I was almost certain the man on the street and the one in the picture was the same man — Daddy's older brother, Leroy, who was blinded in an accident. Where is the portrait now? We had no pictures of him and this would be a great addition to the family history.

I returned to my home in Pennsylvania and weeks went by. I wrote to museums in West Virginia. When I returned to West Virginia I spoke to some curators. One said the painting looked like it was by Lew Raines in his Street People collection.

Blind John *by Lew Raines (c. 1959).*

I went back to Pennsylvania and wrote letters to the Charleston newspaper and other museums. My sister began to help by making phone calls to museums in her area. I made daily trips to the mailbox in anticipation. Finally, an envelope with the Charleston postmark arrived.

The letter told me that the portrait was called *Blind John*. The portrait was stacked behind some others passed on to the library. Tears of joy flowed. I wrote back to see if I could come and view it or even find out how I could obtain it for my family. I soon found out it would be transferred from the Kanawha County Public Library to the West Virginia

Archives and Culture Center. We were very happy it would be preserved.

In 1994, Mary Jane and I stood in the Culture Center before the large, almost life-sized portrait of our Uncle Roy. Even his socks were as we remembered them. The search finally ended. — Barbara Sutphin Witwer, PA, ells94worth@aol.com

Is A Blanket Letter Worth It?

After eight years of doing research on my maternal grandmother, I finally made a huge breakthrough. I found a living relative! I remember very little about my Nana. Her maiden name was Silverstein and she came from a large Orthodox Jewish family. She said that as a teen she had refused an arranged marriage to a man in his sixties. She thought that as an American girl she would find her own husband. She left home and the family might have held the Jewish ceremony for the dead. Apparently she never made contact with her family again and accepted the Christian faith.

She bragged that no one would ever find out about her past and for several years after I started genealogy I believed it to be true. My first breakthrough came when I received her Social Security Application; it listed the names of her mother and father.

Thrilled, I sent birth announcements to some of my genealogy friends announcing the birth of Dorothy (Nana) to Alexander and Esther Silverstein. Finally, I had evidence to trace. I found her with her parents in the 1900 US census in Boston. Now I knew the names of some of her siblings. Only 21 states are Soundexed or Miracoded and Massachusetts is not one of them. By using the Boston city directories, I found the street where they had lived. The front of the directory listed their voting precinct and ward and a guidebook for 1910 census in Boston gave the enumeration district. I went slowly through the microfilm and there was the family with yet another son listed.

I discovered that great-grandfather Alexander came to the US in 1882-83 from the Russian sector of Poland, now in Belarus. He came with his wife Esther and their first-born son Samuel joined him about 1885-86. In the 1920 census, the census taker had written Grodno as place born. Grodno is a *guerbernia* or province in Belarus. I can find no immigration records for them and the census varies for Alexander's citizenship.

In the 1900 census, the entry indicates "PA" (papers applied for?), in 1910 it states that he was naturalized and in the 1920 census he is listed as an alien. Although Boston was their home area, I do not know if that was their arrival port. I found Alexander and Esther's death dates in the Boston vital records. I ordered death certificates and noticed that the informant on one was Louis Silverstein and on the other Louis Silvey, both listed as a son. I was perplexed.

The cemetery became my next goal. I was dismayed to find that the Boston cemetery was large and on both sides of the road. There was no one on the premises and the telephone number listed was no longer in service. Friends and I decided to split up and walk the whole darn place if necessary. Within five minutes, a friend found the gravesite of my great-grandparents. The stone says Elias A., but with other data from children's birth records and Boston city directories, I was not surprised.

There is Hebrew script on the stone and I know that it will probably list their father's names. I took three digital pictures from different angles. Then Ruth took me to another area with eight gravestones for Silvey. There are the names of my Nana's siblings; even Louis, the informant on his parents' death certificates, is there.

Further research in the Boston city directories indicated the name change about 1942 and the Probate Court records verified that.

After locating 13 Silveys in the Boston area through phone search CDs, I wrote a letter with the basic facts, included a self-addressed stamped envelope plus my e-mail address. About 10 days later I received an e-mail titled "Hi Cuz" from Rita in Florida. My letter had been forwarded to Joseph Silvey's widow in Florida and the widow gave it to Rita, my mother's first cousin, the daughter of Nana's brother Harry. She sent pictures of my great-grandparents and their other sons and daughters. For an investment of about $8 I hit gold. — Patricia Bellis Sharp, CA, sharpgenie@earthlink.net

Shoeboxes: Effective Weapons In The Fight Against Brickwalls

I hit my brickwall right at the beginning of trying to trace my paternal grandparents. I was the youngest of their grandchildren, so I didn't have any strong memories of them. I spoke to my elderly aunt, the last surviving child. She only knew that her father was from Quebec and believed her mother was from Montreal.

I knew the family lived in Houghton, MI, from my father's birth certificate, so I began searching the US census records. I couldn't find him anywhere. I sent for my grandfather's death certificate, since I knew what year he had died. All it listed was that he was from Canada. I studied the death certificate and realized he hadn't died in a hospital, but in the home of another aunt. This aunt had recently died, so I could not talk to her, but her daughter lived just a couple of miles away. I decided to talk face to

face with her, so I called her and set up a time I could drop by.

Linda Nordyke's grandparents, Pierre Dallaire and Almosa Rouleau with their first child, Joseph in 1901.

When I went to her home, I brought up my grandfather. She too had been told he was from somewhere in Quebec and grandmother was from Montreal. That was really all she knew except for the typical family stories. After an hour or so, I asked her if her mother might have had any papers from grandfather. She thought for a minute and then remembered a shoebox she had found when clearing out her mother's effects.

When she brought the box and opened it, I almost fell off my chair. Inside, there were my grandfather's naturalization papers, two letters written in French from the 1920s from two parishes in Quebec and a small brown notebook. The two letters were records of my grandmother's baptism in St. Henri Parish and my grandfather's baptism in St. Anselme Parish.

They were both from Quebec and lived only about 20 miles from each other in Canada (they met each other in Michigan). The really exciting part was I now had where they were from plus the names of both sets of great-grandparents.

Baptismal record for Almosa Rouleau.

There was also that little brown book. Inside, neatly written in French, were the names, dates and places where each of my aunts and uncles were born. He had recorded the year my grandmother arrived in Michigan and their wedding date.

My brickwall was down. I was able to go on to trace some branches of the family all the way to France. — Linda Nordyke, FL, ldnord@gte.net

Nicknames

My brickwall plagued me for more than 10 years. I finally scaled that wall and all sorts of exciting things are appearing on the other side. My mother joined me in working on our family tree when she retired from teaching. She was an avid genealogist, dedicated to unearthing all the family stories and documenting them well. I gratefully turned over the branches of our tree that spread into her area of the country, namely Michigan. She spent many hours visiting the State Library in Lansing and collected a great deal of information.

One particular piece of documentation was a biography on my third-great-grandfather, James Anderson. James had come to Michigan and settled in Essex township near the town of Maple Rapids after he was released from the Civil War. In his later years, as it was often the custom, James was included in a *Portrait And Biographical Album* put out by the Chapman Brothers in 1891. They portrayed James as an outstanding citizen of the county and exemplary farmer of the area. In this biography it stated that James "set up housekeeping with the lady of his choice, Phebe Lyon, daughter of Conger and Sarah Lyon, also early settlers of Essex Township". Despite the fact Conger and Sarah were known to be long time residents of the area, no trace could be found of their existence. I had some idea of their birth dates from Phebe's death certificate but very little else as her parents were listed as unknown.

I checked the census, land records, newspapers, death records, everything I could think of, no Conger and Sarah. James and Phebe are buried in the Sowle Cemetery in Maple Rapids, MI. The parents had to be somewhere. While doing some research in the FHC in Westerville, OH, I did run across a marriage entry for a Conger Lyon and Sally Hoyt in Knox county, OH. There was no other information and I could not prove that this was my Conger and Sarah (or some other wife) though the dates were reasonable as to be the same persons. Now I searched the Ohio census, land records and other sources. No Conger and Sarah.

I checked and rechecked every source I could think of in Ohio and Michigan for more than 10 years. Finally I decided to go to the cemetery grounds. I started in the small town of Maple Rapids (about 500 people) and got the cemetery listings from the small library. I had never been able to be in Maple Rapids when the library was open prior to this. I started to walk the cemeteries and write down all the Lyon names and dates that I found. None were close enough until I passed a large marker for Joseph G. Lyon and wife Sarah. I went to the 1850 census for Michigan (James' biography had said Conger and Sally were in Michigan at the time of James' and Phebe's marriage). There they were; Joseph G., wife Sarah and the children, including a Phebe with the same birth and death dates as I had documented with Phebe's obituary.

Now the questions were multiplied. Were Joseph G. and Conger the same person? Were there two wives, Sally and Sarah or just one who wasn't sure what she wanted to be called? When did they come to Michigan? I knew it was probably after Phebe was born as her death certificate states that she was born in Ohio.

It took another year and two more trips from Ohio to Michigan to fill in the blanks. Following the family through the Michigan and Ohio census records was easy once I had the correct name. Joseph G. and family lived in Ohio until after the 1840 census and then turn up in Michigan in the 1850 census. The name of Joseph's wife went from Sally in the 1850 and 1860 censuses to Sarah in the 1870 census. In the 1880 census she is listed again as Sarah, living alone, next door to James Anderson and wife, Phebe. Joseph had died in June of 1871. In the 1860 census I found Phebe gone from her father's family and James Anderson and wife Phebe appear two houses down from Joseph and the rest of the family. This was probably enough evidence that Phebe's parents were Joseph G. and Sarah, but who were Conger and Sally?

Finally I made another trip to Clinton county, this time to the Clinton County Historical Library and waded through the county newspapers near the death dates I got from the grave markers. I found a small mention of Conger Lyon's death and a larger one for Mrs. Sally Lyon, widow of Conger Lyon who died at the home of her son in law, James

Anderson. Finally the connection!

Why did Joseph and Sarah use the names Conger and Sally? There was not a Joseph Sr. to be confused with as far as I know. They did not use Conger or Sally for any other official purpose. I doubt I will ever know. But I do know now that Joseph Lyon and Sarah Hoyt are the parents of Phebe Lyon Anderson. — Jacquelyn J. Danalewich, OH

What's In A Name?

My grandmother told me many years ago before I was into really researching my family tree that her father's name was Natepher Wood and his father was a Jonathan Wood. I knew the Wood family was from the Ansted, WV, area as that is where my grandmother was born. I posted queries looking for Natepher and his father Jonathan Wood. I looked at family trees. I visited just about every query board. I wrote e-mails and letters and visited the state of West Virginia websites. There was nothing on Natepher or Jonathan that matched.

William Johnson Wood.

One day, I stumbled onto a query with the name Nathan Wood on the

Internet. I found that the date of birth and area were very close to what I had. I didn't have the exact date of birth but this was close. But his father was a William Wood. It seemed to be the wrong family. A few months later, I again stumbled into William and his family on the web. This time it was William J. Wood. The birth date and where he lived was again what I thought it could be. Then I found out that this William's middle name was Johnson. Not Jonathan as I was hoping. I thought, "What if his name was Johnson and his descendants mistook Jonathan for Johnson?"

I decided to follow up on this Nathan/William Johnson Wood family. I researched the census for the area and the 1870 and 1880 censuses. All these had him listed as Johnson Wood and not William. Apparently, old William preferred using Johnson as his first name. Now things started really clicking. I found more information on his family with both descendants and ancestors. I posted a query or two on the Internet with these names and dates. In no time, I was hearing from cousins from all over the place.

Some people changed their family names when they came across from the old country or for other reasons while here. But always remember that they may have changed their first names also. — Dutch Meyer, MT

The Gold Locket

I have a beautiful gold locket my father gave me. It belonged to his mother, my grandmother, May Gannuch. The locket is the size of a silver dollar. A beautiful mermaid floats across the front of the locket and the letters, MG, are inscribed on its back. Inside the locket are small faded pictures of my grandparents as young adults. The pictures were cut from a larger picture, but my father neither knew where the original photographs were or when my grand-

mother had acquired this locket. I suspect it was an engagement gift in lieu of a ring, as I remember my grandmother wearing only a gold wedding band. Over the years I'd look at these pictures longing to know more about my grandparents.

The source of the picture in Sandra Ariatti's grandmother's gold locket.

This locket piqued my interest in genealogy. At the NARA and FHC I researched my grandmother's father, Dominic Gannuch. My mother provided his marriage date to Serada Castigliola and the names of their children. In the 1900 and 1910 census I found their birth country was Italy, but no date or town of birth.

My sister-in-law, Ann, discovered a query from an R. Gannuch searching the surnames Gannuch or Cannuscio. She e-mailed him about our Dominic Gannuch. He responded that he was the grandson of Salvador Gannuch, Dominic's younger brother and that he had Gannuch family information.

In the meantime, Ann and I found

a copy of the original birth record of Dominico Cannuscio in Campo Fiorita, Italy. Now I had my great-grandfather's birth and marriage records.

Ann found Rod's telephone number and I telephoned him. Rod said he had pictures of May, Dominic and others. His Aunt Virginia, Salvador's sister, told him that Dominic came alone from Campo Fiorita to the US, as a young boy. While vacationing in Italy, Rod visited Campo Fiorita but was unable to establish a direct relationship to anyone there. We ended our conversation agreeing to meet and exchange research.

From the obituaries Rod mailed me I knew Dominic's burial site was in New Orleans. Rod agreed to meet Ann and me at the cemetery. Hugs, laughs and pictures at the gravesite filled the afternoon. Rod invited us to his home to see family photos.

At his home Rod brought out a photo of Dominic, but he didn't have documentation of Dominic's arrival in New Orleans. To my surprise and delight Rod had the original photograph of the one in my locket of my grandmother, May. A family tree and relationship chart revealed we were second cousins once-removed. We ended our visit agreeing to continue exchanging information. Although Dominic Gannuch's arrival in the US continues to evade me, I am happy to have found a long-lost cousin and the source of the picture in my locket. — Sandra Ariatti, CA

Don't Make Assumptions

My mother started doing our family tree in the mid 1970s. After she passed away in 1994, I opened her files with great anticipation and started reading. In her honor, I took over the job of family historian and started researching the Cooligan surname. Somehow, it didn't seem that she had found the right John Cooligan, her great-grandfather. It took me two years to prove my theory that my mother had the wrong John Cooligan listed as her great-grandfather. She had the nephew of the real John Cooligan we were looking for. Her great-grandfather, John Cooligan, became a farm laborer upon emigrating from Ireland to the US.

I first found John in the 1865 state census for New York in Ontario county. His wife was listed with the name Joint, which was her maiden name, not her first name, which was Mary. I knew I had the right John, after all. In 1870, John and Mary had moved to the town of York in Livingston county. Having heard from relatives that my great-grandfather, Frank, had been born in York, I searched cemeteries in that area, as well as birth and death records. No records existed prior to 1880 and records were very scarce afterwards.

Older relatives knew the names of two of my great-grandfather's sisters. Lillian, who had married Fred Claus, and Louise, who had married a man named Delavergne. I found the Claus family in Rochester, Monroe county in 1890, but couldn't find their father, my second-great-grandfather. In the 1900 federal census, I finally found John Cooligan's daughter, Lilla Belle Claus, living in Monroe county, town of Pittsford. Right there on the page was her father, John Cooligan, but he was remarried to an Agnes. What had happened to his first wife, my second-great-grandmother, Mary Joint? I searched cemeteries all over the southern tier, but to no avail.

Last year, we were lucky to have the vital records index come to our local library. I found John Cooligan had died in Bath, Steuben county, NY. I then drove to Bath and went straight to their town offices. They had no death record for John or his wife Mary. Even though I had the exact date of death, they had no information, or even an obituary in their local paper. As long as I was in Bath, I decided to visit their local history society.

What a lucky visit that turned out to be. The local historian found John Cooligan had been in the US Civil War and he was buried in the Bath National Cemetery. He had enlisted in the Civil War under an assumed name, John Hays. He is actually listed in the 1892 veterans' census as John Cooligan, alias John Hays. I knew his older brother, Philip Cooligan, had fought in the Civil War, but had no idea my second-great-grandfather had also. Perhaps that is why John had to use an alias to enlist.

I then went to the Veterans' Hospital museum and found actual yearly reports listing the soldiers' names, regiments, towns they came from and residents of the soldiers' and sailors' home. John had been a resident at the home with his brother, Philip, and they are both buried in Bath National Cemetery. John came to the home from Pittsford, NY in 1897 and died at the home in 1910. I have since found his Civil War pension papers and Agnes is listed as his widow.

A spur-of-the-moment decision to stop at the local historical society tore down the elusive brickwall. But where was his first wife, Mary? She wasn't buried in any Pittsford cemeteries and she had traveled all around New York's southern tier during her years as the wife of a farm laborer.

One day I was searching our local Catholic cemetery for other relatives, when I typed Cooligan by mistake. Up popped Mary Cooligan and her oldest daughter, Marietta. Of course, she wouldn't be buried less than two miles from my house. I then typed in Agnes Cooligan and found she was in the same cemetery. All the time I had spent in that particular cemetery doing research on other relatives, I had unknowingly passed her gravestone many, many times.

I learned a very important lesson

that day. Never assume that because your relatives moved all over several counties, they might not have ended close to home. Open yourself to the unlimited possibilities before you and those brickwalls can come tumbling down. — Karen K. French, NY

A Day She'll Never Forget

While researching my third-great-grandfather, I found the cemetery where his brother and many of his descendants are buried. I tried to find more information through cemetery records. Since this is a rather small countryside cemetery with no office or apparent director, I could not find any information. I tried the local phone book and historical society with no luck. This cemetery is very well kept, so I knew somebody had to be running it. I called the county courthouse to get the name of the owner of the property. I was given a phone number for the president of the cemetery association. I called, and to my delight, found that I was speaking to the 87-year-old great-granddaughter of my ancestor's brother!

Gravestone of Patrick and Elizabeth Perry, ancestors of Beth Perry found in the well-kept cemetery.

We had a lengthy conversation, followed by a visit. She was born and raised on land that was once the original homestead of her direct line ancestor and baptized in the church for which he donated the land. The church, established in 1854, is still in use — and even has the original pews.

Elizabeth Matilda Mackey Perry and Patrick Perry.

My cousin and her husband took me on the grand tour, which included the church, the 150-acre homestead, three cemeteries and the site of the family cheese factory. We exchanged information, which enabled me to expand the family immensely and share many old photos. It truly was a day I'll never forget! — Beth Perry, OH, bthmbl@hotmail.com

Finding The Parents Of Jacob Brown

My family Bible goes as far back as the birth date of my third-great-grandfather, Jacob Brown who was born on 21 November 1792 in North Yarmouth, ME (which was actually in Massachusetts then). The Bible gives the names of his spouse and children, but not his parents. No record could be found that recorded his birth (church and civil records were searched). The 1790 federal census for North Yarmouth shows seven possible Brown families. There was the brickwall. Which Brown family was Jacob born into?

The first step was to search all the records from North Yarmouth available on film for the 18th century. I literally got to know every Brown in town. The resources include 19 volumes of history compiled by A.W. Corliss. I made family group sheets for all the Brown families I could find in these records. Unfortunately the church records, which were very helpful in identifying parents of children born and marriages, did not offer much after the late 1700s. Therefore, some of my family group sheets had husbands and wives, but no children.

I now had a good idea of who each of the families were in the 1790 census, but not all the family group sheets were complete. The next step was to compare the 1800 federal census for North Yarmouth and surrounding towns with the seven families found in the 1790 census, to determine which had added a son in that 10-year period. Through a process of deduction and omission I came to the conclusion that Jacob's parents were Jacob Brown and Jane Mitchell. Over time I came to realize that there were two Brown lines in North Yarmouth, one from New Hampshire and one from Salisbury, MA. Many of the names in both lines were similar.

The church records in the early and mid 1700s were very helpful in identifying parents of children. This information helped sort which children belonged on each line. The cemetery records provided by the

Maine Old Cemetery Association were very helpful in filling the blanks and providing the history of the members of the two lines. These records also led me to a town just north of North Yarmouth called Freeport. This is where Jane Mitchell is buried. Thus I realized that my Jacob Brown family is the one found in Freeport in 1800 (Jane died in 1804).

Thanks to A.W. Corliss, the Maine Old Cemetery Association and all the record keepers of the 18th century for all their diligent work I was able to knock down my brickwall. — Lynne Henshaw, VA, lynhenshaw@hovac.com

Family Legends

In the family papers I found a birth certificate for Anne Buckley born on 23 June 1930 at Morrisania Hospital in the Bronx. Family legends say that this girl only lived a few hours. A check of the death index was called for. Knowing Anne Buckley's birth date and that she only lived a few hours should have made finding her death certificate easy. It did not.

In the index there was no Anne Buckley listed dying on 23 June 1930 or 24 June 1930. There were no Anne Buckleys that died as infants in 1930. Discouraged I moved on to other research.

After checking with my uncle, we did eventually find her at Calvary Cemetery in Queens. She was 20 days old when she died on 13 July 1930. Further research showed that she was christened on 26 June 1930. The only thing missing was the cause of death. We would need the death certificate to find the answer.

Three years later when I returned to the New York City Municipal Archives, I discovered the problem. Upon checking the death index for 1930 again I saw the death date 13 July 1930 next to the entry Female Buckley, not Anne. Of course when I checked it was my grandparents' daughter. She had died from pyloric

stenosis; a blockage between her stomach and her intestine caused her to vomit and ultimately killed her. She never left Morrisania Hospital.

Timothy Buckley and Christina O'Riordan, parents of Anne Buckley.

She was given a name at her birth. Three days later she was given that name again when she was baptized. Despite living almost three weeks her death certificate listed her only as Female Buckley. A combination of a clerical error and my strong dependence on a family legend caused me to miss the entry.

Be thorough in your research. If you don't find something think of reasons why and check your new thoughts. — Kevin Cassidy, NE, kmct@earthlink.net

Alvin's Legacy

In the early 1990s, while visiting an elderly relative, Alvin Weaver, he told me a story of a man who attempted to walk cross-country to his son's home several miles away. Apparently, the man got caught in a fence he was trying to cross, fell and was found dead almost two weeks later.

Several years later when I was more interested in obtaining some family history, I decided to visit Alvin again and ask him about some of the family. His mother was a sister to my husband's grandmother. Their maiden name was Kieffer and their mother was Sarah Kreider. Although Alvin was now in his 90s, his memory was very keen. As well as remembering details, he also remembered dates by relating them to other events. For example, he knew my husband's great-grandfather died during the flu epidemic in 1918.

Alvin Weaver.

Alvin also was able to supply some stories and details about my husband's mother's side of the family. He was full of stories about people in the area. Again he told me the sad story of the man who died after getting caught in a fence. I asked what the man's name was and he told me Daniel Kiefer. Somehow in my note taking, I wrote Kreider instead and then placed the note in my miscellaneous file, as I was not yet researching the Kreider family.

It was such a joy to visit with Alvin that I went several times over the next couple of years. A few times he would repeat a story or fact, but for the most part he gave new information. Some stories related to the families I was interested in and some related to peo-ple he had known in the same communities where relatives lived.

In researching the Kieffer family, I became confused at times because I had four different spellings in the same general vicinity. Church records, census records, newspaper obituaries and stone markers at the cemeteries didn't always agree. Brothers, whom I knew were brothers, each chose a different spelling even to the present generation. Perhaps they were all separate families after all.

While visiting one cemetery to take pictures of stones, I met another woman there and we talked. Her maiden name was Kiefer and she proceeded to direct me to the front part of the cemetery where her relatives were laid to rest.

"Momma always said these two were the first to come to America." These two were Daniel and Barbara Kiefer. After getting her address and telephone number, taking pictures of the stones and making notes of what she had told me, I decided it was time to visit Alvin once again.

Yes, Alvin was familiar with Center Cemetery where Daniel and Barbara Kiefer are buried. In fact, his grandfather and grandmother, Jacob and Sarah Kreider Kieffer, are also buried there. He also told me that many more of the extended family are buried there as well. He was not sure just how this Daniel and Barbara fit into the family, but he thought that they were probably connected in some way.

"I remember my Grandmother (Sarah Kieffer) took me to a funeral the year I had the accident with my hand. She said Daniel Kiefer was my grandfather's (Jacob) brother and it was very sad because he had died in a field and his body was not found for several weeks."

Now I had more questions. "Was the man's name Kreider or Kiefer?"

"Oh, it was Daniel Kiefer," Alvin said.

"What year did you have the accident where you lost some fingers?" I asked.

"That would have been in 1908 in the springtime of the year. I still had the cast on my arm," said Alvin.

Armed with this information, I searched the local newspapers and located an obituary for Daniel Kiefer in July 1908. With an exact date now, I wrote for a death certificate. There, very plainly written, were Daniel's parents' names — Daniel and Barbara Moon Kiefer. The obituary listed the sons of Daniel. Putting all this information into my history gave me the opportunity to connect the families of Kieffer, Keiffer, Kiefer and Kufer surnames in this locality. And, in connecting this family, I obtained stories and information about others.

Alvin Weaver died on 25 September 1997 at the age of 101. I still miss visiting him and hearing his stories. Not only did I learn interesting facts about family that I was researching, but I realized that we need to listen very carefully to all the things our older relatives tell us and not leave any stones unturned. So I've also learned to ask more questions about names, relations, places and events. — Barbara Sutphin Witwer, PA, ells94worth@aol.com

Late Breaking News

A couple of years ago, while doing research on my husband's family, we knew only that his dad's half-brother had moved to Valentine, NE around 1900. We knew nothing of any descendants this man might have. I found the name and address of the newspaper in that area and wrote a letter to the editor, telling him what I was doing and that I was researching for lost relatives in the area.

The editor printed my letter in the paper and the very day that it came out, I had a telephone call from the great-granddaughter of my husband's father's half-brother. This led to the discovery of all this man's descendants. — Myrna Schosser, TX

A Great Resource

Some families lost touch after the 1918 flu epidemic. In my father's line, five sons and sons-in-law died leaving widows who moved and/or stayed with their own parents thus loosing touch with the next generations of the male line. I wanted to build a family story of my great-grandparents who emigrated from Denmark and include a short biography with photographs of all their children, but couldn't find these families.

During a recent vacation, my husband and I stopped in a very small town and found a wonderful little museum built and maintained by the local residents. It was very well done and they were rightfully proud of the project. I began to wonder if one of these local museums existed in the small towns where I was seeking relatives.

Many of the people I was researching moved to very small towns in Idaho and Montana. When looking for obituaries I could not find local newspapers on microfilm available to borrow through the inter-library loan or FHL system. Using the Internet I was unable to find local historical or genealogy societies. To further complicate the search, local museums sometimes don't use the name of the town as part of their name. Thus I was having difficulty identifying them via the Internet.

I decided my best solution might be to actually talk with local people in the small town I was researching. On the Internet I searched for any kind of local government office, chambers of commerce or stores such as florists, drugstore, library or grocery store for the towns of interest. I then started calling and asking these local people if there was a museum, historical society or genealogy group in town. I found it was important to ask for all three organizations. In one case I had to call the town nearest to obtain a phone number, as I couldn't even find a drugstore in the town I wanted. I was given the phone number for the local village townhall. I found people more than willing to help me. If there was no society they often provided other names or ideas of places to call.

To my joy I found a museum in two of my small towns. One was closed for the winter but the woman I spoke with at a drugstore in the town knew the gentleman who single-handedly keeps the museum and gave me his home phone number. He was thrilled to receive my call.

The second series of phone calls resulted in actually finding cousins. I was searching for three families who were located in Big Timber, MT. Again I called a drugstore and was directed to the Crazy Mountain Museum located in Big Timber. In small towns everybody knows everyone. I sent a letter to the curator at the Crazy Mountain Museum asking about three different families. I always include a family tree with my letters. I've found that this easily explains whom I've seeking and it gets the attention of those not so interested in genealogy. The family tree has been my single most useful item in getting a response.

One of the volunteers read my letter and said, "Oh, this is my sister-in-law she is looking for." I am now in touch with a cousin and have obtained the family tree and photo for a great-uncle who died in the flu epidemic. All my family thought he had died before having children.

Turns out he had two daughters, one who is still living.

Another volunteer was actually a descendant of another great-uncle who had died in the flu epidemic. She is now helping me search for a photograph of her great-grandfather which will complete my family photo gallery.

I was also searching for the location of a grave of my great-aunt who drowned at age six in Deer Creek. A small notice in the Big Timber newspaper said she was buried at the family ranch. It turned out that the curator is well acquainted with the couple now living on the ranch. She sent me their names and phone number and they provided me the location and photograph of the small grave.

These wonderful connections to cousins were all the result of calling the local drugstore. The Internet is a great resource — but for small town searches, get on the phone and call a local business. Start talking to local people to find those small historical museums, historical and genealogy groups. — Ann McClary, WA

Glove Marks The Spot

A great-uncle of mine from Tishomingo county, MS, served in the US Civil War and never returned. I found him listed in a group of

A black glove (center) marks the grave where Irene Barnes' great uncle lies.

Confederate P.O.W.s buried in Mount Olivet Cemetery, in Frederick, MD.

Without knowing if there was a genealogical society there, I sent a letter addressed to the Frederick Genealogical Society (without a street address), Frederick, MD explaining that my great-uncle was buried in that cemetery and in which plot. I said that I would appreciate a member of their society being kind enough to go and take some photographs of the monument and send me a bill for the service.

Gravestone of W.F. Biggs, Irene Barnes' great-uncle.

In less than two weeks, I got six pictures and a bill for just $20. I was thrilled. One photograph was of a long line of markers with the photographer's glove lying on top of the spot where my great-uncle was buried. Another was a close up of the marker that I could read.

With the information I got from the marker I was able to apply for his military record. I learned he was shot in the hip and chest and left on the battlefield at Antietam where he was captured. He died a month later in hospital, without having been paid anything for the last six months. — Irene Barnes, MS

Collateral Line Searching

My interest in genealogy began when my grandmother showed me a book that was published on my grandfather's ancestors. She had long been my only living grandparent and I decided to research her maternal ancestors.

My grandmother knew her maternal grandparents' names, James McMillan and Jane McGill, that they were both born in 1836 and that they emigrated from Belfast to Ontario as newlyweds. She had heard about their thrill as they sailed up the St. Lawrence River to their new home. James McMillan was a schoolteacher. My grandmother's mother had told her how he had walked the frozen rivers from farm to farm to recruit students. She had also been told that they were buried in Carleton Place, ON.

This seemed like an auspicious beginning. However, eight years later, I have researched other lines back for centuries but am still stymied by this couple. I found them easily in the 1871 census (which has been indexed by heads of households for Ontario). The Ontario Cemetery Finding Aid (an online database) led me to the grave of a young son on Amherst Island where I found the family in the 1881 census. My grandmother has her parents' marriage license and she knew that they had been married in the McMillan house in 1888 at Chalk River. I found her father there in the 1891 census. I also found the death registrations of both Jane and James in the Ontario death registrations. However, I could not find their marriage registration in either Ireland or Ontario even though civil registration of marriages was required by law in both countries by 1858, that is, before they were supposed to have been married. A thorough search at the Lennox and Addington County

Museum and Archives provided no further information.

As luck would have it, searching the birth and marriage records for the collateral lines is what produced results. Although my grandmother and her sisters had not heard of it, James McMillan married again after the death of Jane. This marriage turned up in my search for the marriage of his eldest son, James. The names of his parents were included in his marriage registration — James McMillan and Maria Furlong. I also discovered that the youngest daughter of James and Jane had given her eldest child her mother's surname as a middle name — Magill, not McGill. I still cannot find the marriage registration of James McMillan and Jane Magill, but I have finally made some progress on the line I had started first. — Lois Sparling, AB, lsparling@shaw.ca

The Key To My Father's Past And Family

My father's background was always a mystery. The only facts he wanted to impart to his family were that he was born in 1896 in Oxfordshire, England. He also told us that he was orphaned at a very young age, he came to Canada as a boy and that he had an older sister, Mabel, in Ontario. When I was a young boy myself, my mother told me that our family name was not Orr but Hoare. Out of her desire to let me know my true family name, she had handed me the key to my father's past and family. What my mother didn't know was that this simple name change had a far more complex story attached to it.

I had only this small glimpse into my family history until my father's death. Out of respect for my father and the past that he wanted to leave behind, I never spoke to him about his family. It seemed that, while he was alive, my curiosity about my family history would have to wait.

After my father's death, I began my search in earnest. Going on the assumption that these young children (my father and his sister) could not get to Canada without help, I decided to contact the Barnardo Homes in England giving the two names known to us (Orr and Hoare). I received a reply that their names were in the Barnardo archives but that they would not be able to impart any information to us for about a year. My elation at my good fortune was tempered by the frustration of having to wait to find out about my father's family. It was well worth the wait.

Mabel Hoare, before leaving for Canada.

I was told my father was not placed with the Barnardo Homes but that Mabel had been in their care for a number of years having been brought to them by my grandfather in the late 1890s. They included information about the families that she had been placed with in Canada before a doctor and his wife in a small town adopted her. A most precious piece of family history was included with the information, a picture of Mabel. I would have been very pleased if this was all the information that I had been sent but there was more. The Barnardo organization supplied me with the names and dates of birth of all Mabel's siblings (my father's siblings). They gave me other names such as my grandfather, grandmother, aunts and uncles. The documents also spoke of the circumstances that had led to Mabel being placed with the Barnardo Home: My grandmother had died of pneumonia and my grandfather could not care for his children. The older children had been placed with aunts and uncles. Mabel had been placed in the Barnardo Home. But what about the youngest child, my father?

The Barnardo organization could only tell me that my father was in their home for one day but was then removed. They could not tell me where he went. I had instantly found my father's whole family but I could not find my father. The Barnardo Homes were very helpful in supplying me with the names of other orphanages operating during this same time. I contacted them all in search of my father including, what was then called the Church of England Home for Waifs and Strays. The answer came back from them that my father had been put in their charge. They supplied me with the date of his arrival and when he was sent to Canada. They were not as informative as Barnardo but the result was very satisfying nonetheless.

And what about my family name? The Barnardo organization told me that my grandmother's married name was Hoare but that she had left Mr. Hoare and had lived with a Mr. Grange for many years. My father and all his siblings, except for one, were Mr. Grange's biological children. Given the restrictions of the day, they had to take their mother's married name as their surname. So, while my mother told me that my true surname was Hoare not Orr little did she know that it should really be Grange. — Gordon Orr, ON, shirlo@sympatico.ca

Finding The Identity Of An Illegitimate Ancestor

I was confused when I saw Ebenezer Robinson's death entry in the town clerk's old record book. The entry for the parents' names was written in a strange way. It said "Ebenezer Robinson and Abigail" as if her surname was not also Robinson. I had known of an Ebenezer Robinson family in town at the time and was expecting the record to confirm that this was his father. But this Ebenezer was married to a Martha. The Abigail in the old record book was nearly illegible, but it was most certainly not a Martha. Perhaps he remarried, I thought.

I could not find a birth record. I searched microfilmed town clerk records and found a block listing many other children born to Ebenezer and Martha Robinson. There were children born before and after my ancestor, Ebenezer Jr., but he was not listed with them.

I went to the local library and looked at a book on the town history containing a section on local genealogy. I found my Ebenezer listed with the family and next to his name it said "illegitimate son" so at least I understood the reason for the missing birth record. But who was his mother? A search of microfilmed church baptismal records yielded only his father's name.

Then came the clue that would lead me to his mother's identity. I searched a commercial site containing a database of online genealogy books.

I had searched before but got too many hits. This time I used the name of the town as the key word in the search. Up popped a very interesting hit. In a genealogy book on the Whitney family it said that a certain Abigail Whitney named Ebenezer Robinson as the executor of her will. It did not state the nature of their relationship but with her birth date it was not impossible for her to be his mother. I decided to order the probate records anyway.

In the will Abigail Whitney left everything to her beloved son, Ebenezer Robinson, so he was her son. There were four heirs who signed off their inheritance. These names helped to identify the correct Abigail Whitney (there were several in the area), as they were her siblings, legally entitled to her inheritance since she was not married. The author of the book had mentioned the will in connection to the wrong Abigail, but had I dismissed the clue because of his faulty data, I would probably have never found the truth.

I have since searched databases of online books for all names in my tree, sometimes just using a town and a surname and have had great luck with data or clues. What I have learned is that information on ancestors can turn up in genealogies that you might never think to look in. If there is no work published, then try looking for clues in a book on a family in the same area, or try a book on the family of your ancestors' siblings' spouses. — A. Pondaven, Paris, France

The Next Town

My second-great-grandmother was married when she went from Ireland to Ontario. Her first husband died and she married my second-great-grandfather, Thomas Fahey. I spent years looking for her maiden name, as the only ones I could find were here two married names, Julia Fahey or Julia Power. It was a real brickwall

until I began to do research on an old house that one of my sons had bought from my parents in Leicester, MA.

It turned out to be a very old home that I had heard my grandfather bought from his aunt. As I researched, I found it had been left to a Julia Fahey (the name of my great-aunt). I became curious and looked at the will of Johannah Kelly who had left it to Julia Fahey. It really didn't give me much information. However, when I looked up the will of Johannah's husband, James Kelly, he had left a sister Julia Fahey!

Part of the will of James Kelly naming his sisters, one of which was Julia Fahey.

I took the 20-minute ride to the next town and there were my Julia Kelly Power Fahey's parents on her brother's death certificate. After trying for years in Ontario, I found it in the next town. — Mary McCullough, MA, cherrygen1@aol.com

Dear Diary

When my great-aunt died in Columbus, WI, in 1963, her mother's diary was found in her attic. At the time no one realized what a find this was because no one in the family was interested in genealogy. The diary floated around in the family for a few years and someone transcribed it on the typewriter. Still it just sat. Eventually my father sent me a copy of the typescript and I filed it away.

About 10 years after my aunt's death I became interested in genealogy and when I started working on the Nichols line I hauled out the diary and read it with renewed interest. Now the facts in it took on genealogical value and I began extracting names, dates and places. The diary told the story of her romance with, and marriage to, my great-grandfather in New York and his death less than a year-and-a-half after their marriage. It went on to tell of the misery in her life after she married another man. No one in the family liked him.

She described giving birth to five children in the wilds of Wisconsin Territory and of her husband leaving for the gold rush in California, perhaps never to be seen again. Then the diary ended.

What happened to Sarah Nichols after her husband left and she was in a state of shock, almost unable to go on with her life?

Sarah (Nichols) Wadsworth, second-great-grandmother of Pat Darling.

For years I searched for some indication of what happened to Sarah. Knowing that her family had settled in Columbus, WI, I checked there for any possible clue. The 1850 census did not list her in any part of Wisconsin. Her name was not found in the cemetery records for Columbus, even though all the rest of the family was buried there. I read almost all the Columbus newspapers looking for an obituary, but I found nothing. Not a thing could be found to indicate what happened to Sarah after her husband left.

I wrote to the Clinton Historical Society in New York for information on the Nichols, but they were able to provide me with minimal information on when her father arrived in the county and where he settled. In 1980, I decided to enter some of my surnames in the Roots Cellar of the *Genealogical Helper* magazine. This was pre-Internet days and this was the best way to contact others researching your line. One person responded.

She was a descendant of Sarah's sister and she had a lot of information that she had received from another elderly Nichols descendant. We started corresponding regularly, exchanging every piece of data we came across, including letters from our ancestors that had been written more than 100 years earlier. Then in 1984 I received a letter from another cousin who got my name from the Clinton Historical Society. She was also interested in the Nichols family and another correspondence grew.

Together, we discovered that when Sarah moved to southeast Wisconsin, the rest of the family moved to northeast Illinois. By investigating that area for the deaths of Sarah's parents, one of the correspondents discovered a news article in an 1874 Waukegan newspaper about a Nichols family reunion. This story revealed that Sarah was living back in New York and her name was Sarah Wadsworth! I now had a surname and a place to search and it was only a matter of time before I discovered the rest of the story. After living with her sister in New York for a while after her husband left, Sarah eventually returned to Wisconsin, where she lived in Columbus until after the Civil War. Having received word that her husband was killed, she returned to her sister's home in New York, where she married a widower that was a neighbor of her sister. Here she lived out the rest of her life, dying in 1877. I finally knew the rest of the story.

When there are no records to tell the story, contacting other researchers who are related can lead to information that can only be found in family records. — Pat Darling, MT, patdarl@hotmail.com

Look Over Your Shoulder

I work for a public library in my home town. On my day off I was in our local history department doing some research on my family. We had just got a new disc in from the FHL and this was my first chance to use it. After I had been on the machine for a little while, I typed in the name of my second-great-grandmother. I knew nothing about her at all. I just had a picture of her. I then noticed a gentleman was looking over my shoulder

The man looked at me and said, "I don't mean to bother you, but that is my wife's second-great-grandmother."

We talked for a long time and the next week I met his wife. She and I live only a few miles apart and we have both discovered a new side of our family. We have become friends as well as cousins. — Ann Biggs, AL

Web Postings

Versatility has helped me locate almost all siblings of my great-grandmother from Nova Scotia. They moved all over the US. Vital Records listed one sister's husband as from Bangor, ME. I went to various cemetery pages on the web for Bangor until I located her and her husband in one. Census records listed two brothers in Massachusetts, then California. On the California Death Index, I located one brother, his wife and several sons. An obituary mentioned several children unknown to me and gave incorrect town locations for them.

Judy Gillon received this photograph of her great-grandmother's brother's gravestone in New Germany, NS from a relative researching the Nova Scotian lines.

I've joined the mailing lists on RootsWeb.com, which helped me make some good contacts. When I posted my name and the surnames I was researching with a Nova Scotia-based genealogical society, I noticed others were interested in the same name and so e-mailed them. One was researching the same families and needed help in the US — we've been swapping ever since.

I've posted on GenForum.com, RootsWeb.com and GenConnect.com, joined every mailing list with the surnames I seek information about. I sign e-mails with my family website and have launched several web pages with as much information as I can prove.

I also interview relatives, attend parties for distant relations who may fill in blanks, write short letters asking for a little information here and there so as not to overwhelm the recipients. I check the obituary list for my surnames and match them to my locals, swapped GEDCOM files and everything else I can think of to do.

If I wasn't flexible, I would have missed some by not trying something different each time.

Sometimes you just have to sit back and be patient while you let the postings on the Internet work for you. Sooner or later when you least expect it, someone will see it and contact you. — Judy Gillon, MA

Beware Of Misread Records

My brickwall came soon after I started working on my genealogy. I learned my second-great-grandparents were Silas and Elizabeth York. I started trying to find their marriage certificate and with it her maiden name. In just a few weeks I discovered it was listed in *County Marriage Registers Of Ontario 1858-69, Volume 2, Index To Ontario County* (1986). (Incidentally Ontario county no longer exists, it is now part of Simcoe county and Durham region in Ontario.)

In this transcription Elizabeth York was listed as Elizabeth Lupan and her parents were shown as Louis and Charlotte. Using this newfound surname, I began my search for this family and the next generation back. I checked every resource I could find: the 1871 census index, Ontario county atlas, Ontario death indexes, computerized land record indexes, the three volume set of books *The Central Canadians*. I also checked all the French Canadian resources I could

find. Family members had told me that they were told she spoke with a lovely French accent. I found a few names that came close and started to research them, looking for Louis. Nothing came up.

I eventually came to a dead end, so I decided to check the transcription. I got the film for this original record book from the Archives of Ontario and there it was again, Lupan. About this time, I was beginning to suspect someone had misspelled the name. I discovered the original records in the books had been compiled from lists submitted from the various ministers performing the marriages. In most cases, it was a secretary or a wife, who was making these lists for submission to the government. From the original register to this report to the master government books to the book's transcriptions, there was more than ample opportunity to introduce a misspelling. I felt it was hopeless.

Another year or more passed, but at last a serendipitous event occurred to help me past this brickwall. I received a copy of the printed page I had originally found, this one sent to me by a helpful museum curator. On the original, someone had scrawled the name Serpa across from the marriage of my second-great-grandparents. I wondered how this could be the name and only because a microfilm of the 1861 census for Canada West was available to me locally, I decided to look up the name. I easily found the family of Louis and Charlotte Serpaw in the handwritten pages of the census. Looking closely at the flowing script of the census taker, it was easy to see how someone, somewhere, had read the handwriting of the minister and deciphered the name as Lupan.

The brickwall was breached. I have since found several Serpaw (Cherpaw, Chirpaw, Cherpaugh, etc.) descendants and discovered he was from France. — Bill Martin, ON, bmartin@tbaytel.net

A Family Legend Or The Truth?

We never knew much about my grandfather's family. I had only a few facts to begin with. He had 12 siblings and they grew up in Pennsylvania. Then there was the story that great-grandfather, Thomas Miles, had drowned in the Johnstown Flood on 31 May 1889.

Through census records and Grandpa's death certificate I was able to determine the family's home was Canton in Bradford county, PA. Even though I live far from there, I was fortunate that my daughter lives about one hour from the county seat of Bradford county. We made many stops there to see if we could find how great-grandpa Miles happened to die in the Johnstown Flood.

Through county history and census records, I found all 12 siblings. I was able to trace the movement of this family from 1840-80 to three counties in Pennsylvania. But nowhere could I find a clue about what happened to great-grandpa or where he was buried. None of the family lived in or near Johnstown.

Because of the date, the 1890 feder-

Thomas Miles, a musician in Company 1 of the 131st Pennsylvania Volunteers. He served two enlistments and participated at the conflict of Fredericksburg.

al census would have been invaluable, but its destruction in 1921 meant that I was facing a brickwall.

I had just about decided the story was a legend when a flash of insight came to me. What if he died the day of the Johnstown Flood and somehow the story got twisted? If we were correct, I had a definite date to look for.

Great-grandmother Miles was listed in the federal pension lists of 1890 as receiving a pension because she was a widow of a US Civil War veteran. So great-grandfather was living in Canton in 1880 with his wife and nine of his children, but had passed away by 1890. I had earlier found that he was a shoemaker with his own shop in Canton. Chances were that he was still in Canton when he died. But how had it happened? When recounting all this to one of my daughters, she surprised me with her answer. She told me that my mother had told her this story, "The day of the flood, Grandpa Miles left the house to go check on his shop and he never came back." I had never heard that version before.

We were determined to search again at the Bradford County Genealogical Library with the single purpose of finding the answer to where he was laid to rest, so we could put the legend to rest once and for all. We searched the cemetery maps and cemetery records again, but still could not find either him or great-grandmother anywhere in the county. We also searched newspapers for mentions of his death in the 1880s. Finally a librarian noticed our frustration and asked if she could be of assistance. She listened to our story and, when she heard that he was a war veteran, brought us a box of index cards used by the folks who put flags on graves for the holidays. Not only was his card there, but it listed the name of the cemetery, the plot and the particular gravesite. Most gratifying of all was the date of his death — 1 June 1889 — the day after the great flood. The legend was based on fact after all!

We visited his grave that day for the rest of the story. His stone was inscribed "Beloved husband and father. He did his best." I felt I had at last made the acquaintance of my great-grandfather, Thomas Miles, thanks to a flash of insight, a persistent record search and an alert, helpful librarian. — Marguerite Priest Carroll, OH, mcarro1@columbus.rr.com

The Story Of The Good Samaritan

I have been researching my family's history since 1978. I have also enjoyed getting others hooked on the same hobby for many years. On my visits to my home town in Wisconsin I would share my findings with my family. During one visit my aunt asked if I would take her to the local courthouse to find information on her grandparents. I jumped at the chance to get her hooked.

While we looked for the death records, I noticed a death record for Joseph Bennett in 1922. I had a Joseph Bennett in my files, but I thought this couldn't be the man I was searching

for. He was married to my aunt Jane, who was listed as a widow, years before 1922. In spite of this, I checked the death record and found it was the man who had eluded me for those years. It seems Jane did not want people to know she was separated (or divorced) from her husband, so she declared herself a widow.

MRS. JANE SHOOK BENNETT DIES AT NASHVILLE, TENN.

Relatives received word today of the death of Mrs. Jane Shook Bennett, who passed away yesterday afternoon at the home of her daughter, Mrs. L. V. Smith, at Nashville, Tenn., where she had made her home since leaving here in 1897. Death was caused by a stroke of paralysis. She was born March 30, 1844, northwest of town. She was married to Joseph Bennett in 1863. He is visiting relatives in the city at present.

Mrs. Bennett is survived by two children, Mrs. L. V. Smith, of Nashville, Tenn., and C. A. Smith, of St. Paul, Minn. The remains were shipped from Nashville last evening and will be brought here for burial.

Obituary for Jane Shook Bennett, wife of Joseph Bennett. From the Monroe (WI) Evening Times of 8 January 1918.

Being a Good Samaritan has its rewards. Had I not shared my knowledge, I might never have found the death record in the county I had researched for years. — Matt Figi, IN

Mapping Your Ancestors

I was trying to find where my English relatives lived before they arrived in Massachusetts. I only knew their names. I got a highway map of England, Wales and Scotland and broke it up into squares of about four inches in size. Then, one at a time, I searched each square on the map for any location similar to my relative's name. I checked each square as I finished it. This is easier to do than you might think, you just have to be very thorough. When I was done, I had three possibilities. As I knew that some English surnames originated from people taking the names of localities or geographical features, there was a possibility that these towns were the places where my ancestors lived. While not always true for everyone, it was true for me.

National Geographic has published ancient maps of England and France. Other maps can also be found at libraries but *National Geographic* can be found just about anywhere. It is good to scour these maps for your ancestor's name as well, because many old village names no longer exist. It is thrilling and inspirational to walk over land where an ancient village once stood, where your ancestors walked before. — Bill Whitney, AB, wwhitney@telusplanet.net

The Duel

For 40 years, the fate of my great-grandfather, Samuel Jones Darrah had been a mystery to his descendants. It was not a matter that was ever spoken about in the family, thus no one in the later generations had any information. There was only a rumor that perhaps he was shot in a duel!

About 10 years ago, a cousin in another branch of the family (a descendant of one of Sam Darrah's brothers) decided to get in touch with all the living members of the family. With the information gathered, he prepared a genealogy, which he distributed to all that were interested. He also acquired a small, unidentified newspaper clipping with the following provocative opening line: "BANNING, Sept. 17. — (Regular Correspondence.) Evidence given at the coroner's inquest on the body of S. J. Darrah, killed by Frank Milner..."

Fortunately, someone had penciled in the year, 1897, on the clipping. Banning is a small town in Riverside county, CA. When my wife and I were in Riverside on a business trip, we were able to spend a day of research in the courthouse. We found a lot about Sam Darrah, but no information about the murder. However, in the town library, we found almost everything about the murder.

We discovered an extensive and detailed series of newspaper accounts from the *Riverside Daily Press* delineating the killing of Sam Darrah and the two trials of the man who pulled the trigger. Here we found a classic tragedy of unrestrained passions. These men preferred to shoot each

The site of Samuel J. Darrah's Snow Creek Ranch and the adjacent ranch of Frank Milner who shot Darrah in 1897 during a confrontation over water rights. The property is located at the base of the north slope of the San Jacinto mountains in Riverside county, CA, near present-day Palm Springs. Today, the property is part of the city of Palm Springs municipal water supply.

other in the heat of the moment rather than to work peaceably to resolve their differences within the framework of law and the constraints of a civilized society. The results left one man dead, two families broken, a woman widowed, an unborn daughter without a father and three older children orphaned.

The shooting, which occurred 16 September 1897, was the result of an argument over water rights, a volatile subject in that desert area of California near present-day Palm Springs. Milner was tried and on 29 October convicted of second-degree murder. He appealed and on 16 December 1897, three months to the day after the shooting, he was convicted of manslaughter.

Justice was speedy in those days!
— Woodlief Thomas, Jr., NY

The Case Of The Three John Driscolls

My brickwall solution, as it sometimes happens, was solved by the research on a totally different family. However, the researcher was myself. The ancestor I could not find the origins of was one John Driscoll, the grandfather of my wife's paternal grandmother. The fact that there were three John Driscolls in the small area of Hastings county, ON did not help. The existence of each John Driscoll obviously knowing and living near each other to the point where each was in various incarnations the baptismal sponsor for the others' children made it impossible to decipher which John Driscoll was who when their names existed in a record independent of their wives' or children's names.

My John Driscoll was born in Ireland and while I had the family Bible entry that listed his baptism (24 November 1818 in St. Finnbars Parish, County Cork) and that of his wife, his

family and conditions of arrival in Canada were unknown. He had married Mary Walsh in 1849 and her family was part of an entry in the township history book. So I knew she was a Peter Robinson emigrant whose parents had settled in Asphodel township. This was a well-documented emigration of 2,000 Irish to the Peterborough area of Ontario in 1825. To trace your ancestor back to one of these families automatically gives you their townland location in Ireland and in 1825 this fact was virtually unseen in any other kind of source today, even in Ireland. But I did not find anything further about John Driscoll as every route seemed a dead end.

At the time of my brickwall solution, I was researching my father's maternal ancestors in Ennismore, ON, many years later and the story of his origins unfolded with a peculiar twist when it was completely laid bare.

Ennismore is a township on the other side of Peterborough from Asphodel township where Mary Walsh and John Driscoll were raising their family. Grandma was a Harrington whose grandfather William Harrington married one Elizabeth McManus. As fortune would have it Elizabeth's parents were identified in a marriage entry of one of her siblings as Bernard McManus and Mary Driscoll. Now the Driscoll name always filled me with foreboding, as it was a frustrating search for any Driscoll in Hastings. I had no assumption that the two Driscoll families could be related but when Mary Driscoll was reported as being Peter Robinson it moved me to look up her particulars in those Irish emigration records. There was the family in full listing, Mary being the oldest girl but having a younger brother with the dreaded name of John Driscoll. His age: five years and so born circa 1819 in Cape Clear, Cork. An online check confirmed the parish that serves that area; St. Finnbars. I now had John

Driscoll's origins and learned something that I consider a lesson well learned.

If I had tried the assumption I now use for people of this age in the Peterborough area I would have quickly discovered John was also a Peter Robinson emigrant, the assumption being that if one child is a Peter Robinson emigrant check for the existence of the spouse in the same emigration. A study of many of the Peter Robinson children has borne this out. They married others who came in that same emigration in all the townships where they settled. What drew John to Asphodel I can only suppose. Did he remember that lovely little girl he knew as a young child traveling up from the front and spending those harsh months camped on the plains that would someday be Peterborough? They had arrived on different boats but eventually all 2,000 were camped together before they were given their lots. Did he wave goodbye to her family has they went east to Asphodel and his traveled in the other direction to Gore of Emily as Ennismore was known in 1826? He returned to find her at any rate. They were both in their late 20s by then.

The twist to this is that my wife and my father are then fourth cousins both descended from the parents of Mary Driscoll for my dad and from her younger brother John was descended the girl I married. Denis Driscoll and his wife Mary from County Cork then were the common ancestors back five generations. An interesting fact considering I was adopted and so don't share that particular genetic code with my own father. But my children do through their mother. — Blaine Scott, ON

Personal Visits To Counties

My aunt, brother and I had been looking for Isaac Strickland's parents and

siblings for a while. From his obituary we knew that he was born in 1829 in Fulton county, IL. There were no clues to his parentage. With the help of other Strickland researchers, we found his marriage record from Indiana, but no other clues. My aunt decided to go on a research trip to a possible town in Indiana with connections. Before she went she did a people search online for all Stricklands in that town. She wrote to them and came up with a match. My aunt then went out to the county and the person gave her a big box of papers to go through. This person was descended from the same line as us, so most of the documents were pertinent to our line. This included information on Isaac's parents and siblings. — Jane M. Schumacher, WI, jjschu@itis.com

The Little Road Through My Brickwall

I was having a profitable time researching my third-great-grandfather John Tatch. After discovering an entry in a county history book, stating that John Tatch was a Captain of a whaling vessel, I went in search

Rufus Tatch and his wife Thressa (Klein) with their child Arthur Jenney Tatch. Rufus purchased the land which is now Tatch Road in Omena, MI in 1876.

of his ships and whaling logs.

I noticed while searching early birth records indices, that there was another Tatch, by the given name Christian. Christian Tatch had a wife Lydia and two young sons, Rufus and George. The sons were on the 1850 and 1860 federal census records for Massachusetts, but I could not find them after that time. It seems they had just disappeared. I could trace John Tatch's family to central Illinois in the mid-1850s, but could find no trace of Christian or his family.

The original house where the Tatch family lived. The children in front of the house are Irene Tatch and her sister Elsie, granddaughters of Rufus Tatch.

I began using a new Internet search engine. Since Tatch is a rare surname, I entered only the name Tatch. There were quite a few returns, but I noticed one that peaked my curiosity. It was a bed-and-breakfast business located on Tatch Road in the state of Michigan. I thought, and hoped, that maybe this road might have been named after someone in my family. I located the city and county that the business was in and wrote a letter to the local Chamber of Commerce, asking how Tatch Road got its name. The Chamber of Commerce referred me to the Leelanau Historical Museum, so I e-mailed them, inquiring about this Tatch Road. The Curator replied that Tatch Road was named after the Tatch family and referred me to a relative of the Tatch family who had done family research.

I sent a letter to the Tatch relative, explaining my ancestral line to John Tatch, inquiring about Christian Tatch and the mysterious Tatch Road. A few days later, I received a telephone call from the second-great-granddaughter of Christian Tatch! It turned out that Christian's son, Rufus, lived in the county for many years and once owned the land where Tatch Road is located. We exchanged information and I now know that John and Christian were brothers and learned of their parents' names, where they immigrated from and found many puzzle pieces that were so long missing. But best of all, I found a new cousin who also enjoys sharing and exploring the wonderful history of our Maritime ancestors.

All this was possible because of a little road that ran through my brickwall. — Marianne Hale, CA, hhmachshop@aol.com

Even Long Shots Pay Off

I had quizzed all living relatives and searched census data, looked for birth data and death records but could find nothing on my great-grandfather. No one knew his parents' names or any other clue. I subscribed to the online mailing list for the surname Schafer and for Hancock county, IL with no luck. I knew they had lived in a small town in Illinois, I also surfed the Internet every week for clues for more than a year.

One day I saw on a website a volunteer listed who would look up grave markers for people. They had the surname of Schaefer. I sent a short e-mail saying I wasn't interested in a grave lookup but would she by any remote chance be related to a Joseph Schafer born in 1850 in Nauvoo, IL. She replied immediately: "No, but my grandmother is into that genealogy stuff, I'll call and ask her." The next day I received an e-mail that not only was she related but also she had information on several generations back! Great-grandfather Joseph's mother had died shortly after he was born and he had nine half-brothers and sisters, one of whom her husband was descended from.

We've corresponded ever since and I have mounds more information now as well as other family contacts who yielded more information. — CR

Instead Of Going Backwards Go Forwards

For genealogists whether we are just starting or have traveled the exciting ancestral trail through many generations, the direction we aim to go is backwards. Occasionally though, when one hits that brickwall, it may be prudent to travel forwards.

My tree took me back to 1839, two years after civil registration in England began. My ancestor James Payne lived in central London with his wife and family running a small greengrocer's shop in Oxford Market. Also trading in Oxford Market were two other Paynes who I thought might be his brothers. One ran a fishmonger and poultry shop and the other a butcher's shop. The record I had for 1839 was James Payne's wedding certificate, but I had absolutely no records before that or any clue where he came from. I assumed it was London and one should never assume.

I first went forward to look for a will, which I thought might tell me where James was born. Fortunately I found one. James Payne died in 1856. The will stated he wanted the greengrocer's shop to be sold and the money used for his children's education. But that did not give me any clues as to where this elusive man had originated.

I wondered what had happened to his shop after it was sold. On a whim, I went forward to the 1861 census, to find the greengrocer's had become a newsagent and that a Caroline Payne was running it. It seemed too much of a coincidence to find the same surname. I found out she was his cousin. Her birthplace was given as the village of Kings Langley, 40 miles north of London. With nothing to lose I then took on the task of searching the Kings Langley parish registers and to my delight I found the long lost James Payne's baptismal records. Later via other documents, I was able to verify this was in fact my James Payne and the other two Paynes, the fishmonger and the butcher were indeed his brothers, also from Kings Langley. The charming village of Kings Langley in the county of Hertfordshire was positively oozing with a nest of Paynes and I was able then to go back to the 1600s.

My brickwall solution was two-fold; in order to go backwards it sometimes helps to go forwards. Secondly, if you have a whim follow it. — Susan Bogan, Bedfordshire, UK, bogan8848@aol.com

Creative Persistence

I hit a brickwall several years ago when I first started researching the German side of my family tree. My Great-aunt Rosie used to live with us back in the 1970s. She could speak German and often had correspondence with German relatives.

One of the relatives Aunt Rosie wrote to was Hans Kapell. When Rosie became too old to continue corresponding with Hans my mother's sister took up the correspondence, which since she didn't speak German degenerated to Christmas cards once a year. One year, no Christmas card came from Hans. My aunt wrote a few times and gave up.

A few years later I became curious

and tried to find Hans or any relative still in Germany. I wrote to Hans' last known address and received no reply. I had a friend who was originally from Germany translate my letter into German and sent it again. Still no reply. My friend told me that it was possible Hans had moved and that the letters may not have been forwarded and were simply thrown away since they had a US postmark and would be expensive to return. She suggested I write once more, she translated it to German again and on her next trip to Germany she mailed it there.

This time, I received a reply. It turns out that Hans had passed away in 1979. His wife knew nothing about the US side of the family so didn't continue the correspondence. She sent a copy of Hans' death notice and a letter with an address of Hans' brother, Aloys. I wrote to Aloys and received a reply from his son, Martin, who I still correspond with today. At first we used computer programs to translate but his children have grown and they translate for us now. Also, Martin's daughter, Esther, came to visit us for a month in the summer of 2001.

It just goes to show that persistence pays off. I've since gone on to have many more brickwalls but I remain just as persistent and know that eventually I'll get around those too. — Jacque Callis, SD, rjcallis@cs.com

Ask And Ask Again

For two years I've searched for my husband's grandfather, Olof Rappe. My husband and his sister (and their children) are the only living remnants of that family who immigrated to the US from Sweden (his grandfather).

Neither his grandfather nor his grandmother talked about his grandfather's family. He had no old Bibles or letters or anything to provide clues. All he had was a name and a guess at

an age from an old photograph in which my husband was a boy. I began questioning my husband about any scrap of memory. I wrote it all down although much of it seemed useless. I talked to his sister repeatedly. I checked census copies, I contacted counties where he might have died and searched ships lists until I was cross-eyed looking for emigration information. I was facing a brickwall.

I decided to interview my husband and his sister one more time. "Well, there was a lady with a bunch of cats whose name was Karen and we were told to call her Auntie, but I don't think she was related," said my husband. Armed with that sketchy information I reviewed the census for the Tillamook Oregon area of his grandmother and found next door to his grandmother's parents was a Karin with her daughter Linnea Rapp and their ages. Only an E separates Rapp and Rappe.

The upper two lighter entries are for Paul and Helen Ericksons and the lower two are for Karin Rapp Hasalberg and Linnea Rapp. Taken from the 1920 census for Tillamook county, OR.

I talked to my sister-in-law again. She said that Karin had a daughter named Linnea who had a daughter named Sylvia who had two children named Linnea and Adele. I wanted to shout, "Why didn't you tell me this before?"

This was not the end of my good news. I tried the Internet and found a Karin Rapp with a brother Olof born in Sweden with ages coinciding. I also found a record of a marriage certificate for Karin from Oregon confirming her age. From nothing to mounds of information in a few days. I now have 11 brothers and sisters for Olof, his parents and his grandparents all documented from Harnosand, Sweden. — CR

A Brickwall in Greenwich, CT

My aunt had done most of the research on our branch of the Worden family by the time I was in my teens. When I had settled down as an adult and discovered the Internet, I decided to help fill out the names and dates with some stories and histories. Descending from Peter Worden of Yarmouth, MA, I discovered vast amounts of information on the movements of the family. Some of this corrected the earlier material. I found that it helps to actually have the names right. I went on a little detour and later discovered the right family tree. I was home free.

That is until I reached Greenwich, CT. Everything seemed to lead to a dead end. I needed to find how my branch of the family ended up in Arkansas. I visited every website that I could find. I learned about the family forums and the digests.

Eventually, one of the Worden Internet groups called for a roll call to address new issues and old brickwalls. I submitted my request on Isaac C. Worden again. I really did not expect to get a response. Wow, was I wrong! Soon I learned Isaac moved from the Greenwich area to Indiana. There he served in the US Civil War with the 68th Infantry of Indiana. After the war, he moved again to Jasper Co., IL. My great-grandmother was from the adjoining county of Cumberland. Finally, it started coming together.

I also learned about a large volume regarding the descendants

Power of attorney record for Isaac Worden found due to posting information about the Wordens.

of Peter Worden. I ordered that immediately. The one thing I learned is never to give up, a brickwall is just waiting to have a hole knocked into it to provide a door to new horizons. — Robert Worden, KY, rworden@paducah.com

Probate And Estate Files

The probate records of siblings can be very important when confronted by a brickwall. Philip Thomas of Plattekill, Ulster county, NY, left a will in 1856, but it gave no clue to his ancestry. By checking the 1830 Ulster county probate for a John Thomas, who I thought might be Philip's father, I realized John was Philip's brother. In John's estate file, his siblings were listed as Henry of Newburgh (deceased), Jacob of Orange county, William of Wayne county, Philip of Plattekill and, one sister, Susan, the wife of Elijah Townsend.

Learning the names of Philip's sister and her husband were crucial to proving Philip's parentage. Also, knowing some of the history of the area helped. Five towns in Orange county, including Newburgh located immediately below Plattekill, had been part of Ulster county until 1798.

A trip to the Orange county courthouse gave me the link I needed. Another John Thomas, residing in Newburgh at the time of his death, had a will probated in 1801. The heirs listed were wife Eleanor and sons William, Henry, Philip, Jacob and John. His only daughter was Suky, wife of Elijah Townsend.

I have not since found any other documentation that conclusively proved the ancestry of Philip Thomas. Without John's estate file, I would still be searching. — Carol Harris Weber, NJ, chweb@attglobal.net

US Civil War Brickwall Solution

For years people have been trying to find my grandmother's grandmother. Her name, or so we thought, was Pelagie Danis and her husband was Louis Paradis. Because most of our family history is French Canadian, everyone assumed Pelagie's family had the same origins. I have been able to trace most of the family through the American-French Genealogical Society Library in Woonsocket, RI, but Pelagie had remained elusive. I found the record of her death in the Rhode Island Archives. According to the information there I calculated her birth to be about 1832 and she was born in the US. I looked up her obituary and it gave the place of birth as Danville, VT. There are no records of her birth in Vermont.

One day I thought that I would enter names of ancestors into US Civil War databases at Ancestry.com, just to see if anyone was in the Civil War. Louis Paradis' name came up as being a part of a regiment that originated in New Hampshire. I sent for his pension records and found the date of his marriage and the name of his wife. Her name was not Pelagie Danis, but Amanda Dana. They were married in Danville, VT in June of 1852. I entered the name Amanda Dana into

FamilySearch.org and came up with a hit. Amanda Dana was born in Danville, VT in 1832. It also gave the names of her parents, Horatio N. Dana and Minerva Clarke. I did some research on Horatio and Minerva and found the death date of Minerva and the cemetery where she is buried in Bennington, VT. I sent an e-mail to the Bennington Museum and they sent to me some of the information that they have. I now have the names of Minerva's parents and have been able to trace her family lineage with FamilySearch.org.

Amanda Dana, not Pelagie Danis!

Since then I have located the date and place of death, plus a possible birth date of Amanda Dana Paradis' father. He was Horatio Nelson Dana. I placed a query on one of the message boards available and I received an answer from two people. Horatio had been in the Civil War and I now had the regiment that he was in. He is buried in Sushan, NY, and the regiment is on his headstone.

I looked up to see if his name was listed on the Civil War database at Ancestry.com and his name and regiment came up. Even more information! — Norma Smith, RI

Ask The Experts

Early in my research, I had obtained the death certificate of my great-grandmother, Anne Marthea Anderson. I was pleased to note that her parents had been Peter and Anne Holie, both born in Norway. Unfortunately, no place names were included. Also, I knew enough to realize that Holie was the family's farm name, not Peter's patronymic name.

On my next visit to the FHL, I asked at the Scandinavian desk about finding the Holie farm in Norway. I was told that the correct spelling was probably Hole and that there were many farms throughout the country with that name. Not being able to read Norwegian did not help my search, but I persevered and began to collect listings of as many Hole farms as I could find. I recognized that a search of that magnitude would require much more than the one week that I was staying.

Seeking a shortcut, the following day I asked at the desk if there were any records of Norwegians who had come to this country. The staff member, who I had not seen previously, started rummaging behind the desk and came up with an old book entitled *Nordmaendene I Amerika — Deres Historie Og Rekord* (Norwegians in America — Their History And Record). Sure enough, there was Peder N. (for Nielsen) Holie, emigrated from Gran, Hadeland, Norway in 1869.

That was all that I needed to set

me in the right direction. I have now collected so much data on the family of Anne Marthea Pedersen Hole that I am compiling a full genealogy. While I still have problems reading some of the material, I have learned to save my questions and ask the FHL staff when I visit. It pays to get expert advice. — Carol Harris Weber, NJ, chweb@attglobal.net

Old Photographs And Newspapers — Valuable Weapons In The War On Brickwalls

When I started to research my Colpitts family in 1992, I knew nothing about them. While visiting my brother in Nova Scotia, knowing I was searching for information and photographs, he handed me a photo, asking: "Do you know any of these people, standing at the back of Mom and us kids?"

Looking at the photograph I didn't know who the older man was, nor the young woman and man. I could only guess the young couple were husband and wife and the older man was one of their fathers. I brought the photo home and neither of my two older sisters knew who they were.

I studied that photo for hours. Knowing the baby in the photograph was my sister Hilda, who was born in October 1921, she had to be less than a year old when it was taken. A tree in the background was laden with large apples, so I knew the photo was taken in the summer of 1922. But I still didn't know who the three people were standing behind my mother, brothers and sisters. I wasn't in the photograph as I was born seven years later.

Then in September 1992, I sent a letter to the editor of *The Gleaner*, based in Fredericton, NB, asking if any readers knew my aunt, Greta (Colpitts) Sharpe. Her daughter sent me a letter soon after with information on the family.

A few weeks later, her brother, sent me a letter and enclosed some photographs. One was that same picture with the older man and the younger couple with my family. The only difference was, on the back was written, "Uncle Oscar, Mabel and cousin George", the people who were unidentified in my copy.

The picture that began the search.

I asked if he knew who these people were. He said his late mother had told him they were members of the Colpitts family. I had a friend, Pat, who had been helping me with my research since 1992. I gave her the information and she searched all her files and everywhere, but came up empty on an Oscar Colpitts. So we had hit a brickwall.

I decided that as I found the Sharpes by writing to the newspaper, why not try writing to another? Once again I asked if their readers could help me find Uncle Oscar Colpitts, Mabel and cousin George.

I received a letter from Vera Steeves, who told me she had grown up in the area where Oscar and Mabel lived. She also told me his name was James Oscar Colpitts. Apparently, Oscar's first wife died and Mabel was his second wife. Oscar had four boys, by his first wife, and a daughter and son by his second wife, Mabel. I also received a letter from Vera's sister, Dorothy, who verified everything. I sent photographs to both of them and within a few weeks the answer was, "That's them."

In May 1994, Pat found Oscar's granddaughter living in Hopewell Cape, NB. According to her information, Oscar died in early 1940. Pat then found the correct date and I contacted Tuttle Brothers Funeral Home in Moncton, NB. Oscar's death certificate revealed that his father was William L. Colpitts and his mother as Jane Crossman. Later, Oscar's younger brother John Wetmore Colpitts' death certificate in 1925 showed his father was also William L. Colpitts, but his mother was Mary Crossman. Now I knew my great-grandparents were William L. Colpitts and Mary Jane Crossman.

Oscar's first wife, Minnie Clark died in Melrose, MA, in 1905 and, when his oldest son Oscar died in 1907, James Oscar returned to New Brunswick with his four other young boys, and around 1908, he married the young Mabel Crossman, who helped to raise his sons. That young man in the photograph turns out to be Horace Clayton Colpitts, not George. I have located all Oscar's children, grandchildren and second-great-grandchildren.

So if you are up against a brickwall and you know the area a person lived in, take a chance and write to the local newspaper. Letters to the Editor really paid off for me. — Donald F. Colpitts, MA, donaldcolpitts@webtv.net

The Importance Of Wills

A few years ago, a friend who was looking up his ancestors mentioned that he had found my father on the Internet. I looked and discovered a whole branch of my family about whom I knew nothing. After speaking with the researcher who made the original posting, I tried to help him look for clues.

My grandmother supplied the information for my grandfather's death certificate. He was listed as Henry Daniel Moser and was born in Pennsylvania. But nobody knew anything further except that his father's name was Daniel Moser. They had already learned my grandmother, Carrie Louisa Walmer, was probably born in Marne, IA. Later research indicated that my grandfather's birthplace was Sinking Spring, PA. Census searches revealed nothing, so I started periodically doing Internet searches for all the names I had. Since I was getting nothing that seemed to fit, I became discouraged and these became less and less frequent.

One day I got a listing for a Henry D. Moser with my grandfather's birth date and a birthplace of Sinking Spring, Berks county, PA. But his father listed was Frank, not Daniel. Although there were generations of data on the mother listed, Elizabeth Bode, there was nothing further on Frank. Other family members had notes on the subject and one of those had Eliza Body as mother and Franklin as father. However, he had been unable to confirm that information so he set it aside and forgot it.

Finally, the original researcher paid to have the Berks County Historical Society search their records for Henry Daniel Moser's family. That turned up a marriage record for Franklin Moser of Maidencreek township, PA and Eliza Body of Alsace; baptismal records for six children and possible marriages for Franklin's parents. I found more information, like a notice that said in 1822, five bridges across the Maidencreek River washed away during a flood. One of these bridges was the Moser Bridge. That was almost certain confirmation that there were Mosers in Maidencreek, but which Mosers? We still didn't have the final clue we needed to hook it all together.

The original researcher said that what we really needed was a will. Armed with the township name, Maidencreek, and my great-grandfather's real name, Franklin, I searched in the Berks County Register for wills and orphans and found wills for Franklin, his wife Eliza and his father and mother. The Berks County Registrar will send copies of wills if you send them payment and the wills filled in the final connections. We added not just one generation but two with possibilities for more. — G. Gates Sanden, CO

Pages From A Family Bible

I failed to find any records on my Wilson grandmother who was born in 1871 in Scotland. I decided to write to the oldest person left in the family, a woman who was married to the son of my grandmother's brother. She wrote back, enclosing a Bible page that gave birth dates for each member

Susan Peifer Marcus' grandmother, Annie Wilson (back row, far left) and her sisters.

of the Wilson family. She also told me the family lived in Strathaven, Scotland.

I went to my FHC and ordered the 1881 census film for Strathaven. When I went through the film I found the family, but they weren't Wilsons then. They had changed their surname. Using the newly discovered surname, I was able to find Scottish baptismal records at Family-Search.org. I wrote back to the cousin who had sent me the Bible page and she was as shocked as I was. She also told me she had gone to Scotland years ago and tried unsuccessfully to find information on the family. Her son later had similar disappointing results using a professional researcher.

FamilySearch.org.

There is one less brickwall in my research now thanks to a long-shot letter to a woman who was related only through marriage. — Susan Peifer Marcus, PA, smrcus@aol.com

Genealogy Wit

I had been searching for my husband's second-great-grandfather, Vitus Rudolph, for eight years in Maryland by looking through records from 1860 to 1900. He was allegedly born in 1813 in Germany, married to Rosina Altvatter Cronhardt and lived somewhere in Baltimore, MD. I looked at city directories, census indexes, church records and cemetery records when I could find them online. After all this time it began to look like the name or location was probably incorrect.

Then I made a trip to the National Archives. I got my hands on the 1880 Soundex for the city of Baltimore to find Vitus. No Vitus was to be found. I wanted to see if any of his sons, at least, were in Baltimore as young adults and began the tedious process of rewinding the tape to Henry, Charles, Edward or Ferdinand. I suddenly stopped winding somewhere in R and what was before my eyes but "Rosina Rudolph, widow Vitus"!

I was so excited I had finally found proof he existed, I turned to the person in the next booth and said, "I found my husband's great-great-grandfather! The reason I couldn't find him before was because he was dead!"

The man replied, "Aren't they all?"

Bottom line, when looking for ancestors, look for the men and the women by name. You may find yours are also dead. — Leah Ducato Rudolph, PA

An Unlikely Hunch

I had been hitting a brickwall for years searching for my great-grandfather, Joseph Wells in Brooklyn, NY. I was at the NARA branch in Laguna Niguel, CA, and saw an application for Pension Records for military personnel. I had recently read an article about how men who served for 100 days during the US Civil War were eligible for a pension. I had nothing to lose; I filled out the form to the best of my knowledge and submitted it.

About 10 days later, I received a letter telling me to forward a check to cover the price of research and copies. I received a 3/4-inch thick file with more information than I could have ever dreamt about. It had Joseph's death certificate, a verification of his marriage to Margaret Lyle (born in Scotland) and his burial place (which led me to other family members). The icing on this cake were the birth dates of his children.

With all this information, I was able to go to the FHL and find information on the Lyle family in Scotland. I found family letters that told me James Lyle (Margaret's father) had won a lottery — the prize being a plantation in Jamaica. I wrote to Scotland and found out they could not prove that and they told me to contact the National Library of Jamaica. The National Library of Jamaica advised me that it was not James who won the lottery, but his uncle, Robert Lyle. James went to Jamaica with four small daughters and his wife to take over the business and had four boys born there.

At least six of the eight children married Americans and immigrated to the US in the 1850s. I learned so much about my great-grandfather after following an unlikely hunch. — PAB

Name Switching

We are descendants from a family of 13 children. The parents were immigrants from Ireland who lived in New York City for a few years and then in Buffalo. When the family decided to hold a reunion, my cousin and I agreed to get whatever genealogy information we could. She went to the Vital Statistics Department at City Hall in Buffalo and I made requests to the New York City Archives Department. We knew the birth dates of the family members who survived to adulthood and that made the search easier.

My cousin found the birth records and some death records for five of the children in Buffalo. Each birth record listed the father as Patrick J. O'Brien and the mother as Jane Brown. She also obtained copies of the marriage licenses for the three sisters who married. Each of these records listed the parents as Patrick J. O'Brien and Jane Gaffney. Another oddity was noted; on Jane's death certificate, her father's name was listed as John O'Brien. On the 1900 US census record, the birthplace of the three oldest children, Alice, Catherine and Mary Agnes, was listed as New York State. Neither Vital Statistics in Buffalo nor the New York Archives had any record of birth for these three children. In desperation I requested a copy of a birth certificate for Alice Gaffney. And that's how we found a birth record for Alice Gaffney, born on 14 February 1882, child of Patrick Gaffney and Jane O'Brien, residing in New York City. The parents switched surnames. — A. Evans, DC, aaevans@erols.com

Sending Letters

I started to trace my family tree when I had to do an assignment for school. I had the whole history of my mother's side and not much about my father's. My father's mother's family name was Whibley.

At first I just thought it so overwhelming to start tracing and then an idea came to me. I decided to go to my local post office and look up all the Whibleys that lived in Australia. There were 60 families with that name so I sat down and typed a letter and sent it to all 60 families with amazing results. One family that had the same surname but wasn't related to me had found a grave in England that had two young children buried in it. The church and graveyard were just outside the walls of Hever Castle.

I sat down and wrote to Lord Astor of Hever Castle, he sent the letter to someone else that just happened to live in the house that my relatives had lived in some hundred years earlier and they made a video and sent it back to me in Australia. I received many letters from all the families. Most were related to me, which was an amazing success. I was so grateful that I was able to collect all this information from all these people. — KG

*   *   *

Evidence!

John Burnside and his wife, Mary Walker, lived in what is now Pocahontas county from about 1775 until they died in the early 1800s. I am a descendant of their daughter Margaret and the lineage down to me is well established.

Identifying the parents of Mary (Walker) Burnside had me stumped for many years and it is one of my brickwalls. Some members of the Walker family came up the Shenandoah Valley about 1736. By the late 1700s there are so many Walkers west of the Blueridge, especially in Rockbridge county, VA, that it seemed impossible to sort them out. Too many Alexanders, Marys and Johns!

I did have two clues that other researchers had recorded. One historian of Pocahontas county said in his book, written in 1901, that Mary Walker came from Augusta county, VA and was closely related to General James A. Walker of US Civil War fame. Another researcher said Mary was the great-aunt of the General. But she also said Mary was born in 1732. This meant Mary was 60 when her last child was born.

Extracted from the will of Alexander Walker. "Item: I give to my daughter Mary fifty Pounds and the Negro Wench Called Lucey and her Wheel and a young Black Mare a foal of young Jewels and her saddle and her own clothes."

So as I began researching General Walker's family, I found that his grandfather was Alexander Walker who died in 1775 in Augusta county, VA. In his will he named a daughter, Mary, and gave her a slave named Lucy. Mary would, in fact, be the great-aunt of General Walker. Then, I

looked at Greenbrier county's tax list from 1783. It included that part of Pocahontas county where John Burnside and his bride, Mary Walker lived. Furthermore that tax list included the names of the slaves owned. Much to my delight John Burnside's slave was named Lucy, the same slave given to Mary in her father's will – or at least I believe it to be so!

Later I found an Augusta county, VA deed, which named the legatees of Alexander Walker. Among them was the entry "John Burnside and Mary his wife", finally confirming Mary's father. — Wayne Hannah, WA, e170lakewy@aol.com

The Bigger Picture

I'm one of those genealogists who make purists cringe and shake their heads in pity. I get less satisfaction from finding the needle in a haystack than I do from uncovering a 5,000-name GEDCOM. My drive is to paint as broad a picture of my family's history as possible. I don't lose a lot of sleep knowing that a few brush strokes here and there aren't exact.

I'd been researching the Lokker family from Zuid-Holland in the Netherlands for six months. My direct family resources and the Internet had produced about as much as I thought was available. But the taste of having identified 300 Lokker family members, and an additional 18,000-allied members didn't dissipate. I was hungry for more.

Knowing that almost anyone living in Zuid-Holland named Lokker was certainly a relative, I identified 42 Lokker names and addresses in Stellendam, Zuid-Holland (using the directory feature in Ancestry.com). Each received a letter of introduction, a request for information and a summary of the first four generations of my research.

Of five responses, one was from Cor Lokker, a distant cousin. With his help, I discovered what most genealogists already know. It isn't about names, dates and locations. It's the stories, pictures and documents. And even though he had no prior interest in genealogy, Cor had them all. He has shared these with me during three months of correspondence. My fifth-great-uncle's memory book was a diary written by Jan Lokker over a 73-year period, beginning in 1807. It included information about his work in the Netherlands, numerous photographs and information about the marriage and birth of children.

All this has added rich colors to the picture of my family's history. The fruits of my letter writing have broken through a brickwall and given me content to pass along to future generations. It has also given me something even more valuable; a friendship with Cor Lokker that adds richness to my genealogy interests that far exceeds my wildest expectations. — Steve Lokker, WI, stevel183@yahoo.com

The Play's The Thing

For some time, I have been trying to piece together my family history. This particular line was always said to be French. So, I always sought information from French-related sources. I was lucky enough to visit the FHL, but always met a brickwall with the Atlantic crossing.

A few years ago for Christmas, my parents gave my siblings and me each a photo album. It included old family photos they had collected, reproduced and labeled with as much information as they could. This was the basis when searching for one of my family lines.

Shortly afterwards, as I was sorting through the mail, I noticed an advertisement for a play called the *First Ladies Of Ramsey County*. This play was about six early pioneers in Minnesota. I glanced at the advertisement and began to drop it in my recy-

cling bin when a familiar face caught my eye. Here was my third-great-grandmother looking back at me. I had information about her daughter, but not really about her. Imagine my surprise at seeing one of my missing links from my photo album staring up at me.

I contacted the historian at the Great American History Theatre. He graciously shared his information and I shared my family photographs with him. What did I learn? My family, although French, spent time in Switzerland during the French Revolution where several generations were born. I learned a variety of surname spellings and with more research found three missing generations!

Rose Anne Perry (1823-93).

I also learned that missing information can be in the most unlikely spot. I was indeed lucky, for a small piece of information opened the door in my brickwall and the bridge to Europe. — Eileen Lund-Johnson, MN

A Famous Brother

I was at the end of the line in trying to find where William Hayes came from in Ireland. Long searches here in Australia and in New Zealand had ended in failure. I could not find his death record or indeed anything about what happened to William in later life.

What I did know was that William had two brothers named Stephen and Henry who had died in the US. Apparently the brothers were all born in Ireland. Henry went to the US while William and Stephen went to Australia where William prospected for gold and Stephen became a parliamentary reporter. Stephen later went to the US where he served in the US Civil War. He was posted in a confidential capacity under Quartermaster General Van Vliet.

Family legend was that Henry became a senator in the US. We had a copy of a letter Henry wrote from Virginia shortly after the death of William. In it he reflected about life in the US and the career progress of his sons Stephen and Henry. The letter was signed Henry Gillespie Hayes.

I thought this might be the way to find where the Hayeses came from. I decided to trace Henry Hayes the senator. I couldn't find any trace of a Senator Henry Hayes in *Who's Who In America 1932*. However, I did find an entry for a Stephen Quentin Hayes. This was the same name I had seen on the back of an old photograph I had. The entry said Stephen was the son of Henry Gillespie Hayes. At long last I had something to go on.

I then logged onto the Internet and entered "Henry Gillespie Hayes" into the Internet. I was delighted to find a biography for a Henry Gillespie Hayes by the Hawaiian Medical Association. Reading the biography I learned Henry was the medic son of our Henry whom he had mentioned in the letter from the US. In the biography it said he was the son of Henry

Gillespie Hayes, a one-time editor of the *New York Post*. Unfortunately no clues were given as to what happened to Henry or his birthplace. I wrote to the Hawaiian Medical Association who sent me some more notes regarding Henry which indicated his father was dying in the early 1900s. I arranged for a search of his death certificate in Washington, DC but it was not located.

I thought there must be still descendants of this family in the US. The trick was to find them. I searched the Internet telephone directories to see how many Henry Hayeses were listed in the US. There were far too many. I then tried Stephen Hayes. There were not as many. Recalling the unusual second name of Quentin for Stephen. I tried Stephen Q. Hayes. Back came a listing for Stephen Q. Hayes, V. I thought this must be a descendant of our Stephen. I couldn't resist the temptation to call the number.

The person who answered the phone was Stephen Q. Hayes, VI, a young man and indeed he said the Q stood for Quentin! I had found our long lost American family! He referred me to his father who was also still alive. Stephen V did recall that a branch of the family went "down under" many years back.

It was through this connection that I learned about the career of Henry Gillespie Hayes as an eminent journalist who served in both houses of Congress. I also learned his place of birth as Coleraine in County Cavan, Ireland. It said so in Henry's obituary published in many syndicated newspapers after he died in 1906. I was so exited I searched for Coleraine in my atlas to discover that there was no Coleraine in Cavan. In fact it was in County Londonderry! I had found my relatives but still hadn't pinned down the birthplace of the Hayes family in Ireland.

It wasn't until later that the family in the US dug up family papers that proved that the Hayeses actually did come from County Cavan, from a lovely small town called Belturbet. He was the son of John Hayes and Isabel Gillespie. Isabel was the daughter of Sir Robert "Rollo" Gillespie Hayes, a famous career soldier. But that's another story.

It was fortunate through finding William's "famous" brother Henry we were finally able to locate his heritage in Ireland. — Julian van der Veer, New South Wales, Australia.

Different Registered Name

I was searching for my grandmother, Sarah Louisa Presland, in Norfolk, England on the British Census and National Index but I could not find her. I searched for her listing on the 1871 British census for Great Yarmouth and found her with her parents when she was nine years old: On the British census index she could not be found, but there was a listing of a Sarah Louisa Presterland. It was listed in Great Yarmouth, the correct place, and in the correct year, 1892.

I looked then at the 1891 census and found Sarah Louisa Presland age 27 of Great Yarmouth. I subsequently obtained a copy of the birth certificate — it showed the address. I found that, not only was my grandmother Sarah not registered properly, but her brother, Robert was registered incorrectly as Robert Prestland for his birth certificate too.

Sarah Louisa as "Presterland".

I knew the birth date for Sarah and it was correct. I had already obtained the marriage certificate: the marriage date was listed as 2 June 1862. Her father is listed as Henry Presland.

Found at last! Different registered name is all. — Ken Gibbs, ON, ken.gibbs@sympatico.ca

Naming Patterns

After 30 years of hitting a brickwall when searching the family of my Norwegian-born great-grandmother, I had a major breakthrough. I began tracking this line through church and community records to the Middle Ages. Siri "Sarah" Mortensen emigrated from Aust-Agder county, Norway in 1873. She married Tom Nelson in 1876 in Wood county, WI. I had a birth date of 9 February 1840 from Sarah's obituary in the Chetek newspaper. I knew nothing about her family in Norway other than her father was listed as Martin Mortenson on her death certificate.

I purchased a used microfiche machine and bought the IGI fiche for Aust-Agder, Norway from the FHC as this was well before the time of FamilySearch.org. There under Mortensdatter was listed as christened (rather than birth) was my Sarah on 9 February 1840. Her father was Morten Aanonsen and her mother was Gunnild Olsdatter. They did not immigrate with their daughter Sarah. From the date of the christening being the same as the birth date on her obituary I found a record of my great-grandmother by the Norwegian spelling of her name and her parents.

You may wonder how Siri Mortensen could have a father named Morton Aanonsen? In the patronymic naming pattern the child had a first name unique to them and their surname is built from their father's first name and the suffix of daughter or son. Therefore Morten's sons would have the surname Mortensen — son of Morten and daughters of Morten would be Mortensdatter — daughter of Morten. Sarah's mother was Gunnild Olsdatter, or Gunnild daughter of Ole. By having the father's surname Aanonsen we knew he was Morten, son of Aanon. This opened up the IGI records for Gjerstad parish, Aust-Agder for these families with the information of each father's name and appropriate date of birth.

Another vital source are the recently published community records called Norwegian Bygdeboks for parishes within a county. They are written in Norwegian but it is possible to translate names, dates, christenings, marriages and location. This usually gives the listing of the siblings of your ancestors. The records in these Bygdeboks are from censuses, church records and old land records from the Sheriff. If you are still looking at a brickwall perhaps a christening from the IGI, using "datter" instead of "sen" for the last name, comparing parish records with these name spellings and using the Bygdebok source for your parish would help.

If you have a town name source in a North American obituary you can find the parish and county. I couldn't stop in my research until I used this method to study the Bygdeboks, and parish records ended with this family line in 1300. — Earl Ross, MI, earlross@prodigy.net

$50 Well Spent

I encountered a brickwall when I tried to take an aunt's research and build upon it. There were two lines of my Sims family for which I had some names but no geographical locations or dates. These ancestors were listed in the 1871 Canadian census as children but I had no idea where they had gone as adults. By the time I was doing research, my aunt was suffering from a debilitating stroke and could not speak nor write. She died shortly afterwards and I asked to see her genealogical papers. None of her three children seemed to know the whereabouts of her papers. I persisted in mentioning my interest, not knowing if they had been disposed of during the estate clean up. My persistence paid off.

Three years later, one of her children said that he had the suitcase of papers. I offered to reimburse him if he sent the suitcase so I could copy the papers and then return them. About a year and a number of letters later, with no suitcase on its way, I lost patience and sent $50. Within a week I had the suitcase! The suitcase, however, did not contain research records, instead I had in my possession actual old letters written by the children of the people that I was trying to locate.

Addresses in the letters led me to Hamilton and Harriston in Ontario. I matched the locations to cemetery entries on the Ontario Cemetery Finding Aid. I also put queries on the Wentworth County GenWeb website. A helpful person saw the queries and provided me with further cemetery information. I was able to go to the Hamilton Cemetery in search of records for a spouse and serendipitously found most of her children buried in the same location!

One of the gravestones of Alan Campbell's relatives found through the Ontario Cemetery Finding Aid and the Wentworth County GenWeb websites.

As a long shot, I used the Internet telephone directories to locate names and sent letters of inquiry. This method found living relatives in the two lines who fleshed out my information.

Persistence is one way to break down brickwalls. — Alan Campbell, ON

An Old Approach To A New Problem

My success in tracing back my ancestors had been spotty at best. I had spent considerable time searching civil records in England but every quarter turned up several candidates for births and marriages and I could not afford to buy all of the certificates to see which were the correct ones.

When I learned that the IGI had extracted more than 95% of the parish records in Yorkshire and that they were listed chronologically and alphabetically, I could hardly wait to look at them. I searched the computer version but became confused and found it difficult to track from generation to generation and the marriages would not always come up the way I expected.

A friend showed me how to search an older fiche version and I invested $50 in copying all the Wild surnames in Yorkshire so that I could look at them at home. I put them in a three-ring binder and by going back 20 years per generation I was able to find my great-grandfather, his father and then his father. I have since obtained certificates and copies of the parish entries but it was the simple technique of looking at the fiche version of the IGI that allowed me to look at more than a century of parish events chronologically and track births and marriages for three generations. — Ron Wild, ON

Obituary Files

I wanted to obtain the death certificate for an Irish ancestor so that I might find his place of birth and parents' names. He was listed on the Pittsburgh 1910 census with his wife and three children, but his wife was widowed on the 1920 census. I searched city directories, cemetery records and even contacted the Diocese of Pittsburgh with no success. I considered sending to Pennsylvania Vital records, but with a common name and no other data, the outcome was not promising. I put the problem aside.

Many months later, I was looking in another county for some information when I discovered the genealogical library had an Obituary File. Since I knew that my Irish ancestor had lived in that county in 1900, I asked to have his name checked in the Obituary File. His obituary was there and a copy was sent to me immediately. He hadn't died in Pittsburgh or even Pennsylvania; he died in Ohio where he was visiting relatives.

I was able to get his death certificate which did indeed have his parents' names and place of birth. The obituary had information that this man had died under somewhat suspicious circumstances and the certificate was signed by the Coroner, so a copy of the Coroner's Report might yield additional information.

I have since learned that many historical and genealogical societies have obituary files, truly a valuable resource to the genealogist. — Judy H. Swan, CA

Fortune Rewards Those Who Never Give Up

My research hit a snag when I started trying to put together my grandfather's family. As you'll see I didn't use a highly technical or fancy research technique to solve this mystery. Perhaps it was just a little bit of good fortune.

I had been able to find my grandfather Fred's birth entry in the English birth indexes and I had sent for his certificate, which revealed who his parents were, his date of birth and the address where his family lived when he was born.

Fred was born in 1905 and his parents, William and Elizabeth, were married in 1902. I looked through the birth indexes from 1902 to 1912 for George Thomas, which was the name of Fred's brother. I sent for all the birth certificates for Georges that I could find. My mother wasn't sure if George was his name, but I decided to start there. I was hoping it would lead to a new discovery. Unfortunately, one letter after another kept coming back with the same results; it wasn't the George I was looking for. I kept trying to think where I could look next but found I was always getting sidetracked with other lines that were progressing nicely.

Uncle George's birth certificate.

Several years passed and I still hadn't got anywhere with this problem. I volunteer at the FHC and while there on my shift I decided I was going to give it one more try. I pulled open the drawer of the birth indexes and I noticed that there was only the third-quarter of the 1908 indexes, followed by 1911, 1912 and so on. I was going to start at 1911, when I hesitated for a minute and the next thing I knew I was going through the 1908, third-quarter index.

I was putting the fiche into the reader, when I was called to the aid of a patron. When I returned to my fiche I had forgotten where I was. I stared at the screen and found I had left it at the Thomas surnames. I was about to

move to G, because the fiche was left on W, when I saw the name George. It said William George. Could it be? I read on, "Devonport 5b 298". That was the right registration district. It made a lot of sense as his father's, grandfather's and great-grandfather's names were all William.

I sent for the birth certificate and received a response. I couldn't open the envelope fast enough. There before my eyes were the words "William George Thomas, born 23 August 1908". To the far right of the certificate were listed the parents. The names were right. I had found my mother's uncle!

My roadblock was removed by just being at the right spot at the right time, which is not a fancy or technical research technique at all. I am so glad I didn't give up and decided to try one more time. Now the doors are starting to open. I am determined to carry on. — Alison Forte, AB, alison.forte@shaw.ca

Another Brickwall Has A Crack

I posted a query to a Shackleford county, TX website. I was given a name and address of the person who was the primary contact for my family's graves in the Albany Cemetery. I sat down and wrote her a letter. Three weeks later not only did she send a letter but two completed family group sheets. She gave information on a family member's previous marriage and children from it, current information she had on the common ancestor's grandchildren and what she remembered about the family. Her response has given us another few places to look for information.

This line had been put on the shelf for about a year and when I to started work on it again more things were found. Sometimes it pays to let things rest for a while and try again later. If luck and research comes through maybe the entire wall will come tumbling down. — Marcia L. Staunton, OR, mls94@attbi.com

Search Memories

Searching for my husband's Hansen family was a real challenge. His father had passed away and no other family members knew much about the Hansens. We did not even know his grandfather's first name, but did know that he had died in Duluth, MN.

My husband had a childhood memory of an aunt mentioning a cemetery with a statue of Leif Ericksen near by. I wrote a letter to a funeral home in Duluth and asked if any cemeteries in the area had such a statue. The funeral home kindly forwarded my letter to a cemetery. A wonderful lady there did some research and found my husband's grandparents Alletta and Thomas Hansen. We have now been able to trace back two more generations to Norway. — Marilyn Hansen, WA

Far-Out Tangents

My grandfather Patrick Neal (O'Neil/Neil) indicated on his marriage certificate that he was from County Wicklow, Ireland. That was as close as I could get to a location for a long time. The family settled in Lower Town, Ottawa and intermarried with Behans, Bahens and Sinnotts. When reading some literature from Ireland I came across a lady who was researching Sinnotts in Wicklow and Wexford. Wondering if they possibly came from the same area as my Neals, I wrote to her. She replied with the information about the Coollatin Estate of Earl Fitzwilliam that extended from Wicklow into Wexford. She included a wonderful little map of the area. She asked why I was interested. I told her the Sinnott name was not my first consideration but was interested in Neals and wondered if they were

from the same area. She kindly offered to jot down any Neals or O'Neals she found in Kilavaney Parish records. She sent me the notes she had found, but unfortunately, they were not my Neals.

Above: Tomacork Church in County Wicklow.
Below: Interior of Tomacork Church.

A couple of years later during a trip to Ireland, I spent two weeks at the National Library. I asked at the desk about the parishes near Kilavaney in Wicklow. They told me of the records for Tomacork Church. I found my Neals in those records. What a lucky time it was for me. It all goes to show that even the most far-out tangents you might put out can sometimes give you just what you were looking for. — Jean Broadfoot, ON, jeanb@magma.ca

The IGI

After looking at censuses and parish records for years for my father and his father, I finally decided to do what I should have done first. The IGI is one of the largest compiled record sources in the world but it doesn't matter where you look there are always plenty of Taylors.

Imagine my surprise — my father was not on the IGI (might be now), but my grandfather was, his father and his grandfather, along with their wives and children. By my best estimate the information had been there for more than 30 years just waiting and I now knew that I had Taylor ancestors from New York and Vermont.

I'm looking forward to going even further back just to see how many generations of ancestors I and my 12 brothers and sisters have. — Eva Mary Taylor, ON

The American Digest System

The *American Digest System* series is a research tool that is often overlooked. It has proven to be the break through my brickwall, hence I feel it important that everyone know about this wonderful compilation of records.

I knew my mother was born in Germany and my father grew up in Iowa. When I became interested in genealogy, I recorded all the information that I had. I was surprised that when I looked at what I had recorded of my father, I had nothing past his father and mother. I knew that my grandparents married in Jackson county, IA in 1866 and lived in that area while raising their family. My grandfather died in 1892 and shortly after his death my grandmother moved to Wisconsin to live with a daughter. The census records told me that my grandfather had been born in New York. There was nothing to tell me where in New York, when his family had immigrated and how he got to Iowa. He was the only Heustis named in the Iowa census. To make it even worse, my father and mother were both dead by this time and my brother and sister had no interest.

I joined a genealogy society in my home area and attended a seminar where the speaker mentioned the *American Digest System* series. Fortunately I made a note of this — with the thought that at some point in the future I would see what that set of records could do for me in my research efforts.

The *American Digest System* is a central index to all case law in the US. The set allows researchers to find reported cases in any state or federal court. This series is helpful if you have very little information about the case, other than the name of one or more of the involved parties.

The first set of the *American Digest System* was the Century Digest covering the years 1658-1896. This set is followed by the Decennial Digests, which cover the subsequent 10-year periods. The *American Digest System* series can be found in most county courthouses. If not there, larger universities often have a set. The West Publishing Company publishes the *American Digest System* series.

The index of the Century Digest, which is what I used for my research, was in the volumes of 21 through 25 and shows most of the Appellate Court Cases.

The day came when I had to go to Seattle on another issue and I had some time to spare so I headed for the law library. In the index of the Century Digest, I found three Heustises, one being J.B. Heustis (the name of my grandfather). I found that J.B. Heustis sued Daniel Johnson, executor of an estate in Kendall county, IL for not settling the estate in due time. The index showed "HEUSTIS vs. JOHNSON — 84 — ILL — 61." This told me that I would find the court case in volume 84, Illinois, page 61.

At that point I made a quick trip to the National Archives branch in Seattle and there I found on the census a Solomon Heustis in Kendall county, IL, with Elizabette and eight children. Some of the children were born in New York, the others in Illinois. One of those children was John B. Heustis (my grandfather).

I immediately wrote the county seat in Yorkville, IL and was able to obtain copies of the court case, land records, will and probate records. In addition, because I now had found this family, I was able to get the marriage records of the children. With those records, I could piece the family together with documentation. I found that my grandfather had seven brothers and sisters. One brother died earlier and left a small child and wife living with the Solomon Heustis family.

There has been just a bonanza of information available to me — all because I checked the *American Digest System* series. — Emma Heustis Livermore, WA

Searching By An Ancestor's Occupation

Broadening the area of research to both local and national history can be of use when the tried and tested paths of traditional research fail to produce results. Looking at the wider picture surrounding my ancestral family enabled my researches to start again after a brickwall.

My trail led me from London to Oxfordshire. My third-great-grandfather, Thomas Glover, his wife and family, lived in the small town of Woodstock, which is close to magnificent Blenheim Palace, the ancestral home of the dukes of Marlborough. Since the 1600s, Woodstock had been a successful glove-making center and Thomas was a glove master. His family lived in relative prosperity, having a servant. I could not find any sign of Thomas as I went further back.

I began looking at the history of the glove-making trade as I wanted to enhance the family history I was writing. Woodstock was only one of a handful of glove-making towns to survive a terrible catastrophe that hit the industry in the 1820s. The trade plummeted in England due to fatal mistakes by the government of the day who allowed cheaper imports to flood the market.

Woodstock however maintained its industry and it flourished due to the proximity of Blenheim Palace. The sports of hunting and hawking at the palace created a need for quality gloves and the fashions of court life for the duke and his guests created a need for ornate gloves.

I began to wonder whether my Thomas Glover had come from another town that was hit by the glove recession to come to Woodstock to continue his trade. Researching into the history of glove-making I found that the county town of Worcester had more than 6,000 people employed in the industry but overnight it plummeted to just 113. Could my Thomas have left there to go to Woodstock?

Marriage license for Thomas Glover and Mary Mister.

I decided to look in Worcester. I found him quickly, with his wife and family. They had indeed left Worcester for Woodstock when the hammer fell on the glove-making profession. This flight into the history of a trade and how the national history affected it enabled me to kick-start my researches and eventually get back to the 1700s. — Susan Bogan, Bedfordshire, UK, bogan8848@aol.com

*   *   *

Divorced Family Found

There was a line of my maternal grandparents' that had been lost due to a divorce. All I knew was that the mother and three children were in Blairmore, AB, in the 1930s and the mother had remarried a man named Smith.

Her former husband, our relative, had moved to San Francisco and we located a death record for him. Sometime in the summer of 1993, my mother, who lived in Oregon had a visit from her sister-in-law from Alberta. While visiting with my mom she said that she had been to a high school reunion the week before and had run into, of all people, Gerald Brown. Gerald was one of the three children I had been looking for! I checked with telephone information and found a number for him and called that day. He told me a little history and mailed more to me.

A week after the sister-in-law had returned to Alberta she drove to Saskatchewan to visit family, was injured in a car accident and died a week later. — Lois Kullberg, WA

Team Work Works!

Our Varner family Bible listed Robert Whiting Varner as my fourth-great-grandfather. He was born to Elias and Mercy Whiting Varner in Pocahontas county, VA (modern-day West Virginia). He served in the US Civil War and spent the last half of his life in western West Virginia in Tyler, Wetzel and Ohio counties. But between 1832, when he was born, and 1874, when he married his second wife, there was a big void in his life and that of his parents.

I started in Pocahontas county once I realized I couldn't work backwards. I checked census records and found that after 1830 Elias wasn't listed on the federal census in

Pocahontas county. Several other Varners were listed so I went to the local historical/genealogical society there. Again while Varner was not an unknown name, Elias and Mercy were not to be found in any of their records. There was not a newsletter for their organization so I couldn't post a query. A volunteer at the society suggested I write a letter to the editor of their local newspaper asking for direction. I thought that was a very different approach but I was willing to try anything at this point.

Robert Whiting Varner.

Two weeks after my letter was printed, I received responses from three different researchers. Two were working on the Varner line and one was researching the Whiting surname. The Varner researchers were stumped on my line. They knew Elias had married but knew nothing of his family after 1832. The Whiting researcher saved the day. His research started in 1823 and showed the Whiting family in Gilmer county — he was missing Mercy. We checked the census for 1840 and sure enough Elias was in Gilmer county with his family near to his wife's family! Between the four of us we added several branches to each other's research. Luckily all was documented. — Kim Policastro, PA, kpolicastr@aol.com

Published Family Histories

I have worked on various branches of my family tree for about 20 years but it was mostly involving my father's side of the tree. I didn't have any information on my mother's maternal grandfather because he died when my grandmother, Flossie (Bongard) Bovie, was quite young. Since I had sufficient family trees to keep me busy, I didn't worry about that part of the tree until a few years ago when my mother became quite ill.

Over the years Mom had indicated that she would have liked to have known about her grandfather, William Bongard. When he died, the family could not afford to bury him so he was buried in a pauper's grave. Mom remembers going to the cemetery to visit his grave with her grandmother but she was quite young and couldn't remember where it was located. Some years later all the cemetery records were burned leaving no family information or record of where he was buried.

Mom recalled a collection of index cards of information located in the Lennox and Addington County Museum and Archives in Napanee, which was taken from notices in the *Napanee Beaver*. So in April 1998, we drove to the Lennox and Addington County Museum and Archives. While we were reviewing the collection of index cards, we located an index card which showed "Bongard, William Norman, Richmond, 10 December 1889, Pringle, Agnes, Richmond, Clergy, Stratton, F.B., Rev." Since these were the names of my great-grandparents, I went to my local library and requested the microfilm copy of the

marriage through the Ontario Archives. When it arrived, it provided the names of his parents, his date and place of birth, the names of her parents and her date and place of birth.

Using this information, I went to the Quinte Branch of the Ontario Genealogical Society and was able to locate William Bongard's parents, Bernard and Charlotte Bongard and the history of some 6,000 relatives. There were five volumes of family history but William was not in any of them. Shortly after William was born, the family moved from Prince Edward county to Richmond township in Lennox and Addington county. I expect that since he was the youngest of the family and because they moved shortly after he was born, that the person who contributed and prepared most of that family's history was not aware of his birth.

I am certain that if it had not been for tireless work of whoever was responsible for recording this information from the *Napanee Beaver*, I would never have found that side of the family tree. — Mary Culloden, ON

The Search For The Second-Great-Grandparents

My brickwall was my husband's second-great-grandparents. My husband's great-grandfather, William Barth, came to the US as a small child probably around 1864, although we have not found any immigration records for him. We knew from the family that he had a brother, Henry, and a sister, Catherine or Carolyn. The family also thought that his mother's name might have been Catherine or Carolyn. His death certificate provided no clues for his wife, Josephine Roth. She was the source of information on his death record and she did not know his parents, only that he was from Germany. The family had a picture of his sister with Henry and her husband, W. Davis, taken in Ft. Pierce, FL. This was still not enough to go on. We also knew from the family that Henry visited his brother periodically in Columbia, PA, until the 1930s when he dropped from sight. One last clue was a picture of him in uniform.

Since the family knew he was in the Spanish American War, I searched the indexed Spanish American War volunteer records at the NARA with no luck. More questioning of the family indicated that he was also in the West while in the Army. Back to the archives, but this time to the unindexed regular Army enlistments. I finally found him in the enlistment pages. He enlisted in the 2nd Cavalry in 1881. In 1886, after a short break in service, he enlisted in the 8th Infantry. He served until he retired in 1907. While in the Army, he spent time in Wyoming, Colorado, Cuba, California, New York and the Philippines and his retirement papers were sent to General Delivery, Philadelphia, PA.

Josephine Roth Barth (sister-in-law of Henry Barth), her daughters Frances and Anastasia (Anna) and Henry Barth.

By the time I had found that he retired to Philadelphia, I was searching for him in Colorado. I had found him in the 1910 and 1920 federal census for Colorado. I hired a researcher in Colorado to locate him or records of him. She found him in Pueblo city directories from 1911 through 1927 and again he dropped from sight.

Since the family knew he visited his sister in Ft. Pierce, FL, in the 1930s I decided to check there. I hired another genealogist, this one in Florida, to check the indexed death records in Florida. She checked all variations of his first name. Fortunately, I had her check all counties, not just counties near Ft. Pierce as I originally planned. She found one that looked viable and sent for the death record. We hit gold!

Henry Barth died in the Bay Pines Veterans Hospital in Pinellas county, FL. He died in 1950 at the age of 95 and his death record listed his parents as John and Mary Barth. His first enlistment stated he was born in Mannheim, Germany. By his fourth enlistment, he had changed his birthplace to Germantown, PA and became a full American. His death certificate carried on that fabrication listing his birthplace as Germantown. One other problem with his death certificate: he appeared to be six months younger than his brother William. One of them had lost track of their age somewhere along the line.

After having such luck with my genealogist in Florida, I decided to try for a death record for Catherine or Carolyn Barth Davis. Again she searched all variations of the first name. Since Davis is such a common name, she only searched counties surrounding Ft. Pierce, this time to limit the amount of possibilities for my first search. One sounded promising, Carrie Davis in Ft. Pierce. Again, I sent for the death record. Again, we hit gold! Carrie Davis was indeed a Barth before marriage. I got not only her husband's name, but also her parents' names, John and Carrie Barth. It

Headquarters Eighth United States Infantry

Camp Bowman, Calamsa, P. I.

May 16th, 1907.

The Adjutant General,

United States Army,

Washington, D. C.

(Through Military Channels.)

Sir:—

I respectfully request that I be ordered to the United States and placed upon the retired list upon arrival there. My service is as follows:

5 years in Troop H,2nd Cavalry,from Feb.8th,1881,to Feb.7,1886.

5 years in Company H,8th Infantry,from Sept.14,1886,to Sept.13,1891.

5 years in Company H,8th Infantry,from Sept.14,1891,to Sept.13,1896.

3 years in Company H,8th Infantry,from Sept.14,1896,to Sept.13,1899.

3 years in Company H and Non-Commissioned Staff 8th Infantry, from Sept.14,1899,to Sept.13,1902.

3 years in Non-Commissioned Staff 8th Infantry,from Sept.14,1902,to Sept.13,1905.

In Non-Commissioned Staff 8th Infantry since Sept.14,1905.

FOREIGN SERVICE:

1 year,6 months and 4 days in Cuba from Jan.15,1899,to July 18,1900.

1 year,9 months and 3 days in Philippine Islands from Oct.25,1900, to July 27th,1902.

In the Philippine Islands since April 1st,1906.

I had a furlough in the United States from Cuba from Sept.15,1899,to Jan.18th,1900.

Very respectfully,

Henry Barth

Quartermaster Sergeant Eighth Infantry.

Henry Barth's retirement request.

was the same father but different mother. At least I had found out why the family didn't know much about her — she was a half-sister. — Sharon Rea Gable, VA, gables@erols.com

Maternal Lines And Unusual Names

We always thought our earliest traceable ancestor was Samuel Pittard and his wife Rebecca Meredith of North Carolina. When I searched the Virginia/North Carolina border area counties I found no family by the name of Meredith in the late 1700s or early 1800s. However, I always made a habit of copying anything I ran across with the Pittard name on it, whether I knew who they were or not.

Ten or so years ago, after going online, I found a woman who was looking for the Pittard wife of her Davis ancestor in the same area. She had collected a lot of Pittard information, so we sent copies of various documents back and forth.

One day I was looking over some copies I had made 15-20 years ago and noticed Ann Pittard, listed as the daughter of Humphrey Davis whose will was probated in Wake county, NC in 1790. I copied it and put it into an envelope to mail to my Davis researcher friend. As I looked over the information, and tried to figure out what Pittard to whom Ann Davis could have married, it became apparent that her husband must have been the Samuel Pittard supposedly married to Rebecca Meredith. Some of their sons were named Humphrey and Davis! Samuel's brother John's children did not have those names. Although the name Humphrey is not used in the family now, the name Davis is still used, 210 years after the death of Humphrey Davis.

Ann's middle name may have been Meredith. Recently, I was in North Carolina doing research and ran across information about Meredith. Her sisters were Rebecca Davis Tucker, wife of Ethel Tucker, and Frances Davis Landers, wife of Tyree Landers. The Tuckers and Landers went south to Georgia, then Alabama and points west. Only the Pittard children went south, not their parents. Some followed their mother's sisters. As hard as maternal lines are to trace, these Davis daughters have been quite simple, with their unusual married names.

About 10 years ago, I worked with a woman in my area whose ancestor's will was witnessed by one of my ancestors. She knew a woman who lived about 30 miles from us who was also researching the same area of North Carolina. I called the woman and we talked for quite a while about the geographical areas we had in common, then I mentioned the name Pittard, which is not very common. She said her grandmother's first husband was a Pittard. It didn't take long for me to figure out who he was. John Robert Pittard died at Vicksburg in 1863 while the Confederates were holding the town during the US Civil War, a few days prior to the main battle. He and his wife Nancy Elizabeth Lyle had two children, Elvira and Robert Elijah, but I've only been able to find descendants of Robert Elijah.

After her husband died, Nancy Elizabeth married Richard Randall Pace in 1866. They moved to Ruston, Lincoln Parish, LA where they both died. Robert Elijah stayed in Clay county, AL so his mother probably did not move to Louisiana until her children were grown. If I had not been connected to the second woman, I would not know what happened to John Robert Pittard. — Anne Bowden, CA

Local Societies In Other Places

I hit a brickwall trying to find information on my first cousin once-removed who was sheriff in the mid-1900s for Walworth county, WI.

After puzzling about the brickwall for six months, I decided to join the Walworth County Genealogical Society and found all the information I wanted through them.

I am now in contact with numerous cousins and a few are doing genealogy. — Dale Barnes, MO

No One Remembered Him, Until Now

In 1987, my mother gave me pictures for the family album. In one picture there were people standing in front of a bakery. I asked my mother about them. She thought it might be Uncle Carl in front of his bakery. I never heard of Uncle Carl. My mother said he was my maternal grandmother's adopted brother. No one remembered him. I sent my son Joe to the FHC in Mesa, AZ to do some digging. Carl

Gosta Lanner was married, had four children and had a bakery shop.

Joe and I went to our public library and started going through the telephone books looking for any Lanners. We found about 25 of them across the country and decided to start with them. We also mailed form letters and received a response in February. It was from an Arthur Lanner who said he was the last surviving son of Carl Lanner. I called him the next day.

Carl Gosta Lanner was born in March 1875. When he was three days old he was taken to the public orphanage. Three months later my great-grandparents adopted him. I was able to get copies of the information from the orphanage but his birth parents were never revealed. Arthur said his dad thought his birth father was a banker. In 1893, my great-grandfather, my grandfather and Carl sailed for the US and Grandma came later. The men sailed into Boston and Carl decided to stay. The other two went on to Chicago. In 1900, Carl married and he died in 1936. His widow wrote to my Grandma Wendell until 1947 when Grandma died. For 40 years, Uncle Carl didn't exist until I put his picture in the book. Arthur died in 1993. — Ruth A. Gregory, AZ

A Hayle Of A Story

For more than a year we were stuck on our William T. Hayle, born in Mississippi in the mid-1850s when there was no census as they run at the turn of the decade. There was no family before on the 1850 census and no family thereafter in 1860. We thought it was because there are so many variant spellings of the surname including Hale, Hayle, Hayles, Hail and Hejl,

One day, when looking for another family, I came across what was clearly a William Hayle who I knew had not been listed on the federal census for Falls county, TX. I went back and searched the book and he was listed as Hoyle. I began to broaden my search realizing the A could be mis-read. Now, this William was not who we were looking for but this gave me a clue which helped later. Since our Hayle family settled in Texas, we finally went to the Austin Archives. We went through all the death, birth and marriage records of any Hayle in Texas using the correct spelling only. We wrote every one down and came home and studied them. Benjamin is William's brother on the family we know. They lived in Dallas. I had found a B.F. who was not ours who died in Dallas in 1913. I suspected he was a Benjamin and was related. I went to the library and started going through the *Dallas Morning News And Times Herald* microfilm to find infor-mation in the papers a few days after the deaths and had much success in linking him and others to our family.

The obituary on this B.F. Hayle said he died in his brother William's home and listed the address as the same where he was living. This con-firmed he was the brother. Now, when William died, his daughter said she did not know who her grandpar-ents were. But now that I knew B.F. died in William's home, I was think-ing William would have proved the information for the death certificate and of course he would know their parents. I faxed a request to Austin and received the copy of the death record in three days. It listed the par-ents as William Hayle and Maude Belles. B.F. was to have been born in December in Arkansas and he was a younger brother, therefore I had another state to search.

I began to look in Arkansas, but could not find a William with a Maude. However, I did find a William married to an Amanda D. with three children. One of the children was a Benjamin F., who had the same birth date as my B.F. Hayle. This William was supposed to have been born in North Carolina around 1825 and his wife was born in Georgia a few years later. This gave me a clearer migration between states. I went back and checked my marriage records in Mississippi. I found their marriage listed as William Hoyle and Amanda D. Bell in Tishomingo, MI. This was all I needed to confirm this is the fam-ily, so now we have another genera-tion.

I still have not been able to find them in other census records. I have noticed though, that when I broaden my views and do not look so narrow-ly, I have much more success. — B.J. Hayle, TX

Little Clues Solve Big Problems

As far back as I could remember, it was thought that my paternal grand-mother, Lydia (Kirkpatrick) Bozarth, had been adopted. I contacted a cousin that had been closer to grand-ma than myself and found she had a lot of old family photographs and

Lydia (Kirkpatrick) Bozarth, her hus-band, Joseph Bozarth and two of their daughters, Myrtle and Phronia.

other information. When I went to see her, she had a copy of grandma's mortuary record. I took a copy, but didn't really look at the mortuary record until a week later. There before my eyes it listed her parents' names. After more research I found grandma's mother had died when she was a little girl and had subsequently been raised by an uncle.

Alfred and Mahala Kirkpatrick, the uncle and aunt who raised Lydia (Kirkpatrick) Bozarth.

I knew where Grandpa Bozarth was born, but researchers could not place him with a family. I remembered that funeral home file for my grandmother, and my grandfather — her husband — was buried by the same funeral home. I went to the mortuary and the staff found his record: his parents were listed there. I sent the names to the Bozarth researchers and they were elated to find out who my great-grandfather had married. Not knowing her name had blocked the research of that part of the family for many years.

I have learned that it is little clues that solve big problems. — Ron Bozarth, TX, rb623@kc.rr.com

The Help Of The Postmaster

My grandfather Chester Howell was born in 1902, in Tanners Falls, Wayne county, PA. His father, Perry, died very young and Perry's wife Ruby left my grandfather (age two) and his sister in the care of her sister and her sister's husband. Ruby's sister subsequently moved to Binghampton and Ruby never was able to get the two children. We heard she was considered the black sheep of the family. My grandfather was separated from his birthplace and heritage. He did not speak of his unknown father and missing mother or any of his other family that I was to find. My father, an only child, knew nothing.

The area that Chester Howell was born in was a rural area in Wayne county, in Dyberry and Mount Pleasant township. I took a gamble and sent a letter to the postmaster in the nearest town to my grandfather's birth and asked him if he knew anybody who was a Howell or related to them. I was living in Florida at the time and could not get to that location. Amazingly, he replied and gave me the address of a man whose mother was a Howell. It turned out that this man's maternal grandfather and my great-grandfather were brothers.

After going to the location, I discovered that the Howells had been in that area for about 100 years. I took an excursion on some county roads near where my ancestors lived and found a small cemetery enclosed by a stone wall. Here, I found many direct and indirect relatives still in the pastoral farmland where they lived.

Eventually, I met a cousin who still owned an old house and some property. He showed me where my great-grandfather was born and let me look in his attic. There I found a family Bible with information showing a very large family that had been in the area since 1810. I also found my great-grandfather's autograph book — a sort of novelty where friends and family had written little poems and things to my great-grandfather before he died. My cousin allowed me to keep this great family memento.

All this was made possible by just sending a letter to a postmaster in a rural community. — Craig Howell, RI, zenoman@bigfoot.com

My Elusive John Hunter

John was my husband's grandfather and while we have lots of information about his adult life, his ancestry remains a mystery after years of searching. According to his widow, John was born in Mouswald, Dumfries, Scotland in about 1886, the son of an unmarried mother named Jean Hunter. A Hunter in Dumfries is like a Smith anywhere else!

John's mother subsequently married George Guthrie and they settled in Bolton, Lancashire, where they raised a family of three daughters and a son. There seem to be no records of his birth. All experts on Scottish genealogy agree that custom dictated that John be given the surname of his father at birth, but all searches for either Hunter or Guthrie about 1886 revealed nothing.

John was raised in the thatched cottage in Mouswald by his Aunt Serena, sister of Jean. He attended Dumfries Academy, went on to become a ship's captain and died in 1917 off the coast of Africa when his ship was torpedoed. He left a young widow and an infant daughter. After his death his widow and daughter kept in touch with his family in Mouswald and pictures were taken of them sitting at the cottage door with their relatives. I also have letters written between the cousins.

It occurred to me to place a query in the local paper in hopes some of the family still lived there. Much to my excitement, I heard from the son of one of the daughters and the daughter of another. They were very helpful but wanted to point out that their grandmother Jean didn't have a son John, born in Mouswald or anywhere else. To my horror, I realized I had opened up a closet with a skeleton in it.

As tactfully as I could I explained the situation and asked if they could get me any information from the two surviving daughters of Jean and George. Both these surviving daughters became enraged at the suggestion that their mother had an illegitimate son and told my correspondents to have no further contact with the crazy woman in Canada.

The granddaughter who wrote to me thought the whole situation was hilarious and we have become good friends. She made it her mission to find out what she could, making trips to Scotland, etc., to no avail. We both agree that the daughters who have since died, went to their graves knowing the facts but refusing to tell after all that time. Frustrating as it is, I respect them for that. — Pat Greenwell, AB

Female Ancestors

As any genealogist knows finding female ancestors is more difficult because they change their surnames when they marry or worse when they remarry. My family history is well documented, as Horace Mather published *The Lineage Of The Reverend Richard Mather* in 1890, but for me the more recently departed have been somewhat of a challenge.

My grandfather was married four times and had children by all his wives. My cousin said he thought there were 13 children. My dad was the second of his parents' four sons and his older brother had three daughters by his first wife. One of these girls died tragically after falling into a pail of boiling water used to mop a floor. There was evidently blame for this incident directed to my uncle and before long, he was divorced. My uncle remarried and had a son who I met recently. At the meeting he told me that he had never met his two half-sisters and didn't know if they were still alive.

Later, he told me he had a 1935 wedding invitation for one of his half-sisters and gave me her husband's name. I checked the SSDI and found two matches whose age would be similar to what I was able to glean from the 1920 census information. I sent for both SS-5 records. The first one I received was not my long-lost cousin. About six weeks later, the second one came and there she was, Alice Mather Hart. Her death certificate even listed her father's middle name, which was my grandmother's maiden name.

I went to the California death index list and a volunteer found an obituary for Alice who died in 1997 and the informant was her spouse! She died in California. I looked up the address to write for information when a light went on in my head to check the White Pages for the name of my long-lost cousin's husband. There he was alive and well at the same address where Alice was last listed. I phoned and left a message. Later that day he returned my call and we talked for almost an hour. He told me how he and Alice had met in high school, that he had never met my uncle who died 10 years after he and Alice were married. Evidently my father kept in touch with both families and was the information bearer.

And best of all, Alice's sister Marguerite is still alive and also living in California. — GM

Finding
Burial Plots

I have several brickwalls, however, this one in particular, I did overcome. I could not find my great-grandfather's burial spot. I had his son's obituary that said his mother had predeceased him. The light dawned after a few years of endless searching. I traced death indexes from the son's death back and I almost immediately found his mother's death date. I sent for her death certificate, which told me where she was buried. I sent for the cemetery printout and found my great-grandfather along with the

A clue from the death indexes!

names of many family members and even married daughters' names that I did not know. — ERR

Using The Help Of
A Professional

I have been researching my family tree since a distant relative of mine visited my father in 1989 and gave him a copy of the family records from the Dieffenbach au Val Town Hall in Alsace-Lorraine. I've come across a few stumbling blocks in my research but none like the brickwalls I kept running into in researching my paternal grandmother who was from Solingen, Germany.

My first cousin and I started searching for information based on family stories and memories handed down from generation to generation. Some of the stories had a base of truth and others did not. If my grandmother had not lived with my family I would have said, "This lady did not exist."

One of the stumbling blocks we ran into was 1892, the year she immigrated to the US via Ellis Island, when Ellis Island burned down. She resided in an area just outside the village of Brooklyn, New York that became part of New York City in 1898. She went to work at the age of 13 in 1899, one year before the 1900 census. There is no record of her marriage to my grandfather and no record of my father's birth. Of course, if I were still in New York City it would be very easy to do my own research. I now reside in Arkansas and the research facilities here are next to none.

So, in exasperation or desperation, I located a professional genealogist in Germany as near to Solingen as I could determine. I sent him an e-mail and he responded immediately. After giving him an idea of the time frame and location, he sent me a contract that I completed and returned to him. A few months later I received a beautifully made packet of documents and papers with translations on my grandmother going back four generations. — Patricia M. Camajani, AR

thrilled, so I carried it back to J.C.'s grave and placed it on the broken stone. It fitted exactly! Now I had J.C.'s dates and his wife's too.

The next week doors started opening for me. A descendant of his got in contact with me. I can now trace the family back to the 1600s! In a newsletter from RootsWeb.com, I read an article where a woman had found an old gravesite of her ancestors, so she cleaned it and placed some flowers on it and doors started opening for her too. I was very skeptical, until I wrote to a descendant and told him of that story. He told me other descendants had also been looking for that stone.

I couldn't help but feel that J.C.'s wife was thanking me for putting her stone back by her husband's. — Lynne Hanks, TN

Taking Care Of Gravestones Takes Care Of Brickwalls

I had been searching for the Kemp family for more than a year. During a trip to Gibson county, TN, I was looking for the gravesites of my ancestors. I came upon John Calvin Kemp, who I couldn't find on census or marriage records. I wasn't even sure if I had his name right. Next to his gravestone was a broken stone with some dates on it. On the next row farther down I found a stone lying on the ground that said "wife of J.C. Kemp". I was

RootsWeb.com.

Searching For A Maiden Name

My third-great-grandfather, John Vitko, married Anna, daughter of Andrew Gluts in 1791. Searching backwards in the church records (Plavnica, Saros, Hungary now Plavnica, Slovakia) I found this Anna, born to Andrew Gluts and his wife Anna. Several other children were born to them between 1769 to 1785 with some gaps. There was an additional entry in the church records for mixed marriages. My third-great-grandfather, John Vitko married Anna Krajnyak, not Gluts. From the marriage date and other information I knew Anna Gluts and Anna Krajnyak were the same person.

I concluded that for some reason Anna had used both surnames. I had also found an explanation for the gaps in the births of the children of her parents Andrew and Anna Gluts. Some were born with the Krajnyak surname. But I still couldn't find a marriage for Andrew Gluts/Krajnyak and Anna. I did find an Andrew Gluts married to Anna, daughter of Andrew

Stupak and widow of Michael Krajnyak, in 1746, but this would have been too early for my Andrew and Anna. I next tried to find a marriage for Anna Stupak and her earlier husband Michael Krajnyak, thinking that Anna and Michael had a son Andrew who was raised by a stepfather, Andrew Gluts. I could find no such marriage or child.

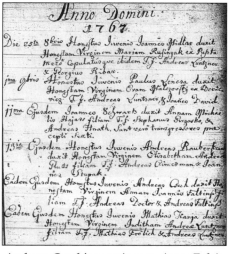

Andreas Csech's marriage to Anna Faltin (second from the bottom) in 1767.

Finally, I found a death record for Michael Csech alias Krajnyak in 1744. Then I found a marriage in 1741 of Michael Csech to Anna, daughter of Andrew Stupak. They had a son, Andrew, born in 1741. When this Andrew married in 1767 he used the surname Csech, but when his first child was born in 1769 the family surname was that of his stepfather: Andrew Gluts. So for two of Andrew's children the surname was Krajnyak. The church records in this time frame did not record the mother's maiden name, so you couldn't tell which Andrew and Anna were the parents, or even if one Andrew was married twice since I initially couldn't find the marriage records.

In the end it was by accident that I found the record. But if I hadn't reviewed the records many times

looking for different aspects of the family and hadn't become familiar with the records in general I never would have made the connection. — Dee Taylor, CT, cpramuka@aol.com

State Archives

My third-great-grandfather, James Clewett, was a fur trader and one of Minnesota's early pioneers. The records I needed were from before Minnesota's statehood. I traced him forward from the state history books, learning that he spoke five languages and is documented as being from England. However, there was no information about him before he came to Minnesota.

I joined genealogy mailing lists, posted to message boards and searched the Hudson's Bay Company Archives in Winnipeg, MB and the FHL. I e-mailed strangers asking for any detail, no matter how small to find anything that would lead me to his past. Nothing materialized.

Well over a year later I began discussing with a fellow researcher how frustrating it is to be unable to locate information about an ancestor who was an early pioneer in Minnesota. She mentioned there might be a roll of microfilm in the Minnesota archives with naturalizations for a group of early pioneers but could not remember any details.

This was rather vague, so I decided to contact the archives. I made a phone call to the Minnesota Historical Society History Center in St. Paul, MN, to inquire about this roll of microfilm. The history library informed me there were thousands of rolls of files in the State Archives Microfilm series with each containing 400-500 items. However, they had no knowledge of the records I was seeking.

I decided not to give up so easily and went to the History Center to begin my search. Upon arrival, I stopped at the reference desk and was again informed they had no knowledge of this particular film. They directed me to the State Archives microfilm as a good place to begin. The section had a wall of microfilm! These files are basically organized by date with the earliest records on the lowest numbered rolls. It made sense to begin with the earliest rolls and systematically review records.

After just a few hours, I happened across a declaration of intent for James in the Wisconsin Territory dated 1847. More searching led me to his naturalization papers in the Minnesota Territory dated 1849. This was a full nine years before Minnesota became a state. Because their naturalization papers are so old, they do not contain many details. Even though some of the facts on the two sets of papers conflict with the others, they have pointed me in a new direction. I now have ports of entry to search, a birth date different from what I previously had and the hope that out of a few meager facts I will indeed locate my elusive ancestor. — Eileen Lund-Johnson, MN

Illegible Records

My parents were born in Norway, but met in Brooklyn, NY. My father came from northern Norway and my mother from southern Norway. I had asked my parents many questions and they gave me as much information as they could remember. They were in their teens when they left Norway, but I knew where and when they were born, the names of their parents and their dates.

I had researched my husband's family and didn't think I would have much luck with my family until I discovered the LDS Church had copied Norwegian church records, which dated back to 1704. I was ecstatic and started on my father's family. Since I can't read Norwegian, I was armed with my mother's Dano-Norwegian-English dictionary she had when she

came to this country, and a copy of the *Norwegian Genealogical Word List* from the FHC.

Starting with my father's birth in 1895, I went from there. These later records gave ages at marriages, parents of children confirmed and a lot of extra information, which was very useful. I found my father's sisters and brothers, the marriage of his parents and names of their siblings and the name of his grandparents. There were two men in the area with the same name as his paternal grandfather. So I copied all the information, children, marriages, etc., on both men, sorted it, became familiar with their farm names and proceeded following the right ancestor. I found my father's siblings and the marriage of his grandparents and then I hit a brickwall.

I researched my father's mother's side at the same time, since they were from the same church parish. I found his father was confirmed with his mother's brother. Again, I gathered information and found his uncles and aunts and his maternal grandparents' marriage and then another brickwall.

I went back to the church records and translated the other categories. I had used the baptisms, marriage, confirmation and death records, so I looked at arrival and departure records.

I found both of my father's grandparents in the arrival records. They had moved to Nesne church parish a year apart and it listed what parish they came from and where they were born. I also looked at the censuses, which filled in more blanks. I found the birth of a sibling in other records.

I couldn't go back on every branch, but I did accumulate a lot of information. I found the names of my father's paternal great-grandparents, full names of his second-great-grandparents and the first name of his third-great-grandfather's line. Not being able to decipher the farm names, or too many people with the same name, another brickwall appeared.

I had better luck with his maternal grandparents. His maternal grandfather's parents ended with a brickwall. Without exact dates, I found five Anders born to Christians in the five-year span. So that wall remains.

But his maternal grandmother's family was different. The pastors' handwriting was legible until I got into the early 1700 records. The names were unique and so easily followed. And the church records contained the two parishes I needed. The pastor went to one church then to the other listing everything that happened in each church. Now the records were not in categories, but were written as the events happened during the church service. A baptism was followed by a wedding or banns announcements, deaths were listed, names of those confirmed and so on.

It was getting more difficult to find but on this line I went back to my father's maternal third-great-grandparents and one of the fourth-great-grandfathers. I found the marriage of one of the third-great-grandparents in 1715, but they were listed as Mons from an unreadable farm name, to Ann from an unreadable farm name. There were no fathers' names.

I am thrilled with the research I have uncovered. All because I went over, around and through that first brickwall. — Agnes Rysdyk, NY

Family Squabbles

My brickwall was finding proof of the descendants of an ancestor who immigrated to Ohio from Pennsylvania and died in 1812. There was no helpful census that listed the family members.

Since my direct line ancestor Griffith Justice's will was missing I checked all possible siblings' wills. A brother, John Justice died without issue in 1821 in Pickaway county, OH and he left his estate to his cousin and

a sister with his written will. But the family squabbles over his property led the family to the Court of Common Pleas in the Pickaway County Ohio Courts. Luckily, the contest between John's relatives over his land had my deceased ancestor's descendants listed including the married daughters and their spouses.

Researchers looked for years to match the family members with the right parent. Another brother was deceased by this time and his children were also listed as possible heirs to this John Justice. So the relationship of the siblings to John, and to the deceased siblings' heirs, were all spelled out.

The top of the first page of the dispute on the will. (LDS microfilm #1303133 — on Pickaway county, OH).

So, don't forget the family squabble over property, even when that ancestor's brother left a will. The courts have the final word and that helped me 180 years later! — Nancy Justus Morebeck, CA

Strength In Numbers

The Ronk family was one of the more difficult lines with which I've ever had to work. It was fairly easy until I got back to about 1800 and then it became impossible to make the connection back to the known progenitor of the line in Ulster county, NY. There were four known sons but little information was known about their wives and the names of their children. Additionally, each of them seemed to have had a John Ronk and sorting one from the other seemed a daunting task. Over the years I had only met eight other people who were researching this Ronk name and each of them had the same brickwall in front of them. None of us were making progress.

With the advent of computer technology, our little group decided to form the Ronk Group. We put all our heads together and through our e-mails to each other meshed all our collective information together, informally, in a huge database. One brave 70-year-old lady did all the compiling while another person created a Ronk website. Next, we all put forth arguments to the group about the constructions of these four sons' families and how our lines connected to them.

We collectively searched for evidence to support our positions and were fortunate to find a few wills and other pieces of information for each other. Whether the material we found applied to our own direct line or not, it didn't matter; we worked for the collective good. All Ronk material was admitted and shared because we knew it would help one of us. By working cooperatively, we were able to find a lot of new information that helped each of us work out which son we descended from.

I think many heads working together in this challenging case was so much better for me than if I had continued to tackle it alone. We needed information from each other's lines to know what the possibilities were for our own lines. I know that I was previously working down the wrong line. Now I have the confidence that we are as correct as we can be given the information available.

Incidentally, we still keep each other alerted to any new tidbits of information or Ronk family members that come along. And exciting news as a result of this Ronk research! I have a new maternal line back at least another five generations. I also know that my direct ancestors make up about half of the original founders of the Kingston Dutch Reformed Church in New York, which was founded in 1660. This was a real family effort and one of which I was proud to be a member. — Judy McAuliffe, CA

Message In A Jar

My cousin Julia and I were searching for the gravesite of our second-great-grandparents, John C.J. Selvidge, Sr. and his wife Elizabeth Bryant. From land records of 1840, we established they had lived in a nearby area from where they are buried in the Price Chapel Cemetery, located four miles southwest outside the town of Cleveland, Bradley county, TN.

Julia and I decided to walk the approximate 50-family cemetery and grounds checking each gravestone. However, not finding the Selvidges, we wanted to check again. Finally we

John Selvidge's gravestone.

located two gravestones that had been broken and were laying on the ground mostly covered with grass and weeds. After cleaning them, we were excited to discover we had found our second-great-grandparents' grave site. We went into Cleveland to check if any company could repair the markers but they said they were unable to do what we wanted. It was necessary for us to end our visit, but agreed we would return and try to resolve the broken marker project.

Elizabeth Selvidge's gravestone.

Some months later we returned and to our surprise the gravestones of Elizabeth and John had been repaired. We couldn't imagine who had done what we had tried to do. After contacting all the stonemasons and monument companies in the area and finding they had not worked on this project, my cousin and I decided to leave a note. We got an empty jar with a top and wrote the following message: "The Selvidges are our great-great-grandparents and we are interested in finding out family history on

them, also, on other generations. We are very curious as to who had their gravestones repaired. Please get in touch with us." We signed our names, addresses and phone numbers, put the message in the jar and taped it to the gravestone, hoping the right person would find it.

Many months later we were contacted by a new Selvidge cousin who along with two other new cousins had repaired the gravestones. We also found out there was an upcoming Selvidge reunion to be held in Sweetwater, TN, so of course we made plans to attend.

Our message in a jar solved our brickwall problem and gave us the opportunity to meet extended families and to share what genealogy we had and to learn more about our Selvidge line from those at the reunion. — Leona McKenzie Carder, GA

Working And Dying On The Railroad

One of our family stories involved my great-grandfather, Joseph Schmidl. He was killed while working for a railroad, but no one seemed to agree on the details. After I began working on my family history, I contacted my uncle, Alexander Schmidl. He shared what he knew and pointed me to an old cemetery. I enlisted my brother, Eric and we visited Flowerhill Cemetery in West New York, NJ.

Although we visited the location of the grave of Joseph and his wife Anna, the stones were long gone. But the cemetery staff were gracious enough to allow us to examine and copy down the burial information contained in the original ledgers. It read as follows:

"Joseph Schmidl, age 41, died 6 April 1907, buried 9 April 1907. Mortuary: Volk. Cause of Death — Railroading Accident. Plot Purchased By: Lackawanna Railroad, New Jersey."

Now that I had a date, I could check the newspapers for an obituary. I went to the Archibald S. Alexander Library in New Brunswick, NJ. A review of the available local newspapers for a period of several days before and after turned up a single article in the *Newark Evening News* for 6 April 1907.

"Killed At Kearny Crossing: Victim Apparently Walked In Front Of Approaching Train Had Gateman's Ticket In His Pocket.

"An unidentified man was struck and instantly killed at Sanford's crossing of the Lackawanna Railroad in Kearny about 8:30 o'clock to-day. The man evidently did not see the train approaching the crossing as he was traveling along the Turnpike road in the direction of Jersey City and walked in front of the engine, which struck him and hurled him nearly 30 yards. The train was stopped and the crew placed the body in the baggage car and removed it to the Hoboken station and from there to Volk's morgue.

"The body is that of a man about forty-five years old, four feet six inches tall, dark hair mixed with gray. He was dressed in the garb of a workman with dark clothing and overcoat and weighed about 150 pounds. The only thing found in his clothing was a gateman's ticket of the Pennsylvania Railroad. There was no name on it. At the crossing, little information could be learned about the incident, except that the regular gatemen was not on duty when the man was killed, his place being taken by an Italian who, it is said, did not lower the gates when the train approached."

There was no follow-up story identifying the victim or an obituary. Despite similarities between the cemetery records, the newspaper story and family lore, the unidentified man was not necessarily Joseph Schmidl. Further proof was necessary.

First, I wanted to establish the location of Sanford's Crossing.

Writing to the Jersey Central Railway Historical Society produced a map and photographs. Next, my brother contacted a friend who was a mortician. He told us the funeral home had relocated and had transferred all records to their new location. They were able to locate the appropriate ledger and after reading the information over the phone, mailed photocopies. The essential information is as follows: "Joseph Schmidl, died 6 April 1907; age: 41 years, 18 days; place of death: Kearney, at Sanford Crossing, R. R. Road. How Long in State; 15 years. Birthplace: Germany. Father's Name, Joseph; Mother's Name: Eva. Chief Cause of Death: Accidental railroad injuries; Place of Burial: Flowerhill Cemetery. Services at: residence on Tuesday 4/9 at 2 pm. Total cost: $168. 10 (the specifics are itemized in the ledger). Goods Ordered by: Annie. Bill Charged to: Annie"

By identifying the specific location and date of the accident, I had the linkage needed to establish that the unidentified victim in the newspaper was indeed my great-grandfather Joseph Schmidl. — Gregory Schmidl, NJ

Connecting The Brothers

My second-great-grandfather, Adin Burt, stated in his Civil War pension papers that his father and mother were Joseph Burt and Emily Tucker of Morrow county, OH. Joseph, a farmer born in Pennsylvania in 1818, never seemed to have made it into documents of any kind besides the census and a deed or two. Joseph left Morrow county for Paulding county, OH around 1853 with a Mark M. Burt. I felt sure that this Mark M. Burt was the same person who had a lovely autobiography printed in the *History Of Paulding County* stating that his parents were Ebenezer and Sarah (Leonard) Burt of Washington county, PA.

Back row: Willis Burt, Ellen/Alice Burt (Willis' wife), Arminta (Burt) Dunham, Marion George Burt, Adin Burt, Almira (Burnham) Burt and Imogene (Burt) Hodges.

Front row: Ruth Burt (daughter of Ellen and Willis), Charles Hodges (grandfather of Jane Peppler), Irene and Imogene Dunham and two unidentified boys.

My big break on making the connection between the siblings came when I read this amazing little article in the *Morrow County Independent* for 27 December 1882, which I quote in its entirety: "A pleasant reunion was held at the home of Mr. Adin Burt, on Christmas. Mr. Burt's father, Joseph Burt, and uncles Mark, Merritt, George, and Ebenezer Burt were present. This is the first time in 30 years these five brothers have met together and it goes without saying that the occasion was greatly enjoyed."

My great thanks to the librarian, Ms. Conant, who pointed me in the direction of this excellent resource, the small-town newspaper. — Jane Peppler, NC, jpeppler@duke.edu

Marriage Websites

After several months of researching my grandparents and coming up with little information, someone sent me a website address for marriages for the boarder area shared between France and Belgium. I found my great-grandfather and an uncle I was not aware of before then.

I joined two online groups pertaining to the area and within two weeks I had more information than I could have dreamed of receiving. I had information on my great-grandparents, their parents, the town in Belgium they came from and information for two uncles. I was so thankful to the nice gentleman from Belgium who spent his Thursdays viewing microfilms to extract this information for me. There are many helpful people out there. — Marie Van Laeys, CA

Go Back To The Original Sources

I have been searching for about three years for the parents of a John E. Deese, the great-grandfather of my daughter-in-law from Dale county, AL. John E. was married to a Gerona Joiner, called Dee, and they were in the 1900 and 1910 US census for Dale county. She was listed as a widow in the 1920 census living with her daughter and son-in-law. The tombstone for John E. Deese said he was born on 29 October 1853 and the census said he was born in Alabama and the parents were born in Georgia.

The Deese family descends from Emanuel Dees born circa 1675 in Scotland. The family is mentioned in *Historical Southern Families* and there are many John Dees(e)s in there but none seemed to fit and I needed one more generation to make the connection to this line.

There are many Dees/Deas/Dease/Deese researchers in the south and I have been in touch with several trying to find where John E. fits in this family. There were other Deeses in Dale county but I could not seem to find the connection. Recently I e-mailed a lady in Dale county, who is a Snell descendant who has a Snell/Deese connection. I knew she was interested in Dale county history. She happened to attend church recently with the aunt of my daughter-in-law and the aunt said that her mother (Vasste Deese, daughter of John E.), was a first cousin of Frank Deese, who was the son of Sidney S. Deese of Dale county who was a brother of John E. Other brothers were Edmund Wiley (Doc) and Malcolm Deese. This family was listed in *Historical Southern Families* as the family of Isham and Milly Ann Hester Passmore Dees who married 1839 in Troup county, GA. They had several children but there was not a John E.

With these names in mind I read a microfilm of the 1860 Barbour county, AL census. However, the left-hand pages were faded and almost unreadable. I found a family with children named Riley, Doctor, Milton, Sidney, an unreadable name, Nicolas and Malcolm (barely readable) and the mother's name as Anna. The surname was impossible to read. I put this film on a reader/printer and magnified it, then I darkened it before printing. The name after Sidney now becomes barely readable as Emory, age six, and not Henry as recorded in *Historical Southern Families*! Since John E. was born on 29 October 1853 he would have been six at the time of the 1860 census in July. He moved with at least three brothers across the county line to Dale county. The E in Emory is quite fancy and matches the writing of Eufaula, which was the place of enumeration. So I am sure I have found John E.

What I learned from this is to go back to the original source and interpret it for yourself. Someone not knowing a family can easily misread a name. Also people were sometimes listed by one name in a census and in the next census may be listed by the middle name or a nickname. — JMJ

Local Newspapers

It's far too easy to focus on what you can get for free on the web and on mailing lists, but for a little money and a couple of stamps, you might find the answer you're looking for.

I live in England, but found a wonderful woman in Buchanan county, IA who collected 100-year-old newspaper clippings of the local residents. She gave me more information than I could ever hope to find on my maternal side. This included names, dates, obituaries and stories. It's fascinating to learn a second-great-uncle used to be well known for his gopher-catching ability at the age of eight. Or that a few of the young married couples went west and often returned, preferring Iowa!

Local newspapers can be an excellent resource for genealogical research.

The obituaries were invaluable because they often listed surviving family members and where they were living. At the time of my third-great-grandfather's death, I knew which children were still living and where, thanks to the obituary. Another obituary confirmed the year a brickwall ancestor immigrated to the US. If only they could have thoughtfully added his parents' names and his home village! — Lisa Laurent-Michel, UK, lm-.lm@ntlworld.com

And So It Enz

Having done genealogy for almost 30 years, I have encountered numerous brickwalls. My most recent success at getting through a brickwall was on my wife's side of the tree. All her ancestors came to the US from Germany between 1850 and 1885 and I had been able to trace all her lines except one.

To trace her family, I usually started with the local Lutheran church where her ancestor lived in the US and I would typically find a record of marriage or birth with the town name in Germany where the person or parents were from. This worked in all cases except one where, even though the name of the town was given, I wasn't able to find it in Germany.

The ancestor's name was Anna Marie Klaiber and the records in St. James Lutheran Church in Lafayette, IN said she was from Insthal, Nagold. I had seen this name written in cursive in the birth records of her children and typed in other records. So for 20-odd years I searched for Insthal. I looked on numerous maps of the Nagold area and it was nowhere to be found. Knowing that "thal" means valley, I thought the river Inns, which flows through Insbruck, might be a clue. But the Inns River is not near Nagold, which is in the Black Forest area of Worttemberg. I hit a dead-end.

My big break came when I visited Nagold. I was determined to find Insthal. So while eating lunch one day I went table to table in the small restaurant and asked the patrons if they knew where Insthal was located or had ever heard of it. No one knew of an Insthal but one of the diners said that there was an Ins River nearby. I asked her where and she showed it to me on the map. It was spelled Enz.

After that it was only a short time after returning to the US before I looked up Enzthal in my local FHC and ordered the films for Ensthal, Mittelenzthal and Enzklsterle. I was able to find my wife's parents and grandparents after a 20-year search.

Never give up and, more importantly, check early for possible alternate spellings of any name. — Bob Young, OK

Online Searches Lead To Contacts

I was looking for my husband's grandmother's family. I knew her name was Bernice Lindsley. My sister-in-law had given me the names of a few brothers, but no dates or other factual information. I knew that Bernice was born in Fond du Lac, WI. I went to a people search on the Internet and put in the names of her brothers and Fond du Lac. I figured at least one person in the family had a son named for his father or a brother. I came up with a match. He turned out to be the nephew of Bernice. He led me to a distant cousin who has taken the Lindsley line and several related lines back three or more generations each. — Jane M. Schumacher, WI, jjschu@itis.com

The Discovery In The Dresser Drawer

My husband is from Swedish parentage on both sides of his family. The patronymic naming system makes it very difficult to trace lines. When his grandfather, John Kullberg immigrated to the US in the late 1880s he had changed his name.

He didn't have any close blood relatives but we talked to my husband's mother. Previously, we had hired a professional genealogist and he had not been able to locate anything either.

One day while we were at my mother-in-law's home, she was looking for rent receipts. While searching a dresser drawer, she casually said, "Oh do you want to see John Kullberg's passport?" Of course we did! Actually what she had was his Declaration of Intent to become a citizen under the name of John Kullberg and a payment receipt for passage on a ship to North America under his Swedish name of Jan Jansson. Then the professional genealogist was able to make headway on this line. — Lois Kullberg, WA

*   *   *

The Lees Of Texas

When my mother and I started the search for my maternal grandfather's family, we put forth several questions to my grandfather about his grandparents. He told us that his grandfather "was a Lee who married another Lee." The walls went up and the search began.

The first wall came down when my mother and I ventured to the small town of Eckert, TX, to visit a cemetery where we had heard through the family grapevine that maybe Laura (my grandfather's grandmother) was buried. No Laura was found, nor was Clark, my grandfather's grandfather. But there were two very large tombstones proudly bearing the name Lee. Were they our Lees?

A lady living down the road from the cemetery, herself bearing the Lee name, met us at the cemetery and proclaimed that they were the very Lee family that my grandfather descended from and more importantly they were Clark's parents. She substantiated those facts with a letter that told the tale of these two people, John and Ann Lee. We left that afternoon with more names and dates and certainly more family history than we knew what to do with. Some walls had fallen, but more had gone up. We still knew nothing about Laura.

We went back to my grandfather.

Clark Johnson Lee.

"Isn't there just anything you can remember your father saying about his mother? Just anything?" He replied, "I seem to recall my dad saying her father's name was George and they lived in Medina. She had brothers who were large and rough and, considering my dad said that, they must have been rough."

I was doing some non-specific research on USGenWeb.com, which ended up knocking down a wall that afternoon. I found a date of marriage for Clark and Laura in 1878 and discovered that they had been married in Blanco county, TX, which neighbored the county of Gillespie where they had lived and raised their children.

My mom and I went to Blanco for a copy of their marriage certificate and hopes of finding Laura's Lee line. There was no such luck. There was only a record of their marriage, which of course was still enough. From Blanco county we decided to go to the Gillespie county courthouse and discovered through a land search that Clark's family had acquired their land in 1873.

A search of the census at the library was next. We knew that since my grandfather had been born and raised in Fredericksburg, as had his father, we knew they had to be there in all those reels of microfilm. And they were. Clark's parents (John and Ann) were in the census with their three remaining children as were Clark, Laura and their first child. The surprise came when we found Laura's family living there as well, George and Artemice and her siblings Mitchell, Laoma and Robert.

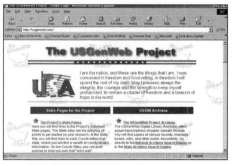

The USGenWeb Project.

We still have many walls to crumble. Clark has long since been located in the records. However, after his and Laura's divorce in 1900, she disappears. My mom and I probably won't ever consider this research done (if it ever can be considered done) until we find her. Meanwhile, I still hit the libraries, courthouses and Internet every chance I get. Every visit to one of those usually yields one further piece of information. Unfortunately, it usually raises one or two more brickwalls at the same time. — Lee Ann Schwarz, TX

Always Keep Your Eyes Open

My great-grandfather left home when he was 18. He never told his wife or children much about his background. All we knew was that he was born and raised near Boston, MA. I wrote to the Boston City offices requesting a copy of a birth record, telling them that my great-grandfather, Robert Lewis had lived in the Boston area. I received a notice that they didn't find him in any of the records at their disposal. I then wrote letters to the editor of newspapers in the area and to postmasters of the small towns around Boston. Nothing gave me any results

and years had slipped by with nothing happening.

Then one day as I was reading through *Everton's Genealogical Helper* I noticed someone named Lewis, who lived in Boston and had sent in a query, although she was looking in Canada and for a different name. I thought if she lived in Boston, it was possible she had done research on Lewises there in Boston. I wrote to her explaining my problem and what I had done. She wrote back and said that she would check all the birth records. Anyway, she found Robert in Lynn, MA.

She also looked for the marriage records of his parents and on that record found the names of their parents. It was just what I needed to send me to the FHC looking for records in Lynn. I found a marvelous book *Edmund Lewis Of Lynn, Massachusetts* which even had my great-grandfather listed in it. — Elizabeth Schooler Watkins, WA

An Off Chance Pays Off

Our family record states that my great-grandfather emigrated from Michelstadt Baden, just outside of Heidelburg, Germany to Ontario via New York City in 1850. I looked at a couple of detailed German maps and found two Michelstadts, one north and the other east of Heidelburg. After hitting a brickwall with this information, I wrote a letter to the Saskatchewan German Council in Canada on the off chance my history was wrong.

A very nice person sent my letter to Sinsheim Baden, Germany. After some correspondence with the Protestant pastor in Angelbachtal, he not only gave me records on my great-grandfather, but also records on his siblings, my second-great-grandfather and second-great-grandmother from a second marriage, as well as their status and occupation in Michelfeld, which had been merged with Angelbachtal south of Heidelburg. — Clark Lauman, BC

A Brickwall Solution In The Åland Islands

I was researching my husband's maternal grandfather's line, the Erholms. Unfortunately, I had little to start with other than bits of information that had been passed down over the years to my mother-in-law which were as follows: Andrew George Erholm immigrated to the US from Sweden where his family were wealthy shipbuilders. There were numerous brothers, two who went to Washington state where they set up a successful laundry business and another went to Wisconsin. Andrew had married in Sweden and had numerous children with his first wife, Maria Olivia Nylund, who died in childbirth. Andrew then married Albertina Wilhelmina "Mina" Schilling or Schelin, (my husband's great-grandmother), the daughter of the Erholm cook, who was also a family maid. Andrew and Mina settled in New York and then New Jersey where they had children. Nothing was ever said about what happened to the first-marriage children left behind in Sweden.

With this information, I spent nearly two years trying to find where in Sweden the Erholms came from. One breakthrough that provided quite a bit of information was locating the family on the 1900 federal census for New York and then on the 1920 federal census for New Jersey living in Jersey City. There were indeed many children so that part fitted, however no reference whatsoever to stepchildren. Both Andrew and Mina gave their birthplace and that of their parents as Sweden. However, I could

find nothing on that surname on various US websites, Swedish websites, ships' passenger lists and other non-Internet research. I even tried applying for Andrew's naturalization papers (he came over in 1887 with his first wife) but as he was naturalized in 1907, the papers could have been processed in a New York or New Jersey court or through the US Department of Justice in Washington DC. I had no luck with those searches.

About a year later, I had a conversation with my mother-in-law where she mentioned the names of Andrew's brothers who went to Washington State: Charles/Carl and Hugo. She also mentioned there was a son from the first marriage called Cleve whom she believed Mina raised (but where was he on the 1900 and 1920 censuses?). I found Charles and Hugo on the 1900 census living in Bellingham, Whatcom county, WA, where they ran a laundry business.

I knew I'd found the right Erholms but both men stated they were born in Russia and their parents were born in Russia also! My mind was reeling. I then found a Sophia Erholm living right around the corner and she was born in Finland. Living with her was her grandson Cleve Erholm, born in Wisconsin in 1888 and his parents born in Finland. I knew I had found something important but it was all so confusing.

Obtaining a book on Finland from the local library, I found that Finland was occupied and ruled by Russia for many years until just after WWI when it gained autonomy. Could it be that the Erholms were actually from Finland, not Sweden? By accident I found a website on Whatcom county, WA and on looking through a website on obituaries found about five related Erholms, including Charles. There, part of the mystery was solved: "Charles J. Erholm b. 1868 in Åland Islands, Finland, parents John and Sophia Erholm also born Åland Islands, Finland." Further research led me to the location and history of the Åland Islands or Ahvenanmaa in Finnish, which are equidistant between Sweden and Finland.

Apparently, there were once major disputes between Sweden and Finland over who claimed the islands. It was decided they should be part of Finland, but with autonomous rule, as the Åland Islanders consider themselves Swedish as they are of Swedish origin, culture and speak Swedish and have lived on the islands for hundreds of years. I found a Finnish website that has parish records for the Åland Islands and it unlocked numerous records on the Erholms and Schelins. I've now traced both Andrew and Mina's families back to the 1700s.

What about all those children from the first marriage? Andrew's first marriage lasted only five years when Maria died of lung disease in 1892 after leaving Andrew in the US and returning to Finland with Cleve, her only child, who was born in Wisconsin. Further research on the Whatcom county website led to the information that Andrew and his brothers originally immigrated to Merrill, WI, where Cleve was born (the family also founded a Swedish Lutheran church there). That same year Andrew married Mina who had immigrated to the US in 1890, and before the birth of their first child in September 1892, they settled in New York while his brothers also went their separate ways. In 1893, Mina fetched her five-year-old stepson Cleve from Finland so that he could live with them in the US. By 1900, Cleve had moved to Washington state to live with his grandmother, Sophia Erholm. I found Mina and her stepson Cleve on the Ellis Island database. So much for the numerous children from the first marriage.

And the shipbuilding dynasty? That was also a myth. Andrew's father Johan Erholm was actually a captain of a merchant ship. Most Åland Islanders were either sailors or farmers.

One brickwall down, many to go!
— Elizabeth Ball Kaufmann, WY, ekaufmann@vcn.com

An Empty Grave?

While at a conference a few years ago, I met a gentleman from Canada with whom I exchanged genealogy stories. We each had a brickwall in the other's country and agreed to see how we could help.

The problem I had to work on was to find the death and burial place of my friend's great-aunt, Emma. She was listed on a gravestone in a cemetery in Montana, along with her mother and husband, with the dates of 1873-1945. However, the cemetery officials said Emma was not buried there.

The gravestone for Emma Hutt.

I knew that Emma's husband, David, died in 1955 and was buried in the plot and at the time of his death was married to a woman named Sophie. Emma and David had three children. The search for Emma's death certificate was to take me on a two-and-a-half year odyssey to Seattle, Tacoma, Spokane, New York City, Los Angeles and a few other places where I learned about many available resources.

I checked the 1920 US census and found that Emma was listed as divorced and had two children with her. David was in another county with the third child and was listed as widowed. A search of court records netted 105 pages of lawsuits against David for non-payment of debts. Some of the cases listed Emma as a defendant; later ones mentioned his wife as Irma, apparently a second wife. This moved Sophie to the status of third wife. One case was filed for the child support due Emma for her minor child.

At this point, I decided to research the three children to see if they might be alive or had descendants who might be alive. I found that one had died while a resident in a retirement home and one had died while living with his sibling. Both were buried in a National Cemetery. I contacted all the places and people listed on the death certificates for these two, but could not find where they might have lived in 1945 when Emma supposedly died and neither had left children.

The third child, a daughter, was much more difficult to locate. Not being listed in the SSDI, I hoped she might still be living. Various searches on telephone listings were not successful. I found her listed on her father's probate records in Washington state at the time of distribution, so I asked a genealogical society there to check their obituary file for her. She was listed there and with the date of death of 1966. I was able to get her death certificate with a listing of the mortuary, cemetery and informant. A check of the mortuary and cemetery records netted the telephone number of the informant and cross checking with telephone listings showed the person to have the same telephone number after 30 years. A call to the informant's number elicited the information that the informant had died, but her husband remembered her friend, the daughter of Emma. Combining what he knew

with a piece of information from the initial heirs list of her father's probate file proved to be the battering ram that broke the brickwall.

Emma had died in New York City in 1945 while residing there with her daughter. Her name was most likely on the stone in Montana, as the plot had been purchased for her mother, her then-husband, David and for Emma. I am sure her children saw to it that her name and dates were inscribed there.

At long last, the brickwall came tumbling down. — Judy H. Swan, CA

A Brickwall In Christina Street, Cardiff

The 1861 census for 11 Christina Street, Cardiff, Wales was where I fully expected to find Sarah Elizabeth Denham and William Gage, my second-great-grandparents.

This was where Sarah Gage, the oldest sister of my great-grandmother Louisa Caroline was born to Sarah Elizabeth and William in 1857. I was aghast to see the family not there. Looking closely I noticed that the head of the house was a young woman named Caroline with a surname I am still not able to read and the other occupant was a 57-year-old woman also claiming to be head of the household, Jane Denham, the same surname as Sarah Elizabeth.

Could Caroline be a married sister of Sarah Elizabeth's arguing over who was head of the household and the 57-year-old Jane Denham their mother?

The 1861 census lists places of birth and it showed Caroline was

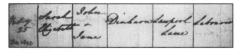

Baptismal record for Sarah Elizabeth Denham.

born in Wells, Somerset and Jane Denham in Totnes, Devon. I followed my hunch and checked the church records for Wells, Somerset.

I found Caroline and her maiden name was Denham! With all fingers crossed I then began to look for Sarah Elizabeth Denham, who was born in 1835 according to her death certificate. There she was!

Following the clue of her possible sister's place of birth, I found Sarah Elizabeth's birthplace. After hunting for 20 years this was a sight I thought I would never see! — Pamela Voss, BC

Finding Opa John

I had been searching for information on my great-grandfather or Opa, John Martinka, for some time, but I could not find the correct town of origin. I had three different places mentioned in records for John Martinka's birthplace, family lore named another and I knew that the name Martinka was Slavic. So the question was — what was the best type of record to search to determine place of origin?

I looked at some ships' passenger lists for 1881, John's year of arrival, but that was a daunting task due to the tremendous number of immigrants entering the US through New York City at that time. I looked into records for the Alsace-Lorraine area because that was still my focus for a European origin, but the records

were very sparse for this period. I joined a number of RootsWeb.com mailing lists for this area and for Bohemia, but found nothing. I did learn that Martinka was a fairly common name in the Czech Republic and the surrounding regions. No known family connections were established.

I bought a cd-rom called *Germans In America* and searched for the name Martinka. There were seven Martinkas and the fifth one was John Martinka, followed by Marianne Martinka. They arrived in New York on 12 April 1881 on the ship *General Werder* from Bremen, Germany. Their nine-month-old son Anton was also on the list. So I had now made a connection across the Atlantic to a port in Germany. But the ship records for New York at this time did not contain any information about the city or town of origin of the passengers, only the country, and most of the records for ships leaving the port of Bremen had been destroyed. I noticed that there was another Marianne and John Martinka included on a ship that arrived from Hamburg in 1884. And their ages were listed as about three years older than the 1881 Martinka record. Could these be the same people?

What made me unsure was that their son Joseph, my grandfather, was born in New York City in 1883 and he was not on the list. Also the Martinkas' country of origin was listed as Prussia

John Martinka and family in New York City, c. 1886.

rather than Germany as it had been on the ship record for 1881. But the most important piece of information for the 1884 record was that the ship — *The Rugia* — had originated in Hamburg. Hamburg passenger ship records were readily available and often contained the town of origin of the passengers.

It didn't take long to locate John and Marianne on the Hamburg's ships' list. Their town of origin was listed but difficult for me to interpret. I figured out that it was Schneidemühl, Posen, which is a larger town in the northwestern part of present-day Poland

I joined the Posen list hosted by RootsWeb.com and it proved to be a crucial component of my research. I learned that Posen was a province of Prussia and Schneidemühl was the German name for the town and if I were going to get anywhere I would possibly also need the Polish name. The latter turned out to be Pila with a ~ through the l. When I looked on a Polish map, I thought this was actually Pita but soon learned the difference.

I ordered and spent hours reviewing church records, civil records and directories for Pila/Schneidemühl, but to no avail. I found some Martinkas but none with the correct given names or dates. So I again turned to the Posen mail list and posted a query seeking help in locating my Martinkas. Almost immediately I received a reply from a researcher who was pursuing the name Martynka in the same area. She passed along some information about three Martynkas who were listed in a 1772 land registry from the town of Rzadkowo that I found out a little later was only about 10 miles from Pila.

I did not immediately pursue this potential new avenue. The researcher then found several people with the name Martynka/Martinka/Martenka. I then ordered a film of the Friedheim

Parish Church records that she recommended. This film included the time frames when John Martinka was born so I immediately went to his birth date — and although the record was in Latin, there he was! I now knew the town — which turned out to be a small village — of origin of my great-grandfather. It was named Rzadkowo. This film and others covering earlier time frames contained numerous records of Martinkas that lived in this area and nearby villages. I tallied more than 100 birth, marriage and death records for this family. Apparently depending on what priest recorded the events, the name was spelled Martenka, Martinka, or Martynka. The records also took me back three generations.

I have since located distant relatives who had information about the family including a picture of John. — Bob Martinka, MT

The Search For Robert Garner

My father, James Parker Kirkpatrick, was 43 years old when I was born. I was very close to him and I knew about his immediate family, but I did not think it was important to know any more. When my father passed away in the 1970s, I began to wonder about the history of my family. Too late to ask him what he knew, I turned to his sister, Jennie.

My aunt told me of my great-grandfather, Robert Garner, who fought in the US Civil War and had been a prisoner at Andersonville. I was on active duty with the US Air Force at the time and it piqued my interests to learn that my great-grandfather had fought in the Civil War and that he was a prisoner of war. I wanted to know all that I could about him.

I was an Air Force recruiter at the time and I knew that the US Government kept service records on just about everyone who had been in service. The NARA would be the agency to contact. My aunt stated that Robert and his family had lived in Unionville, Putnam Co., MO, but did not know from where he originated. We believed that it was logical that he served from that state on the side of the Union. We completed the form for Order and Billing for Copies of Veteran's Records in September 1979 and asked for Confederate soldier records, just to be safe and again in November 1979 for Union soldier records. Both searches came back unsuccessful. We continued to search for Robert in libraries and books about the Civil War and Andersonville.

We thought he might have served from Iowa and then settled in Missouri after the war. We asked for Union soldier records serving from Iowa. That request came back unsuccessful again.

We were up against a brickwall. We only knew that he had received a pension for his war service and that he had died in Unionville, MO. Furthermore, the Andersonville Records did not indicate that a Robert Garner was incarcerated there. We hired a Unionville professional researcher to help us with the search. I was transferred to Portugal and would not be able to search for three years.

The researcher found newspaper accounts of Robert and his brother, Henry, having attended a reunion of Union Soldiers and that they had served from Illinois. She also found he had a will probated upon his death and his pension file number. We

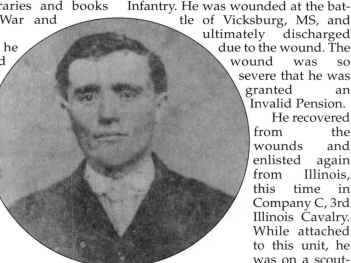

Robert Garner.

quickly filled out another records request with all the discovered information. This time we received his Civil War pension file and his military file. After reviewing the file, we found that there was an additional military file for a previous enlistment early in the Civil War.

It took us five years and five attempts to finally get all the information on my great-grandfather's participation in the Civil War. We learned that he lived in Illinois and volunteered from there to serve in Company K, 47th Illinois Volunteer Infantry. He was wounded at the battle of Vicksburg, MS, and ultimately discharged due to the wound. The wound was so severe that he was granted an Invalid Pension.

He recovered from the wounds and enlisted again from Illinois, this time in Company C, 3rd Illinois Cavalry. While attached to this unit, he was on a scouting patrol near Lawrenceburg, TN and was captured by Confederate forces and sent to Andersonville Prison. But the records of Andersonville did not contain his name as being a prisoner there.

In 1999, I went to Atlanta and discovered that Andersonville was not far from there and went to see if I could solve that mystery of his incarceration. I used the database at the National Monument and still could not find his name. I purchased an interactive cd-rom called *The Prison Camp At Andersonville* by D.L. Hutchinson. I also talked with the staff at the Andersonville National Monument. I told them that I had his pension file and that it clearly showed the date he entered Andersonville and the date that he was paroled/exchanged. They stated that they would add his information to the database if I provided them with copies of the file.

It was after my return home and going through the cd-rom that I found the mistake in the database records that excluded my great-grandfather from it. He was listed as Ganer, not Garner. All the unit information and the dates were correct. I contacted the superintendent of the National Monument and asked if the name could have been copied incorrectly from the original sources and sent them copies of the pension file. Their comment was that I was correct and that the records would be corrected. I also contacted Mr. Hutchinson about my discovery.

I have traced my family back to Scotland in 1580. I have found that my family has participated or fought in every war from the Revolution to the Persian Gulf War. I am very proud of my family heritage. — John P. Kirkpatrick, MO, jpkirkpatrick@earthlink.net

Don't Let A Clue Lead You Astray

I had reached a brickwall on my Garner line in Kentucky in 1836. My great-grandfather was James Anderson B. Garner. We had tried all the spellings for Garner that we could think of including the common Gardner and even Garnier. In looking for clues, we thought the B stood for the mother's maiden name, Brown.

We finally visited the Bath County, KY Courthouse and was told that there were still some Garner ladies living in the area and that we should knock on their door. We were greeted by a couple of wonderful ladies that told us that the name originally was Baumgardner, then Bumgarner/ Bomgarner and eventually shortened to B. Garner. It had not occurred to us that we should be looking under B instead of G.

While clues are definitely worth checking, sometimes they can lead us astray. — Shirley Garner deCoup-Crank, CA, sdcc9@pacbell.net

Getting Back To The Old Country

When I began researching my Italian ancestry, I didn't think I would ever be able to make the leap from the US to "The Old Country". Every document that I found listed my grandfather's birthplace simply as Italy. I searched for a city for years. My father and his siblings were all deceased, but I remembered hearing that their father had come from "somewhere near Naples", in the province of Potenza. Somewhere near Naples — that really narrowed things down!

When I located my grandfather's Petition for Naturalization, I was elated to find his birthplace listed as Stellaino, Italy. Paying special attention to the province of Potenza and the area around Naples, I immediately sought this city on maps, atlases and pre-WWI gazetteers, only to come up empty-handed. No such city existed.

I searched for cities close in spellings; I even searched for cities beginning with St. as in Saint. I searched for years, checking and rechecking resources with no luck. A

View of Stigliano, Italy, where Nancy Boudreau's paternal family originated.

very complete and comprehensive list of Italian cities and villages failed to list Stellaino and the closest match I could find was a city called Stigliano located in the province of Matera.

When I posted my problem to an Internet Italian Genealogy mailing list, I was encouraged to investigate Stigliano. Learning that the name of the city was pronounced Steelyano, I now realized that the "Stellaino" of my grandfather's Petition for Naturalization was a misspelling of someone's attempt to spell the city as they heard it. In addition, the city of Stigliano was in the province of Matera, southeast of Naples, but before boundary changes, it had been in the province of Potenza!

Entrance to cemetery in Stigliano, Italy.

My next step was to order the FHL film containing births that corresponded to my grandfather's birth date and cross my fingers. I found my grandfather's birth certificate, recognized his mother's name and knew I had the right guy.

In a relatively short time, armed with new information, I have been able to track my family from my brickwall at 1859 all the way back to 1740.

On a dream trip to Italy, I visited Stigliano and met cousins who put me in touch with other relatives who were in the US. The family continues to grow. — Nancy Boudreau, WI

The School Project

I still haven't made it all the way through my brickwall, however, I have made a large dent in it. My story begins several years ago, when a cousin of my mother started my interest in genealogy. They lived in Texas and would occasionally visit my mother in Iowa while on their genealogy treks.

They were researching my mother's Bauman relatives from Indiana and talked about her grandmother Cintha Stokes, whom everyone knew was part American Indian. They weren't sure which tribe or which side of the family was American Indian. They spent a lot of time in the Indiana counties of Clay and Owen searching for information on Cintha, but had come up empty handed, with the exception of her birth and death dates and her marriage license to Levi Bauman.

When my own children were in school, they came home with a project, to go back as many generations as they could. So, this was my key to start doing some research. I contacted my mother's cousin and got a copy of all the information they had acquired, which included the children of Levi and Cintha, as well as the brothers and sisters of Levi and some of their spouses.

I started doing some research in the Indiana area, as well as leaving queries in various locations. The first response I received was from the son of my mother's cousin, who had found my query and had recently found a possible name of Cintha's parents. While I was looking at land transactions for Levi, his father and grandfather I found a Lovina Bauman and her husband, William Stuck, listed. I quickly decided that Cintha and William were probably brother and sister. I then put a query out for information on William Stuck and was contacted by a descendant, who sent me his death certificate with the names of his parents David Stuck and Elizabeth Rader. He also sent a picture of Levi Bauman and some of his children and one of William and Lovina and their children. This picture of Levi happened to be the same picture my mother and her cousin had of Levi, so we knew we had a match.

I then found David, Elizabeth and children in the 1850 census. Among the children were William and Syntha. I have placed more queries regarding the descendants of William Henry and have since received more information on other descendants. All have the same information regarding the Indian blood in the Stokes/Stuck line but not which tribe or parent.

We have found the possible parents of David Stuck, Walter and Mary Francis. Now, I have started to rule out different lines. — LaVonne Hallberg, GA

Back To Basics

For years I had a brickwall that seemed impenetrable. I had the marriage certificate for my great-grandfather, Pacifique Lippe, and his wife, Virginia Cloutier. They were married in St. Jean Baptiste Church in Lowell, MA on 23 November 1879. While living in Lowell, they had two children, one who was Pierre Lippe. He was baptized in the same church. On Pierre's baptismal certificate the sponsors' names were Pierre Cloutier and Julie Lemire. This seemed like a relative of Virginia's, but no one could prove it. The family moved to Bay county, MI by 1884. The 1900 federal census lists Pacifique's family and said that Pacifique and Virginia were born in Canada. I had no clue where to start looking in Canada because there were no clues to follow. On Pacifique and Virginia's death certificates the parents' names were listed as unknown. Also, the documents said place of birth was Canada.

I have a few relatives across the country researching the same family. Now and then I'd ask if anyone found the parents of Pacifique or Virginia. No one had. I decided that I would not stop until I found them, going to every known avenue available to me.

I scoured the Internet for weeks, never once finding any mention of my great-grandparents. I was starting to think that these people were invisible or that they never even existed. Since I was caught up in the search for so long, I lost sight of the basics. I decided to act like a beginner in genealogy.

I went to the library and got a few books with ideas on where to locate information. It was then that I got back on the Internet and located the Pollard Library in Lowell, MA. They have a genealogical section and I inquired about this couple, asking if the staff could look through their records for anything pertaining to Pacifique or Virginia. What they found was a marriage record on microfilm listing the first names of their parents. I paid the fee and they sent me a copy. Pacifique Lippe was listed as Pacific Lupee and Virginia as Virginie. Pacifique's parents were listed as Benjamin and Genevieve. Virginia's parents were listed as Pierre and Julie. I jumped on the Internet and found Benjamin Lippe and Genevieve Breau at WorldConnect on RootsWeb.com. I wrote to the person who submitted this information, but he didn't have Pacifique listed as a child to this couple. There went my hopes again.

I found many websites listing Benjamin Lippie, but still, no Pacifique listed as a child. I went to my local genealogical library and found a book listing Quebec parishes and their locations. Since Benjamin and Genevieve were listed as being in Lavaltrie, I followed that as a lead. As a last attempt on this, I left a message on the Quebec-Research-L mailing list on RootsWeb.com asking if anyone could help me with Lavaltrie research. A lady saw my posting and e-mailed me telling me she could look. Shortly after that, she gave me wonderful news. She found Benjamin Lippe and Genevieve Breault with a child listed as Gabriel Pacifique! I can't ever thank her enough for what she did for me.

Marriage record for Pacific Lippe and Virginie (second from the bottom).

People often lose sight of the simple things such as city directories, local libraries in the towns where their ancestors lived and so on. Sometimes we need to take a step back, slow down and think it all out. We won't always find our ancestors on the major websites. — Julie K. Haynes, OH, budmom@aol.com

The Scraps We Save

In researching my family tree I had a fairly easy time with my mother's side. On the other hand, there was my father's side, the Hays line (without any trace of an E). Everyone remembered Grandma Richardson, Dad's mom. She was born in Kansas, or so someone recalled. Her name was Bessie Mae Richardson. Grandpa Hays? Grandma Richardson? There was a pickle.

We all have document collections in drawers and boxes. In going through my collection of numerous pictures, papers, letters, articles and items turning yellow from age, I wandered across a newspaper clipping from 1941. This gave me the information about my father coming home, after finishing Navy Machinist Training in San Diego. His parents were listed as Mr. and Mrs. C.B. Hays along with their address in Alhambra. He was married at the time to Kay Palmer and she had just given birth to their daughter. My grandfather, C.B. Hays, became a sticking point. My older sister believed his name might have been Clarence.

Also in my collection was another item, which was yellow, tattered and somewhat illegible. However, certified as a Delayed Certificate of Birth from the state of Kansas was the name of my grandfather, Clinton Burhl Hays. There was Grandma Bessie listed on the certificate, but more importantly, this was a delayed certificate, which meant affidavits had to be used. Also within my collection were scraps concerning Great-grandma Hays, Aunt Alma and more people, including cities, counties, dates and treasures.

The 1920 US census for Greely county, KS, produced a family of Hays that goes back to the late 1600s in Wales and Scotland. Their neighbors happened to be my Grandma Bessie's Davis Clan. There was not just one but three households.

Never overlook the collateral families associated with your main surname focus. Most of our ancestors existed with collateral families. These were neighbors, friends and cousins. Established trust and bonds of blood ran between them. Find one and you will often find many. — GCW

*   *   *

Read The Neighbors' Tombstones Too

For years I tried to find the parents of my second great-grandmother, Eliza Jane Schwenk. I had found no records of her birth, baptism or marriage to my second great-grandfather, Anthony Lory. The only record I had was a death record and an obituary notice.

On a recent trip to Pennsylvania, I visited the cemetery where she was buried. On the same plot were buried other Lory relatives. On the adjoining plot, were buried a couple who were of the approximate ages of Eliza's parents. I thought this couldn't be a coincidence. Their names were George and Mary Schwenk and they died in 1895 and 1892 respectively. Eliza died shortly thereafter in 1896. My next step was to find the ownership of the Schwenk plot. It was owned by a Sarah Lory Shaffer. That's all I needed to hear to continue my research of George and Mary. I didn't know who Sarah was but the Lory name is not that common.

George and Mary Schwenk's gravestones.

After many inquiries, I was able to obtain an obituary of George Schwenk. It stated that the funeral services were to be held at the residence of his son-in-law, Anthony Lory. That completed the circle for me. I now know that George and Mary were Eliza's parents.

I am so glad I made the trip to Pennsylvania to see the gravesites. I solved two mysteries by just reading the names on the neighbors' tombstones and with a little bit of follow-up. — Theresa M. Corbett, FL, tmcorb@aol.com

The Shotgun Approach

I was searching for a relative in California but I did not know his name or where he lived. I only knew the names of his parents. Using a shotgun approach, I got a telephone book of San Diego and wrote to every Whitney in the city, including a SASE, asking for their help. I knew many would not answer, but I got enough replies to help point me in the right direction.

A few more letters and I narrowed my search and eventually had success. — Bill Whitney, AB, wwhitney@telusplanet.net

How Well Do You Know Your Funeral Director?

I have been researching my family for several years and have used the records of funeral homes to solve some of my biggest obstacles. The death date and burial location of my great-grandfather had eluded us for years. Searches of the local cemeteries proved nothing. Census records only showed that he died sometime between the two census years, giving me a 10-year period to work with. Use of the state census records narrowed it to five years.

I then turned to the funeral director of the town where my great-grandfather was last known to live. My heart sank briefly, as he explained that his records didn't cover the dates that I was seeking, as it was before they were in business. He was able to give me the name of the funeral director who preceded him. He believed that even though this gentleman had passed away several years ago, his son who was also a funeral director, had his father's records. I called him and explained who I was and what I was looking for. Thanks to his help and his father's records, I was able to find the death date and burial location of my great-grandfather.

The cemetery location is now part of the church parking lot, much to the disbelief and horror of many. The graves and stones were plowed under and paved over, with very few moved or relocated.

In similar research scenarios, I have found a wealth of information in the funeral home records. In one such record I found names and birth locations of the deceased's parents. These records are as varied as the funeral directors who kept them, but are well worth the effort and time to research, as they may provide that crucial piece of evidence needed to get over that brickwall. — Carmon D. Rust, NY, psgen@yahoo.com

Wasting Time

I was stuck on a family brickwall for a long time. I knew my third-great-grandfather was Jacob McKee and that he was born in 1781 in South Carolina, however, I couldn't prove it. Death records on his children had no information on parents. The county courthouse in Wedowee, Randolph county, AL had burned in 1896 and had no records prior to that point.

I was in Randolph county doing research when I decided to go to the current courthouse to see what they might have. While rummaging through the records department I found an envelope titled "War Letters of John V. McKee", a son of Jacob McKee. The person who left this information had stapled his business card to it. I called him and he turned out to be a distant cousin who put me in touch with his aunt who put me in

touch with someone else who had a family Bible of John V. McKee. Once looking through the family Bible, it listed Jacob McKee as the father of John V. McKee. Also, in these letters, which John wrote home to his wife during the Civil War, he mentions his brother, Milton McKee, my ancestor.

If I hadn't decided to waste time going through those courthouse records, I would still be pondering the question of if Jacob was really the father of Milton, Lindsay and John. — Mark McKee, VA

A Connection Between Variations In Spellings

My grandmother, Maude Conkwright Perry, died in 1946, and my grandfather died when I was nine years old. I was never able to trace my grandmother's line back because when I started doing this research, the only census in Oklahoma which was indexed and available was the 1850 census and I had no way of knowing where her family came from. In the meantime, I wrote down every Conkright and Conkwright I could find in every record I came across. As indices for each census came out, I did the same. I also moved a lot. I lived in several different states and had access to several different libraries and historical societies. Everywhere I went, I wrote down anything related to anyone with any of these spellings. This was pre-computer days, but I kept all this data in the hopes that someday something would come along that would help me sort all this data.

Then I came across a note in a Kentucky historical journal that said that all Cronkrights, Conkwrights, Cronkhites and Cronkites were related. I started piecing together all the data I had gathered from all over the US and was able to trace the line back to New Amsterdam to Harck

Syboutszen and Wyntje Theunis, who were married in 1642. They were Dutch and their sons went by the Dutch patronymic Herricksen. However, they acquired the surname Kranckheyt, spelled numerous ways later in life, most likely as a way to appease the English. The will of their son, Jacobus, allowed me to link all the descendants together.

So not only have I found her line, but I almost have enough documentation to prove that all Cronkhites, Cronkites, Conkwrights and Conkrights (and many other spellings) are all descended from the same couple. - Vickie D. Peterson, OK

Online Memoirs

A genealogy request for help by a Brian Schaller of South Africa blossomed into a full-fledged search for his long lost relatives in Omaha, NE.

The Schaller family appeared in the 1870 census and eventually the 1890 Omaha directory, which furnished us with occupations of some of the family and the street address back then. After that we lost all trace of the family. Alas, that street address is now the center of a physical fitness building at our local Creighton University.

When I arrived home one evening after investigating the address and finding it smack in the middle of the university, I ventured onto the school's website. In the online memoirs written by of one of the university's founders, there is a mention of how the Schaller father was greeted with great gusto by the family after work. Apparently the university staff and students watched the family's comings and goings.

The date was 1894, fours years after the 1890 directory listing. Further along in the memoirs in 1905 the writer noted that the family now consisted of only two women who couldn't keep the house and that the university had bought the property. It was alleged that father, son and other

Creighton University's website.

family members had passed away during a bad flu season. One of the remaining females was traced to the California Death Index. The other is still a mystery along with the burial sites of the rest of the family.

Just by chance the brickwall we faced after the 1890 directory was torn down by the online memoirs of a college administrator. — Unknown Submitter

Finding Old Friends

I was trying to find an old friend of my mother-in-law who was still living in England from the time of WWII. She has had no contact since then. The man was a pilot from Poland but she had no idea where he ended up. I didn't find a name on the Internet phone directories.

I started with the Polish hall in the city nearest to where this man used to live and asked for help. The pilots' associations have lists of their members and the Polish hall can contact someone who has the list and can tell you where that person lives. Then I wrote to the Polish hall where the man lived and asked for his address.

After a phone call from my mother-in-law, they decided to give out the name and address. — Bill Whitney, AB, wwhitney@telusplanet.net

*   *   *

Linking The Family

After hearing for some 20-odd years that my dad was going to do his genealogy, I decided to see if I could just get it done for him. I started with a couple of names, dates and places. I hopped onto the Internet and typed in "genealogy" and I couldn't believe what came up. Among other things, I found some information that included a name that I recognized. The person who posted the information was my dad's cousin. Through this person, I made contact with their uncle who was almost 90 years old. I also made contact with another person who happened to have old church records. I started writing e-mails to people just to see if there was some way to connect the information I was gathering. In just seven months, I had connected eight generations before me. It was great, but how was I to cross the Atlantic back to Germany?

I knew that the name Shiffler had been misspelled in the US records. I figured that since everything I checked showed nothing, maybe the name was misspelled when my ancestor left Germany. I find out that SS and FF in German could possibly be mistaken for each other. I purchased a cd-rom that showed a Schissler leaving Germany in 1742 and it referred to a book that was actually information someone translated from German records.

My father and I took a day trip to the FHL to try to find the information. While I was there, an employee helped me find a microfilm of Steinbach in the Saar district, which was listed as Johann Georg Schissler's town of origin. I decided to show another employee the signature of Johann Georg Schissler on his permit to leave Germany and asked her what she thought the signature said. She was German-born and had been hired for her knowledge of old handwriting and the language. She had no idea of what I was looking for and she said,

"Johann Georg Schiffler". I had to grab my dad's arm and squeeze it to keep myself from making a jubilant noise.

When we found the microfilm and I located the name, she translated the text for me. It turned out to be a church record of the marriage of Johann Georg Schiffler! Then we found the church record for the christening of their first baby shortly after.

The biggest thrill for me was that in one year, I was able to coordinate the efforts of myself and nine other people into a volume of information that was a total of 350 pages! Half was data and half were the documents, records, pictures, census images and other source information used to put the data together.

German marriage record for an ancestor of Leslie Twogood.

Several of the contributors had been doing genealogy for almost 30 years and had not been able to get to Germany. It was a great discovery and I was thrilled to be able to find the links and people to bring it together. — Leslie Twogood, UT

Go To The Mortuary

When I was trying to find information on all the children of my husband's great-grandmother, I ran into what I thought was a brickwall. There were 11 children in the family. I found the birth records and baptismal records for the children by writing to the church they attended. The civil birth records did not include two children who had died young but the church records did. These children were also listed on a chart, which had been passed down through the family and was in the possession of one of the descendants. This was written by the parents in old German script and contained the births of their children and the deaths of those who died while the parents were still alive.

In the courthouse records and newspapers of the day, I found the marriage records of the children. But one of the daughters, Matilda, baptized Maria Matilda, seemed to have disappeared after her marriage to Leonard Schmidt. A relative told me she had died in California in 1933. I checked the California Death Index and found a Matilda Schmidt who died in 1933 but she was not my Matilda. When I checked the obituaries of other relatives that gave survivors names she was listed as Matilda Smith. She had anglicized her surname. When I checked the California Death Index I did not find a Matilda Smith but found a Mary Smith who had died in 1933.

I sent for the death certificate and realized it was the correct person. But in checking census records, I could not find this family from the time they left Illinois where they married, to the time they moved to California. The death record stated how long they had lived in California.

This was my solution: the death certificate also gave the name and address of the mortuary. I checked in a Los Angeles phone directory but the mortuary was not listed. However, another mortuary was at the same address. I wrote to that mortuary and requested records for Mary Smith who had died on the particular date given in the Death Index and on the death certificate. The secretary included information that there were others buried in the same plot, but it was not known what the relationship of Mary was to the persons buried there. I wrote back to obtain the information on the other people buried there. It turned out to be her husband and two sons. When I checked the 1900 census, which tells how many children a mother has given birth to, I learned she had given birth to only two children. The death records I obtained on the sons showed they had been born in Wisconsin and Iowa. I had no knowledge that she had lived in these two states after her marriage or any information on her family. Now I had her whole family!

If it had not been for the information given by the mortuary I would not have able to obtain the names of her children or even know how many she had had. — Marjorie Alderks, PA

Seeking Anna

The only thing my father and his siblings knew about their mother was that her name was Anna Skibinski and that she came from Poland with her two brothers when she was 16 years old. Later a sister came and met them in Scranton, PA. Anna married Blasej Rejman, my grandfather, while there and bore several children before moving to Lackawanna, NY where they lived until their deaths.

Everyone took the names as facts. From my aunt that is still living, I found my grandmother's sister had married a Skoronski and they had moved to Gaylord, MI. The family had been to visit them years ago but hadn't been in contact for quite a while.

One day I was searching through RootsWeb.com for the Skoronski name. I found an e-mail address of someone researching that name. I e-mailed her and it turned out that her great-grandmother was my Anna's half-sister. She then proceeded to explain the information her grandmother had told her. Anna's mother had died and her father, Frank Strinkowski, remarried a widowed woman, Michele Skibinski, who had two sons. Because of the prevailing conditions in Poland of war in the early 1890s, Anna and her two stepbrothers were sent to the US, with Antonia following a few years later. I have read that single women were not allowed to travel into the US alone. I figured that the authorities at the time would not have allowed a single woman to travel with unrelated males including stepbrothers so they probably called Anna Skibinski instead of Strinkowski, so that she could come to the US with these stepbrothers, no questions asked. She never told her family this information.

Anna Skibinski (Strinkowski) and Blascj Rejman on their wedding day in 1895 in Scranton, PA.

I have not verified this information in Poland yet, but on the marriage records in Scranton both Anna and Antonia list their parents as Frank and Michele. I have not found the stepbrothers' records yet.

So, sometimes the names we think our ancestors had weren't their names for various reasons and this reason is a new one to me. I hope it might help others. — Rosa Raiman, NY, rosaraiman@adelphia.net

Middle Names

I was having a hard time finding the parents to my great-grandmother, whose maiden name was Craig. I knew of her, Mary, a brother, John, and that they were both buried with their spouses in Andrew county, MO. According to the obituaries and funeral records, they had a brother, Thomas, in Oregon and two sisters, Ann Adams and Betty Strong of Council Bluffs, IA. Additionally, they were born in Holt county, which is next to Andrew county. I looked in the available censuses in Holt and Andrew counties but couldn't find them. Living in Buchanan county, which is right next to the other counties, I found their obituaries in the *St. Joseph NewsPress* and funeral records at the Northwest Missouri Historical Society. Neither had their parents listed. I tried to find the remaining siblings through the Internet, but to no avail.

Finally, I began searching anything on Craigs in Buchanan county just to see if there was someone in the family not listed. I went through every probate record until I discovered a William T. Craig. What a find!

William T. was the Thomas from Oregon. Seems he moved back to Missouri shortly before he died and was living at the home of John's daughter. He left no will and had never married. His estate in Missouri and Oregon was left to his living heirs. This consisted of a multitude of nieces, nephews who were children of his already-deceased siblings and the still-living siblings. Additionally, his funeral record listed his parents' names, David Craig and Jane English.

I still couldn't figure why I couldn't find the family in Holt county. I decided to go through again and burst through another brickwall. There was my Craig family with David, Lucinda J., Martha E., Alena A., Mary F., William T. and J.F.H., in the 1860 census listed in Holt county.

I had seen it before, but I could only connect with one name, Mary, a too-common name. Apparently Jane's younger sister, Rebecca English, was living with them. It seems the family had a penchant for using their middle names in everyday life and in their obituaries.

Finding William Thomas Craig's probate record in a county and state where I didn't expect to find him broke down a piece of the brickwall that I'd been hammering against. Sometimes you have to search through records you may not think pertain to your family. — Jan Coy, KS, jec1945@ccp.com

A Valuable Lesson

My great-uncle was our family genealogist and I inherited from him extensive correspondence going back to the 1940s. Uncle Don and his correspondents were all absolutely sure the wife of our ancestor Isaac Metcalfe was Joanna Baker. Unfortunately, there was no documentation.

I was determined to settle the matter of Joanna once and for all. I decided the key might be the death record of Joanna's youngest child, Miles Jackson Metcalf, who was my second-great-grandfather. Miles died after the advent of death records, which I thought

Miles Jackson Metcalf in the late 1880s.

might provide the clue. He died in a little town in Iowa named Hornick. I grew up about 15 miles south of Hornick and my mother was born there, so I knew that Hornick is in Woodbury county. But repeated trips to the Woodbury county seat yielded no death record, probate record or will. Miles was buried in Woodbury county, he lived in Woodbury county and he died there — or so I thought.

I decided to try the Internet. The Woodbury county webmaster, upon my query, asked if I had checked surrounding counties. Well, why would I? I know what county Hornick is in. Finally, I found a note in a county history, which said that Miles died on his son's farm "just south of Hornick".

In a conversation with my mother a few weeks later, I casually asked, "Where is the county line for Woodbury county?"

"Why, about a mile south of Hornick." she replied.

I checked the death records for the next county south, Monona county, and there was the death record for Miles and there was his mother's name, Joanna Baker.

I was so sure of my knowledge. This taught me a valuable lesson, which has since stood me in good stead. — Mary Ellen Boyd, CO

*   *   *

A Brickwall In St. Mary's, ON

My father told me that his paternal grandfather, Robert Sparling, was born in County Tipperary, Ireland and immigrated to St. Mary's, ON as an infant with his parents, John and Mary Jane Sparling. My father also said that John was married three times and, so he told me, John went on his honeymoon with his third wife and was never heard from again.

My research in St. Mary's revealed that John Sparling was indeed a colorful character. *The Illustrated Historical Atlas Of Perth County* recorded that he was one of the original pioneers of Blanchard township in 1842. He was elected to the District Counsel and was the first clerk and Justice of the Peace in St. Mary's when that village was established. I came across a local militia muster roll, which revealed that John Sparling was the Captain. I purchased gravestone transcriptions from that local genealogical society for the main cemetery in St. Mary's and a pioneer cemetery. This pioneer cemetery was called the Sparling Cemetery. How could I miss?

I found transcriptions of the gravestones of a number of relatives, including that of John's first wife, Mary Jane. I found her obituary in volumes of birth marriage and death notices from an Ontario Methodist periodical, *The Christian Guardian*. I also found an announcement of John's second marriage to Rachel English. In the Wesleyan Methodist Baptismal Registers for Ontario I found the baptisms of a number of their children. The family was farming in Blanchard township at the time of the 1851 census. John Sparling and his family had moved to a two-story stone house in St. Mary's at the time of the 1861 census. By the time of the 1871 census he was gone. His older children were established in their own households but John, his second wife and the younger children disappeared. No further birth, marriage or death registrations in all Ontario. No further baptisms. No graves. No will. John sold his land and moved on. Where did he go?

My father joined the Ottawa branch of the Ontario Genealogical Society and submitted the surnames we were researching. Another member of the Ottawa group contacted him because she had an interest in Irish Palatine families. Sparling is a distinctively Irish Palatine surname. She put us in contact with another genealogist in Toronto, ON who in turn put us in contact with a cousin in Joshua Tree, CA. Our newly discovered cousin knew what had happened to John Sparling because she was descended from a son from his second marriage. He had moved with Rachel and the younger children to Washington Courthouse, OH and then Chillicothe, MO. Then Rachel died and John remarried for the third time but died himself in 1871. His third wife had no children herself but raised the many children from his second family.

John Sparling's St. Mary's house, built in 1858.

Our California cousin had been researching the Sparling family for 20 years. Through her I was able to join the informal network of Sparling researchers around the world. Now I know how the other Sparling pioneers of Blanchard township and St. Mary's are related and am able to help others sort out their ancestors' marriages with Sparlings and, if they, too are of Irish Palatine descent, they can help me with my other lines. — Lois Sparling, AB, lsparling@shaw.ca

The Mysterious Guardians

Early in my research I found my great-grandfather, Henry Elton Bozman, in the 1880 federal census for Logan county, OH. I wanted to know why he, at the age of seven, was living with the storekeeper/postmistress Amanda McCall and her sisters. Was he really a cousin to the head-of-household as the record indicated?

I requested and received Elton's death certificate, from which I learned that his parents were Madison Bozman and Eudora "Dora" Carson. In the 1880 census I had found Madison, but living with wife Martha. A letter to the Logan County Genealogical Society resulted in three marriage records for Madison: to Lucy Johnson, to Dora Carson and to Martha Hickman.

Then a trip to the Logan County Genealogical Society proved to be more fruitful. I found Dora's family in the 1870 census, giving me her parents' names, Henry and Mary. But in the surname file, along with obituaries from local newspapers, there was a letter from a woman who wanted to know more about her grandparents, Matthew and Martha Hickman Bozman. This led to correspondence with an elderly cousin who shared everything she knew about Madison, including a photograph. From Madison's death certificate I learned he was born in Licking county to an unknown father and Elizabeth Parr. Despite years of searching, these people are still a brickwall for me.

But I have been able to discern how Elton Bozman ended up in the McCall home and later with the Gordons. In my pre-Internet days, I'd learned the names of Dora's parents, Henry and Mary. Soon after we got a new computer I was off and running. I also discovered RootsWeb.com and joined several surname and county mail lists. Then I found a wonderful resource at RootsWeb.com; the list archives. I could search any message that had ever been posted to any of their lists!

In the Carson list archives I typed Logan into the search box and brought up a message from 1998. I e-mailed the submitter. This kind woman offered to send me a copy of a letter that she received eight years ago that mentioned my Henry. The letter gave Mary's maiden name as McCall. Again I searched the old messages on GenForum.com with this new information and learned that Mary McCall's brother George was the father of Amanda. So Elton really was a cousin, or more accurately, first cousin once-removed to Amanda. But I still didn't know how Elton ended up in the Gordon home.

One day, while surfing the Internet, I found a link to Tammy's Genealogy And More, with information on several Logan county families. Her page is easy to search and on it I found a record of the marriage of John E. Gordon and Amanda McCall. John Gordon was married to Barbary Keller, who died after having several children. John then married Amanda McCall. Apparently she took Elton with her to live in her new home.

The key was to find messages that were already written down. The first one a letter in a genealogical society surname file, the second one posted a few years ago and kept in the RootsWeb.com list archives and the third one a letter saved for years by another researcher, even though she doesn't know if her family connects.

With persistence, the right tools and the kindness of others, I was able to solve this mystery. — Jeanne Crews, OH, jeannecrews@attbi.com

*   *   *

Going Out On A Limb

My Treichel line was a real difficult one. All that I knew took me as far back as my grandmother had been able to tell. She didn't know from what town or village the Treichels had originated, only that they came from Prussia. She could take the family back as far as her immigrant grand-parents who were my second-great-grandparents.

On a lark, one day, I decided to be radical. I went to my web search browser and plugged in the name "Treichel". I received several commercial websites, each associated with a person named Treichel. I decided to pick the first three and send them e-mail messages asking them about their family names. One of the three was a nuclear physicist working in Switzerland, but he took the time to reply to my letter. He said his father, living in Berlin, was interested in family matters and he would give him a call soon. It wasn't long after that I heard back from him. He told me that his father had a book about the Treichel family and he wanted to know which Treichel family I was searching. I wrote back about the information of my immigrant Treichels that my grandmother had given me. Within a couple of days, he wrote back to tell me they were in the book. It even said that my second-great-grandfather had "ausgewandert nach America".

Treichel parish record received from a stranger on the Internet who was researching Judy McAuliffe's family.

Many letters and conversations later, I now have a major break-through in my Treichel line and now know exactly where they lived in West Prussia. All because I thought I would go out on a limb and contact a stranger. — Judy McAuliffe, CA

Brickwall Conquered By Bookworm

Many years ago, my father, a second-generation Irish-American, once told me the first Catholic Mass ever said in a certain Massachusetts town was said in his grandfather's house.

Years later, I mentioned my father's comment to my wife who is an avid genealogist. She asked me if I knew the name of the town but I told her I couldn't remember. I tried, but to no avail. She urged hypnotic-age regression, scopolamine, the rack, etc., but I demurred and the issue was shelved. The truly strange, serendipitous part follows.

My wife, on her genealogical quests, makes many trips to Boston. One day, she stopped into a second-hand bookstore on her way home and purchased an old two-volume *History Of The Archdiocese Of Boston*. Being an inveterate swoon-reader, I picked up Volume I and started reading. It soon became apparent that the Roman Catholic entry into Puritan New England was essentially a missionary movement and the date of each and every Catholic establishment in the New World was clearly chronicled. Noting this pattern, I persisted, hoping to correct my memory lapse and to thereby delight my wife.

Finally, on page 148 of Volume II, I found it; "At Pittsfield [MA], when detained over Sunday while traveling, [Father O'Callighan] learned that there were a few Catholics in the place, and gathering this little flock of ten or twelve in the house of a man named Daley, he offered the Holy Sacrifice for the first time in the chief town of Berkshire County (1835)."

That's it, Daley, my father's mother's maiden name!

Further research in a Pittsfield, MA's library provided more details. — Edward L. Fenton, CT, scfen@aol.com

Being Up To Date In The Past Lane

Searches for Charlie Hallett and his wife Gaetana Ross, supposedly married and living in Winnipeg, MB in the late 1800s, had turned up nothing. It was believed they were born in England and Scotland respectively, but an extensive search of databases, censuses and parish records had produced only frustration. I was at my wits' end and had just about spent as much time as I cared to looking for this couple when a newspaper clipping from another branch of research on the same family suggested that they may have moved to Thunder Bay, ON in the early 1900s.

I prepared to search the 1901 Canadian census but knew this census was poorly filmed and the prints are very light and difficult to read. Within a week of becoming aware of the possible move to Thunder Bay, the National Archives of Canada very quietly announced the availability of the 1901 census online. Within two minutes of surfing the website I had Charlie and Gaetana Hallet and their eight children on the screen. They were not born in England and Scotland; Charles was born in New Brunswick and Gaetana in Quebec.

I then decided to look at the 1881 Canadian census index as I might find Charlie and Gaetana as children with their parents. Imagine my delight when I found both Charlie and Gaetana with their families. Weeks of fruitless research had suddenly paid off by finding three generations in five minutes.

These two resources have only been made available recently. Both the 1881 Canadian census and the online 1901 Canadian census were launched in 2002.

Without the knowledge of the location from a newspaper clipping and the online 1901 census, there would have been hours of intense film search required to point the way to the 1881 census, which would also have required hours of searching.

These newly formatted resources paid big dividends and turned hours of film research into a five-minute electronic success story. — Ron Wild, ON

Spelling Mistakes And Phonetics

"I'm happy to meet you Mrs. Vorpul," I said when I was introduced to the woman who would one day be my mother-in-law. "Dear, it's 'Vor-paul'," she said, correcting my enunciation.

Mispronunciation of such a good Prussian-German name as Vorpahl is bound to happen. Fanciful variations of the name of Frederick Vorpahl appear on nearly every legal item, including his marriage certificate: Frederick Worphal married Augusta A. Miseler on 12 April 1858. I assume the marriage was legal, regardless of the incorrect spelling, since there are no records to dispute the fact. But then, maybe I just haven't come

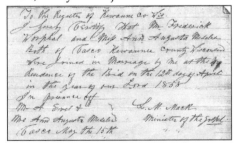

Maybe Frederick Vorpahl was too excited on his wedding day to notice that his name had been misspelled as Worphal. That little slip of the pen may not have bothered him, but it sure made it hard for descendants to find.

across another county clerk's innovative rendition of the name.

Census misspellings through the years include Vorpel and Vorphal. The 1860 census taker in Wisconsin recorded it as Tripfall. No wonder it took years to find these people in the census records. I knew they were living somewhere in Kewaunee county, WI, but I simply couldn't find them whenever the census was taken. It was as though they left home every 10 years. I found land records, with the correct spelling, so I knew he was there, but...

The corner of that stubborn brickwall was finally turned when I came across the Vorpahl family on a Soundex. I have never been a big fan of Soundex — but that was before I saw the light. There they were, where they were supposed to be every 10 years, in Casco, Kewaunee, WI — just under a variety of spellings.

The McDowell brothers, McElroy (left) and Dabo. McElroy was named for his mother's maiden name, he spent a lifetime having his name mispronounced, even his own family called him "Uncle Muck".

McElroy McDowell was a second-great-uncle of mine; his first name was his mother's maiden name. I tracked McElroy and his brother Dabo, my great-grandfather, for years in Ripley county, IN, until the older brother disappeared. I couldn't find McElroy McDowell under Mc in the alphabetized census index books. But looking further down, there he was in Howard county, Indiana as Muckelroy McDowell.

"Uncle Muck", they called him.

He evidently went along with the moniker because after his death, his wife legalized the misspelled name as Muckelroy to settle his estate.

Be inventive with spelling your ancestors' names and use phonics to the maximum. — Beverly Smith Vorpahl, WA, dbvorpahl@earthlink.net

Hit-And-Miss Methods

My family's brickwall was finding the ancestral home of my great-grandfather Johann Fellner. He came to the US from Germany in the 1870s and married my great-grandmother Margretha Rinke in 1876. Throughout the years my relatives believed my great-grandfather came from Bemberg, but I had no proof.

In 1985, my father John Fellner and I were preparing for a trip to Germany to visit my sister whose husband was stationed in Heilbronn. My father decided to bring copies of some family documents along on the trip in case we had time to find the ancestral home. After we arrived in Germany my father and I studied one of the documents and determined that the correct city was Amberg not Bemberg.

The day before we were scheduled to leave Germany, my father decided that my sister and I would go with him to find the ancestral home. We went to Amberg and headed for the town hall. In Germany, town halls are closed during the noon hour. A lady who worked at the town hall took pity on us and looked at our documents. The documents were written in old German script and she was able to decipher that our great-grandfather's village was Massenricht. She gave us the directions to Massenricht, which was a short distance from Amberg. We arrived in Massenricht and decided to stop at the church. I went inside and found a lady cleaning the church. I asked her if she knew any Fellners that lived in the village. She said her name was Fellner. She took us to her home and introduced us to her family. Her husband showed us the old Fellner house, which is still occupied and in very good shape for being built in the 1700s.

It was a short visit but my father continues to keep in contact with our German relatives. I have now traced our lines back three generations. Our hit-and-miss method paid off for our family. — Patricia Fellner, WI

From Buried Twice To Buried Four Times

My goal was to find out what my wife's granduncle, a bachelor, did in WWI. When I started, his siblings and his nieces and nephews were dead. All I had was oral tradition that he was killed shortly after he arrived in France and that he was reburied in Minnesota after the war. A fire at the National Personnel Records Center had destroyed his service record and the center was unable to reconstruct any information on him.

I contacted the Minnesota cemetery in which oral tradition held he was buried. It provided one good piece of evidence and one worthless piece of evidence. The good piece was that his gravestone reported that he was killed in action on 20 October 1918 and that he served in the 341st

Infantry. The worthless piece was he was reburied in 1937, which turned out to be incorrect.

Based on the date of reburial furnished by the cemetery, I requested the Newspaper Library of the Minnesota Historical Society to search for an obituary. It did not find one.

I asked the Army Military History Institute at Carlisle Barracks, PA for a history of his regiment. It sent me a history that led to a dead end. The 341st Infantry arrived in France in October 1918. Rather than committing it to battle as a unit, its members were transferred to other units as replacements for casualties. My wife's granduncle was sent to a replacement depot on 9 October 1918. The trail ended there. The evidence gathered at this point supported that he was killed shortly after arriving in France. But where?

On a hunch, I asked the NARA whether it had files on the soldiers whose bodies were returned from France for reburial in the US. It did, so I requested my wife's grand-uncle's file.

From that file, I learned he was transferred to the 310th Infantry; that he was killed on the 18th, not 20 October 1918, during a German counter-attack. He was buried in a shallow grave where he fell because his unit was forced to withdraw and was unable to take its dead with it. Ten days later when the hill was taken, his body was exhumed and reburied in a temporary military cemetery in Saint Juvin. In April 1919, the Army again exhumed his body and reburied it in the permanent military cemetery in Romagne. In July 1921, at the request of his parents, the Army once again exhumed his body and shipped it to US for reburial at his home and on 1 August of that year, his body was reburied in Minnesota. — Thomas E. Ross, CA, tross666@earthlink.net

*   *   *

Success In Scandinavia

My families came from Norway and Sweden and my wife's families came from Sweden. I have found that the most important source of family history will come with finding the living families in Norway and Sweden. In most cases they are working on the family history, but have not heard from some family branches since they left in the 1800s.

I have used a number of ways to locate the living families. In most cases it just requires making the right contact. My paternal grandfather, Albert Lundquist came from Oland, Sweden and I personally visited the island Oland twice but could not find my family. After many false starts, I looked in a travel book for a hotel on Oland and wrote the owner for help to find a local person who could help me. It turned out he knew my family and put me in direct contact with the living family. When I later visited my new-found cousins, they gave me the medal my great-grandfather, Nills Magnus Lundquist received from King Oscar II.

My maternal grandfather, Ole Andersen, came from Vallset,

This medal was presented to Nills Magnus Lundquist by King Oscar II of Sweden for a lifetime of service to the Church and people of Grasgard, Oland in Sweden.

Norway. I wrote to the Statsarkivet in Hamar, Norway and they referred me to a historian in Stange, near Vallset. My biggest problem was that I did not know the family name was Haraset, but the historian recognized the family from the information I supplied.

In Norway and Sweden many areas have written chronicles of the regions. The historian in Stange had been involved in preparing the Romadal Chronicle, which included the area around Vallset. With these chronicles it was easy to trace the family back to 1535.

I had a lot of difficulty in tracing my wife's grandmother's family, Nordfeldt family. In an effort to make a contact with the living family in Sweden I wrote to the House of Emigrants in Vaxjo and requested the names and addresses of all the Nordfeldts in the Vaxjo region. They faxed me three names. I wrote to them and was able to make contact with two of my wife's cousins, who supplied me with a very expanded family tree.

When we visited the Emigrants Museum in Vaxjo, my wife found a copy of her maternal grandmother's Carlsson family tree on display. We got in touch with the man who prepared this and he turned out to be a cousin to my wife.

With all our newfound family contacts we have obtained many pictures and books about the family. I have a regular mailing to our families, newfound members as well as those we had known. I supply them with copies of all the new information and pictures I obtain. I now have pictures of my great-grandparents and my wife's great-grandfather. In this way I spread the information to many family members so when we are gone there will be a base of information spread across the family. I want them to be as proud of their families as we are. — Burton R. Lundquist, AZ

*   *   *

Finding Ancestors' Friends

I have definitely found the birthplace in County Carlow, Ireland for my second-great-grandfather, Thomas Byrne (Burns in the US). I always knew it to be County Carlow, but couldn't find any townland until last year. I typed in his name as well as his parents' names, Charles Byrne and Johanna Nolan (his parents' information, including his mother's maiden name, are mentioned in my ancestor's published biography), in the LDS website search and up popped a baptismal record with those three names. The date was 9 December 1822, which was the right month and day, but the year was four years off from what I had. His biography says that his birth date was 4 December 1826. I ordered the microfilm of those parish records (Roman Catholic Parish of Bagenalstown, the townland is Ballyloughan) and I found the entry. While doing the search, the baptism of a female infant, Mary Byrne, also came up, with the same parents. That was a surprise. I filed that information for a later time.

The earliest record I had of my second-great-grandfather was the ship's manifest. Most of that information was found in his biography. The date he sailed to the US was June 1848, the age given was 25 and so he was either born in 1822 or 1823. However, his biography says he was born in 1826. The baptismal record says 9 December 1822. I have always looked for multiple records and then compared dates. I wondered if my second-great-grandfather sailed to the US alone or with someone he knew. There were no other names on the manifest that I recognized, so I put that thought aside.

Recently, I found a third obituary for Thomas. It was a long one, front page, in the newspaper of the Illinois town where he died. Considering that so many of those old newspapers no longer exist, it was a stroke of luck that this particular issue was available. I read the obituary, seeing things I already knew, when an unknown name appeared. Daniel Gahn, a boyhood friend from Ireland, was mentioned in the obituary. My second-great-grandfather had visited him in the last year of his life. The gentleman lived in Elgin, IL. I wondered if the newspaper had got the information correct.

Once home, I checked the ship's manifest again. My second-great-grandfather's name is the second-to-last on the list; the last name was Daniel Gahan of Ireland. David's age was also listed as 25. Again, I was keeping in mind variations in ages.

I went to the Illinois State Archives to read the Soundexes for the 1900 and 1910 US censuses. There was Daniel Gahan, living in Elgin. One of the Soundexes gave his date of birth as March 1824, so it was the right time frame at least. I found death certificates for two of his children, noting the name of the cemetery where they

Thomas (Byrne) Burns and his granddaughter. Taken c. 1900 in Chicago, IL.

are buried. Their father is likely there too, but I do not have a death date for him. I noticed that on the daughter's certificate, the birthplace of her father was given as County Carlow. Before leaving the State Archives, I found an index for the 1870 census and found Daniel listed for Elgin also.

At another library, I looked up Daniel in those census records. There he was with his family in 1870. I checked 1900 and 1910 and his year of immigration was given as 1848.

There are some websites for Elgin and I found a business listing for Daniel (same business that the census gives) as well as some burial and probate information for a few members of his family. My next step is to find the date of death for Daniel and then look for an obituary and any local histories. I am hoping to find something about Daniel's life in Ireland, as well as his first years in the US, that would also give me clues about my own ancestor's life.

I think it's safe to say I found the birthplace of my second-great-grandfather. — Debbie Lubbert, IL, gainebyrne@aol.com

Church Archives

My father knew his maternal grandparents as "Gramma" and "Grandad". Fortunately, his sister recalled a lot more. The usual sources (census, death registrations, church records) took me back another generation or two. However, I could not find the family of origin of my second-great-grandmother, Ruth Willoughby.

I tracked her to West Gwillimbury township in Simcoe county, ON from the church record of her marriage. There were several Willoughby families there and in nearby townships but no indication of her connection to them. Two lucky breaks put it all together.

Through the *Genealogical Research Directory*, I found someone in my own city that was also descended from Ruth Willoughby. My great-grandfather was Ruth's eldest son and my newfound cousin is the great-granddaughter of her youngest son, Nicholas Kenny. Her family recalled that Ruth had a brother who was a Methodist minister. I wrote to the United Church Archives in Toronto to ask if they had information on a Reverend Willoughby. (The United Church of Canada is a union of Methodists, Congregationalists, most Presbyterians and the Evangelical Brethren.) A few weeks later, the archives sent me photocopies from their biographical files of two Rev. Willoughbys, one of which was my second-great-grandmother's brother. Rev. Nicholas Willoughby was the son of John Willoughby and Isabella Ramsey, early settlers of West Gwillimbury township. I found John Willoughby's will which named both my second-great-grandmother by her married name and her eldest son, my great-grandfather.

Willoughby gravestone found in the Newton Robinson United Church cemetery in Simcoe county, ON.

A year or so later, I was contacted by a genealogist in Ontario who had been told by the Simcoe County Archives that I was researching this family. E-mails went back and forth between us and some of her contacts. One of the contacts found the will of her ancestor, a married sister, which named her three brothers: my John, Hugh and Ralph Willoughby. This connected most (but not all) of the Simcoe county Willoughbys and provided valuable information on this family's movements in Ireland. — Lois Sparling, AB, lsparling@shaw.ca

Bill And Ted's Excellent Genealogical Adventure

Bill Garrett of Ontario had a dilemma. He had traced his lineage back to a William Jackson and was stuck. Who were William's father and mother? There were four Jackson families in the Kingston area in the late 1700s and early 1800s. None had a William Jackson registered whose dates corresponded to Bill's information. Although he suspected Jethro Jackson, Sr. was William's father, he had no proof. Ted Murphy in Manitoba had also traced his line back to William. Ted also felt Jethro Jackson, Sr. was William's father, but had no better luck than Bill. Both Bill and Ted were close to giving up.

Then Bill found that I was researching one of the families and contacted me. I informed him that Jethro was my third-great-grandfather and I had his children well documented. I had not found a son William for Jethro in my research. To say Bill was disappointed was an understatement.

We continued to correspond, and when I told him I was going to Wallingford, VT to do some research, he asked to come along. Jethro's father, Deacon Abraham Jackson had founded Wallingford. If William was Jethro's son the proof should be there. In Wallingford we searched old records in the town hall and library. Most of Jethro's children were born in the US (one born in Canada) and were

recorded there, but no William.

According to the year of his birth, he could not have been born in Canada. If William was a son of Jethro why was he not registered? The other children were recorded, why not him? Maybe William belonged to one of the other families after all. Bill's hopes were dashed and he seemed ready to call it quits.

Land grant for William Jackson.

Bill was talking to a member of the Kingston Genealogical Society and was told if Jethro was a United Empire Loyalist (UEL), the Loyalist land grant records may be a source of information. Apparently children of UELs were also eligible to receive a land grant. Bill searched the land records and found the proof he needed. William had applied for a land grant as a son of a UEL. He had named Jethro Jackson as his father. When the application was made, Jethro Sr. and Jethro Jr. (William's brother) had both died. He was therefore forced by the Crown, to present sworn statements from two individuals who knew his father, his brother and knew him to be the son of Jethro Sr. who was a registered UEL. The statements were attached to the application. Bill was able to make copies of the land grant application and the sworn statements.

William got his land grant, Bill Garrett and Ted Murphy got their ancestry and I welcomed new cousins to the fold. We still do not know why he was never registered or where he is buried. Maybe some day we will have the answers. Persistence can work miracles. — George C. Jackson, ON

Mashey, Mashey Not

I knew my grandmother's maiden name was Mashey. It was on her birth and death certificates. I had my grandmother's burial records but nothing for her parents. I kidded my mother about it and told her they must have been criminals or something and changed their name.

My friend and I went to the FHL for a week and my goal was to find any information that confirmed their name was Mashey. In that week, I found only one census entry from when my grandmother was an infant. I came home and started to work on other lines where the information is more plentiful. I put most of my mother's lines on hold.

About a year ago I was browsing the Internet. I went to one of the bigger genealogy sites and once again I put in my surnames. I typed Mashey and several responses came up. I noted the possibilities, including one that did not look promising. It was about a book that had been published on German handwriting. The author's name was Mashey. I copied the address anyway, as it was within 30 miles of my home and maybe the author could lead me to other Masheys who might be related. I sent a letter to the author requesting the book.

Several weeks later I got a telephone call from a gentleman who said the letter had been delivered to him. The former occupants, Mashey, were both deceased. Knowing I was within 30 miles, he decided to call me to let me know the Masheys were dead. During our conversation, he mentioned he had purchased the house "as is" with all its contents. The only surviving son had come to take the few items he wanted and left the rest. Most of what remained had been disposed of over the years, except for a filing cabinet that was too heavy to move. If I wanted it, he would contact the attorney who handled the closing to get permission to give it to me.

About a month later I received a 20-page fax from the surviving son, now in California, as the attorney had forwarded my information about my interest in genealogy. It turns out the author, his mother, had done their family history for years. He didn't know if we were related, but was sending some of what he had. As I pieced the pages together to form the pedigree chart, my eye fell on a familiar name — my mother's.

I began to cry as I realized the chart took the lines back another four generations and included children's names, dates, places and burial information. It also listed the eight different spellings the family used over 100 years. They are buried only about 30 miles away under the names Maschi and Maschie.

Had I not perused the book written by an author of the same name I was searching, I would never have found this information. I visited the man who now lives in the house my relatives owned and he gave me the records and pictures he found. The filing cabinet turned out to contain records of their dairy business, not her research as I had hoped. I plan to someday visit the son, as he has offered to share the rest of the information he has. — Helen McCandless Staiger, PA, helen@geniespeak.com

They Changed Their Name

My brickwall comes from my mother's family. My maternal grandmother was Alice Maud Jones. She was a remarkable woman. She lived to be 96 years old, outliving two husbands, her seven brothers and sisters and two of her children. Her father was in the British Army and as a child she lived in India, Africa and England before coming to Canada. Luckily, she kept original documents. In her personal effects I found pages from the family Bible, her baptismal certificate and her parents' marriage certificate. I found a lot of information to start from.

After sorting through this information, I still did not know very much about her father, Frederick William Jones. I checked the IGI and I found noth-

Frederick William Jones with his wife and children. Taken in 1897 in Cairo, Egypt. Janyce Mann's grandmother is the girl on the far right.

ing to help me there since I did not know where he was born. When I checked the Index for civil registrations I found 14 possible Frederick Joneses, but I still had the same problem of not knowing where he was born. I knew the way to proceed would be to hire someone in England to check the Army records, but that was too expensive. A friend knew someone in England who would look for about half the usual price. It was within my budget.

This gentleman looked through the files but couldn't find the right Frederick William Jones. On a hunch

he checked the unburnt WWI records, something I would not have thought of. Sure enough there was Frederick Jones. He had reenlisted at the age of 53 during WWI. The information, including his death certificate, was bountiful. Children's birth dates, places he had been stationed, the medals he had won, when he was hospitalized and most importantly where he was born. I now had a place — Chichester in Sussex.

Back I went to the civil registration ever so excited, only to find no Frederick William Jones in Chichester. I tried the 1881 census and found nothing there or in the IGI. I had been so happy but now I was frustrated. I went back to the Army records. There had to be something there to help. I got a magnifying glass and finally found it. Under next of kin was his wife's name but crossed out there had been written "Mother, Sarah Harding". I had his mother's name.

I decided to look for Sarah Harding. When I looked in the 1881 census, I found her and Frederick too, but not as I expected. The listing was: "Stephen H. Harding, 44 years, sawyer; Sarah Harding, 53 years, dressmaker; Stephen H. Harding, 20 years, woodsman; Frederick W. Harding, 19 years, blacksmith; Kate C. Harding, 16 years, at home; Alice H. Harding, 7 years, scholar". I had the family but why did Frederick join the Army under the name Jones? On his marriage certificate his father is listed as Stephen Jones, sawyer, and Kate C. was even more proof I had the right family as my grandmother's sister was named Kate Ceclia. My mother said that her great-grandmother was a dressmaker and Frederick was a blacksmith. There he was Frederick William Harding, not Jones, in the civil registration. However, Stephen was under Jones.

Then everything fell into place. The IGI turned up a marriage for Stephen Henry Harding and Sarah Jones in 1863: the two boys were born before the marriage and were given her maiden name. I researched the branches of the Harding family and got back three generations.

In 1999, I took all the information I had found and wrote a family history. My mom sent a copy of this family history to Kate Ceclia's daughter, my mother's cousin in England. Her cousin was very happy to receive it and wrote back with additional information that I didn't have! — Janyce Mann, ON, eeks.place@sympatico.ca

Two Down, Two To Go

I have hurtled two brickwalls in my genealogy research and a newspaper death notice was the boost I needed in both cases.

I received a copy of a newspaper article from one of my husband's cousins. It stated their great-grandfather was born in Schwedelbach, Germany. I used the German telephone book on the Internet to find people with that surname still living there. I wrote to them and was happy to get a response. They said they would look into the possibility of a connection. Their next letter contained a copy of the great-grandfather's baptismal record obtained from a church in a nearby village. There have been many letters back and forth in the last four years. The connection was found five genera-

tions back and we are currently able to list 12 generations of my husband's family.

My second breakthrough came when I found a death notice for my great-grandfather in the newspaper archives at the library. It was in an 1873 edition of a German paper that was formerly printed in Cincinnati and needed to be translated. I learned he was born in Oberrieden, Bavaria. I have been able to view church records on film at the FHL and I have found birth, marriage and death records of my ancestors going back 11 generations.

Death notice for John George Huber from the 22 February 1873 edition of the Cincinnati Volksfreura.

I still have two brickwalls to conquer. I can't find much information about my mother's family or my husband's mother's family. However, I am no longer boxed in, two sides down and two to go. — Marian Huber Dietrich, OH, marian_dietrich@my-family.com

* * *

Contacts! Contacts!

Successful genealogy is all about contacts. Sometimes another researcher will share some research documents with me. I always try to accumulate documents that I can in turn share with them. I have made exciting discoveries by contacting the source people who are mentioned in the documents. They usually have even more data they are ready to share with an interested colleague. But always remember to thank them for their generosity. — Joan L. Mooney, HI, jmooneygal@aol.com

Tracing Your Ancestors On Maps

This item took place pre-Internet; these days it would have been a lot easier. I was researching the family Halbritter. I had found my US Civil War ancestors and the immigrant Halbritter. Unfortunately, all available records indicated origin as Germany, with no clues as to city or state. Ultimately, I went to the city library where they have telephone directories from all over the world. I searched every German telephone book and copied down the address of each Halbritter listed (about 120 hours total). Then I created a form letter asking for information on the Halbritter family and particularly any Halbritters who had come to the US. I had a German fellow at work translate the letter in German and sent several hundred copies. To save money I sent them surface mail so it took months before I began to get responses.

I was soon overwhelmed with data, but none of it seemed to have anything to do with my branch of the family. I had file drawers full of data and still had not found the source. In the meantime I had located a large map of Germany and was sticking pins in the locations where I had received answers to my mailing. I connected the "before" and "after" pins with a thread. One day I realized my map looked like a daisy, all the pins and threads were starting at a central point and leafing outwards. That central point was Nurnberg.

Focusing on Nurnberg, I discovered the family Halbritter had lived in Nurnberg from 1345 until 1634. In 1634, the family exploded outward, away from the Black Plague. Now all those file drawers of letters began to make sense. In time, I was able to find my direct ancestors in the city of Crailsheim where the family has lived in the same house since 1634. The key to the entire puzzle was that daisy effect of the threads and pins on my large wall map.

Here is a solution to someone else's brickwall. According to the church records at Gossmaul, Germany, (present-day Czech Republic), Andreas Halbritter was born in 1680 and married Catherine. Their children were Johann Georg Halbritter born in 1710 and Georg Mathias born in 1716. The Church record also states the family left for Amerika.

According to Rupp's *30,000 Immigrants*, the following arrived: Hans Georg Haldriter (age 33), Peter Haldriter (age 25) and Phillip Haldriter (age 18). R.B. Strassburger's *Pennsylvania German Pioneers: A Publication of the Original Lists of Arrivals in the Port of Philadelphia from 1727 to 1808* has the passenger lists including: Jurgen Kaltreuter, Philip Kaltreuter and Philip Kaltriter. Strassburger continues with the immigration lists, Hans Georg Kaltriter, Philip Kaltriter and Peter Kaltriter, and concludes with the Oath of Allegiance administered to Hans Georg Kaldriter, Philip Kaldriter and Peter Kaldriter.

It's obvious that some mistakes

were done in reading or writing or both. This is especially noteworthy as the names Kaltreuter, Kaltriter, Kaldriter and Kaltreider are not European names. They are not found in the current telephone books of Berlin or Vienna.

This is going to be an insurmountable brickwall for anyone not aware the German H looks similar to the English K and the German B looks like a D or T to the English reader. — Ron Halbritter, CA

Searching The Records Of A Second Marriage

When I first started researching my father's family in 1988, I learned my grandfather had two brothers I didn't know about. I soon found a granddaughter of one brother, John McMichael. She had researched her family, so that solved one problem. The other was not so easy.

It seemed every time I contacted a family member, they asked about James D. McMichael who had been missing for years.

By the time of a 1991 reunion, I knew James D. McMichael had married Libbie Kugler in Dallas county, IA on 7 September 1881. My grandfather, W i l l i a m McMichael and his brothers, Joseph, John and James D., had all

James D. McMichael,
the missing family member.

left Dallas county to homestead near Wellfleet in western Nebraska. Early attendees of the 1991 reunion in North Platte, NE went to the Oak Grove Cemetery near Wellfleet. When I arrived, people asked me if I knew about Lulu May McMichael who was buried at Oak Grove. I knew that my grandfather donated the land for the Oak Grove Cemetery and the Oak Grove School. His brothers homesteaded nearby. After the reunion we went to the Oak Grove Cemetery where several members of the John McMichael family were buried. On the opposite side of the cemetery we found a marker for Lulu May McMichael. Buried in the same plot as Lulu May were her grandparents, William and Sarah Kugler (Libbie's parents) and an infant son of Theodore L. and Libbie Baker. Libbie had remarried! I was certain Lulu May was the child of Libbie Kugler and James D. McMichael, but had no proof.

Nothing I tried gave me any more information on this family, so I decided to try the Kuglers. By now I had accepted the family story that James D. left for Omaha, NE with a shipment of cattle just before Christmas 1887. He was never heard of again. The cattle were sold and it was assumed he had been robbed and killed. Checking Omaha newspapers for an unidentified body yielded nothing. I contacted several Kuglers in the Maywood and

Wellfleet area with no success.

I finally found a woman who had been a Kugler in North Platte. She knew Aunt Libbie, but insisted she married Ted Baker. When I explained my theory of the Oak Grove markers, she called an elderly aunt who verified Libbie had been married to James D. McMichael before she married Ted Baker.

I found a copy of the divorce papers in the Lincoln County Courthouse at North Platte. It gave full particulars of the Iowa marriage to James, date of Lulu May's birth and the story that he had left for Omaha in December 1887 and never returned. The divorce was granted on 27 August 1892 and Libbie married Theodore L. Baker on 20 May 1893. By going through the family of his spouse, I found answers to James D. McMichael, except what happened to James. — (Mrs.) Erdine McMichael Nugent, WA, enugent@alveus.com

Budding Researcher

When I started my family history research back in the fall of 1995, I made notes from older family members as a base for further research. My sister had learned from a great-aunt she had an uncle or grandparent who had been a Methodist minister. Since the Budd family ancestors I knew at that time had lived in Trenton, Mercer county, NJ, I assumed this minister would have lived in New Jersey. But before I was able to do any research, I talked with the curator of the Barratt's Chapel and Museum near Frederica, DE. This museum is a repository of artifacts and history of Methodist Churches on the Delmarva Peninsula.

From the small library at the museum the curator found a book for me that contained the name of a William Budd who had been a minister in Pemberton, NJ. This led me to look at the 1850 US census for

Burlington county for the parents of my great-grandfather. In addition to learning where to find great-grandfather Abraham I learned the Rev. Budd traced his ancestry back to the Budd men who had arrived in Burlington, NJ during the period 1675-80.

In finding my great-grandfather's name in the 1850 census I then knew my second-great-grandparents' names, Samuel C. Budd and wife Hannah. Living with them was a Rachel Pippitt, who appeared to be Hannah's mother. My next approach was consulting an AAA Tour Book for New Jersey. Here I found a telephone number for the Burlington County Historical Society. I called and was able to talk with their librarian. I stated I was looking for information that would connect Samuel C. and Hannah (Pippitt) Budd to William Budd who was a minister for many years beginning about 1771 through 1807. The librarian offered to look for the Budd family book that the Historical Society had in its library and promised to send me information.

Budd gravestone in Riverview Cemetery in Trenton, NJ.

In three days I had the information in my mailbox. This gave me the opportunity to purchase *Three Centuries Of Budds In America*. So now I know the Budd brothers who came to the US were the sons of Thomas Budd born in 1615 and his wife

Susannah Prigge born in 1611, of Montacute, Somersetshire, England.

It was a wonderful feeling to go from a second-great-grandfather to an eighth-great-grandfather. — E.T. Wall, DE

The Truth Behind The Family Legend

My great-grandfather, John William Pring, married Mary Jane Beer on 15 July 1865. He had been in the building trades and was a cabinetmaker for Queen Victoria. The couple came to the US in 1871 and established a small furniture factory in Rock Falls, IL before moving on to Colorado Springs where he established a large cattle ranch and also owned several mines. As in most families, legends had been passed down.

The Pring family had owned a great estate in Devonshire called Poppleford. Also, great-grandmother Mary Jane Beer always parted her hair in the center, just like Queen Victoria. The reason was that as a young girl she had been a lady-in-waiting to Victoria and had been responsible for arranging Her Majesty's hair each day. Mary Jane had been placed in a very exclusive school called Blue Cape School for Young Ladies where she was taught the finer things such as sewing, tapestry work, reading and writing.

I knew the couple had been born in Devonshire and had married in

Mary Jane Beer, c. 1870.

London but that was the extent of my knowledge. In 1988, my wife Joan and I made a trip to the lovely city of Exeter. In the library of Rougemont Castle we checked the current telephone book and found Prings, a comparatively rare name, were spread all over the area. We found a complete set of city and post office directories going back more than 100 years, listing Prings and Beers in towns with such wonderful names as Hatherleigh, Iddesleigh, Otter, Awliscombe and Newton Poppleford. Newton Poppleford?

I found there was not and never had been a Poppleford estate. It was the area from which great-grandfather had come. One legend gone.

Next we went to the Hall of Records. It was there I learned John Pring had been born on 22 June 1845 in Aylesbeare, Devon. I managed to prove John Pring's ancestry back for another three generations. After dealing with the records that may or may not be found in the US, I was truly amazed at the extent and completeness of the records in even the smallest shires of England. Also in the library I found the Mormons had been through the records microfilming every record they could get and had left a copy of the IGI with the librarian. This was a big help. I found Mary Jane Beer was born in Iddsleigh, Devon on 29 May 1843. She grew up in Exeter and I was able to find the house she lived in and the park across the way where she must have played in as a girl. I was able to carry her family back six more generations. However I'm afraid along the way, I exploded another family legend.

Joan and I were passing a lovely mall area in which stood a small statue of a Blue Boy. The plaque said that on this spot had stood the Blue Boy School for Boys. I went back to the library to check and found there had also been a Blue Maid School for girls. "In this establishment girls are maintained, clothed, and instructed in reading, sewing, and knitting. They are admitted between the ages of seven and ten and discharged at 14 when they are bound apprentices with a premium of a half pound each, or become servants in respectable families". There went the family myth.

Baptismal record for Mary Jane Beer.

Now for one of the most exciting parts! Mary Jane was the daughter of William Brook Beer and Elizabeth Tucker Thorne. In going through the records I found Elizabeth was buried in Bartholemew Cemetery in Exeter. We went looking for the cemetery but none of the townspeople had ever heard of it. We were about to give up when an elderly gentleman asked if he could be of assistance. We told him we were looking for Bartholemew Cemetery. He smiled and pointed to a spot 30 feet away. He said it was damaged badly during the Blitz and wasn't used very often. We thanked him and found the gate leading to the graves. The markers were in great disarray but they had been gathered up after the war and were lined along the wall. We had no luck finding Elizabeth's markers. However, I man-

aged to get a map of the cemetery from the library. We had the cemetery location we were able to find my second-great-grandmother's grave.

What a wonderful experience. — Frank Bouley, NJ, fbouley@prodigy.net

Mary Ann, The Missing Mormon

I was researching the Jose family and I needed to find my great-grandmother's sister's family. The Jose family left Cornwall, England for Australia in 1846. They spent a few short years there, where a wagon accident killed the mother, Mary. William Jose joined the Mormon Church in Australia and headed for the US in 1855 with four children, Grace, William, Mary Ann and Thomas. Grace, who was my great-grandmother, was easy to trace, but not so for Mary Ann. She, too, was a Mormon and married Jacob Terry Jr. I tried to locate them in Mormon records, but they apparently did not remain Mormons. They were not to be found.

A family letter mentioned they moved to Seattle. I did not locate them in the 1920 federal census for Washington, which was not indexed. I looked at two rolls of microfilm of Seattle but did not find them. Finally, I decided to search a few Terry family names, and using the telephone directory for addresses, I wrote three letters.

Shortly thereafter I received a telephone call from a great-grandson of Jacob and Mary Ann; and he supplied me with all the information I needed to complete the record for Jacob and Mary Ann Jose Terry. I then included them in my book, *The Jose Family — Utah By Way Of Australia*. Mary Ann was the last of all 16 of William's children to be located, including those by his second wife. — Corlyn H. Adams, TX

*   *   *

Helpful Hints

I am the Microfilm Office Supervisor/ Records Manager in the Prothonotary and Clerk of Courts office in Indiana county, PA. My job is to oversee the microfilming, preservation and management of our records dating back to 1806. As part of my job, I do a great deal of genealogical research. We hold the Naturalization and Immigration records which are the main attraction. However, the court records themselves can be of immense help in family research. Though tedious, the nuggets of information gleaned may contribute an invaluable part to a family history and fill in gaps.

For example; in a case from the criminal dockets for 1867, Commonwealth versus Joseph McAfoos, the defendant was accused of beating his wife, Elizabeth. McAfoos was acquitted on grounds of insanity and released into the custody of his father, John McAfoos. This establishes, as a matter of court record, the relationship of father, son and daughter-in-law. As another example, a civil case from the 1840s involved a dispute over property in which a man died without a will. There was disagreement over whether he truly owned the property to begin with. The resulting depositions named three generations of relatives of the man and his wife dating to the late 1700s. It gave places of residence of parents, grandparents, aunts, uncles, cousins and children that included towns and counties in Ireland, Scotland, Pennsylvania and Ohio. This would be a treasure trove for someone researching that particular family name.

As any family researcher is aware, it is often difficult to find information about female family members. Women's names appear surprisingly often in the early court records. Before the early 1900s, a husband, father or uncle represented a woman. Under the name of the plaintiff, it may read "Mary Smith *by her next friend*, John Jones". Usually in the text of the case it will clarify the relationship between the two people.

Divorce cases often yield names, dates and places. Equity cases involve disputes over property. The court records include change-of-name cases especially among immigrants, coroner's inquests, applications for guardianship (of a child or an aging parent) and applications for tavern or peddler licenses.

Schedule a day (or two) to go through the court records. You may be surprised at what you find! — Kathy A. Dean, PA, history1@adelphia.net

Clue Found In A Riddle

I wanted to locate the maiden name of my third-great-grandmother Gracie who married my third-great-grandfather John Sellers. I figured the easiest way to do this was by the marriage certificate. I knew most of their children were born in Saint Clair county, AL. An extensive search of the marriage records for this county turned up nothing. My next idea was to search the Alabama counties where the Sellers had kin. I checked the records of Coosa, Talladega, Clay and Tallapoosa counties, but to no avail.

I knew John Sellers was born in South Carolina. I didn't know when he moved to Alabama. So I first started checking the census records for South Carolina. He left the state around 1830 but he didn't show up in the Alabama records until 1840. Where was John during those 10 years? It really had me stumped.

I went back over my records and my collection of family stories. Nowhere could I find mention of any other state of residence other than South Carolina and Alabama. It took me a bit to think what to do next. I had to find a new angle. I knew the Sellers married into two other large lines, the Allisons and the Riddles. I also knew when one group moved the other groups normally moved with them. I started with the Allisons. They started out in South Carolina and then moved to Alabama. That was of no help. So I tried the Riddles and that was when my brickwall started to crumble.

I located where the Riddles had settled in Newton county, GA. In the same county, just two towns over I found the missing 10 years of John Sellers' life. But more importantly I found a marriage certificate with Gracie's maiden name of Huff. I even found enough information on the Huffs to start a whole new limb on my tree. — Laura Bryant, AL, buclau@gulftel.com

State Death Indexes

Most genealogists know of the SSDI, but it seems most do not know about state death indexes. I use the Washington State death index a lot helping others and I know RootsWeb.com has the Texas and California death indexes online.

I was trying to find where my great-grandfather Stanislaus P. Dillingham died so I went to the FHC. I knew he had lived in Illinois, so I checked under Illinois Vital Records and they had a death index (and the death certificates also). The Illinois death index was on 191 fiches, which I ordered. A while later the fiches came and I found not only my great-grand-father Stanislaus, but also his wife Eliza M. Dillingham. I then ordered the film that had their death certifi-cates and was so excited when I finally found Eliza's mother, Rhoda's maiden name, which was Preston. I knew that Rhoda had been born in Canada and now I had a maiden name.

In September of 1999, we went to a reunion of my father's Army Air Corps unit, close to the town where

Stanislaus and Eliza died, so we stopped by the library there and copied the obituaries. As a bonus we found the newspaper article on the marriage of Stanislaus' and Eliza's daughter, Anna to Anton Hansen, who was my grandfather.

The gravestone in the Union Cemetery in Crystal Lake, IL.

Then we headed for the Union Cemetery and found the gravestone for Stanislaus and Eliza. We took lots of pictures while we were there. When I showed the pictures to my uncle, he told me why Stanislaus was not a US Civil War veteran. He was not able to stand very long because of medical problems with his legs. All this came from the Illinois death index. — Charles Hansen, WA

From Someone Who's Been There

One method that has helped with a couple of brickwalls is to go sideways. That is, if your direct line cannot be traced, go back down at least one generation and try to follow a sibling or a child. I reached a dead end with my second-great-grandfather. But I knew about the spouse of one of his children. So I went and tried to follow that spouse's birth and parents. It turned out they came from the same place in Ireland and people in my family line were mentioned as godparents as well as marriage witnesses.

Obituaries are often a source of more information than the official entries, again following a sideways line. I looked up an obituary at the Ontario Archives which has microfilmed newspapers from the 1800s. I found the person I was tracing was identified as a sister of the second-great-grandfather I was interested in and she had two brothers still living in Ireland when she died. This led me to the exact town and a couple more generations.

Another piece of advice is to go over any old family photographs you might have. (And be sure to ask other people in the family what they have.) Look on the back of each one. You may find a photographer's name or possibly the city where it was taken. In the best instance, someone will have written who, when and where. If the photos are in frames or cardboard folders, gently taken them apart to see if there is any identifying information on the back. — Lynn Blaser, ON

Use Your Imagination

As I was starting my genealogy work everyone was giving me surnames to research. I was able to find leads and gather complete families and go back several generations on some names.

I was only having problems with one family name. The name given to me was Bitleus. I thought that name would stand out but I could never find any clues. I finally put that name

in the back of my mind and was concentrating more on the other names.

Several years later I was searching another surname in the census records. In searching I saw the name of the married daughter of Bitleus from whom I descend. She was listed with a child and not the head of the household. There were several other people I didn't recognize. I looked to see who was the head of the house and the surname was Betten. This man was the age that her father could be. Quickly copying this, I took it and went to some books on the history of this area and there was the family, Bettens. The book proved she was the daughter of this man. Her husband had died and she returned home and the youngest child was listed with her in this census.

Further study proved a son was living at home and a daughter-in-law was there with her children. It seems the daughter-in-law's husband died and she moved in with her in-laws. I have been able to trace them back two more generations to Switzerland and through the FHC have seen microfilms of records for this family.

1850 federal census for Switzerland county, IN. Philip Bettens' daughter, Amelia Duplan, was the clue to finding him.

I was asked by some of the family how I could just change the name of a family like that. I had done my homework and could show them the proof. I now look at a name and imagine any number of ways it could be spelled. — Barbara Kirkpatrick, IN

*   *   *

The Water Meter Reader Brickwall Beater

A few years ago after the passing of my mother, I inherited some family pictures. Minimal descriptions were written on the back of some pictures, while others had nothing.

Two of the pictures were the oval curved-glass type, quite obviously of different people, but the couples in the two pictures had a striking resemblance to one another, stiff and proper, quite possibly wedding pictures.

I knew one photograph was of my great-grandparents and the other was marked "Uncle John and Aunt Edith". I had been studying this picture trying to figure out whose aunt and uncle they were, who they were and why they resembled so much the picture of my great-grandparents.

I had these pictures spread on the ping-pong table in the basement, where I could walk by and keep the thought process working.

Above: Wedding picture of Isaac Bice and Mary Catherine Brannaman, married 9 November 1864. Below: Wedding picture of John Bice and Edith Brannaman, married 1 January 1879.

One day when the water meter reader came to check the meter, he saw the pictures and looked at them. He asked briefly about the pictures and then commented, "She sure looks like a younger sister to that one," pointing to my great-grandma and "Isn't he related to the man too?"

That did it! It triggered my thinking. She was indeed a younger sister to my great-grandmother and by further checking, he, in the second picture, was a nephew of my great-grandfather.

Moral of the story: Let others have a look at your information, including photographs, because they are not hindered by previous notions.

They can sometimes be more objective and can see the forest in spite of the trees. — Joan Bice Underwood, IA

Criminal Court Records

No one knew anything about my husband's grandmother's sister Rosa except that she died young. Seven-year-old Iowa-born Rosa was listed with her family in the 1880 census in Audubon county, IA. Nothing more was found on her until a cousin came across an old letter dated 23 May 1891 to my husband's grandmother, Annette, from her brothers and father.

This letter told Annette of her sister, Rosa's, death on 21 May 1891. Her brothers and father had been working in Nuckolls county, NE when they learned Rosa was very ill. The letter writer (probably the father of Rosa and Annette) wrote Annette that Rosa's husband, Fred, and his mother had starved Rosa to death. Rosa lived three days after a baby boy was born. The baby was still alive when the letter was written, but I have been unable to find whether or not the child survived beyond that. The letter went on to say Fred was in the county jail charged with murder in the first degree. This was the first we knew Rosa had married.

Fred had turned Rosa's body over to the county for burial by the time the men arrived. They purchased a lot and gave her a decent burial. I could find no record of her burial. The Gage County Genealogy Society, NE said she was probably buried in a cemetery near her home in Indian Creek. This cemetery had many graves with no markers and was later abandoned. Identifiable bodies were moved to the Scott Street Cemetery in Beatrice, NE. I wrote to the County Clerk of Gage county hoping to find a marriage record and obtain her husband's full name. I sent a copy of the 1891 letter that apparently intrigued a worker in that office as much as it had me. She found a record in the Brides Index for a Rosa Fagan to a Charles Carpenter. No other information was given in the index.

She called to ask if I wanted a copy of this record although no mention was made of Fred. She explained these records were in the courthouse basement and there would be a charge for a copy. I felt money was no object and soon had a copy of a mar-

riage certificate for Rosa Fagan (age 18) and Charles Fred Carpenter (age 22) on 4 August 1889. It then occurred to me that if Fred had been in the county jail, there had to be some records. I again wrote my new friend in the County Clerk's office. She found and sent copies of the warrant issued by the Coroner's Office charging him with manslaughter. His bail was set at $750, which he was unable to pay, and so waited in jail until the June term of the District Court. The doctor who was called to attend Rosa in childbirth reported her death to the Coroner as being due to confinement (childbirth), nervous prostration and general debility caused by exposure and general neglect. A coroner's jury was called and Fred was found guilty and held for trial. A court-appointed attorney to defend him was paid $40.

The clerk referred me to someone with a collection of old newspapers and I obtained a copy of the *Gage County Democrat* for 28 May 1891. It had a lengthy report on the Coroner's Jury and witnesses' testimony. These same witnesses gave testimony at the June trial in the District Court. The actual trial testimony could not be found, but I received a list of court costs and names of 25 witnesses who were served with subpoenas to testify. Many of the witnesses testified Rosa appeared weak and half-starved and she did not have adequate clothing. They said Fred worked only occasionally and was frequently drunk. Neighbors testified they had invited Rosa to their homes for meals because they had tried giving her food, but Fred sold it to obtain his drink. Despite all this testimony and that of the doctor on her condition, the verdict was not guilty. He later remarried.

Rosa Fagan Carpenter was only 19 when she died. With the help of a sympathetic and curious worker in the County Clerk's office who found marriage and court records and referred me to a newspaper collection,

Rosa's short life story was recorded. — (Mrs.) Erdine McMichael Nugent, WA, enugent@alveus.com

Chaplains' Returns At The Public Records Office

Searching in the Public Records Office in Kew for the records of a soldier in the British Army is seriously hampered if the number or name of his regiment is unknown. Sometimes if a person can supply a series of genealogical events such as births, baptisms, etc. with dates, one might be able to narrow the search by looking at only those regiments in the appropriate locations on the dates given by the family.

The Public Record Office in Kew. Photograph courtesy of James Pratt.

However, if the family does not know the regiment and has no knowledge of any genealogical events, then the brickwall is looming. The Public Records Office has a set of microfiche records known as the Chaplains' Returns or General Register Office Regimental Returns which record from about 1790, those events at which an Army Chaplain officiated. Although these records are not complete by any means, sometimes when the birth of a soldier's child was recorded, the father's regiment was shown.

Unfortunately, the marriage and death records have still not been indexed so that it is only birth/baptisms that are really useful. But with a bit of luck and tightly crossed fingers, we might have managed to find a chink in the brickwall. — Bob O'Hara, London, UK, searcher@dircon.co.uk

Changing Tactics

I was looking for the surname Marlin. I did all the easy steps first to find some information on my ancestor, Sarah Marlin.

I checked FamilySearch.org, the IGI, Ancestry.com and other surname databases. I rarely found, if ever, the surname listed. I knew Sarah married out of a Quaker meeting in colonial Virginia, so I changed tactics. I began looking at early Quaker records and early Virginian records.

I did not find a Marlin family, but I did find several references to a Malin family. I think I have found a likely family link that does exist. — Donna Potter Phillips, WA

It Just Didn't Make Sense

Just finding the state where my grandmother died was almost a brickwall but eventually I did find her death documented in Elk City, OK in October 1917. However, her burial site was a mystery; that part was left blank. I wrote to cemeteries and funeral homes but to no avail. Each response denied the existence of any records for Mary Ann Dunn Hall.

I also had a death certificate for my grandfather Charlie stating he had died on 20 December 1925 in Mangum, OK but didn't have any better information on his burial site. My grandparents were separated for several years before her death, so that seemed like another brickwall.

Since the only clue was the date and town of her death, I decided I had to go to Oklahoma to look for myself. My sister joined me in what seemed likely to be a wasted effort. When we arrived in Elk City, OK, we hit one brickwall after another. There were no county records, no church records or records from funeral homes. Published cemetery records in Elk City did not show anything for Mary Ann.

Finally, we decided to go on to Mangum to see what we could find out about Charlie. We found the funeral home that had records for Charlie but the spot that named the burial site was blank. Foiled again.

We decided to try the Mangum Public Library. They did have some cemetery records but again, no reference to Charlie. Almost as an afterthought, I asked the librarian if they had any old newspapers on file or microfilm. Eureka! We found Charlie's obituary, which said he was buried in Elk City.

We went back to Elk City but this time we were a bit more efficient and asked for the newspapers on microfilm. Sure enough, there was Mary Ann's obituary stating that she was buried at East Fairlawn Cemetery on 12 October 1917. Back to the cemetery we went. The managers of Fairlawn Cemetery in Elk City were amazingly willing to help us. They seemed to know everything about the cemetery. While they had no records for Mary Ann they did show that Charlie was buried in lot 97, east addition.

Although there was no marker they helped us find Charlie's grave. We stood there staring at the site and it just didn't make sense. Given the difficulty of transportation as well as the time of year, why would his friends have taken him all the way from Mangum to Elk City for burial unless a plot had already been purchased?

We were ready to give up but the managers had a better idea. They suggested we go to the office where they could check their database to see who was buried in the plots next to Charlie. The manager checked plot 97; sure enough there was Charlie. Then he found Mary Ball was in plot 96. I asked him if the date was 12 October 1917. He said that was the date. The truth dawned on him as it did on me. As he gazed back at the computer screen we all knew what had happened; Mary Ann Hall's records had been written as Mary Ann Ball.

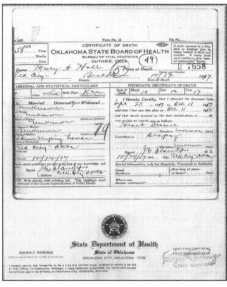

Mary Ann Dunn Hall's death certificate.

Today granite markers are installed for lots 96 and 97 in East Fairlawn Cemetery in Elk City, clearly marking the final resting places for Mary Ann Dunn Hall and Charles Samuel Hall. — Marion Keefer, OR

Ukrainian Ancestors

My family immigrated to the US from the Ukraine beginning in 1884 through 1923. They were poor Jewish immigrants fleeing from the Pogroms. They didn't document their family history. Their surname in the old country was long forgotten until I began doing family research.

Searching for any formal documentation was a brickwall. Here is one of the more difficult walls I had to hurdle:

For 15 years I have been trying to locate the Ukrainian town where my great-grandfather was born. Before my uncle died he told me the name of the town was Hertzikov. I poured through old atlases with no luck. I even tried Poland and about the closest I got was a town called Herby.

When doing research at the FHL, I spoke to the supervisor of the microfilming being done on the Ukraine. I casually mentioned the problem with my grandfather's birthplace. I told him I had tried Hertzivok, Herbilov, Chorikov and others with no luck.

He pulled down a gazetteer and told me the town I was searching for was Gorikov! It seems the letter G and letter H are interchangeable as are many consonants in Soundex. — BB

Help From Afar

Although I have traveled to Minnesota several times to research my family, my great-aunt Catharina's line remained a mystery. Living elderly relatives could remember only three things about Catharina: she had a large family, she lived in the St. Paul area and her sister Susanna kept a photograph of Catharina's daughter, Florence DeGraw, on top of her piano

On one trip, I brought a St. Paul phone book home with me and wrote to every DeGraw and DeGroh listed. No one knew if DeGraw was the daughter's married or maiden name. I received no responses. A few years later, I again got a current St. Paul phone book and sent letters to the appropriate surnames. This time I received a response from a Bob DeGraw who was descended from the first wife of Henry DeGraw — it turns out that my Catharina was the second wife of Henry DeGraw.

Through Bob, I was able to contact an elderly granddaughter of Catharina, with whom I had several

fruitful conversations — Catharina Weyrens DeGraw inherited three young children when she married Henry; she herself bore nine children, five of whom predeceased her and only one had descendants. I now had information about Catharina and many avenues of research opened.

Back row, left to right; Math, Anton, Joseph, M.D., Michael and John. Seated, from left to right; Susanna, mother Elizabeth and Catharina. Picture probably taken in 1911 at the time of father Peter Weyrens' death as all are present and dressed in black.

I wanted to know more about my maternal grandfather, Catharina's youngest brother, who died when I was a baby. I placed an advertisement in the Scottsbluff, NE newspaper saying: "Anyone having known Joseph P. Weyrens, M.D., Scottsbluff resident 1926-1939, please contact…" Many elderly people who, as children, had been his patients, contacted me and I was able to get a feel for what kind of a man he was through their memories.

Don't underestimate what you can accomplish long distance. I live in California! — Carol Fitting, CA, caroljeanf@aol.com

Under A Rock

When I was about 10 years old my father's family was gathered together "down at the ranch". The adults were talking and a sudden burst of loud laughter made me ask my uncle what was so funny. Apparently they told granma she was born under a rock.

He explained that in Portuguese it means she was a bastard. That thought stayed with me.

A few years later I asked her what her name was before she married granpa. She snapped back, "The same as Granpa's of course!" I didn't pursue it any further.

After my retirement I started researching my family history. What about my paternal grandmother? I knew granpa had gone back to the old country to find a bride, I knew which island he came from, but not where they were married. Years later I sent for her death certificate. Her name was given as Mary Vierra (a spelling change from the original Vieira) and everything else was unknown. The informant for the death certificate was her oldest child. How could there be so little information? Perhaps no one knew.

I floundered about with passenger lists, found the original document hand-written by the purser in the logbook of the *Barque Sarah* from Fayal in July 1888 at the archives in Waltham, MA. Granma arrived as Maria Emilia Vieira, the 18-year-old bride of Manuel R. Vieira who was returning to the US. With them was the bride's mother, listed as Maria Emilia Vieira aged 58. Were all those names really the same?

A few years later, Aunt Amelia (in her late nineties) and I were spending a day sitting around talking. Amelia, as the youngest daughter of Maria Emilia, knew nothing of her mother. We talked about Tia Mariana — known to me only as a lovely elderly lady who had lived her last few years with Granma. I thought she might be my grandfather's aunt, or perhaps it was just a polite way for children to address her. She told me "Tia" had not been just an honorary courtesy title, Mariana was indeed an aunt, my grandmother's aunt and godmother.

I sent for Tia Mariana's death certificate. The informant was my grandmother and had completed every sec-

tion. There was all the data for Mariana and her parents.

The secret had to have been my grandparents were cousins. Manuel and the elder Maria Emilia were first cousins, the younger Maria was a once-removed cousin. To add to the confusion, the elder Maria Emilia had married a man with the same surname that I discovered later through church records. From there it was to the FHC to the baptismal and marriage records and ever onward and further back into the past. — Anonymous

American Revolution Websites

A family story and the Internet helped me trace my Wolf ancestors back to William Wallace Wolf, who was a US Civil War soldier in Clinton county, NY. He enlisted on 8 May 1861.

Pension papers from the NARA indicated a birth date of 19 August 1837 in New York. I would have been stalled here except I met a distant cousin whom I had never known. He contacted me via the RootsWeb.com surname list where I registered my William Wallace Wolf. He put me in touch with another cousin who had done extensive research on her Lucy Ann Wolf, a sister to William Wallace Wolf. She went back two more generations.

Through FHL films for Saranac, Clinton county, NY she found a town clerk's register of soldiers in the Civil War that listed William Wallace Wolf as a resident of Schuyler Falls, Clinton county, NY. His parents were Elizabeth and Orin Wolf. She also found Orin's father, John Casper Shana Wolf, as listed in Lyman Hayes' book *History Of The Town Of Rockingham, Vermont*. This town history stated "John Casper Shana Wolfe, (s. of Casper and Catherine [Young]

Wolfe), b. about 1750 in Germany; was a Hessian soldier, and probably one of those surrendered by Gen. Burgoyne in 1777. They were called "Conventioners" and marched to Boston where they were kept for a time, later being allowed to work among the farmers who needed help. Mr. Wolfe went to Leominster, Mass., and concluded to remain permanently in this country. In 1778, when the officers called for him to join his companions in their march to Virginia, he hid in the cellar of his employer's house, until the officers gave up the search for him and departed…"

This is where everyone was stalled for several months. We researched Hessian soldiers and the American Revolution. We checked Leominster, MA websites but it wasn't until I placed a query on the Windham, Vermont RootsWeb.com site, listed the above synopsis and asked if anyone knew about John Casper Shana Wolfe, that we found success. The webmaster responded to my query, stating I should check the Kaspar Schoenewolff at RootsWeb.com's American Revolution, Hessian Soldier queries. Now it all made sense — John Caspar Shana Wolf was really Kaspar Shoenewolf from Rotterode, Hesse, Germany.

NARA pension paper of William Wallace Wolf giving his birth date.

Through e-mails with the Kassel (Germany) Archives, using AltaVista's BabelFish translator, I was able to pur-

chase copies of Johann Caspar Schoenewolf's baptismal record, among other data. These records stated he was born on 26 January 1755 and his father was Conrad Schoenewolf and the godfather was Johann Caspar Catrinawts; thus we were able to go back another generation.

Maybe your ancestor's middle name is really part of his surname. — Gail Krause, WI

Post To Get
The Most

During a telephone call with my mother in March 1997, she told me that she had been trying to find a family member of her sister's first husband. He was a WWII Canadian RAF pilot who was killed in France in September 1944 when his plane was shot down. Mom's sister had died in 1996 and some medals that had been awarded to her first husband were found in her belongings. We felt these medals should be passed to his family. No one knew anything about his family and we weren't sure how to find any living descendants.

The only thing anyone could recall was that there was possibly a nephew who might have been an artist. Mom told me she had written letters to some Canadian military veterans' groups as well as the National Archives of Canada in Ottawa and was unable to find any information.

I decided to use some of the resources on the Internet. She gave me the information and I spent some time checking quite a few Canadian genealogy sites. In April 1997 I posted a query on one of the Internet genealogy sites. Within a couple of days I had a reply from a lady living in Calgary who was sure she had gone to art school with the nephew. She told me she was trying to contact mutual friends who might know where he was living. I sent letters to the addresses she had given me and a few days later I discovered a message left on my answering machine from the nephew. I returned his call that night and we visited like long-lost friends instead of strangers. He remembered his uncle, even though he was quite young when he was killed and he was really excited to learn about his uncle's medals. He had no idea they existed.

He must have thanked me at least a dozen times and assured me over and over again that he would treasure them.

It was definitely a rewarding and worthwhile mission and taught me how valuable the various resources available on the Internet are. I've knocked down quite a few other brickwalls through query postings since then. — Mary Lindbo, NV

Clues On Photographs

I was given a set of pictures taken at my aunt's funeral. The pictures were sent from Accrington, Lancashire, England, however, I had no idea where the burial took place. I found an entry for my aunt at the FHC but the first names did not match. I decided to pursue it anyway and sent for the death certificate.

I still wanted to know where my aunt was buried. I looked closely at the folders for the pictures. Printed on the front was the name of the professional photographer who took the pictures. It was a shot in the dark. I entered the name of the photographer on the Internet in a directory, but found nothing. I decided to use the Lancashire Message Board on the

The photographer's name and address from the picture.

Internet. I posted a query looking for anyone who might have known the photographer and what would have happened to his records. I received a few replies directing me to someone at the Family History and Heraldry Society. I contacted a woman there who was very interested in my query and offered to help. I scanned the photograph for her and sent it over the Internet. The next day she replied that she recognized one of the pall-bearers.

This discovery led her to the funeral home where this gentleman worked and he was able to supply me with the location of my aunt's plot. A few weeks later, I received a copy of my aunt's death certificate and all the information matched.

The Internet and a kind lady helped me jump over the brickwall. — Natalie Lisowiec, ON

The Mystery Of The Non-Existent Grave

During my childhood my family occasionally drove to the town of my mother's birth. The highway passed the cemetery and sometimes we asked if grandma and grandpa were buried there. Mother always replied, "Yes" but said she probably couldn't find the gravestones.

When I became interested in genealogy, I was told that mother's brother, Gordon McNab, purchased a marker for his mother's grave but not his father's. Uncle Gordon was dead by then so I could not ask him why he neglected grandfather. Since grandfather died in 1928 it seemed to me the county clerk should have cemetery burial records so I wrote for the information. The courthouse cemetery records did not start until 1935. Prior to that the cemetery was a private, profit-making organization that eventually failed. Records were incomplete and handled by a local undertaker.

I wrote many letters and several months passed without progress. Both the undertaker and register of deeds were convinced my grandfather was buried in Potter's Field. No records were kept for indigents and the records the undertaker did have did not show a grave for Daniel McNab.

I discovered my grandparents had been divorced and that grandmother died six years before grandfather, so I did not expect to find them buried in adjoining graves. Knowing where grandmother was buried would not help find grandfather's grave.

I decided to conduct personal primary research on location at Britton, SD. There were several tasks I wanted to accomplish while there, including a search of register of deeds records, newspaper announcements, church funeral records and cemetery records. I also wanted to tour the cemetery and interview the sexton. Several visits to the register of deeds office failed to find any data concerning grandfather's grave.

Newspaper records were very disappointing. Several searches were required to locate a short entry mentioning grandfather's death. There was no obituary and nothing regarding his funeral.

It was not possible to review church records because the pastor was away and time was running out. I determined grandfather's funeral was held at the Methodist church. The local undertaker's records consisted of a plywood board which had slips of paper glued to it showing where burial plots were, who purchased them and when. There was also an index of persons buried there. I asked if the records showed a Daniel McNab and the answer was no, but there were other McNabs and uncle Gordon owned a plot. I knew Gordon was buried at Bremerton, WA but that he had a young son buried in the Britton Cemetery so I thought nothing of this at the time.

In a dejected mood, I went to the cemetery searching for clues. Grandmother McNab's marker was easy to locate, as was the family plot for Gordon's first wife's family. I noticed Gordon's son, Eugene, was buried in the Stroupe plot and he had died in 1926. Then I located the large plot that contained several small markers for the McNab family and another large plot with a huge Morgan family marker.

Then on to Potter's Field. It depressed me immensely and I simply could not conceive grandfather being buried there. During a second visit to the undertaker, he let me look at the records myself. I was especially concerned about the period around 8 December 1928, when grandfather died. As I looked at the entries, one leaped out at me, "Gordon McNab — 9 December 1928." I knew of no reason why Gordon would purchase a cemetery lot the day after his father died unless it was for his father's burial. I had just seen his son's grave in his in-laws' family plot. Besides, his son died in 1926 so I knew the plot was not for that purpose.

Daniel A. McNab's gravestone in Britton Cemetery in Britton, SD.

Although Gordon was dead, Aunt Dorothea, still lived in Britton. I immediately wrote down the lot location and rushed to her house. She knew of no reason for Gordon to buy that lot and never knew he had done so. She agreed with me it must have been for grandfather.

The next day I returned to the cemetery with a tape measure and stakes to mark the location. Later that day Dorothea drove to the cemetery and saw where I placed the stake. She told me, "That is where your grandfather is buried. I remember it well because I was standing by that big tombstone when he was buried."

Today, a simple marker nestles in the grass over grandfather's grave. — David L. Perkins, CA

When You Least Expect It

My brickwall came into being when I was looking for my grandmother Nevada May Longwell's grandfather. I had looked for several years for him.

My grandmother's father was William Henry Longwell and I was always told he was illegitimate. Nevada May was from Tyler county, WV. I found a birth certificate for William Henry in Wetzel county, WV, although he was born in Monroe county, OH on 7 June 1866. Wetzel county was just across the Ohio River and maybe his mother, Canrissa Longwell, gave birth to him at a relative's home.

The birth certificate lists his mother as Canarissa Longwell and his father as B. Longwell. A distant cousin gave me the original marriage certificate of William Henry's parents. They were married 12 March 1865 in Monroe county, OH, further proving he was not illegitimate.

Remember at this point, I am looking for William Henry Longwell's father and I have B. Longwell. The marriage certificate states his parents' names as Canarissa Givens and Benton Longwell. On the census there was no Benton Longwell with family in this time frame. I learned he was in the US Civil War so I sent for Civil War records for the name B. Longwell. The answer came back with no B. Longwell records. I sent for Benton Longwell records. The answer came back again with no

records for Benton Longwell.

I went to the Tyler County, West Virginia Court House and looked at the Fiduciary Orders. In the 1881-1902 book I found where Hannah J. Longwell who was over the age of 14 years and a minor of Thomas B. Longwell, deceased, had made the choice of her guardian, Mrs. Canarissa Longwell.

One more time I sent for Civil War records, this time with Thomas Benton Longwell and some records came. In the records it stated Canarissa Givens was his wife and his two children were William Henry Longwell and Hannah J. Longwell.

Finally after 20 years of searching every record I could get my hands on I found my grandmother's grandfather. It was a great day! Since then I have found his grave in Monroe county, OH. I have found him in the census with his parents, listed as Thomas Longwell.

Finally a brickwall was solved. There have been a few since but not as hard to solve as this one. — Christine Brookover, WV

The End Of The Line

Evangeline "Bridie" Fording was married to Charles Byron Hopkins in Seattle in 1919, and they had two sons before they were divorced, Martin Harvey and Byron Oliver.

In 1925, Bridie married Gottlieb Theodore "George" Wuertz and they lived in El Monte, CA. Bridie and George Wuertz moved to Utah after WWII and were good friends of our family. George died in 1974 and Bridie continued to live in St. George, UT. She had never mentioned her sons to us, although we did know she had two boys.

In 1997, Bridie passed away and a few months later I inherited her genealogy. She had no other family of whom we were aware. She had a wealth of information, including an article about Harvey who died in 1932 in El Monte in an accident. No wonder she had never mentioned him, but what about Byron?

There were some school papers that showed that Byron had also taken his stepfather's name Wuertz because they were living together in 1932. I found a drugstore photo-developing envelope, dated 1936, that said Byron Hopkins, so by then he had gone back to his birth name. There was an unlabeled photo of a teenage boy on a bike and another photo that showed the boy playing a musical instrument, but nothing else about him. I assume those photos might have been Byron and these pieces of information were all I had.

AL. RUIZ PHARMACY
935 Temple Street   MAdison 5192
Los Angeles, California

Columbia Quality Photo Finishing

Name
Address

DEVELOPING ORDER
Rolls
Packs
PRINT ORDER
Negatives
Prints, Each
Enlarge
DULL   GLOSSY
NOTICE—In Case of Error This Envelope MUST be Returned. Responsible for Retail price of film only

Have YOUR FAVORITE
NEGATIVE ENLARGED

COLUMBIA PHOTO SERVICE

1936 photograph envelope showing the name Byron Hopkins.

I wanted to share with Byron some knowledge about his wonderful mother and give him her genealogy. I searched through Bridie's papers and found a typed genealogy, dated 1957, that had Byron's birth date. I looked on Internet sources of the SSDI and found no deaths of a Byron Wuertz. There were several Byron Hopkins, but none matching his birth date. I wondered if Byron had died in military service and I searched Internet sites that had deaths of veterans but found nothing for either Wuertz or Hopkins.

I found a letter from an aunt of Bridie written in the 1960s that asks about Byron. Bridie kept copies of a lot of her genealogical correspondence, but I never found a copy that mentioned the boys. I found a letter of inquiry from some Fording genealogists and sent letters to them at the old addresses. The letters got to their destinations, but they didn't know Bridie had any children.

Since Bridie was 96 years old when she passed away, I figured her aunt would no longer be living and there was no more recent communication than 1964.

I looked up the name of Byron Hopkins in several Internet sources that listed names and addresses, but he could be anywhere.

In June 2000, I received an e-mail message that said the California death index was available on the Internet. I immediately looked up information and found some possible answers. There was a Byron Hopkins that died on 11 July 1970 and the birth date matched my Byron. There were no parents listed. I sent to California for a copy of the death record. There was Byron's death certificate with the mother's name, Bridie Fording. It was her son! He had died in a Long Beach hospital. His address looked like an apartment and his body was cremated. The certificate said he had never been married.

It was time to close the books on this brickwall. Bridie had left no blood descendants and she had no siblings who left posterity. — Cheryl Whitelaw, UT, whitelawcs@suu.edu

*   *   *

The Missing Veteran

When my grandfather was nine months old his maternal grandparents took him from his parents. His mother had two more children with her husband and then left him. None of the children had any further contact with their father's family as they grew up. My grandfather looked his father up as a teenager and visited him at his place of employment. That was the extent of their relationship.

Fifty years later I began working on our family history. I asked hundreds of questions about my great-grandfather, but got very few answers. Grandpa remembered that his great-grandfather's name was Samuel Zane Wilson. He had lived in Martins Ferry, OH in 1922 when my grandfather was born and he had served in the Army during WWII.

So I began at Martins Ferry. There was an entry in the city directory for Elsie Wilson, my great-grandmother, but not for Samuel in 1924. I wrote to the NARA for his service record. While I waited for that answer, I checked with Ohio vital records for a death date and came up empty. I checked courthouse records in Martins Ferry for deeds, wills or any legal action but found nothing. I talked to some of the older members

Samuel Zane Wilson.

of the local historical society who lived in the area during the time Samuel had lived there. One man thought he might have been a mechanic during the 1940s, but wasn't sure he was the right guy.

In the meantime the answer on his service records came. They had been among the records lost in a fire. They were able to forward a copy of his Final Statement, which gave me his rank and induction date as well as where he joined the service. A helpful file clerk had attached a note that he had a Veterans Administration claim number that may be of help to me. Maybe Samuel's records could be accessed through the Veterans Administration. By using his claim number I was able to use another route to find out about my great-grandfather.

I wrote to the Veterans Administration and explained the situation. My grandfather was 74 at the time and had never been able to find his father's final resting-place. He wanted closure and I was determined he was going to have it. After I explained that all I wanted to know was where Samuel was buried the Veterans Administration became very cooperative. I received a copy of the Application for Burial Allowance that had been completed by the funeral director in Fairmont, WV and was signed by Samuel's sister and a copy of his death certificate. Samuel passed away on 20 June 1949. He was buried in Woodlawn Cemetery in Fairmont, WV. After two years of letter writing and phoning local veterans' offices, I had found my great-grandfather.

My grandfather was able to stand at his father's gravesite and say goodbye. — Kim Policastro, PA, kpolicastr@aol.com

Hush-Hush

Mother was orphaned when she was 14 years old. She was born in 1900. There was something hush-hush about my grandmother's death. I later learned she had died due to an attempted abortion. She was young and had three children and did not want more. My grandfather was so distraught that he died from pneumonia brought from lying all night in a ditch after a drinking binge.

When I became interested in learning about the family, people older than me were either dead or did not know much. I had remembered my relatives talking in whispers about the name being Irish — Farren or O'Farren. I knew my mother's maiden name was Bunnell. I also knew my grandfather's full name was Charles Bunnell and that my grandmother was called Maggie. They had lived in Boston in the early 1900s.

After much thought, I finally remembered going to my mother's cousin's house in a town in Massachusetts and remembered the name Gallagher. I called several Gallaghers in that area and finally found my mother's cousin had a daughter still living in the town so I called her. She told me her mother's people, as far as she knew, were buried in Holy Cross Cemetery in Malden, MA.

My husband and I took a trip to Massachusetts. We visited my first cousin who lived near the Cape. He told me that someone had called him asking for information on a Lucy Jackman who was related to the Bunnell family. My cousin and I remembered aunt Lucy. My parents would visit her on their annual visit to Massachusetts. She was my maternal grandmother's sister and my great-aunt. I then went to the Department of Vital Statistics in Boston as I had a name: Lucy Jackman. I asked for her birth and death certificate. Her maiden name was Farren. I tried to find Charles Bunnell who had died around 1912-15. I could not find any such person. I then tried to find a Maggie or Margaret or Magdalene Bunnell or one such name with a Farren in the middle and still could not find any such person.

Then I went to Holy Cross Cemetery in Malden. I found several Farren names in a particular area of the cemetery. Two were the names listed as Lucy Farren Jackman's parents on her death certificate (Hugh Farren and Mary King). I was fairly certain then they were my great-grandparents.

But I still could not find my grandparents. I went to the library and looked in a city directory. I found a Charles Bunnell listed at an address in Boston in 1914. I decided to go back to the Vital Statistics. There a very nice, helpful lady who looked into all sorts of spellings close to Bunnell. She found a Charles Brunnell listed at the same address as Charles Bunnell in 1914. She also found a death certificate for a Margaret Jane Brunnell at the same address only earlier. Margaret Jane had died of bleeding during childbirth and they were buried in Holy Cross Cemetery. Their parents' names were correct. I went back to Holy Cross and found there a gravesite for Charles and Margaret Brunnell.

Apparently their families had been disgraced with the attempted abortion and the drinking death so the families must have tried to hush-hush the disgrace by changing the name. They were buried in paupers' graves outside of hallowed ground.

The funny thing is that the cemetery has grown so much since then that they are now in the middle of the cemetery. — Donna Talbert Doscher, SC, talbunn2@aol.com

Class Rolls

While growing up on a farm in Grant county, OK I attended a one-room school. A few years ago I decided I would try to reconstruct the class rolls from the time the school was established in 1894 until it was closed in 1940. This is really no different than researching your own family history, except you are looking at about 36 families in a school district.

I knew all the county school records had been destroyed. However, at the county courthouse I found the county commissioners had retained all the school census enumeration's records, starting from statehood in 1907. The school enumeration census was conducted each year to record all school-age children in each school district. This included all children from ages five to 20 years old. This census was then used to distribute school tax funds proportionally to each school district. I copied all these lists. Naturally, some of the older children were not active students. I knew these families and could easily eliminate the older children that had not attended school. I also knew those families who had lived in the area between 1894 and 1907, but had no idea if they had homesteaded in the Cherokee Outlet Land Run of 1893 or arrived later. The 1900 federal census naturally provided a mid-way starting point.

In the register of deeds office I hit the brickwall. I found their land records didn't start until about 1900 when the homesteaders began to receive their land patents. After the homesteader staked his claim he registered it at a government land office where he received a claim number. He then had five years to "prove up" and

file an application for patent, whose number is different than the claim number. It took four to five years for the federal government to process his application and issue a patent of land ownership that has a different number. This last form is usually the first record of entrance in the county land registers. During this period of time the land ownership might have changed a number of times, but this is not of public record. It was done through a bill of sale, which was submitted with the patent application. The originals of all these forms are in the NARA. To access these files one must have the claimant's name, land description and form numbers. So where do you go from here?

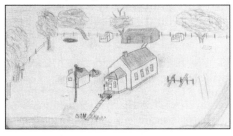

Drawing of the Grande Valley one-room schoolhouse in Grant county, OK, by Ivan L. Pfalser, as a young boy.

I visited the local licensed land abstract company. They had no idea of where to go as they never had needed to go past the county ownership records. A local old time real-estate agent and lawyer stated that in his career he had never needed to search past the registered land patents at the courthouse.

Some time later I visited the Cherokee Strip Museum in Enid, OK and asked what they knew of any land claimants lists. They said that they had a list of about 1,000 names, but it was far from complete. Potentially there would have been at least 15,000 registered claims. They referred me to a member of the Garfield County Genealogical Society who graciously gave me a computer printout of their listing. He referred me to the Oklahoma State Historical Society Library in Oklahoma City.

We found the Oklahoma State Historical Society Library had all the original register books on microfilm but all their viewers were presently occupied and it would be late afternoon before they would be available. The original books were over in the State Library and Archives Building, which was three blocks away. We proceeded to the Library Building and went to the Archive Section. No one was in the research room except a clerk. Within 10 minutes she produced five huge ledger books. In two trips to the library we completed the Garfield County Genealogical Society list and continued on to claimant #3000. Would you believe the very first name on the list had been copied wrong!

We had uncovered the brickwall, but there remained some 12,000 names to transcribe. Luck has been a factor in a lot of my experiences in clearing brickwalls and sometimes I didn't know it was a brickwall until luck hit.

For example, on the last day at the archives my wife turned to the last ledger book labeled "Other Land Transactions". As she thumbed though it she said, "Here is your grandfather!" He had leased one of the restricted school quarters in December after the run in September. All such transactions had been recorded in this last book. — Ivan L. Pfalser, KS

The Cost Of A Few Stamps

When my mother died, I was only 12 years old. Shortly afterwards my father remarried and our new family cut ties with my "former relatives". I never questioned where these former relatives were. But as I got older, I felt the need to know.

By that time, my father and his mother had died and I was living in Texas (born and raised in Pennsylvania).

I went through all my boxes of treasures and found an old address book that was given to me when my grandmother went into a nursing home. I wrote to all the people in the book (20 of them). I explained who I was, asked for information about whether we were related and sent a SASE. I got only one reply, but what a gold mine she turned out to be. She's a cousin who lives in Lancaster, PA and she invited me to come and stay with her and discover my past.

In the three-day visit, I met at least 10 relatives that I didn't remember, but they knew me (and all my family). One of these cousins had already traced the family back to 1680 when they came to Philadelphia from Switzerland. We also visited the cemetery where most of the family is buried.

The original deed to the Yorty farm hangs in the parlor.

As a bonus, they took me to a 100-acre dairy farm built in the early 1700s. The land for this farm was given to our family by the Penn brothers (the original deed is framed in the parlor). The farm is still lived on and run by a member of the family.

My family tree is pretty impressive — at least on my father's side. And I was able to discover all this for the cost of a few stamps. — Doris Anne Roop-Benner, TX, darbey@att.net

The Luck Of The Irish

My great-grandmother, Mary Shee-han, came to the US from Ireland in about 1850 with two sisters, Margaret and Bridget. When I started my research, I had the names of their husbands and children. In my mother's generation, Mary and Margaret's families were in close touch. Margaret lived in Chicago and Mary (my line) in DeKalb, west of Chicago.

After researching all the US sources I could find, the only clue I had from Margaret's death certificate was that she was born in County Kerry, Ireland. Everything else said simply Ireland. I wrote letters to 40 of my great-grandmother Mary's descendants, asking if they had ever heard of a more specific origin for Mary, and more importantly, had anyone ever heard her parents' names. No one had an answer for me.

I then wrote to all my mother's surviving first cousins, asking if any of them were still in touch with any of Margaret's descendants. One lady gave me the address of one of Margaret's great-granddaughters. She wrote to say that the girls had come from Listowel in County Kerry. She was sorry, but she didn't know the parents' names.

Unfortunately, Sheehan is a fairly common name in Kerry. So I started a project that took me more than a year to complete. I spent one day a week in the Irish microfilm collection at the

Mary Sheehan O'Brein, taken in 1890 in DeKalb, IL.

FHC. Using the Listowel Poor Law Union as my geographic boundary, I searched the Tithe Applotment Books, *Griffith's Valuation*, subsequent valuation lists (up to about 1910), Civil Registrations and the 1901 Irish census. For every Sheehan entry I found, I made an index card, including all the information available on that record, particularly townland and parish (civil and/or Roman Catholic), dates, ages, relationships, etc. I sorted the cards by parish and townland and soon saw family groups emerging.

Because of traditional Irish naming patterns, I ruled out families with frequent occurrences of names that were never given to their children by the immigrant girls. That left me with plenty of families with lots of Patricks, Jameses, Johns, Timothys and Daniels, just like my Sheehan girls. Encouragingly, they were all concentrated in three Roman Catholic parishes in or near Listowel.

Then luck took a hand. One of my first cousins who lives in a Chicago suburb was buying a raffle ticket at church one Sunday when the ticket seller saw his surname (Diedrich) and asked if he knew any Diedrichs in DeKalb. My cousin told him that he was from there.

The man told him that as a boy during WWII he had spent one summer working on a Diedrich farm in DeKalb. He said, "One son was flying in the Pacific, one was in the Army in England and one was in the Navy." "I'm the one who was flying in the Pacific", said my cousin. This man is another great-grandchild of Margaret Sheehan. He wrote to me, "I'm sure I don't know anything that you don't already know. I don't know where they came from. All I know is that her parents were Timothy Sheehan and Johanna O'Donnell!"

When I finally went to Ireland to search the Roman Catholic records, I knew from my card project which parishes to search and found the baptisms of six daughters of Timothy and Johanna, including the three immigrants, occurring in two of the three parishes I had isolated. Without the parents' names I might have identified the family from the three birth dates, but I would not have been certain.

Sadly, these baptisms are the only records I have found anywhere for Timothy and Johanna. They appear on none of my index cards. I have some evidence, however, that indicates that Timothy is related to one of the Sheehans in my collection and I am pursuing this trail. — Mary D. McKinnon, CA, mdmckinnon@earthlink.net

Great Scott!

For years we could not go any farther back than my third-great-grandmother, Lucy C. Scott and her husband, Dr. Joseph Scott, of Lexington, KY. Since we did not know Lucy's maiden name, we could not find the names of her parents. One of our few sources of information was her will dated 1868, in which Lucy named her deceased husband, her married stepdaughter, Elizabeth Fullerton of Chillicothe, OH, her deceased son, Matthew T. Scott and her seven living children.

I remember being confused because we seemed to have the names of eight children instead of seven. Later I realized the typewritten copy of the will I was looking at listed one child as J. Webb Scott, which should have been I. Webb Scott. In another place the same son was referred to as Isaac W. Scott.

One day when my husband took his father to a doctor's appointment in Liberty, I asked him to drop me by the Clay County Archives. While looking through a book, *The History Of Fayette County, Kentucky*, edited by William Henry Perrin, I found an article about Matthew T. Scott. I knew this was the name of Lucy's deceased son but the dates were wrong. This Matthew was married in 1810 to Winnie Webb, daughter of Isaac Webb, "lately emigrated from Virginia." I suspected there must have been another Matthew T. Scott because I had found some references to him that were dated in the early 1800s, too early to have been the son of Joseph and Lucy.

I read through the list of the names of his children. I discovered several that were the same as the names of Joseph and Lucy's children. I was really confused now. I had the right names but the wrong parents.

Suddenly the fog lifted and I realized there was a strong possibility that Matthew T. Scott and Joseph Scott might be brothers married to sisters, since Winnie was the daughter of Isaac Webb and both Winnie and Lucy had sons named Isaac W. Scott.

Several months later, I found a book called *Virginia Genealogies, the Glassell Family Of Scotland And Virginia* by Rev. Horace Edwin Hayden in the Ray County Genealogical Association library in Richmond, MO. This book had an article on the Ware/Webb families of Virginia. It was rather difficult to understand, but it stated that Lucy Ware was married to Isaac Webb and their son, Dr. James Webb, was the father of Lucy Ware Webb, who married Rutherford B. Hayes. It also stated their daughter Lucy C. Webb was the second wife of Dr. Joseph Scott. It took me a while to comprehend that my third-great-grandmother was quite possibly related to the wife of a president of the US.

I began searching for more proof. I found an encyclopedia article about

Hayes. One of the sources listed was a book by Emily Apt Geer, *First Lady, The Life Of Lucy Webb Hayes*, published in 1984. I ordered a copy through the inter-library loan from the Kansas City Public Library. In the book there were several references to people I believed were related. However, the most important clue was the mention of Lucy Webb Hayes' cousin, Lucy McFarland who later married Lt. Eric Bergland. I had a copy of a lawsuit by the heirs of John McFarland, who were suing the children of his wife's sisters in order to clarify the terms of his will. The plaintiffs listed were mainly grandchildren and great-grandchildren, including grandson Eric L. Bergland and great-grandson Eric Lloyd Bergland. I also had a copy of a wedding invitation to the wedding of Eloise Beale Bond to William Scott Bergland, scheduled for 17 August 1912.

Middle Spring Church in Shippensburg, PA founded in 1738 by pioneer Scottish-Irish Presbyterians.

I first called the Rutherford B. Hayes Library in Fremont, OH and talked to a Mr. Ransom. I asked for a copy of some pages from *The History Of Ross County, Ohio*, which stated that Lucy Ware Webb's mother, Maria was the daughter of Isaac Cook and Margaret Scott, who were married in Shippensburg, PA. The article about Matthew T. Scott had mentioned that he was also born in Shippensburg and

the 1880 federal census of Ray county, MO stated that Lucy C. (Scott) Holloway's father was born in Pennsylvania.

When I mailed a check for the copies, I wrote a letter to Mr. Ransom telling him that I thought my third-great-grandfather, Dr. Joseph Scott might be a brother to Maria (Scott) Cook. Mr. Ranson wrote back and offered to copy approximately 48 pages of the *Scott Family History* compiled by a former volunteer at the Rutherford B. Hayes Presidential Library. These pages confirmed Maria (Scott) Cook, Joseph Scott and Matthew T. Scott were the children of Matthew Scott, a soldier in the Revolutionary War and his wife, Elizabeth Thompson.

The pages also gave the names of Dr. Scott's grandparents, John Scott and Margaret Mitchell, who were married in Edinburgh, Scotland, and emigrated around 1725. I also learned the names of Dr. Scott's first wife and the children of that marriage.

Later, I received a copy of Isaac Webb's will from the Kentucky Archives which listed Lucy Caroline (Webb) Scott as a daughter. With all this information, I believe that my second-great-grandmother Lucy C. (Scott) Holloway, daughter of Joseph Scott and his wife Lucy Caroline Webb, was a first cousin to first lady Lucy Ware (Webb) Hayes through her mother, Lucy Caroline Webb, and also a first cousin, once-removed, through her father Dr. Joseph Scott.

My next project is to attempt to prove Caroline Scott, wife of President Benjamin Harrison, is also related. — Jenne Holloway Layman, MO, jhollay@yahoo.com

Sharing Information

I found sharing information can have unexpected rewards. I was researching my Short ancestors in Hampshire county, WV and was having difficulty tracing any further back than my great-grandfather.

At the genealogy section of the Hampshire County Library, I found that someone had written a short history of a different Short family. Although none of the people mentioned in that history were my relatives, I nevertheless decided to send a copy of my research to the author.

To my surprise, he sent me information that added two generations to my family tree, including a copy of a will probated in Ohio that I probably never would have found on my own.

He also put me in touch with another researcher who sent me documentation that showed that my ancestors were in Maryland before the Revolutionary War. — Carolyn E. Fields, VA

Persistence

I have been searching for proof and place of my husband's grandparents' marriage. I knew they could have been married in Hudson Heights, QC as that was where the grandmother was born and the marriage is usually in the bride's home town and church. But not so! I bought three books with the births, marriages and deaths of the congregations of two churches in the area but they stopped short of the 1895 marriage. I asked relatives if they knew but that information was lost as no one could remember or ever knew.

At an aunt's 100th-birthday celebration, I mentioned the search and a son-in-law came up with the original marriage certificate. However, the corner of the paper with the place name was missing. I ordered another book of the church registry for a different church, as in the meantime I found the original church had grown too big and the congregation was split. I decided to write to the Archives Nationales du Quebec in Montreal with the name of the last church and included every small piece of information I had gathered, including the county name from the certificate. In three months I got a copy of the church register with the marriage of the grandparents! So persistence pays off and I am thankful for the kindness of the researcher in the archives. — Nola Reid, BC

Slowly Climbing The Ladder

My Plumb brickwall has been with me far beyond my tolerance for ambiguity. I have been looking for the parentage of Samuel Plumb who married Catherine Allbright. The census indicates Samuel was born in Ontario. Family statements indicate Pennsylvania, New York or New England.

Two of his children, Sarah and Martha, were both married at the Primitive Methodist Church in Reach township, ON. Land records show that in 1837 Samuel bought property in Pickering, ON and before the 1861 census he lived in Thedford, ON. He died in Lambton county in 1875 and was buried in the Thedford Baptist Cemetery but no records have been found other than those contained in his wife's obituary and in an old letter from a relative written in the early 1900s. The Ontario Genealogy Society has been particularly helpful in locating much of this information.

Vital records, land records, church records, surname postings, censuses, area histories, obituaries and other

The original marriage certificate of Nola Reid's husband's grandparents with the missing corner and place name.

genealogies have been searched, with some success. As information became harder to find, I began building Plumb families by combining the information found in the above records, giving special attention to those groups that used the given name of Samuel.

Lambton county, ON land records.

I looked for familiar surnames to identify possible religious communities moving together. Since I knew Samuel's wife was a Mennonite when she died in Brown City, MI, I made timelines trying to match generations. I was able to find nine of the 11 children of the Samuel/Catherine Plumb family by piecing together the information from the Ontario Genealogy Society and other sources. The Plumb families grew slowly and sometimes connections were found between distant cousins. It was still a step higher on the ladder even if I discovered there was no possible connection to my family. Some day that ladder will be complete but the story will never end. — Dorothy P. Heimnick, FL, djheim@nut-n-but.net

Road Trip

With a surname like Brown, I had a sturdy foundation for my brickwall. That impossible surname was made worse in that my relatives were dead, so I couldn't ask them what they knew about our ancestry. I had waited too long to begin my search. However, somewhere back in time, a stubborn streak became part of the Brown genetic makeup and I had inherited it. I was not to be discouraged.

The only clue I had was a mysterious family Bible that turned up in my father's effects. Pages in the middle had birth, marriage and death dates and towns for a bunch of folks named Brown. Just one problem: I had no idea who those particular Browns were.

I posted the names on GenForum.com, figuring it was my only hope, if a slim one, and promptly forgot all about it. I came back from a trip to find two e-mails from distant cousins I hadn't known existed in, of all places, my home town. When our mutual excitement died down, we learned that we had no clue as to the identity of those Bible Browns, as we dubbed them.

The cousins did give me the e-mail of another Brown researcher by the name of Ethel who had contacted them. Thinking that Brown researchers probably number in the thousands, I wrote her just in case, but truthfully held little hope.

We compared notes by e-mail. Ethel had traced her Browns to Massachusetts and Vermont in the late 1700s and early 1800s, which was very similar to the Bible Browns' locales. We felt we had at least three genealogical clues in common: an impossible surname, the same time frame and general neck of the woods. However, we couldn't find anything to actually connect our ancestors, despite our suspicions. We exhausted every route we could think of: searching censuses, vital records, which are slim or none that early in history and, again, puzzling over that mysterious Bible. Letters we wrote to towns where the ancestors had lived yielded only negative replies — "No record of those people."

Ethel came to pay a visit to a friend in San Diego and included a day with me. She mentioned that she dreamed of going to Vermont to retrace a route her father had driven many decades before, on a sort of genealogical quest of his own. Ethel had his written account of that trip. Out of that day grew the seemingly crazy plans for both of us to do Ethel's dream drive in a last-ditch attempt to trace our separate Browns. In July 2000, after researching the cheapest airfare, we met in the Manchester, NH airport, rented a car and set out for northern Vermont.

A stop in Concord, New Hampshire's library for Ethel to look up an ancestor left me with time to kill. One name in the Bible, not a Brown, was a Laura Grout, who'd married Stephen Brown. Idly, I looked along the shelves and was startled to see a book about some Grouts. Curious, I leafed through and found brief mention of Laura Grout and Stephen Brown's marriage. They had to be the same as those in the Bible.

Our plans were to work our way south through towns that appeared in our skimpy data, even if the only result was to see where Ethel's people and mine had lived so long ago. In Troy and Jay, towns nuzzling up to the border of Quebec, we looked through old town record books and found frequent mention of her second-great-grandfather and mine on the same pages. We still couldn't establish if they were related, nor if the Bible Browns had any connection to these Browns. We bounced from town to town checking Westfield, Johnson, Cavendish and Montgomery, sometimes finding meager information but no solutions.

And then came Wolcott, VT, where the Bible said Stephen Brown (who married Laura Grout) had died. In the tiny two-room town hall, in a huge old record book, we found Stephen Brown's death recorded and there beside his name were the names of his parents, Stephen Brown, Sr. and Betsy Day, the names of Ethel's third-great-grandparents. Our high-fives startled

the clerk, but with a grin she photocopied that telltale record, a precious copy for each of us. It satisfied us that it was true what we'd felt in our bones, that my second-great-grandfather Ammi Brown, was the brother of Stephen Brown, Jr. and Ethel's second-great-grandfather Levi Brown.

Like Joshua and his trumpet, our own Jericho, our Brown brickwall, came tumblin' down. It took a dream road trip to do it. — Gloria Diane Brown Altona, CA

Mass Mailings Overseas

My Swiss family, the Wernlis, immigrated to Texas in 1905 and 1907. The entire family immigrated: my great-grandfather, Gottlieb and his wife Rosa, his two siblings and their wives. My great-grandfather's parents, Jacob and Frena Wernli (my second-great-grandparents) immigrated two years later. My Wernli grandmother saved the family Bible, obituaries, funeral books, all of which provided valuable information. However, I was completely stuck on my second-great-grandfather's family for more than 20 years.

I had information that Jacob Wernli was born on 28 November 1848 in Thalheim, Switzerland and that he died on 9 February 1926. I found later that part of the reason why my search was so difficult is

Wedding photo of Gottlieb and Rosa (Kaiser) Wernli taken in Switzerland in 1902.

because Wernli is among the most, if not the most, prevalent surnames in Thalheim. I was able to find information from sources in Texas about my Wernlis' immigration (their immigration papers provided their Swiss home towns) and information after they moved to Texas. The only information I found about my Wernlis before they immigrated was from the Church of Latter-day Saints. I found from the IGI records that a Jakob Wernli had been born in Thalheim on 21 November 1848 and one had been born on 27 November 1848. Obviously I was unable to tell which Jakob was mine.

Theresia and Hans Wernli (back row) and their children. The man seated center is Jacob Wernli.

I met with a cousin who had purchased a Wernli surname book. The book did not provide any useful information except for the addresses of all Wernlis world wide, including a countless number in Thalheim. He suggested I write to some of them. I had no idea who to select and I was not willing to write hundreds of letters.

On the Internet, I found a Swiss version of Switchboard.com, called tel.search.ch. It was in German, which I do not know, but having enough familiarity with Switchboard.com, I managed to perform a search for all Wernlis in Thalheim, Aargau Canton. I printed the list and compared it to the list in the Wernli surname book, which was surely some years old. I was able to narrow the list to 45 Wernlis. I decided these represented the Wernlis most likely to still be residing at the addresses listed, so that my letters would not be misdirected or thrown away.

A friend's mother, originally from Germany, translated a letter for me that included all the Wernli information I knew. I sent the letter with English on one side and German on the other. I included my e-mail address. My mother and I stuffed envelopes and mailed the 45 letters for little more than $36.

About two weeks later I heard from a (somewhat removed) cousin in Thalheim who had found my family on his family tree. One of our 45 letters just happened to reach the right person. He told me Jacob (Jakob) was born on 21 November 1848 and that the 28 November date was a baptismal date, which helped me identify which IGI record represented my Jacob. The cousin also provided me with Jacob's ancestors back to Wilhelm Wernli, born in 1750 (in Thalheim). — Karen Monsen, TX

A Small Note

I was in the process of completing my historical file on my great-grandmother. I needed a death certificate, but was uncertain of her date of death. At that time there was no published index to the state death records as there is now. A relative who knew of my research provided me with a mass of items retrieved from our grandmother's trunk. However, within this assortment of items was a small sympathy card with the following penciled notation: "Miss Georgia's funeral May 8, 1940."

This information provided a wellspring of evidence, which not only led to the location of a death certificate, but the birthplaces of her parents and the identification of the next generation in my family that had previously been unknown. A small note led to a new realm of genealogical exploration. — John H. Whitfield, MO

Family History Societies

Every genealogist should belong to the Family History Society at the location where his or her ancestors originated. For example, if you are resident in Canada or the US but your roots extend back into Lincolnshire, England, you should join the Lincolnshire Family History Society. One of many advantages in doing so is that you will obtain the magazine or newsletter published by that society.

One inclusion in most society newsletters is the section detailing members' interests — i.e. the surnames that others are researching. Personally, I eagerly await each newsletter edition to see who might be researching my Milson surname. Alas, it may be months or years before I see such a researcher. I'm sure many people experience this frustration.

However, another benefit is also available from these lists: If your ancestor is from a little town or village, try looking up a member of that society who now lives at that location and contact them. Despite them not being related to you or researching your names, I find that person is often more than willing to help you. You share a common interest — genealogy.

I contacted one lady in a small village in Lincolnshire who readily agreed to photograph various aspects of the village (church, old pub, school, etc.) and also wander through the graveyard looking for names on gravestones. This provided me with some photos to add to my history and some useful dates from the headstones. Another person, in a different small village in which I had ancestors living in the 18th and 19th centuries, forwarded various historical booklets and information about various aspects of the village.

The Parish Church (St. Denys) in Killingholme, Lincolnshire, where Rob Milson's ancestors would have been baptized, married and buried.

I have had great genealogical luck by this method which fleshes out the geography and local history of the relevant area, all adding to the reality of my ancestors. In addition, I have met some wonderful fellow genealogists. — Rob Milson, AB, rrs@compusmart.ab.ca

Leaving No Stone Unturned

My ancestors came from Italy. It's not difficult researching records written in English; but what do you do when you want to communicate in a foreign language and you can't speak or write it? I wanted to research relatives that might be living in Italy. I already knew the city and province they came from, but how could I reach out?

There were no family members to assist me in this endeavor and the chances of any family members in Italy being able to read and write English were slim.

My parents and I were all born in the US. We had stopped using Italian and the only language I spoke was English. It would take years for me to begin to learn another language. Then I had an idea.

I typed the word "translate" into my search engine and came upon various links for translating from English to different languages and back to English. The online translator program was free. I began to experiment with sentences and found the program couldn't handle difficult sentences. English grammar and foreign grammar are very different. Using Windows Notepad, I typed short, simple sentences, making sure to put a period after each sentence. I then copied and pasted my message into the translator and converted it.

Soon I was sending letters to Italy and posting messages on genealogy boards in Italian. I also experimented with copying and pasting Italian written messages I came across on these same boards and translated them into English. Since then I have communicated with relatives and non-relatives. I have destroyed a brickwall that was in my way for researching my Italian ancestors. — Joseph Salvia, NY

The Case Of The Accidentally Sent Obituary

In a reply to an inquiry sent to the Fillmore County Historical Society, MN, several photocopies of data were sent to me. One piece I had not requested was also sent. It was an obituary of a 20 year old from Illinois with our family name. This obituary was from a local paper in Minnesota and referred to the deceased as being a relative to the family there. This was in my early days of research and it did not pertain to my inquiry. So I read it and set it aside thinking if they were a relative, then they were some distant cousin. As far as I knew then, the only ancestors from there were the three who settled in Minnesota. I had never heard of nor had any information regarding any family in Illinois.

Quite some time later, I ran into this obituary again. I wasn't working on any particular puzzle at the time and thought I would see if any of the family was listed in the telephone directory for Jacksonville, IL. There were four listings of our surname in the book. I wrote to all four. One responded and referred me to another cousin in nearby Springfield who had been researching our family's history for more than 20 years.

A piece of initially unwanted information led to Pat Lain's eventual discovery of the family's ancestral farm in County Clare, Ireland.

The cousin in Springfield had traced the family back to County Clare, Ireland and to the original family farm. My sister and I were able to visit Ireland and the family farm, and meet our cousins. We also visited a cousin in England for a few days on that same trip. I can't find the words to describe the warmth in my heart when I met my family and walked on the land of our ancestors. — Pat Lain, AZ

My Common Sense Approach

I began my ancestor search about two-and-a-half years ago. My brickwall was my great-grandfather's parents. Who were they? I had two boxes of old papers and photos. My great-grandfather, Isaac Newton Poston's papers included deeds, bills of sale and even the deed to his family cemetery plot — all in his name. I contacted relatives that might know who his parents were, but no one did. I did not have a Poston family Bible, but I did have an obituary dated 7 August 1907 from *The Enterprise* newspaper in Livingston, TN.

From his obituary, I learned he was born in Overton county, TN, on 2 October 1826. He moved to Pulaski county, MO with his parents when he was 17 years old and that in 1851 he moved to Montgomery county, IA where he died on 27 June 1907. Although his parents were mentioned, their names were not given. It did state he was one of 17 children.

I sent for his death certificate from the state of Iowa Department of Vital Statistics. The blocks for the names of his father and mother were left blank. I checked the 1850 federal census for Pulaski county, MO. It showed Isaac Newton Poston living with a family other than parents. The 1900 federal census for Montgomery county, IA showed his father and mother were both born in Virginia.

I remembered that a Poston relative had given me a Poston genealogy about 25 years ago. I finally found it and read that John Poston (our Poston immigrant ancestor) was born in England around 1688 and immigrated to Maryland in 1703. This genealogy appeared to be quite complete until about 1775, when there seemed to be missing information and there were many suppositions. After reading two more genealogies by other Poston researchers, I concluded that no one was certain about the generations after about 1775. The Postons all had very large families and there were so many descendants named John, William or Richard it was hard to tell who belonged to whom.

After trying these various ways to get over my brickwall (who was Isaac Newton Poston's parents?), I finally decided to use what I call my Common Sense Approach. Even though the censuses for 1820, 1830 and 1840 would only list the head of household by name, I would examine these three federal censuses for Overton county, TN and see the most likely Poston who could (at some point) have 17 children.

All the Postons in those days had large families, but luckily only one Poston in Overton county seemed to fit my criteria — Richard Poston — and he was born in Virginia. After reviewing several microfilms at the Yuma FHC, I felt certain Richard Poston was Isaac Newton Poston's father.

Richard Poston had married (Amelia) Elizabeth, daughter of Colonel Stephen Copeland and Sarah Townsend of Overton county. I found several published articles about Stephen Copeland and some lines of his ancestors. The next stop: who were Richard Poston's parents?

After rereading the Poston genealogies, I concluded his parents were Richard Poston (Sr.) and Anne Campbell of Washington county, VA. Anne, according to the Poston genealogies, was the daughter of Charles Campbell and Margaret Buchannan.

One thing I noticed was an apparent naming pattern. The mother's maiden names were given to the male descendants, usually as a middle name. Some examples were Richard Poston and (Amelia) Elizabeth Copeland's sons were named Campbell, John Townsend and Alexander Buchannan. Apparently, Richard Poston and (Amelia)

Elizabeth Copeland's son, Isaac Newton Poston (my great-grandfather) continued the tradition by naming one son James Buchannan and another John Townsend. After I decided that the above lineage was reasonable, I went on the Internet. I found that some other researchers have come to the same conclusions I have. Meanwhile, I am sending for any legal documents that are available, such as copies of wills, probate packets, pension files, land records, etc., to further confirm my conclusions.

A deed to the family cemetery plot found amongst Patricia Ann Poston Weaver's great-grandfather's collection of papers.

I feel that the boost that got me over my brickwall was deciding to check the 1820, 1830 and 1840 federal census for Overton county to see which Poston could have 17 children. In other words, it was my Common Sense Approach. — Patricia Ann Poston Weaver, AZ

*   *   *

Cry Across The Ocean

Our researcher had found the grandmother's family but had no luck in finding the grandfather. Up to this point she had, via our instructions, looked for a Karl Wilhelm, the German version of Charles William. In a letter from our researcher she said, " I hope that soonly [sic] I can cry across the ocean: I found your Karl Wilhelm!" Lo and behold, on 28 January 2001 she sent us a letter saying, "Did you hear my cry across the ocean? I am sure that I could find the Carl. I say on purpose only "Carl", because this one, which I found, is Carl Ludwig."

The clue was Durlach. A cousin wrote us telling that she remembered her grandfather's family lived in Durlach and operated an engineering firm. She found the family in Durlach and the engineering firm which closed in 1965.

We found that Carl Ludwig and grandmother had had a child out of wedlock (who died at age seven months). We received the records from the Parish Books confirming all dates and other data. It turns out there were two other brothers in the family. One brother Wilhelm Friedrich was grandfather to a Marianne, who unfortunately passed away at age 50 shortly after we found her. She knew that she had family in the US and we had written to her before her passing. The other brother we found, had corresponded with the American family and was the recipients of clothes and money from the US after the end of WWII. This connection ended with the deaths of the grandparents and none of us younger generation had any knowledge of this. My wife, June, recalls her grandmother giving her a drawing of a hill in an area near Durlach and saying, "This is where I grew up." But regretfully the drawing has been mislaid or lost forever. After describing this hill, our researcher's husband sent us a post card showing this hill as it looked in the late 1800s. We always have hoped that we will find this drawing again as we now know who drew it.

Marianne gave our researcher a photo of Carl Ludwig's parents, Carl Ludwig and the brother Friedrich Wilhelm and the wedding photo of Friedrich Wilhelm and his wife, Luise Sophie. There is a strong family resemblance of the brother to one we have of grandfather at about the same age.

We feel that having the out-of-wedlock child was why Karl Wilhelm and Karoline left Germany to come to the US. He might have changed his name from Carl Ludwig to Karl Wilhelm for the same reason and might have picked Wilhelm as a way of remembering his father and older brother, who were both named Wilhelm.

It is important to note we have received copies of pages in the parish books for all communities concerned with our German families. We also received maps of all the areas mentioned with the important towns and communities highlighted. All pertinent data that had been written in German were translated for us, making the job of placing everyone in the right place much easier. We feel that we know everyone much better now which is an accomplishment, as we had nothing before! — George and June Dimmig, OH, autumnwheat@dragonbbs.com

Jumping Over The Brickwall

When researching my great-grandfather, Henry L. Reed, I found him listed in the 1880 federal census of Baker county, FL. He was married to Mary J. —. Who was this woman?

The old Baker County Courthouse had burned to the ground years ago and the fire destroyed marriage records as well as many early documents for the county located just west of Jacksonville.

I had found that Henry L. Reed was from Alabama and had served in the Confederate Army as a private in Company E, 2nd Battalion, Alabama Light Artillery, from October 1862 until May 1865. After Henry's death in Dade county, FL, Mary applied for a widow's pension claim. Upon requesting a copy of the widow's pension claim from the Florida State Archives in Tallahassee, I was provided a copy which certainly jumped over the brickwall.

The Reed family. Mary Jane Greene (mother) is seated in the front row (left).

The pension application states Mary J. Greene was lawfully married to Henry L. Reed in Baker county, FL on 19 October 1871 and that she was not divorced from him. She had not remarried after his death, which occurred on 4 December 1907 in Dade county, FL. It also stated she was a resident of Dade county and had continuously resided there.

In addition, it stated the property owned was 25 acres in Arch Creek, valued at $2,000; personal property was $200 and her post office address was in Arch Creek, Dade county. This document was signed by Mary J. Reed, notarized and witnessed by two citizens, L.K. Reed and H. C. Reed (sons). — Weymouth W. Reed, FL, reedbb2@aol.com

Niece Solution

I had been searching for John Clayworth who married Hannah Slater of Belper, Derbyshire on 5 March 1838 in North Wingfield, Derbyshire. They moved to Liverpool, Lancashire in around 1844. One of their seven children was born at Cleveland Square in Liverpool before John died on 25 November 1849. Hannah and her children were still in Liverpool in 1851 but were back in Brampton, Derbyshire by 1861.

The hurdle I came across was finding the birthplace of John and who his parents and siblings were. In the IGI there was only one John Clayworth that fit the dates I had and that was the one christened 13 September 1817 in Newark, Nottinghamshire and whose parents were John and Alice Clayworth. John's death certificate stated he was 34 years old when he died, making his year of birth either 1814 or 1815.

While I was trying to figure this out, I was contacted by a Jack Clayworth who was just beginning a Clayworth One Name Study and had heard I was also researching this line. It turns out that Jack is my third cousin and between us we were able to gather a large amount of data from all available sources.

Jack had pieced together all the Clayworth lines he could from this data and found that two of the children of John and Alice Clayworth of Newark, Nottinghamshire had married and moved to Leicester, Leicestershire. Thomas married Mary Pollard and George married Zeruiah Beall.

Thomas and Mary had six children who were accounted for, but we were unable to find any further information about one of their children named Jane who was born in 1845. From the General Register Office indexes we found a death registration for a Jane Clayworth in 1848 in Liverpool. So I mentioned to Jack that this could possibly be our Jane and that we should purchase the death certificate to see who she belonged to. As no ages were given in the indexes before 1865 we were hoping that the certificate would state that she was about two years old and that her parents were Thomas and Mary.

The 1848 death certificate for Jane Clayworth, niece of Hannah Slater and John Clayworth.

Well, you can imagine how ecstatic we were when the certificate not only stated that she was two years old but that her father was Thomas and the informant was Hannah Clayworth of Cleveland Square, Liverpool, her aunt. So through the death certificate of his niece we were able to discover that our John was the one christened in Newark, Nottinghamshire on 13 September 1817 and that his parents were John and Alice Clayworth and Thomas was his brother. — Jayne McHugh, ON, spiregen@webcomcreations.com

Separation Of Church And State

While researching for an ancestor's proof of birth (including parents' names) we ran into a problem: the person had been adopted at around eight years of age. The only birth certificate we could obtain showed only the name and date of birth — no listing of parents. A request to the Surrogate Court for the release of adoption information gave us only a polite letter saying all adoption records were sealed.

It was then we remembered — separation of church and state. We imagined our ancestor had been baptized and believed the family was Catholic. We also had our research narrowed down to a specific city. We then checked the Catholic Churches there and to our surprise, we obtained a copy of the baptismal record, complete with parents' names and sponsors. It was a wonderful find for us! — Rick and Dolores Rodgers, NY, pp1955@twcny.rr.com

Check Out The Irish Festival

I had tried all the usual ways to find where in Ireland my husband's family had come from. The name O'Brien was like looking for a needle in a haystack. Recently my husband and I were in Chicago for the weekend and there happened to be a Celtic Festival going on. Having about two hours left before we were to depart, we decided to go.

Hurrying down the last row of tents before leaving we spotted the sign "Irish American Heritage Center" and decided to peak inside. There were only a few books on tables, but knowing that Bill's great-grandparents had lived in Chicago in the late 1800s I decided to take a look. The first book I picked up was *Irish Obituaries 1890-1910*. Flipping through I quickly found Bill's great-grandparents' date of death, where they were buried — Calvary Cemetery in Evanston, IL, and best of all where they were from in Ireland — County Kerry.

On my husband's next business trip to Chicago, he paid a visit to Calvary Cemetery where his great-grandparents were buried. On the headstone were all the family names and the names of the town, Dingle in Garfiny Parish in County Kerry that the family had belonged to.

In the spring of 2002, we took a trip to Ireland and visited Dingle. At St. Mary's, the Catholic church in Dingle, we located the marriage records from 1852 for the great-grandparents. It was an overwhelming feeling to be in the town where they had lived so many years and to visit the church where they were wed.

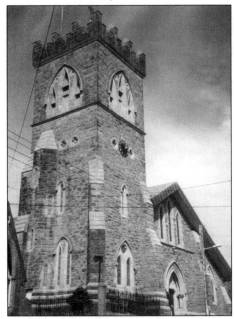

St. Mary's, the Catholic Church in Dingle, County Kerry.

All thanks to an Irish Festival in Chicago! — Kathy Monaghan Weibel, NH, kweibel@cheshire.net

Mob Connections

Carole, now in her mid-50s, had been trying to find her father since her late teens. She'd been raised to believe she was the natural daughter of her step-father. It wasn't until she needed her birth certificate to apply for a marriage license that she realized she was adopted by her stepfather. When she asked her mother about this, her mother would only tell her that her father left them when Carole was six months old.

Through the years, Carole continued to ask about her father, but to no avail. Her mother died taking any knowledge of her father to the grave.

Carole tried to obtain information on her father through a maternal aunt. The aunt staunchly indicated that Carole would be better not knowing and refused any further conversations on the subject.

Years went by and Carole became more curious about her father. In the early 1990s, Carole decided to try again. She went through the paperwork she received after her mother's death and realized her father had served in WWII. Armed with his name, birth date, branch of service and serial number she wrote to a senator in Washington, DC asking for assistance. The senator forwarded the letter to the National. Personnel Records Center in St. Louis for research. When a response was finally received it verified his military service but gave no indication of his whereabouts. Carole gave up any hope of locating her father.

I met Carole in 1999. I shared my love of genealogy and she shared her story and wondered if I'd help her find her father. I was hesitant, but she was persistent and I finally agreed to try. She brought me all her documentation (her birth certificate, a picture of her father in uniform in the 1940s and several newspaper articles on reputed family members). Family tradition says her father had been the brother of a famous mob moll (girl-friend). This couldn't be substantiated as no one was talking and none of the articles mentioned her father, but it definitely had my interest.

I studied the information and searched all I could think of: telephone directories, county and state searches, SSDI, family names. I consistently came up empty handed.

One day while looking at her father's military picture, I thought that, if he were deceased, as a WWII veteran he would be entitled to burial in a national cemetery. I explained the theory to Carole and suggested she write to the National Cemetery System in Washington, DC, in search of a record of burial. We discovered that he had indeed died in 1991 and was buried in a national cemetery in Texas.

I recommended she write the National Cemetery and request the name and address of the funeral home that handled the arrangements. Upon receipt of this information, I recommended she write the funeral home asking for copies of the funeral home record, the death certificate and the obituary. I cautioned her not to expect the death certificate and explained that she may have to order one from the county courthouse. The funeral home was extremely cooperative and sympathetic and provided all three documents requested without charge.

With only three letters in six weeks, Carole had learned quite a lot about her father and discovered she has a half-brother, a half-sister and many other relatives. Although, she hasn't yet contacted her new family, she can take that next step when she's ready.

As to whether Carole's father was related to the mob moll. Yes, he sure was! Our research has taken us thus far to Chicago, New York (Kefauver Hearings), Hollywood (murder), Las Vegas (building and opening of the Flamingo), Mexico and Austria.

This has been a truly incredible family to follow! — Deirdre "Dee" Gore, SC

Brainin Storming

I have been trying to research my maternal grandmother's side of the family for many years, but she has been resistant (she has not said why) and would not give me any contact information for living relatives.

However, I was dealing with an uncommon name (Brainin) and I knew that there were supposed to be relatives in Florida and New York.

I decided to try a web search with some of the telephone directory sites.

I found seven Brainins in Florida and 14 in New York. Since it was such a small number, I decided to call every one and work my way down the list. I had no success with the Florida ones, but the 13th one on the New York list was a cousin!

Not only that, his niece had also been working on a family history for that line. So I have been able to fill in lots of information about the current generation and get some additional information about past generations.

Sometimes the brickwalls you find are put up in the current day, but there are still ways to tear them down. — Janice Sellers, CA, janice@seismosoc.org

The Sally Ann To The Rescue

My search for Aunt Anna started when I had a new hobby: genealogy. Aunt Anna had become a ward of the state of Connecticut at age one and her sister (my mother) Aurore at age four. Anna's adopted parents went back to the orphanage to get Aurore but she had already been placed with another family. The agency could not give any information on the adoption so they had no way of finding her sister.

Anna searched all her life for my mother, the sister she never knew. In 1995, at the age of 75, Anna wrote a letter searching for information on her

Anna with parents Anna and Sam Buttacauoli.

sister. She sent out 131 copies and mailed one to each Probate Court in Connecticut. With the help of a dear friend, I came across Anna's letter in 1999 and started my search for Aunt Anna. The address on the letter belonged to Anna's daughter and she had moved the same year the letters were sent. The owners of the house couldn't be found and the new tenants thought that the daughter had moved to New York. The letter gave Anna's adopted parents' names so I had more information to use in my search, but all my efforts were in vain. Then I heard that the Salvation Army had a Missing Persons Department.

I asked for a form and sent my request. They started the search four weeks after the letter was mailed and were able to find Aunt Anna four weeks after that. When Aunt Anna was found she said, "Is this a joke? My husband just died." She was assured that this was not a joke and that her niece was looking for her. She was very happy and called everyone to tell them the good news.

Anna was born in Massachusetts and did not know that she was the ninth child of her mother, as the Massachusetts birth certificates do not list this information. She knew she had a sister but didn't know she had more siblings. Anna's mother, Regina, was married previously and had five children, with four living, when she married Adelard, Anna's father. Together, they had five more children, the last born in April 1921. Regina died of pneumonia two weeks after the birth of her youngest child.

Her father had lost his wife and had nine children including a newborn to be raised. It must have been overwhelming. The father was able to place seven of his children with other families but had to give two children away through the court. Anna knew only about Aurore and herself.

Theresa Giroux's mother Aurore at age five.

Anna's sister Aurore had died in 1985 but she was able to enjoy the reunion with her sister's children. It was a very happy time for all.

Having found Aunt Anna I continued my search for the rest of the family. I knew that the first seven children were dead. So the next one in line to find was Aunt Clara. I had Aunt Clara's adopted name on my baptismal certificate, as she was my godmother. I remember Aunt Clara visiting us back in 1947 with her husband and two sons. I had searched most of

eastern Connecticut for her birth certificate with no results. So now the search was moved to Massachusetts, as that is where Aunt Anna was born. Aunt Clara's birth certificate was found, so I sent another request to the Missing Persons Department to start a search for Aunt Clara. They found Aunt Clara three weeks later.

I enjoyed our phone conversation with Aunt Clara and told her that her sister Anna had been found. She had not known Anna, or about her other siblings. I called Aunt Anna and gave her Aunt Clara's phone number so she could call her. They met for the first time in March 2001. Aunt Anna finally had herself a sister! Aunt Anna is age 82 and Aunt Clara is age 83. — Theresa C. Giroux, GA, tgirouxt@wmconnect.com

Join A Society

One of the best ways to break through a brickwall is to make new contacts. After one has exhausted the memories of the living family members, the next step is to turn to the bulletin boards, query lists, mailing lists and newsletters. There is an abundant supply of these on the Internet. However, in my experience these prove to be hit or miss — a few juicy responses and long, long periods of no significant contact. After having experienced this, I realized that most of my branches came from southwest Missouri. In that area was a local genealogical society, the Ozarks Genealogical Society. They are a group of researchers who concentrate on my very family background area, southwest Missouri.

Joining the society required a nominal fee and the act of listing the branches I am researching, which were then published in their newsletter. Because of that exposure, I have received numerous contacts, become reconnected to some relatives I did not even know about and one of my branches was advanced to the late 1500s.

Do not pass up that little genealogical society located nearest to the area of your ancestors. You never know what connections are there, waiting quietly for you. — Joan L. Mooney, HI, jmooneygal@aol.com

The History Found Him For Me

As I was tracing my Taylor line back generation-by-generation I hit a brickwall. My third-great-grandfather, Joseph B. Taylor, suddenly disappeared in his late thirties, leaving behind his children and extended farming family. By using the tried and true genealogical principle of putting my ancestor into historic context, I quickly broke through this brickwall.

Before hitting the brickwall I had successfully documented that my third-great-grandfather, Joseph B. Taylor, born circa 1813 in Kentucky, had migrated in the early 1830s with his extended family of farmers to the Bear Creek Neighborhood, Mendon/Ursa township, Adams county, IL. I easily found documentation showing that Joseph was married three times, had three sons and lost all three wives within 11 years from 1836 to 1846.

Then I hit the brickwall. There was no 1850 US census listing, land ownership records, tax list, will/probate records or death information for Joseph B. Taylor in Adams county, IL — it was as if he had disappeared.

I went back to the 1850 US census and made an in-depth study of his extended family (since the 1850 US census lists each individual in the household) and discovered that his three sons were all still living in Adams county, IL with three families who were Joseph's relatives or neighbors. So it appeared that only Joseph, not his entire family, disappeared sometime between 1846-50. Relying on my training from the American Genealogy seminar led at Chicago's Newberry Library, I figured my best

chance to break down this brickwall was to put Joseph in his historic context (knowing this might give me ideas for other records to search).

I found an 1879 *History Of Adams County, Illinois* book that covered the county happenings since its inception in the 1830s. I thought it might tell of any military conflicts, diseases, social influences, etc. in the late 1840s that might explain Joseph's disappearance. About 15 minutes into perusing this history I came upon a section entitled California Gold Fever.

I thought this could be a possible cause for his disappearance and kept reading: "The excitement continued throughout the year [1849] and many emigrated during that period and we give below a list of as many names as we have been able to obtain, who went prior to May 1st, 1850. There are neighborhoods in the county from which we have been unable to obtain information, and the list is necessarily incomplete... From the Bear Creek Neighborhood... Joseph Taylor"

Joseph was listed as a member of a California gold rush caravan leaving from Quincy along with a first cousin and two neighbors prior to 16 May 1850.

Now there's an ultimate brickwall solution: in trying to put my ancestor in his historic context, the history found him for me! — Marsha Peterson-Maass, IL, somethingco@hotmail.com

Technology — Isn't It Wonderful?

I have just solved another brickwall with the help of the countless FHC volunteers that have put together the CD transcript and national index of the entire 1880 US census. For years, I have been stumped by one of my Davis lines. Like any common surname, it can be extremely frustrating trying to sort out which person belongs to you in censuses and other records. I had an old newspaper clipping that showed that the parents of my second-great-grandfather, Arthur S. Davis, were Joseph C. and Mary S. Davis from Oxford, MA. From that information, I managed to find their marriage record and records of the births of their seven children up to my second-great-grandfather Arthur, who was born in 1852.

I found a listing of Joseph and Mary Davis in the 1850 census in Oxford, MA with their first six children.

However, extensive searching of the 1860 and 1870 census indexes for Massachusetts showed no entries for my Joseph and Mary, although Arthur was located in Oxford, working as an 18-year-old farm laborer in the 1870 census. The 1880 Soundex only had entries for families with young children. I searched the 1880 Massachusetts Soundex, but did not expect to find an entry for Joseph and Mary. My expectations were correct.

I was beginning to believe that I would not be able to trace this line back past Joseph. Then I received my 1880 census transcript CDs in the mail. The national index in that set allows you to search nationally for an individual using a variety of criteria. I plugged in Joseph's name and birth date (I had conflicting information about place of birth, so I left that blank) and searched. There they were, in Connecticut! Actually, they were living not far from Oxford, MA, just across the state line.

I found a cemetery listing for Joseph C. Davis on a Connecticut website, which noted his service in the First Regiment Artillery Connecticut Volunteers Company G during the Civil War. The website also had a summary of his US Civil War service, noting enlistment and mustering out dates. My family had no knowledge of this military service. In a half-hour I had made more progress on this line than in the previous four years of searching!

I have, of course, verified the information I found online. I received a nice, thick pension file from the NARA and have obtained birth records for Joseph C. Davis, his wife, Mary S. Worsely and their nine children. This information has led me to Joseph's parents and grandparents and has connected this line to an old Davis family in Oxford, MA about which pedigree information has been published. The brickwall has crumbled!

One truly ironic part of this story is that my great-uncle is an avid Civil War buff. He knows more about the Civil War than any other person I have met. But he didn't know his great-grandfather fought in it! Boy, was he surprised! — Christine Whittaker Sofge, North Yorkshire, UK, sofge@yahoo.com

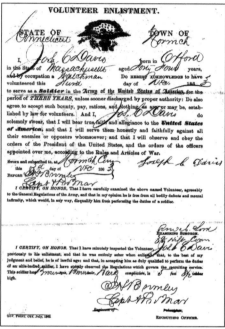

Private Joseph C. Davis served in the Connecticut Heavy Artillery from December 1863 to September 1865. (Enlistment document from the military service records at the NARA).

*   *   *

Early Bible Records

Forty years ago, after talking to my grandmother about her ancestors, I started to puzzle over the family of my third-great-grandfather, Philip Lockwood. Grandma told me that he was the first Baptist minister in the Western Reserve of Ohio. I researched in Geauga and Lake counties and was successful in uncovering considerable information about him.

When I wrote to the Morley Library in Ohio, I was referred to a woman living in Lake county, a relative, who had a scrap of an old calendar which listed several of Philip's children and apparently some of his siblings. The notes jotted on the calendar seemed to indicate that Philip was the son of James Lockwood, Sr., of neighboring Ashtabula county. James and Philip had come to Ohio from Cortland county, NY.

Land records in New York showed that James' wife was Elizabeth and I began to see the names of other relatives appearing in the land records. I started to try to construct a family group sheet for James. Because he died before the 1850 census and because his will made statements such as, "I leave to my stepson (name) to share equally with my own children (no names)", this seemed a discouraging task. But as I wrote many letters and searched lots of films, I began to compile a list of possible children for him. There was a Jonathan Lockwood that died early in

A page of James Lockwood's will.

Cortland county — he was a possible son. James mentioned children of Mary Gifford in his will — I was not certain where they fit.

Some of James' children left a better trail than others. Two daughters were not listed in the marriage records available, but there were two Lockwood girls of the right time period who had marriages listed in the local newspaper. Finally, I discovered one of those terrific "et al" land records that named these two daughters and their husbands. Yet I did not have that conclusive document for all the children that we hope to find that makes us secure in the knowledge of a relationship.

After writing to the Cortland County Historical Society in New York, I made contact with a woman in New Hampshire who had also written a letter to them about 25 years before. Her husband was related to the wife of my Philip Lockwood — Anna Owen. In this letter the New Hampshire researcher stated that she had access to the family Bible of James Lockwood. I called telephone information for New Hampshire and obtained a phone number for her. (Amazingly, she was still alive and still living in New Hampshire.) She mailed me a typed extraction of names and birth dates and marriage dates for James and his 11 children. I was elated to see that the children listed matched my list and confirmed at least two about which I had no absolute proof.

I was frustrated, however, to observe that the birth dates for the two oldest children (including my Philip) and the marriage date for James and Elizabeth (his first wife of three, I had supposed), seemed to indicate yet an earlier wife.

The Daughters of the American Revolution Library in Washington, DC, held a photocopy of the original pages for this family Bible. I urged my daughter who was living there to call the copying service at the library to see if she could get me a copy of the original. I needed to check the dates. James Lockwood's youngest daughter, Sarah, had married an Amos Green, whose father Joseph had served in the Revolution and had also left a family Bible. Sarah, as the youngest, must have inherited the Bible, passing it down to her descendants. The Lockwood Bible pages were actually in a file labeled Green. Of course there were several files with that surname and a few with the specific name of Joseph Green. But one of them was labeled Joseph Green of New York and Ohio. My daughter, remembering that I talked a lot about needing to visit New York and Ohio, picked the right file over the telephone, the one containing the Lockwood pages and ordered a copy of James' Bible record for me.

The confusion in dates occurred because the numeral four looked like a nine in the Lockwood Bible. Once I had determined that, I could see that James and Elizabeth were married in 1784, not in 1789, as the typed copy showed. James was born in 1764, not in 1769. He had had no earlier wife and Philip was their second child, born in 1787.

I feel extremely fortunate to have located such an early Bible record relating to my ancestors. I am still seeking to establish James' parentage and I am hoping that the Stephen mentioned in the Bible record, born in 1768, is a sibling of his and thus will provide me with a needed clue for pursuing yet another earlier generation. — Marcia W. Green, CA, mwverde.mwg@verizon.net

A Little Bit Of Luck Helps

After many years of trying to find where my great-grandfather, Athanase Roux, was married, we were ready to give up. We knew that he was born in Canada and that he died in Lewiston, ME. After searching Maine we thought he might have been married in Canada. Relatives had conflicting stories about him being married in either place. His wife, Philomene Lacombe, was also born in Canada so it seemed likely that the marriage might have occurred there. Fruitlessly we poured over all the records in Canada. It seemed that his marriage record was completely lost and we despaired of ever finding it.

One day we were in Manchester, NH visiting the archives there. My father had moved from Maine to New Hampshire where he married my mother at St. Augustin Church. Since the research center had records for St. Augustin we decided to see if my parents were listed. They were! But even better, so was the marriage for one Athanase Roux and one Philomene Lacombe! For some reason they had come to New Hampshire to marry and had (luckily) done so at the same church my mother attended.

A lot of research narrowed down where the marriage wasn't. A little bit of luck showed us where it was. — Larry Roux, NY

Russian Mennonites

My Dad's parents were Mennonite emigrants from Czarist Russia who came to the US and had all their children here. Whenever Dad would ask them about the old country, they would always say, "Vee aww Amewwicans now". My grandparents both died while my father was growing up in the wheat farming area of Washington State. Soon after this, Dad left for the excitement of the big city and lost contact with many of his relatives. This was the brickwall that I bumped into.

Here's how that wall was breached: One day, I was staying with a cousin who lived near the old family farm. The next day his Dad asked me if I wanted to visit the Mennonite cemetery nearby. I never knew one existed, so he took me there and he and his wife began to tell me about our common ancestors. From there, I learned how to find the passenger list of the *S.S. Vaterland*, which brought over several shiploads of Mennonites. Then I learned where to visit the usual courthouses, cemeteries and libraries. I also had the good fortune of meeting many relatives and attending two large family reunions. I am still meeting distant cousins and having them occasionally send me family pictures. The Internet has been a great tool because I have been able to research school, church and land records going very far back. — George Ensz, WA, gaensz@hotmail.com

What If?

I ask myself, what if I hadn't looked for that surname in the telephone directory of a small town in Ohio?

I was working from an old family chart showing my great-grandmother's sister had married a Zimmerman. Eight Zimmermans were listed in the directory and I made an educated guess hoping for a descendant to respond. A return letter said that this gentleman had died, but the respondent knew of a local married daughter. I was delighted to learn my letter was forwarded to her.

Helen, my second cousin once-removed, was 21 years older than I, but we clicked and wrote each other for more than two decades. Our common ancestors stemmed from Pennsylvania and immigrated to Ohio in 1847. Her branch remained there, while mine moved to Iowa and then to California. The families stayed in touch and frequently sent family items to each other: informative letters, photographs of themselves and their children, clippings from newspapers. These have ultimately traveled down the lines of cousins.

One of Helen's Ohio correspondents made a generous gesture. When she heard of my pursuits, this widow of a distant cousin provided me with three precious items: the gold-trimmed 50th-wedding-anniversary invitation of my great-grandparents, one of those ancestors' original obituary and a four-page letter the survivor wrote to the Ohio sibling. "I want the great-granddaughter to have them," she wrote.

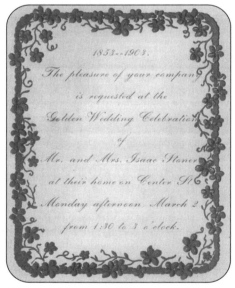

The golden wedding anniversary invitation of Mr. and Mrs. Isaac Stoner of Toledo, IA.

Helen also presented me with an original quit claim deed showing my great-grandparents as grantors in 1877. Looking at county cemetery records she located the graves of my second-great-grandparents in a small obscure place, sending me a photo. Subsequently, I attended a family reunion in Ohio and have been able to assist many others in their quests.

Yes, sometimes I ask myself, what if I hadn't looked for that surname in the telephone directory? — Marjorie Stoner Elmore, CA

A Picture Says A Thousand Words

Our family has a tiny vacation cottage on the shores of Chesapeake Bay. When my grandparents were no longer able to provide for themselves, my dad painted, papered, renovated and provided our little getaway as their home.

Whenever we visited, Daddy would get upset because Nana had pictures nailed to every wall: living room, bathroom, hallway, basement stairwell, even over the kitchen stove. There were holes everywhere and she wouldn't let us clean or make repairs. Nana liked things cluttered.

My grandfather died and a few years later, Nana followed. When both were gone, we went to the house to clean and repair. The first thing Dad did was take down all the pictures and pull out all the nails and spackle those offensive holes. Most of the pictures went to either Goodwill or the dump. I saved only two or three that interested me.

When I got involved in genealogy, I decided to put one of Nana's pictures in a binder. There within the cardboard padding of the frame was a note: "We left Gettysburg on March 6, 1908 (Friday) ~ Mama, Daddy, brother Billy, sister Pearl, and me." So that's where they had lived before coming to Annapolis! I can only imagine the clues that went to the dump.

Never throw away pictures in frames. Always check to see what's behind them. — Anne Nemeth-Barath, VA

*   *   *

Picture To Become A Family Heirloom

My problem was getting pictures of my grandfather's home. I had been trying for a long time to get pictures of the place my father was born and raised in (built by his grandfather). The home is on the other side of the country.

A great-grandfather of Bob Quinn built all the houses on this block, giving four of the houses to his sons.

I monitored Internet postings from the city where the home is located and one day a lady submitted a query. Her e-mail address suggested that she was a realtor. I e-mailed her about my problem and asked if she was in the neighborhood and if that area was safe for a woman to travel in, would she take a picture for me. She promptly went and took pictures and sent them to me. — Bob Quinn, CA

It's All In How You Pronounce It

Many years ago when working as a research coordinator for a genealogical research firm, a Mr. Grayshaw presented me with a very interesting problem. He was then living in New York but his family was from Michigan. Family tradition was that their distant ancestor had come from Canada to work in the lumber business in the upper peninsula of Michigan and since Michigan borders on Ontario, much research had been done in Western Ontario. It was felt that Grayshaw was an English or possibly Scottish name and since Ontario was filled with English and Scottish immigrants, this would be the logical place to find the lost Grayshaw ancestor.

Search after search proved futile and the brickwall loomed higher and higher. One day while browsing in the library I came across a book called *Families Of The Rouge River* that dealt with the early emigrants to this part of Michigan and the area between Detroit, MI and Windsor, ON that are divided by the Rouge River. I was a little disappointed when I realized that most of the early residents were French Canadians who came to work in the logging trade.

I couldn't resist looking through the index of names for Grayshaw but was again disappointed, until following my finger down the G page, I came to Grandchamps and my heart skipped a beat. My knowledge of French acquired in school and refined during a two-year stint working in Montreal had given me an ear for the correct French pronunciation of names of which I am still proud. Grandchamps spoken by a French Canadian sounds exactly like Grashaw to a non-French Canadian ear, which is close enough to Grayshaw to be worth following up.

It turned out be the correct link and our New York Grayshaws were really Grandchamps, which both delighted and amused them and helped us to climb over this brickwall.

This situation is not unique. I had another incident happen to me when I received a telephone call from a lady in Rhode Island who had a query on an ancestor she had been stumped on for several years. She felt that the ancestor was of French Canadian origin but had been blocked in every inquiry she ever made with the ances-

tral origin of Joseph Gemmis, who might be Joseph Jemmis. I offered all the advice for searching in Canada that might be useful but it wasn't until the lady hung up the phone that the solution kicked in and I can only hope that the lady calls back sometime or reads this.

The identification of her ancestor is a classic example for French Canadians whose names frequently get spelled phonetically and this was the solution to this brickwall. The ancestor's name was Joseph Jemieux and only when spoken by a French Canadian does the untrained ear hear Gemmis or Jemmis and this was obviously what happened. I found Joseph living on a farm on the 1871 Canadian census in Eastern Ontario.

I chastise myself for not having taken down the lady's name so that she could move on with her search. If she does chance to read this she will be pleased to know that French Canadians have some of the best genealogical records in the world and it is often possible to research back to the early 1600s in the Tanguay Index widely available at FHCs. — Ron Wild, ON

They Were Always On Her Mind

My brickwall story involves the Baine family on my father's side. It was strange to hit a brickwall with this family because they had been in Hamilton, my home town, since at least 1871, but I was having less trouble researching my other families who lived much farther away.

From the 1871 census, I learned that my third-great-grandparents, John and Mary Baine, were born in Ireland, both around 1835. At the Hamilton Public Library I looked up funeral records, cemetery transcriptions and city directories, but I found too many couples named John and Mary Baine to pinpoint which were my ancestors. I recorded all the information I found, even though I wasn't sure which of, or if any of, the people I found at these sources were related to me.

A few months went by and I continued researching my other families, but the Baines were always on my mind. I took a chance by assuming that John and Mary Baine were buried in the Hamilton area. I called the Catholic cemetery and found more information that had not yet been transcribed. One of the John Baines that seemed to fit had passed away in February 1902. I was sticking with this person because his age and other information sounded right.

All night I couldn't sleep, wondering where to look next for confirmation of my hunch. I got up and went straight to my file folder. There was a section at the back of the file folder where I kept the information I had collected on the many Baines I found in funeral records, cemetery transcriptions and city directories. This was where I stashed the information I had on people who I thought might be related, but I was not really sure how. Pieces from all these sources fit together to give me the confirmation I needed. The funeral records listed a John Baine whose death information

The Baine gravestone did not have John's name on it, but a call to the cemetery confirmed he was buried there. John's date of death and his last known address, along with census and directory records confirmed that he was the John Baine that Kimberly Muldoon-Staley was looking for all that time.

matched that of the cemetery. Looking at the city directories is what really made it clear. The one address similar throughout all my different sources of information was listed for both John Baine and his family, but also members of the Hinchey family. John and Mary's daughter Johanna married Edward Hinchey.

Since then I have found many other sources to confirm what started as a hunch. From census records, death registrations and newspaper obituaries, much has been discovered about both my Baine and Hinchey families.

I hope my story will help people to realize that it's important to write down everything you find that could relate to your family, even if at the time you aren't really sure how. By piecing together bits of information from different sources you may overcome a brickwall in your research. — Kimberly Muldoon-Staley, ON

Combined Knowledge

Caroline Stehle was my paternal great-grandmother and the wife of William Seeman. They were married in May 1866 in Belleville, IL. Her death certificate states that she was born on 10 October 1847 in Stuttgart and that her father was Christ Staley, although my father's records show it spelled Stehle. No mother's name was listed. My father also told me that she came to the US as a young girl.

For years I have tried to find out more about my Great-grandmother Caroline and her parents, with no luck.

In 1999, I received her obituary from a distant cousin. It listed a sister, Mary Christianson, who survived her. My great-grandmother was almost 82 when she died so I assumed her sister was younger. At our FHC in Washington, MO we have a book of the *St. Paul United Church Of Christ, Belleville: Church Records, 1839-1939*. I looked up Mary Stehle and Mary Christianson. I found a Maria Stehle who married Franz Christian. Could Maria Stehle Christian be Mary Christianson?

The director suggested I check the Evangelical church records from Mary's birth place: Moeglingen, Wuerttemberg, Germany. We checked the library catalog and found a film for the Evangelishe Kirche, Möglingen (OA. Ludwigsburg), Kirchenbuch, 1558-1956. My excitement upon receiving that film quickly dimmed, as I was unable to read most of the records. The director offered to try to find a Maria Carolina Stehle born on the same date with a sister, Maria Rosina Stehle, born three years later, which he did. The film showed her six brothers and sisters, her parents (her father was not Christ Stehle but she had two brothers, one Christoph and one Christian), her grandparents and more family back several generations. Across the bottom of their family page is written: "Nach Amerika Mai 1853".

It is absolutely amazing to me that the information on my father's records, the obituary and the Belleville church book at our FHC, combined to enable me to break through this brickwall. — Anne Hixson, MO, anneshixson@hotmail.com

Widen Your Research

I am researching my family name Stuttard. When I started I believed my family name to be sufficiently rare for me to not just concentrate on my own immediate descent but the history of the whole family. We are primarily UK-based and mainly from the area of Lancashire bordered by Colne and Burnley. I found that a typical year in the 19th century would have 25 Stuttards born across England and more than half of those would be registered in the district office of Burnley. The rest were almost all descendants of former residents of that area with just a few oddities that did not fit this rule.

St. Bartholomew's Parish Church in Colne where Geoff Stuttard's earliest known ancestors married and their son was christened.

Then my ambitions changed — I now wished to trace the whole family history back to a common point of origin. I had traced my own ancestry back five generations to a family in the small town of Gisburn on the Yorkshire/Lancashire border. Of the nine children born to William and Susan, my own ancestor Thomas was the only one to completely leave the area. My research found William's birth in 1804 to a Richard and Mary who married in Colne in 1800 and that was my brickwall. Whatever I did I could not find which of several Richards was William's father and my ancestor as none of them had a suitable date within a sensible range.

In the course of my research I had made contact with many Stuttards around the world and was tracing their family trees in parallel to my own. I was was plowing through the St Catherine's Index of UK births and had reached the births of individuals still alive today and many of the people I was in contact with.

On Ancestry.com I found a page of UK names, addresses and telephone details that listed more than 300 Stuttards in the UK.

I used my computer software to run a mail merge on all these addresses with the exception of those I was already in contact with. Many of the addresses were duplicated so the final run amounted to 177 letters. I drafted an introductory letter explaining my research and my objectives and sent this to all those addresses. I was rewarded by almost 50 replies by letter, telephone and e-mail. Not only did I discover several other Stuttards who had endeavored to research their own ancestry but I found several descendants of my own ancestor's brothers. I also found people who had postulated my missing Richard as possibly being a brother of their own ancestor (although so far I have not been able to prove this). However I did find someone with census details of my missing Richard in 1841 at age 60, pinpointing his birth in 1780 or 1781 and that he came from an isolated community in the Colne area which founded its own church, thus explaining his absence from the normally available parish records of the area.

I have visited the area around Colne, Burnley and Nelson, which encompasses the area where my ancestor Richard originates. I did find

from various contacts where he is buried and indeed a churchyard holding almost 60 Stuttards in the area once known as Great Marsden. I have yet to visit it though — nor have I yet been able to visit the small rural communities where the family lived. This is due to 2001's foot-and-mouth disease restrictions so I confined my pilgrimages to the libraries in the towns involved.

I now know where to look for his details and bridge the gap between my brickwall and my data of generations before that. Best of all, through the range of my research I was able to demolish the brickwalls of many of my fellow researchers — something I have done on several occasions already.

Use a collateral line to bypass the blockage. One should not be afraid to go further than that and widen the research even further. Don't forget the value of identification by process of elimination. It worked for me. — Geoff Stuttard, West Yorkshire, UK, geoff.stuttard@cwcom.net

Library Guest Books

I had been researching my mother's family for more than 20 years and had not done much on my birth father's family; my parents were divorced when I was eight. My father's last name was Williams and I knew from experience that it would be quite an undertaking when I started so I just kept pushing it back.

On a trip to Indiana my cousin had some old pictures and in one of these pictures was a list of family names for that side. So I went to the county library a few miles away, with only a few hours to spare. Knowing that I could spend lots of time on this venture I checked the family files and found there were three William Williams families in the same county at the same time within 10 years of age with children all nearly the same names as the others. I copied all I had time to do and started to leave. On my way out I stopped to sign the guest book in the genealogy section and the second name on the list was Baxter and he was looking for family names Williams and Kemp; these were my names on the new found list! Then, I remembered a story told by an aunt that three Baxter brothers married three Williams sisters.

I contacted the man in the guest book and received five generations and 160 pages of information. This would have taken years for me to sort out, but thanks to the guest book I found family that I knew nothing about.

Now the first thing I do when I go to the library is look in the guest book, fill it out with my surname interest or write and ask if someone in that county can look up researchers that have visited the local library. Not everyone has Internet available so don't pass up this valuable tool. — Elaine Acosta, LA

The Case Of Henry McTee

Henry McTee has been a difficult ancestor to trace. The 1910 census said that he was born to Irish-born parents. His 1920 obituary said he was born on 1 November 1859 in Chicago. Therefore he should show up in the 1860 Illinois census in Cook county. This census is indexed but the only McTee listed did not have a son named Henry, Hank or Harry.

Finding Henry's marriage certificate became a challenge. He had married Daisy Hubbard in the early 1890s in western Kansas. Or so it was believed. Calling each county in western Kansas led to nothing. Ultimately his widow's obituary said they were married in Trenton, Hitchcock, NE. This was incorrect but after checking adjacent Dundy county, NE, we final-

ly found it. Since Dundy county is very rural, the clerk checked the record over the phone and we got the certificate later for $1. This piece of information was crucial for later research in the Chicago city directories and the US census.

Henry McTee's death certificate lists him as Charles Henry McTee. It states that his parents were Charles and Anne McTee, which disagrees with the 1891 marriage certificate which listed them as Samuel McTee and Mary Taylor. An 1860 census was found that agreed with the 1891 information and the 1920 information.

Ann Taylor McTee McCauley Dier (1837-1910).

Knowing that Henry McTee was born in 1859 in Chicago made a search of the 1860 Illinois census a necessity. However, the one McTee in the index was not a match. The index listed Robert McTee, Cook Co., Illinois, 844 PALOS. When checking the family it listed: Robert McTee, 33, born Canada, Ellen McTee, 36, born Ireland, Jeremiah McTee, eight, born Illinois and Ronald McTee, one, born Illinois. When Henry's father was listed as Samuel we decided to check every Samuel Mc___ in Cook county in 1860. There were eight. Of course, upon checking the first seven there was no match but the eighth was a hit.

Samuel and Ann McIntire were living with their eight-month-old son Henry in the eighth ward. Unfortunately, there was no Samuel McIntire or Ann McIntire in the 1870 census index. We got a huge lead as to what the unadulterated form of McTee was but it is still proceeding at a snail's pace.

Ann was found in the 1880 census with her third husband Andrew Dier and her younger children; 11-year-old John McTee (listed as Dier), eight-year-old Sadie McCauley (listed as Dier), Amelia Dier, William Dier and Maude Dier. It appears that Samuel was around until at least July 1868. Second husband Richard McCauley fathered Sadie in June 1871. He died in October 1871 and his daughter was born in March of the following year. Ann appears to have married Dier circa 1873. Henry McTee has not been found in the 1870 or 1880 US census.

We had checked the 1860 Chicago city directory looking for McTees but there were none. After finding them in the 1860 census as McIntire we rechecked but still no luck. Finally, we checked the neighbors listed in the census for their address. Abraham Schick could be found on North Dearborn Avenue in 1859 and 1865. In 1865, there was a Samuel McAndee on North Dearborn. In 1868, there was a Simon McTee on North Dearborn.

This has been such a pain-staking process because we get such little success. We believe that the McTees lived in Holy Name parish in the 1860s.

Unfortunately this parish lost its records in the Chicago Fire of 1871. — Kevin Cassidy, NE, kmct@earthlink.net

Secret Identities

My search for my great-grandfather, Harry C. Salisbury, began when I was a novice at genealogical research. My grandmother told me her father had changed his name and she thought it had originally been Helmer Solberg. She didn't know why and I was left with the impression that it was a secret. I also felt he probably didn't go through any legal channels to have it changed.

My grandmother had a copy of Harry's and Anna Matilda Brouse's marriage license where my great-grandfather was listed as Harry. No parents' names were provided. I considered sending for his death certificate, but knew that it would only be as good as the informant's memory. If Harry's former identity was a secret, I assumed my great-grandmother wouldn't have relinquished Harry's parents' names.

I knew Harry's birth date, but a birth certificate for a Helmer Solberg would provide no tie to Harry. A search of the online SSDI yielded nothing appropriate for my Harry or Helmer. Fortunately, my grandmother also knew he was born in Spring Grove, MN and had a brother named Albert.

Switchboard.com, an online telephone directory.

I was looking through the online phone directories to see how many possibilities lived in Minnesota and I decided to narrow my search to Spring Grove itself. I sent four letters. Months later I received a letter from a woman who said she found my letter in her deceased brother's belongings. She was sure that she had uncles named Helmer and Albert. She sent me a list of all the siblings, their birth dates and Helmer's parents' names: Christen Solberg and Berthe Hagen. This was wonderful, but I still needed proof that Helmer and Harry were the same person.

After my grandmother moved into a retirement home, I helped to sort through her papers. To my surprise, I found Harry's Social Security card. I immediately sent away for his registration. He was listed as Harry C. Salisbury and his parents were Chris Solberg and Bertha Hagen.

If I had it to do over, knowing what I know now, I would probably begin by searching the census for Houston county, MN. But then I may never have made contact with my distant Solberg cousins. If I had sent those letters much later than I did, the one that went to the right Solberg, may have been sent back to me because of the addressee's death.

Sending those letters was the key to getting over my brickwall concerning my great-grandfather. — Marcy (Hennum) Hoover, WA, faeriecats@hotmail.com

Ask A Librarian

This is a solution that worked twice with libraries. I had been trying to find information on my grandmother, Charlotte Morton Fakler.

Her brother Morris lived in Hudson Bay, SK, when I was about four years old and I have pictures of myself at his farm. Hoping to find a descendant in the area, I wrote to the Hudson Bay librarian.

Several weeks passed before I heard from anyone. A librarian passed the letter on to someone who also passed it on eventually to a woman named Elsie. She was married to a Morton. She wrote a letter to make sure we were talking about the same people. Once that was established the information came forth like a waterfall. She and her husband had been researching this line. They had correspondence and copies of docu-

ments from their research in England several years prior that dated back to the 1700s and a soldier in Napoleon's Army. She had the stories about Charlotte's adoption and name change that opened up another line. I will forever be indebted to that wonderful librarian in Hudson Bay.

This same thing happened when my husband was looking for ancestors. He knew they had been in Kelvington, SK and wrote to the librarian there. She sent him copies of pages from a family book that had been written a few years before. It listed one person as living in Langley, BC. The next day he drove to Langley and found her in the phone book and called and left a message.

A few days later she returned the call and once it was explained, it opened up another line. Again, thanks to the wonderful librarian. — Phylis Jorgenson, WA

The Heart Of A Genealogist

When I started doing research in the 1960s, I talked to my grandmother about her family, but she did not know her maternal grandmother's maiden name. Her own mother had died when she was 18 and she had never known her grandmother.

I was very excited when I finally discovered in a local history, 20 years later, that she was Angeline Miller from New York. Then I wanted to know the names of Angeline's parents. I figured she would be at home with them in 1830, so copied all the Millers in Monroe county, NY, from the Accelerated Indexing Systems Index — since that was where she married. One of the Miller heads-of-household in that county in 1830 was named Justin. Angeline had a son named Justin and I knew it was not a name from her husband's Titus line. So I settled on Justin as a possible name to research.

The Monroe county, NY, surrogate's court wanted $40 just to check the surrogate index for one name through the mail and, as I later learned, Justin didn't leave a will anyway. I wrote to the town historian in Rush, Monroe county, where I had found the family in 1830, 1840 and 1850. (Though Justin was dead by 1850, I found a family I thought was his: a widow Sarah Miller, with a probable son next door named Calvin Miller; Angeline had named a son Calvin Miller Titus.) For $5 the historian offered to check the surrogate index for me when she went to the courthouse for other business. She came up with an entry for a Sarah Miller, dated too late to be our Sarah, we thought.

Sarah Driver Miller's gravestone in Monroe county, NY.

Later, the historian wrote to me that the entry bothered her, so on her next trip to the courthouse she checked the file. Briefly, the Millers had had two spinster daughters who inherited their parents' little house and lived there. After they died, a niece petitioned that the estate be settled and in the process they looked up anyone and everyone who might have had a possible claim on the tiny little amount concerned. The resulting estate settlement listed all the descendants of Justin and Sarah, including deceased daughters and their descendants and including Angeline's 12 children (Angeline had actually died before her mother did, so she was a deceased daughter), one of whom was my own great-grandmother, given by name, so I had absolute proof that I had the right family. (There actually was a short little will of Sarah's, just naming a couple of grand-daughters and her two spinster daughters.)

The historian only charged me that original $5 for her efforts, saying that she taught classes and wanted permission to use the story as an example of following up and of the possible wealth of information which might be gathered from a tiny estate settlement.

I think of the town historian today as a good example of "heart" and the sharing of one's time and one's proximity to records to help a fellow researcher. — Marcia W. Green, CA, mwverde.mwg@verizon.net

Good Deeds Do Return Rewards

I was stuck on the maiden name of my third-great-grandmother. I was searching from 1,000 miles away and couldn't seem to locate any source documents that listed her maiden name. I had taken all the usual routes: collected wills and church records and checked the census, but I still could not find her maiden name.

At the same time, I was a lookup volunteer for the 1870 census index CD for Schuylkill county, PA, the area where she had lived. I had done thousands of lookups for people, but one day I received a lookup request from someone for my second-great-grandfather (the son of my third-great-grandmother with the elusive maiden name). The woman who had written asking for a lookup was my previously unknown second cousin once-removed. She asked for information about her great-grandfather who, although she had no idea at the time, was my second-great-grandfather.

It was an exciting day when we found each other. She had that elusive maiden name! I was able to give her information she had been seeking and a 100-year-old family rift was healed. Good deeds do return rewards! — Kathi Reid, FL

Kindness Is Remembered

We had my great-grandfather's obituary, long entries in several local history books, old reunion records and dozens of tales about his life including him walking to California during the Gold Rush and as the father of 10 who celebrated with his wife, their 50th-wedding anniversary.

His birthplace was always listed as Kurhessen or a variation thereof. After many years of looking in vain for his exact birthplace, we checked the death record at the church at which he was buried in 1927. There it was!

A brief life story was written in German and though the village's name was misspelled, it was enough to narrow it down and locate the church. The village is now part of another town. We asked the pastor to copy the record as no microfilming has been permitted. The pastor was kind enough to also send photos of the church to us.

I am so grateful to that 1927 Illinois church secretary who could easily have just written that this old fellow was born in Germany. — Gilda Kinzer, IL

Pictures From The Past

My maiden name is Robbins, which is fairly common but added to that no one in my family was even remotely interested in family history. The only information I had was what my grandmother had recorded in my father's baby book — a bunch of names, no dates and no places.

When I began my search, my grandfather, Wayne A. Robbins, was still alive so he provided the information on his parents, but he knew nothing on his grandparents, Henry and Alice (Murray) Robbins. Knowing that they were living in Minnesota by 1900 I was able to find them in the census. Finally, approximate birth dates! But where did they go after that?

Wayne Allison Robbins as a child.

At this point I knew that they were born in New York, probably in

Livingston county, and were living in Mindon township, Benton county, MN, in 1900. While going through some photographs, I found one of my grandfather as a baby, a typical 1910s postcard picture. The card was addressed to his grandmother, "Mrs. H. W. Robbins, Emerson, Iowa C/O Mr. Arthur McClain." Not having any idea who Arthur McClain might be, I decided to write to the Mills county Genealogical Society in Glenwood, Iowa.

Not very long after a lovely lady answered my letter. She included an abstract of an obituary for Alice, her sister and brother-in-law, Caroline and Arthur McClain, and her mother Mary Wyman Murray Young. Finally something to work with.

Reverse of picture of Wayne Allison Robbins: Julie Robbins' great-grandmother signed the back saying "I look nice and fat and healthy, your loving grandchild, Allison Wayne". His proper name was Wayne Allison, but his mother desperately wanted a daughter and called him Allison until he was about five, when his sister Alice Lenoe was born.

According to the obituary Alice died in Minneapolis so I immediately sent for her death certificate. The death certificate stated that Alice was buried in St. Cloud, MN. So off I went writing to St. Cloud and discovered that Alice, Henry, two daughters and Henry's mother were all buried in Northstar Cemetery. From the cemetery office I also learned that Henry died in Racine, WI. These people moved around a lot. Finally I had

found my family, all because of a picture of my grandfather addressed to his grandmother. — Julie Robbins Dresser, IL

Orphans

My mother, Fern (Ensign) Gregerson, learned she was adopted in the spring of 1937. I still remember when she read the letter to my brother and me. Her birth mother wrote asking if she would like to meet her. The day we met mother's birth mother, Dot Lyle, was a great day, one I will never forget.

Dot's parents were James Cline Lyle and Ida Floyd. After the Civil War, James suffered with a bullet in his leg, but did not want it amputated. So James and Ida were sent from Iowa to the Sherman Texas Army Hospital for his treatment in 1880. Dot was born in 1881 and four weeks later, Ida died. We have the letter asking Ida's parents to take Dot, so she was raised in Lisbon, IA.

In 1883, James Lyle married Laura Bell and they had three children. Then, around 1890, they moved to Lake Charles, LA. In 1896, Laura deserted her family. The youngest child, Edith, was adopted by Orrin L. Smith and his wife. In 1899, Orrin, his wife and Edith went to the La Crosse, WI area. Orrin became ill and died a few weeks later. Orrin's wife took Edith to the Sparta, Wisconsin Children's Orphanage in 1899. Edith's second adoption was in 1902 to the Prosser family of Kendall, WI.

James took his other two children, Lillian and Algernon, to Florida. Then he went to Tennessee and became ill with the bullet in his leg. He was placed in an Army hospital there and later transferred to Marshalltown, Iowa Soldiers' home in 1900. When James Cline Lyle arrived in Marshalltown, he only listed two children of his four children, Dot, as living in Lisbon, IA, and Edith in the state of Wisconsin Orphan School in Sparta.

In 1902, Dot married and became pregnant, but before her child was born the marriage was terminated. Dot went to Arnes, IA to work for her keep and have the baby, my mother. There were now five children orphaned in the family; Dot and her three half-siblings and Dot's daughter.

We began searching for my grandmother's siblings. We began with Edith, who last known to be in Kendall, WI.

Armed with all my information, we went to the officials for Madison and Sparta, WI for Edith's adoption records and were told all records had been destroyed years ago. I went to the courthouse in Sparta, WI and other offices looking for Edith's adoption dates. At the fifth office, Monroe county in Sparta, WI, the clerk said she'd look for Edith Lyle and found her records in the index cards of the state orphan school. Obviously, the records had not been destroyed. I had been told the adoption took place in 1910, but it turned out to be 1902.

As an adult, Edith was located in Michigan as the Superintendent of the Higland Park General Hospital in Detroit. She had since married twice. After the second marriage she changed her first name to DeDe and moved to Detroit, MI.

With Edith, if we knew her birth date, we could have found her in the Wisconsin odd-year state census of 1905 by checking every family, as there is an abbreviation beside some names meaning the the person was adopted. I've found that the federal censuses missed a lot of people and the state censuses are very helpful for these types of of searches.

Had I read the obituaries in the old newspapers, I probably would have saved myself a lot of time and money. I should have also checked the cemetery records, especially the funeral reports, to see where people died and where they were buried. This would have also given relatives' names.

There were a lot of children named Edith in 1905 in Wisconsin. — Merle Gregerson, WI

A Brickwall in Roundup

Sometimes the way over a brickwall is to take the wall down one brick at a time. I decided this was the only way to proceed with my grandfather after interviewing family and employing other usual methods of research.

My father knew nothing of his father as he abandoned the family before my father was born. My grandmother knew little of her runaway husband or chose not to share what she knew.

My aunt, their oldest child, provided me with a copy of the marriage certificate for her parents, which stated they married in 1909 in Salt Lake City. I attempted to acquire their marriage statistics, but they are missing for that time period. Based on further information that my aunt was born the following year in Roundup, MT, I believed I would learn some of what I needed from the 1910 census record of Yellowstone county. I sent for that microfilm through the local FHC. They weren't there.

The second child, another daughter, was born in Grant county, WA, 13 months after the first child so I checked that 1910 census also in case they had moved there soon enough to be counted in that county's enumeration. They weren't there either.

I placed queries, checked city directories and attended seminars focusing on brickwalls. Wondering if he might have divorced my grandmother and remarried, I investigated that possibility and invented one scenario after another trying to figure where my grandfather had come from or where he went. After a few years, I determined I would have to start taking bricks out of that wall by hand.

Plotting any possible course a family might take in moving west from Yellowstone county, MT to Grant county, WA I made a list of counties where they might have been enumerated and headed for the nearest library that had the entire 1910 census on microfilm. I began reading the counties alphabetically and crossing them one at a time from my list.

In Fergus county, MT, I found another town named Roundup. The census line, not the county line, ran right through this little town. There they were with just enough information to smack me right into another brickwall, but I really only had to remove two or three bricks from the first wall once I plotted a course. — Claire A. Bardwell, WA

Library Phone Books

This situation happened to me in 1989. My mother had traced our family to my third-great-grandparents, John and Elizabeth (Morrison) Corbett in County Down, Northern Ireland. Through correspondence and visits with relatives, she was given copies of old letters that had been saved by John and Elizabeth's daughter, Eliza. From the letters dating back to 1856, we knew the village in County Down was Ballyward. One letter written by a niece told of John's death in 1877 and burial at Drumgooland Cemetery.

At the time, I was searching for information on the family of the oldest daughter, Mary (Corbett) Bell, many of whom had not come to the US.

One day while in the San Diego

The old Corbett home in Ballyward.
Photograph courtesy of John and Marilyn Chalstrom.

Public Library, I noticed they had phone books from around the world. I opened the Northern Ireland phone book to the surname Corbett and scanned down the list until I found a Corbett with a street address that sounded familiar from some of the old letters.

I wrote Mr. Corbett a letter outlining our family history and asking if any of it sounded familiar to him. I enclosed money for return postage in hope of receiving a reply.

I couldn't have been more pleased! He was so kind. In his letter he answered many of the general questions I had asked of the area and as it turned out, he lived just down the road from where my third-great-grandparents had lived. He could make no direct connection to my family but said perhaps farther back in generations there was a connection.

In subsequent letters, he sent a picture of his family, postcard pictures of the area and a picture of his niece's wedding inside the Drumgooland Presbyterian Church where my ancestors attended. And best of all, he put me in touch with a living relative, Ann, still residing in Northern Ireland! It was through Ann and her cousin Betty that I gained information on that line of the family. I also learned that the original home in Ireland is still being lived in by a descendant. I was able to pass along that information to a first cousin and he and his wife were able to visit the home on a recent trip to Northern Ireland.

While this may not be a solution for everyone, it was one of my most memorable! — Jackie (Swink) Creighton, CA, jcr8on1@cox.net

Always Check The Neighbors

I had only sketchy information on Paul, my mother's brother. I knew his first and last names, that he was born in either Nebraska or Iowa and that he was approximately eight years younger than my mother. Mom always said was that he was Retired Navy. Because of this, I thought this would be an easy task. I thought I could just write the Department of the Navy, explain who I was, what I was doing and they would either send me his address or forward my letter. I spent a year trying to fulfill their numerous requests for additional information and returning the documentation to them, only to have them ask for more.

Finally they wrote and said they could not release the address nor forward my letters without the signature of next of kin. This is who I was searching for all along, his family. Why they didn't let me know in the beginning and save all our time, I do not know.

I had two aunts living in Denver where Paul was raised. One aunt knew the church where Paul was married, so I wrote there and they had birth information, parents and the full name of Paul's wife, Betty. Then I contacted the Veterans Administration. The clerk put his first and last name in the computer. Three names came up, only one was Navy and he was too old. All her life, Mom had talked about Paul retiring from the Navy, so I knew this was no mistake. The clerk asked for a middle name, which I did not know, however, I guessed Edward after his dad, my grandfather. There he was. The clerk couldn't explain why it didn't come up before with the first and last name only, but there he was.

From there I went to the FHC and checked for Paul in the SSDI. I needed his birth date before checking here. This verified the date of death, where it happened and it gave me the zip code area (southern California) where he was living at the time of his death. After finding this information, I ordered a death certificate and an obituary.

The obituary listed his family: a wife, two daughters and a son. I looked for his son as the daughters might have married and changed their last names. I sent letters to all the people in the California directory with the same name living in central to southern California. I got a reply from the son of one of my grandfather's brothers. He connected

Pat Lain's Uncle Paul, c. 1945.

me with his three sisters who live in northeastern Nebraska. He also knew of another family living in Minnesota. The husband, deceased, was the son of another of my grandfather's brothers. I wrote the wife and have since visited the families of both the cousins in Nebraska and Minnesota. The cousins living in Minnesota are in the same town our original ancestors settled in after emigrating from Ireland.

I decided to write to the Santa Clara County Genealogy Society to see if they could come up with some information on Paul's family. The death certificate I ordered showed his last address, but that would have been 25 years old. One man at the society decided to check the address for me because it was only a few blocks away. The lady who lived in Paul's old home had lived there 10 years and did not know of Paul or his family. She, however, referred him to neighbors a few doors away that had lived in the neighborhood for about 25 years. This couple turned out to be the godparents of Paul's son. The neighbor gave the man the son's phone number to give to me. I called him right after hearing from the society. It was so wonderful after all the years of searching to finally find Paul's family. — Pat Lain, AZ

North American Vital Records Index

In the many years I have been working on the family history there have been many brickwalls. However, most of them tumbled down when I went online in 1997. I have met cousins from all over and with each other's assistance we have broken down many barriers.

In April 2000, I began volunteering at our local FHC. During a slow evening I thought I would become familiar with their collection. One set

in particular, seemed very interesting. The North American Vital Records Index contains birth and marriage records. I started putting in names into the index that I have been working on, with little result or information I previously had. I then typed in Crittenden. I proceeded to search under the two first names I had, Truman, born in Canada and William, born in New York.

For some reason I looked under the marriage records and found a William Crittenden married to Hannah Brandow in Talbot district, Walsingham township, Upper Canada in 1851. Could this be my William? The 1870 federal census for Michigan listed William Crittenden and wife Hannah in Mecosta county. The CD provided the film number, I ordered it and made a copy of this new information.

While waiting for the film, I went to the State Historical Society of Wisconsin and found a book titled *The Marriage Registers Of Upper Canada* by Dan Walker. William Crittenden was not listed, but Hannah Brandow was listed as marrying William Outtenden. Other information this book provided was the name of the pastor and the denomination.

The film was taking a while and I had a research vacation planned for Fort Wayne at the Allen County Public Library. It was noted that they had the 1851-52 Walsingham township, Norfolk county census. For three days I attempted to hunt down that book. I happened on the microfilms of the census. I settled in at the film reader, the copies were dreadful and, of course, there was no index.

I found Walsingham township and looked individual by individual. There was a Crittenden and several Brandos. At the top of page 20 I found Hannah Crittenden and below, Truman Crittenden. On the next page I found William Crittenden. They were in the household/homestead of her father. Finally the film arrived and the marriage record was there, though difficult to read. William Crittenden married Hannah Brandow.

Unfortunately, I'm still at a brickwall and have not been able to go further back, or even forward. The last notation for William Crittenden is a church record in May 1876 indicating, "Gone to the Weslyans". Truman went west, but William, Hannah and son, Walter, have fallen from the face of the earth. I have been unable to locate a probate or cemetery record.

Going backwards would be an attempt to connect to the descendants of Abraham Cruttenden, who is noted in family documents to have set sail with the *Mayflower* but on the sister ship, *Hopewell*. There were many William Crittendens/Cruttendens born in approximately the same time frame as mine and they all appear to have been the end of the line in the information. — Christina Zahn, WI

The Elusive Mattie

The information I had stated that Mattie S. Clayton died in Los Angeles shortly after her granddaughter, Opal Rose Clayton, was born on 14 July 1914. Opal's sister, Pansy "Pat" Violla Clayton remembered that Opal was a baby when Mattie died and that Mattie was buried in the cemetery in downtown Los Angeles. Pat thought that Mattie might have had a second husband. She knew that Mattie had two children, Augustus (Gus) and George. Gus was Pat's and Opal's father, but he and their mother had divorced years ago and he had died somewhere in Oregon.

Armed with this bit of information I started my search. I tried to get a copy of Mattie's death certificate but nothing was available under the name Mattie S. Clayton. I located the cemetery that Pat remembered but they had no record of her. Pat was sure we had the right cemetery. I sent to the state of California to see if they had a marriage record for Mattie to

anyone. I received a copy of Mattie's marriage to David Pierce. I went back to the cemetery to find Mattie's gravesite. I also sent to the state for her death certificate.

As is so often the case, this was not as easy as it sounded. There was no death certificate for Mattie Pierce and no gravesite for her in the cemetery. The marriage license I received gave me the state where she was born, but did not list her parents' names. She had married David Pierce on 27 October 1901 when she was 37 years old.

A city directory pointed Carolyn Hutchinson Brown in the right direction.

In the Los Angeles city directories I found her under the name Mattie Clayton from 1895 to 1901, a widow. Her husband was John or J.M. Clayton. Under the name Mattie Pierce I found her from 1902 to 1910. This led me to believe she either remarried or moved, as I was certain she died sometime in the summer or fall of 1914.

I sent a letter to the state to see if she remarried. Sure enough, I received a marriage license for Mattie Pierce to James M. Smith dated 21 September 1910. This license said her parents were John Brown, born in North Carolina, and Mary Wilson, born in Kentucky, and Mattie was 45 years old. I went back to the cemetery to find her gravesite and sent another letter to the state for her death certificate. There was no gravesite and no death certificate for her under the name of Mattie Smith. A search through the city directories for Mattie Smith showed she lived in Los Angeles from 1910 to 1913. Since she died in 1914 it was possible that she was living with family and not listed in the city directory for that year.

Certainly she would not have married again only three years after the last marriage. I needed a different method. I researched the *Los Angeles Times'* obituaries page by page, since they were not indexed for the summer and fall of 1914. I started with 14 July, Opal's birthday, and researched all obituaries for anyone named Mattie. I didn't care what the last name was, only that the person's age was close to 49. I located a Mattie Thomas, age 50, who had lived at the right address based on the city directory information, in the obituaries on 6 August 1914. I checked several days later and found nothing more on Mattie Thomas.

I again went to the cemetery to locate her gravesite. This time the clerk found the interment record, signed by her son George Clayton. I then got both her marriage license, to Charles C. Thomas dated 12 November 1913, and a copy of her death certificate. The marriage license said her parents were Vinson Brown and Martha J. Mosteller, both born in South Carolina. Her death certificate listed her age as 50. There were no names for her parents on the death certificate.

Now I wanted to find Mattie's parents. My census record search showed nothing. After I got the marriage license to Charles Thomas I found in the census records that they were Vinson Brown and Martha J. Mosteller. Since that time I have found a lot of information on the Mosteller family and I found that Vinson was killed in Vicksburg, MS in the Civil War. — Carolyn Hutchinson Brown, OR, sidcarol@escapees.com

Revisit The Information You Already Have

Trying to find the naturalization papers for my ancestor had been my brickwall for several years.

According to church records, Meinrad Fakler, who was born in 1843 in Germany, came to the US in 1864. He stayed in Winona, MN, for more than three years before settling in Olmsted county, Rochester, MN. Olmsted county sent their naturalization records to St. Paul's but the years I was searching for were missing.

Ancestry.com.

I gave up until I tried Ancestry.com on one of their trial periods. When I checked for his siblings' records, I was very surprised to find Meinrad's name under Winona county. For some reason, this obvious source escaped me.

Ancestry referred me to Iron Range Research Center in Chisholm, MN who sent me the record for a very small fee. After many years of frustration, this proved the obvious was there all the time.

It pays to revisit the information you already have. — Phylis Jorgenson, WA

Second Enumeration

One of the most important tools for tracking down American ancestors is the US census. Since the people I was looking for lived in New York City and were listed in all Manhattan directories for the years from 1869 to 1878, I believed I would find them on the 1870 federal census. The 1870 census index for New York was searched, but one name of interest was missing and the other possible matches on the index did not match the known age, marital status and occupation of my ancestor.

These ancestors were known to have lived in Ward 16, Manhattan, as determined by all the directory entries for a period of 10 years. An actual search of the census taken for that ward in 1870 was done, but the family was not found. I knew that the family was living there in 1870 because a baptismal record of a daughter born in June 1870 had already been obtained. It appeared that this family had not been counted in the 1870 census. This does happen, especially in a large city.

My next step was to attempt another search of the 1870 census to consider the possibility that an unusual spelling of one of the family names or some other mistake prevented me from finding them. This time I noticed that there was a second enumeration taken of the 1870 census for New York City. I then searched the microfilm of the second enumeration of Ward 16 and found my missing ancestors.

I was able to learn several new facts about them that would provide leads to follow for future research. It is not common knowledge that a second enumeration was taken for the 1870 census for several cities. The cities that have a second enumeration are: Indianapolis, IN; New York City, NY and Philadelphia, PA.

If you cannot find your ancestors on the 1870 census indexes and you know they lived in one of these cities, consider searching the second enumeration for them. You might have the same success that I did. — Maura McLeod, FL

You Can Get More From A College Than Just A Degree

In order to obtain the death certificate for a great-grandmother, I had to know her year of death. Unfortunately, I had exhausted all the usual repositories and was faced with a brickwall.

At a family gathering, I questioned an elderly aunt about her grandmother. She mentioned her grandmother had died a few days after her father had graduated from college and because of this, he was unable to go on for an advanced degree. Finally, a clue! I learned from her that her father had attended a small liberal arts college in New York. I quickly sent a request to the Alumni Office of the college. I asked what year this man had graduated. I received an immediate reply with the year he had graduated and the degree he had earned.

Armed with the year of her death, I pursued the death certificate from the Vital Records Office and received it by return mail. Great-grandmother had been buried in a different county from where she had died, which was why the search of burial permits had not been successful. The death certificate listed her parents who I soon found buried in the plot where great-grandmother was laid to rest. — Judy H. Swan, CA

When Ancestors Lie

For about 20 years, I searched in vain for evidence of my third-great-grandfather Robertson in Lanark county, ON.

I searched through the census but found nothing. When my great-grandmother died she had many scraps of paper and old postcards in her possession. She had an obituary that her own mother had possessed from 1906, which concerned the death of this third-great-grandfather Robertson.

> **Died Suddnely**—The following is from the Era, of Lanark, Ont: Old friends and neighbors in this locality will learn with deep regret of the death of Peter Robertson, which occurred at his home in Perth, Monday, February 5. Death came very unexpectedly and a gloom was cast over the entire neighborhood by the sudden taking away of the aged gentleman. While attending his daily business he was suddenly stricken with a paralytic stroke, and although all was done that kindly hands and medical aid could do, the spark of life was extinguished. The deceased was one of the oldest settlers of Perth, and had reached the advanced age of 86 years. He was greatly esteemed by all who knew him as a man of honesty and uprightness. Mr. Roberson was a native of Scotland, born in the city of Glasgow. He came to Canada 56 years ago and settled on a farm in Perth. Before leaving the old land he married Miss Sarah Todd, who also was a native of the old city in Scotland. Mrs. Robertson died in 1889. Nine children were born to them, of which four survive—Willim, at Cedar Springs; Mrs. Annie Johnson, Bay City, Mich.; John, of Lanark, Ont., and Abraham, a well-known young man of this village. The funeral, which was largely attended, took place yesterday afternoon at 2:30, from his late home, Rev. Mr. Scott officiating."

Judy McAuliffe's third-great-grandfather's obituary.

It said that he was born in Glasgow, had a wife named Sarah Todd, whom he married before immigrating from the old country and he had had nine children. He died quite suddenly in the streets of Perth. This obituary had been written in Bay City, MI, to inform the local residents that second-great-grandmother lost her father in Ontario. But where was he?

I searched all the censuses from 1841 on and could not find a trace of him. I decided that since I had such a precise date of his death, I would just send to Ontario for his death certificate.

No luck they told me. All they could come up with was a Peter Robinson and I knew that wasn't correct because grandmother was emphatic about the Scottish origins and the name Robinson was Irish. Third-great-grandfather was Scottish. Why, there were even Robertson relatives, whose names were marked on the back of ancient pictures that were still in her possession!

About 10 years ago, I began thinking about this problem again. I rechecked my research data and decided I needed to try a new angle, but wasn't sure what. I went to the local public library and I searched for a way to locate old newspapers in Perth, where this grandfather died. It took a few trips to the library before I hooked up with a helpful reference librarian who told me I could order old newspaper articles. I wanted to find one for Perth for an obituary of a Peter Robertson in January 1906. She searched and found a source at a medical hospital library at a military base in Texas and sent for it. The appropriate edition was obtained and so was the obituary I wanted. There in front of my eyes the truth fell forth: third-great-grandfather Robertson, or rather Robinson, died exactly as had been described in exactly the same city as had been described, widowed to Sarah Todd and having left the same children. He was born in Belfast and he and his bride were married there before leaving.

What was second-great-grandmother trying to hide in writing the obituary the way she had? Why did she want to be Scottish? Why did she lie about the family name and change it? Why did she hide this from her family for so long? I'll never get to ask her these questions, but the point is that sometimes there are ways to get around even the roadblocks set by your own grandparents.

I went back to those Ontario censuses and found numerous Robinsons. But there in Lanark county was third-great-grandfather, Peter Robinson, and his wife, Sarah Todd. They were still there waiting for me when I finally came back. — Judy McAuliffe, CA

Big Foot

Nearly four years ago at a small family gathering my mother stated, "I was told all my life that we were related to "Big Foot" Wallace through my maternal grandmother."

Naturally, we asked her who Big Foot Wallace was and exactly how we were related. William Alexander Anderson "Big Foot" Wallace was a legendary frontiersman and one of the original Texas Rangers.

Unfortunately, my mother was not certain of the exact relationship between Big Foot and her grandmother, Sara Catherine Wallace Beach, thus presenting a brickwall. She thought Big Foot was possibly a brother or an uncle to Catherine.

My mother believed the answer was probably among the old papers and photo-

William Alexander Anderson "Big Foot" Wallace.

graphs in Catherine's trunk stored in her attic.

Since that announcement I have spent countless hours sifting through the contents of Catherine's trunk, which included her journal recording the names and deaths of her parents and two of her brothers.

The back of an old photograph of Nettie Wallace Needham, Catherine's older sister, recorded that Big Foot was an uncle. A letter from Catherine's daughter-in-law recorded Big Foot as a brother to Catherine.

I telephoned the Chamber of Commerce in Taylorsville to see if any Wallace descendants might still live in the area. They furnished me with a woman's name whose number I called and she provided me with the name of Myrtle Mae Wallace Fidler. I wrote to both women and included copies of some of the photos of unidentified Wallace family members. Myrtle responded with a letter that revealed she was the granddaughter of Catherine's older brother, Samuel Alan Wallace.

More telephone calls were made to the Taylorsville library and the Bullitt County Historical Society, which produced limited information but did provide me with the address of the Filson Club, the historical society of Kentucky. I wrote to the Filson Club and they provided me with enough information to uncover the exact relationship of Big Foot to Catherine.

The truth was Big Foot was first cousin once-removed to Catherine.

Big Foot was the son of Andrew Wallace and Rachel Jane Ann Blair. Andrew was the son of Samuel Wallace and Rebecca Anderson. Samuel and Rebecca had another son named Anderson who had four children. One of them was a son, named Samuel Anderson, who married Cecilia Durham and they became the parents of Catherine, Nettie and Samuel Alan Wallace. This made Catherine a first cousin once-removed to Big Foot.

When you discover a town where you believe your family was from contact the Chamber of Commerce and their local library and you too may find the solutions to overcome genealogical brickwalls similar to the brickwall of Big Foot. — Cheryl Owens, TX

Death Books

John Houser was the first police chief in Arnold, Westmoreland county, PA and a US Civil War veteran. I sent for his pension paperwork, hoping to find something about his wife and his other children. He was a widower when he got his pension. He listed all his children along with their birth dates and his wife Fanny Taylor, along with the date they married. He left no will and his death certificate listed a funeral home but no cemetery.

The funeral home was no longer in business. I checked with the local historical society to find which funeral director bought the business. The next funeral director was also no longer around, but the third to own the business knew where the records were from 1923. The son of the second funeral director still had all the records that were in the files when his father took over. Not only did he know that John Houser was buried in Union Cemetery in Arnold, PA but that his daughter Charlotte Krieger had reported her father's death. One mystery was solved.

Now I could go to the cemetery and find out about Fanny, his wife. All I knew was that her name was Fanny. Beyond that she was another mystery. John Houser had a headstone that listed his military service. He was buried on the plot with a couple named Patton. There was no headstone on the plot for a Fanny Houser. The cemetery office had no interment records for the old portion of the property. So I could not find if Fanny was buried in the plot near her husband or not.

I went back to the courthouse. Fanny left a will and property but not a trace of where she came from or where she was buried. I had all but given up on finding anything else on Fanny Houser.

While doing volunteer work at the Westmoreland County Courthouse I stumbled across a death book. It contained deaths for 1893 until 1906 when the record keeping was switched to New Castle Vital Records Office. Few people reported deaths before it was legally required. Those who did usually gave only as much as necessary.

I was looking up a surname that began with H when I happened across Frances Houser, daughter of Charlotte and Dennis Taylor born in Mercer, PA. She died of a heart attack and was buried in Union Cemetery. Her husband, John Houser, reported the death. The entry listed both a birth and death date for Fanny. I now have a starting point for her branch of the family. — Kim Policastro, PA, kpolicastr@aol.com

Migration Patterns

Several of my family members could not find one great-grandmother. We knew her husband came from Kentucky and we think we know which county. This grandfather was said to have been married seven times, and that figure appears to be right. Finding his second wife, my great-grandmother, was a two-year experience.

Just searching when we could let us go around the one county, then branching out. Even though we searched the county where she was found, we did not find her. A person outside the family found her in a funeral record book.

My hint would be to first stay in that state and then check all censuses for all those counties. If the person is not found, then start looking at migration patterns out of that state. In my case I knew that north to Ohio was the migration pattern for most. If you were to farm more than you could eat, you moved out of Kentucky, but if you were aged by 1866-90 you probably stayed in your home state. If you were young, you left for greener fields.

Always get yourself on a mailing list for the county you think that family member is listed in then rotate out of that county after a roll call is done because you might need to check another new county. Keep rotating and sign up for several counties at once then go for the migration patterns.

I figured out mine as I was finding cousins in Ohio and Illinois so I called the courthouse where I knew some of the family records were found and checked to see if I was right on migration. My own grandfather moved from Bath county, KY to the middle of Illinois because Illinois gave or leased land out until 1890 to get people to populate the state. — Roxanne Garrett, OR

The Eyes See What They Expect To See

Psychologists know that it is really the brain that determines what we will see. The eyes will be receptive to those images. My brain woke me up at two a.m. one morning recently to put together facts my eyes had seen

earlier but passed right over.

Here was my brickwall: Though I descend from the second marriage of Zenas Chapman (my second-great-grandfather), I have the Bible listing the births of children from his first marriage to Anna Randol. Their last child, Katherine was born in 1803, after they had moved to the town of Otsego, in Otsego county, NY. Zenas re-married in 1812, so Anna had died between 1803 and then. Since I haven't found Anna's death date and had never found her daughter Katherine, I presumed Anna died in childbirth and Katherine along with her. The probate of Zenas' will mentions children from both marriages and three girls with unfamiliar names who must have been his granddaughters: Emeline Bliss, wife of Seth; Lucy Fay, wife of John; and Mary Veber, wife of Israel. I never found a clue linking them to any of Zenas' children.

Two pages from the small leather-bound Bible in possession of Jean Chapman Snow. Left page is title page, right page has entries made into the Bible; two-thirds down, barely visible, is the record for Katherine who was born on 14 April 1803.

I put queries online, searching for the names. I found nothing, until the Otsego county website posted cemetery records. There were Emeline, Lucy and Mary and their husbands, birth and death dates for all in Exeter, a town close to Otsego. There still was no connection to Zenas.

Last summer I was in Cooperstown, NY, seat of the New York State Historical Association's library. A rented laptop held my genealogy files. I was determined to break through this brickwall.

Right away I found a pedigree file with Emeline, Lucy and Mary. Though their birth and death dates were what I had found online, I was terribly disappointed when I found their maiden name was Rider. Their mother was a Catherine Chapman born in Exeter, obviously from one of those other unrelated Chapman families in Otsego county. I'd come across quite a few of them. I still had no connection to Zenas.

But that night my brain woke me. It made me get up, turn on the laptop and pull out the copied pedigree and study it again.

Suddenly the brickwall crumbled. This time my eyes saw that their Catherine of Exeter and my Katherine of Otsego had the same birth date! Someone must have guessed at Catherine's birthplace, but she was definitely my Katherine. Zenas and Anna's daughter had lived. Emeline, Lucy and Mary were their granddaughters. — Jean Chapman Snow, CA, snowstar@earthlink.net

Explore All Possibilities

One of the things I have noticed about some researchers is that sometimes they are unwilling to look at variations in both names and dates. I have a lot of luck when I'm stuck by going to the IGI and downloading onto a disk all the persons of a certain name and just studying it for a while. This site includes variations on names so it will also give you an idea about other search variations to look for.

Additionally, when I look for a name I will search for individuals who have baptismal dates that are close to the known birth dates.

Sometimes it is forgotten that the information we have collected from our families may not mesh because we are looking at two different events, the birth and the baptism. This happened to me once. My second-great-grandfather Frederick Treichel was born on 2 November 1854 according to my grandmother. I looked but couldn't find anything initially but then some time later when I was more desperate I noticed a Frederick Treichel baptized on 6 November 1854. As it turned out, this was the correct individual but I was initially stuck because I insisted on 2 November 1854 and was not thinking about baptisms.

> 3. **Friedrich Alexander TREICHEL** - International Genealogical Index / GE
> Gender: M Christening: 13 Nov 1853 Stadt-Und-Landgemeinde, Kulm, Westpreussen, Preussen
> ▶4. **Friedrich TREICHEL** - International Genealogical Index / GE
> Gender: M Christening: 6 Nov 1854 Gross Leistenau, Westpreussen, Preussen
> 5. **Friedrich TREICHEL** - International Genealogical Index / GE
> Gender: M Christening: 12 Mar 1854 Rehden Graudenz, Westpreussen, Preussen
> 6. **Friedrich TREICHLER** - International Genealogical Index / GE
> Gender: M Birth: 11 Mar 1854 Dombrowken, Westpreussen, Preussen
> 7. **Friedrich Wilhelm TREICHEL** - International Genealogical Index / GE
> Gender: M Christening: 4 Nov 1857 Evangelisch-Lutherische, Strasburg, Westpreussen, Preussen

Treichel IGI listing.

Something else I have also learned from the IGI is that you shouldn't be discouraged because you cannot locate your individual under a birth search or even a marriage search.

One time the only way I located and found my family in Corsham, Wiltshire was because I looked for them in a parent search. Their marriage and their own baptisms as individuals, interestingly enough, were not given in the IGI. Initially I had overlooked that there are many avenues of getting at information.

You need to explore everything and not give up when it seems that the computer does not have the name in its database. — Judy McAuliffe, CA

*   *   *

Confirming Family Stories Through Old Newspapers

In our Lenox family Bible record there is mention made of William Lenox. He was a sheriff in St. Joseph, MO during the 1860s. A prisoner shot him during an arrest.

We contacted a researcher in Missouri who found an article in the *St. Joseph Gazette* dated 22 June 1869. William was indeed a Deputy Marshall. He died of exposure after being shot by the prisoner somewhere in Missouri. They also found an article on my grandfather, James Lenox, who was involved in a barroom brawl in St. Joseph on 24 January 1882. He almost died from the injuries. For the following week, the paper ran an update on his condition. — Gene Stevens, WA

Take Advantage Of Every Piece Of Information

We couldn't find any information about our grandfather, William Roy Stillman, so we decided to pursue information about his sister May. In our grandmother's Bible there was an article about May's death. She'd been hit and killed by a train. But the article, clipped from an unidentified newspaper, had no date or place in it. It did, however, have the name of the minister who conducted the funeral service and that proved to be a key piece of information.

My cousin Maryellen and I traveled to Nova Scotia, allegedly our grandfather's birthplace, to dig up our roots. Maryellen was looking at a microfilm when she came across the name of the minister from the article, the one who conducted our great-aunt's funeral. She discovered that the minister was at St. James Church in Kentville, NS. We got the microfilm for St. James Church. There was the death record. Now we had a date and discovered that May's name was really Hattie May. Our grandfather told Maryellen that his mother's name was Hattie. In fact, that's all he knew about his mother. Now we knew that his sister had been named after their mother. Maryellen checked on newspapers in Kentville and got the microfilm for those papers. We scrolled to the date of Hattie May's death and there was the article that matched the article from our grandmother's Bible. Now we had the source and date of the article.

With an actual death date for Hattie May, I went to the Vital Statistics Office in Halifax to request a copy of her death certificate. We were in for a surprise. The certificate showed that she had been born in the US and the informant had been her father. We knew that there had been connections to Massachusetts. Our grandfather moved there as a young boy, became a citizen, married and raised a family. So when I got home, I went to the Berkshire Athenaeum to check vital records. The death had occurred in 1916 and the article said she was 23 (the certificate said she was 22), so I looked at births 1890-95. There was Hattie May Stillman, born 1892, in Brockton, MA. But the big prize was her parents' names, Frank and Hattie (Foley) Stillman. After all these years, we finally have our great-grandmother's maiden name!

Take advantage of every piece of information. — Aggie Stillman, NY

Old Scrapbooks

I'm new at genealogy and have only been seriously researching for about three years. I work with a team, two from Ontario and one from Alberta. We have been searching for a lost aunt for two years. One evening after mulling over the information we had about this aunt, I had an idea. I know several people who have old scrapbooks that have been handed down by grandparents and great-grandparents.

I borrowed several of these books and photocopied every brittle page. Some of this material went back more than 100 years. I spent many delightful hours reading every bit and scrap. Not only did I find the elusive lady's obituary complete with her family but also I found lots of little snippets on many relatives that proved to be very helpful. I was amazed at the information you can find if you take the time to reread them. Our team has been lucky to find several old family diaries and daily journals that our ancestors recorded. They are a wealth of information. — Doris Jones, MI

Marry Me Times Three

I had been looking for my grandfather, Major Stephen Moore (Major was his first name, not a title), who had fought in the US Civil War for the Confederacy and not deserted.

The information appears to have become almost hidden, until one day there it was. I learned to look in places

Major Stephen Moore.

that I might not have looked by finding him in a book that had him with his second wife and not my grandmother. It also had the wrong number for the regiment.

So, look at extended families, of which there were many, due to childbirth deaths of women in the past. My third-great-grandmother was married three times, the last marriage was to my third-great-grandfather who went on to have two more marriages of his own. — Rosemarie Arredondo Kidd, VA, rebelrose@hamptonroads.com

Finding Adopted Ancestors

Because my grandmother, Edna Calderwood, had been adopted at six months of age, I had very little to go on. I thought she had told me that her birth name was O'Neil, but I couldn't be certain. I discovered that McNeil meant the son of O'Neil and therefore began to research for O'Neil and McNeil and various other spellings of the name. The only other information I had for my grandmother was that she was Catholic, poor shanty Irish and from Oakland, CA.

I learned RootsWeb.com had the records for St. Mary's Cemetery in Oakland online, where grandmother was buried. I calculated the dates and discovered a Mary McNeil was buried there in February 1897. This date was six months after my grandmother's birth. I sent a letter to the cemetery and they sent me information back on Mary McNeil and five other McNeils buried in the family plot. They also noted a church name, St. Francis in Oakland. I discovered that the church had been destroyed during the last San Francisco earthquake. A telephone call to the Diocese revealed that St. Mary's Immaculate Conception had in its holdings the records for St. Francis. The records from St. Francis had a wealth of information including baptismal records for my grandmother's siblings who were buried in St. Mary's cemetery.

I contacted the person who had posted the information for St. Mary's on RootsWeb and she volunteered to search Oakland early birth records at the Oakland Library. There she discovered my grandmother's original birth record. To my surprise, it had never been expunged. Now I knew for sure that Edna Mary Calderwood who was born on 10 September 1869 was in fact Mary Jane McNeil and the daughter of Mary Jane Hart and John McNeil.

Later in my research on the Hart side of the family, I noticed all records except one stated Illinois as the birthplace of my great-grandmother, Mary Jane Hart. The one record that was different was the birth record for her first child. It listed Kansas for mother's place of birth. After not finding Mary in the 1860 census for Illinois, I turned to Kansas. I found Mary Jane Hart born in Illinois, age one years old, daughter of Jane and Robert Hart.

Besides the age being correct, I also knew from both church and cemetery records that my grandmother's older brother had been named Robert Hart McNeil. It was a perfect match. — Linda Hahn, CA, lynatorcas@aol.com

The Quest For Lea And Bedford

In planning a trip to England, a large part of the anticipation involved finding the home where my father was born. I had the street address, which was listed in the town of "Lea & Bedford near Manchester". My atlas search achieved nothing but frustration. A variety of maps on the Internet couldn't reveal this elusive site.

During my map quest, I ran across a website called Virtual Manchester. Being a novice in the world of computer use and genealogy, I never

Above: Leigh.
Below: Bedford.

considered adventuring into the world of message boards. Deciding it was now or never, I quickly typed my request. The answering e-mail came from Brisbane, Australia! The information, and accompanying map attachment, quickly corrected two of my preconceived facts. I misspelled Lea and Leigh and Bedford were actually two neighboring communities, not one town.

We found my father's Leigh birthplace and were even invited in for tea. Further exploration allowed us to find the church in Salford where my grandparents' 1893 wedding had taken place. — Marion and Don Caldwell, WA, mardon@olympus.net

Willing To Share

My brother Dale and I had been doing family tree research since the late 1950s and we had gathered many names and information on all branches of paternal and maternal lines. We were not just looking backwards for our ancestors, but for all the cousins and other relatives.

We knew that in the 1870s a Margarett Standen had married a man by the name of Borton and moved to Iowa. They had at least 10 children, but we did not know where to begin looking.

In 1994, I decided to concentrate on finding this branch. We found a newspaper clipping of another relative that stated that survivors included Margarett Borton in Marshalltown, IA. I addressed a letter to the "Mayor or Manager or Librarian, Marshalltown, Iowa" explaining what I was looking for. I specifically asked for a photocopy of the local phone book. I enclosed some money and an envelope, stamped for return.

Three weeks later I received a reply from a library volunteer, containing copies of the 1880 federal census and the 1885 Iowa census for Marshall county, the 1935 directory and the Minerva township, Iowa phone book list. She also included a list of all the Bortons buried in the Clemons Cemetery in Minerva township. Twenty-two names and dates of birth and death. What a resource all that was! The extra effort of the library volunteer was certainly appreciated and I told her so in a return letter.

I then wrote a letter to a dozen Bortons on the telephone directory list for Minerva, saying who I was and what I was seeking. I offered to share my information on the Standens that stayed in Ohio, if they were a grandchild or one of the relatives of the individuals I was seeking. I also asked them, if they were not interested in genealogy, to pass my letter to a family member that may be.

In January 1995 I received my first letter from an Iowa relative, George Borton. In February I received a letter from Lucille Glenn. She said that a copy of my letter was sent to her nephew who forwarded it to her. She said that they have a family reunion

every year and she is the historian. She was a treasure trove of information. She sent me information on more than 700 descendants of the two that moved to Iowa. It was very detailed, with dates and places of birth, death, marriages and children. She continues to send me updates after each family reunion.

So there is always a way to solve problems in your research. Be patient, follow leads and maybe you will find a person that has the information that you need and is willing to share. Show appreciation if only in writing. In return be willing to share your information. — Jack C. Stranden, OH

Read Local Histories

I have puzzled over the identity of one of my ancestors, John Onorton of Sussex county, DE for quite some time. I could not find anything anywhere, except for a probate abstract that told me no more than I already knew. I researched the Swedish settlers to Delaware, hoping that perhaps something would come of that. I had to finally fall back on the premise that if all else fails, read the history of the area.

I discovered that this area of Delaware was part of Worcestor and Somerset counties of Maryland and went back and forth for a time. From here I consulted records for that area and began to pick up bits and pieces, such as his wife's will that revealed her remarriage after his death. I began searching every resource having to do with this area of Maryland and I quite fortunately came upon the break I needed.

In one reference I found "O'Norton's Lot", a land grant in Somerset county records issued to William O'Norton. I saw this grant in Worcestor county land records but it was called Norton's Lot there and I didn't make the connection. I didn't imagine Norton to be connected to an Irish name. From here I did a web search for O'Norton and discovered a website for the O'Noughton/ Naughton/O'Neachtain royal family of Ireland. From there I learned of the name change that occurred often to Norton or Onoughton. When I searched records on genealogy websites and the library, the O'Norton world opened up for me.

I found wills, court, land, marriage and immigration records and maps of the locations of land grants. Now I know that William O'Naught, (Onaughton/Onoughton/Onorton) arrived in Accomack Co., VA in 1655. He received his first land grant in 1664, his next in 1672. He was frequently in court for various reasons and apparently did not like or get along with his British neighbors. He married Katherine Newgent in Maryland in 1672 and received his first grant there in 1687.

It always pays to take the time to read local and area histories. — Diana Thornton, TX

Just Spend A Little Money...

For 34 years I have been collecting my family's information, mostly word of mouth from older relatives. It was not until my grandfather died that I finally charted the information and realized there was a lot more information I could have obtained from him had I been organized enough to know what questions to ask before he was gone.

From then on I became very serious in my search for relatives, but I didn't want to have to spend money to accomplish my goal. On my husband's side there was little information known and no one left to ask. We were only able to go back a couple generations.

After years of feeling frustrated with the search, my daughter decided to send for a birth certificate I had

Linda Pauwels learned the marriages, occupations, addresses and names of all four parents from the marriage certificate.

been reluctant to spend the money on. It cost $4. When we received that certificate, we found the mother's maiden name, whose spelling we had been unable to determine in years of searching. That encouraged us to send for the marriage certificate based on the obtained information which again gave us new information, a date and the parents' names taking us back a further generation for just $6.

Now that we knew that the family lived in the same city for many years, I had a census search done for $10. This search gave us birth months, immigration dates and country of origin. By having the immigration date from the census, I could guess at a naturalization date, so I sent for naturalization papers ($12). From those I was able to get birthplace and exact date of arrival and sometimes the name of the ship. Since I keep biographical sketches on each family member in addition to basic birth, marriage and death information, all these sources added to my biographies. I had finally learned that spending small amounts of money on an occasional basis could send my research into whole new areas. — Linda Pauwels, NH, cap@cyberportal.net

You Came To This Country When?

I ran into a completely unexpected brickwall while doing research at the Northeast Regional Branch of the NARA in Pittsfield, MA. I had made the trip with a wish list of both easy and difficult tasks to accomplish but decided it would be best to start with what I thought would be the easiest of projects. This was simply to make a copy of the passenger list which contained my maternal great-grandfather, Theodore Hampel Sr., who came to the US through New York City on the ship *Trave* from Germany on 23 August 1888.

I knew this because it came from my great-grandfather himself who had

Theodore Hampel, Sr., age 29 in 1896.

written this in his autobiography. The 33-page text had a wealth of information from his early childhood to the exact date and even time he set foot on American soil for the first time.

However after searching through the correct microfilm reel for the date in question, I could not find either my ancestor or the vessel he arrived on! Could my great-grandfather have forgotten the date of one of the most important events of his life? Then I remembered that he had written his life story in segments beginning when he was 64 years old. In fact the last entry that included his immigration to the US was written the same month he died. As this was nearly 50 years

after his journey, maybe he had been a little off on the date. With this in mind, I began checking the days just before and after 23 August 1888. Still I found nothing.

I then considered checking naturalization records which if found would settle the question of the exact arrival date. However Theodore Hampel Sr. had lived in several towns in eastern and western Massachusetts before settling in Cohoes, NY in 1897. Therefore this would prove to be a time-consuming and probably unsuccessful venture because as this was a regional Archives branch it would have an index to New England Naturalization Petitions which excluded New York.

I then referred to the multi-volume *Germans To America* which contained lists of passengers arriving at US ports from 1850-93 and which was even indexed by family name. Unfortunately only the volumes up to 1886 had been compiled at this time and my ancestor was not among those listed.

Willing to try anything, I then proceeded on the premise that the date of 23 August was correct but the year was wrong. Therefore I then searched through the microfilm reel containing the ships arriving through New York City on 23 August 1887 but again found nothing. At this point I was getting frustrated but decided to retrieve the microfilm reel containing the 23 August 1889 passenger lists.

I finally found the ship *Trave* with

my ancestor's name among its many passengers. To say I was overjoyed is an understatement.

In looking back I realize now that if I had been unwilling to be so flexible and creative in my search that day, I would not have been successful. — Edward John Dudek, Jr., NY

A Little "Bridie" Told Me

In 1997, Evangeline Wuertz passed away in St. George, UT. We always called her "Bridie". Her husband was Gottlieb "George" Wuertz. George had passed away 20 years before and they are buried in the St. George City Cemetery. Bridie and George were almost like another set of grandparents to us.

Bridie lived in a rest home and we always thought she and George had no children together. When Bridie died, a bishop of the Church of Jesus Christ of Latter-day Saints and his wife took care of the funeral arrangements for Bridie. A few months later they gave us several boxes of belongings, including photographs, genealogical research and military information. We had known Bridie had two sons from her first marriage and that one had died as a young boy, but we didn't know where the other son was. We had never known the boys. Bridie had never mentioned children to me and I had known her for about 30 years.

Bridie worked in the FHC in St. George for many years. In the boxes given to me were many letters and research they had done. As I was looking through George's box I found a pedigree that said he had a daughter, Stella Mae. He had never mentioned a daughter. I kept looking and found a letter that he wrote to Mr. Alva M. Haines in 1957 that mentions Stella Mae, who was Alva's first wife. He also states that Stella Mae had died in 1946 or 1947 and that there

were two sons but he didn't know their names. The letter asks Alva to send him the information so he could complete his family history book. I never found an answer to that letter. It occurred to me that there really may be some descendants of the Wuertz family and I wanted to find them.

George married Myrtle Jane McEwan in 1915. Their daughter Stella Mae was born in 1916. George went to serve in the military and apparently came back to find Myrtle had divorced him. Myrtle Jane married a Basil A. Seymour and Stella Mae took the surname of her stepfather. Meanwhile, George married Bridie.

Both George and Bridie wrote many letters of inquiry in their research and some of those letters say they were writing a history "to share with my descendants." They did a lot of work finding ancestors but hadn't found their children.

If I could find their descendants, I could give them this research of their ancestors. George and Bridie had information going back several generations to Norway and Germany in the 1800s and Virginia in the 1600s. There were also photographs and military certificates and even George's identification tag from the Army. These would be valuable to descendants.

When I found out about Stella Mae and Alva Haines, I took on the challenge of finding their two boys. I was able to find Stella Mae's death date by writing to somebody on the Internet who did a lookup for me in the California Death Index. I looked on the SSDI and found that Alva Haines died in 1994. I have not been able to get obituary information and Los Angeles county is so large I was stumped. George's 1957 letter to Alva indicated he couldn't find a death certificate for Stella Mae. That 1957 letter was my only clue about the sons and it had an old address.

I have been looking at online cemeteries to see if I might find where these people were buried. I've written letters to the Haineses that I found in Whittier, CA, but neither of them knew of Alva. I posted queries on several Internet genealogical message boards. I subscribed to genealogical mailing lists and periodically asked about possible descendants.

Not all newspapers for Los Angeles county are online or available on microfilms for inter-library loan. I got a list of possible newspapers for Whittier and Pico Rivera and I also got a list of cemeteries. I felt it would be better to travel there to search in person. I got maps and planned a trip but knew I couldn't take a trip for quite some time.

In June 2000, I got an e-mail message that California birth and death indexes were online. I went to the birth index and did a search for Haines born in Los Angeles county with the mother's surname and found Terry and Warren Haines, both in the right period. I was quite sure that Warren had to be one of the sons; his middle name was the same as Alva's. I finally found some possible names of Stella's sons!

Next I looked at several name and address files on the Internet. I found some entries for possible Terry Haineses and Warren Haineses and wrote down the ones in California. I looked up the addresses on a map and found a Warren Haines not too far from Los Angeles. I had a phone number to try and decided to try on a Sunday.

I was so anxious to find out if this Warren was the right Warren Haines. If it wasn't the right Warren Haines he might know other Haines named Warren. I said a quick prayer that if this was the right person I would be able to say the right things so he would understand me and wouldn't hang up on me, then I placed the phone call.

Warren answered the telephone and I introduced myself. I told him I was looking for the sons of Stella Mae Seymour and Alva Meredith Haines. He hesitantly said he was their son. It's probably a good thing he couldn't see me jumping up and down with joy and I was trying to keep a calm voice. I mentioned Stella's mother and he recognized her name and said he knew Myrtle Jane. He mentioned names and dates that I recognized from George's pedigree charts. This really was George's long-lost grandson. Warren confirmed that Terry is the other brother and gave me his mailing address and phone number.

Eventually I was able to visit them in person to tell them about the friend we knew. — Cheryl Whitelaw, UT, whitelawcs@suu.edu

Find Lost Cousins Via Alumni Lists

I have found several cousins via the alumni lists on the Internet.

Classmates.com.

For example, I looked in Carrollton High School, Carroll county, Ohio's list of classmates with the surnames that I have been looking for. I found a married name of Yeager and knew that she was married to a Yeager cousin. So I e-mailed her and gave her the information that I had on that family group. She e-mailed back with updates on her husband's family and her children.

On Classmates.com I found a Blazer listed from East Liverpool High School, Columbiana county in

Ohio. So I contacted him and told him of the Blazer relations that I knew used to live in that area. As it turned out, this Blazer from East Liverpool High was living in Florida. He contacted his aunt who was doing family research and who lived in Salem, Columbiana county, OH. We haven't linked but I am sure that after we keep working on it that we will connect.

There are various college, high school and even elementary school lists available. I have had most success in using the Classmates.com site because alumni are listed by maiden and married names and locations by country, state/province and city. I had to run through each letter for the first name; A Blazer; B Blazer, etc. It shows all the Adam, Amy, Angie Blazers with the school and location listed.

I feel this is a great, but little-used resource. I plan to look in other locations where I know relatives have lived. — Elizabeth Stookesberry, CA

Day-By-Day History

I wanted to find out what my granduncle did in WWI. When I started, he, his wife, his siblings and his nieces and nephews were dead. He did not have children. All I had was oral tradition that he served in WWI and an obituary that stated that he served in a medical battalion. A fire at the National Personnel Records Center had destroyed his service record and the center was unable to reconstruct any information on him.

On a hunch, I asked the Minnesota Historical Society whether Minnesota had any records of soldiers who served from Minnesota. The society sent me a copy of a state questionnaire that my granduncle had completed after WWI. It provided dates of enlistment and discharge and the name of his unit, a hospital train.

I then asked the Army Military History Institute at Carlisle Barracks, PA, for a history of his unit. It had none but it suggested that I contact the Old Military Records Section of the NARA. The NARA initially reported that the unit had not prepared a history. However, it sent me an extract from the multi-volume work, *The Medical Department Of The United States Army In The World War*, published in 1927, that provided information on what hospital trains did (took wounded from the front to hospitals and transferred wounded between hospitals).

I then went to the local Medical School Library to search the entire work from which the NARA had sent the extract. I found a footnote that stated written histories of hospital trains had been prepared and that they had been submitted to the Historical Division of the Surgeon General's Office.

The crew of Hospital Train #55 with Thomas Ross' granduncle.

I went back to the NARA and asked it if the files of the Historical Division of the Surgeon General's Office were still available. The NARA sent me a copy of the written history of his unit.

Its history consists of a narrative summary of its operations and an attachment listing the day-by-day movement of the train during its service in France. — Thomas E. Ross, CA, tross666@earthlink.net

The Precious Gift Of Family

I have been pursuing my second-great-grandparents from my father's side for many years. I first started genealogy looking for Daniel Lipe and Eliza Beaver in the 1970s. While we had a lot of information on their family of 10 children, we barely knew anything about them. Daniel was born in 1811 and Eliza in 1812, places unknown. According to 1850 and later censuses, they lived in North Carolina. We worked sideways, backwards and forwards, trying to get around this brickwall.

At one point in 1980, I was corresponding with an elderly woman who was their granddaughter but all she remembered was that her grandma was Pennsylvania Dutch and that they were buried in the Salisbury, North Carolina Cemetery. She put me in touch with another woman who was working on related lines and who had quite a bit of genealogy done on the Lipes, but it didn't tie in with what I had. In the past 20 years, I have collected a lot of names from Rowan county, NC. I just knew that they must all be related; I just didn't know how.

In 1999, my daughter was on the Internet and signed up on a mailing list for the Beaver family. She was sent a notice of a family reunion in Statesville, NC in the fall of 1999. Now I didn't know anyone from this family, but I knew that if I was going to find anything at all, I was going to have to go there, so I talked my sister into accompanying me to the Beaver Family Reunion. I spoke with one of the organizers named Buford Rimmer, who is married to a Beaver. He collected and organized the genealogy of many generations into a computer program. He mailed me a copy of his book, but upon searching it, I still found no mention of Daniel or Eliza. We arrived early at the church social hall in Statesville that day in October 1999 and began mingling with others who were there.

Buford approached us and said, "This is the only copy I have of this, but you are welcome to look to see if your ancestors are in it." He handed me a thick sheaf of papers on which was printed a descendants' list from their common ancestor. Anxiously, I thumbed through the descendants' chart and stopped quite unexpectedly on page nine where I found Daniel Lipe married to Eliza Beaver and the list of children's names, which were now so familiar to me. I couldn't believe I was actually seeing their names! I showed my sister — we didn't know whether to laugh or cry.

We photocopied the book at a local library. While there we were able to look at some local records which have never been microfilmed and were therefore only available to local patrons. When we got home and looked at the information we had, we realized that we had suddenly advanced the research six generations on the Beaver line! The other information we found at the library tied into previous research, which gave us six generations on the Lipe line. Both families came from Germany in the 1600s.

What a wonderful gift the Internet is — if we hadn't made that first contact, we'd never have known about the reunion and never received the precious gift of family. — SC

The Priceless Will

One of my second-great-grandmothers was Lucy Jane Miller who married William M. Reeves in Trumbull county, OH. They later settled in Ingham county and later Gratiot county, MI.

I was going through the census records on William and Lucy and found an Ira Miller with wife Sophia. The dates would be about right for them to be Lucy's parents and the two couples were always close together in the 1850, 1860 and 1870 censuses.

I was at the Library of Michigan and took a closer look at the Ohio indexes for 1840 and there were only two, one in Trumbull county where Lucy married William. Again this information was consistent with my previous information. I knew that it was likely they were in New York in 1830 and found only one Ira Miller listed and in Essex county. Still nothing was proven. A friend and I were combing the Oak Grove cemetery in St. Louis, MI for the headstone of William Reeves. We knew he was in the old section and, not even a stone's throw away, was the headstone of Sophia and Ira Miller. I was beginning to think these were, indeed, my third-great-grandparents. I then came home and ordered the probate index to Gratiot county, MI on film. There was Ira. I followed up by ordering the film with the full record. Ira's estate was limited to his land and was contested. The administrator was William M. Reeves and Lucy J. Reeves was among his heirs.

After all the debts were paid, the heirs received $31.50 from the sale of the property, but what I got through this will was priceless. — Christina Zahn, WI

Use Local Newspapers

My great-grandfather, Charles Young, came to the US in 1894 and married my great-grandmother in 1901. My grandfather, his only son, was born in 1903 and great-grandfather, Charles Young, died in 1905 of typhoid fever. Though my great-grandmother remarried, it was known that she never forgot Charles. When she died in 1964, she left mementos of her life with Charlie, including a prayer book, shreds of letters from the beginning of the century and a number of unmarked photos.

When I took up genealogy one of the first things I wanted to know was about Charlie's family in England, but I wasn't sure how I was going to find anything when the man was long dead. No one knew much about Charlie. He had died so early and my grandfather didn't know anything about his father, except what his mother told him. Looking through great-grandmother's things I found a book on Berkhamstead, England, and I thought that might be a clue to great-grandfather's origins. But of course, that was more than 85 years ago and I wondered how I could ever begin to look for anyone in England who would know anything about my great-grandfather.

Some of Charles Young's belongings, including the book on Berkhamstead (upper left).

I went to my local public library and asked if they could help me locate a present-day newspaper that would be circulated in Berkhamstead. The librarian gave me the address of the *Berkhamstead Gazette*. I then copied all the unlabeled portraits I owned and photocopied the shreds of addresses of my great-grandfather's sisters.

Next I sat down and composed a letter to the editor of the *Berkhamstead Gazette*. In the letter I told of the book of Berkhamstead written in the last century that I had in my possession and the portraits of persons that may have lived there. Lastly, I mentioned the names of my great-grandfather and my great-grandfather's sisters and asked that if anyone knew descendants of these sisters, to please contact me. I was very ecstatic to receive a letter not long after from a local historian who had written an updated version of the book I owned about Berkhamstead. He wanted to send over an updated version of this book. At least I accomplished something in my quest and it wasn't a complete waste of time. So I ordered the book and was delighted to see tucked in it a copy of my letter to the editor as it had appeared in the *Berkhamstead Gazette*.

About three months later, I opened the letterbox and there was a letter from a lady in Berkhamstead by the name of Olive Verney. I opened it and amidst the tears flowing from my eyes I read that she had opened her paper and had seen the name of her mother, Rose Young, and her aunts listed in the paper! She was so shocked she couldn't imagine that the source of this letter was from the US since the family story had always been that he went to Canada and was basically never heard from again.

Over the course of the next few months I sent her the portraits I had. They included pictures of her mother, her father, her sister and even Olive as a little girl! Unfortunately, Olive died two years ago, but we are going to bridge a 100-year gap in the Young family. That letter is still working! — Judy McAuliffe, CA

Were you a Young?

Sir, — My great-great-grandparents, Henry and Sarah Young, lived in Berkhamsted, in Kitsbury Road, in 1900, and were buried in Berkhamsted cemetery, in 1911 and 1901, respectively. Their only son, my great-grandfather, was Charles Frederick Young, who emigrated to the U.S. in 1894, and died a premature death of typhoid fever in 1905. Six Young sisters survived him in England.

My special request is to make contact with anyone knowing the descendants of these sisters, which are as follows: G and Dolly Smith, Berkhamsted; Ted and Rose Fisher, Hemel Hempstead; F. and Sissie Plested, Great Missenden Bucks; V. and Pollie Woods, Surrey; Alice and Harry Chapman, Middlesex; and Lily Young, Berkhamsted.

I would be pleased to share copies of 80 year old correspondence from this Young family in England in return for any information concerning them.

The letter to Berkhamstead Gazette.

*   *   *

Synthesize For Solutions

I have hit many brickwalls in the 10 years I have been tracing my family's history. The best tool I have found for solving brickwalls is to check my assumptions. I carefully review all the information I have on an individual or a family, checking all the copies of the original and compiled sources. I try to determine if I have made any assumptions when I originally read the sources. Once I assumed the name of a county was the name of a town in a record, sending me researching in an area hundreds of miles from the location where my ancestors actually lived. When I finally realized the error, I was back on track quickly.

If that does not solve the problem, I carefully consider whether the facts agree. If they don't, I try to consider as many alternatives as I can devise as to why there would be a discrepancy. I test all the alternatives, including those I had previously discarded based on contrary facts, best guesses and hunches. In one case, I discovered one ancestor who seems to have absent-mindedly neglected to file paperwork to divorce a first wife before acquiring a second, an alternative I had not originally considered. As a result, I had rejected a census record of a man in the right place with the right name, ethnic origin, profession and age, only because he was living with a much younger wife and several children. When I researched him, I found him to be my ancestor and I also found another genealogical researcher, from the second family, who has been a marvelous source of many family stories.

If the first two don't give me a lead, I write a "chapter" of my family history featuring the person or family. I try to synthesize all the information I have and weave it all together so that it makes as complete and logical a picture as possible. I send copies of this chapter to everyone who might have any information at all on the people, time period or locations discussed. This includes family members, historical society members and genealogists working on the same lines. I ask them all if the synopsis fits with what they know about the subject(s) of the chapter and the time and place in which it occurred.

Frequently I have found that I misunderstood what an informant said to me, that one or more people have information they had forgotten, or that several people have pieces that fit together to explain something none of us individually knew. While tracing a Walker ancestor, I found a chapter sent to several people brought out an oral tradition from a genealogist in another part of the family. When I repeated it to a great-aunt, she remembered a story about the children visiting their father's store in town every week. Finally, a piece of a pension application document clicked into place. The father had been injured so badly in the Civil War, he had to operate a store in town, while the wife ran the farm. A mystery was solved as to why a mother-in-law left her farm to a daughter-in-law rather than to her only living son.

While checking my assumptions has not helped me break through every brickwall I have encountered, it has eventually helped me around most of them. — Terry Terrell, CO

The Search For John Gallagher

I wanted to find out about my paternal grandfather, John Lawrence Gallagher. My father barely knew him as he died when my father was very young. We knew very little and we didn't have the most basic vital records. We knew he was born in County Sligo, Ireland and immigrated to the US as a young man. He had two siblings who also came to the US. He

married and had seven children. The first two children were born in Passaic, NJ. This made us think that the wedding probably took place there also. That is where John's brother, Dennis, lived as well.

The family story was that he was working as a night watchman at the construction site where he had a fatal accident. A cousin told me that he died on 30 or 31 October 1925. He fell into a ditch and died the same night. His widow died on the anniversary of his death in 1953. We thought that the story of his death should have been in the local newspapers but we found nothing.

Meanwhile, we found his entire naturalization file. Included in those documents were the ship's name he came to the US on and the date. The ship was the *Lusitainia* and the year was 1908. The name of his home town in Ireland was apparently written phonetically and could not be found in any reference book or gazetteer. The most experienced volunteers in the FHL had to admit that they were stumped. Various records have his date of birth as anywhere from 1882 to 1888; but always on July 3.

The ship's name and date led to the ship's manifest in the FHL. This looked like a significant break. He listed a relative in Ireland as Francis Gallagher. John's intended destination was his brother's home in Passaic, NJ. This led to the 1910 US census and the listing of both brothers and Dennis' family. A total of 15 people lived in that house on that day. Since ages were listed, it was apparent that Dennis was John's older brother. With 16 years difference in age, I thought they might be half-brothers.

Even with all this new information, his age, birthplace, parents and the circumstances of his death remained a mystery. Draft cards, New Jersey and US censuses, naturalization records, his children's birth records and ship manifests had not given us a break in Ireland. All the records thus far were made during his life in the US. As a result, there was no hint of how he died.

While in the FHL, I quizzed every volunteer I could find. One man asked about the name on the headstone. I told him it only says "Gallagher". He told me to look for the cemetery records in the FHL. Checking under Fort Lee, NJ I found there were cemetery records. Several members of the family who were buried in the cemetery were listed. Finally John Gallagher was listed.

John Gallagher.

The date of death we were all expecting to find, 31 October 1925, was not there. John died on 31 October 1924 and was buried on 4 November 1924.

That explains why there was no newspaper story in 1925. I called my cousin and told her that we had a problem because the cemetery said they buried John in 1924, not 1925. She quipped, "I hope he was dead."

I returned to New Jersey to find the 1924 newspapers. I found the story; it said that he was a night watchman who fell 25 feet into a utility trench. He fractured his skull and died instantly. Three days later, there was another front-page story dealing with his burial and background. This story reported that he was married in St. Nicholas Church in Passaic, NJ.

A kind church secretary said that she would need a few days to check the records but was sure that she could find something. She called back to report that she found a record of a John Gallagher's wedding on 23 June 1910. He married a woman named Mary McHugh. I told her that was probably the same couple. His address was the same as the one given as his brother's address a few weeks earlier and in the 1910 census. His birthplace was given as Gurwain, County Sligo, which appears to be the phonetic spelling of Gurteen.

His parents are listed as Francis and Margaret McKenna Gallagher. John did not list a complete date of birth. The only entry is 3 July.

The church also has Dennis Gallagher's marriage record. Dennis reported that his parents were Francis and Bridget Harkin Gallagher. Dennis and John had the same father, but different mothers. They were half brothers after all.

With his parents, her parents and a place in Ireland to look we finally have a toehold in Ireland. This break resulted in locating them in the 1901 Irish census and *Griffith's Valuation.* — Jim Gallagher, AR, jimg20@earthlink.net

Cousin Dieter

About 20 years ago, when we were both working, we did considerable research on George's family with the assistance of a nephew who had Internet access. He was able to do a lot of the research for us. We had great success with this research and were able to find family in the US and in Germany.

Until recently, we did not do any research on June's family. We had no data, except for the fact that her paternal grandfather followed his bride-to-be to Buffalo, NY to marry her. Then we got a letter from a cousin mentioning the town in Germany where the grandfather was supposed have to emigrated from and the fact that he was of Huguenot ancestry. We wrote a letter (in English) to one of the regional archives in Germany for information. The response was in German, which required us to find someone who could translate the letter. We found a German-born Lutheran pastor who translated the letter for us.

Karoline and Charles Legler.

The letter stated that they did not have the personnel to do research for us but recommended a former archives worker who may do the work for us. We wrote to this lady and she said that she could not find any data of the people we were looking for but did find information on my family — some of which was new to us.

At some point I had gone to the FamilySearch.org website and typed in the names of June's grandparents and got nothing. A genealogy column in the *Columbus Dispatch* said that when going into FamilySearch.org, not to tell them too much, so that more hits will be returned. So, we went back to the website again and typed in grandfather's information, Charles William Legler, and got nothing. Then when we typed in grandmother's (Karoline Schneider) and the whole world opened up — with the grandmother, her parents and her six siblings, two of which we knew about.

I sent a copy of this report to my researcher in Germany and she found the family. She sent a copy to us of the grandmother's birth record from the parish record in the archives. She said that, for a fee (and not an exorbitant one at that) she would look further. So soon after we received a whole packet of family records, all the way back to grandmother's great-grandparents. She sent not only the copies of the records, but even gave us a shortened version of the records in English!

In the packet was a letter from the researcher's husband who evidently did all the translating of our letters back and forth. In this letter he told us that he found a connection of his family with June's family with an ancestor in common, a seventh-great-grandfather. This man said, "Please call me Dieter, dear cousin!" — George and June Dimmig, OH, autumnwheat@dragonbbs.com

Bless Those Volunteers!

My husband was interested in his Simms family and had acquired several books about them. His mother, Thelma, somewhat petulantly, wondered why he didn't look into her side of the family. I decided to try to uncover some of her ancestry as a gift to her. She was 85 and had wonderful recollections of dates and places. Her mother's side seemed to fall in line with the help of two other researchers, but her father's line was not as easy.

Ten years ago, I knew very little about my mother-in-law's paternal side. My mother-in-law told me that her father was William Lemon Godfrey, who was born in 1865. She also knew that her Uncle Joe died young from tuberculosis and there were three spinster aunts: Mabel, Mamie and Lydie. She also said there was an uncle "out west" and an Aunt Mary who had married a man named Wright, but that she had never known them. Her grandmother and the three aunts lived together in Washington, DC. Her grandmother died when she was 10 and might have been named Mary.

I found where a Joseph Godfrey, at age 29, had died of Tubercular Enteritis and was buried at Rock Creek Cemetery. I was successful in obtaining Joseph's death certificate but it did not list his parents, only DC as birthplace of father and Hagerstown, MD as birthplace of his mother. Letters to the funeral home and the cemetery were never answered. The service had been performed by the Masons and I made contact with them. He was initiated in August, died in September and raised in October 1898. I was assured that I would receive a copy of his application to their organization, but that never came through.

I also had a copy of William's DC National Guard discharge paper and wrote for that record, again to no avail. How could I find out William's parents' names?

The 1860 federal census for Washington DC's Georgetown, listed a Joseph Godfrey, 26, bricklayer, born in DC, married within one year. Also in the household was Mary, 23, born in DC; Martha, 50, born in DC; and Virginia, 28, born in DC. Could Martha have been his mother, Virginia his sister, Mary his wife (with a mistaken birthplace) and no children yet born?

The 1870 census for Georgetown, DC listed Joseph and Mary with children: Thomas, Lydda, William, George and Mary. Mabel, Mamie and Joseph, Jr. were born after 1870. Knowing William's birth date led me to believe I had found his parents, but I still didn't know his mother's maiden name.

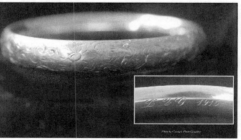

The bracelet that solved the brickwall. Insert shows L Q G and 1915.

In the summer of 1999, Thelma showed me a bracelet that had been her aunt's. She explained that her aunt Lydie willed it to her sister-in-law, Nina Godfrey, who in turn willed it to her, as the only natural female Godfrey descendant. Inside the bracelet were the initials "L Q G" and a date 1915. I realized that L was for Lydie and G was for Godfrey. But what did the Q represent? A distant cousin of my husband's suggested Mary's maiden name was possibly Lekron as her sister's middle name was Lekron. I found an IGI record for Mary Eliza

Leckron born 1834 in Hagerstown, MD to Daniel H. Leckron and Eliza. Was this my Mary?

A few days later, at the Washington County, Maryland website, a volunteer offered to do lookups in a couple of her books. (Bless all lookup volunteers!) I e-mailed her with a request to look for Leckron with various spellings. What a goldmine she shared with me! Daniel H. Leckron's wife was Eliza Quantrill. Daniel's father Simon Leckron had married Sarah Lyday. Chills ran through my body.

Within a matter of days I had opened up a puzzling part of my children's ancestry: their second-great-grandmother and any number of family members. I had discovered the initials on the bracelet stood for Lyday Quantrill Godfrey. I made contact with others who are researching the Lydays and Quantrills. And most important of all, there was the pleasure it gave to my beloved mother-in-law who died just one month later, just five days before her 96th birthday. — Tosca K. Simms, VA, tkwhsimms@hovac.com

Lovers' Quarrels

My great-grandfather came to the US in the 1870s and married another immigrant in Brooklyn in 1879. I had already gathered a lot of information in the US and moved toward the next step of identifying the town of birth in Europe. The marriage certificate said Kalme, Germany. The family said both he and his wife spoke German. No member of the family knew any further information. European church records for towns similar in sound were checked without success.

Interviewing my uncles and aunts (now in their late 80s and 90s) brought forth memories of their grandparents, but no knowledge or family papers to show place of birth for my great-grandfather. Apparently, they did not recall times when their grandparents talked about their European families or where they grew up. While talking to my uncle, on a whim, I inquired if he could recall what they argued about. To my surprise, he recalled that they argued about whose town was better!

Since my great-grandmother's town was listed as Carnikau, Germany on the marriage certificate, I began to search towns within 20 miles as I figured there would be no point in that type of argument if they were not very familiar with each other's birthplace. One nearby town fit perfectly!

Carnikau is in Posen, which was Prussian at that time. The nearby village of Chodziez, Posen was known as Kolmar during the Prussian period. Church records from Chodziez were obtained and there he was! — M. Tuck, NY, tuck3@mail2world.com

Shots In The Darkness Of Cyberspace

I was tracing my grandfather and his family through the census records. I did this by estimating where they may be. Each census record I saw sent me back to another state. I used the census database on Ancestry.com and when I found the surname it gave me a county to look in. I then went to RootsWeb.com and asked on the page if someone had the record. Someone always answered and gave me what the census record said, and if it was online someone usually gave me a link. I had traced the family back to the 1800s this way, when I couldn't do any more.

I wanted to figure out when a second-great-grandfather had come to a county. I asked if anyone in the county had a record of his marriage. I was in luck, someone e-mailed his marriage date from a county book on marriages. I was then able to write to the county to get the record.

I then couldn't figure out where he

was born. So I proceeded to look at more recent census records after he died and his children said he came from North Carolina. I was lucky that the later census records recorded their parents' birthplace. — Catherine Livezey, CA

Missing In Action

My surname is Lignowski, a rare name even in Poland. The objective of my research is to unite all the Lignowski lines into a common lineage. A number of years ago I began research on a family of Lignowskis from the Bronx, NY. It began when I found the enlistment record of Teodor Lignowski on the Polish Genealogical Society of America website. Before the US became officially involved in WWI, a number of Polish societies assembled approximately 25,000 volunteers who formed the Polish Army in France, or the Blue Army. I became quite interested in the story of this erstwhile soldier.

From the information on the application, he did not seem like the soldier type; he was five feet, two inches and weighed only 120 pounds. He would have probably blown over in a stiff breeze. He listed his next of kin as an aunt who had a different surname.

I had a number of questions: Were his parents dead? Did he go to fight? It seemed unlikely that Teodor made it overseas, since he enlisted on 31 July 1918, was sworn in a few days later and WWI ended in November of that same year, a mere three months after Teodor joined the Army. If he did see the war, did he make it back?

In an online index I found a naturalization record in Westchester county, NY for a Marion Lignowski, whose home was the same as Teodor's. Sending away for Teodor's birth certificate confirmed my theory that this was his father and it also gave me the name of his mother (Kathi). It also revealed he had brothers and sisters. I located information on some of these siblings from Social Security records and then from birth and death certificates. Looking up Lignowskis in New York in the 1920 census also gave me some more answers. I found three of Teodor's brothers and sisters living with their eldest sibling and her husband and children and one living in an orphanage. I found Teodor living in an apartment in Manhattan with a friend. So he had survived the war and his parents had died sometime between 1910 (they had their youngest child Stanley that year) and 1920. At this point I started trying to contact other Lignowskis. I found descendants of the family on Long Island, but they had little information about the family. A divorce had sundered the family and they had cut ties. Similar circumstances existed with another descendant in Washington state.

St. Raymond's cemetery record for the three Lignowskis buried there; Kathi, Marion and Teodor.

The last individual I contacted was Stanley's son who was now living in Florida. At first he was hesitant, brushing me off and asking me not to call again, but minutes later he called me back and explained his reluctance. He then allowed me to ask him questions. He said he thought that Teodor had gone to Europe and came back, but that Teodor drowned in New York City's East River sometime during the 1930s or 1940s

How could I find out when Teodor had died with such a range of years, especially in such a large city as New York? I had hit a brickwall.

One day I got an e-mail from Stanley's son stating that he was going to talk to his sister who still lived in New York. She was the custodian of all the family records. Among other things, he told me that his sister

The Lignowski gravestone, showing Kathi, Marian and Teodor's names.

pened to the soldier, now no longer missing in action. — Stephen Lignowski, NJ, pakrat98@aol.com

A Lovely Family Story

There was a lovely family story that involved my third-great-grand-parents, Elisha and Martha Inman Chastain.

The story goes that in late October 1793, a wagon train left South Carolina for Tennessee to settle in unexplored territory. They rose as early as two a.m. to start their long cold day's ride to go as far as they could before night fell. The wagon train arrived in middle Tennessee in November. Elisha Chastain of South Carolina, born 1778, was going to ride a few miles with the wagon train to say goodbye to his Tennessee-bound girlfriend Martha Inman. This was what he told his parents but the further he rode, the more he knew he could never say goodbye to Martha.

So Elisha joined the wagon train bound for Tennessee. He was later granted many acres of land at what is now Shop Springs in Wilson county, TN. He operated a wood shop and cotton gin. Together Elisha and Martha had 16 children and his oldest son John helped in the wood shop making furniture and caskets.

I had relatives who lived in Wilson county and they told me Martha Inman had been born in 1779. Then I heard from a researcher of this same family who gave me the names of 16 children. The youngest child would have been born when Martha was 63 years of age. Not only that but she would have waited until she was 37 to have her first child. There was something wrong.

I was returning to Washington, DC from a trip home to Texas with another lady and we stopped at a distant cousin's house in Lebanon, Wilson county, TN. This cousin took us to see

remembered that the parents (Marion and Kathi) were buried in St. Raymond's Cemetery in the Bronx. I called St. Raymond's immediately. They told me that for records going back that far I'd have to send my question by mail (their computerized records only went back to the early 1980s). I could also only give them a range of three years or so. I asked Stanley's son to pin down the date any closer and he said that he thought he remembered that his father had been placed in the orphanage about 1913. I sent away to St. Raymond's using the information I had and that they had died between 1912 and 1914.

A few weeks went by and I finally got an answer. In the same plot were buried Kathi (died 1912), Marion (died 1917) and Theodore (died 1926). Later I was able to make a trip to the cemetery and photograph the gravestone. I finally found out what hap-

the gravesite of Elisha Chastain and Martha Inman Chastain. We waded through weeds onto the property of the current owners. There in the grass was a stone propped against a tree and another laying on the ground. I found my answer. The stones read: "Elisha Chastain — born 1 August 1778; died 1 March 1851" and "Martha Chastain — born 4 October 1799; died 1 January 1848". She was 21 years younger than Elisha.

Martha Inman Chastain was born in 1799 not 1779. She wasn't even born when the wagon train left South Carolina. Well, the mystery of her age was solved and she did have 16 children but another problem took the other's place. If Elisha left South Carolina at age 15 with a wagon train and continued on to Tennessee in 1793, who was the girl he didn't want to say goodbye to? Did they marry? Did they have children?

None of the relatives that still lived in Wilson county, TN ever heard of another woman in Elisha's life and they were a close family.

I have thought that perhaps the wagon train was attacked and the girl was killed or perhaps they did marry even though they were so young and perhaps the girl died in childbirth. Who knows? So I solved the brickwall of how many children the couple had and Martha's age. However, I am now trying to solve the brickwall about this family legend. — (Mrs.) Loyce Coolidge, AR, loycec@aol.com

Baby Books

We had grasped at many straws in trying to discover the name of my great-grandmother. The search for details of my grandmother's birth and marriage had been difficult. When they were finally resolved, they had offered no clues to her parentage except for her father's name, which we already knew.

One day I was tidying papers and photos from my research; I wanted to put all my family history collection together in a safe place. I had another look through my baby book; I discovered that my mother had written the name we sought in it. My great-grandmother's name was Jeanette Hutton.

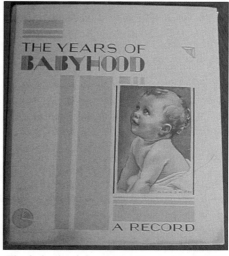

The baby book began in December 1937.

We have since been in contact with a branch of that family who provided some excellent research for our records. — Annabel Taylor, SK

Treasures In The Attic

Finding an old family photo in that dusty attic brings excitement and anticipation to a genealogist's heart. But turning over that picture and finding no names or dates written on the back will plunge you into despair. You realize you will probably never find any information or at best only find when a picture was taken by the clothes and hairstyles of the subject.

I experienced this problem recently. I turned a recently found photo over and the only information I had was the photo company, the town and state where the company had been located. This struck an idea. Could this little information lead me to the information I desired? I knew the identity of the photo but nothing else. I took the city and state to mean that possibly the subject had lived there for a time and inquired into the libraries, newspapers and churches for any information regarding this man.

After writing many letters and a few checks for research, I was able to find reliable information as to where he lived, worked, the property he owned and that he had been married in this city. The result of this search led me to other avenues, new family members and has found a new branch to our family tree.

The upside is not to look at an unmarked photo as a dead end but as a possibility of new and exciting genealogical search. Remember to look for any company names, cities, states or dates that may lead you to family information. — GiGi Simons, IL, gigibob450@aol.com

Know Some History

A good brickwall tip is to try talking to everyone in the family to gather every possible clue. My parents divorced when I was a child and I hadn't been in touch with my aunt in nearly eight years. But I got her e-mail address from my dad. It turns out she had several dates I needed and even more fascinating, she recalls stories that her father told her. I wanted to make sure I wrote every one down, as my paternal grandfather died before I was born.

In one story, my Chicago-born grandfather talked about visiting relatives in Germany at the age of seven. They had a huge house that had a ballroom. After the war the house was in the British sector of Germany and when the British soldiers arrived, they gave the family 20 minutes to leave as they were taking the house for officers' use. Knowing some history, this sounded to me like it was Berlin. After further research with this clue I found out it was! — Lisa Laurent-Michel, UK, lm-.lm@ntlworld.com

Originals, When Read, Produce Golden Information

Many years ago, I received a typed, transcribed diary written by my second-great-grandfather as he traveled the Oregon Trail to Multnomah, OR. I did not have a copy of the original diary and did not even know if it existed. My quest in learning more about this ancestor began by searching for his birth information — everywhere I searched produced brickwalls.

Throughout my search I took the transcribed name William Willie Cooke to be his name and never questioned it. I knew he had originally lived in North Carolina before going west but did not know where. Did you know that North Carolina has more counties that any state in the union? Through the FHL I found his second marriage dates — yes, two different ones two days apart.

One day I was searching North Carolina books and found a listing for a William W. Cooke in an index published by the state of North Carolina archives. Gold! Soon I visited the archives and held in my hand the original diary. I did not read it carefully because after all it had been transcribed.

Two years later, I looked at a letter written by William as I was preserving it in an archival folder. Much to my surprise, I observed, in very clear handwriting, his name: William Willis Cooke. No wonder I had not found any more information on him — I didn't have his correct name. I had taken the diary transcriber's word and had not checked it. I found the gold mine when I also discovered that the letter was addressed to his parents, Mr. and Mrs. Howel[l] Cooke in Franklinton, NC. With another generation and a location to search I was rich in new information and convinced that from this day forward I would do my own transcribing. — Caryn Johnson, VA

Brides Index

On 8 November 1894 my maternal grandparents, John and Mary Lannon, either descended from a spaceship on West 47th Street in New York City or emerged from underground caves. One thing is for certain, there was no sign of them before that date when my great-uncle, Hugh Lannon, died from acute pneumonia at 424 West 47th Street in New York City.

I first had a verifiable sighting of my maternal grandparents in the 1900 federal census for New York. Before that date I had been led on a chase through Vermont, where family legend said the family originated. Like many new researchers, I had figured to skip a few steps in my research by hopscotching from New York, where my generation and the two before had lived, right to Vermont.

In this case family legend attested that John Lannon, a cooper and fourth-generation Yankee, had married Mary Sherry, also a Yankee. This legend both obstructed and advanced my research.

When I couldn't find the family in the 1880 federal census for Vermont, I searched the 1900 Soundex for both Vermont and New York. In 1900, the population of New York City had reached such a proportion that common names were sectioned by country of origin in the Soundex. Among the US-born there were a considerable number of John Lannons living in New York City in 1900, but none had both a wife named Mary and sons named Louis, Charles, Hiram and Albert. The next group of John

Lannons hailed from Ireland. I began to think that he might have been filed incorrectly. I started through this list and I found him living on West 96th Street. According to the census the oldest son, Louis, was born in Vermont. Before leaving New York, however, I checked vital records in the Municipal Archives. I found death certificates for my great-grandparents, marriage records for my grandparents and two siblings, and the death certificate for my great-uncle — which was the earliest record I could find for the family.

Ellen Paul's great-grandfather's death certificate.

Needless to say, the information on all those vital records conflicted. My grandmother's marriage certificate said she was born in Rutland, VT, one great-aunt's marriage certificate said she was born in Brandon, VT and a second said Yonkers, NY. My great-uncle's death certificate gave Buffalo, NY as the place of birth. My great-grandfather's death certificate listed "United States" as his place of birth and my great-grandmother's listed "Ireland". New York City is fortunate in that a Police census exists for the borough of Manhattan, which somewhat replaces the destroyed 1890 federal census for those lucky enough to have a relation listed there. However, there is no finding aid and it is accessible only by address of the listee. I searched by the two addresses I had to no avail.

Since Vermont's vital records begin in 1790, I decided to write for a marriage record for a John Lannon marrying a Mary Sherry circa 1870. When that failed I wrote for a birth record for an Eleanor Lannon, my grandmother, circa 1880 and when that failed I drove to Montpelier and began searching the roomful of index cards. It didn't take long to exhaust all the Lannons and come up empty. Crestfallen, I was actually leaving the building when I decided it couldn't hurt to search under the Brides Index for marriages. There I found a Mary E. Sherry marrying a Michael Landregon in the town of Brandon, county of Rutland, on 13 May 1867. I would have bypassed it except for the notation of the groom's occupation, which stated that he was a cooper, the one true part of the family legend.

The 1870 census for the town of Brandon later confirmed that these were, indeed, my great-grandparents because it listed the names of my two-great-aunts as their oldest children. — Ellen Paul, CT, paul868@rcn.com

Sibling Information

I had a lot of information about my second-great-grandmother, but her mother's maiden name was unknown to me. Nothing I could find in the local records (New York, 1800s) left a clue.

One day I was looking at some US Civil War records for someone else and found the registration information for my second-great-grandmother's brother. Sure enough, his mother's maiden name was there. While it was a rather common name, I did by chance come across some of her family history through a mailing list for her home state. If you know anything about the siblings check them thoroughly. — Betty Wilson, NY

Irish Brickwalls

In 1999, my sister and I went to Ireland with very little information about our family. We were hoping to find more information about our William Laverty and his parents, John Laverty and Rachel McFall. We understood he came from the village of Castleagree, which we could never find on a map, but learned it is actually the townland of Castlenagree, just east of Bushmills.

We checked some cemeteries in the area and found a number of Laverty names, but none fit. We learned later my family were Catholics, so we had gone to the wrong churches!

Islandoo, the Laverty family home in the townland of Castlenagree.

We went to the Records Office in Belfast, certain we would find census records, but didn't find anything that applied as we were not aware of the Names Index there.

We found a Laverty family in Portballintrae by checking the phone book and knocking on their door. They were quite excited about our quest and tried to be helpful.

I sent a letter to the editor of a newspaper in Ballymoney and was delighted to receive several e-mails and letters from people who knew my grandfather, from which I got some great information — names, dates, burial places and the name of grandfather's second wife. Recently I

Rachel (McFall) Laverty's family home.

received pictures of my grandfather's house and grandmother's family home.

Everyone was so helpful and we really appreciate it. I wish I had written to the paper before we made our trip as we would like to have met these kind people and could have found the appropriate cemetery stones. As we get older, our background means more to us. — Amy Work, ON, awork@sympatico.ca

Verify Online Census Records

Mary Cobb was born in Camden, ME to Thomas and Lucy Cobb. No records have been found to provide me with a birth date. Her marriage to James Howlett is documented in Lynn, Essex, ME on 25 April 1824. The Howletts are later found in the censuses of 1830, 1840 and 1850. In 1860, I found James Howlett in the federal census of 1860 in Vacaville township, Solano county, CA. This information coincided with her son, Alfred Cobb Howlett's obituary, which stated that Alfred and his father migrated west to California in 1852.

What happened to Mary? Had she died in Maine after Alfred's sister Lucy was born? Were they separated by the trek west? I hired a genealogist to search Maine records and she found nothing to indicate Mary had died in Maine. She did find two deeds of trust with James and Mary Howlett as signers.

I had found James in the 1860 census online and I decided to order an actual photocopy of the census.

Always excited to get genealogy mail I ripped open the envelope with excitement. My jubilance came when right after James' name was Mary Howlett. Somehow she was never transcribed to the online census records.

Use online census records as a beginning with actual photocopies as evidence. — Caryn Johnson, VA

Inspiration And Luck

For a number of years, I have been researching the family of my maternal grandfather, John William Howard, born 1857 in Southport, Lancashire and who died in 1934 in Edmonton, AB. I knew something of his life from several documents: his birth registration, his marriage registration, his obituary and a brief history written by a now-deceased cousin of mine.

Although I knew a great deal about John William Howard, his siblings were elusive and I could find almost nothing about them. From John William's birth registration, I had determined that his father was Henry Howard and his mother Elizabeth Bolton. John William's obituary mentioned two surviving brothers, Herbert and George of Manchester, but were these the only siblings? What were their birth dates? I could not find answers to these questions.

The obvious place to look was in the census and I began with the 1881 British census and national index, a digital copy of which I purchased from the FHL. Try as I might with the Resource File Viewer, I could not locate a family headed by Henry and Elizabeth Howard (or Howarth or any of the usual alternate spellings) in England. I did locate their son John William and his family.

Since I could not locate the family in the 1881 census, I decided to look at the 1861 census. Here I was successful and I located the Henry and Elizabeth

Howard family that comprised three children including the eldest, John William, but included neither a Herbert nor a George. This progress spurred me to look again at the 1881 census but still to no avail.

I tried a new approach. From the 1861 census, I knew Elizabeth's approximate year of birth (1836) and that she had been born in Southport. I decided to look for all the Elizabeths born in Southport who were around 45 years old in 1881 and still living in Lancashire. If she had remarried, she might show up in a search under a new surname.

The Resource File Viewer came up with nine Elizabeths (including Elisabeths and Bettys) born in Southport in the years 1834-38. One was Elisabeth Havard (age 45) living with her husband, Henry Havard, and a family of seven, the two youngest named George and Herbert. This was surely my grandfather's family and somehow the name had been recorded mistakenly as Havard, either by the census taker or by the person who compiled the index. A check of the birth records in the Civil Registration indexes confirmed that the children were indeed Howards, not Havards.

A bit of inspiration plus a generous portion of luck helped me to find seven more members of my grandfather's family. — Donald A. Faulkner, BC

Uncovering The Truth

My brickwall had a big sign on it that read: "Who was my great-grandfather, the Rev. James DeBuchananne?"

According to his 1896 obituary, he was a descendant of French royalty and buried at sea in a silver casket with the inscription "James De-Buchananne, D'Orleans, de Bourbon, LDP". Other claims in the obituary reported his service in the US Civil War was a secret duty with General Morgan and that he accompanied the General on all his raids. Additionally, he was said to be a Congregational minister, serving the Belknap Congregational Church in Dover, NH for 20 years, but ejected from the ministry as a heretic. When he died he was a Spiritualist lecturer. He also freely admitted to using an assumed name, "to thwart the emissaries who had been sent to assassinate him." The obituary gave his date of birth as 4 June 1838 in Haverhill, MA.

Several attempts had been made by family members to validate the family history of royal descent and James' Civil War service. No one had ever been able to learn any more about this man, other than what the newspapers reported at the time of his death. My brother challenged me, a novice researcher, to prove we were of royal descent.

I searched the Haverhill, MA birth records and found no references to any DeBuchananne individuals. Then I decided to try to learn more about the Belknap Congregational Church, only to discover the congregation had been disbanded. I contacted the American Congregational Association Library in Boston. They confirmed that Rev. DeBuchananne had served at the Dover congregation for four years, not 20 as the obituary claimed. The next step was to contact the New Hampshire State Library, asking if any records existed for the Belknap Church. The librarian provided me with copies of minutes of the Belknap Society containing references to my great-grandfather, taken from a book, and referred me to the book's author. The author, who had transcribed the church records, provided a new item of information — DeBuchananne was married while in Dover. No one in the family had known he had a first wife!

I searched Dover newspapers and found an article noting the divorce petition of DeBuchananne had been denied. I then requested the divorce records from the courthouse. The divorce records revealed the date and place of the first marriage. I requested a copy of the original marriage record and intention from Massachusetts for James DeBuchananne and Caroline Woodwell on 3 January 1876. He gave his age as 22 and she was 38. James' birthplace was shown as Haverhill, MA and his father's name was Philanza.

This indicated that James had not been born in 1838, as the obituary stated. I returned to the Haverhill birth records for the 1830s to 1840s and again no DeBuchananne entries. I decided to review the records one last time. I looked for any male child born to a father with the name of Philanza. There was one: James B. Ricker, born on 4 June 1856, his father was Phylonzo Ricker.

The next step was to examine *A Genealogy Of The Ricker Family*. This book shows the birth of James Buchanan Ricker to Phylonzo Ricker on 4 June 1856 in Plaistow, NH (the town adjacent to Haverhill, MA). The book also revealed James' mother had died shortly after his birth. The obituary reported that James was left an orphan at an early age. Census work has located James with his father in 1860, but not in 1870. In 1880, James was in Dover, married, reporting his age as 30.

I feel confident James Buchanan Ricker, for whatever reason, decided to become James DeBuchananne. However, I have no idea why he added years to his age, married a woman 15 years older than himself, invented tales of royalty, heroics in the Civil War and assassination attempts and then deserted his second wife and two young sons to lecture as a Spiritualist.

We learned from the divorce record that James had been accused of improper associations with females of the Belknap Church. He left Dover abruptly, when his request for divorce was denied and later obtained a

divorce in Missouri. He charged Caroline with desertion.

I found the Missouri divorce record with pure luck. Another researcher on the Internet and I were sharing information on the Francis family of Bonne Terre, MO, as Bessie Francis was James' second wife. While the Internet researcher was examining St. Francois county records, she noted the DeBuchananne name and asked me about it. I never would have thought to look in Missouri for that divorce record.

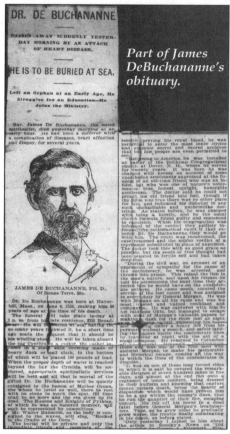

Part of James DeBuchananne's obituary.

There is still a lot we don't know, but at least we do know that James DeBuchananne was not a bigamist, was not of royal descent, could not have served in the Civil War and that he was almost certainly James Buchanan Ricker. — Jean D. Hurst, PA, genea4001@aol.com

Siblings And Children

Always uncover everything about siblings and children of your brickwall. Censuses are excellent for this. You never know where the extra information could lead you, to another town, another country, or another previously unknown person could appear. I have found that elderly parents and the widowed often went to live with family.

I searched everywhere for the census record of my great-grandparents in Chicago in 1900 and it turns out they were living with one of their daughters and her husband. It paid knowing all the children's spouses' names. — Lisa Laurent-Michel, UK, lm-.lm@ntlworld.com

Masonic Homes

My maternal grandfather was a taboo subject while I was growing up. No discussion was ever allowed about him. Even my father confessed that he knew nothing about my mother's father. The information we had indicated that he just appeared in Indianapolis, IN and assumed the name William Jones. Later, he reportedly said he liked the name Larkin and took that name as a middle name. This seemed an impossible dead end.

Mother had said that her father was buried in a distant section of the huge cemetery. After Mother's death, my wife and I visited the cemetery office. There were no William Joneses buried where Mother had indi-

William Larkin Jones, c. 1968. Photograph provided by the Masonic home.

cated. We reduced the list by eliminating all with incorrect first names, unlikely birth/death dates, etc. There were five remaining. I had a hunch about one of the names, so we visited the funeral home listed for that one. Their records indicated that he had a child with the same name as my mother's brother and that he had died at a Masonic home in southern Indiana.

We visited the Masonic home and found the specific Masonic chapter where our William Jones had been a member. A letter to this lodge resulted in no information, except that he had indeed been a member there. However, the Masonic home agreed to search their records if we would send a request by letter.

A few weeks later, they sent us a substantial file. The Masons had formed a committee to review my grandfather's history with the aim of determining whether any descendants were living that could help with his expenses. This file included an interview with him regarding children, marriages, life history; this included the verification of his wife, my grandmother and their two children, my mother and my uncle. The Masonic home letter also indicated it was unusual for the file to include a photograph of him — but this one did! They sent us the original print.

His birth name really was William Larkin Jones. He was born in southern Indiana in 1879 of parents Ance Jones and Laura Cooper. After the age of about seven, an aunt and uncle, Dr. and Mrs. Augustus Tulley in Brazil, IN took him into their care. He is actually buried

William Larkin Jones' gravestone.

within 40 feet of our family gravesites.

The Masonic home solved our brickwall about William Jones. — W. Gene James, OH, genejames@aol.com

Check Every Lead

My mother-in-law provided her parents' names and knew quite a lot about her father's side of the family, including accurate references in Ireland. Her mother's family, however, was vague. She knew her mother and her brother were born in New York City of Irish-born parents, John and Rose (Denning) McDonnell. She also knew Rose died at a young age, presumably of appendicitis. John also died while the children were fairly young. No other information was available.

I did find John and Rose, as married, arriving in the US, at the Port of New York, in 1879. They were not on the 1880 census or the 1900 census, nor the other censuses and substitutes that are available. Since I reside a distance from New York City and could not search their records in person, I tried other ways to obtain records for a family whose name is often misspelled McDonald.

The 1900 census showed a child, Rose McDonald, age nine, in the New York Catholic Protectory. Since it was the only Rose on the census and could be named for the deceased Rose McDonnell, I pursued the records. Another brickwall — the records of the Queen of Angels Home (Catholic girls' home name) are located in Lincoln Hall in a contaminated area requiring a court order for extraction! I requested a death certificate search and found that Rose died in November 1900 and was burial in Calvary Cemetery. Calvary Cemetery is indexed chronologically, not alphabetically. With the date, I contacted the cemetery, found her burial with several Denning family members — a connection at last!

Next, I requested the name and address of the purchaser of the cemetery plot. It was Mary Denning McDonnell, mother of the deceased. Using the address, I plotted the location of the nearest Catholic churches, and, on my first try, located the marriage record in 1890 of John McDonnell to Mary Denning, sister of his deceased wife.

Eventually, a check for pre-1890 death records developed the rest of the story. John and Rose actually had seven children, five of them dying before 1892. Rose died in 1889 and John married her sister, Mary, who helped him raise the children. John died in 1892 from a fall. The family knew little about this because of family division caused by a marriage outside of the family faith back in the 1890s! — M. Tuck, NY, tuck3@mail2world.com

Finding Family

My grandmother, Lula Whitacre, was an orphan and all we had of her relatives was a picture with names written on the back. These were her mother's relatives from North Carolina. I had no idea which part of North Carolina.

Using the names from the picture, we recently found cousins in Georgia using RootsWeb.com. Luckily, they have a family Bible. They were able to give me all eight of the Howard children's names. (I only had six of them before.) I now also have the birthplace of my great-grandfather, John Thomas Howard. — Rose Lane, VA

Curiosity

I grew up thinking my maternal grandfather died before I was born and neither my maternal grandmother, who lived with us, nor my mother told me otherwise. My grandmother died when I was 12 and my mother died when I was 22.

When I was nearly 40, my grandfather's sole-surviving sister died. Her attorney inquired about my mother's sisters and brothers as potential heirs.

It was only then I learned my grandparents had been divorced and that my grandfather had remarried and had a second family. My search for them began with questions to my father and my mother's cousin — my grandfather's niece. Both knew about the second marriage, but didn't know anything else about my grandfather's movements after the divorce. I didn't even know in which state to search. That was in the late 1960s and all the people who could have helped me were dead.

I searched unsuccessfully until 1994. In the FHL, I found only two references to him. One was as my grandmother's husband on her pedigree chart, the other in the 1920 federal census in

A.O. Helms, Bob Hartsell's grandfather, assumed to have died before Hartsell's birth.

Kentucky, where he was listed with his wife and three of the children mentioned in my aunt's attorney's letter. I knew I had the right person. But I could find nothing else.

In 1997, I went to the town in Kentucky where the family had lived, confident I'd find something in courthouse records. Two days of searching were completely unproductive. It was as if they had never lived there. (Later, I learned that they had stayed there only a short time and had only rented a place to live.)

Although I have worked with computers since 1982, I didn't have one with Internet capability until 1999. In early 2000, I noticed an icon on my screen that my Internet service provider installer had left there. I didn't know what it was, so clicked it out of curiosity. Suddenly, I was in the state death record index maintained by the University of Kentucky. Remembering that my grandfather had lived in Kentucky, I typed in his name. Almost instantly his name, death date and death place popped up on my screen.

With the date and county of his

death before me, I called local libraries, got a copy of his obituary and identified his burial location. This led me to his widow's death date (45 years after his), her obituary and the married names of their daughters.

Another day of computer work led me to their daughter, my mother's surviving half-sister. Forty-seven years after my mother's death, I was talking to her half-sister on the telephone, 66 years after their father died. I learned that my grandfather had not died before I was born. He died when I was four; my mother and grandmother had simply never spoke of him in my presence.

I also talked on the telephone to my mother's surviving half-brother. A few weeks later I visited my aunt and her family in Kentucky. They took me to my grandfather's grave, the first direct link with him I had ever had — finally, at the age of 70! My computer and the Internet got me past the brickwall to living flesh-and-blood kin. — Bob Hartsell, AR, u4eah@hsnp.com

It Began With A Picture

My father told me that his mother was orphaned at about age two and that she had lived with various families in Athens, TN until about age 18. She then went to Colorado for about three years. He also said that she had no relatives; certainly none that he knew. He had tried a couple of times to find someone in Athens who remembered her, but had no luck. Her name was Margaret Irene (Maggie) Stegall.

I was working on the First Families of Tennessee Project and was looking for an ancestor who lived in Tennessee on 1 June 1796 to qualify. I did locate Maggie in the 1880 census at age two. My father always talked about a couple from Athens with whom visits were exchanged. I always assumed that Maggie and the lady were girlhood friends as my grandfather was from Knoxville. The man was Miles McCuiston. After my father died, I found a picture of his parents with another couple in a photographer's frame folder with "Athens, Tennessee" printed on it. My father was in the picture also. He was about four years old. A piece of paper clipped to the picture said, "This is Miles McCuiston"; the other man in the picture. As I looked at the picture the resemblance between my grandmother and Miles was so similar that they had to be related.

I did a name/address search on the Internet for McCuistons in Athens, TN and found two. I wrote a letter to one who called me almost immediately. He said that the name Miles sounded familiar but that I needed to talk with his father who lived in Athens, AL. I called him.

He said that I needed to talk with his aunt in Melbourne, FL. She had to be approaching 90, but I was told that she was very much with it. I wrote her and enclosed a copy of the picture.

She called back as soon as she got the letter to tell me that she had a copy of the same picture and that Miles was her father! Her mother wrote on the back of the picture "this is Miles' cousin, Maggie. She was quite a dresser"!

I now have a copy of that picture and am almost there in my First Families of Tennessee Project. This was all due to a picture and some very nice distant relatives. — Parke Brown, Jr., MD, plb.ksb@erols.com

Registry Book

I was trying to find the person who submitted a short narrative story about some of my relatives and some family group sheets to a library close to the area where I was born. I questioned the librarian in charge of the genealogy room and she could not tell me where the information came from. I contacted everyone in the area that I knew (which are very few now) and could not find this person.

The next time I was at this library I got the sign-in register and copied every person's name and address who over the last three years had been researching the same surnames that I had. I wrote six letters and got six responses and lots of good information from six distant relatives that I did not know existed. I have added more than five hundred names to my database just from these connections.

I still have not found the person that submitted the original information but I am still looking and am confident that I will find them. Keep looking and sometimes you may find something better than what you were looking for in the first place. — Clifford B. Johnson, GA

Hi, Great-Grandma Emma Jane!

In 1996, all I knew about my great-grandmother, Emma Jane Spinks Smith, was that her parents came from England and that my middle name, Melbury, supposedly came from a park in the town where she lived in England. None of our family Bibles nor her widowed husband's diary of 1863 recorded any information on the Sprinks family.

Family diary records showed great-grandfather Dr. William Mervale Smith was from Short Tract

Emma Jane Spinks Smith.

in Granger township, Allegany county, NY. Dr. Smith would later practice in Angelica, serve as a surgeon in the US Civil War and then retire as Health Officer of the Port of New York in 1892. By 1894 he moved to Redlands, CA where he died eight years later. More family papers and records showed Dr. Smith had been married three times, first to Adaline Weeks, then to my great-grandmother, Emma Jane, then to Frances Lyon, who survived him. But neither Dr. Smith nor any of his wives are buried in the Redlands Cemetery.

A letter from my father to his sister in 1972, shortly before his death, recalled that he thought Dr. Smith was buried in Angelica, NY. However, the list of US cemeteries didn't include Angelica.

The federal census records for 1850, 1860 and 1870 in Allegany county did not produce any Spinks family reference. San Bernardino county probate records produced Dr. Smith's will, but there is no mention of Emma Jane. My call to the town clerk of Angelica, NY revealed that there was no list of cemetery records, but I was referred to the town librarian. The town librarian said she did not have the cemetery records.

My wife and I took a trip east to visit Angelica. In a book on the history of Allegany county was a list of ministers of the Angelica First Methodist Episcopal Church, including a Rev. John Spinks in 1858-60. Could this be Emma Jane's father?

At dusk we drove to Short

Tract, about nine miles north of Angelica, just to see the area. We happened upon the Short Tract Cemetery and immediately proceeded past the modern gravestones to the back of cemetery.

After a brief walk with the mosquitoes, I soon found a row of

Short Tract Cemetery.

gravestones, including my second-great-grandparents', Dr. Smith's first wife's and Emma Jane's! She was born in 1838 and died in 1859 at age 21 years.

We returned to Short Tract the next day and local residents referred us to the Granger town clerk. She had the original census records for 1855, but the records showed nothing of Emma Jane or John Spinks.

We then returned to Angelica, where Dr. Smith relocated his practice in 1863 and proceeded to the Angelica Cemetery. We found the small, but architecturally attractive Smith Mausoleum. Naturally, it was locked, so we checked with the town clerk to see if he had, or knew who had the key. The town board was contacted and they said it was the responsibility of the next of kin, which, as it turns out, was me!

So, we cut the lock, took pictures of the tombs of Dr. William Smith, wife Frances, son Frank and Frank's wife Clara. We installed a new lock and left the key with the Angelica Inn.

A written request and small fee sent to Drew College of Theology in Madison, NJ, where the Methodist Episcopal minister records are kept, produced the record of church assignments for John Spinks. This included Wellsville, NY in 1856-58 where William and Emma were married in 1857! A trip to the Methodist Church in Wellsville produced only a

Women's Fellowship record of 1858 where John and Elizabeth Spinks donated 50 cents. This was the first clue that Emma Jane's mother was named Elizabeth.

Further records found that John Spinks immigrated to Rochester, NY in 1841, when Emma Jane was three years old. I also discovered that he was a builder when he moved to Nunda, NY and he made a career change when he studied for the ministry in 1846. The Granger town clerk did a subsequent follow-up on John Spinks and found that his and Elizabeth's graves had been moved in 1902 from Bradford, PA. A new e-mail contact from Palmyra, NY found Elizabeth was born in 1815 and died in 1872.

Emma Jane appeared in the FHC microfilms of English births from 1837, released in 1999. I sent the form to England and received the record of the birth of Emma Jane Spinks to John and Elizabeth Rupell Spinks of Charminster, near Dorchester, England!

Hi, Great-grandma Emma Jane! — Mel Smith, CA

The Kindness Of Volunteers

In 1991, I had been attempting for some time to locate four paternal first cousins, who I hoped were still alive. No other family members had been in contact with them for almost 50 years. It was thought that their last whereabouts were in Grimsby, England.

From a fellow member of the genealogical society where I now live, I obtained the name and address of the Secretary of the Lincolnshire Family History Society and wrote explaining my brickwall and requesting her assistance.

This gracious lady looked up the phone numbers of the four names I had provided her in the Grimsby telephone directory. She was successful in reaching one of them by telephone, explained my request and obtained her address. My cousin said if I wrote to her, she would reply and put me in touch with remaining family members. She kept her word.

As a volunteer, the Secretary would accept no payment, but suggested that if I wished to make a modest donation to the Lincolnshire Family History Society, that would be most acceptable.

One amusing and puzzling item of information that has been revealed through this new correspondence is that one of the four cousins who is shown on a genealogical chart, compiled by another cousin, now deceased, as married with three children, is in fact a 60-year-old bachelor. This goes to show, every item should be checked carefully for accuracy. — Joan Iris (Gooch) Rutter, ON

Keep An Open Mind

My third-great-grandfather was a Seminole War veteran and farmer by the name of Emanuel D. Mott. From two family Bibles, I knew immediately upon commencing my family history research that he was born in East Florida on 16 March 1800 and died in Jacksonville, FL on 28 October 1858. Emanuel was unique in that he was born a non-Spanish, native Floridian of such vintage as that of the Second Spanish Occupation of Florida (1783-1821). There were factors in my favor: the excellent record keeping by the Cathedral Basilica of St. Augustine of non-military inhabitants of East Florida and Emanuel's somewhat-rare surname. However, I still could not prove his parentage.

I did find Emanuel in the Spanish land grant records. These were grants that the US would honor, with proof, after Florida became a territory in 1821. These records and testimonies proved his early life in, or near, St. Augustine. Several possibilities existed: the Jacob C. Mott family of Long Island, NY that had invested in land and citrus crops in Mandarin, FL; a Matthew Mott who arrived in 1793 from VA; the widow Hannah Mott who came prior to 1786 from SC and a Jonas Mott of London who arrived in the 1760s when Dr. Andrew Turnbull settled his Smyrna Colony.

Despite some promise in each of the four Mott families, none provided a proven, direct connection to my Emanuel. However, one of the four had to be that of my ancestor. I read and re-read the Spanish records of the Basilica written by the priest, but the name of Emanuel (Manuel in Spanish) just did not appear. Years went by and hours were spent on old East Florida Papers of Spain's Second Occupation; but no further proof of Emanuel's family emerged.

Finally it dawned on me to revisit the Basilica's records for children baptized on or immediately after Emanuel's known date of birth. I found him and opened up the trail of his ancestry back to 16th-century England. Emanuel was there, not as Emanuel D. Mott, but as Manuel Joséf Resoy, the illegitimate son of Manuel Resoy, a Cuban Army soldier and Anna Maria Mott (spelled "Moot" in the record). Manuel's date of birth matched exactly the date in the two family Bibles.

Never take too literally the exact name or spelling of the name of the person for whom you are searching. — Bob Nichols, FL, bnichols@tfn.net

*   *   *

Dig Deep And Ask Questions

My mother and I overcame a brickwall regarding her great-grandmother Helen Shearer Duncan. We knew little about Helen other than family stories that she and her husband, Thomas Duncan, were born in Scotland and that her middle name may have been Marion.

Helen and Thomas had three children, born in Trumbull county, OH: Agnes, George and John. We also knew that Helen had an older son, David McNair. A search of the 1880 census found Agnes listed as a domestic with the Richardson family in Scott township, Fayette county, IA. Agnes married John Wesley Hazen in 1883, in Scott township. In 1891, John Duncan moved from Greenville, PA to Fayette county and married J.W. Hazen's youngest daughter, Rachel Anne in 1891.

From our cousins, we learned that Thomas was an alcoholic and unable to support his family. A search of the 1870 census found Thomas Duncan, 47, living in a boarding house with 15 other men in Hickory township, Mercer county, PA. David McNair, 22, was living nearby with another family. The younger boys were both found with foster families: George in Cool Spring township and John in East Lackawannock township. The first concrete information we had about Helen was an

Helen Marian Duncan's gravestone.

extract from the *Brush Creek Mercury*, dated 5 February 1892. It read: "J.W. Hazen and John Duncan and their families tender their sincere thanks to neighbors and friends who rendered them assistance and sympathy during the sickness and death of their mother Mrs. Duncan." The only known copies of the *Brush Creek Mercury* are in a private collection, so we were unable to search them for more information.

A search of the death index in Fayette county came up blank. The Work Projects Administration Grave Index listed a Helen Duncan born in 1822 and buried in Oelwein, with a death date of 31 June 1892. Was the day wrong or the month? Mom was sure that this Helen belonged to the other, unrelated Duncan family in Fayette county. Besides, we had no known connection to Oelwein. I just had to see this grave marker for myself, if for no other reason than to eliminate this Helen as our ancestor.

When we found the grave, the marker was covered with moss. I brushed off enough to read the inscription and Mom and I were elated when we realized this was our Helen Duncan. The marker revealed the day of birth as 18, but the month was unreadable.

Energized by this discovery, we went back to the Fayette County Courthouse to search the death records again. A search from 31 January 1892 and forward several years still came up blank. A trip to the Historical Society to view newspaper microfilms yielded nothing. When I asked the volunteer about other newspaper microfilms, she knew of none available, but another volunteer passing by suggested contacting the small library in Arlington, which was formerly Brush Creek. The small village of Brush Creek had not one, but two newspapers in 1892 and the *Brush Creek News* was available on microfilm. It took just minutes to find Helen Duncan's obituary.

We now know that she was born 18 June 1822 near Glasgow, Scotland, that she came to the US as a young woman and married Thomas Duncan shortly thereafter. We were surprised to learn that she lived with daughter Agnes and J.W. Hazen after 1883. She was not listed with them on the 1885 Iowa census.

My brickwall fell after we dug deep for the answers. — Mary Mittelstadt, MN, mary.mittelstadt@ptk.org

Follow The Siblings

My quest for family history began with a typed family history of our direct line given to me by my great-aunt. She had received an earlier, handwritten copy from her aunt. I thought that I wouldn't have any work to do on this line.

Years later I still hadn't made progress in finding where and when my third-great-grandparents died. Although I already verified their parents and other ancestors dating back to 1630 in New England, I still wanted the complete facts on this couple.

Then I remembered what my genealogy teacher and countless genealogical periodicals had said: If you can't make headway with your direct line, track the siblings. My ancestors chose some unusual names for their children so I chose the daughter with the most unusual

name and began tracing her.

I found Arley Cossitt and her siblings in the Congregational Church records of Pompey, Onondaga county, NY but it only listed them as children of Calvin and Mary Cossitt. Marriage records weren't kept in Onondaga county at this time period. The 1850 federal census of Onondaga county, NY did not list Arley as a member of the Cossitt family. I looked at the entire Onondaga county census searching for any female named Arley. I found none.

At this point, I made copies of what I had collected and wrote to the Onondaga Historical Society asking for someone to go over what I had to see if I had missed any records. Several weeks later a large envelope arrived. Material from the society included the same church records I had collected, township maps of Pompey, cemetery records of Pompey and two pages copied from the 1855 state census of Onondaga county, NY. I quickly read the pages from the census. There was Arley right at the top of the second page. My heart first beat with excitement at finding Arley then quickly sank when I read her surname. It was Smith.

1855 state census for Onondaga county in New York. Page 23 shows Arley Smith and the two children in the household. Credit: the collections of the Onondaga Historical Association.

I looked at the last name on the bottom of the previous page. There was Arley's husband. My outlook brightened when I saw that his first name was Lanson. I also learned that the couple had two children. The older one was too old to be Arley's daughter so I concluded that Arley was Lanson's second wife.

Coincidentally I took out a library book about the history of Onondaga county. I did not find any mention of the Cossitt family, but in the back of the book in tiny type was a list of the US Civil War soldiers who had served from Onondaga county. There was Lanson Smith listed as serving the Union in the Civil War. It even listed his unit. I used the forms from the NARA to obtain Lanson's pension records.

Several weeks later Lanson Smith's pension records arrived. It took a few minutes to get used to reading the old handwriting, but I continued. One paper in the packet indicated that Lanson Smith had died in Portville, NY. Remembering the notation in the church records that Calvin and Mary Cossitt "removed to Portville," I decided to write again to the town clerk this time asking for cemetery records.

I didn't write that letter right away because I hadn't finished reading the pension records. The pension records also included Arley's application for a pension at the death of her husband Lanson Smith. A widow must prove she had married the US Civil War soldier and that she was his only wife. There was a letter from Arley to the pension office that gave her marriage date and then went on to explain that she was Lanson Smith's second wife.

1855 state census for Onondaga county in New York. Page 22 shows Lanson Smith as son-in-law of Calvin Cossitt. Credit: the collections of the Onondaga Historical Association.

She also gave the marriage date for Lanson's first marriage and explained that Lanson Smith's first wife was Arley's older sister, Juliette. The older child listed with Lanson and Arley was Juliette's daughter, Arley's niece and now stepdaughter.

I wrote to the town of Portville. It wasn't even a week later that I received an answer. Yes, Calvin and

Mary were buried in Portville, but the gravestones only listed the year each had died. That was fine with me because it confirmed the place and year of death. In addition, the town clerk reported that Calvin and Mary's daughter, Mary, had married a "pillar of the community" and the town still celebrated the man once a year. The town clerk enclosed copies from the town history about this couple.

My suggestion to those with brickwalls is to follow the siblings and get their pension records if necessary. — Beth Hanson, CT, rabgen@earthlink.net

Broken Family Ties

My mother always says her birth certificate read, "Girl Child". Other than that and an occasional story, she refuses to talk about her past and forbids any further research or inquiry. Well, I am an adult and I've wanted to know about my ancestry for a long time.

For two years I searched for a birth certificate for "Girl Child" without luck. In the meantime, I transcribed 100 years of the San Francisco city directory. Analyzing the entries, I could identify at least two families that were possibilities. One was related to a dentist, obviously not my mother's poor Irish-French family. The other was a family that was constantly moving around. By tracing who lived with whom through the years, I was able to identify nine names in one family. They lived in Butchertown, the poorest neighborhood in San Francisco. My half-brother remembered once driving with our mother in San Francisco past Silver Avenue. She muttered how much the neighborhood had changed since she was a girl.

One day, sitting at a computer terminal, I absent-mindedly entered my mother's first name, instead of "Girl Child." Up popped an image of a revised birth certificate. In 1952, she had revised her birth certificate to include her full name, required to receive a passport. The birth certificate contained my grandparents' names, John and Dora.

The 1927 city directory lists my grandmother as living in Butchertown on Quesada, one block from Silver Avenue. It also lists her father, my grandfather, living on the corner of Silver and Quesada. Later, Uncle Albert lived one block away at the corner of Silver and Paru while he recovered from an industrial accident.

I now knew which family was mine, but I had still not found them. My next breakthrough came at the Catholic Church in the neighborhood. In their baptismal book, I found a record for a cousin. There apparently had been some question if the father was actually Catholic. The priest had checked on the father's marriage and noted it had been at "Old St. Mary's".

There have been three St. Mary's Cathedrals. The first burned and was called "Old" after the second was built. The third is a modern landmark on Geary Boulevard. I found nothing at Old St. Mary's (the second), but finally found the record at the new cathedral. The parents of the groom were my grandparents, John and Dora.

Further searches on Roots-Web.com disclosed Uncle William's death place as San Mateo. Driving to San Mateo county, I found the record, which contained a last address. I knocked on the door that afternoon. I told the woman about my grandmother and she said, "We must be related," and invited me in. When I told her my mother's first name, she almost screamed, "Sister Evelyn!"

She told me how her late husband had spent his whole life wondering what happened to his sister. His mother, Dora, had spent the rest of her life searching for Evelyn, without luck. She gave me the name of one of my uncles in Clearlake and called to let him know to expect my call.

That evening, I called Uncle Albert. A couple of weeks later I drove to Clearlake and interviewed him. His only clue to the split in the family was that the oldest brother had tried to prevent my mother's marriage to her first husband. He also told me of Aunt Dorothy who lives "in an old age home on top of a hill on the east side of the freeway in Vallejo."

Using the phone book and a map, I plotted the locations of all the old age homes in Vallejo. When I found the right one, I was directed down a long hall to a door, which I knocked. Introducing myself, I went to sit on a rocking chair. To do so, I had to pick up a doll and hold it in my lap. After telling her who I was, Aunt Dorothy told me that she had sold her large doll collection except the one I held. She said she kept it "because it reminded me of your mother."

When I returned a few weeks later, I discovered likely clues to the cause of the family split. First, Aunt Dorothy said, "you were just a small child then." I was born in 1950, after the split, so I knew she was mistaking me for my older half-brother. That would have put the split sometime after 1943. Then Aunt Dorothy spilled the beans, "We did not get along. She was going to the college and all the kids were talking communism. Those people in Oakland were talking communism. When she came to the door, I said my husband worked for the post office and she should not come around talking that stuff."

After working in the shipyards during WWII, my mother took a job in Washington, DC and then returned to the Bay Area. My parents met when someone arm-twisted my father into giving her a lift home from a meeting. They were together during the Oakland General Strike. My parents were activists in the old Technical Engineers, AFL union. My father says he never met my mother's family.

Putting all this together I realized

that my mother apparently attempted to interest her sister in some union activity, perhaps even early support for the retail clerks strike that led to the general strike. The family break was probably in 1946, just before the Oakland General Strike of 3-5 December 1946.

But this leaves one question: Why would both my mother and aunt forbid me from exploring further with the exact same tone of voice? My father was blacklisted in 1952 for union activities and the family passports were taken away. Did my aunt rat on her sister and live with the shame for 55 years? Has my mother lived 55 years with the shame that she might have betrayed her union friends by talking to her sister?

Perhaps a Freedom of Information Act inquiry will reveal the truth. It is one more possible source of information to break down a genealogical brickwall. — Martin Schaaf, CA

RootsWeb.com Mailing Lists

My ancestor Martha Jane Harper married Henry C. Sowers on 27 July 1843 in Muskingum Co, OH. I followed Henry and Martha through several states to Atchison, KS where they both lived until their deaths. In all materials I looked through I could not find the names of Martha's parents or siblings. I have been to Muskingum county three times. I also have been through all possible records.

On her marriage record it states with consent of her father (no name). All references to her birth list Virginia, no help there. There were a large number of Harpers in the Muskingum county, OH area, let alone the entire state of Virginia. Looking through wills and probates gave no clues.

I talked to genealogy groups, left cards in index files, all to no avail. It was probable that her family was

Henry and Martha Jane (Harper) Sowers — from Stephanie McBrayer who was one of the five people who responded to the request on RootsWeb.com's Harper mailing list.

never in Muskingum county, or was in another county or another state.

In this instance the written records did not give me any help. The brickwall solution was for me to post a request on the Harper Mailing List on RootsWeb.com.

Within a week, five people had responded to my request. I not only received information on her parents, John and Hannah Gilham Harper, but also possible grandparents. As with all information these names, dates and places need to be verified. But I now have names, dates and places to research when before I had nothing but a brickwall. — Connie Ohlman Bradish, TX, bradish@escapees.com

The Lure Of Free Land

In the early days of my research, I couldn't find anything out about my great-grandfather. I sent for several death certificates including his, his wife's and their children's. When I went to my great-uncle's, I found the death certificate that stated where that part of the family had lived. Then I checked that county in Ohio and found where my great-grandfather had lived. Since that time I've used Bureau of Land records to add more information. Many people came to an area because of free or cheap land — Myra Wright, AZ

Working On The Railway — Genealogy Style

My children chipped in and bought us a computer including a genealogy software package. I started school when we still dipped pens (and girls' pigtails) in the inkwell. I quickly became fascinated and presently have a family tree that spans eight generations and 22 pages of banner paper.

My grandfather died in 1913, a few months before my father was born. All that we knew was that he worked on the New York Central RR and my uncle remembered going to Minnesota for the burial. We presumed that since he had died while working the New York Central buried him in a company cemetery.

My nephew was getting married in St. Paul, MN, and since we were going to the wedding I decided to see if I could find anything on my grandfather. I wrote to the New York Central Historical Society, but their records only went back to the 1930s. They had no information about a company cemetery.

We had no idea where in Minnesota he was buried, but I decided to take a chance. I e-mailed the Minneapolis/St. Paul Chamber of Commerce and asked if they knew anything about a cemetery owned by one of the railroad companies. They responded that they could not find a

cemetery owned by the railroad, but they gave me the address of one in St. Paul that they said was surrounded by railroad yards. I wrote to the cemetery and they responded that they did have a John Geary who was buried in May 1913.

Clockwise from lower left: Joanne Wilson, Jennifer Lennox, John Geary, Kieran Geary and Robert Geary at their ancestor John Geary's gravesite in 1999.

While we were in the state for the wedding my wife, brother, sister, niece, nephew and I went to the cemetery to see if we could find the gravesite. The Administrations Office gave us a map with the general location and we were off on our hunt. There were a number of small stones set even with the ground and covered with grass. The six of us spent about an hour pulling grass, trying to find a chronology to help us. Finally my brother wandered off and came back with one of the maintenance men who were working that day. He looked at the site map we had and told us that the road we were using as a guide had been relocated since the time of the burial. Directly across the road, we found a very large headstone with the name "Geary". Also buried there were my great-grandmother and three of my great-uncles.

Apparently, the family had immigrated to Minnesota and my grandfather ended up in New York because of his job with the railroad and not the reverse that we had assumed. — Robert Geary, NY, we2gearys@aol.com

Who Lives With Whom?

Family records listed my great-grandmother as Telitha Jane Caldwell (married George Collier) and her father as Hampton Caldwell. In a search of census records I could find no record of a Hampton Caldwell.

As I scrolled through the microfilm of the 1900 census Soundex, I scanned every Caldwell listed but found no Hampton. Then I saw it — a breakthrough! Elizabeth Caldwell had living in her household John Collier, a grandson. That's my Uncle Johnny, my grandfather's brother.

On reviewing earlier census records I found a family group of James H. Caldwell with wife Elizabeth and among the children a daughter Jane. The H must have stood for Hampton! I had found my family by carefully looking through the Soundex and finding out who lived with whom! — June Collier, MS

There Is Always Another Variant

My family name, Kenneison, is rare and often misspelt. My father has always said that although he thought his father, Ernest James Kenneison, was born in Woking in Surrey, the family originally came from Scotland. If you look up Kennison (the nearest variant) in a book of clans, it is given as a MacFarlane name.

My father only had very sketchy details about his family: his mother was born in Ceylon, his parents were married in Singapore, his father had

been in the Army and was killed in 1942. Owing to WWII, there are no papers and few photographs.

I obtained my grandfather's birth certificate and found he had been born in 1877, just outside Woking and had been, as my father had believed, the survivor of a pair of twins. I found his first marriage in Madras, in the Army returns. So far so good, I thought. My next step was to find him, a child in England, in the 1881 census index, so I would discover his parents' birthplaces. I didn't think this would be easy, even though my great-grandfather gloried in the name of Cornelius Kenneison; my name has come back to me as Kenneifon, Kerrison, Kennelson and Kenniston to name a few. I tried all these on the index as well as all the others I could think of. There were Kennestons and Kenisons in Dorset and Hampshire, but not a single set of Kenneisons and no Corneliuses.

I tried the Birthplace Index for the 1881 census. Still no luck. The best I had for the 1881 census concerned a Caroline Kennison. Someone of this name, given as cousin, had registered Ernest's twin brother's death and someone of this name also appeared in the 1881 census, living at Mortlake and married to a John Kennison who was born in Brentford in Middlesex. I paid great attention to the ramifications of this family, as I felt sure they were connected to me somehow.

Searching for the death of Ernest's father Cornelius in the indexes at the Family Records Centre, I came across the death of a Thomas Kenneison in the district of Chertsey, just down the road from where Ernest was born. This chap seemed be the same person as a Thomas Kennison in the 1881 census, who had been born at Brown Candover in Hampshire. I felt sure he must link too; the spelling was just too coincidental and so was the location. I began to doubt the Scottish hypothesis. I became tied up in patterns of given names amongst these people — James, George and Thomas all cropped up regularly. I went to the Surrey FHC; I found my grandfather's baptism and not much else and asked the lady at the desk for advice.

"Normally," she said, "it's the John Smiths you can't find. You wouldn't think someone with a name like that could vanish."

I spent long hours trawling through the 1891 returns for Woking; I had obtained Cornelius' death certificate by then (he died in the 1900s) and found the right street, but they weren't there. I searched lots of the 1881 for the area and parts of the 1871. Still there was nobody. It took hours and I was bug-eyed and despondent by the end. Not one to give up easily, I went back to the indexes at the Family Records Center. I had already tried to find my grandfather's parents' marriage, searching through 20 years (that's 80 volumes) of indexes, without success. My father had given me the names of his father's siblings so I went through index after index, noting every variant of Kenneison I came across. I wanted to see if a pattern emerged.

One did emerge; they were concentrated, as in the census index, in Dorset and Hampshire and Kenneston was a popular spelling. Of course, I had no idea if this was of any relevance, or whether what I had was an outlying branch of the numerous Shropshire Kynastons. I applied for all the certificates with the spelling Kenneison (even though Ernest's hadn't been spelt that way) and every single one came up trumps! They had been a very mobile family, Cornelius seeking laboring work all over Surrey and Berkshire. They had moved from Bray to Easthampstead to Horsell, where Ern was born, to Cobham. The Cobham birth of his baby sister Lilian, was in August 1881. I was delighted — a census year! I resolved that, at the first opportunity, I would search the fiche of the original Cobham return.

Before I got a chance, my distant cousin, with whom I was in regular e-mail contact, mentioned that he had a searchable CD of the 1881 census index. I had never heard of this, despite extensive reading and asked if he would have a look for Ern, Corn and company. I e-mailed him everything I had.

The next evening I logged on with baited breath. My husband has never understood my interest in my family tree and was totally bemused by the yell of joy that emanated from the region of our computer.

"He's found them! Chalky's found them! It's them! He's found them! He's a star!"

There was an odd specific of a birthplace as the children didn't tie up, but the ages were right and so were the names. I was ecstatic.

It was no wonder I hadn't been able to find them in the index. The surname was given as Kemreison. — Rebecca Kenneison, Surrey, UK

Families Often Traveled Together

Solving my brickwall required both persistence and determination. I had a copy of a letter addressed to Miss Samantha Gleason, Wyoming, NY. Her future husband Joseph Peck sent the letter on 27 May 1849. By the 1850 federal census, Joseph and Samantha were married and living in Allegany county, NY. The question was who

Joseph and Samantha Peck.

were Samantha Gleason's parents?

I began by gathering all the census records for individuals with the name Gleason in western New York. I also joined the Western New York Genealogy Society, submitted a query to *Everton's* Roots Cellar and obtained a copy of the genealogy of Thomas Gleason of Watertown, MA. The next step was to extract information pertaining to my research on index cards, one for each Gleason name found.

I then used the data to narrow my research, eliminating those who did not have a daughter in the correct age bracket. After writing to the New York county historians, I had two candidates. Samantha's father could either be Chester Gleason or Thomas Gleason of Middlebury, Wyoming county, NY. An article sent from the Wyoming county historian indicated Chester had a daughter Samantha. But how could I be sure this was my Samantha? A cemetery record indicated Chester Gleason died in 1847. No probate could be found. In addition, I could not find his widow, Eliza, in the 1850 census.

When I found nothing further about Chester Gleason, I decided to search for Thomas Gleason. He turned up in Kendall county, IL in 1850 — the same township where Joseph and Samantha resided in 1860. But Thomas Gleason was no longer there in 1860.

While thinking about this problem, I noted that the second daughter of Samantha and Joseph was born in Michigan. As I knew families often traveled together, I set out to find the birthplace of Zorada Peck. My breakthrough was the 1860 federal census index for Michigan. I found a Thomas Gleason residing in Lapeer county. When I looked at the record I received a major surprise. I not only had located the right Thomas but also with him was Eliza Gleason, widow of Chester Gleason, and four of her children. Fortunately, Eliza left a will in Lapeer county listing all her living children

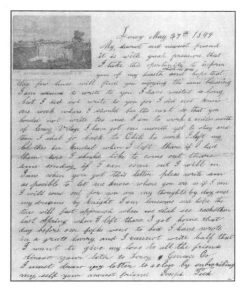

1849 letter from Joseph Peck to Samantha Gleason.

including daughter Samantha Peck.

Another bonus was a Lapeer county history article for Eliza's youngest daughter, Emma Gleason Potter, identifying her parents as Chester and Eliza (Hewett) Gleason. — Darlene Stone, WA

Lost And Found

I'd been researching for 30 years off and on, but decided to get serious. I began by going over all the letters and documents I have collected over the years. I ran across an article published in Chapman's *History Of St. Joseph County* about my father's grandfather. One sentence caught my eye. It said that Mr. and Mrs. Anderson had eight children, seven of whom are living.

Then I found a blurb written by my father's mother saying that Grandpa Anderson came to the US with the two oldest girls. Mama came a year later with the other four children and then had two more in Indiana.

I found all the family's records in Indiana but no babies. So I armed myself with a Swedish word list and went to the international floor of the

FHL and started to look at Swedish church records. Five hours later I emerged from the film reader with a new baby for our family.

Not only did I find where he was born in 1862 but I also found where he died in 1866 of scarlet fever. Just another crumbled brick in the wall. — Norrita Sanders, ID

The Elusive Great-Grandfather

I was searching for a few years for information on my great-grandfather, who had a child with another woman in Jersey City while still married to my great-grandmother. My great-grandmother divorced him in 1893 and I was unable to find him in the 1900 census. I sent for divorce papers that told the story of how my great-grandfather got a young girl pregnant at the same time his wife was pregnant with my grandmother. He brought this young girl to a boarding house in his own neighborhood. The owner told his wife about this situation when she noticed the girl was pregnant. My great-grandmother left him and divorced him when she found out about his infidelity. I was unable to find any information on this girl or what happened to my great-grandfather after this incident.

While looking in the Jersey City Public Library for information, I was seated in front of some card catalogs that looked very old. I had never looked at what was in them, until a man came over to use them. Since my seat was blocking the drawer he wanted, I got up to move and he saw that I had old city directories. He asked if I was doing genealogy and he said that I should look in these drawers. They were marked Births, Deaths and Marriages. I looked for a few names of my ancestors to no avail.

Then I looked in the marriage index under the name of my great-grandfather. There was a handwritten card with his name on it and that of a woman I had never heard of, along with a local newspaper name and date. I went down to periodicals and found the newspaper article with information about how he had divorced because of religious differences and married a woman from New York City. It gave me the name of my great-grandfather's second wife and I was able to get the marriage certificate to find out her parents' names.

The woman he married was not the same one named in the divorce papers who was pregnant by him. — Mary Schwarzenberger, NJ

In 20 Words Or Less

In 1973, I decided to tackle my Scott line. It was the shortest pedigree in my collection and my grandmother had already given me the names of my second-great-grandfather and his wife (William Scott and Elizabeth Gray) and the place of their marriage (Belmont county, OH).

In her brief personal history, Grandma had also written, "I never had the privilege of knowing my grandparents. My Grandfather Scott went to California during the gold rush in 1849. He never returned and was thought his life was taken by the hand of a prospector."

I had success with the very first record I searched that morning at the FHL. Whereas most marriage records give the name of the father of the bride, that of William Scott and Elizabeth Gray in 1835 in Belmont county identified the father of the groom as David Scott. At that instant, pushing one more generation back to find David's father became my obsession.

I found other records for David Scott in Belmont county. The tax records confirmed his first known land purchase in 1820 and payments for following years. The land records also indicated that David's wife's first name was Catharine. Another land record, accessed less than a month after first finding David's name, indicated that he had sold land along with a Samuel Coleman, both serving as executors for a Brice Collins. I naïvely assumed that David was simply a trusted neighbor of Mr. Collins and completely dismissed that morsel of information.

For the next 24 years I pursued this family through the records. The census from their subsequent Des Moines county, IA, residence gave me an outline of the rest of the family members along with David's birthplace as either Ohio or Pennsylvania.

Coordinated efforts with some other Scott descendants supported William's conjectured October 1867 burial in the Stockton Rural Cemetery in Stockton, CA. William's family Bible was also located. One entry for William confirming the cemetery's information and a death date for a David Scott likely placing William's father's death in the year preceding his own.

In April 1997, two good friends came to visit. Because they were both professional genealogists and kindly agreed to look at my research problem, I prepared a detailed summary of much of the information I had collected. After duly acknowledging all my floundering efforts, they offered some discouraging counsel. It would be advisable, said one, to read each and every deed during the same time period as David's first deed in order

David Scott, Sr. (1791-1886). Photograph courtesy of Norma G. Griswold.

to determine the major points of origin for those who were moving into that area. Believe me, I was hoping for a much simpler assignment.

As I obediently read page after page of the deeds, I became familiar with the names in the area. It was particularly thrilling to see a collection of Grays in the vicinity, as I suspected Elizabeth's father was among the number. Sadly, although there were indications of preceding locations for many of the new landowners, none of them seemed to yield any clues about David's prior residence.

However, there were two interesting entries for a Brice Collins. The first indicated that he had purchased land from a John Connell on the waters of Wheeling Creek, Barr's Run, in October 1817. David's land bought in 1820 was also on the waters of Wheeling Creek! In addition, the neighbors listed were a John Coleman, a John Baker and an Alexander Gray. These names began ringing some bells since the grantor for David's land had been Joseph Baker, Samuel Coleman was the other executor for Brice and there once again were the Grays.

The second entry in June of 1819 showed John Connell selling more land to another grantee, but this time the "heirs of Brice Collins, dec'd" were included among the itemized neighbors. All the pieces — executor David Scott, Collins, Coleman, Gray, Baker, Colerain township, shared township and range designations, identical waterway locations — everything began falling into a tantalizing pattern.

Obtaining Brice Collins' will took on a whole new urgency. A few weeks later, in a darkened room in front of a FHC microfilm reader, I began to examine the will of Brice Collins. As the document continued, I was getting discouraged because so much of it mentioned other children whom I did not recognize. Doggedly I persisted in deciphering the handwriting. There it was, at the bottom: "to my beloved daughter Catharine Scott, four hundred Dollars, and to her son William Scott, fifty dollars."

I wandered into the next room, stunned and overwhelmed by what had just happened. After more than a quarter of a century looking for some piece of information that would allow me to go further back on this family, there it was in less than 20 words! One single record revealed Catherine's maiden name, confirmed the relationship between her, David and William, outlined her own parental family's structure and eventually allowed me to place them in Pennsylvania. Thankfully, the researchers in the other room were very patient with my tearful recitation.

This experience taught me a valuable lesson — pursue every shred of evidence until it yields its full harvest. Had I followed up on the Brice Collins connection in 1973, I might be a lot further past my brickwall. — Lorraine Indermill Quillon, VA, lorraineq@juno.com

The Shorter Distance

In researching my Tyldesley (and variants) line from Farnworth with Kearsley, I came upon my brickwall with Betty Taylor, the wife of James Tyldesley, who died in 1840 at the age of 30. Checking all the Betty Taylors born circa 1810 proved to be fruitless. There were too many possibilities in Deane by Bolton and Bolton. I revisited the copy of the certificate of death

and used the informant information.

Since the 1841 census took place in close proximity to the date of death, I followed up with Jane Taylor, informant, who was a resident of Kearsley. I had assumed that Jane might be Betty's mother. Much to my surprise there was only one Jane Taylor living in Kearsley with her husband, Lawrence, and his widowed mother Mary. As it turned out, Jane was Betty's sister-in-law. From the names of the family members and their ages, I was able to identify Betty's father as Lawrence Taylor and to continue with research on both her maternal and paternal lines.

The death certificate for Betty (Taylor) Tyldesley.

Betty's baptism was never found at Deane by Bolton or Bolton. Her family was in the habit of baptizing their children at Ringley, which was a much shorter distance to travel! — G.J. Hersak, MB

Checking Family Lore With Newspapers

My mother, my aunt and their cousin all told stories about their grandmother Guy's brother, Job, who had, according to his gravestone, "Departed this life by a kick from a horse" at the age of eight. The stories varied, from the sparse to the fanciful.

So at the record office at Lewes in Sussex, I decided to check this. I knew, from a photo of the gravestone, when this event had taken place and, from family lore, where (Chalvington). I found the film of the *Sussex Express* newspaper that covered the relevant weeks and soon found it: "Chalvington: Child killed by a kick from a horse."

There it was, the whole story taken from the inquest, including quotes (or the clerk's rendition thereof) from the boy's mother. It was nothing dramatic, just a tragic accident, but it was satisfying to have a few facts.

A few hours later, I packed my papers and drove to the churchyard, through fields where my line had worked for generations.

It was an amazing experience, finding that grassy grave, with Job on one side and his parents on the other. It was then I knew I was hooked on family history! — Rebecca Kenneison, Surrey, UK

Eastern Cherokee Reimbursement Applications

For years family researchers had researched the Hackworth family and arrived at various conclusions as to the wife of Augustine Austin Hackworth, a Revolutionary soldier and the wife of his son, Austin Hackworth. It was a known fact that Austin's wife was Elizabeth Rigney but Augustine's wife was allegedly Mary Ruth or Ruth Reed. It had always been said in our family that the Hackworths were part Cherokee.

On one occasion, I had an opportunity to check the index to the *Eastern Cherokee Applications of the United States Court of Claims* by Guion Miller (1906-09), which contained persons who had applied for reimbursement from the Federal Government for land lost in the removal of the Cherokees in 1834. I found 27 Hackworths who had applied for these reimbursements. I ordered rolls of microfilm that contained the applications of the oldest individuals who

Shirley Hopkins-Landen tracked down ancestor Elizabeth Rigney Hackworth using Eastern Cherokee Reimbursement Applications.

had applied, which included my second-great-grandfather. In these applications, the applicant had to give the parents, grandparents and siblings of all and to tell where they had lived. What a treasure trove!

Two applicants were born in 1822 and 1828 so they certainly knew their grandparents. These applications gave us the name of Augustine's wife as Ruth Keeth. There were Keeths in the Bledsoe county, TN, area as early as 1815 with the same names as some of Augustine and Ruth's children, Gabriel and Nichodemus. Elizabeth Rigney's parents' names were given as Rigney and Sirena Huffman, born in Virginia. All siblings were listed.

All applications were denied, as they could not prove that their ancestors lost any property or land in the removal. However, they did break down several of my brickwalls!

This just goes to show that we should never overlook any unlikely source. I think there are 337 reels of applications in this collection. One must be cautious when looking at the index as it first has a small list of Cherokees residing east of the Mississippi River, then west and then again east, which is the majority of the Eastern applications. — Shirley Hopkins Landen, KY, landtec@kih.net

Simple Solution

My brickwall was trying to get a birth certificate for my father. My sister and I had tried off and on for 20 years. Our father had always said he was born in Louisiana. I checked the SSDI but he was not there. I had his Social Security Number so I sent directly to the Social Security Office. When the application arrived it showed he had been born in Warren, AR. I wrote to various places in Arkansas but was told they didn't register births until 1914. He was born in 1905.

Then one day I heard the word *delayed* connected to a birth certificate. I got a delayed birth certificate from the County Clerk. It had been filled out in 1941 by my father's sister-in-law. I just hadn't asked for the right kind of certificate! — Norma Foltz, WA

Brickwall "Story"

My great-grandmother was born Sarah Woods Kear. She was born near Fredricktown, MI in 1839, apparently while her family was in transit from Sevier county, TN. I was unable to find the family (James and Polly Kear were her parents) in the 1840 census, but in 1850 I did finally find them in the St. Louis area.

Sarah married Joseph Story in 1859, but I wasn't sure where. Joseph had left White county, IL, after the death of his father in 1857 but I did not know where he had gone. When Sarah applied to receive a Civil War widow's pension after his death, she stated they were married in Wayne county, MI, but the courthouse had burned and there were no records.

In my grandparents' old pictures was the photo of a man with a long white beard in a suit standing next to a buggy with a sod house and little more in the background. The photo was inscribed on the back, "Give one to Aunt Sarah." From this I guessed he was either Sarah's father or brother and the photo taken in either Kansas or Nebraska.

I had corresponded with some Kear searchers but none were from the southern states and were not related as far as we could ascertain. However, one said she had a 10-year-old letter from a man named Vernon Kear and from what he had written she thought that was my long-lost Kear family. He founded the Sod House Museum in Kansas, which is still in operation.

I wrote to Vernon Kear but he had since died. However, I did hear from a close relative of his and they turned out to be my long-sought Kear cousins. From them I learned that James had been a Justice of the Peace and lawyer in St. Charles county, MI, and after the death of James, Thomas (Sarah's brother) had taken the entire family in a covered wagon to Kansas, stopping to wait for his Civil War pension check to catch up with them. He also kept a journal throughout the trip. This family had a ledger from the time Thomas ran a wood yard on the river to supply steamboats with fuel. They also had old Bible records, which gave birth and some death dates for all Sarah's siblings. They confirmed that the old man with a long white beard in the picture I had was Thomas Kear, Sarah's brother.

And as a postscript, Sarah's memory had lapsed and she gave the wrong county as their marriage site. She and Joseph had moved back to White county, IL, which is near

Wayne county. In Missouri, Wayne county is about 150 miles from St. Charles county but Warren county is immediately adjacent to it. So she confused the two and it was in Warren county that they were actually married! — Jack Story, IL

Helping Other Researchers

My brickwall has been one that has lasted since the beginning of my research. According to every document and census I found my third-great-grandmother was Alice Ellen Armstrong. But I did not know her mother. She was the daughter of Wheeler Cuffe Armstrong, yet there was another interesting problem; Ellen first appeared living with Wheeler's parents, simply as one of the children. Her age did not match up with being John and Eliza's child. In a family history written for a local township, I discovered a relative who said she was Wheeler's daughter. According to family legend, she was an illegitimate child. The Armstrong family was a very wealthy family in Peterborough county, ON, and any notes on them had their son as never married and no children.

George Patterson, husband of Alice Ellen Armstrong.

I later tracked down Ellen's death certificate, which listed her as the daughter of Wheeler Armstrong. I found Wheeler's will which had him leaving his property to her eldest son Wheeler Patterson. In 1861, Ellen married a George Patterson. George and Wheeler worked together settling the lands of northern Peterborough and Haliburton county. There was never any mention of Ellen's mother's name. I searched for birth records, but being in the early 1840s, records are hard to find.

My first break came when I decided to transcribe a set of marriage records for Peterborough county. As I went through the records I came across the marriage record for George Patterson to Ellen Armstrong. Again, her father's name was Wheeler C. Armstrong. This time a mother's name was listed, Mary Ann. Mary Ann's last name was so badly written I only knew it started with a D. At least, I thought, this was a start.

However, for years I couldn't get past it. I even tried using a scanner and graphic programs to isolate her last name and at least get an idea. I consulted fellow genealogists. We came up with the possibilities of Dwyer, Dever, Duire and Dwven! Frustration had reached its peek and I had all but given up.

I joined an Internet site called Helplist Canada. Using the resources I had at home, I could help people around the world with local genealogy questions.

I started helping a gentleman in Australia research his family in Peterborough. He asked me if there was anything he could do for me. I thought this was unlikely as he was in Australia and all my research was in Peterborough county. I sent him the information and sure enough months later he had spoken with another gentleman via e-mail who researched old letters of the Peterborough county pioneers. The gentleman told him in one of the old letters from the Armstrongs there was mention of the maid who had a child by Wheeler. Her name was Mary Ann Dwyer!

She being Catholic Irish and the Armstrongs being Protestant Irish may have something to do with her being omitted from the family history. Or was it because she was the maid? From there my friend in Australia also discovered her baptismal record in Asphodel township in Peterborough county, something I had searched high and wide for!

In helping others, it is not just rewarding in itself but also can unearth those lost ancestors! — Tina Marie (Patterson) Hansen, YT, idigupfamily@hotmail.com

Try, Try, Then Try Again

My ancestor, Nicholas Questel, was one of the French Five Hundred that left France in 1790 and settled the town of Gallipolis, OH. The earliest proof I could find that he lived in Gallipolis was the 1800 census. For several months I tried to find a document that proved he was a resident earlier than 1800, but found nothing and gave up. Meanwhile I wrote to the NARA in Washington to see if they had the military records of another ancestor — Francis Questel served in the Kentucky Calvary during the Civil War. The NARA had nothing and referred me to the Commonwealth of Kentucky. They had no military records for Francis and referred me to the Ohio Historical Society. I decided to write this one last letter.

The Ohio Historical Society responded and had no military records, but they did furnish a burial record for Francis. Then as I read further in their letter it said, "We found the enclosed material indicating that Nicholas Questel was one of the original French Five Hundred." Enclosed was a copy of the list of lot owners in Gallipolis in 1795. This was exactly what I was looking for and I had not even asked for it. The lesson I learned is: Try, try and then try again. You may find the information you are looking for out of the clear blue sky, like I did. — Nick Questell, IL

A Brickwall In Liechtenstein

About 10 years ago I actively started researching my mother's paternal family, whose surname was Eberle. I had discovered an obituary for my great-grandfather Louis (Alois) who immigrated to the US as a child from Liechtenstein. I had no clue as to where to begin to find records about this family and the country. I started my search by working on my pedigree chart and tracing back to Louis Eberle born in Liechtenstein. I made a list of what it was I wanted to find out about Louis and his family. I thought the typical things, like vital records, obituaries, cemetery records, photos, census records and maybe a ship list, would be good to have. I never dreamed to get much further past the time of arrival to the US.

I began what I thought to be an

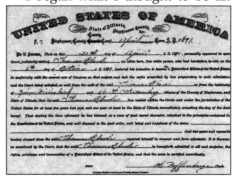

Thomas Eberle's Naturalization paper from Stephenson county, (Freeport) IL.

impossible task, looking through ship lists. I started guessing the date of arrival, port of departure and port of arrival. One fateful day in the library I came across a gold-colored, paperback book in the genealogy department titled *Passenger And Immigration Lists Bibliography 1538-1900; A Guide To Published Lists Of Arrivals In The United States And Canada* edited by P. William Filby. It was a bibliography of ship lists that were indexed into nationalities, years, arrivals, departure and arrival ports.

Magdalena Eberle's gravestone in St. Joseph Cemetery.

I really did not expect to find anything but thumbed through and copied the title for future reference. Before returning it to the shelf, I looked through the extensive index in the back. What I found told me that someone else had heard of Liechtenstein! In the book's Liechtenstein entry it explained that the list was a book written in German by Norbert Jansen, entitled *Nach Amerika*. The book is about families who immigrated to the US and where they settled. Through inter-library loan I was able to get a copy from another Wisconsin branch library. It was in German, but that did not deter

me, especially when one of the chapters was titled, "Freeport, Illinois".

As I scanned down the chapter I saw familiar names of my earliest known ancestors and became increasingly excited. I had the chapter and introduction translated and came to find out the year of arrival and port of embarkation. With this information, I found Thomas and Magdalena Eberle with six children, one of them being Alois.

Notations made in the book told the address of the archives for this country. I wrote them immediately and they sent me my family lineage back to the mid-1600s. While I know this is an exceptional thing to have happen, it just took that one right reference to find what I obtained.
— Susan A. Schlosser, WI, sas46_99@yahoo.com

Genealogy — The Cure For The Blues

While visiting my sister in Longview, TX shortly after Christmas a few years ago her neighbor came by to say "Hi!" and tell of her trip home to Nebraska. She had brought her dad back after heart surgery. He was very depressed having to leave his wife in a nursing home there, having never spent much time apart. I asked her where her father lived in Nebraska and she mentioned a town I was not familiar with. I said I had family in Dundy county since the 1880s.

She was startled to find I knew where Dundy county was since it was so sparsely populated and rather remote. In fact it was the county she grew up in. I had contacted family members there but they were not really responsive to my queries. After mentioning some family names she said I needed to talk to her dad since he was county commissioner there for more than 40 years. I spent the next few hours with him. He got his home town phone book and suggested I write or call the family members he knew and mention his name. From there I was able to catch up with several family members that had previously been elusive to my research questions.

What a break! The real up side was it apparently broke his spell of depression. He started eating more and interacted with other family members, discussing the old days with them. — Elaine Acosta, LA

A Genealogist's Delight!

My brickwall was an unknown name. My maternal great-grandmother's name on her death certificate was Alice Debora Tarrah. I had received many family tree papers and notes from a distant cousin regarding this family when I first started my family history hobby. One of the notes stated that they had never been able to discover any more about my great-grandmother. There were no Tarrahs that they could find. Now, they had been doing their research before the advent of the Internet, so I thought it would be a piece of cake; I would just put the name into the search engine of choice and voila, there it should be. How wrong I was. There are no Tarrahs — at least as a surname.

A couple of years later I helped a family member move out of the family home of three generations. There were several sheds just full of papers and photographs — a genealogist's delight! Because I am the family historian, I was able to bring what I wanted home with me, a whole pickup load! There were two children's books in the collection that had inscriptions ending with "with love, from your cousin, Katie Parsons". These books came from the box of Alice's collection. So now I had another name to work with. Also in this same collection I found enough information to figure out that maybe Alice had come

from Holmes county, OH or at least Katie did. So I joined the Holmes county mailing list and started reading everything that was posted. It took about a year, but finally someone posted a query regarding a Parson who had married a Tarrh. What a difference that A made! I was able to reveal further back into my maternal great-grandmother's family with this post. — Elizabeth Jay Davis, WA

Chance Meeting

When my aunt started secretarial school in 1942 she met another girl with the same surname of Cassidy and both fathers were Joseph Cassidy. They went home and discovered that they were second cousins. The families got together for a visit and then fell out of touch until 1997.

Kevin Cassidy's aunt and uncle, Joseph John Cassidy and Sarah Alice Goodwin before their 1919 wedding.

I gleaned what I could from my aunt that the non-related Joseph Cassidy had a wife Lillian and siblings, Joseph, Mary (who married a McRory) and Frank. They lived in Bayside, Queens. After trying to find Cassidys in the Bayside section of Queens from the phone book I decided to use the 1920 federal census. I found Joseph and Lillian Cassidy living in Queens with her parents named McGorry. When I checked the phone book I found a McGorry in Bayside and called. Sure enough they were related to the Cassidys and gave me a contact name. Surprisingly they were also related to me because Mary Cassidy married a McGorry not McRory. Siblings Joe and Mary Cassidy married first cousins Lillian and Bill McGorry. Joe and Mary Cassidy's parents had married in Ireland in 1877 and had two sons there so it was possible to identify the place of origin in Ireland down to Ruddle's Row, Newry, County Armagh.

A chance meeting and a story passed down from my aunt helped me fill out some of my family history. — Kevin Cassidy, NE, kmct@earthlink.net

Back On The Trail Again

My paternal grandmother's family, the Sharps, presented the greatest challenge in my family research. All I knew about her family was from her obituary. It gave the name of her parents, including her mother's maiden name, Devlin. However, there was no indication of where in Scotland they came from, what year they came to the US, where they were naturalized or if there were any other children besides my grandmother. My 75-year-old dad didn't seem to know much about his mother's side of the family. I assumed she was an only child. One day, my dad told me he remembered hearing that his mom had a sister, Annie, and a brother, James. He further remembered that James had gone to Canada during WWI and joined the Army there.

It took me several weeks before I decided to try using the Internet to locate the enlistment papers of James Sharp. I looked for Canadian Military Records and under the category of Soldiers of the First World War, 1914-1918 — Canadian Expeditionary Force, I found many James Sharps. I checked every James Sharp and, screaming with joy, found the scanned attestation papers of my great-uncle James Sharp! These papers included his age, birth date, place of birth, last place of residence (Bismarck, ND) and occupation. It also listed my grandmother as his next-of-kin. It included James' height, weight, eye and hair color as well as his religion. From these records, I could trace James from Scotland to Pennsylvania to Bismarck, ND and then to Canada.

Furthermore, after learning where they came from in Scotland (Hamilton, in Lanarkshire), I joined the Lanarkshire, Scotland mailing list. I was soon contacted by a helpful gentleman who had found the names of James' parents in the census records. It listed when and where they were married, where they resided and the names of two older siblings who, apparently, stayed behind when my grandmother came over here. Suddenly I have a wealth of information about my grandma Sharp's family that has broken down my brickwall and put me back on the trail again. — Kathy A. Dean, PA, history1@adelphia.net

Unlocking The Past With Ziploc Bags

After years of trying to locate information and records on my Doherty family in Montana, I made the long trip from Washington to the small town of Boulder. Not knowing for sure which cemetery I should start in, I decided to check the one at the Catholic Church, as my family had been Catholic.

With dowels, Ziploc bags and a short description of the people I was looking for, I set out to find John and Margaret (Campbell) Doherty. The cemetery was very small, so walking up and down the rocky rows was fast and easy. There before me on the second row were two small granite headstones. Carved for all to see were the names of John and Margaret Doherty. It was overwhelming to see, as I had hunted for them for so long.

At the graves, I planted the dowels with Ziploc bags taped to them. I included a short note about John and Margaret, their children and my name, address and telephone number. I wanted to let people know why I was looking for living family. As I walked away I thought it would be a real miracle if any family members would ever walk the same rocky path and read my message.

Within a day of placing the message, I received a call from a cousin in Butte, MT. She and another cousin had been in the cemetery placing flowers that afternoon and they saw my message. They were very excited to find someone looking for their ancestors.

We have since then met each other and shared my pictures and records. What a find and all because of a note left in a Ziploc bag at the cemetery. — Shirley Penna-Oakes, WA

Grandpa, Where Did You Live?

Early in my research I discovered that grandfather, Daniel Archibald McNab, lived in Spink county, Dakota Territory for about three years. He then sold his homestead and returned to Wisconsin briefly in 1886. While there he met and married my grandmother, Martha Cecil Myers. Beyond this the only information I had was a memoir written by a son, my Uncle Gordon, about the family's move to DeSmet, SD.

Since DeSmet is the county seat for Kingsbury county, I wrote the county's Register of Deeds to obtain homestead or other land records. No reply. I wrote also the postmaster at Erwin, the State Historical Society in Pierre, the editor of the DeSmet newspaper and the County Auditor to see if school census lists existed for the children. All gave me little or no new information.

I concluded Kingsbury county would require personal on-site research. Before my trip I was gratified to receive school census records, which listed the McNab children beginning in 1894. At least I knew they lived in the county — somewhere.

Spirit Lake District #6 School in Kingsbury county, SD. McNab children attended this school from 1888 to 1902.

My first research stop in DeSmet was the Register of Deeds office to look for homestead, birth and death records for the McNabs. It only took a few minutes, with a county map, to locate the one-room school the McNab children attended. From past experience I knew the McNab farm should lay within a two-to-three-mile radius of the school. There simply was no property registered to Daniel McNab for the period 1886-1904.

Next, I visited the auditor. We looked at records but nothing new turned up except I discovered all county offices had additional records stored in the basement. Immediately I went to the basement vault where the old Register of Deeds records were stored.

I determined Grandpa McNab lived in Hartland township (Erwin) 1890-94 and in Spirit Lake township 1895-1902. He was assessed personal property taxes (not always paid) but no real estate taxes. Next, I visited the clerk of courts and the treasurer to see if they could offer any advice. The treasurer suggested that I research mortgages since just about every farmer back then was poor and borrowed from next year to pay this year's bills or took loans out on anything of value.

I went to the Register of Deeds to look at mortgage records books. There were mortgages for horses, a harrow, $1800 to International Harvester and so on. Still, with all this data, I did not know where the family lived.

Suddenly, I spotted an entry mortgaging the crops on NE 1/4 of S11 T112 R56. This meant grandfather farmed that land. Imagine my elation — the first and, as it turned out later, the only entry in the entire courthouse records to tie any land to grandfather. I raced up the stairs to the register of deeds office and located that piece of property. It was less than a mile from the school attended by the McNab children.

The next day I visited the schoolhouse and tried to find the McNab property. I was ecstatic to see my grandparents' home from 1895 to 1904 — but I still lacked proof.

I realized that some of the children on the list of school attendees, provided by the auditor, may still be living in DeSmet. So, I grabbed the local telephone book to see if any were listed. Four of the surnames did appear and I immediately tried calling them all. Two were not related and two did not answer.

I went to the library and looked at newspapers on microfilm and talked with the librarian. I asked her about the two people, who may have been schoolmates of my aunts and uncles, which I had tried to telephone. She suggested I contact another person who lived near DeSmet. This person was one of the girls on my list and the librarian knew her married name.

This woman confirmed she was a schoolmate of Archie, Robbie and Jennie, my uncles and aunt, without me mentioning their names. When I asked if she knew the buildings I felt were the McNab home, her reply was, "Yes, of course. They have always lived there."

McNab family prairie farm house in Kingsbury county, SD.

Proving where my grandparents lived depended on four things: Use of primary records, personal on-site research, detective work and perseverance. — David L. Perkins, CA

Hunt For The Age Instead Of The Name

In researching microfilm of an 1880 census of Iceland to find my husband's grandfather I used a process that speeds up the search. I knew his birth date and figured he was about five years old at that time, so instead of attempting to read the names first I followed the age column down, checking each child's name who was listed as four, five or six years old.

In this way, Grampa Johannes was found quite easily along with family we never knew he had! I consider this a very helpful tool in researching any film that is not English or that is just difficult to read. — Bonnie Johannes, WA

Pay Attention To Contract Witnesses

In 1818, John Coy married Deborah in Sullivan county, IN according to the Oregon Donation Land Records. I worked for eight years and tried everything I could to find Deborah's maiden name. John Coy was from Hardin county, KY and in about 1818 his entire family left for Trigg county in the western part of Kentucky. Only John went to Indiana. Logically John migrated with his wife's family.

I copied the 1820 census pages for Sullivan Co, IN. I did the same for William Coy, his father, in Hardin county, KY. I studied both counties looking for similar names. I actually found two that I followed until I knew that Deborah did not belong to either family.

In Oregon, I noticed that John House (Hawes/Haws) seemed to have a close relationship with John Coy. They signed for one another for the Oregon land and witnessed each other's daughter's weddings. John Hawes was about 15 years younger than John Coy so I figured that he might have married one of John Coy's daughters. I was able to prove that this was not so. I had to finally conclude that they lived near each other in Johnson county, MO and came on the Oregon Trail together and therefore must have been good friends.

Finally not long ago, I decided to review the 1820 census records for Sullivan county. I looked at the name above John Coy and it was John Hawes. I had been reading the name as Hayes for seven years. The census copy was not good and the writing very flowery. The C was quite fancy and it hit the name above making it look like the letter was below the line like a Y. Once I saw that, I knew that John Hawes in Oregon was the brother of Deborah. I then rechecked Hawes in Hardin county. I found none but did find them in Nelson county, which is next to Hardin.

There are three things I learned from this brickwall: Recheck your data periodically. Sometimes during subsequent readings you pick up things that you missed previously or simply see things differently. Also, copy the entire page of census records. Last, pay attention to any name you see associated with your ancestor, such as witnesses for marriages, land or wills. Often relations signed for other relations. — Carolyn Peterson, CA, corkster@attbi.com

Have A Little Faith

When I was 14, my mother and stepfather moved away from my birthplace. They settled in Conroe, TX next door to a family named Faith, who were said to be my mother's cousins. My family lived there for about two years and decided to move back. My stepfather and I did not get along, so at 16 I decided I was going to stay while my family moved. I was disowned, but I stayed in contact with some of the other family members. My mother said I could not write, phone or see her. Later I settled down and had a family.

Eventually I remarried and when my new wife asked about my family, I realized I didn't really know much about them. We started working on my family tree and when we reached the Myers, my mother's family, we hit a snag. We were able to find all the siblings of my grandfather, except one, a woman named Mariah (according to census records).

When we began trying to find the association with the Carl Faith family, we found that his great-grandfather was married to a Meyers, the sister to my third-great-grandfather. So I thought I solved that one — not quite. Carl's mother was named Rida Meyers, according to Myers family records, but no one knew what Meyers she was related to. We searched in vain to find some record of her.

One day I was talking to someone in Florida about the Myers and Faith families and he said that there was a Glenn Faith in the same town we live near. Our Carl Faith had a brother named Glenn who would be in his 90s if still living, but I thought he had already passed on. I called anyway, hoping he would be a relative and found it was the Glenn Faith I remembered! He had moved from Houston several years ago and now lives about 20 minutes from us. Glenn has just turned 93.

We called and set a time for a visit. Lo and behold, we found that his mother Rida Meyers was actually Rida Myers, sister of my grandfather, Ora Wendell Myers. This Rida was evidently listed on census records as Mariah. After checking birth and Social Security records, we have proved this fact. The best part is that we now have many long-lost cousins we are establishing contact with. — Wilson League, TX, leaguetree@aol.com

Message Boards Find Long-Lost Relatives

The brickwall I had was with George Collier, my great-grandfather. Family records did not list any of his relatives. I noted on the 1880 federal census for Leake county, MS, that he was living next door to William T. Collier who would be old enough to be his father, but I had no proof.

For several months I read the Collier message boards on the Internet. One day it appeared, a query

Collier message board on RootsWeb.com.

about a William T. Collier who came from South Carolina through Alabama to Leake county, MS.

Through this query I established contact with two distant cousins (each of us from a different son of William T. Collier). By pooling our information we concluded that George T. Collier's neighbor in 1880 was indeed his father. I had found the relative names of relatives of my great-grandfather and some living cousins! — June Collier, MS

My Genealogy Fairy Godmother

My most successful way for getting around a brickwall is by networking, but not in the usual way.

I placed a query in an issue of *Everton's Genealogical Helper* asking if anyone had information regarding a Slagle ancestor of mine who seemed to disappear around 1865. I received a response from a retired professional genealogist who had done work on my Slagle family several years before.

Based on her extensive notes, she was able to answer my question regarding what happened to Margaret Slagle as well as provide me with additional information. She also taught me, an amateur genealogist, about the value of deeds, particularly estate deeds, for tracing female ancestors when they marry or remarry and seem to disappear.

This genealogy fairy godmother

was kind enough to help me with additional branches of my family where I was having trouble. She checked some of her out-of-print books for me; she found how an ancestor of mine had started to use his first name instead of his middle name when he enlisted in the Civil War, thus leading me to additional family information in his Civil War Pension File. Before her help, he was another ancestor who seemed to disappear.

Although networking seems like a very general solution, my situation was helpful in my research and a learning experience for me. In addition, I made another friend through this effort and still keep in touch with the researcher. — Lisa Kerr Ilowite, NJ

Jewish Funeral Service Records

I am relatively new to genealogical research. I've started and stopped, getting nowhere, many times in the past. But this time, I had a helpful start from a posting on a genealogical website. Due to this posting, I have been able to get a lot of information from an unusually rich source at the Western Reserve Historical Society: the Burial Books of J.D. Deutsch Funeral Home and Crematory in Cleveland, OH. All the record books from this popular Jewish Funeral Service have been turned over to the Society.

However, not everyone used Deutsch as their choice of funeral parlor. According to obituaries from the early 20th century, a popular one that no longer seems to exist is Cohn-Margowski Funeral Services. I had not found anyone, even those involved for quite a long time in this area, who knew who this service was and/or how it is related to current combined services functioning in this area.

Then one day, I was checking an old microfilm issue of a Jewish week-

ly, the *Jewish Independent*, and looked around the page, rather than just focusing on the article of my interest. Logically, since I was in the Obituary section, there was an advertisement for Cohn-Margowski. In the advertisement it mentioned the Berkowitz chapel and listed the two funeral directors, both with the name of Berkowitz. Jackpot! One of the main currently functional Jewish funeral operations in this area is Berkowitz Kumin so I now know where to check for more Cohn-Margowski records. — Sue Weiser, OH, sue@weiserweb.net

You Scratch Mine And I'll Scratch Yours

I answered a query on the Oneida county, NY, website to help a person with the surname Hamlin as it is also in my family. Imagine my great surprise when I found that this man had books from Germany with my Baechle/Bachle family in them.

Through these books, I finally found the parents and grandparents of my second-great-grandfather. I

One of the items given to Carol Michaud by someone she met through answering a query on a genealogy website — the death certificate of Catherine Schelorn Baechle.

MR. AND MRS. REINHARDT BAECHLE.

On Monday next Mr. and Mrs. Reinhardt Baechle, two well-known and highly respected residents of this city, will celebrate the golden anniversary of their wedding with a mass in St. Joseph's Church at 9 o'clock in the morning. In the evening the happy event will be celebrated at their pleasant home, 178 Columbia St, and there they will entertain a number of friends in addition to the members of their family. Mr. and Mrs. Baechle have been residents of this city for more than half a century and that they will be able to celebrate other events of the kind is the wish of many friends.

Mr. Baechle was born in Jungholz, Baden, about 75 years ago, and Mrs. Baechle, whose maiden name was Catherine Schellhorn, was born in Schleidthal, Alsace. Mr. Baechle came to this country in 1852 and a short time afterwards Mrs. Baechle came here. They were united in marriage in St. Joseph's Church on June 26, 1855, the church then being a wooden building on Lafayette street. The ceremony was performed by Rev. Father [...] C. Well[...]

who was then pastor, but who passed away a number of years ago. Mr. Baechle was employed at his trade of shoemaker by Jacob J. Hamlin for over twenty-two years and later worked for himself. He retired from active business six years ago and has since lived a quiet life at home. Directly after their marriage Mr. and Mrs. Baechle went to live in the house at the corner of Columbia and Varick streets, but for the past thirty years they have resided in the house where they now make their home. Both Mr. and Mrs. Baechle are faithful members of St. Joseph's Church, being among the oldest attendants there. Mr. Baechle is also a member of the Roman Catholic Benevolent Society and his wife belongs to the Altar Society of the church and the St. Elizabeth's Home Guild.

The venerable couple have four children and ten grandchildren, all of whom will be present at the celebration. They are: Catherine, widow of George Goppert; Mary, wife of Louis Stenger; Veronica, widow of Michael Go[...] Albert [...]

Another one of the items concerning Carol Michard's family that was given to her by someone she met through answering a query on a genealogy website.

didn't know them before because all his and his brothers' records had parents listed as unknown.

He had been naturalized under the old law, thereby he didn't have to give his parentage. This man and I shared information on the Hamlin/ Hemmerle names and I did research in Oneida county on them for him, thereby finding also my second-great-grandmother's parents, grandparents, etc. — Carol Michaud, NY

Go Forward In Order To Go Back

Two months after I began my family history research I knew my second-great-grandfather was James B. Sidbury from Onslow county, NC. I also knew that he either was the son of James Sidbury and had a wife named Elizabeth Hines, or he was the son of John Sidbury and his wife (and

cousin) was named Elizabeth Sidbury. Both men and both women were the same ages and both marriages occurred in Onslow county within two years of each other. After five years of diligent research of all available documents of early 19th-century Onslow county, I still faced this brick-wall and still could not place my James in the correct family.

I leaned towards James being the son of John Sidbury since his son, John Sidbury, Jr., came to Jacksonville, FL just prior to the Florida 1845 statehood election and that city is where my James also settled as a young man at about the same time. I easily was on the brink of accepting the fact that John, Jr. and James were brothers, even though there was no proof. The early (1820-40) census records just didn't quite fit with my known date of birth for James Sidbury of 1819-20.

My James had one daughter who he named Rhoda Elizabeth for the given names of the daughter's two grandmothers (Rhoda Collins and the unknown Elizabeth). However, the name of Elizabeth did not offer any proof since that was the given name of the mother of both men. Despite the balance of my figurative and literal substantial weight of evidence pointing ever so slightly towards the family of John and Elizabeth Sidbury, I still held off committing to that family as being my ancestral line.

In one last, desperate search for proof, I planned a tactic that had proved successful in other past, similar situations: to look forward at sibling descendants in order to go backwards. By progressing forward through the descendants of my James Sidbury, my notes revealed the unusual surname of Fridell when his granddaughter, Ida Fallana married Orien P. Fridell in Jacksonville. The only surviving children of this marriage were two sons, John Louis and James Alvie Fridell.

I had an old Jacksonville telephone book, so I looked up the name of

Fridell and was shocked to find a John L. Fridell, Jr. A quick telephone call later I had discovered a new cousin, John Louis Fridell, Jr., who not only knew of our Sidbury connection, but also had the family's old (circa 1848) Bible. Johnny, as he preferred, read to me the first entry in the Bible that stated: "James Sidbury, son of James Sidbury and Elizabeth, his wife, was born the 15th day of November 1820."

I know, to this day, I would never have been able to prove my correct Sidbury lineage were it not for Johnny and our family's old Bible. I would never have torn down my brickwall had I not looked forward at the families of descendants of my ancestor's siblings. — Bob Nichols, FL, bnichols@tfn.net

Rewarding Work

In 1983, my paternal first cousin, Bertie, sent me a copy of a genealogical chart of our ancestors, dating back to 1516 in England, which he had painstakingly compiled over a period of 15 years. The chart is about 20 feet long and three feet wide and has to be rolled out on the living room carpet to be read. It is most inaccessible for regular reference.

Following Bertie's death in 1990, and knowing I was the sole recipient of a copy of the chart, I resolved to continue his research and locate every living member of my paternal line. I wanted to make available the stories of our colorful family, in written form to them. The result is a 372-page book, copies of which were sent to 50 surviving family members all over the world.

I met my brickwall with two first cousins; an illegitimate son of my father's sister and his half-brother: No family member had been in touch with them for almost 60 years and Bertie's chart did not show them. Their last known whereabouts was in Birkenhead, near Liverpool, in England.

I obtained the name and address of the local newspaper there and wrote a letter to the editor, asking any of their readers who knew my cousins to contact me. Friends of one of the brothers saw my letter, told him and he wrote to me. He had no children, was then 70 years old and had lost touch with his only brother who had moved to Ottley in Yorkshire in 1933.

So I followed the same procedure with the Ottley newspaper, with similar success. My cousin hadn't moved far in the intervening years, saw my letter and wrote to me. He was now 78, married with one daughter, who had three sons. I gave each of my cousins the other's address and a great reunion was held. They have also received a copy of my book, with annual updates of births, marriages, deaths and changes of address.

As one of them wrote to me: "I never knew any of my mother's relations, and suddenly I have my brother back, and a huge family: it's wonderful."

All my roots are in England and research from this distance can be very time consuming and costly, but the rewards are enormous. — Joan Iris (Gooch) Rutter, ON

Mortgage Applications — More Fun Than You Can Ever Imagine

I searched for years for my grandfather's (Erich Otto Stutzke) naturalization date. I knew he and his family came to Wisconsin from Europe in about 1903, but there were no records in Wisconsin. They moved to Mt. Vernon, NY in around 1912, but there were no records there either. They then moved to Carteret, NJ in about 1922 and I finally found them in Middlesex county, NJ records.

I had a copy of the deed to their

home purchased in Carteret in 1924 and evidently he had to be a citizen in order to obtain a mortgage. He was naturalized in 1924! With that group of papers I found all the information on his immigration record, plus my father's name (Eugene August Frey.) At that time my father was 16 years old and working as a clerk at Carteret Town Hall. He signed his future father-in-law's petition as a witness! Grandpa became a citizen of the US 21 years after arriving.

Ilsa Frey Lezgus used mortgage applications to find information on her grandfather Erich Stutzke, here with Augusta, his wife.

My advice is not to give up looking for your record. Also, check every locality your ancestor lived in and check for mortgage applications. — Ilsa Frey Lezgus, FL, maxdog29@comcast.net

Dying Young

I was researching my husband's great-grandfather, Allen Gow and his wife, Lucy Brown. They were married in Portland, ME in 1825 and had five children, all born in Portland.

We traveled back to this area and I was able to get a copy of their marriage license and birth certificates for three of the five children. Two of the children, Frankie and Willie, died in Portland and therein lies my problem.

There were no records of the birth or death of these two boys. One died at the age of one and the other died in infancy. My mother-in-law told me that they were buried in Portland but did not know where. There are a lot of old cemeteries in Portland. Additionally I didn't know when they were born or died.

I researched the FHC, corresponded with the Historical Society in Portland, the library and the newspaper, all with no luck in finding these children. After I had searched microfilm after microfilm, I sent for a death index in Maine for 1877 and there was Frankie Gow. He died in September 1877 at the age of one and there was a listing of the cemetery where he was buried.

So I found information on Frankie, but I am still looking for information about Willie. — Patricia A. Heumann, CA, i436643@thegrid.net

The Benefits Of A Rare Surname

My genealogical problem was that I had no contact with my father's side of the family as my parents divorced when I was three. My paternal grandfather died when I was three, my father, an only child, died while I was in school and my grandmother died when I was in college. I only established contact with my grandmother after my dad's death. I flew to meet her before she died and was informed I was the only living relative. After she died I received a picture of her mother and a list of my father's siblings with birth and death dates.

I first requested my grandparents' SS-5s to see what they said. To my disappointment they filed incorrect information about their parents and birthplaces. None of the information for my grandfather's SS-5 matched what he had written for his family records. I looked up his brothers in California that I could find using the old records. I found them all in the Social Security database. I then proceeded to request his brothers' data on their SS-5s and this information perfectly matched the data my grandfather had written on his personal information. Birth and death dates matched and I located counties where they resided and verified his mother and father's name. I then proceeded to trace my name to the 1700s.

I was able to trace everything through census records. I was lucky I have a rare surname and they were in states where the census is now on the Internet. I've traced about 10 lines to the 1600s to Germany and England.
— Catherine Livezey, CA

Broaden The Focus

"Focus on your direct lines," said my genealogy instructor. Or at least that's what I heard her say.

For at least 10 years, I recorded information I obtained from the census about my ancestors' siblings, but otherwise I ignored their existence.

This changed recently when I faced a dead end while researching my great-grandparents, Joshua and Elmira (Fannin) Blanton. Joshua was a coal miner, who lived in Kentucky, Arkansas and West Virginia. They had one daughter and three sons including Joshua, Jr., my grandfather. I never knew my grandfather.

My mother shared stories about her father, but she could remember very little about his family. I wanted to learn more about my great-grandparents.

As I unsuccessfully searched the SSDI for my grandfather, I discovered

his brother, Edward. Based on the date and place of death listed, I obtained a copy of his death certificate. From that certificate I learned the name of the funeral home that handled the services. Online, I found a funeral home in Ashland, KY with a similar name and was able to obtain a copy of the papers that were completed at the time of the funeral, listing the names of the survivors. There was the married name of his surviving sister and her place of residence. Another online search turned up two listings for her married name. I wrote to both of them.

Edward Blanton's death certificate.

One morning I got a call from her grandson. We had a wonderful chat as I learned that my great-grandfather was killed in a coal mine accident in 1915 and is buried in Henryetta, OK. This grandson put me in touch with two of his aunts who told me how and when my great-grandmother died and where she is buried. I also learned that Elmira had often talked to their mother (my grandfather's sister) about a twin sister. I have since been in touch with a Fannin descendant on the Internet whose great-grandfather had a sister named Elmira. He said the stories he's heard about the family are that Elmira and her sister Amanda were twins!

I now know so much more about this family than I did just a few months earlier — all because I broadened my research to include my grandfather's siblings. Of course, there is still much to validate about the information I received and I still haven't located my great-grandfather's ancestors. But by including my grandfather's siblings in my research, I at least feel like I've been able to climb a wall that once looked so ominous — Dora Hildebrand, CO, dmhildebrand@aol.com

A Brickwall... Almost

I started looking for information on my great-grandfather, Fred John Stulken, more than a quarter century ago. A county history recorded that he came to Freeport, IL in 1870 and he married Helene Lammers in 1875. I checked with several churches and historical societies in the Freeport area and adjacent counties and never found a record of him being in the area, nor have I ever found a record of their marriage.

I checked passenger lists and found Helene Lammers' passage in 1875. I checked every passenger list that my great-grandfather would logically be on and never found anything. His death record at the church simply lists the date he died and the date of the funeral. Helene Lammers Stulken's death record indicates she was from Grossherzogtum Oldenburg — the Duchy of Oldenburg. Since Lammers is a patronym and most with that surname are not related, that wasn't much to go on. Their respective death certificates list their places of birth as Germany and the names of their parents as "not known", except that Helene's father is

listed as James (it was really Herman).

Two bits of good fortune have made the solution fairly simple. First, my grandparents and then my aunt and uncle lived in a little house for a total of 45 years. When the house was sold, the man who purchased it noticed a slip of paper about the size of a check in a corner of a closet. It was Helene Lammers' confirmation certificate from Bockhorn. I shall be forever grateful to him for taking the trouble to give it to one of my cousins. A genealogist working in Bockhorn has traced Helene's lineage going back five generations.

Second, since my dad's cousin had no children, he gave me a box that included two letters written in German in the 1920s. One of the letters was signed by Diedrich Hedemann in Bad Zwischenahn.

A translation of the letters convinced me that the writers of the letters were relatives. I tried the Internet and sent a letter to Bad Zwischenahn. A distant cousin replied and sent me three generations of my great-grandfather's line. — Marilyn Stulken, WI, mstulken@discover-net.net

Soundex Magic

Several of my early family members "disappeared" from the family farm in the mid-to-late 1800s. I had no idea of how to go about finding them and we went without any information for more than 20 years. Then I used the US federal census Soundex for a branch we knew had gone to Kansas.

I realized that I would be able to use the Soundex like an index to scan the whole US. Soundex cards generally list the person's date or year of birth and where they were born. I got the Soundex reels from my local FHC for several likely states and quickly went through them noting Canadians with the right name and approximate year of birth. I located my Graham — they had moved to Stanley, WI, following the lumber trade. I confirmed this information later with an obituary. — Heather Boucher Ashe, ON, h_boucher@sympatico.ca

Unearthing Relations In The Graveyard

My brickwall story makes the point that there is often no substitute for traveling to the places where your ancestors lived to just take a close look around. Especially in the case of cemeteries, you can sometimes pick up hints that you will never find in a simple cemetery listing.

I had a brickwall with my third-great-grandfather, Lewis Gordon, who had died in Kentucky. Most of what I knew about him came from some old family stories that said he had come into Kentucky from Virginia. I had therefore been spending a lot of time searching Virginia resources without having much luck.

I had a cemetery listing for him in the Old Washington Cemetery near Maysville, KY, and took a trip there just for the experience of finding his gravesite. When I eventually found it, there were stones there for both Lewis and his wife, Keziah. Keziah's maiden name was not indicated, so there were no leads there. However, on inspecting the site, I noticed there was a marker immediately adjacent to the Gordon family plot. That stone was the same style. In fact, it was so close to the others that it seemed to be part of the same grouping. The name on the marker was Jonathan Stout. Who was Jonathan Stout?

Using various Internet search tools, I looked up some Stout family resources. Amazingly, within just a few minutes I had found a site with an online tree that showed a marriage between a Keziah Stout and a Lewis Gordon! There were no reliable dates or sources cited, but within a short time everything fell into place. The big breakthrough was that this Stout branch had originated in New Jersey, not Virginia. After switching my research focus to New Jersey (an area that I was not familiar with), I quickly found my Gordon connections going back at least two more generations and with a possible link to Scotland. Not only that, but I found myself descended from the Stout line, which has its own rich and well-documented history.

Keziah Gordon's gravestone.

I have since found similar clues in other old cemeteries. Related families often had gravesites close to each other, or perhaps a husband and wife might be buried in the wife's family plot. By taking a close look around, it is often possible at least to pick up some related surnames for further study.

And the relationship of Jonathan Stout to Lewis and Keziah? He was both Keziah's second cousin and brother-in-law, being married to her sister, Rachel. A group of Stout families had immigrated to Mason county, KY from the Hopewell, NJ area in the 1790s. — Doug Gordon, MI, doug@wdgordon.com

How To Make A Tombstone Come Alive

My normal research techniques seemed to be steadily yielding fewer results in obtaining information on my second-great-grandparents and my grandmother's brother. Then I hit upon an innovative and unorthodox research technique.

Memorial Day was fast approaching and departed loved ones' graves are visited to pay personal respects. Around this part of Kansas, we always leave flowers at the gravesite and often say a few quiet words to each of our relatives. For many years at this small cemetery, where I am secretary/treasurer, I place a book at the cemetery entrance that allows visitors to register. It is interesting for all to look at the list of visitors. You might find a relative's name on the list. It was then that a brickwall solution came to me.

A few years ago I took my mother to the Mountridge township cemetery in McPherson county, KS, on Memorial Day to visit the graves of her great-grandparents, William and Anna (Goshe) Vogt. We found flowers at the gravesite, but from whom?

The following year, I left a package that included a pedigree chart, family group sheets and highlighted how I was related to the deceased. I also included a cover sheet containing the surname I was searching, my name, address, telephone number and e-mail address. Since I have a computer I typed in bold letters and printed the cover sheet in red and blue ink. I placed the sheets in a clear, gallon-size Ziploc bag with the introduction cover sheet showing through the plastic.

On the Tuesday before Memorial Day I traveled to the Mountridge township cemetery and taped the packets on the Vogt tombstones. I also visited the Newton Greenwood Cemetery in Harvey county and left a packet there with a different surname cover sheet on a Mead tombstone.

Carol Burke Peterson attached genealogical information and her contact information to an ancestor's gravestone.

It worked! To my amazement I received a phone call from a cousin who had retrieved my packet from a loved one's grave in the Greenwood Cemetery. Before she called me she had already sent my information to two other family members in California and Kansas. Since then we have met and shared photographs and information. Also, in the mail that week I received a letter from another newly found cousin, whose brother picked up the packet at the Mountridge township cemetery and was kind enough to make a copy and return the original packet back on the stone for other family members to find. She sent me family group sheets and invited me to a Vogt family reunion, which I attended that July.

As a result of these packets I have netted many new cousins, priceless old photographs, information and friendships. — Carol Burke Peterson, KS, peterson@kanokla.net

Several Sources Needed For Verification

According to family history my second-great-grandfather, George Washington Cramer, was born in Pennsylvania to Pennsylvania Dutch parents. The only other information I had concerning him was that he was married to a Mary Ann Raycroft in Ontario. I had no birth dates, no marriage date or place, nothing. I couldn't find any record of George in Pennsylvania, so I turned my search northward to Canada.

A distant relative sent me a copy of an excerpt from *The Centennial History Of Arygle*, *"Come into Our Heritage"* that stated that George Washington Cramer's family was from Ireland and settled in Pennsylvania. George then married Mary Ann Raycroft near Kingston, ON. This book gave me the first major break in finding George and his family.

From there I checked with Canadian online resources for Kingston. A volunteer named Jen found my George Washington Cramer married to Mary Ann Raycroft in 1858, in the 1858-69 County Marriage Register of Ontario, except Mary Ann's name was spelled Reogcraft. Not only did Jen e-mail me about George but she also sent information for his parents, Abraham and Mary and that George had two brothers, Abraham and

Clockwise from left: George Washington Cramer, daughter Margaret Elizabeth, wife Mary Ann Raycroft and son Charles Abraham. Taken c. 1878 in Kingston, ON.

Edward, who were also listed in the marriage register as well. This gave their wives' names and Mary Ann Raycroft's parents' names, as well as their ages at the time of marriage and their birthplaces too.

From this I found that George Washington and his brothers were not born in Pennsylvania, but in Kingston. Another volunteer, Ruth, found Mary Ann's parents and siblings in the 1851 census for Kingston. She also found George Washington and his brother, Abraham, Jr. (both listed as Cremer) working for other families as laborers at the age of 15 and 17. Their brother, Edward, was still too young and would have been living at home. But Edward and his parents were nowhere to be found.

Then I was lucky to find a posting on one of the message boards from a Cramer descendant of George Washington. After corresponding with Bryan, we were delighted to find that we were third cousins. He put me in touch with his sister who is doing more of the family research and after locating another one of the Cramers from a separate branch of George Washington descendants, another Brian, I found I was no longer working alone.

I still was wondering what happened to Abraham Cramer, Sr., when I submitted a search on World Family Tree and a lookup for the Canadian Genealogy Index 1600s to 1900s. I found Abraham, Sr. was a yeoman bondsman in 1833 in Kingston at another yeoman's wedding. So then I knew that as of 1833, he was in Kingston. Abraham, Jr. was born in 1835, George in 1836 and Edward in 1839.

Two of my cousins found that Abraham Cramer Sr. was listed as deceased as of 1841. That would have explained why the older Cramer boys were working for other families by the 1851 census.

A friend of one of my Cramer cousins was making a trip to Kingston, so she went to the cemetery where Abraham was buried. There she found an area that was not part of the main cemetery, with stones covered in dirt and moss, while one had fallen over. Not only was Abraham, Sr.'s stone there, but other family members too... more names, birth dates and death dates.

With that information, we posted information on RootsWeb.com in the belief that Abraham was son of Peter Cramer, a Loyalist during the American Revolution. Abraham was not the son of Peter, but of Lorenz Kraemer of Essenheim, Germany. Lorenz deserted while his regiment was in North America during the late 1770s and later married Gertrude Clapper in New York. The couple had several children, including Abraham in New York. The family then moved to Quebec. Abraham stayed in Canada, moving to Kingston, while his family once more moved across the border. The earliest record for Abraham being in Kingston is in the Return List of Men from Age 19 to 39 Years of Age, Frontenac Regiment of Militia, Kingston.

So despite false starts, George Washington Cramer was really born in Kingston, ON. And though the article in the book states that George was of Irish descent, we found he was of German descent. All censuses except one indicate he was of German descent. Mary Ann Raycroft's family, however, was of Irish descent.

Through the help of lookups,

newly found family members, posting to boards, joining lists, that brickwall finally came down. — Terry Wilde Spear, TX, tspear@flash.net

Tracing The Immigrant's Trail Using Church Records

My husband's paternal grandfather arrived at Ellis Island, headed straight for the west coast and promptly completed his Declaration of Intent to become a US citizen. With the ship manifest and naturalization records, finding his roots in Finland was simple. Tracing his ancestors back eight generations using Finnish parish records was incredibly easy.

I naturally assumed that information on grandfather Sommarstrom's wife would be as easily obtained. Twenty years later and much wiser, I now know that one should never assume anything in genealogical research.

Matts Felix Sommarstrom, my husband's grandfather, married Esther Matilda Mattson on 18 June 1907 in Oakland, Alameda county, CA. Esther was born in Manistique, Schoolcraft county, MI to Gust and Kate Mattson on 11 May 1886. After searching for Gust's naturalization papers through Schoolcraft and neighboring counties as well as federal court records, I was stymied.

After trying many other techniques, I had a chat with my mother-in-law about her in-laws and how she met her husband. She told me that when she first moved to the San Francisco Bay area, she attended the local Swedish Baptist church in Oakland with relatives of her mother's. The Mattsons and Sommarstroms were both active in Lakeside Swedish Baptist Church. It occurred to me that, given the importance of the church in record-keeping in both Sweden and Finland, if I could find records for the church, I might just get the information I needed to track the Mattsons back to the appropriate parish in Finland.

Of course, nothing in genealogy can be simple. My mother-in-law informed me that Lakeside Baptist Church had changed its name several times, split off new Swedish Baptist churches as its members moved to the suburbs and merged with other Baptist sects as its membership in Oakland dwindled. Calls to the church office of what was left of Lakeside Baptist revealed that all the old records had been sent off somewhere — no idea what exactly was in the records, when or where they were stored. In other words, a dead end.

I had been a member of several Swedish genealogy lists for several years and knew there were many knowledgeable people reading and responding to requests for help on them. So I posted a message asking for help locating church records and was answered by the Head of Genealogy at the Swenson Swedish Immigration Research Center in Rock Island, IL. Much to my delight, the Swenson Center has collected Swedish-American church records from a number of denominations. They maintain a research library at Augustana College, which includes microfilmed copies of numerous church records from throughout the US, along with many other records pertaining to Swedish immigration.

The next summer I went to the Swenson Center to view the microfilmed records. Since I knew that the Mattsons joined Lakeside Baptist Church sometime after their arrival in Oakland in about 1901-02, I started with those records. The meeting minutes began with the organization of the "First Swedish Baptist Church of Oakland, California" on 1 February 1885 and are written in Swedish until 30 January 1930, when "It was decid-

ed to have the minutes of the business meetings written in English." Included in the minutes are notations about all new members admitted to the church, all members requesting transfers, member deaths (including those who had previously moved away), elections to church positions and any other business matters that came up at the regular meetings. Even for someone not fluent in Swedish, it's fairly easy to find family names in the minutes. However, it's more difficult to figure out *why* they've been named. Gust and Katherina Mattson begin showing up in the minutes in mid-1901, with Gust first elected to church office in 1904.

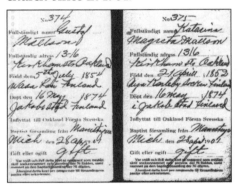

The transfer records.

At the very end of the roll of microfilm are a series of cards, four to a page, which are clearly the transfer records for members joining this church from another, in numerical order by member number. There we finally found some useful information for tracking Gust and Kate Mattson back to Finland. The list was filled with names, places and dates in Finland for my ancestors. We now knew that Gust and Kate were probably living in Jakobstad, Finland in May 1874, at the time they were baptized there. Kate was born in Nya Karleby and Gust somewhere else in Vasa county (not very specific information for him).

Armed with this information, I was able to find the couple in the

Jakobstad church records which are available on microfilm from the FHL. Many of the Finnish vital records are also now available on the Internet through the Genealogical Society of Finland's Hiski Project website. There is no indication that they ever returned to Finland. I did eventually also find where the church records for the Swedish Baptist Church in Manistique are located. The original paper records are in boxes in the archives of Bethel Baptist Seminary in St. Paul, MI, as are those for many other Swedish Baptist churches affiliated with the Bethel Synod.

Finding the key to link my husband's Mattson ancestors to their birthplaces has taken much trial and error. Had someone pointed me in the direction of US church records 20 years ago... — Ginny Sharp Sommarstrom, WA

Dead Men Do Tell Tales

I was stuck with a 20-year-old brickwall, so I decided instead to check out two identical family stories in two different parts of the country and nearly one hundred years apart! This way I thought I would at least have something interesting about the family.

My brickwall was my great-grandmother's parents. I know they left London, England for South Australia on 31 October 1863. William and Sarah Elizabeth (Denham) Gage had two daughters at the time they immigrated. The second daughter, my great-grandmother was born in Haggerston West, London on 13 November 1861 and I have her birth certificate.

Twenty years and no one has been able to obtain the birth certificate for the older sister nor the marriage certificate for the parents. If the second daughter was born in London and the immigration papers state the family was from London, how come no doc-uments can be found in London? Even the address of my great-grandmother's birth did not find the family at that address on census day a number of months prior to her birth.

Researchers were then asked to check all England and Wales for the parents' marriage certificate and the birth of the oldest daughter, Sarah Jane. None were found. Even St. Catherine's House admitted that some documents do get lost, but not two for the same family.

The photograph labeled "Aunt Sarah Pedler in Geelong".

So I gave up this quest and instead decided to find the truth about the two identical family stories of the dead grooms. My mother sometimes spoke of how her sister attended a wedding of a cousin in the 1930s and stayed on a few days later for the groom's funeral. Imagine my surprise when I asked an elderly distant relative for a family story and she told me of the same story happening in a different location and in the 1800s! The odds of a groom dying within days of his wedding happening twice in one family were certainly worth looking into.

A distant cousin had given me a

photo of a lady in front of a house named "Denham" (my second-great-grandmother's maiden name) and the photo was labeled "Aunt Sarah Pedler in Geelong". Could this be the sister of my great-grandmother and the mother of one of the grooms that died within days of his marriage? My mother said my aunt went to Geelong for the wedding and funeral.

I wrote to the Geelong Family History Group giving full details and asking them to look for the death of the Aunt Sarah in the photo and the possible marriage and death of her son in the 1930s.

The reply was a surprise. I was not only given the death of Aunt Sarah, but, yes, her son had died within a year of his marriage and he had only been ill for two days. Not quite as the family story went, but one could see how it all began. I sent for the two death certificates of the mother and son as I thought it would be interesting to see why the groom died and from his mother's death certificate I may find out more of her background, as Australian documents do contain more information than most other countries.

It turned out that Sarah was born in Cardiff, Wales! I sent for her birth certificate, although I have lost count of the other times I have tried, but at least this time I had a definite location. The birth certificate came back and Sarah Jane was the daughter of William and Sarah Elizabeth Gage. Next I sent for William Gage and Sarah Elizabeth Denham's marriage certificate for Cardiff, Wales and finally received it.

It turned out that the groom died of liver problems and I have been so busy working on my brickwall that came tumbling down that I have not researched the other groom's death! — Pamela Voss, BC

*   *   *

The Linix To The Solution

For years we were stumped on James Lenox from Ireland. He supposedly came over in the early 1800s. We found an article concerning the purchase and sale of the Lenox family farm on Manhattan Island. It turned out not to be our James Lenox. The information contained at the FHC turned out to be incorrect.

Finally, my brother went to the NARA's Pacific Alaska Region branch in Seattle and searched the census roll for 1850 in Ross county, OH as that is where James Lenox settled. He went through the entire roll, page by page and on the last page there was our James Lenox. All the family names and dates matched what we knew to be correct. The problem was the name was spelled Linix. — Gene Stevens, WA

Build A Timeline

I first used this tool when I was researching my Richardson family. They lived in colonial Louisiana around the time of the Louisiana Purchase in 1803. The records for that period are few and rather disjointed and this was my first attempt at researching Louisiana records.

I occasionally found myself searching for records in the wrong parish and coming up empty. This was because the political boundaries changed so frequently in the early years. As a reminder, I made myself a timeline:

Louisiana Timeline
1803: Louisiana Purchase;
1810: St. Tammany Parish formed from part of St. Helena;
1819: Washington Parish formed from part of St. Tammany;
1832: Livingston Parish formed from part of St. Helena;
1869: Tangipahoa Parish formed from parts of Livingston, Washing-

ton & St. Tammany.

I began collecting data from all the usual sources: Bibles, census (earliest is 1820), land sales, military, marriage, tax and succession records. I looked for anything that might be even remotely related to my ancestor, Samuel Richardson and his daughter Elizabeth. I gathered data not just on the Richardsons, but also on the related families.

After a few months, I had gathered quite a bit of data, but it was unorganized. I use a genealogy database program, which allows me to list the facts connected with individuals. I needed a way to see how all the individuals might be connected to each other. I decided to build a timeline, placing each fact that I had uncovered about the various family members in chronological order.

Richardson Timeline

1780-89: Samuel Richardson born (census);

1795: George Richardson born in Georgia (obituary);

1800-05: Enoch Richardson born (census);

1804: Elizabeth Richardson born in Georgia (census);

1804: Samuel Richardson settles land in Louisiana, west of the Pearl River;

1805: Samuel Richardson marries Rachel Hamilton (no proof);

1807: Elizabeth Richardson born in Louisiana (daughter of Samuel and Rachel);

1809: Augustus Richardson born in Louisiana (son of Samuel and Rachel);

<1812: Micajah Spiller Spanish land grant for daughter Eliza;

1813: Samuel Richardson overseer of road from Myers Landing to Ponchatoula;

1813: Skipworth Durbin overseer of road from Ponchatoula to Tangipahoa;

1814: James Durbin in War of 1812;

1814: Jeremiah Durbin in War of 1812;

1814: Samuel Richardson in War of 1812;

1815: Enoch Richardson, Sr. dies in Georgia; leaving widow Mary;

1816: Jeremiah Durbin marries Jane Headen/Hayden;

1819: Samuel Richardson business at inn in Montpelier, St. Helena Parish;

1819: George Richardson business at inn in Montpelier, St. Helena Parish;

1819: George Richardson marries Margaret Hamilton in Louisiana;

1819: Mrs. Mary Richardson buys land from Absolom Traylor (neighbor of Samuel R.);

1820: Mary Richardson, widow, gives permission for daughter Elizabeth to marry Spiller;

1820: Elizabeth Richardson marries Jeremiah Spiller in Louisiana;

1820: Samuel Rankin buys schooner from Micajah Spiller;

1831: Samuel Richardson buys mulatto slave, Eliza from Jeremiah Spiller;

1823: Samuel Richardson gives permission for his daughter Elizabeth to marry S. Rankin;

1844: Samuel Richardson's estate is partitioned between his heirs

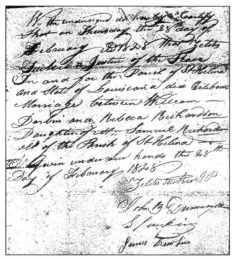

Document certifying the marriage of Samuel Richardson's daughter, Rebecca, to William Durbin, and witnessed by Samuel Rankin.

The timeline was extremely useful in letting me see the big picture. It organized all the seemingly disconnected pieces of data into a logical progression that could be easily understood. New facts or speculations could be added to see if they fit.

A couple of times, I discovered I had a bit of data that I hadn't realized was connected until I viewed the timeline. It pointed me in the right direction for further research and kept me from going in the wrong direction. I have used this tool on other families I am researching and have found it to be extremely helpful.

Eventually, the timeline led me to find the proof I needed that Samuel and George Richardson were brothers and Elizabeth Spiller was their sister.

I was able to get together enough information to write a biography of my ancestor, Samuel Richardson and his family. The timeline was extremely useful for that task as well. — Shirley Rankin, CA

The Power Of Message Boards

When you've hit a brickwall never underestimate the power of the message boards. A cousin of my husband, with no prior interest or experience in genealogy, decided to find his father's family. He began interrogating me on the finer points of researching family history. I sent him to my favorite genealogy websites, the best genealogy library in our area and the local vital records office to request birth and death certificates. His only knowledge of his father's family was his father's full name and birth and death dates.

While he was busy getting the birth and death certificates of his father, I decided to post a message on the Dawson message board of Genealogy.com. Once at the message board, I thought, "Why not browse through the board and look for something familiar?" Off I went into the current messages of Dawsons.

Finding nothing, I thought, "I'll look further back and see what's posted." In moments my eyes were drawn

to a post that said "Dawson Family Bible". I told myself, this couldn't be our Dawsons. There were a couple of messages to the person who posted about the Bible and one of the messages actually had the name and birth date of my cousin's father. After a couple of e-mails to the persons posting the messages, I knew I'd found a treasure via the Internet. I'd found the family Bible of our cousin!

Shirley D. Horn-Bray found this posting on an Internet message board and located the family Bible.

We confirmed the information in the Bible with the birth and death certificates my husband's cousin received that same week. A couple of telephone calls to the lady in Florida (who had received the Bible from a previous employer who was cleaning an old warehouse) and plans were set for the Dawson family Bible to be on its way to Oklahoma... back to the family whose history it records.

What a find! From the brickwall of only one name to a Bible full of family information. — Shirley D. Horn-Bray, OK, sbrayokc1@netzero.com

A Toast To Genealogy

Researching my husband Tony's line in northern Italy seemed overwhelming, even though we knew his grandfather Ferdinand Revelant was born in 1854 in Magnano, Udine province. We made several trips to Udine, where we searched parish records stored in the lower floor of Monsignor Don Lavaroni's home adjacent to the old parish church at Artegna. I extended Tony's line back several generations, which actually pleased me far more than it did Tony. Claiming that I was only interested in the dead relatives, Tony would walk around the town and chat in his limited Italian (which was a lilting version of Spanish) with shopkeepers that had the name "Revelant" on their signs.

Tony grew increasingly frustrated that he could not tie his line into the local Revelant families. He wanted to trace the descendants of any siblings his grandfather might have had, since we surmised that Ferdinand had siblings who remained in Italy even though he went to Austria as a young man, settling in Arnoldstein, an hour's drive north of Magnano.

I felt we had hit a brickwall, but our daughter suggested a way around that brickwall. Returning home from a business trip to Italy, she brought us a telephone book for Udine, with a name highlighted — DR. SSA Irene Revelant, owner of a translation business and language school in Manzano, about an hour south of Artegna.

So now we knew of someone with Tony's surname who lived in the province his grandfather came from and who spoke English. Preparing for another trip to Italy and hoping we had found someone to help us find living Revelant relatives, Tony sent Dr. Revelant a letter via DHL. She responded because she was impressed that he would pay $20 to send her a letter. She agreed to meet us during our trip, even though her father told her we were probably selling encyclopedias. She arrived at the Costantini Restaurant near Artegna with her father. I looked in surprise at Adolfo Revelant, whose face bore a strong resemblance to my husband's face. Surely Tony was related to this

Revelant family! Fortunately both Irene and her father spoke excellent English and, after exchanging pleasantries, they agreed to meet us the next day to try to learn more about the Revelant family.

The following day we drove on narrow roads through heavy rain to several towns. We talked with Adolfo's relatives, trying to learn more about living family members, but no one knew their family history.

Irene and Tony became increasingly frustrated. I knew we needed to have Irene assist us in looking at the Monsignor's records and we drove to his home, only to find him out of his office. Eventually, Irene arranged an appointment for us to visit the Monsignor's archives. While there, I saw that Irene, like Tony, was too impatient to sit for hours reading through old church records. I did the research and was able to find the births of two surviving siblings of Tony's grandfather, Antonio and Tomaso Revelant.

Tony Keihl (left) and his Italian cousin, Adolfo Revelant, taken on trip to Italy.

Once we returned from Italy, it took a while for Irene to understand genealogy, but as we worked with her via letters and e-mails during the following year, she assisted us by hiring a professional genealogist. We were able to put together the data from the church, civil and cemetery records to complete the families of the siblings Antonio and Tomaso Revelant. And it wasn't too surprising to find that the living relatives Irene helped us find were herself and her father, who are descendants of Antonio Revelant. There is no doubt about the relationship — and Tony is very pleased to have living Italian relatives to joke with and to share life stories with.

To celebrate the success of the research, Tony arranged a luncheon at Costantini Restaurant near Artegna and brought together Austrian and Italian Revelant family members. They met for the first time and have continued to visit each other in the year since the luncheon. It was an exciting event for Tony, as he looked around the table at the smiling faces of American, Austrian and Italian Revelant relatives — all very much alive and toasting each other! — Lynnet Auker Keihl, CA

A Walk In The Cemetery

When I first started to research my great-grandfather, Friedrich Steinmeyer, I had a report to go by that my sister had written for a school project many years before. Unfortunately, my grandmother had since died. When my sister wrote it, she was able to interview my grandmother about her father's background. Grandmother had said her father was born in Ablon, Germany. For several years, I could not find anything by that name in Germany.

One day I went to the cemetery where my great-grandfather was buried. As I walked around looking at the stones, I found one stone that said the birthplace of another person was Apelern, Germany. Thinking about my grandmother's accent and that she barely spoke English, I thought this must have been the town.

After writing to Apelern, Germany for the records this indeed did turn out to be the correct

Church in Apelern, Germany, where Jeanne Schwimley's ancestor was baptized.

place. — Jeanne Schwimley, IL, cricket1@mc.net

Adopting A New Family History

In the middle of the 1930s, a baby boy was born at a Mission Hospital in a southern state. At the age of five hours he was taken into the home of a loving couple and later adopted by them. He was cared for as one of their own and, for their own reasons, he was not told he had been adopted.

After both adoptive parents died, a cousin, Ed, told the young man that he was adopted. Questions began forming. Are my birth father and/or birth mother still in this area? It was beyond him to even think of not pursuing the quest of finding out.

Thus, having in hand his birth certificate on which his adoptive parents were named and a picture of his mother that Cousin Ed had passed on to him. Tony (not his real name) began his quiet search for facts. Ed also told him his mother's name and the name of the man she was supposed to have married.

He traveled to the courthouse of the county stated as his birthplace. There he readily obtained copies of the adoption papers and related items. However, he met discouragement when the clerk in the State Vital Statistics refused to unseal his birth certificate and give him a copy of the original one. He needed a court order. Tony obtained the court order from a willing judge. The Vital Statistics clerk made a copy, but she had blocked some information. This was not acceptable, for he needed all the information — after all it was about him. He asked for a supervisor and then the supervisor's superior.

Finally, pointing to the court order that said he was to receive a copy of "the complete original birth record without alterations", direction was given by the superior for copies to be made without blocking any information. That information was what he needed.

Perusal of the local telephone directory turned up many listings with his birth mother's family surname. There were just a few of the family Cousin Ed said she married into. Did he want to call any of them? No, not until he was more certain; and then again, he did not want to be found if his birth family did not want to be found either. However, he decided to continue his investigation.

Because I was out of the immediate area and was interested in family history research, Tony asked me to make some discreet inquiries for him. I did what I could via telephone, correspondence by mail and e-mail, inquiries at FHCs, local historical societies and other means.

After checking courthouse records of marriages in the county, we reached another brickwall when my contacts with his mother's supposed married name turned up no record of her marrying into that family. A sister had referred me to her brother, the family historian and he willingly spent many hours searching his family records. Upon his direction, I even put a query in their family newsletter and several historical newsletters in the surrounding counties without any response.

We spent time looking over the pieces to our puzzle and asked more questions. The SSDI was little help at that time for we did not know whom she might have married.

I decided to begin searching online with the birth mother's maiden name. Finally after several months, a result was recorded. There in the middle of another surname family history was an identical name of a woman who had married into that family and with a birth year near the same for which we were seeking. Could we have found the right person?

Before telling Tony and getting his hopes up with the possibility of another brickwall, I continued looking at the history. I checked the SSDI for some of the places of death for listed persons in that history. Again, we were pointed back to an adjacent county with great hope. Taking my findings, Tony contacted the local newspaper for obituaries and then went to the county courthouse and found very informative records of marriage, birth of children and a subsequent divorce. We were getting warmer.

Much thought went into deciding whether or not to make inquiry of the birth mother's whereabouts. Tony chose to have his wife call a woman's home. After several inquiries back and forth during the telephone conversation it was felt there was enough information confirmed to tell some of Tony's story. The conversation ended with the woman saying she would gather more information if possible and get back to Tony.

Several weeks passed and one evening the woman called. She had received information from her mother's sister that would be of interest to Tony. Would he come and visit her? A time was set and just two weeks later Tony and his wife met this woman face to face at her home. Tony was indeed her half-brother. She gave him some pictures of their mother and told them more about her and let them read the letter from the aunt that knew the story of Tony's birth and his father's name.

The sad part is that the birth mother died only recently and some answers to Tony's questions have no doubt gone with her to the grave. However, Tony, who was raised an only child and the woman who lost her only known brother will be able to enjoy their remaining years getting acquainted. — Barbara Sutphin Witwer, PA, ells94worth@aol.com

The Sherlock Holmes Within

My first genealogy brickwall was dealing with a box of unidentified family photos. Successfully working through this dilemma launched my interest in family research. I hope sharing this experience will suggest new ways to unlock the stories hidden in a family photograph collection.

Mother passed away in 1982 leaving me with a small wooden chest containing a substantial number of various-sized sepia photographs. Although Mother lived with our family from 1968 until her death, my children had not experienced the adult storytelling I had enjoyed as a young girl. My children's memories were only of their Nana's life with them. Now that Mum had gone I felt a great weight placed squarely on my shoulders. What was I to do with these lovely old photos?

As I searched each photo I felt ashamed at the few faces I could identify. I felt depressed, blaming myself for not taking more interest, for not asking more questions and for not listening more closely to those stories. Checking a few of the photo backs for written hints produced nothing. Most were void of captions except for the identifying mark of a developer's stamp.

I remember thinking, "I could turn away, ignore this nuisance, put the box back on its shelf and let time deal with its contents or I could rise to the challenge." A childhood of memories spoke loudly, prompting feelings of loyalty to family. I picked up the chest and headed for the kitchen and the Sherlock Holmes within me said, "Yes!"

I cleared a space on the kitchen table, proceeding to pile pictures face down, sorting the photos according to size. This exercise helped attach the photos to a camera and perhaps to the person who took the pictures. From there, I sorted the piles by the developer's mark stamped on the photos' back. This collected pictures belonging to individual films that in turn might identify all the photos taken on an occasion or within a time frame.

I soon found the table space too confining so moved the project to the living-room carpet. After the task of sorting was complete I looked at each group of photos, comparing them to each other. I then transferred informa-

Linda Sokalofsky used photograph sizes and the information on the backs of the pictures to overcome her brickwall.

tion from one photograph to another, noting and recording all deductions. I studied carefully each person, each background, each notation (I discovered there were a few) written on a photo's back, interweaving the clues with what I remembered. Photo by photo, I bridged the gap from what I knew, back to the unknown. Then I built a timeline incorporating these notes. As the photo stories unfolded my mind began to recollect some of the people's names our family talked about when they visited.

I discovered some of the photos were from my grandfather's brother, Tom Plowright, who made several trips back to England to visit family and took pictures to preserve these special occasions. He then sent those photos to my grandfather Edward in British Columbia. We should be grateful for family members like our Uncle Tom, who had the heart to preserve family ties. Because he cared, he labeled his photos so his brother would easily identify the subjects in each picture. Little did he know his labeling would serve as the bridge to identify unlabeled photos and the link between his generation and that of my grandchildren. — Linda Sokalofsky, BC, vesey@dccnet.com

Use Every Bit Of Information

Since I first started doing genealogy, a major goal of mine has been to do research in Ireland where all my mother's side lived. To locate anything in Ireland you need to know the county your ancestors came from and even the parish if possible. Sarah and Michael Cartan, my maternal second-great-grandparents, emigrated from Ireland to Canada with the first two of their six children around 1852. I traced every possible record I could find in Canada for the parents until they vanished around 1896. Three sons remained in Canada until their

deaths. No investigation of Patrick, Michael Jr. or James provided any clue from where in Ireland the Cartans came. The two daughters and youngest son also seemed to vanish between 1885-96. The only scrap of information I had was that my grandmother used to write to a Cousin Sadie in Chicago. I knew the name on those envelopes I saw as a child wasn't Cartan.

I inherited two large boxes of family pictures and other things after my parents died. I thought I'd gone through everything in them. One more look through the collection led to an old address book of my mother's in which the only Chicago address was for a Sadie Meehan. By applying for a copy of her Social Security application, I found out that her parents were John Meehan and Bridget Cartan, the eldest daughter. This small gap in the brickwall led me to Chicago where I found my second-great-grandparents' graves and the marriage and death records of the two daughters. Sarah and Michael must have moved there to live with their daughters when they were too old to take care of themselves.

Social Security application for Sadie Meehar showing parents' names.

But still no clue as to where to look in Ireland. However I did find another family of Cartans in Chicago who came over about 1847 and who could be related. I believe my Cartans emigrated, trying to join their relatives in Chicago, but they were too poor to get there right away so settled in Toronto. So far obituaries of the other Cartans have named a county (Wexford) and two towns (New Ross and Dublin).

With the brickwall partly down, I'm working on establishing a firmer connection to the Chicago Cartans. If I do it I'll be ready to set off for Ireland.

One solution to brickwalls is to ask yourself what information you have and haven't really used and how might you use it. — Lorraine Green, ON

Oh Brother!

St. Raphael's Catholic Church is one of the few Manhattan parishes available from the FHL. The records are in English and I was able to gather a great deal of information I needed. I checked here for Sarah Goodwin's baptism in 1896. I also found her half-brother's baptism in 1905. The most interesting things I discovered in St. Raphael's records were the baptisms in 1903, 1907 and 1912 for the children of Owen McGinn and Mary Mahoney. From the 1900 census I knew that Sarah Goodwin had a maternal uncle called Owen McGinn. Family legend held that this uncle moved out from their apartment and married a much younger woman.

Here was an Owen McGinn in the same parish having a family. If the wife was truly much younger one would expect that they would have children. I decided to write down the information and check it later against other sources. My aunts remembered an uncle named James McGinn but not an Owen McGinn. The census clearly established an uncle named Owen, but was this him and his wife?

A check of the 1920 census found this family and it showed that Owen was 20 years older than Mary. This too agreed with the family stories. A check of the SSDI led nowhere. There were no marriage notations, so I could not try and track their marriages and spouses.

A few years later I tried the SSDI again and hit it big. I found a John McGinn with the same birth date as the one in the St. Raphael's register.

He had died in New Jersey and I got his obituary by calling the local library there. A fellow historian was there researching and since I had a date she obliged me and searched for the obituary.

I called the funeral home and asked them if they could confirm John's parents' names. I gave them the names Owen and Mary McGinn and they confirmed that those were the names of the John McGinn whom they buried.

Following up on newly found names in a church register helped me find another branch to my family tree and contact them for their oral tradition. — Kevin Cassidy, NE, kmct@earthlink.net

Fishing For Clues

I was seeking for the birth date and place for my grandmother Mary Jane "Molly" Fowler.

I was told that grandma was an Indian girl raised by her adoptive parents. No one knew where she was born but I remember that grandma told me that her brothers used to fish on the White River in Indiana.

I got a map and looked where the river flowed. It was a long winding river. On my fourth research trip I was surprised. She was not an Indian girl. She was born in Morgan county, IN to Samuel and Sarah (Ludlow) Fowler and I found her and more on the family. — Mary J. Craig, IN

Stepping Out Of Line

I found that studying great-uncles and great-aunts, rather than just direct ancestors, can yield a solution. I knew that my grandfather Goss' parents came from Germany, but for a long time I didn't know where in Germany.

From the 1920 federal census, I found that John Goss (Hans Goos)

emigrated from Germany to the US in 1858 and that my great-grandmother, Margaret Sophia Wieben, came to the US from Germany in 1862. At my local FHC, I found their La-Salle county, IL marriage license showing their marriage on 20 May 1865. I also located my great-grand-father's declaration of intention to become a US citizen. He signed it in German script in 1876, renouncing his allegiance to Wilhelm, Emperor of Germany. The obituary for my great-grandmother stated that she was born in Germany, but not where in Germany. The death notice for my great-grandfather did not say where he was born.

Back row, left to right; Catherine, Martin, Frank, Arthur, Anna, Margaret, Thomas and John. Seated, John (Hans Goos) Goss and Margaret Sophia (Wieben) Goss. Photograph taken c. 1902 in Illinois.

Curiosity about my grandfather's four brothers and three sisters led me to the answer. I have only dim childhood memories of one of my great-uncles, but I have a photograph of them all with my great-grandparents taken around the beginning of the 20th century. I obtained obituaries, death certificates and other information for my great-uncles and aunts. The death certificate for one of them, Thomas Peter Goss, had the birthplace for both John Goss and Margaret Wieben recorded as Klinerider, Germany. It looked like I finally had an answer, but I couldn't find Klinerider in Germany in a European atlas.

I assumed that Klinerider was an anglicized version of the name of the German town. A friend from work had spent many years in Germany and had some very detailed maps of Germany. He found a town named Klein Rheide in the very north-ernmost area of Germany (Schleswig), just a few miles south of the border with Denmark. To confirm the origins of my great-grandparents I wrote to the Schleswig-Holsteinische Gesellschaft für Familien-forschung und Wappenkunde (Schleswig-Holstein Society for Coat of Arms and Family Research), a genealogy organization. I sent them the names and birth dates of my great-grandparents. I was overjoyed when they wrote back with baptismal information for my great-grandparents from parish records, along with other information concerning their siblings and three generations of their ancestors. My great-grandparents and their ancestors were born and lived in farming areas and small communities in the vicinity of Klein Rheide in Schleswig.

Thinking outside the direct line helped me find my ancestors. — David A. Goss, IN

Small Evidence Adds Up

John H. Coy was a brickwall for me for a long time. I managed to learn several important facts early in my genealogy. He was born about 1796 in Hardin county, KY and married Deborah in about 1818 in Sullivan county, IN.

Using the Oregon Donation Land Claim information and census information, I was able to trace his migration pattern from Hardin, KY to

Sullivan, IN to Gallitan, IL to Johnson, MI to Marion, OR and then finally to Curry, OR. I was able to do this by the birth location of his children. Unfortunately, there were several Coy families in Hardin county, KY and they all had children named John.

I focused on Johnson county, MI because there were four Coy families in and around the area, Matthew, John, Isaac and Peter. I looked at their ages and they were about two years apart. I assumed that they were brothers. Then I looked at the 1810 census to see who could have four sons the ages of the four in Missouri. The only one was William Coy. William did not leave wills or any paper work to make it easy so I had to go a round-about way to prove things.

William and family moved to Trigg county, KY in 1818, the same time John married and went to Sullivan. I managed to find marriage and tax records that clearly tied them all together. The hardest was John but during his travels he went to Trigg county for about three years before going to Missouri. I found him in the tax records and that time was confirmed by the birth of a daughter there.

Collect all data although it might be very small. If you take that small piece of evidence along with another small piece and put them together it is a big piece of evidence. — Carolyn Peterson, CA, corkster@attbi.com

Locating Jens Brodsho

My problem was locating where my great-grandfather was born in Norway. All I knew was that he married and lived in Norman county, MN and died before I was born. My first task was to view plat maps to locate his property and then to see which church and cemeteries were close to him. I found those cemeteries and walked the grounds looking for his

plot, but could not find it. I ordered his death certificate and found his death date of 8 February 1937. Also listed were a birth of 1862 and a burial at Wild Rice Church. I contacted that church and found his burial date and the location of his grave. (It was and still is unmarked.) I borrowed microfilm of the local paper of that area but only found a tiny statement concerning his death. Still no clue to his birthplace in Norway.

Jens Brodsho in Norman county, MN.

I checked the Minnesota state census of 1895 and it told me his length of stay in Minnesota. From that information I obtained his naturalization papers to see if a specific place in Norway was mentioned. It told of him leaving the diocese of Kristiansand and arriving in New York in 1883.

I thought this would narrow the search to the areas around the two Kristiansund/Kristiansands of Norway. I ordered and looked at maps of Norway and found a Broske near Kristiansund and a Brosjo near Kristiansand. I contacted the genealogist for the Norwegian-American Association that was researching the area around Kristiansund and found no Jens. I contacted the historical society in Norway near Kristiansand and they found no Jens. While waiting for my responses, I read books about the area and near the time period Jens was alive in Minnesota.

One summer I was visiting other relatives in Norman county and telling them about my brickwall. My great-aunt mentioned a person still living in a nursing home who was a neighbor of Jens. She was in her 90s when I interviewed her. During the interview, she mentioned Jens had the notion that people, including family members, were trying to poison him. She remembered he would go to Fergus Falls sometimes. Remembering from my reading that Fergus Falls had a mental facility at that time, I contacted the facility, which led me to the Minnesota Archives. The archives sent me the admission and discharge papers of the mental facility in which Jens was placed in Fergus Falls. Still no specific place in Norway but the records did give me his father's name: Johannes Aslakson. In desperation, I pleaded on the Norway-List message board giving the dates and information I had accumulated. Ole Bjorn sent me an e-mail concerning the 1865 Norwegian census of a Johannes Aslakson, age 46, with his son Jens Johanneson, age eight, born in Drangedal. As the date of birth I had was 1862, it did not seem to be the proper fit as well as no mention of Brodsho.

I thought I would prove the information wrong. I ordered the Drangedal parish records from the FHC. The parish records were so obscure

that the FHL had to make the microfilm from its original. After waiting a couple of months, I looked through the birth records of the eight-year-old Jens and found him on 5 November 1858 with the right parents.

To double-check the date, I found the confirmation records of Jens and it also had the proper parents and date of birth. The place of birth was Holte. Brosjo is a farm about 12 miles south of Holte. I contacted Ole thanking him. He then proceeded to research and send me the lineage of Jens back five more generations as well as Jens' brothers and sisters.

However, I still do not know why Jens took the Brodsho name. — Richard Line, CA

Wills Of Acquaintances As A Brickwall Solution

I traced my father's line back to my ninth-great-grandfather Thomas Malbon, felt-maker and thrice mayor of Congleton, Cheshire, England. Thomas was born in 1629 in southern Cheshire and arrived in Congleton in 1646 to become an apprentice. He died in 1711, aged 82, and was buried in Congleton with his wife Mary, who predeceased him in 1705, aged 81.

My brickwall: Who was Mary? Her first name, engraved on the tombstone, was the only clue I had as to her identity.

From other sources I knew Thomas and Mary had at least three sons born before 1660. From this, and from the fact that apprenticeships generally lasted seven years, I deduced they were married between 1653-55. But I could find no marriage record in Congleton or nearby, probably because most parish records are spotty or non-existent for the Civil War and Commonwealth period (1642-60).

In my search for Thomas' parents, still not positively identified, I checked every Malbon will in the Cheshire Record Office. I found a couple of good leads for his ancestry, but nothing for his wife.

I wondered if he married his master's daughter, as did many apprentices. I searched Congleton's town records for his apprenticeship record but only found a gap between 1632 and 1650. But from those records and two Congleton histories, I listed all known felt-makers and sent for their wills if they existed. None of them mentioned Thomas. One, William Mottershed, had a granddaughter named Mary, but there was no indication in his will that he, or she, had any connection with Thomas Malbon.

As a last resort, I tried to guess where Thomas might have met Mary. He was an apprentice from 1646 to 1653 and presumably kept very busy, yet somehow he managed to marry almost as soon as his apprenticeship was over. So he must have met Mary in Congleton or somewhere close by. Since I couldn't identify her as a felt-maker's daughter, I decided to send for the wills of anyone he might have known during his early years in Congleton, men in other trades, the minister, who might have been old enough to be his father-in-law. Again I met with no success but then it was always a long shot.

I was about to give up when I realized I had overlooked two distinct possibilities. In 1653, as soon as he was qualified, Thomas took on two apprentices of his own: John, son of alderman Thomas Spencer of Congleton, and Benjamin, son of yeoman Randle Cliffe of Bidnall. When I first read this in the town records, I had wondered at the trust these fathers apparently had in such an inexperienced master for their boys. Then it struck me — someone with a son old enough to be apprenticed might also have a marriageable daughter. I checked and found that

Randle Cliffe left no will, but alderman Thomas Spencer's was proved in 1663. I sent for it.

When Spencer's will arrived, there among his bequests was this wonderful sentence: "I doe give unto Thomas Malbon and Mari his wife, my daughter, the some of one shilling for and in the name of all her dowry." How much clearer could he be?

The record (at top of page) showing Thomas Spencer's son John's apprenticeship to Thomas Malbon.

Apparently Thomas got the girl, with a dowry to set him up in business and her younger brother thrown in for good measure. It turns out the Spencers were long established in Congleton, so now I have a whole new family to follow up.

I realize that my solution of sending for non-family wills is at best a hit-or-miss operation, especially since so few people left wills. I was lucky that Thomas's father-in-law left a will. I was also lucky that my research was in Cheshire, where all wills at the Cheshire Record Office are listed on the Internet; in most English counties, a personal visit to the record office or the services of a researcher might be required. I was also lucky that Thomas Malbon was a public figure, mentioned frequently in Congleton records, although I must admit that those records are not easily accessible if you live in Canada.

But, if you're lucky as I was, checking the wills of friends and neighbors can be a great brickwall solution. — Barbara Lynch, BC, pblynch@telus.net

Internet Translations

I was researching my in-laws' family tree and had a lengthy tree from Sweden starting in 800. It had a member of the family who immigrated to the US, Gustaf Ádolf Kebbon, born in November 1790, died in Manchester, NH in 1838. He had seven children and one of them was Rudolf August Kebbon who was born around 1834 and died around 1887 in Cadiz, Spain. From his third marriage with Johana Carol Dorotea Ripa, he had a daughter Alma Louise Vilhemina Kebbon, born around 1870. He emigrated to the US and then to Cadiz. His daughter Alma married Georg Scharfhausen around 1895. This is all I had for the Spanish line.

I tried looking at phone books and contacting relatives in Europe. I told them I was in search for somebody called Scharfhausen in Spain. I had a couple of positive matches on the name but the names were set the Spanish way, like Scharfhausen-Perillo or Scharfhausen-Ramon, as the husband and wife carry both their names. I had an idea that I should look for Scharhausen-Kebbon but these names might have evolved through the years.

Every time I surfed the Internet I made a search on the names Scharfhausen and Kebbon to see if there are new hits from Spain. Finally, I got a hit. I don't remember too much of the Spanish I learned in school, but I went to the site anyway. It was a site from the Spanish Navy. I got the URL and went to Babelfish.AltaVista.com and used their translation program. The page turned out to be the logbook of a Spanish research vessel in the Antarctic. It said that they had three persons aboard from the same village of 6,000 people. The captain's grandfather, D. Christian Scharfhausen-Kebbon, spent his summer in the same sea resort.

Whoever wrote the logbook did not leave a name or e-mail address and no mention of the captain's name. I kept searching through the site in Spanish, as the translation is a little cumbersome to handle. I then went to Go.com, which also has a translating section. This program was able to read the site and I got a translation from Spanish to English. It was not the best translation program, but it did work.

Babelfish.AltaVista.com.

I found the story of the new commandant assigned to the boat. His name is Carlos Cordon Scharfhausen. I knew that his grandfather is Scharfhausen-Kebbon, so my next step was to write to him.

I sent a letter to him care of the Spanish Office of Science and Technology who is sponsoring the expeditions. Carlos replied and put me in contact with some of his family members who were interested in genealogy. I was then able to complete a great deal of that side of my wife's family with these contacts. — Jacques Travers, MA.

The Search For My Mother

I was born in Cleveland, OH and my mother died when I was only seven months old. Very little was known of her or her family, except that my birth certificate and her death notice revealed she was from Bohemia.

These were the only documents in my possession from childhood. My father didn't seem to know very much about my mother or her family and was reluctant to talk about them.

My mother's maiden name appeared to be spelled Pohanceny on her death certificate and listed Bohemia as her birthplace. It noted her father's first name as unknown and Bohemia as his birthplace. Her mother, my grandmother was Mary Ola (misspelled) and Bohemia listed as her birthplace as well. I wrote to the Cleveland Public Library for her obituary. "Sole, Josephine, beloved wife of Fred, and mother of Donald Sole" were the only names on it.

A visit to the Federal Records Center in Kansas City, MO, to use their Soundex/Miracode card system allowed me to obtain a copy of the 20 April 1910 Cleveland census record, which listed my mother as Josie Pohanceny, working as a domestic taking care of Joe and Helen Glick's eight-month-old twins. She was shown as 15 years old and her birthplace was shown as Hungary/Slovak.

I asked one of the volunteers at the center where to find my mother's family. She suggested further research was in order as it could be on another date. Sure enough, further 1910 Cleveland census research revealed 18 April, two days prior to my mother being listed at the Glicks' home, she is also listed with her father, John Pohanchani, stepmother, Johanna, sisters Mary and Margaret and, of course, Josie. Her and her family's birthplace was shown as Austria/Slovenia.

Having spent a considerable amount of time getting to this point I joined the Czechoslovak Genealogical Society International (CGSI) in Minnesota, thinking if my mother and her family were from Bohemia this would be an excellent research source. I had a Pohanceny/Olla query published in their March 1996 newsletter with no response. However, one of the CGSI newsletter's articles was on the Western Reserve Historical Society in Cleveland, OH and their Library Research Service. I signed up for their service, as it appeared I had hit one more brickwall being unable to find any trace of the Pohanceny family beyond 1910.

Western Reserve asked for any and all records I had, including my mother and father's marriage license. I didn't have a copy and so ordered a copy. When the marriage application arrived, close scrutiny not only revealed Josephine and Frederick being listed, but another Pohanceny, Sophia and a Michael Branik, and my mother's place of birth, Bohemia. I then ordered Sophia and Michael's marriage certificate, thinking it would also include place of birth and father and mother's names. It so happened that Sophia and Michael were married 9 May 1916 and only the Rev. L. Necid was listed.

Further research by Western Reserve revealed in the 1936 Cleveland city directory, which was too fragile to photocopy, the following entry: "Branik, Michl (Sophie), labor home, 8818 Buckeye Road, Cleveland, Ohio." The Cleveland Necrology File showed "Branik, Michael, born 1886, died 1937, age 51, buried Calvary Cemetery, Cleveland, Ohio." All that was needed was Sophie's obituary, which could list her birthplace.

I contacted the Cleveland Public Library and they sent me an obituary dated 3 July 1957 from the *Cleveland Press*. It contained her sister's name, Pauline Bruncak and a church name, St. Ladislas Church. I wrote to St. Ladislas Church and received a copy of Sophie and Michael's sacramental record of marriage and information of the baptismal location. However, this was written in Latin, which the local priest kindly translated into English.

I sent the translated copy of Sophie and Michael's sacramental record to the CGSI to identify the location and postal code of Tvrdosin and Dolni Stefanov, which are both located in the Orava area of northern Slovakia. The Society also enclosed copies of Slovak form letters along with its English translation and suggested writing the town mayor.

From left to right; Tanta Soubriet Sole, Magda Trstenska, Eric Sole, Lou and Don Sole, Kosto Baros and the full-time interpreter, Marcel Veselovsky.

The Mayor of Tvrdosin's return letter was written in perfect English and the first paragraph stated: "We have found out that your relatives live in our town. They are your mother's half-sisters." This culminated more than 20 years of intensive genealogy research, becoming a detective along the way.

We exchanged pictures and letters and accepted my cousin Magda Trstenska's invitation to visit Slovakia. This turned into an emotional, excit-ing and sensational gathering of two aunts and 21 cousins. — Donald F. Sole, KS, soleconcern@juno.com

Did You Hear The Brickwall Solution Involving...

Over the years I've hit several brick-walls trying to research the Akerblom family at the Los Angeles FHC. My first brickwall was trying to find the parents of Eric Akerblom. Luckily my in-laws traveled to Sweden and got the birth certificate of John Herbert Akerblom. On it was the birth date of his father, Eric Wilhelm Akerblom. I went to the FHC and looked in the Swedish Clerical Survey for the birth date in the town of Falun, Sweden. I found the name and date and the town where his parents came from. It was abbreviated and hard to read. I asked for help from a Norwegian vol-unteer at the FHC but she was not able to help me. The abbreviation looked like Asbo.

I ordered the Clerical Survey microfilms for that town but could not find any Akerbloms. Then I looked on a list of all the towns in Sweden and found the town of Aspeboda, a possible lead. There were quite a number of films on Aspeboda in the library. I looked on the films and found the family. By ordering some more films I was able to trace the family back to 1659. I thought that was as far as I could go back.

After that, we were planning a trip to Sweden and my husband wrote to a pen pal he had during WWII who lived in Falun, Sweden, which we were going to visit. He had not writ-ten to his friend since the end of the war so we put "(or Occupant)" on the envelope. The pen pal had moved but the occupant recognized the name Akerblom as someone working at the newspaper. The woman at the newspaper was not related but she printed the letter in the local paper. A librarian recognized the name and contacted us. It turned out that she had been researching the family with a study group who were all descendants of Mans Nilsson, the patriarch of the family. He has quite a historical background. I bought the book they had published. It contained the names of 2,500 related individuals. I have kept in contact with the librarian and with her help have traced the family back to the 1400s in the Judgment books. The best part is that all the information is documented in the Swedish records, which are very complete. — Dorothy Akerblom, CA, dormarak@aol.com

Tracing Sarah Overocker

My family knew little about my great-grandmother Sarah (Overocker) Titley. She died when my grandmother was an infant. Family lore related that she was of Dutch origin and that she was from the Saratoga region of New York. After Sarah's death, my great-grandfather remarried. My grandmother's death record identified her birth in 1878 in Fort Ann, NY.

There were a few obstacles to tracing the origins of Sarah Overocker. New York didn't start a system of statewide vital records until the early 1880s and the information I wanted was for earlier dates. The Saratoga region is

Sarah (Overocker) Titley, taken c. 1876.

characterized by having many small towns, each with its own set of vital records, which were begun at different times and some were non-existent for the period I was interested in.

I obtained the Civil War records for my great-grandfather, William A. Titley. These provided very useful information. Sarah and William married in Fort Ann but no date was given. Sarah's maiden name was listed as Shortman and as Overocker. I suspected that William was Sarah's second husband. A copy of a death certificate showed that Sarah (Shotman) Titley died on 24 December 1879 in Maynard, MA, but was buried in Hart's Falls, NY. Also, town historians were available throughout New York State. I called the historians in Fort Ann and Hart's Falls (present-day Schaghticoke) but was advised that neither town had the records I wanted. Further, there were no extant church records for the period I was interested in.

I set out on a four-day visit to the Albany/Saratoga region for a first-hand investigation. I was aware of the usual genealogy guidelines that recommend one should search progressively backwards through the generations. In this case, I opted to skip a search of my grandmother's birth record; instead it seemed more productive to concentrate on her mother, Sarah, even though I would be looking for older records

The first stop was a search of cemetery records in Schaghticoke (Hart's Falls), which Sarah's death certificate identified as the place of interment but nothing was found. Next I went to the State Archives/Library in Albany, which has a full set of census records for New York. A review of the 1855 state census for the town of Schaghticoke, Rennselaer county, identified the family of John and Catherine Overocker and seven children, all who were born in Rennselaer county. The list of children included Sarah, age six and Oscar, age four. This looked promising, as Sarah's age was in the range and Schaghticoke isn't that far from Saratoga or Fort Ann.

Then I turned to the 1880 US census for which there is a Soundex. However, I didn't find any Titleys and there were so many Overockers in the region that it would take too long to find any of Sarah's family that had been identified in the 1855 census for New York. There was no point in looking for Sarah, since she died in 1879.

At this point I followed a hunch. On the chance that Sarah Overocker had first married someone named Shortman and that there were children from this marriage, I searched the 1880 New York Soundex for Shortmans. In the Saratoga region I found that three Shortman children were enumerated with their grandfather, John Overocker, in the town of Greenwich in Washington county. Their ages indicated birth dates of 1869-72. A fourth child was enumerated with his uncle, Oscar Overocker in the town of Saratoga.

The children's birth dates were consistent with a first marriage of Sarah. Their relationships to John and Oscar Overocker, in combination with the 1855 census data, strongly suggested that Sarah (Overocker) Shortman was their mother.

Playing another hunch, I searched the state's death index, dating from the early 1880s and also located in the Archives. I found that Ada Shortman

died in 1888 in Greenwich, NY and George Shortman died in 1890 in Mechanicville, NY. Death certificates obtained from the respective town offices showed that the deceased were buried in Schuylerville, NY. The Greenwich records also included a death record for John Overocker, showing his death in 1891 at age 82, with burial in Schuylerville.

William Alderson Titley, taken c. 1862.

Traveling to Schuylerville, I received assistance from town officials and a local funeral home, which provided burial records and directions to the Shortman plot in Prospect Hill Cemetery. Laid to rest there were Sarah Titley, her first husband George Shortman, two Shortman children, Sarah's sister, Margaret (Overocker) Carr and Sarah's father, John Overocker.

I was overwhelmed by my success. I not only located my great-grandmother's gravesite, but those of her father and other family members. With all the information obtained during my visit, I have a good basis from which to research earlier generations of the Overockers. — John A. Worton, DE

Phonetics In Family History

I never knew my grandparents. They died before I was born. My parents knew very little family history, just bits and pieces of stories. Thus, not much was known before I began my genealogical search. Stories had passed down through my family regarding the death of my great-grandfather, but I had no concrete evidence with which to begin a search. I was told his name was Arthur Albrecht but that he always went by the name Otto. He worked as a florist in Brooklyn and was born in Germany. His wife's name was Helena Kopp.

After a great deal of searching, I located Arthur and his parents on the 1880 federal census and then as Otto with his own family on the 1892 New York state census. The latter was not indexed so I had to first locate the family's address using a city directory. The family did not show up on the 1900 federal census or on the 1905 state census.

I found out my great-grandfather's full name was Charles Arthur Albrecht, but that he also went by Carl, Carl A., Carl Arthur, Charles, Charles A., Charles Arthur, Arthur and Otto, his nickname. Thus whenever I did a search for him, I needed to check every variation.

I was told Otto died before his son, my grandfather, reached adulthood. That put his death between 1892, when I had last found him on a census record, and around 1909, when my grandfather would have been 21 years old.

New York City is separated into boroughs, which are similar to counties. I knew the family had lived in Brooklyn in 1892, so I began with Kings county where the borough of Brooklyn is located. I searched all the death records under the letter A for Otto Albrecht. These indices are not alphabetized so I had to look through thousands of names for each year. I did the same for New York county and last for Queens county. I found about 10 death certificates that looked promising.

From the 1880 federal census, I learned Otto's father was named Charles, Carl or Karl and his mother's name was Amelia or Emilie. On the back of the license of Otto's marriage to Helena, I learned his mother's maiden name began with a K, but the rest of the surname was illegible. On some of the death records I looked at, either the parents' names were incorrect or the place of birth did not fit. This helped to narrow down the possibilities. There was one filed in 1908 that caught my eye even though some of the information was incorrect. It was filed under Arthur Albrecht in Long Island City, Queens county, NY. His age was off by a couple of years, but that wasn't important. His father's name was correctly listed as Charles, but his mother's name was listed as Ann Miller. I knew his mother's name was either Amelia or Emilie, but did not know her surname. Was Ann her actual first name by German custom, or possibly her middle name? Was her last name Miller or did it begin with a K as Otto's marriage license had indicated?

I found there were court documents attached to this death certificate, so I obtained copies of them. In the court documents was another death certificate filed under the name Charles Albrecht with the same filing number as the one I'd found listed under Arthur Albrecht. An affidavit signed by his wife, Helen Albrecht, stated that Charles and Arthur were one and the same person. Also, on the second certificate his New York burial location was crossed out and written in as Baltimore, MD. My mother had told me that we had a connection to Baltimore from New York, but she didn't know exactly what that was. Well, here was that connection.

From all this information, I knew I had the right person, but Otto's mother's name still puzzled me. Why was Ann Miller listed as his mother, when I knew her to be Amelia K.? I began to say the words, Amelia… Ann Miller over and over again until it hit me. When my great-grandmother, Helen Albrecht, gave the information to the clerk filling out her husband's death certificate, she stated her mother-in-law's name as Amelia, but what the clerk had heard was Ann Miller. Amelia… Ann Miller.

Under duress and possibly in a slight German accent, the clerk had heard the wrong name and thus it was recorded as such. — Judy Place Maggiore, AZ

Calling All Relatives

My wife and I had reached a stalemate in locating her McCracken family line. We contacted one of her oldest living relatives that might know something. All she could tell us was that they came from Bolivar, MO.

I called information for a telephone number of any McCracken in Bolivar. The phone company gave me three names and numbers to call. The first one I called was not my wife's line. However, she said there was a lady in Bolivar that was doing genealogical research on the McCracken line that I was inquiring about. She assured me that this person was very knowledgeable about the McCracken line going back. After expressing my deepest appreciation to the lady for sharing this information, I called the individual she had suggested. I was so excited I could hardly wait to make my next telephone call. To my amazement, this

person's husband was one of my wife's long-lost cousins.

Carroll McCracken, a long-lost cousin from Missouri, and Jill McCracken.

This was the beginning of a long and productive relationship. We spent hours sharing family information. We both decided that the telephone, when used to its fullest potential, was still an excellent tool for getting valuable genealogical information. Now, with the Internet, I don't have to pay the phone company to get a telephone number for me. It's all available right on the Internet. — Clayton Hicks, TX

Combine Proofs To Find The Truth

When I searched the Daughters of the American Revolution Registry I wanted to prove the maiden name of my third-great-grandmother from South Carolina. I searched for years in the Edgefield county probate court, census records, wills, obituaries and everything else I could think of, to no avail.

I sent in a form of Preponderance Of Evidence listing the following: Artemesia's first son was named for her father. There was not another person named Artemesia in the entire probate records except for her daughter. Third son was named after her maiden name.

The Daughters of the American Revolution accepted those proofs. However, before this was verified, a cousin wondered into a funeral home in a nearby county asking for old records. They handed her several old books. There was an obituary for a son of Artemesia giving her maiden name and listing her as mother. Her husband was listed as father — thus proving her maiden name along with proof of her marriage! — Dee Redkevitch, GA

When People Change Their Names

What happens if someone decides to change his or her whole name? For those researching these people it is often very difficult to prove their ancestry. The good news is that many people who change their name leave some information around about their family. Locating that information may take a lot of searching, but it is worth it.

I had this situation with my husband's grandfather, William B. Brown. I had received a copy of a piece of paper from my husband's Aunt Nettie listing her father's parents and sisters. Her father, William B. Brown was born on 21 August 1872, in Radok, MO, and his father was James Monroe Brown, who she thought might have been James Monroe Winn. William Brown's mother was listed as

Georgia Ann Hampton. Three sisters were listed, Lizzie Winn, Mary Dysert and Grace Thomason. There were no birth dates and no brothers were listed. Looking at the sisters' surnames led me to believe that these were all their married names.

At the time of my search Nettie was dead so I could not question her about her father's family. My father-in-law, Sidney, was not interested in me taking on this search and said he knew nothing about his father's family. Nettie's husband did not know a lot about the family, but said he would try to help. I later learned that he did not want to talk about his father-in-law and he gave me as little information as he could just to keep me searching and not asking questions.

From family photos, I learned that Grace had married Forrest Thomason. There was one photo I located that had "Mother and Dad" written on the front and the family was sure these were the parents of William B. Brown. There was also a photo of two women cutting a Daughters of the American Revolution (DAR) ribbon at the dedication of a statue in Lexington, MO. The date of the photo was listed. The names on the back of the photo were "Mrs. Winn and Mrs. Walton". One of the women looked like the woman listed as Mother on the other photo, but I was not sure if they were the same people.

From Carolyn Hutchinson Brown's original photograph of DAR ribbon cutting.

Armed with this information I started looking in the 1880 census for James Monroe Brown. I found nothing. Then I looked for James Monroe Winn and located the family in Lafayette county, MO. The names of the children in the census fit for the girls and both parents, but there were also four boys with them but none were named William. There was a son, Sidney, of the right age bracket, making it very obvious that Sidney Winn was probably William B. Brown, based on the fact that William had named his first son Sidney.

Research in the Lafayette county, MO history book revealed a biography of James Monroe Winn, listing his parents, his wife's father, his children and a lot about the family. All the girls I had on my list were in the biography, Mary was married at the time the article was written so her surname was given as Dysert. Grace and Lizzie were not married at that time. Everything in the article fit with the information I had on the family.

However, this article did not identify a son William, or any reason why Sidney might have chosen the name William Brown. The biography of James did list a son Albert Sidney Johnston Winn. It also made it clear that Sidney, who was listed on the 1880 census, was A.S.J. Winn. From what I had it seemed obvious that Albert Sidney Johnston Winn, a.k.a. William B. Brown, had named his first son, my father-in-law, after himself, just turning the first two names around.

This seemed like I had the right family, but I was still looking for proof. A few years ago my husband and I visited Lafayette county and located a Dysert cousin. When we went to visit her I took all the papers and photos I had on William B. Brown. It turns out that she had known her uncle Sidney Winn and when I showed her a photo taken in

Newspaper picture of DAR ribbon cutting.

California of William B. Brown she identified him as Sidney Winn. I also showed her the photo that was taken of Mrs. Winn and Mrs. Walton at the DAR dedication.

Just two days before we arrived in town, the local newspaper had printed a photo taken at the same dedication of Mrs. George Ann Winn and her cousin, Mrs. Clemmie Walton. Along with other photos we shared, we proved that the photos I had were indeed of George Ann Hampton and James Monroe Winn.

This led me to research in the DAR records for the ancestry of George Ann. The article in the county history listed George Ann's parents as Joseph J. Hampton and Elizabeth Ray Cox. The DAR records showed that Elizabeth Ray Cox was the daughter of Solomon Cox and Rebecca Jordan Parks and carried the Parks line another generation back. The information in the article made it possible to connect to several written genealogies of the Winn family. While in Lafayette county, I located a marriage announcement in the local paper that showed that Sidney Winn married Pearl Hicklin on 24 January 1900 in Kansas City, MO. Albert Sidney Johnston Winn left Missouri and showed up in the city directory of Sacramento, CA in 1902 as William B. Brown.

We are still not sure why he changed his name. I have not located a divorce record for him in Missouri. I also have not located the town of Radok, MO where he was supposed to have been born. William B. Brown was supposed to have married Sylvia Smittcamp in California, but no record of that marriage has been located in California or Nevada. He was also supposed to have divorced Sylvia in Sacramento. There is no record of the divorce in Sacramento county.

We might never know exactly why he left Missouri and changed his name, but it is always fun looking. — Carolyn Hutchinson Brown, OR, sidcarol@escapees.com

Hitting The Mother Lode

My father was separated from his family when he was five years old. He stayed in contact with an aunt, his father's youngest sister. He always corresponded with her, but she would never discuss his family with any detail. She only told him that he came from a well-known family and never to be ashamed of who he was. She would never tell him anything about his father or mother. The sad thing is that she was killed in a car accident while en route to his wedding in February 1942.

At one point, my father had also met an uncle, his father's brother. So when I started my genealogy search the only names I knew were the two names on my father's birth certificate and his aunt and uncle's names.

I was lucky. The family was very well known and I found out a lot very easily. However, there was still a lot missing. I had no oral history to go on and I had never been able to find any photos of these people. I have seen two portraits that were in museums. My desire was to meet just one person who is related and to just hold one object in my hand that belonged to this family.

On the Internet I had read that a family member had done a complete genealogy search in 1878 but no one had ever seen or read it. I wanted to go to the genealogy library hoping against hope that I would find the information. I went to the library and among their files was a copy of a family tree done by this man in 1878. Here was the entire family, all its various branches and every single name.

Then we went to the cemetery. While at the cemetery I found the burial sites of the man who did the chart as well as his wife. Right next to his grave was their son and his wife and right next to them was their son and his wife. Then we noticed that the son's wife was still living.

I looked her name up in the phone book, got her address and wrote her a letter. I was so frightened about writing to her. I know from research that she is living in at least a third-generation home in a very exclusive neighborhood. I also know from research that one of the sons had donated his entire art collection to the local college. This was way out of my league.

I was careful how to word my letter. I began by telling her how I was related and that I realized it was a really long stretch but did she by any chance know where the 1878 genealogy research was kept. I asked to please tell me that they were safely in either some museum or library. Then I held my breath and mailed the letter. Then a week went by. It wasn't returned, so I figured at least it got to somewhere.

Then one evening while I was doing dishes after dinner, the telephone rang. It was the woman. She sounded so pleasant and wonderful that we talked for quite a while. She told me that I would be glad to know that not only did she have the original chart, but also she had all the 120-year-old research documents in her house. The most amazing part was that she asked if I would like to come and have a look at them.

Well, I finally hit the mother lode. I cried. Finally, I may get to hold an object that they held. — Catherine Comeau, NY, cats14818@yahoo.com

Breaking Grandmother's Silence

I was 16 when I started work on our family tree. Dad was born and raised in Atlanta, GA. His father, Hiram Charles Proctor, died when he was a boy (around 1914 or 1915) and he never really knew much about his father's family including the first names of his paternal grandparents.

He did know Hiram had grown up in Rome, GA, and that Hiram's parents had died before Dad was born. And he remembered hearing his father refer to his "Rome relatives". My one hope for getting the names of Hiram's parents was his widow, my grandmother, who was still living in Atlanta. So I wrote to her.

Grandmother refused to help. "The past is past," she said, "Let the dead rest in peace." Even Dad's follow-up plea didn't help. And her two sisters wouldn't help either. Sadly, I had to settle for what little that I had.

Twenty years later, Grandmother Proctor and her sisters were gone. My parents were retired and still lived in Phoenix. My attention once again turned to Dad's childhood and family. One day I asked him if he would write his autobiography up to the age of 21. He said he'd try.

Soon Dad's manuscript arrived — 27 single-spaced typewritten pages packed with details. A particularly poignant memory was of his father's death from kidney failure. Dad described his last illness and the closed-casket Atlanta funeral. He even remembered the attending doctor was Dr. Hawthorne and "the mortician was Autrey and Lowndes." Seeing Hiram Proctor through the eyes of his son increased my curiosity about him.

In the late 1980s, I was living in the Vancouver area. Once again I decided to pursue my father's ancestors. (Dad had died in 1985.) This time I began using the local FHC, ordering microfilms of the US censuses of Rome, GA, and nearby counties in the late 19th and early 20th centuries. I found many Proctors. But nothing connecting anyone to my dad. I even hired a Rome genealogist to search local records. He came up with more information on Proctors, but no links here either.

Then in 1988, my husband and I went to Alabama. We decided to add a trip to Georgia to visit the important places in my dad's childhood. We drove to Atlanta armed with Dad's autobiography. We explored his old neighborhoods. And as I stood in each place that had molded him as a child, I let his words transport me back to his youthful experiences there.

The Autrey & Lowndes Funeral Home record. In 1988, it was Lowndes & McLane Funeral Homes in Atlanta.

That morning, at our motel, I had looked in the phone book for the funeral home that had arranged Hiram Proctor's funeral 70 years earlier. No Autrey and Lowndes was listed. But I did find a Lowndes and McLane funeral home. I called and they confirmed that they were the same group. "Yes," the man said, "our funeral records go back to the beginning. We opened in 1916."

So we visited Lowndes and McLane that afternoon. There I saw the original order for Hiram Charles Proctor's funeral, with information provided by my grandmother. The order stated Hiram Proctor had died of acute uremia in Grady Hospital on 12 July 1916. The funeral was the following day. Grandmother had paid cash for the arrangements. And it showed the names of his parents: H. Proctor and Eliz Hill.

With the date of Hiram's death, we drove to the Fulton County Health Department for a copy of his death certificate. Once again, his parents were named — Hiram Proctor and Elizabeth Hill. They were among the Proctors unearthed by the genealogist and me in our census and record searches. It took 35 years, but I finally had what I needed to proceed with my family-tree research. — Sharon Proctor, BC

Family Memories

When I began my ancestry search, I had little hope of locating any members from my mother's family. My mom was a Jones; this common name is difficult to trace. As a child, we spent 10 years in Michigan away from all family members. When we visited Kentucky it was with my dad's family and mom's mother and father; although I was aware that my Grandma Jones came from a large family and had many brothers and sisters, I had never met them.

Early success with my husband's and my lines kept me busy for a while. I invested many hours, and continue to do so, on my dad's grandfather, George W. Renfroe. My Renfroe ancestors liked to travel around in the 1800s; not to mention the many various spellings of their name.

Right when I felt I would never know another Jones who was related to my grandfather, I remembered that my mother used to call her grandfather Ole Dock Jones. I contacted my uncle and asked him if he remembered the name Dock Jones. Elated, he replied. "Yes, I remember the name Dock and now I remember that his father was a blacksmith in a place called Rock Creek, NC. I remember going there once when I was eight and it was even rockier than Kentucky. My great-grandfather was in his 80s and still running a large farm and taking in blacksmith work."

Uncle Paul was born in 1924, so that means he visited his 80-plus great-grandfather in 1932. That also meant the elder Jones must have been born sometime before 1852, hopefully in North Carolina.

I decided to post a query on GenForum.com: "Looking for a Jones born around 1852 who was a blacksmith in Rock Creek, North Carolina".

GenForum.com.

Two days later I was rewarded with a message from a gentlemen from Bakersville, NC. He had the complete line of Solomon Jones, father of Austin, father of James, father of Dock. Within two weeks, I was able to locate the Jones family I needed. On a trip to Bakersville, I found documentation proving the family ties and placing my grandfather, David Jones in the family with Dock, son of James and information regarding Dock and James. I also had an opportunity to meet the man who shared this information with me.

Sometime later, I decided it was time to dispose of my mother's belongings that I had kept since her death. Before adding an overnight bag into the pile, I felt it might be wise to see what was inside. Inside was a small old address book. Thumbing through the book, it looked empty. Just as I decided to toss it, something told me to take a better look. Sure enough, I found one address penciled in the book. It was an address in Grafton, IL. I recalled a trip my mom had made to Kentucky in the 1970s and her speaking of a visit to Illinois to visit her mother's sister, Goldie.

With a hope and a prayer (the address was more than 20 years old), I wrote a brief letter explaining who I was and that I was looking for any family of Edith Jones Green. The day after Christmas of that year, I received a call from Goldie's daughter, Barbara. We had a wonderful visit and she informed me that I have a very extensive family in Kentucky.

I have since traveled to Kentucky and met this family. One of them is also a genealogist and she has provided many wonderful family pictures and me with ancestry back into the early 1800s. — Sue Willey, CA

Maiden Names

My brickwall story involves finding the maiden name of one of my ancestors, Martha, wife of George Hill, of Haldimand county, ON. According to census records and her death registration, Martha was born in Ireland. Because parents' names were not required for Ontario death registrations until 1907, that document did not reveal her maiden name. I searched through every available

marriage index in the Haldimand-Norfolk area, but could find no record of a George Hill marrying a Martha. Likewise, all records pertaining to their daughter Mary Ann Hill (my second-great-grandmother), failed to identify Martha's name.

Mary Ann's marriage record in 1859 to John Hosner gave her birthplace as Walpole township, Haldimand county, but listed her parents only as George and Martha Hill. Mary Ann died in 1911 but my hopes of finding Martha's maiden name on her daughter's death record were dashed when I discovered her death had not been registered. Of course, no obituary exists for Mary Ann either. I then turned to Mary Ann's siblings hoping to find this information in records pertaining to them. Her two sisters who died in 1907 and 1909 had no parents listed on their death registrations and I could not locate a surviving brother. Another brother died in 1858 at the age of 16. I concluded there was going to be no record available to tell me Martha's maiden name. I decided to search for Martha's possible parents in census records, by process of elimination.

I knew that Martha was born in Ireland, circa 1809, and that her husband George Hill came to Haldimand county as a child with his parents about 1820. Therefore, Martha was also single when she came to Canada and must have been living somewhere in Haldimand county when she and George were married. I knew their eldest child Mary Ann was born in Walpole in 1839 where the Hill family lived, so I made the assumption that Martha was probably a Walpole resident as well. The earliest Ontario census that lists everyone in the household, with ages, is the 1851 census. Although George and Martha Hill were living in nearby South Cayuga township on the 1851 census, I decided to start with the 1851 Walpole township census to find Martha's parents. My search criteria were simple enough. I was looking for a couple, or widowed person born in Ireland, old enough to be Martha's parents. By examining ages and birthplaces of any children still at home, I had to determine if they were in Canada before 1839. I narrowed it down to five candidates. One of the five even lived next door to George Hill's parents, which looked really promising.

My next step was to locate any available records for members of these families. Before I began, I decided to reexamine the entry for George and Martha Hill on the 1851 South Cayuga township census. I found again the Hosner family (Mary Ann Hill's future in-laws) living next door to George and Martha Hill and family. The next family was that of a George Steen, born circa 1810 in Ireland, with wife Elizabeth and five children. Living with George was presumably his widowed mother Mary Steen, age 73, born in Ireland. I quickly put aside the five possibilities in Walpole and began looking up every Steen reference I could find. I realized George and Martha's son Robert George who died in 1858 at age 16 is buried in the South Cayuga cemetery, also known as the Steen cemetery. Of course that alone did not indicate a relationship, since other neighboring South Cayuga people are also buried there. I recorded all the Steen names from that cemetery, but it wasn't until I found the will of a John Steen, who died unmarried on 2 April 1863 in South Cayuga, that the pieces of the puzzle finally came together.

In the Surrogate Court Records of Haldimand county, John's will dated 31 March 1863, leaves property to his brothers, Robert and George Steen, and a nephew, Samuel, son of his deceased brother Samuel. In addition to these bequests, John gives to Martha Hill, the wife of George Hill, of South Cayuga, 10 pounds.

While the will itself does not actually identify Martha as a sister, I am convinced that she indeed must have been a Steen, since she appears in a will where siblings are the beneficiaries of the estate. John Steen's will has been the only shred of evidence I have ever found pointing to Martha Hill's maiden name. — James L. McCallum, ON

The Odyssey

For some time my cousins and I had been looking for our second-great-grandfather, Greenberry Smith. One cousin mentioned that they thought he might have died in Ohio, as he was coming from Indiana, and going to West Virginia. About 1852 he had gone to Indiana, where as a blacksmith he worked on building roads. He had enlisted in 1862 in the 99th Indiana Infantry and was discharged in 1865, so he served in the Civil War.

I had been at a dead end for about eight years, so remembering what my cousin has said about Ohio, I looked at a census index and found him. He was listed in the 1880 census for Montgomery county, OH, in a National Soldiers Home.

Greenbury Smith's grave registration card.

I ordered a microfilm of records for the Soldiers Home. He had entered the Home in 1876, his death was listed as 3 September 1883 and his burial was in the Soldiers Cemetery across the street from the home. It also confirmed his birth date as 1814 and that he was born in Baltimore, MD. — Betty L. Jones, AZ

A Brickwall In Forgue, Aberdeenshire

I have been researching my Minty family for 12 years and found a helpful way of sorting all the names and dates in their parish in Scotland. There were so many James and Williams and others that I kept putting it aside. Using this method, I was able to establish a connection between them all.

William Minty (standing at back beside his mother), with his parents, James Minty and Ellen McLean, and his seven siblings. Photograph taken in 1883 in Ontario.

My area of research for this family is Forgue Parish, Aberdeenshire. I obtained printouts from the IGI for all Minty, Minto, Mintoe, Mintie and Mynto entries after seeing spelling variations in a Scottish dictionary. I entered all Forgue entries on a Quattro Pro spreadsheet program on my computer. Using the date/sort command, I was able to sort them into chronological order. A family pattern appeared. I then made a list, family by family, and was able to tie most of the entries back to the original William Minto, who had eight children.

Some time later, I was checking Scottish monumental inscriptions done by the Aberdeen and North-East Scotland Family History Society. I found William Minto and his spouse Jannet Cruickshank are buried in Iverkeithny, Banffshire, just down the road from Forgue. Many other family members are buried there, right down to Margaret Jopp, mother of James Minty, who is my husband's great-grandfather. These burials gave me spouses and other family members.

It was very exciting to see how all this linked together so easily. Try it with your family data and see how much fun it is. I can't guarantee it will work in all cases, but it sure helped me to overcome a huge brickwall. — Leonie Hooper, SK

The Mystery Of William Fairservice's Birth

A few years ago I started to trace my ancestry on my father's line. It was not very difficult to get back to the marriage of William Fairservice and Margaret Brownlee at New Greyfriars church in Edinburgh, Scotland on 2 April 1813. I had a small problem when I tried to find the birth date of his grandson, William, who was born about 1837, just before civil registration. I found a reference to a birth certificate for a William Fairservice born 20 August 1837. I sent for this, but was disappointed to find that the father was a William Fairservice, when my research had indicated that it should be John, the eldest son of William and Margaret.

This William was born in Bethnal Green in East London, which was the right place, but the wrong family. Examination of the 1841, 1851 and

1861 censuses revealed that there were two separate William Fairservices living in the same area. The "wrong" William's father was born about 1811, in Scotland (the English censuses do not give parish of birth outside of England and Wales). William Senior's English death certificate did not help. He died in 1891 and his age was given as 80, which again suggests that he was born about 1811. I now was puzzled. Who was he and how did he fit in, if at all?

I put a general inquiry into the 1995 *Genealogical Research Directory* for Fairservices in Scotland. My copy arrived and I quickly found an entry for Fairservice. About four months later, I was idly studying this directory, when I actually read the entry and, to my amazement, there were two queries under Fairservice; mine and one other. This was for a Fairservice in Bethnal Green, London in 1836 and 1810 in Scotland.

This got my attention and that day I wrote to the inquirer who lived in Melbourne, Australia. She replied instantly and explained that she was descended from the mysterious William and was stuck. We corresponded and brainstormed all sorts of possibilities, but they all drew blanks. Then my wife and I went for a trip to England and diverted to Edinburgh in Scotland to see what other records we could examine.

We found many interesting records at the Scottish records office. These records provided additional information about the Fairservice family. From the marriage entry in the New Greyfriars church records, we knew that Margaret Brownlee's parents were Archibald and Laurie Brownlee of Cambusnethan, Lanarkshire. I had also found Margaret's baptism there. We therefore decided to see if the Kirk Session Minutes for Cambusnethan had survived and if we could look at them for any clues about Margaret and the mystery William. To our joy the minutes existed and we could look at them. We started by going backwards from 1813 and during the year of 1809 we found an entry on 20 August that Margaret Brownlee had appeared before the congregation to be rebuked for her sin of adultery with James Ferguson.

As we read back through the minute book the whole story came out. Margaret had married a James Ferguson, soldier, in a civil ceremony before a Justice of the Peace at Hamilton, Lanarkshire on 27 July 1807 and a child was born on 22 April 1808. About this time, James Ferguson left her and she subsequently discovered that his real name was Peter Graham and that he was already married and had two children. The marriage, although it would have been legal, under Scottish Law, if it had not been bigamous, was an Irregular Marriage as far as the Church was concerned and they would not baptize a child until the couple had confessed their sin and been absolved. Margaret was absolved from the scandal and the child was baptized two weeks later.

I now had some information, but not enough, so I went to London and to the South Kensington FHC, where I looked at the Scottish old parish records index. Sure enough, I found the baptism of "William Brownlee Ferguson (or Graham)" on 3 September 1809 and when I got home I obtained a microfilm of the Cambusnethan parish records and found the full entry.

Margaret Brownlee, after the desertion of James Ferguson/Peter Graham, married William Fairservice in 1813. Her son William took his stepfather's name Fairservice from that point.

It pays to advertise and the Kirk Session Minutes can be a valuable source of genealogical information about the people, particularly when they get into trouble with the church. In reading the minutes from other churches I have found various useful references, particularly regarding children born out of wedlock. — Robin A. Fairservice, BC, r&b.fairservice@telus.net

Do Your Homework

Do your homework before making that phone call! Robert Gustavson remembered his dad had mentioned some cousins that moved from Sweden to California and may have become longshoremen. Now retired, Robert was working on his family tree. But he hit a brickwall when looking for the cousins.

Then he found me in Pennsylvania, a second cousin on another branch. I remembered a brief correspondence with a woman in California in 1980 who wrote that her daughter and son-in-law had purchased an auto parts store in Davis, CA. Perhaps there was a connection.

Johan Magnus Gustavsson and his wife Lena Lisa Petersdotter of Korsberga, Sweden. Robert's half-grand-uncle and aunt and Norma's great-grandparents.

I looked up addresses for auto parts stores in Davis and eliminated the large franchises. There were four possibilities. An Internet map showed three were in town and one on the outskirts.

I called one in town. "No," the young man who answered the phone said, "it had never been owned by a couple, nor had the other two in town. We are a small town with only three stores."

I asked, "What about the one on the edge of town?"

"Oh! I forgot about that one. Call Randy, he'd know. Randy knows everyone."

I called Randy at that store. He was there. "That would be Marilyn and Ray. Call me back in half an hour." When I did, he gave me their phone number and I called the couple. Marilyn was thrilled to hear from her newfound relatives and supplied names of the lost cousins and many more relatives. We still keep in touch. All thanks to searching the Internet and doing some homework. — Norma Bittler Smith, PA, smithno@aol.com

Fleeker Really Pflueger

With help from my two sisters, I searched for our great-grandfather Fleeker for about 10 years. We didn't know his name or anything about him. My mother didn't know and had never been interested enough to ask her father. The only clue she could remember was that her father said he had been baptized by a Catholic priest and was born in Elkhart, IN. I found my grandfather, Fred Fleeker, on the census in Kansas, the earliest year being 1870. He lived with his brother-in-law along with his mother, half-sister and brother. His mother's name was Christina Rauschenbach Fleeker. At that point I searched the 1860 federal census for Indiana, wrote to the Catholic mission at Elkhart, Notre Dame University and the Indiana Catholic Diocese and went to Elkhart to search the cemeteries.

We finally determined the spelling was probably different and maybe he was born in Elkhart county, not necessarily the city. We then began searching baptismal records in Indiana. I found an early one in Goshen written in German, but I could easily read the name Christina Rauschenbach.

We got some help reading the record and found that Christina and Georg Pflueger were the godparents attending three baptisms from one family and it stated they were from Middlebury, IN.

Baptismal record showing Christina and Georg Pflueger as godparents.

At that point we went back to the 1860 census with our new spelling and found them, including my grandfather at the age of three months. We also noted the parents of the three children were probably neighbors. I have since found his Civil War record and discovered that they moved to Indianapolis. — Jean H. Proud, CO, jeanhproud@aol.com

It Only Costs Time And Postage

One of the brickwall surnames on my family tree is Weber (Webber). I had little information to start when beginning my research and I figured this endeavor was comparable to finding a needle in a haystack. I knew my family originated in Baltimore, MD and moved to Hancock county, IL then moved again and ended up in Sedgwick county, KA. My trail ended in Kansas. I knew that the Webers spent quite a bit of time in Hancock county so I focused my efforts there.

After exhausting all leads and questioning relatives with no luck, I was at a loss and extremely frustrated. I didn't have the money to travel or hire someone to find my elusive ancestors. I knew there was information out there, but didn't know how to find it and at this point I thought I might never find it.

I took some time away from my research. I hoped I might revisit the situation with a fresh perspective. I began to wonder if there were still Webers living in Hancock county. I did an Internet white pages search for Weber and Webber. Yes, those names were listed in Illinois. I decided to write a letter to each person listed. It was a standard inquiry; I stated my objective, gave details about what information I had and thanked each person, in advance, for their time. I listed my mailing address and e-mail address.

Within two weeks, I had two responses. The first letter detailed the writer's family tree, which I couldn't connect to my line; the other person promised to keep my letter in case they would stumble across anything pertaining to my ancestors.

Finally, I hit the jackpot. One man sent me a detailed family tree with a wonderful narrative — it was my direct line. I wrote him back and thanked him repeatedly. His letter helped the brickwall crumble allowing me to find even more family members.

I have done mailings on other surnames and met with success. I have kept all the responses, even if the information doesn't directly pertain to me. I have also been able to lead others in the right direction. The people I have been able to meet through this process have been wonderful and so helpful. The only costs are one's time and postage. — Julie Bahr-Kostelac, KS, jbahr_kostelac@hotmail.com

*   *   *

One Response Is Enough To Reveal The Past

I was searching for the family of my grandmother's father, Don Carlos Self. I had very little information. He had buried his wife in McAlester, OK in 1917 and left his two children with her parents. My grandmother was only eight at the time and had no recollections of her father.

I had hunted for more than a year when I decided to flood every message board with what little I knew. Just a few days later a woman contacted me to tell me she was a descendant of one of his half sisters. She had been looking for us and thought she would never find us. It seems he had a huge family (his father had married three times) and I have an incredible amount of relatives.

It was worth all the time I spent putting my messages out there just to have one person read it. Most people underestimate how important it is to put the information where others, even just one other, will see it. — Kimberly Dempsey, TX

Be A Respectful Researcher

I was researching my grandparents and ancestors around Boston, MA and in the course of doing so went to the NARA (Federal Records Center) in Waltham, a suburban town west of Boston. There, I was able to sign into the archive libraries and access many of the usual Federal records, as is the legal option available to researchers. After frequent visits and numerous sign-ins, I asked the staff if there was an easier way to gain admission for my ongoing and detailed research projects. I was cheerfully advised that I could request and receive, with proper identification, a researcher identification card that would allow access without repetitive sign-ins.

I applied for the card and was given a wallet card with the Federal Seal on it, my name and the title of "Official Researcher, National Archives." This gained me immediate access there at any time I wished. The work progressed.

Later, on one of my frequent and frustrating trips to Boston or surrounding area City Halls, I asked to see an actual Record Book, in order to verify an entry was as reported. I sensed that the clerk had hastily extracted erroneous data. She replied that only Official Researchers were permitted in the vaults. I was a tad miffed and then a light bulb went off in my head!

Extracting my wallet, I flipped it open to the "Official Researcher, National Archives" card. I suggested that if the Federal folks in Waltham seemed to consider me trustworthy enough to grant unlimited access there, might I be able at least to look at the original page? The counter gate flipped up and I was happily escorted into the vaults. I was in genealogical heaven!

I treated the material with extreme caution and respect, often carrying the larger ones into the main office, where they let me use a spare desk (one of those great, massive, oak ones), in order to be in decent light and under minimal dust clouds. I found so much information and climbed over a few brickwalls.

Returning visits were just as pleasant and fruitful. Respect as a researcher is earned with civility to personnel and display of an obvious respect for the records. — Tom McKeever, FL, tomm@spacecon.net

*   *   *

Don't Discount The Veterans Administration

While trying to research my grandmother family, I realized I had all the information back to the Revolutionary War except for my great-grandparents McCracken.

We visited their two daughters in the state of Washington many years ago. At that time, I was not doing family research. After I retired and had time to do some genealogy work, my parents, grandparents and these great-aunts were already dead. I knew my great-grandfather McCracken was in the US Civil War and fought in the Union Army. One of his daughters in Washington had a disability and drew a veteran's pension on her father's Civil War service. I contacted distant relatives but they could not give information except the listing of the children. The county courthouse where the McCracken records were had burned and the records were destroyed.

I needed documents and finally decided to go the Veterans Administration Regional Office in Waco, TX to see if they had any information on my great-grandfather. Their computer showed they did have records on him. I filled all the necessary forms so I could receive copies of documents from his file.

Some weeks later, I received a package about an inch and a half thick. This had all the documents relating to his birth, death, service record, wife's birth and death and his children's records. It had everything I needed but was unable to get due to the courthouse fire. These documents helped me complete my McCracken/Holmes line back to the Revolutionary War. The Daughters of the American Revolution accepted my material and I qualified for a supplemental line.

Copied sheet from the Veterans Administration papers for Fawn McCracken, a great-aunt who received a veteran's pension for her father's Civil War service. The pension continued until Fawn's death in 1982.

When doing family research, do not discount the power of the Veterans Administration and their ability to provide documents that might be needed. — Selma Hicks, TX

No Matter How Small A Clue, Follow Through

I overcame my brickwall when I was trying to find my paternal grandmother's parents' names. I sent for her death certificate. When I got it back everything was wrong on it, even her name! The only thing I recognized was her youngest son that had given the information.

This was very disturbing. I had looked for her funeral records, but the funeral home had flooded and the records were destroyed. Then it dawned on me that her brother had come to visit us often and during his last visit he was killed by a drunk driver. I was only about five years old at the time but I thought if he had no family who would have furnished the information for him? I realized that it would have been my own father and immediately sent for his death certificate. Sure enough, my father was the informer and he had the father's name but no mother's name. I had a name to follow.

I started an intense census search and three very nice people sent me the census that my great-grandfather and family were on. No matter how small a clue follow through. — JH

Try The Classifieds

I found an obituary stating that my ancestor's sibling was buried at Sires Cemetery in a county in Missouri. I tried the local library, the state historical society and several other resources. All said there was no such cemetery in their records. Finally, I placed a small classified advertisement in the local newspaper. I gave the names of my ancestors who had lived in the town and asked if anyone remembered any of this family or had knowledge of a Sires Cemetery.

I received several responses to my advertisement. Sires Cemetery is a small family cemetery in the middle of a pasture. One person walked the entire cemetery, recording all the names and information on all the stones for me!

Another couple made a trip to the courthouse and sent me all relevant papers they could find on my family!

The responses to my classified advertisement helped us find another generation in our direct line. — Kim Shafer Crayne, NE, bkwoman222@aol.com

Kim Shafer Crayne tried the classifieds.

Morlaix city, France **JEANNE PASFERE** wedded **HENRI CAZAUX** before 28 August, 1830? Contact **Richard Morrissey**, 28656 Murrieta, Sun City CA 92586

NICHOLAS MORISEY wedded March, 1755 **MARY MAJOR**, Suffolk, Boston, Massachusetts! Data Higginson Pub. Salem, Mass. *1789 Gravestones (Boston)* Descendants contact: **Richard Morrissey**, 28656 Murrieta, Sun City, CA 92586 or e-mail <dawnmac@ix.netcom.com>

Seeking information abut **ANNIE ELIZABETH MINES**, died circa 1909 Virginia, married to **ROBERT B. GREEN**. Please contact **Dawn MacDonald**, 3128 Barkley Avenue, Santa Clara, CA 95051 or e-mail <dawnmac@ix.netcom.com>

Seeking information about balloonist **JAMES ARCHIBALD MACDONALD**, probably born February 14, 1898 in Cambridge, Massachusetts. Please contact **Dawn MacDonald**, 3128 Barkley Avenue, Santa Clara, CA 95051 or e-mail <dawnmac@ix.netcom.com>

I.D. Rupp and Robert Barnes *Md. Marriages* 1778* **JOHN FILLINGER** wedded **MARY EMMA STILLINGER** circa 1788 Baltimore Cathedral. (Ludwig Fillinger). **ELISABETH TSCHIRHART** (1724-1775), Thann, France wedded **JOSEPH DIETRICH** 4 June, 1742. Contact: **Richard Morrissey**, 28656 Murrieta, Sun City CA 92586.

In Newtownberry, county Wexford, Ireland seek 16th century ancestors. **ANNE MORRISSEY** (1787-1851) Mrs. **DOYLE**, **JEREMIAH MORRISSEY** (1787-1861) brother. **JAMES MORRISSEY** (1750-1846), Occupations? Contact: **Richard Morrissey**, 28656 Murrieta Road, Sun City, **CA 92586**.

Using The Postal Service To Find Your Ancestors

When I was newly married, on-site research was a financial impossibility. I solved my problem by composing a one- or two-question letter, which I would then enclose, with a SASE, in a second, blank stamped envelope. Then I would write a letter to the postmaster of the small town where I hoped to find long-lost relatives. After explaining my intentions, I would ask that my blank stamped envelope be directed either to a relative or to someone who might have known my relations. (This is legal because I was not asking the postmaster to divulge private addresses, just to send my blank stamped envelope on to another individual.) Finally, I would address the outer envelope to the postmaster of the small town. This method worked beautifully in three separate states.

Concerning my West Virginia relatives, I heard from a woman who attended school with my grandfather and his brother after their parents died. She gave me the name and address of a man willing to make free copies of tombstone records in a small cemetery in Doddridge county, WV. The letter I directed to Hawkins county, TN, was sent to Georgia where a distant cousin, happy to share family information, lived. My third attempt using such an approach was in Breckenridge county, KY. This time, I was contacted by another distant cousin who had addresses, pictures and stories of ancestors.

Whenever utilizing the postal service, I suggest the following tips: Always make your initial request short. Small towns are best, since postal workers have frequently lived in the community all their lives and know the region's population and its history. Never fail to send proper thank-you notes to all involved. Finally, always phrase the end of your request to postal workers and anyone else with words such as these: "If you cannot help me, could you please direct my letter to someone who can." This ensures that your letter reaches its desired destination.

Two letters, three envelopes and three stamps can solve a multitude of research problems. — Larre White, TX

Fraternal Society

I was researching my mother-in-law's family and came to a dead end with her grandfather. I had found him listed in the census and city directories in St. Louis, MI but did not have any actual vital information on him. I had no primary birth date or death date.

My mother-in-law's brother had been down to St. Louis to see if anything remained of the family homestead. It had been bulldozed for an expressway. He was interested in what I was doing. He found an old photo with his grandfather's death date written on the back in his mother's handwriting and sent the information to me. Armed with this death date, I wrote to the St. Louis Public Library and asked the reference librarians to look for an obituary for him. They were able to do this and sent me a photocopy of it. According to the obituary, my husband's great-grandfather had been a member of a fraternal organization called the National Slovak Union.

I went to the Internet and was not able to find anything by that name. I did find a reference to the National Slovak Museum in Cedar Rapids, IA and to the National Slovak Society located in Canonsburg, PA. I wrote to these organizations and was successful with the Pennsylvania connection.

The National Slovak Union was once a fraternal organization and insurance company and was now the National Slovak Society still dealing in insurance. Some wonderful person in their office took the time and effort to pull a box from storage and to copy the entire file for me.

The file included several documents including death certificate, marriage certificate to his second wife, the list of her children and their addresses in 1947. It was his whole life in one envelope. I sent a thank-you card to the dear worker who took the time to do the searching and copying for me.

I still can't believe how everything just connected. Using the information in this packet I was able to go to church and civil records and fill in quite a bit more on this line. — KAT

Don't Believe Everything You Read

This story plays out in the Netherlands. My second cousin once-removed, Adriaan Westerhof, was a genealogist. He worked on the family tree of our mutual forefather, Hans Heinrich Hanhart. I inherited his working papers in 1964 and continued the genealogy research as time permitted.

It was known that Hans Heinrich came from Steckborn, Thurgau, Switzerland. According to the extract from the register of deaths, Hendrik Hanghart (Hans Heinrich Hanhart) died 16 August 1812 at the age of 62. This suggests that he was born in 1749 or 1750. Adriaan therefore contacted the Steckborn City administration. The Steckborn office had no record of Hans Heinrich's birth and suggested he might be a descendant of Christoff Hanhart born in 1731, who moved to Goes, Netherlands in 1752. The Goes Archives did contain a record of a wedding of Christoff Hanhart. No records were found of children being baptized in Goes or any other vital statistic. Christoff and his wife later returned to Switzerland and

Adriaan's attempt of linkage ended in failure.

After I took over the research, I contacted a genealogist in Switzerland and asked him to help me find the parents of Hans Heinrich. I shared with him all my findings to date. He reported he had found Hans Heinrich, who was baptized on 27 March 1749 and had married Hendrika Jansen in the Netherlands. I was elated, but also somewhat suspicious about the accuracy of his report. I contacted another genealogist, shared with her my misgivings and that I was looking for a second opinion. We decided to reconstruct the whole family tree of the Hanharts in Steckborn. She took special note of all the people named Hans Heinrich Hanhart, especially those born around 1749 or 1750, the approximate time that my forefather was born. Hans Heinrich, born on 27 March 1749, showed up on this family tree. However, this person was married in Steckborn and had two children. It was impossible that he was the person I was looking for. The new Steckborn family tree of the Hanharts (covering a period from approximately 1500 to about 1775) showed that the name Hans Heinrich was very common.

Since Hans Heinrich was a soldier in the Swiss Army, serving in the Netherlands, I contacted the General Government Archives in the Netherlands for Army records. They confirmed Hans Heinrich had served in the Swiss regiment and they found a muster roll dated 16 April 1781. On this roll Hans Heinrich was listed and was reported to be 23 years old. This new information suggested that Hans Heinrich was born between 17 April 1757 and 16 April 1758, instead of 1749 or 1750. It also brought into question the validity of the information on Hans Heirich's death certificate.

In 1998, I wrote the archivist of the Statsarchiv Kanton, Thurgau, Switzer-

land and shared the new range of dates for Hans Heinrich's birth. The archivist wrote back and advised that he found three persons by the name of Hans Heinrich Hanhart baptized on 22 May 1757, 26 May 1758 and 27 August 1758. He eliminated two for several reasons. The third Hans Heinrich fit since he was baptized on 27 August 1758. It was not unusual in those days that infants were baptized several months after birth. No further information was found of this person in any of the records in Steckborn. Thus ended the search for a link between the Hanhart family in the Netherlands and Switzerland.

Death certificate for Hans Heinrich Hanhart.

Written records are not always dependable. The efforts to link my forefather with Steckborn, Thurgau, Switzerland provided me with quite a bit of additional information about Hans Heinrich Hanhart in Holland that I otherwise would not have found. — Peter Hanhart, AB, phanhart@telusplanet.net

First Name Hints

For those with Dutch heritage it helps to know the spelling of given names as they appear in a variety of different records. This also holds true for most European searches. For example, the name Peter appears as Pieter in Dutch, Petrus in Latin and Pierre in French.

On the Internet the Dutch Reformed Church has a list of given names that helped me in searching for a second-great-uncle who migrated from the Netherlands long before my grandparents left France to come to the US. I would have never known that Jan was another version of John without that list. — Marie Van Laeys, CA

Tracing Family Naming Traditions

My father was named William Kinsey Carr. His first two names were the first names of his two grandfathers. As I developed an interest in my family history, I assumed the name Kinsey must be a surname back in time somewhere. There was also a family legend about an ancestor who fought in the American Revolution and who carried a 13-pound sword. No one knew that ancestor's name.

Through census records I learned Kinsey Carr was the son of George Washington Carr who had married Gitty Daniels, daughter of Kinsey Daniels. The Daniels clan in 1849 left Mercer county, PA and moved together to Jackson county, IA. This included relatives by marriage like my second-great-grandfather, George Washington Carr. The Daniels always named one of their sons Kinsey. The name Kinsey Daniels became so common it was hard to tell uncle from father, nephew from son.

I kept searching census and probate records in Mercer county, PA carrying the line farther back until it led to Jonathan Daniels in New London, CT in colonial times. Jonathan had 10 children and his eighth, Jonathan, was baptized on 23 September 1733 in New London. Jonathan Daniels grew up to marry in 1756 a woman named Johannah Kinsey. I had found the beginnings of the Kinsey naming pattern.

Jonathan served as a private in the Second Battalion NJ Continental Line. We wonder if he could be the leg-endary ancestor who carried the 13-pound sword. Many of Jonathan's descendants have proved Daughters of the American Revolution membership through his service.

No one has been able to find out anything about Johannah Kinsey. Some speculate that she was a Quaker and, when she married a military man, her name was removed from Quaker records.

Will of Jonathan Daniels from 1764, husband of Johannah Kinsey, source of the family naming tradition of Kinsey.

It thrills me to think that through perseverance I was able to trace back a name that sounded like a surname. Johannah named her second son Kinsey Daniels and that was the start of the naming tradition. When my grandmother named my father William Kinsey Carr, she thought she was naming him for his paternal grandfather. She never dreamed that the name Kinsey came from a woman who was born in 1724 — a woman who was found only because she gave her maiden name to her son. — Jean Cummings, MI, jcumming32@aol.com

The Coal Miner's Granddaughter

My wife's grandfather came to the US from Lithuania. He was a coal miner in West Virginia and had children there, including my wife's father. That was the extent of our information. We had no dates and we weren't sure of his correct name. It was further complicated by the fact the records office containing vital documentation for the area had burned down, destroying all the records and the local church where the family attended was no longer functioning.

I looked for census records but found nothing as he came to the US after the 1900 census and died before the 1910 census. I wrote and called the state archives in Charleston. People were cooperative, but there wasn't anything to help me.

My wife joined local historical and genealogy societies in an attempt to see what information might be available from them. We also wrote letters to them, indicating everything we knew, which wasn't much.

Months later, a postcard arrived in the mail from a West Virginia school teacher. She had researched the mining town in which the family had resided called Century, WV because her grandparents had lived there too. She wrote a lengthy and excellent story on Century. Because of her interest and knowledge of Century, a local society passed along our letter to her.

The postcard contained her telephone number and we immediately called her. We had a very nice conversation. She made one very important suggestion that would crack the case. She suggested contacting a church miles away in the county seat of Buckhannon, WV. She felt the Century church records might have been moved there. We promptly sent a letter to the Buckhannon church.

A long time elapsed when a letter finally arrived. It contained notations on the original letter we had sent to the church. They gave the correct spelling of my wife's grandfather's surname: Mazeika. It provided the complete maiden name of my wife's grandmother, who had remarried three years after the death of her husband. In addition, it gave the name of her parents in Lithuania.

While previously I was not successful in locating their ship's passenger record, armed with better information, a new search found it. It gave the town he came from in Lithuania and it revealed he was joining his brother-in-law in Thomas, NY. I immediately suspected New York was an error and it was. He went to Thomas, WV. I then found corroborating information from the church in Thomas.

I now had sufficient information to write the Lithuanian Archives. For a hefty fee we received a wonderful report documenting the family for four generations in Lithuania, with towns, dates of birth, marriages and deaths.

We did not go through the brickwall but we were able to go over it. — Richard G. Horvath, NJ

Mailing Lists For County Query

In searching for my grandmother's mother, father, grandmother and grandfather I tried all the surname searches on the Internet I could think of. I was beginning to think (in a joking way) that maybe my Nana had made up these four names. Then I had an idea that seemed like a long shot: I posted a query to the county where they had lived. In the meantime I went to the local FHC and continued to search through books, films and fiches.

It took a while, but finally someone answered my query. I gained a lot of information from the answer. I now have the three companies that my second-great-grandfather served for in the Civil War, his many occupations, obituaries and his will. I also have the cemetery and plots where the four of them are buried, as well as the obituaries for my second-great-grandmother.

From my second-great-grandfather's will I discovered the names of his two other sons and where they were living at the time of his death. I posted queries to those locations. I have received no reply to one yet, but for the other I was sent pictures and diaries of his wife, obituaries for him, his wife and five of their six children. I am also getting a copy of a family file submitted to a historical society by a family member

All I can say is don't forget to look in the area where they lived. — Nancy Brown, CA

The Search Started With A School Project

When my mother-in-law, Lois, and her mother died within a year of each other, my daughter became interested in knowing more about that part of her family. Lois' only brother had died many years before and so there was no one to ask about the family. As part of a school project, my daughter started researching her grandmother's family. My daughter knew that Lois' father, Gurney McBain, was buried in a cemetery only about 10 miles from home and so we made the trip to find more about dates. Buried next to her great-grandfather was her second-great-grandfather, Donald McBain. Next on her list was a trip to the county next door to find a death certificate for both men. It seemed that we would be stopped in the process since the death record of her second-great-grandfather listed his birthplace as Scotland.

Interested in seeing if we couldn't

find more about the family, we then looked for an obituary. We finally found one in a small town library with a surprisingly large genealogical section. Imagine our surprise when the obituary listed Donald's wife, Margaret, five daughters and adopted son, Gurney Shultz. Now we had a new problem. We knew from other sources that Gurney had been born in Marshall county, IA.

A letter to that county returned an unnamed Shultz boy with the right month and day for his birth but four years earlier than we though Gurney has been born. No mother was listed on the birth certificate and the occupation of the father, Jarvis Shultz, was listed as pauper. No other children were found with the same father. Checking federal and state census records resulted in conflicting ages.

Gurney Shultz McBain in his WWI uniform.

Periodically over the next five years we would check the daughters of Donald McBain, but the descendants of these women had no idea about that part of their family history.

Finally we took a trip to Marshall county, IA. The entire day was planned to search for the elusive Gurney and his natural parents. We spent time in the courthouse, in the historical society, in the library and finally back to the courthouse. I had recently read about using court records in family research. Doubtful that we would find anything and having only an hour before the courthouse closed, we started looking through the indexes. We copied any record with the surname Shultz that occurred between two years before Gurney's birth and five years afterward.

The clerks were very helpful and patient as we looked through record after record that they set before us. It was about 10 minutes before closing and my daughter and I had about given up when the record of a divorce was found. There, in 1893, was given in detail the personal lives of two people and the divorce. Four children were involved and neither parent was given custody. The children were put into the care of the Iowa Educational Aid Association. As we turned the pages, there was listed Gurney, as a four-year-old boy. Also listed were three other children. His father's name was James, not Jarvis. His mother's name was given as was their marriage date and place in Illinois.

In the seven years since then we have found Orla Otto Shultz in a work home in Lee county, IA. He married and raised a family in that area. We're still looking for Lizzie Etta and Nathanial. Gurney kept the name Shultz until after Donald McBain died. Gurney's father, James Shultz remarried and raised a family about 25 miles from the McBains, but as far as we have been able to determine, they never knew about each other's lives. Lucy (Hutzel) Shultz remarried, but her husband was abusive and she was again divorced. From the marriage date and place in Stephenson

Part of the divorce record that gives the names of the children and what will happen to them.

county, IL we have been able to trace both of Gurney's parents and their families back several generations. — Carolyn Jensen, IA, cjteach@cfu.net

A Long Shot

I hit the wall looking for family members on my maternal grandfather's side of the family. I often heard my grandfather talk about an Aunt Virlea and a cousin named Mildred Ketchum. While taking care of my grandfather before he passed away I ran across a paper from a funeral home. It was a memorial notice of Mildred's death. On this notice it listed both Pastors that officiated the service and addresses. Another part of the notice listed Mildred's children's names.

I took a chance and wrote the pastors and asked them that if they had an address for any of the children if he could forward my letter to them as they were my cousins and we had never met. I told him I was doing my genealogy and would love to hear from my cousins. It took a little while but I got a call from my cousin and we have been in contact since.

It was a long shot but it paid off. — Connie Kester DePalma, MI

Hyde And Seek

My grandfather, Park Smith Hyde, was a problem. I believed his birth date was in 1883. I sent a request to Prescott, AZ for his birth certificate and was told they had no record of him. I corresponded with a lady who worked for the genealogy society and she did her best but couldn't find any information on him. Then I sent a request to the state and was told they only have records going back to 1884, so I thought I would never get a copy of his birth certificate.

I searched the Social Security records and found nothing. I had a certificate from the Railroad Retirement Board so I knew he worked for the railroad. I wrote to them and was told they could not send me any information unless I had his social security number, which I didn't have. I went to Prescott with the hope of discovering more information, but found nothing.

I researched at the local FHC with no luck. I went to Utah and researched at the FHL with the same result. I searched a number of microfilms and found nothing. After all the research and hitting brickwalls all along the way I decided to send for his death certificate as I knew he had died in California. When I received it I discovered that his social security number was on his death certificate. So I sent the information to the Railroad Retirement Board and they returned 10 double-sided pages of information on everything in his file. With this information I found out that the family moved to Kansas and were recorded on the 1900 census for Kansas.

I also discovered that his birth date was 1884 not 1883. So I again sent to Arizona for his birth certificate. After sending the necessary proof I finally received it. I discovered it was a delayed birth certificate, probably made up so he could get his railroad retirement because there was no birth

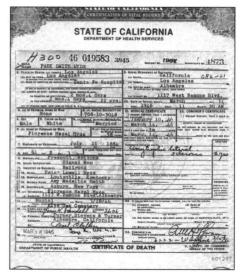

Patricia A. Heumann's grandfather's death certificate where she found his Social Security number and the correct year of his birth.

certificate at the time of his birth.
— Patricia A. Heumann, CA, i436643@thegrid.net

Name Changes

Our great-grandfather, James Edward Whitelaw (son of Edward Whitelaw), married Melissa Jane Smith of Van Buren county, MI. Melissa Jane was born 20 March 1849 to Peter Smith.

Family records have Peter born in March 1808 in Scotland, dying on 7 July 1862 and buried in Thompson Cemetery, Bloomingdale, Van Buren county, MI. Some records have Peter's wife born "about 1816" and most of the records had her name as Matilda. One of Dad's family group sheets had Matilda typed, but penciled in "Sabin" and "born 27 October 1815". One record had Peter and Matilda married in Pennsylvania. We did have their children Nancy Ann, Katie, Duncan and Melissa Jane, with possibly another child born about 1857. The birth dates of Melissa Jane's siblings varied among the records. I got curious about that Matilda that has been reproduced on all the family records for the last 20 years.

We had also hit a brickwall on connecting our Edward Whitelaw ancestor to Scotland and, if Peter was from Scotland and a family friend, perhaps he could lead us to the Whitelaw ancestors.

In June 2000, some descendants from Edward Whitelaw's other children were gathered in Michigan to see where Edward was buried and where he lived. I asked them if they had time could they try to find the cemetery where Peter Smith is buried, even though they don't descend from him.

Shortly afterwards, I got an e-mail from them. They had found the cemetery and headstones for Joan Smith and Duncan J. Smith. They almost gave up finding Peter but decided to take photos of the other Smith headstones there. They found a headstone that was lying down and a little over from these. It read "Our Father, Peter Smith, died July 7, 1862, 54 yrs. 5 months." I asked for a lookup of cemetery information for this plot from a person listed on the Van Buren county Internet site and was sent this information a month later; "Smith, Peter died July 7, 1862 — 54 yrs. 5 mo., Phebe Ann born Mar. 8, 1805 — died Oct. 25, 1867, Peter born Jan. 25, 1876 — Feb. 26, 1901, Joan born Oct. 27, 1845 — Nov. 15, 1898, Duncan J. 1848 — 1923."

It looked like Peter Smith's wife's name could be Phebe Ann. I started checking census information. I knew Peter had purchased land in Columbia, Van Buren county, MI. The 1850 census for the township of Columbia had the information right there. Peter Smith, 48, was born in New York married to Phebe and had four children, Nancy, Duncan, Catharine and Phebe.

Katie could certainly be Catherine and baby Phebe must be our great-grandmother Melissa Jane. The 1860 census again shows Peter and Phoebe Ann with Jane age 11. So that baby Phebe changed to Jane and that

matches our Melissa Jane a little closer.

I searched in the IGI records at the local FHC and found that Peter Smith married Phebe Ann Duncan on 21 November 1835 in Washtenaw county, MI. The 1840 and 1850 census lists some Duncan families in Washtenaw county with James born in Scotland. There's another Scotland tie.

Based on census information, Phebe Ann Duncan could have been born about July 1807 in New York and Peter Smith was born about March 1808 in New York. Our Matilda now has the name of Phebe Ann Duncan, and we have a little more information to carry forth more research into these two lines of family history. — Cheryl Whitelaw, UT, whitelawcs@suu.edu

I Drove A Volvo Through My Brickwall

Having come to genealogy only recently I missed the opportunity to tap the memories and thoughts of my parents and any older relatives. After exhausting my own scant memories and those of my older sister, I was left with a very sketchy picture of my Kaufman family history. All that we knew were the names of my father's parents and those of his three sisters and that his parents emigrated from Russia right after the beginning of the century. With my aunts deceased, the only Kaufman descendants who I was aware of were my cousins, Jay and Sally. I had not seen or heard from Jay in at least 20 years and it was at least five more since I last spoke with Sally. I became determined to find them, believing them to be my only link to that line of my family.

The 20-years-old telephone numbers that we had for Jay and Sally were either disconnected or belonged to other people who had never heard of them. I turned to the Internet in hopes of finding their current telephone numbers, using several of the telephone search engines. I found several Jays with my cousin's surname and many Js. He had settled in Long Island, NY and I believed that in all likelihood he still lived there, so I concentrated on the numbers on the list from Long Island. After many messages I realized that I was not going to find Jay this way. I met with the same lack of success with the listings that I found that could have been for Sally. I kept searching the Internet, but finally put Sally and Jay aside.

One day I took a piece of paper and I wrote down everything that I knew of Jay and Sally. All I knew was very old and ended in dead ends. I had two pieces of information that I thought I could follow-up. Twenty

Left to right: Sally, Rocco, Dotty and Jay Gentile.

years earlier Jay had been an auto-mechanic in a Volvo dealership on Long Island. Sally was as a nurse in a Manhattan hospital. The hospital proved to be no help.

For Jay, it was back to the Internet. I searched for Volvo and Long Island, NY. It only came up with one listing. Considering my information was 20 years old I was not optimistic. I called the number and was concerned when the person answering the telephone said, "Good morning, Karp Buick." I believed that my only lead had just closed down. I said, "I'm sorry, I thought this was a Volvo dealership," she replied, "Yes we are. We sell

Buicks, Saabs and Volvos." I breathed a sigh of relief and asked for the Service Department. A voice on the telephone said, "Service. Harvey. Can I help you?" I asked if they had a mechanic named Jay Gentile. He replied that they did not. I asked if he was aware of any other Volvo Dealerships and he said he was not. I thanked him for his time saying that I was a long-lost cousin of Jay's and that I was trying to find him.

There was a hesitation and then Harvey said, "I know Jay." Not only did he give me Jay's place of employment and the number there but also he gave me a brief update on Jay's family. I thanked him profusely, hung up and immediately called the number for Jay.

The number was for an automotive service center in Woodbury, Long Island. A lady answered the telephone, I asked for the service department. A man came on the line and said, "Service." I asked to speak to Jay and the gentleman said, "Who is this?"

I told him my name and said that I was Jay's long-lost cousin and that I had been told that Jay worked there to which he replied, "Hi Cary, it's Jay." My brickwall had fallen. — Cary Kaufman, FL, cjkinfl13@cs.com

* * *

Dealing with Incorrect Data

My great-grandfather, George Walter Cullen, immigrated to New Zealand in around 1858. I deduced from his death certificate that he was born around 1838. He is listed in the 1841 British census for Bath, again the same year of birth was indicated.

However searches of all the parish registers from Bath and surrounding parishes did not disclose a birth/baptismal listing. I learned the period 1836-38 is somewhat of a gray area in the UK. Many births were not registered in the parish registers and notification was to be sent to Somerset House, now the Central Registry. I have found in many cases there is no record of a birth for this period. Therefore, I had to rely on the census data. I found the marriage lines of my great-grandfather's parents, George and Mary Cullen. They only had George, my ancestor, and another son, Henry, who was listed in directories for the time. Father George stated in the census record that he had been born in Weston Zoyland, in Somerset, which I had never heard of. The records I wanted were not in the IGI, so I spent a week in Taunton at the record office for Somerset.

I found George Cullen was baptized on 19 July 1827 and he had, in fact, been born on 14 November 1809. There was a tiny note in the margin of the register, he was not baptized until he was almost 18 years old. The dates in the census and on his death certificate matched. His parents were given as William and Anna, so I worked back through the records to find he was the last child born to a family of eight. Then I stumbled upon the marriage.

Earlier I had found a birth of a child born to William and Rosanna and ignored it. Then when I read the marriage lines I realized Anna was in fact Rosanna, also William had been a widower, so found his first marriage and the birth of two daughters along with the death of his first wife. I would not have been able to sort this had I not been searching the original records.

William Cullen married Mary Sawtell at Huish Episcopi Church, Somerset.

An all-counties search revealed William was born in Cornwall in the parish of St. Keverne, on 17 February 1750. Coming back to Somerset, William married in the neighboring parish of Huish Episcopi. His wife Mary died in 1785, leaving William, a laborer, with two youngsters. He remarried in the December of that year to Rosanna. I traced the family in St Keverne back a further four generations when the second-great-grandfather of William of 1750, is identified as a gentleman. Yet by the time William was born the various branches of the family were fishermen and laborers. I wondered if Leonard Cullen and wife Mary were dispossessed Irish gentry? That is a brickwall I have not been able to scale.

Rightly or wrongly, after researching for almost 15 years, I check everything back to original records without fail! — LC

A Jolly Good Tale

I was searching for information on a Mary Jolly Birket, living in the Weeton/Kirkham area of Lancashire,

England. Family history said Jolly was her maiden name.

A birth certificate for her son, born in Weeton, listed her name as Mary Birket and beneath her name a notation "formerly Kirkham". Weeton and Kirkham are small villages within a mile or two of each other and I assumed she was formerly from the village of Kirkham.

I had been searching with no luck for the Jolly surname and one day, looking yet again at the birth certificate, it dawned on me that perhaps the notation meant her maiden name was Kirkham and not the village from which she came.

After pursuing that avenue, I found that indeed her maiden name was Kirkham, not Jolly and I finally had found my Mary Kirkham Birket. — Gail Birket, FL

Don't Dismiss The Land Records

I had been searching for the maiden name of my second-great-grandmother for more than a year. The only mention I had of her was in the 1883 birth record of her son, my great-grandfather, in the microfilmed records of Bernardston, Massachusetts Books. I had scanned through published birth records of Bernardston and several adjoining towns for anyone with the unusual first name of Theoma. I found nothing. I knew the pre-1850 census records would be of no help, listing only heads of household.

I took a genealogy vacation to Franklin county, MA, and spent a day in the courthouse in Greenfield. I found no listing for Theoma Foster in court indexes, where I hoped I might find her listed, as beneficiary of a parental will. The land records office was just down the hall, but up to then I had not seen a land deed that mentioned relationships, even when I knew the transactions to be between

family members. With a feeling of futility, I thought as long as I was there I might as well check for records of Foster lands. Theoma G. Foster was listed several times in the index. The first record I checked, for a parcel in Gill, contained the magic words: "set off to me as a part of my portion of the real Estate of my late Father, Joel Munn, deceased."

Foster land record.

Never again will I denigrate the possibility that land records might prove useful! Once past the brickwall, I went the next day to the town clerk's office in Gill and found a previous town clerk had gleaned his records and compiled the genealogies of all the old families in town. I had the Munns and several collateral lines back to the 1600s. — Ellen Foster Monroe, OH, efoster@config.com

Letter To A Postmaster

This episode happened more than 30 years ago. I was researching a relative's family history from Nebraska. We had already written to relatives but nobody knew much about his maternal grandmother's family. The relatives thought she had come from Bartley, NE.

After searching all the death records available at the time and then looking for a historical society, I still didn't have a clue. So I wrote a letter to the postmaster at Bartley, NE asking if he knew of anyone related to her. I got a reply that there was no one in Bartley who was related to the grandmother, but that the postmaster's wife was related to them. He sent me the address of an elderly man in another town in Nebraska and he in turn sent me the name and address of his daughter, a family genealogist living in Littleton, CO.

This genealogist had researched the Sanders/Saunders line back into New England and then I found all kinds of names, dates and places. — Lois Kullberg, WA

The Ballad of The Brosses

My father, Edgar John Bross, Jr. grew up in the Newark Orphan Asylum in New Jersey, after the untimely death of his mother when he was six years old. My father knew very little of his ancestry and because he died when I was 11 years old, I wasn't yet old enough to know what questions to ask. It seemed my father's only relatives were his father, Edgar John Bross Sr. and a childless uncle, Arthur Henry Bross.

In my early teens, I asked Arthur about his ancestry. He wrote down the names of his parents and grandparents but no dates or places of resi-dence. I filed it away. Before I was 30, I was serious about researching my paternal ancestry. I don't remember how I knew the Brosses lived in Newton, Sussex county in New Jersey, but that is where I began. After all the normal avenues of searching for my second-great-grandparents, including joining genealogical societies, I had no answers.

A few years ago, I was offered a computer. With the use of the Internet the door opened wide. I put queries on genealogical websites. An unknown distant cousin, sent me an obituary of second-great-grand-mother Bross' sister's death in which Christiana Bross was listed as a survivor and residing in Newark, not in Newton where I had been searching for more than 30 years. My next course of action was to make a trip to the Allen County Public Library at Fort Wayne, IN. There I researched Newark city directories where I found Abram Bross and his wife Christiana, as residing there as early as 1868.

Next I wanted dates and places of death. There were no records of Abram's death in Newark. Christiana was noted in the late 1890 Newark directories as widow of Abram, but he was not deceased. One day someone put the obituary of Abram Bross on the Sussex County, NJ RootsWeb.com list. I was ecstatic! He died in Newton at the home of his sister, Sarah Ann Bross Case, yet the obituary stated his wife and surviving sons resided in Newark. I was able to put many pieces of the Bross, Crabtree, Givens and related families puzzle together.

Then there was the brickwall of dad's mother, Frederica Braun. Her death certificate did not give helpful information. Her parents' names were first names only and Germany was listed as the birthplace. Through researching Newark city directories and additional census records, I learned more about her parents. Her mother, also Frederica Braun, was a midwife and was the medical attendant and signed the birth certificate as such at the birth of my father. He was born Louis Edward Bross on 4 December 1899. In 1942, he legally changed his birth year to 1900 and his name to Edgar John Bross, Jr., I don't know why.

I knew grandmother Frederica Braun Bross was buried in Woodland Cemetery in Newark. Through contact with another person working through those cemetery records, I learned the dates of death of my grandmother's parents. The 1900 census record stated that great-grandmother, gave birth to six children, but only three were living at the time of the census taking — my grandmother, Frederica Bross and her sister Bertha Braun, who married Edward Leckie and a third child who was unknown.

I sent an e-mail requesting obituaries from Newark newspapers, giving the dates of death as I had them. From the obituary of Bertha Braun Leckie I learned her funeral service was held at the home of her sister, Frida Schnepf. There was the third surviving child who was noted in the 1900 census. During a trip to the public library at Fort Wayne, IN, I learned Frida was a widow by 1905 with two young children. She was a laundress in a private home. I found the son's name, Charles Schnepf, in the SSDI. — Mona Bross Hylton, IN, monamusic@aol.com

Changing Names

I located the parents and siblings of one of my husband's ancestors in the 1885 state census for Minnesota in Red Wing. They were using the surname Larson. I found several siblings in later censuses but was not able to find the parents, even though I knew the mother was still living in 1929. I had a picture of her and I knew she was living with one of her daughters in Minneapolis, MN.

I did find one of the other siblings in the Social Security death records and sent away for a copy of her application. In that application her parents were listed as August Lidblom and Elizabeth Anderson. No wonder I could not find them, they had changed their surname!

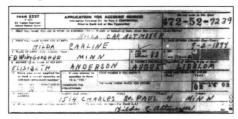

Application for Social Security by one of the Larson daughters which lists her parents' names.

I was then able to track them through the rest of their days, using the state and federal censuses along with city directories. The Minneapolis city directory actually listed the death date of August Lidblom. Some of the children kept the name of Larson and some used the name of Lidblom. — Marcia L. Johnson, MN

The Mystery Of Calcutta

I began tracing my husband's ancestors by writing hundreds of letters. I only had minimal information from my mother-in-law about his grandparents who lived in New Brunswick, NJ and had come from Birkinhead, England to the US.

With the bits of information available, I contacted a researcher in New Jersey who found the cemeteries where his grandfather and grandmother were buried and copies of the death certificates. I contacted the cemetery's custodians who provided information on the gravestone of his grandmother and great-grandmother. They were buried in the same grave, along with a child. The stone showed the birthplace of his great-grandmother as Calcutta. I was fairly certain she was not born in India.

Giving up on that line, I wrote for a copy of census records for Birkinhead for the years, which based on their ages at death, I felt they would have been there. For a fee of $450 I received six microfilm reels. Persistence and money paid off, I found his great-grandparents listed in the 1851 census. There was great-grandmother, showing she was born "At sea, Bajay Hobart Town". The only Hobart I knew was in Tasmania, Australia. I thought maybe Calcutta was a ship. A letter to Lloyds Ship's Registry in London provided a page from their records showing the ship *Calcutta* was sailing during the years she would have been born.

I posted a query about *Calcutta* and an answer stated it was a convict ship. From information obtained from the computer search, I e-mailed a query to Hobart, Tasmania about birth records for my husband's great-grandmother. I received a photocopy of the baptismal record of great-grandmother listing names of the second-great-grandparents.

The researcher in Tasmania looked at old newspapers and military records to discover that the great-grandfather was not a convict, but a soldier in the British Army who served in a regiment that guarded convicts sent to Australia. The researcher was even able to pinpoint that great-grandmother was most likely born on the ship *Urania* on route from the Australian mainland to Tasmania. Second-great-grandfather's regiment was transferred to India when great-grandmother was about four years old. It is my belief that she or her family thought that she was born in India and hence the Calcutta on her tombstone.

I subsequently found out that the *Calcutta* did not sail to Australia or Tasmania during the time that great-grandmother was born, so that brickwall has been re-erected. But I have now traced my husband's second-great-grandfather to Caven in Ireland

in 1813 where he enlisted in the British Army and gained from his enlistment information a detailed description of him.

Enlistment record with physical description, from 1813 for Leah Beth Simpson's husband's ancestor, John Reily

So, in a period of about five years, I have discovered mountains of information about grandparents, great-grandparents and second-great-grandparents. — Leah Beth Simpson, LA

Team Work

In my 20-plus years of tracing my family tree I have found and used many different brickwall techniques. Sometimes they work, sometimes they don't. On one family line in particular, I had been against a brickwall for several years when I discovered a great solution.

One day while surfing the Internet, I came across an Internet group researching this same troublesome family line. The research group has now grown to more than 100 members. I know there are a lot of specialty Internet and surname groups out there, but this group is different from any other I've come across. Just like other groups, we have pooled our information, each of us gaining new information in the process. The information, along with further research, gave us new leads and still more questions.

We now have our own website containing information about our group, which extends an invitation to others researching our line. It also includes some of our in-depth research, as well as many family pictures and stories we have accumulated. We hope this will bring more new cousins to our membership, along with new information.

Here is where we differ from other groups. We have divided into small groups, with each group assigned certain areas and time periods to research. Each group has a leader to whom those on that particular team report. Then each team leader reports to the Captain. After the new information has been sifted and sorted we reorganize into small teams again, depending on the combined findings and start over again with our separate new assignments. Many minds working together, in an organized manner, all with the same end goals in mind, is much more efficient than each of us slugging away, picking up tidbits of information once in awhile.

Using this method we have found many answers to questions we'd all but given up on. — Donna Tice-Carnall, KS, dcarnall@earthlink.net

Victory At Vimy Once More

I knew my grandfather, William Hugh Gourley, had three younger sisters, Elizabeth Mary, Sarah Ann and Rosina Minerva. However, the only one with whom I was acquainted was Elizabeth because we lived near one another. The other two lived out west and I had never met them. By the time I became interested in family history, all the relatives that might have known where I could find the two western sisters and their families had passed away. Although I knew their married surnames, Runions and Walden, I had no idea where to look for them.

My brickwall began to crumble in an unusual way. I was reading *Vimy*, a book about the magnificent victory won by Canadian troops at Vimy Ridge in northern France during WWI. Near the end of the book the author, Pierre Berton, briefly relates how a young sergeant in the Winnipeg Battalion just reached the crest of the ridge when shrapnel from an exploding shell tore into his upper body. It appeared to be a fatal wound. However instead of penetrating his heart the shrapnel was lodged in the New Testament in his pocket. He sustained only a minor shoulder wound.

The sergeant's name was Wesley Runions. Suddenly, I had a flashback. I had heard this story many years before. When I was a child, my father told me how his cousin escaped death during WWI because he was carrying a New Testament in his tunic pocket, over his heart. Furthermore, the uncommon surname Runions rang a bell.

My next step was to obtain Sergeant Runions' service records from the National Archives of Canada. I scanned the online index of the soldiers in the Canadian Expeditionary Force for his name and regimental number. On a hunch, I also searched for anyone named Walden. Two names popped up: Wesley Douglas Gourlay Runions and Loftin John Gourley Walden. Both soldiers had Gourley(ay) as one of their middle names. I knew I was on the right track. This was confirmed when copies of their service records arrived from the Archives. The records revealed Wesley Runions' mother was Sarah Runions and Loftin Walden's mother was Rosina Walden. Both were living in Manitoba during WWI.

I then obtained from the Internet names and addresses of nine persons, living in Manitoba, with the surname Runions. I sent each a form letter asking for information about the family of Wesley Runions. Only one response was received, but that was enough. It came from Ken Runions who is a fellow family historian. He has been a tremendous help in filling the blanks in both the Runions and Walden families. When my wife and I took a trip to Manitoba, Ken arranged for us to meet descendants of both families, including the two daughters of Wesley Runions.

That chance reading of the book *Vimy* provided the clue to a major breakthrough in a search that at one time seemed hopeless. — Desmond R.H. Gourley, VA, desgourley@aol.com

Funeral Homes

While researching my family in Baker county, OR, I met with many brickwalls. Since a lot of these people lived prior to the county taking records on death, birth and marriage, I decided to look into what funeral homes were around during the time frame. There was only one, which was still in existence and operational.

I contacted the funeral home and they gladly shared records on everyone they had in my family without question or cost. These records included death dates, parents, siblings and obituaries. The obituary for my second-great-grandmother mentioned she was a *Mayflower* descendant and a Jamestown, Virginia settler descendant too. Most of these families were also Oregon Trail Pioneers. This information would be a gold mine for any genealogist. — Mark McKee, VA

You'll Find It As Soon As You Stop Looking

I wanted to see if David Craig and Lucinda Jane English were married in Holt county, MO, since their children were apparently born there. I sent letters to Holt county with their names and an estimated time when I thought their marriage would have taken place. They sent me a marriage record for David Craig and Lucinda Davenport. There were no Davenports or English surnames to be found on either the Holt or Andrew county censuses.

I got through the brickwall of Lucinda's surname by doing something that I do quite a bit. When searching on the Internet, or going through indexes, or just taking my finger down a page of names that are not indexed, I keep a list of surnames in my head. Even when I'm searching for a certain one, my eyes latch onto any of the other surnames if they'd appear. This is what happened when I was searching the Buchanan county marriage records for another surname. I found James Davenport and Lucinda J. English, who were married in 1851 in Buchanan county. Two years later she married David Craig in Holt county.

Marriage record of James Davenport and Lucinda English.

This is how I broke through brickwalls, but I've still got more bricks to crumble. I have yet to find anything on David Craig's parents for certain and I'm still searching for where David and Lucinda Jane died and were buried. However, I have found Lucinda's parents through queries on the genealogy sites. Some things seem to fall into place once you break into that brickwall. — Jan Coy, KS, jec1945@ccp.com

Probate Records

Ten years ago I was in Michigan researching my father's line. I found the cemetery where my third-great-grandparents were buried. The gravestone read "Elish Farnum and wife Sally". I went to the county courthouse and found the death records for both of them. They both died in 1883 but the death records listed their parents as unknown.

I found an obituary for Sally that read, "Mrs. Sally Farnum, 92, died last Wednesday" but this wasn't much help. I didn't find an obituary for Elisha. The cemetery records were lost some years before I did my research. A year later I found a book in the FHL about the Farnum family, which said Elisha married Sally Mandeville. But there was no proof.

I contacted some of the people in the book and found they had a will for Francis Mandeville, which said he had a daughter Sally Farnum. Farnum was a common name at the time but at least it looked like I had found Sally's maiden name.

Three years later I still didn't have the evidence to prove it was Sally. I planned a trip to New York to do research. When I got to the courthouse where the will was located, I found it listed in the probate index book. There were no other documents. It seemed strange there were no other papers listed for the estate because he had six daughters and three sons. Other listings in the index had other papers listed for quite a few other estates so I knew there should have been more. I got a copy of the will and left.

The next day I was still researching in the area so I went back to the probate office and told the clerk about my dilemma. She said she would look in the basement for any records with a date in that time period. She came back with a packet of documents for that year. In the packet were three documents from Francis' probate along with documents from other estates from that year. One of them was what I was looking for. It listed all the children and where they lived at the time of the death. That was the proof I needed. — Harold Godley, AZ, harold.godley@gte.net

A Darling Story

I have been interested in my family history for as long as I can remember. My mother was a good storyteller and made me feel part of a long line of people who had a can-do attitude.

My brother, who has a passing interest in genealogy, was the conservator for our dad's older half-sister in her last years. Aunt Helen was not one for sharing family traditions and I only met her once or twice as a child. After her passing, my brother was thoughtful enough to send along a letter he found amongst her belongings. Carlos P. Darling wrote the letter to my aunt asking her for information on her branch of the Darling family. Carlos Darling was a genealogist and his return address was at the top of the letter. I decided to pursue this clue. The letter was dated 1947 and so my chances of finding him alive were slim. I hoped he joined a local, or even a national society.

Just some of the contents of seven cartons, including handwritten journals, compiled over a lifetime of genealogical research.

I called the historical society in the Pennsylvania town where he lived and the woman who answered the phone remembered him. He had passed away years earlier. She told me he wanted his research to go to the New England Historic Genealogical Society, but his family never followed up and it was all discarded. Greatly disappointed, I hung up and thought that was a brickwall.

A year or two later, I had an opportunity to visit the New England Historic Genealogical Society Library. Remembering that conversation about Carlos P. Darling, I thought, somehow his research might have made it to this location. I looked in the general catalog cards, the manuscript catalog cards, the name-file catalog card files and the location catalog card files with no luck. The librarian suggested I try the miscellaneous cards. I found a card that read "Carlos P. Darling, 7 Cartons". I asked if I could see the cartons. Many of the cartons contained notebooks; one had envelopes of letters and questionnaires. In one of the notebooks I found some names that looked very familiar. These were my Darlings. I found my grandparents, my father and me! This notebook listed my family back to colonial Boston in 1660.

I learned not to take anyone's word for lost records. Look for yourself. What was a brickwall turned into a bonanza for me. — Alice Darling Strom, NV

Memories Of Sweden

My paternal grandmother's mother is Maude Anderson. When I started my family history, I had slim hopes of tracking her family as Anderson is quite a common name. Years before my interest in genealogy flowered, I spoke with my grandmother and recorded that her maternal grandparents (Maude's parents) came from Sweden and they had the surnames Anderson and Danielson. She told me her birthplace of Ong, NE was also the residence of her grandparents at least in 1906. Her grandparents were farmers there. More recently, I was informed great-grandmother Maude was born in Galesburg, IL in 1884. From my aunt I learned the names of Maude's sisters and their spouses. A check of the SSDI showed Maude's youngest sister Ellen, spouse of Carl Benson, died in Ong in 1983.

I searched the 1900 census and found my family, correlating most of the facts about Alfred W. Anderson,

his wife and their children. I looked up Ong in the 1990 census and found there were fewer than 100 people living there. I checked the white pages telephone directory online for Anderson and Benson in Ong. Two Andersons and four Bensons were listed. After a number of telephone calls and correspondence, I sorted the names, approximate birth dates and general birth locations of my ancestors, Alfred Anderson and Sophia Danielson and their children, as well as accumulated more information about their other descendants who would be my cousins. One of my grandmother's cousins, now living in Nebraska, recalled her grandparents Alfred and Sophia came from Stockholm, Sweden.

At this point I felt stuck. I needed reliable information about this town in Sweden from where Alfred and Sophia came. Their death certificates added no new information. I had not even located Maude's birth record. A copy of Maude's Social Security application showed her birthplace as Galesburg, which was the same as my family's oral history. However the clerks at the Knox county courthouse could not find any record of her birth or of the marriage of Alfred and Sophia. Occasional searches of sources such as recently released (or discovered) cds or library reference books covering the right time and place went nowhere until two search hits happened almost simultaneously.

The first hit was in the Illinois marriage index from 1851-1900 and the other was in the North American Vital Records Index cd-rom series. Maude was born in the township of Clover in Henry county, about 20 miles from Galesburg. Her parents were married in Woodhull, also in Henry county. The marriage records identified the names of parents of the bride and groom and the birth locations. Alfred was born in Adelof, Sweden and Sophia was born in Morlunda, Sweden.

Seeking and regularly checking index sources as they became available and obtaining copies of original documents overcame this brickwall.

I have since learned Alfred and Sophia were buried in the Stockholm Swedish Cemetery in Shickley, NE. So, there was something in my grandmother's cousin's childhood recollections. — Gary Shea, WI

Lots Of Telephone Calls Pay

Back in the early 1960s my father and his eight sisters compiled a 16-page document covering many of the family traditions mixed with some hard information about the family's history. They had little material in writing but among them they had an amazing variety of traditional lore. They covered only two generations.

I began a traveling sales job about the same time covering, over a few years time, every state west of the Mississippi. My interest in the family history increased after the publication of the work completed by my father and his siblings. I started calling Sleepers in the telephone book in any town I visited. None of us had any idea how widely spread the family was. No one seemed to have any information about where the family came from, beyond the fact that my grandfather, Oren Alphonso Sleeper, was born in Plymouth, NH.

Finally, I connected with an Air Force Colonel in Texas, who thought his father might have something. The elderly gentleman told me there was a book titled *The History of Bristol, N.H.* in which there were Sleeper genealogies.

I wrote a generic letter of inquiry to the public library in Bristol. I got a reply from a board member of the Sleeper-Minot Library in Bristol offering to photocopy the relevant pages from the now out-of-print book. The resulting copies took us right back to

1640 to the first immigrant Thomas Sleeper. We discovered the town of Bristol was founded after the American Revolution by some of our ancestors and it was a treasure trove of information about the family.

Oren Clough Sleeper, who is mentioned in The History of Bristol, N.H.

I found a copy of the two-volume work, which is still, nearly 40 years later, referred to frequently as I work at connecting other branches of the family into my own. I have a couple of thousand ancestors identified in this line now and every time I indulge in a burst of research I find more.

I'm sure the whole job would have been simple had I started my research on the Internet but I would have missed a lot of pleasant contacts with nice people. — Richard David Sleeper, OR, dick@sleeper.us

*   *   *

The Search For Lorrane

I hit a brickwall as I attempted to complete the Labahn vital statistics for the family page on my genealogy program. In the early 1970s, when my mother, Hedwig Labahn, supplied data to someone who was researching the Reuss family history, she did not include the name of her eldest child Lorrane Henry August Labahn who died as a baby. When I was a youngster our parents mentioned we had an older brother, who died in infancy. Other than that, they furnished no details.

By 1997 I had a complete vital history of all the descendants of my mother and father and my brothers and sisters, except the data for Lorrane. My parents were deceased and no living relative could offer any information about Lorrane. The records of the First Evangelical Lutheran Cemetery in Alsip, IL indicated that only an infant was interred in the family plot early in the century. This lead fizzled because the cemetery lost burial records in an office fire.

I contacted the city of Blue Island, IL to determine whether they had any birth or death records for Lorrane. They told me there were no records of birth or death prior to 1920. I checked with the County Clerk of Cook County in 1988 and again in 1997 for information. No records were found at either office. In addition, I checked with the secretary of the St. Paul Evangelical and Reform Church of Blue Island and was informed the records were written in German and the information was too difficult to decipher. I did not press the issue at that time. Sometime later the congregation disbanded due to a declining membership with the remaining families joining other churches.

In late 1998, while discussing my predicament with a friend he told me the vital statistic records of St. Paul's church are in the care of the Christ Memorial United Church of Christ in Blue Island and I should write to them. I did not receive an answer to my first letter. I then wrote to the pastor of the church. She replied and enclosed copies of the record book for the St. Paul Evangelical and Reformed Church of Blue Island. She stated the records were written in German and difficult to read, but they did show Lorrane Henry August Labahn was born on 7 June 1910 and died at the age of three months and three days.

Church birth record for Lorrane Henry August Labahn.

Perseverance, even though it took a number of years, broke through the brickwall. — Marvin F. Labahn, Sr., IL

Ask Cemetery Officials

Years ago my grandmother had mentioned the name of the cemetery where her father was buried. At the time I was interested in family history and decided to check the information in the Philadelphia telephone book and wrote to them. My letter was returned as having an incorrect address and when I called the telephone number was no longer in service.

A few years later while working on a high school reunion, I realized one of the women I had known was living in Philadelphia. I wrote her to inquire about the cemetery. She gave me the name of the neighborhood where it is located and an updated telephone number.

Another friend living in the area made the call for me and obtained the date of my great-grandfather's death.

I obtained the death certificate from Philadelphia. The certificate listed a widow who was completely unknown to me — apparently she was wife number three. Nothing I did provided me with any marriage record. I have no idea of the year but I figure it had to be after 1903 considering what I knew. A trip to Philadelphia was impossible at the time.

Years later, a friend took me to Philadelphia to visit the grave. We found the stone with no trouble and took some photographs. We then went to the office where I asked what they could tell me about my great-grandfather. The man was kind enough to photocopy the records for me. In the grave are my great-grandfather and his widow and two others who I believe to be her sister and brother-in-law.

There was a letter with the cemetery records from my great-grandfather's daughter with an address that was 18 years old. I checked the telephone listings on the Internet and she was still listed at that address. At first I wanted to call but decided that, because she might not even know her father had another family from an earlier marriage, I would write. Three weeks later I received a telephone call from my great-grandfather's granddaughter. Now I have information that continues to lead to other family details.

I recommend to anyone visiting an ancestor's grave to inquire at the cemetery office to learn what information is available — my experience has led me to far more information than I had hoped to learn. — Nancy Anne Rougvie, RI

Search Military Records

My second-great-grandparents, Middleton and Elizabeth, were married in 1853 in Sciota, OH. They had a daughter, Narcissa, in 1860. Then Middleton joined the Army for the Civil War. Middleton died on 15 May 1863 at the Battle of Vicksburg. Elizabeth had given birth to a son only 10 days before in Scioto. In 1868, Elizabeth remarried. I lost them for almost 20 years. I finally found the daughter, Narcissa, at the time of her second marriage in 1885 in Harlan county, NE. I looked and tried all kinds of things. I sent to the Federal Archives in Washington and received a lot of information about the family, but couldn't figure where they were and why there was a pension for Narcissa and not the brother.

Finally I saw an advertisement about a soldier search. It was going to cost me, but I knew this was my last chance to locate them. I told them as much as I knew and I already had a lot of the war records but that I couldn't locate them. I received a folder back with a lot of the same information but at the back of this folder were three separate bits of interesting information.

First there was a copy of a form that was an "Increase of Minors Pension". It was dated in 1873 and it had the residence in Beatrice, Gage county, NE. Then there was a copy of a form and it stated in small print that all the witnesses declared that Narcissa was the true child of Middleton. Then it stated Middleton was not the biological father to the son and the mother would not name the father. Also in the folder was a letter dated 1919. It stated the death of Elizabeth and it listed the son and that he lived in Waneta, NE. These three things were wonderful news and helped me open a new avenue to research. — Teresa Olson, IN

Keep Everything!

I was beginning to think my Baird family was simply a figment of an overactive imagination. I was trying for several years to get a line on my Baird ancestors, but they had been successfully eluding my efforts.

"If you're really interested in this family stuff, get hold of these people," my Uncle Walt said, tossing me a large envelope. "They seem pretty involved in this family business."

Volume 1   an on-going publication   January 1993

Family newsletter for the Baird family, which helped Barbara Peters find relatives.

The return address read, "Sage-Valentine... Denver, Colorado". I never heard of these people. The letter read: "Baird Bulletin! Dear Family, as a result of our vote, August 1992 has been set aside for our next gathering... at a cost of..." I read no further because I thought it sounded like a business. Normally, I'd throw a letter like this away. For some reason I tucked it into my purse and later filed it in my Baird file.

"I'm putting my Baird research on ice to concentrate on the Day family," I told my husband on the way to visit my cousins, Evelyn and Galen. While chatting with Evelyn, the subject turned to genealogy.

"I have the last letter Ida Day wrote," Evelyn said. "She names all 13 brothers and sisters and their spouses and children! I'm amazed she could remember all that information. She was over 90 when she died!"

"I want to read that. I've been trying to find names of Grandpa Day's siblings for ages. I know about Aunt Ida and Will, but that's all I know."

Evelyn disappeared into the other room and began searching through every drawer of their two desks. About 15 minutes later she emerged victorious, waving several sheets of paper in the air. Handing the letter to me, Evelyn sat across the table and began going through some notebooks I'd brought.

I began reading Ida's letter.

"Martha Rachael Day (Fiedler) died 11 Dec 1959. Bessie Mary Day (Wolbert)... Bertha Alma Day (Baird), born 11 Aug 1874." Wait a minute — Bertha Baird — I had an Aunt Bertha! I read on. "Married to Merle Baird... had four children: Kenneth... Eldon... Gwen married Joe Sage..." Wasn't Sage one of the names on the mysterious envelope?

"I didn't know my Aunt Bertha Baird's maiden name was Day. That was my grandma's maiden name. Or that Bertha Day married uncle Merle Baird, my grandpa's oldest brother. And, it says here, one of the children, Gwen, married somebody named Joe Sage."

Several weeks later I found the mysterious envelope Uncle Walt had given me and wrote a note to "Sage-Valentine... Denver, Colorado". One Saturday morning the telephone rang.

A voice on the other end said, "Barbara Peters?" The excited woman said, "I think we're cousins!"

"Who am I talking to?" I asked, confused.

"I'm Eldonna Valentine. My fathers' name is Eldon Baird and his father was Merle Baird!"

My Bairds weren't just a figment of my imagination after all. Eldonna and I talked for at least an hour. She told me her sister had a genealogy of the Bairds and would send me a copy.

True to her word, in two weeks I received a copy of the *Baird Genealogy* that took my direct line back to Moses Baird, born in 1736. — Barbara Peters, WA, bj.peters@earthlink.net

Due Diligence

I knew nothing about my Colpitts family. In 1992, a friend in Riverview, NB found the death notice and obituary of my great-uncle John Wetmore Colpitts in the *Moncton Times & Transcript* of 22 July 1925. John, 48, died as a result of a gas explosion in a house he was visiting. John had four sons, Fenwick, Lotty, Fred and William. Over the course of several years I was able to locate information on everyone except Lotty.

DEATHS

COLPITTS—At the City Hospital, Moncton, N. B., on Tuesday, July 21, 1925. John W. Colpitts. The funeral will be held on Thursday afternoon from Tuttle Brothers Limited Undertaking Parlors. Service at 2 o'clock, funeral cortege leaving at 2.30 for Elmwood cemetery where interment will take place.

Obituary from the Moncton Times & Transcript.

Lotty was reported to be living in Detroit, MI in 1925. When I found William's widow and a son, they knew nothing about Lotty. That was in 1994.

It wasn't until October 1997, while at the Lynn Public Library viewing films of the Moncton, NB School Records, sent from the Provincial Archives of New Brunswick in Fredericton, that I found additional information.

I was really searching for the school records of my father Howard Colpitts. But the name Lotty kept appearing and I made copies wherever I saw his name. It dawned on me that Lotty must be John Wetmore Colpitt's son. The only one I hadn't found.

I located the address of the Detroit Public Library. I sent a letter asking if they would have a Lotty Colpitts listed in a Detroit street directory from 1925 onward. About two months later I received the following entry from 1928: "Colpitts, L.F. (Valida) home 5803 Loraine Ave." This looked promising and if it was Lotty, I now had the first name of his wife.

Some years ago, I bought some books about Colpitts with addresses in the US and Canada. Checking Michigan, I found nine living there. So I sent each a letter. Four days later, I received a telephone call from the last remaining daughter-in-law in Ferndale, MI. She gave me some information and told me that a grandson would call me.

The next night, the grandson called me. Lotty was really Alotus Fletcher Colpitts, who underwent heart bypass at the Henry Ford Hospital in 1957, but died. Valida's maiden name was Melanson, and she happened to be born in Fitchburg, MA. Alotus met Valida at a skating rink in Moncton, NB, and they were married on 27 June 1920 in Lewisville, NB, and had three children.

Donald sent me all birth and death certificates and even a photo of each of them on their citizenship papers. — Donald F. Colpitts, MA, donaldcolpitts@webtv.net

The Lost Tribe Of Abraham Pennington

I am a member of a small group of Pennington researchers in Louisiana. We are descended from Absalom Pennington and one of his three wives. We work in conjunction with the nationwide Pennington Research Association.

Absalom was the son of Abraham Pennington and an unknown mother. This Abraham was first found in the Mississippi Territory in 1796. He came via Briar Creek, Burke county, GA. The courthouse in Burke county burned down and all records were lost. What scant information we have of his family during this time came from published family Bible records, which show Absalom was the son of another Abraham Pennington who was born in 1718 in Cecil county, MD. His mother was Mary Anderson, born in 1721 in Chester, PA. At this point, we were stumped.

Ruth Dickey, author of *Penningtons Of Big Buffalo* opens her book with the will of another Abraham Pennington. This will was probated in 1756 in Berkeley county, SC. Bible records show his first wife was Katharina Weister and his second was Catherine Williams. We have long thought this Abraham was possibly our ancestor. We worked diligently, gleaning information about the families of these two Abrahams and came up with several clues.

The Abraham of South Carolina (SC Abraham) was born in 1722. The Abraham in Mississippi (MS Abraham) died in 1802. If these were the same people, he would have died at age 80, so the age fits.

The brothers of SC Abraham received land grants in Kentucky, Tennessee and Georgia, so we thought he might have also received one. SC Abraham was a Lieutenant and his brother, Isaac, was a Captain in the South Carolina Colonial War in 1759-60. The grants might have been given in recognition for their service.

The abundance of Bible names in the families of both men shows both were descended from Quaker Penningtons. In all our years of research, we have never found anyone, outside of ourselves, who claims descent from the SC Abraham.

Although some of the Pennington branches are famous for their Bible names, the name Absalom is only in the families of the SC Abraham and the MS Abraham, as far as we can see.

Toby-LeRoy and LeRoy-Toby is a rare name combination. It is found in the families of both men. Both the Abrahams had grandsons who married women with the surname Craig. Men with the surname Prince witnessed documents in the families of both men.

In 1818, in South Carolina, LeRoy Burns bought a tract of land known as Maple Swamp Creek, which empties into the South Tyger River. A brother of the SC Abraham once owned land on the Maple Swamp Creek. LeRoy married Mary Pennington, a niece of the SC Abraham. LeRoy and Mary are found in Tishomingo county, MS in 1850. The MS Abraham signed an Oath of Allegiance to the US Government in nearby Starkville in 1798.

Another rare first-name combination found in the families of both men is Abraham Anderson. A son of the SC Abraham married Mary Anderson. Land records in the book, *Amite County, Mississippi 1699-1890*, show that there was an Abraham Anderson Pennington in the Mississippi Territory at least by 1802, along with Courtreys, Hickmans and Curtises, all whom are our allied lines.

Adjacent to the SC Abraham's property on Little River, was a Peter Martin. The MS Abraham's grandson, Isaac, married Martha Martin. Each of these links, standing alone, is weak, but when put together, they indicate strong evidence that the SC Abraham and the MS Abraham are one and the same. We have found our man. — Juanita Cline, LA, clinej@cox.net

*   *   *

Using the White Pages

I had taken an Elderhostel class on genealogy and had a chance to investigate my mother's side of the family. But I needed to find out about my grandmother Mary Johanna Budden who was born on 27 August 1859 in Canford, Dorset. I knew she came from a large family because she had been fostered out when she was about 12. I contacted a friend in England and asked that they send me the page from the telephone book listing Buddens in Canford, Dorset. Budden is a rather common name there and there were more than 40 names in the phone book. I wrote to all the listings and none of the replies were helpful.

A month later I got a telephone call from a Margaret Budden in Canada. Someone had forwarded my letter. The whole Budden family, with the exception of James, the oldest son who was already married has immigrated to Ontario in 1871. Further, Margaret was an avid genealogist and had researched the family back to 1709. — Rosemary Swayne, MO

My Grandmother's Family

A distant cousin sent me a GEDCOM file with 4,200 names and stories about my grandmother's side of the family. She died when my father was seven years old and I went from knowing nothing about her to knowing more about her family than any other branch.

After working on my genealogy for about two years, I hit several brickwalls. I decided to make solving two of those brickwalls my priority. I chose my maternal great-grandparents, Felix Charles Kienlen and Bertha Whipke Kienlen. My mother did 20 years of research with limited access to records but from that

research I found Felix had come from Alsace-Lorraine, France. His father, also Felix, came from Alsace at the same time with his wife Magdalena Spenleyhouer. I could find nothing but US records for the family. I could not get them back to Europe.

Bertha Kienlen.

I decided to visit some French websites and found a list of living Kienlens, some who were online. I sent an e-mail to the first two and letters to the others and was lucky enough to hear from two of them. The first family and I have not been able to connect although I am still trying. The second respondent said he had an aunt who did genealogy and when she came to Paris he would give her the information I had sent. He e-mailed me after her visit to tell me there was a connection and sent me his aunt's address. I mailed a package to her containing everything I found as well as the only picture that we had of Felix Charles, my grandparents, my parents and my family.

Three weeks later I heard from her with information taking my family back to Johannes Georg Kienlen in 1636. As a bonus she also sent information on the Spenleyhauers. My great-grandmother's name turned out to be Madeleine Magdalena Spenleyhauer not just Magdalene as on her tombstone and all other records.

Another brickwall in the family was my maternal grandmother Bertha Whipke, who was born in Fort Madison, IA. She was a mystery lady. My mother knew nothing about her other than her great-grandmother, Bertha's mother, was married before and had other children including a Thomas Dropple, who my mother remembered quite well. My mother was positive her name was Whipke and I could find nothing concerning that name. I was quite sure the spelling of the name was incorrect as there was no one with that name anywhere in any records.

I joined a genealogy society and told them about my problem. I received a nice letter from one of the researchers in the society. It turned out Bertha was actually Anna Catherina Hubertina Wupke according to her baptismal records.

I later learned Bertha is often used as a nickname for Hubertina. Wupke in a lot of the records was also Whippke and Whipka. The researcher also found her parents, John Henry Wupke and Anna Maria Mansheim. I have since found 87 of my Mansheim relatives, although John Henry is a new brickwall. I have climbed two brickwalls. — Judith Henderson, CO, blkuni42@aol.com

Keeping The Faith With Parish Records

In my census research I had discovered another group of Goodwins, who were a part of my family history. John Goodwin had a brother Peter who married Mary Cunningham and had several children — including Peter, Thomas and Kathleen —

between 1894-98. These children and their godparents were listed in St. Raphael's records. The notation records were inconsistent as Thomas had a marriage notation, while my grandmother did not. Both were born in February 1896. Both married in 1919.

I wrote to the Church of the Holy Cross because I could not find my grandmother's three older brothers in the St. Raphael's records between 1890-94. Holy Cross was the most likely parish in the neighborhood to have these records. I received a return letter saying that they had searched but found nothing.

The old Goodwin homestead in Tullanafolie Townland in Clogher parish, County Tyrone in Northern Ireland. The information gleaned from the Holy Cross records led Kevin Cassidy across the Atlantic to contact cousins still in the Clogher area.

I wrote to Holy Cross again because another branch of the family was married there in 1881. This time the return letter informed me that there was a $5 charge per certificate. So after searching every other parish in the area I wrote back and asked Holy Cross to search the records for Goodwins between 1890-94 and sent the money. They found five baptisms for Patrick, Owen and Hugh Goodwin and their cousins Owen and Francis Goodwin.

Be persistent in your research especially in parish records. — Kevin Cassidy, NE, kmct@earthlink.net

Bricks Of Multiple Spellings, Many Names and Wrong Locations

I always believed my mother and that is how I hit a brickwall: A wall with a multiplicity of names, a variety of name spellings and the wrong geographical locations.

My mother told me that when her father came to Texas from Germany in 1893 he wrote to his brother, who left home in 1857 to immigrate to St. Louis, MO. This uncle, who owned a brickyard, replied he was far too busy to travel to Texas to see his brother. My grandfather then wrote to say he had time but had no money and would his brother send him some. The answer came back, "Money doesn't grow on trees." There was no further contact between them.

I looked through parish records in Wehdem, Westfalen and found the family. Heinrich Friedrich Wilhelm (the one I was told lived in St. Louis) was followed by a Carl Heinrich Wilhelm and by my grandfather Heinrich Wilhelm Carl. My grandfather was known as Carl. But I could not assume that the third of the given names was used as the legal name, because the third name of both his older brothers was Wilhelm. Furthermore, my mother told me the last name was spelled Niemeier. If the name was spelled Niemeyer, it could not be the same family. I soon disregarded that piece of information.

I searched St. Louis records. The city directories contained many Niemeiers and Niemeyers, many with names of William or Henry or Frederick, as well as the German equivalents. So did the cemetery lists. Some almost matched the age of the elder brothers, but none had anything about a brickyard.

Finally, I decided to try other states and began searching in Illinois as it was close to Missouri. There was a William Niemeyer who owned a brickyard in 1870. I traveled to the little town of New Memphis, IL. The church records had been destroyed in a tornado some years before. There was no death date on his tomb stone, but using the probable decade of death, the funeral home records were found, which showed the birth dates matched. I had found my great-uncle. — Mabel Loesch, FL, mloesch@bellsouth.net

The Story Of Aunt Sally

During the years I grew up in rural northern New Jersey, I heard stories about Aunt Sally Van Dien. My aunt and uncle remembered Sally as an old woman. She was the grandmother of some of the kids they had gone to school with in the one-room schoolhouse at Postville, a small village in present-day West Milford township in New Jersey.

One of my uncle's school chums, whom I interviewed many years ago, related how all the old families in the area of Postville were related. He said Sally was indeed a daughter of Jacob Post, a brother of my ancestor Peter Post.

I was able to locate the Van Dien family in the 1850, 1860, 1870, 1880 and 1900 census records. I could not locate any birth or death records for Sarah "Sally" Van Dien in the archives of the state of New Jersey. Many doctors in rural New Jersey never forwarded their birth and death records to the county and state authorities.

The city of Newark, NJ, built the Newark Watershed in the period of time from 1880 through 1920. The city purchased most of the land and forced the inhabitants to sell and relocate elsewhere outside the watershed area and even out of New Jersey. By 1920, Postville was no more and only cellar holes and over-grown fields remained.

But what happened to Sally — a woman of 82 years in 1900? Her home had escaped the watershed buyout, but had new owners in 1930. By the time I was doing my research even the children and grandchildren of Sally had passed away. The Van Dien family members I spoke with all said Sally had died long ago and no one knew where she was buried.

I have in my personal file records of the headstones in all the old graveyards in the area now West Milford township, NJ. These records were made between the 1920s to the 1950s before some were vandalized and destroyed. Nowhere could I find Sally's final resting place.

In the late 1980s I was corresponding with a member of the Frederick family, who also had a Post ancestor, trying to connect various Fredericks families together as one. Later research proved they were two separate families, one of Dutch origin and the other German.

I was reviewing this correspondence in 1998 as some question had arisen as to this Fredericks-Post ancestor. I found in this correspondence a clue that I had overlooked. A sentence at the end of a letter said a mutual friend, also with a Post ancestor, had some old funeral home record books. I contacted this mutual friend and months later received a letter. He did have a funeral home record book, *Book #2* dated February 1890 to May 1898. I visited this friend in April 1999 and was able to get copies of some of the records and a copy of the book's index.

On 16 March 2000, I received a package in the mail from my mutual friend's sister containing funeral record *Book #3* dated May 1898 through December 1908. She wrote she had found this book in her late mother's belongings and thought I could put it to use. In *Book #3* I found a record of the funeral of Sally Van

Dien, which listed her death as 15 November 1900 and notes she was the daughter of Jacob Post and his wife Sophonina. Sally was buried in the Oak Ridge Presbyterian Church Cemetery in west Milford township, NJ. Sally must be in an unmarked grave, as she doesn't show on the cemetery records.

Burial record for Sally Van Dien.

A clue, overlooked years ago about some old funeral records, helped me solve my mystery as to when Aunt Sally Van Dien died, who her parents were and the location of her final resting place. — Leslie L. Post, AZ, genealogist@penaguin.com

Looking For My Second Great-Grandfather

My brickwall was one of my maternal second-great-grandfathers, William R. Pate, born about 1828. I had looked for him and jokingly told my mother that he was hatched in Duplin county, NC, because that is where he and all his children had lived and died.

One day I learned that a person surnamed Pate from a nearby county,

Wayne county, had visited the library where I worked. I requested and received his address. I wrote the visitor and explained I had been unable to locate my second-great-grandfather. He kindly wrote that he did not have any information, but had sent my letter to a person in Florida who had also worked on the Pate family. In fact, this person had published material on his Pate family.

Soon I received a letter from Florida telling me that there was an estate record in the North Carolina State Archives for a William Pate who died in 1828. By that time, I had become acquainted with a second cousin on the Pate side who lived nearby and with whom I shared information.

Soon thereafter he went to the State Archives in Raleigh and came back with the estate record, which was almost negligible. But that was not all. Somehow he had found that William Pate's father was Lewis Pate and that William's wife was the daughter of Jacob Herring, all of Wayne county, so my second-great-grandfather was not hatched after all!

Both grandfathers of young William R. Pate had included him in their wills. His paternal grandfather's will reads "to my grandson William Pate, son of my deceased son William Pate." His maternal grandfather's will reads "to my grandson W. R. Pate and his mother Cressy Cherry."

Excerpt from estate record for William Pate, died 1828.

It was probably the Monday after my cousin's trip to the State Archives that he called me at work to tell me of his great find. Unfortunately, by the time I found out, my mother was no longer living. — Billie F. Evans, NC, bevans@intrstar.net

* * *

Finding Phebe

Phebe Jane Andrews was my second-great-grandmother. For many years I was unable to get beyond her. I knew that her maiden name was Andrews from the death certificates of her children and that she was born in New York state on 10 July 1817 from census records and death certificates. She married Joseph Avery Langdon about 1836. Andrews is a common name in the north-eastern states. There were about 50 Andrews families in New York in 1820.

I found the family in Carroll county, IL in the 1850 census. I found Joseph in Stephenson county in 1840, but was unsure it was him. I decided to check the local genealogy library for county history books for Stephenson county and found one that did mention Joseph Langdon being an early settler. By chance I decided to see if there were any Andrews. There was "Anson Andrews lived in Yellow Creek" and a light went on. That is the same place that Joseph Langdon lived. I wrote to the Stephenson Genealogy Society to see if there was anyone who was working on the Andrews family. They immediately put me in contact with a man who had a copy of an old Andrews' family Bible. Anson had a daughter, usually referred to as Jane, who was born 10 July 1817, just like my Phebe. I knew it was the right family.

From this Bible I knew that Phebe Jane Andrews' mother was also named Phebe Jane and was born on 3 March 1793. I checked Andrews families in New York state for Anson in 1820 and there were two. The Anson in Tioga, NY, looked like a better possibility for my Anson so I decided to check the county history there. I did not find anything on Anson but I did find some information on the members of the First Baptist Church. Among the members were Joseph and Phebe Barker and Thomas and Jemima Andrews. I thought perhaps these were the parents of Phebe Jane and Anson. I then decided to check Ancestral File to see if I could find anyone.

I found Phebe Jane Barker, born 3 March 1793, who was the daughter of Joseph and Phebe Barker. — Carolyn Peterson, CA, corkster@attbi.com

Preponderance Of Evidence

My brickwall involved my wife's (Donelda Jane Bennett) second-great-grandmother, Lydia Beckley. Who were the parents and grandparents of this Lydia Beckley? The grandfather of Lydia Beckley seemed to be Abraham Beckley. He is reported in Caroleen Beckley Sheppard's *The Descendants Of Richard Beckley Of Wethersfield, CT*, with a son, Isaac from a second marriage. There were no dates, no places, no documentation listed in this report. Was Isaac the missing generation between Abraham and Lydia?

We could not find a record for Isaac Beckley's birth. We found no additional information in the Connecticut State Library. But we found other records that made the tie. A probate record dated 24 May 1790 in the town of Berlin, stated the distribution of the estate of Abraham Beckley to Deborah Beckley, widow of Abraham Beckley, late of Wethersfield and also to Isaac Beckley. Deborah Beckley is buried next to her husband in the Beckley Quarter Cemetery.

Now we had a tedious collection of census data to create a census track of Isaac Beckley and reconstruct the family from that information. From the table we constructed, the family fits the known data very well. Isaac Beckley resided in two counties of New York. He had several children, apparently by two wives and finally moved to Michigan, where he lived with his daughter and son-in-law. Isaac Beckley died in Washtenaw

county, MI on 29 April 1853, but left no will. Mary Beckley, the wife of Richard Hall, died in Washtenaw county, MI on 8 August 1856 and is buried in the Reynolds Corner Cemetery noting she was the daughter of Isaac Beckley and his wife Polly. This confirms she was Isaac's daughter and fixes her year of birth at 1809. A similar certificate for Laura Beckley, who died in Washtenaw county, MI on 27 June 1851, states she was 39 years, nine months, 19 days old, fixing her date of birth as 8 September 1811.

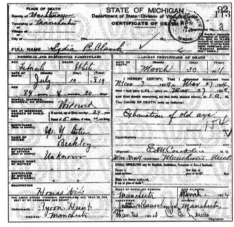

Death certificate for Lydia B. Clark. It gives the birth and death dates and the surname of her father.

Lydia Beckley married Charles Clark on 21 May 1844. She was 24 years of age at the time, which would place her date of birth in either 1819 or 1820. A certificate of death for Lydia B. Clark shows a date of death of 30 March 1904 and reports her date of birth as 10 July 1819. Her father is listed as Beckley without a given name. An obituary for Lydia states she was born in Rome, NY, the widow of Charles Clark and she came to Michigan when she was about 16 years of age with her parents, which would have been around 1835.

A marriage for Celestia Beckley took place on 2 January 1854. It notes Celestia was 27 at the time of marriage, thus almost definitely born in 1827. More importantly it states the witnesses to this marriage included Lydia Clark. Would not an older sister be a witness to a younger sister's marriage and thus add further weight that Lydia is, in fact, a daughter of Isaac Beckley?

The obituary states Charles Clark's widow was Lydia Beckley and that she was born in New York and came with her parents to Michigan in 1835, which she did when 16 years old. This was the same time that Isaac sold his Oneida county land and acquired his Washtenaw county land from his son-in-law. Richard Hall with wife Mary Beckley, Isaac's eldest daughter, preceded them to Michigan.

Donelda Bennett in Beckley Quarter Cemetery where Abraham Beckley is buried.

Lydia's death certificate gives both her dates of birth and death and importantly states that her father is a Beckley. Since all other Beckleys have been removed as a possible candidate and since all the data fit the profile, we concluded Isaac Beckley was the father of Lydia Beckley. This evidence is of great weight since someone who had witnessed the events and persons supplied it or had that information from someone who did. The fact that Beckley is given as her father in this death certificate may be due to the probability that the information giver for this role knew no other Beckley. The negative results of the searches

reported merely confirm data the information giver already assumed. — The Rev. Frederick W. Pyne, CGRS, MD, revredpyne@compuserve.com

The Search For Jeanie Brown

When I started to research my grandparents' ancestry, I found the Brown family had been well documented. Little was known about my grandmother's family. The only information available to me came from a newspaper account of her wedding and a copy of the marriage certificate. The certificate recorded that Jeanie Masterton was 26 years old, a spinster and resident of Shallow Bowells, Essex, UK, and the daughter of John Masterton. The newspaper account added that John Masterton was deceased, that he had lived in Dundee, Scotland, that Jeanie was his only daughter and that she had lived with a family named Coubrough since childhood.

Questions to my mother and her siblings revealed no further information except that my great-grandmother's maiden name was Simpson.

The next research step was relatively straightforward. The IGI provided a birth date of 1 July 1865 in Dundee, the daughter of John Masterton and his wife Jeanie Simpson. Their marriage took place on 24 February 1863 in Stirling, Scotland. A copy of the marriage certificate showed John Masterson was 35, a bachelor, a grocer and his place of residence was in Dundee. The family was rounded out by a search of the IGI and the Index to Births in Scotland. Four other children, one girl and three boys were born between 1864 and 1873. It should be noted that Jeanie Simpson appeared in the records as Jeanie, Jean or Jane.

My vision of a complete family unit was shattered by the 1881 census. That census has been well indexed and hence makes the record finding easy if people are where you expect them to be. To my surprise Jeanie Masterton was not listed in the 1881 British census for Angus nor was she in Essex. Where was she?

A county-by-county search starting in Angus and moving outwards produced an index entry for her in Perth county. She was living in Tulliallan parish, which includes the town of Kincardine. She was 15 years old, a boarder and a scholar living in the household of John and Elizabeth Coubro, a variant spelling of Coubrough. The census record confirmed the newspaper story that she had lived with the Coubroughs for many years. The 1881 census for Angus provided an entry for a Jane Masterton, widow. Her household consisted of an aunt, Jane Crawford, a daughter, Jane Geekie, and two sons, David and John Masterton. David and John were two of the boys that I had counted as brothers of my grandmother. Now the question arose: Who were they?

The search had to get back to basics. A search of the database available online from the General Register Office in Edinburgh showed that Jean Masterton had died in 1867, age 36, Jessie in 1865 and Alexander in 1867. Jeanie Masterton had lost her mother, a sister and a brother by the time she was two years old. Her father married a widow, Jane Crawford, on 16 March 1870 in Dundee; John Masterton died 30 July 1872. Two sons, David and John, were born to his second wife. My grandmother was an orphan shortly after her seventh birthday. She went to live with the Coubros who were related to the Simpsons.

Basic research, increased availability of data and some luck all helped me scale the brickwall of my grandmother's family background. There is a real necessity of linking data from a number of sources. All these sources, particularly the census, are important. But the real secret to success is persistence. The file should be kept open and periodic checks made of databases to see if new information has become available. — Gordon D. Taylor, ON

Local Historians Can Produce The Most Unexpected Results

For many years, I was stumped by the maiden name of my second-great-grandfather's mother. He was Barton F. Brainard, a US Civil War veteran from Stockholm, St. Lawrence county, NY. I knew from census returns that her first name was Sylvia.

On a whim, I wrote to the town historian of Stockholm. She sent me a photocopy from the original war registration book. It gave the maiden name of his mother, as well as his full middle name, which I did not know. That turned out to be his grandmother's maiden name.

The record included his birth date and birthplaces as well. It was a unique and fact-filled record and one I did not expect to find in a small town historian's records. — ARC

Re-Read Records

No one in my family knew the name of my fourth-great-grandfather. Before I started doing family history seriously, two people were already doing the family history. One had hired a professional genealogist but still could not find anything about my fourth-great-grandfather. To search him out was one of my main goals.

My third-great-grandfather, James Sisler, was born on 18 November 1822 in the village of Sharon, East Gwillimbury township, York county, ON. I searched church, land, probate and various other records. I searched not only in East Gwillimbury township, but in the surrounding townships as well. I found nothing. One of the records I had searched was a microfilm of early marriages registered by the province of Ontario. My third-great-grandfather's second wife, Sarah Starr, died in 1888. James then married Emma Shenwood. James and Emma appear in the 1901 Canadian census for East Gwillimbury township as husband and wife, therefore James married Emma between 1888 and 1901.

I just happened to reread this film for another purpose and I found an entry for a James Sisler married in Mount Albert on 25 December 1889. I found the marriage record on another file. Were the parents of James mentioned in the record? Yes! James' father was also named James. James Jr. was the only child they had so that made the search harder too. James Jr.'s mother's name was Elizabeth.

The lesson is simple and effective; re-read records when searching them. Re-reading worked for me and it will work for you too. — Ken Sisler, ON

O Jacob, Where Art Thou?

My brickwall was trying to find my maternal great-grandfather Jacob Maxwell. Facts about my mother's family were difficult to come by. The obvious ones were there — my grandparents' names, ages and dates of birth. I knew Grandma's sister and three brothers and Grandpa's brother and son. My grandfather, Jacob Junior, was a carpenter, my grandmother, Katherine, a housewife. My mother had two sisters and a brother who lived about 15 miles from us, which simplified things.

I recall sitting on my grandfather's lap fascinated by the tattoo on his arm, which was his initials JWM. Over and over I asked him what his middle initial stood for and he always replied the same way: Work. In truth, it stood for nothing — just a letter.

However, while sitting there he did tell me about working with his father making coffins but I never thought to ask where.

I did find great-grandmother Harriet, who lived with Grandpa and determined that she was buried in the local cemetery, along with my grandmother's four infants who died at birth. Ultimately, my grandmother and grandfather and aunt and uncle were buried there also. But why wasn't Jacob Senior there too?

Jacob Maxwell Senior and friend.

I haunted the local library and courthouse, since they lived in the county seat, and ran microfilm after microfilm for obituaries — but no luck. This went on for several years and I just could not imagine there was not an obituary for Jacob — there was one for Harriet.

My brother and I were in the

courthouse, downstairs in the vault looking for other ancestors. It was getting late and I proceeded to hurry him telling him the meter was about to run out. He asked that I wait one more minute as he had just found an old dusty ledger high on the top shelf titled *Records Of The Alms House*, which contained records of people from the early 1800s living in the poorhouse. I definitely didn't feel there was anything in it that we needed to know — but was I wrong! There was not only Jacob Senior, but also Jacob Junior (my grandfather) and his siblings. It turned out the book had been missing for years and it had been meticulously written with names, birth and death dates and, most importantly, where they were buried with grave marker numbers. Now it all fit into place. The reason for the reticence on my family's part as that they were ashamed. At that time being in the poorhouse was not something you bragged about, but they didn't know me.

The abandoned cemetery was right across from the alms house and when my brother and I walked up the hill, as strange as it might seem, I walked directly to Grave #105! He was waiting for us. I am sure if he could have talked he would have said, "What took you so long?"

According to the ledger, the reason he was not buried with his wife was that he and his wife and children had left and he was working in a nearby town raising his family. When his wife died, he went back to work at the alms house doing carpentry. When he became sick and died they buried him there.

According to the ledger, Jacob Senior had entered the Home with his mother when he was eight years old — apparently his father had died and they had no family. The alms house was in fact an honorable place to be. Whole families went there as it was a working farm and everyone worked together and they learned trades.

Photograph of the alms house when it was first built in the mid 19th century.

There was a school, medical care and good food. Jacob Senior and Jacob Junior became carpenters (explains the coffins) and one of his brothers became a baker. When you were able you could leave and become part of the community.

Welcome home Jacob Senior. — Phyllis Mowder Stanaback, NJ, rstanaback@aol.com

Often Answers Are Not Where You Expect To Find Them

I spent a full day conducting research at my local FHC. I checked a microfilm for the town in Hungary that was supposed to contain the Catholic church records of my great-grandparents' marriage. I was not sure of the date, so I had to do a thorough search in the approximate time period. This was exhausting.

I was ready to pack it in for the day when I gave the microfilm crank a quick twist, leaned back and rubbed my eyes. When I glanced back at the screen, right before my eyes was the very information I needed. It was the marriage record, but it had a line crossing it out.

I moved the screen to see where I

was in the record book and found myself in the death records.

Obviously the priest had entered the marriage in the death section by accident. I turned to the marriage section for the date that was entered and there it was.

Needless to say I took copies of both entries. This was a good lesson learned that day. Now I never fail to check places were records should not be but sometimes accidentally entered. — Sharon I. Dickson, IL

Sometimes Doctors Have Good News

My mother's family arrived in Boston from Germany in 1893, but her parents moved to Pasadena, CA and I never met any of her relatives. I did know one of her cousins, now deceased, was a physician and had directed a research department in a southern medical school. I remembered being told he had two sons, but one had died young.

I was able to find the doctor in *Who Was Who In America*. It confirmed he did have two sons. On the chance that his surviving son was also a physician, I did a computer search of physicians in the city where the medical school is located. I found one with the right initials, wrote him and, after a month, I received a telephone call and a written reply listing many of the current relatives. It turned out seven of them are Harvard graduates, so I spent a day at the New England Historic Genealogical Society photocopying Harvard yearbooks. In one day I learned a huge amount about this branch.

Since then my wife and I attended a wedding of one of the relatives and we were asked to arrange for a family reunion soon. There are still many more relatives to locate, but it sprouted some new branches on our family tree. — Edwin M. Knights, Jr., NH

My Great-Grandfather's Grave

One memorial day while visiting the National Military Cemetery in Mobile, AL, I gazed at my great-grandfather's grave. The marker on it read "Walter Braziel, U.S.C.T." I knew the initials meant he had served with the US Colored Troops during the Civil War. My father told me stories of his grandfather's service in the Civil War. Since he was born and lived behind the Confederate lines in Georgia, I wondered how this could be.

A few years later, I had the opportunity to go to Washington, DC. When I passed the NARA Building, it dawned on me that perhaps here was the place where I might learn how my great-grandfather served in the Civil War. I went to an assistant and asked for help and received instructions on how to do my research. My excitement turned to sorrow. I searched and searched the US military records but there was no Walter Braziel. When I returned home, I realized he could not be buried in a military cemetery unless he had military service.

After thinking about this, I recalled my father had talked about his grandmother receiving a pension. I decided to search her record and maybe that would give me a clue. I wrote to the NARA and requested the pension record of Frances Braziel. I was elated when a huge package arrived from the NARA. Inside that package I found a gold mine! In that pension file was a three-page letter from my great-grandfather, in his own handwriting. In the letter he explained how he had left his home in Georgia at age 18. Traveling by night, he moved through the Georgian mountains and crossed the Confederate troop lines and made his way to Chattanooga, TN. There he found the Union troops and enlisted in the Union Army.

Several people had witnessed the letter as he was using this letter to explain that he had enlisted under an assumed name of Walton Phillips to protect his family who were still in Confederate-controlled Georgia. He was providing proof of his correct name so pension benefits could be made available to his spouse. In that letter he had also included his personal history, family, birthplace and other facts.

Now with his military name I had a record to request. I received from the NARA his complete military record under the name of Walton Phillips, who was discharged as a master sergeant in the US Colored Troops.

Proof of service for Walter Braziel.

Then with the proof of his service I was able to provide the facts to have his name as one of those inscribed on the National Memorial to the US Colored Troops in Washington, DC. I am grateful that I remembered the stories my father told me about my great-grandfather. Now when I visit his grave in the military cemetery, I feel like I know him personally. — Rosemary Butler, AL

A Brickwall In The Azores

My brickwall came early in my ancestral search for my grandfather on my mother's side whose name was Manuel Damaso Pereira. It appeared I would not be able to follow his line any further because I did not know from where in the Azores Islands he came. It is important to know not only from which island he came, but also the city or town and the freguesia (parish) in which he was baptized. Every religious and/or civil document I have on him gives only the Azores as his place of birth. Sometimes, the record only says Portugal. I was fortunate to find on his marriage certificate that he came from the island of Sao Miguel, Azores, but no city or town and no freguesia were listed.

On one trip to the National Archives branch in Waltham, ME, I was looking through a microfilm of ship passengers for the year 1889. I was not looking for him as my hopes of ever finding him had diminished by that time. But as I continued through the reel, my eye caught a family of five with the name Pereira — husband, wife, two sons and a six-month-old baby girl, who were coming from the Island of Pico to Boston.

Since Pico was the island from which my grandmother came from, it seemed possible that this family was mine. I remembered my mother's sister was born in the Azores, but again, it wasn't clear on which island. Having lived in Lowell, MA since they migrated here in 1872, it is unknown why they returned to Pico. But the baby girl was born there.

I sent away to the Archives in Horta, Faial Island, for the baby's baptismal record. They did not have it but suggested that I write to the Registo Civil in Lages, Pico Island, where my grandmother was baptized. If I was lucky enough to get this baptismal record, I knew it would list the parents' birthplaces, as well as the names of the grandparents of the child.

The baptismal record showed the place of birth of my grandfather as the freguesia of Sao Yicente Ferreira, city of Ponta Delgada, Sao Miguel Island, Azores.

My brickwall no longer existed. — Anne Sousa, MA

The Mysteries Of Soundex And Miracode

Over the years I have listed the many spellings of my surname Sellnau. Listings from some sources show spelling as Sellnau, Selnau, Selnow, Sellman, Selman, Sellnan, Selnan and Sellnoin. So why couldn't I find my grandparents in the 1900 and 1910 federal census for Cleveland, OH? The Cleveland city directory had them listed every year under one of the above names.

Using Soundex codes S 450 and S 455, I began my search and made the first finding in the 1920 census. There was the Sellman family: Gustie was head of the family, Minne Brady listed as the mother with children Leonard, Herman and Irma. Grandfather Emil Teodor Sellnau did not appear, as he had died in 1915. I found Emil's birth certificate while at

the FHL. He was listed in the Lipno, Poland Evangelical Church Polish language birth records. His name was spelled Emil Teodor Sellnau and his date of birth as 13 February 1865. That is my family and Herman is my father.

Continuing Soundex searching in the 1900 census and Miracode searching in the 1910 census revealed nothing. I know that they had not moved from Cleveland; that Grandfather Emil Sellnau immigrated to the US in 1890; that he had married Augusta Schewe in Cleveland in 1895; and that most of my relatives had not moved from the Cleveland area.

I devised a plan to scale this brickwall. Using the Cleveland city directories from 1895 to 1920, I created a spreadsheet by directory year and the numerous Sellnau spellings recording the street address for each listing. I was able to see what persons lived where and with whom by street address. I found cousins living with uncles and aunts. I found some named as widow.

Then going back to the 1910 census first, I used an enumeration district guide to locate the residents at a particular street address. Checking my spreadsheet for Sellnau in the 1910 city directory I found them at one address. When I looked through the 1910 census for the occupants at that address, they were listed as Emil Zelnoh and his children as listed above. Minnie's maiden name was

Amil Ralnro in the 1900 US federal census.

listed as Braetie. Sellnau was listed under Zelnoh. I never would have considered looking under Soundex Z 450. The census enumerator spelled the name phonetically.

But what about the 1900 census? My spreadsheet for the family showed them living at a different address 10 years earlier and when I cross-referenced for the federal census, I found an Amil Ralnro listed. Why did they enumerated my family under the letter R? Checking across the columns of the 1900 census led me to the M or S entries for married or single. Under every entry on sheet 15 those single entries were shown with the letter R. The enumerator wrote in (cursive) script the letter S and it appears as the letter R. Never would I have guessed to check the family under Soundex R 456.

But, what about Minnie/Minna Brady/Braetie/Braetro? She was listed as mother, mother-in-law and head. Who was she? Within the last few years I learned my great-grandmother had remarried. Her new husband at the time was Carl/Karl Breitag as identified by his listing in the various Cleveland city directories. Last year I found my great-grandmother Wilhelmina Breitag buried in the Schewe family plot in Lutheran Cemetery in Cleveland. Had she been buried alone I might not have been certain of her identity, but her burial with my Schewe family members proved that she was family. Obtaining her death certificate from the Ohio bureau of Vital Statistics in Columbus, OH verified this person. Her date of birth on the 1924 death certificate matched earlier information I had. I was surprised to find a correct birth date on a death certificate given as secondary information and which many times can be inaccurate. Carl Breitag had died before 1899 and Minna Brady was shown as a widow in the 1899 city directory. — George A. Sellnau, TX, gsellnau@aol.com

1,200 Miles Away

Fifty-five years ago, my parents moved from Long Island to Kansas City, MO. At that time, I had little interest in my ancestors. That interest came about, as it does for many of us, after my parents and their siblings were deceased. My mother had given me a list of relatives from my father's side of the family, which took my paternal grandmother's family back to the mid-1850s in Belfast, Ireland. As my interest grew, I became intent upon finding my paternal grandfather from whom my grandmother was divorced, at least so I thought. I knew he was *persona non grata*, but I didn't know why, nor did I know anything more than that, other than my parents and my uncle went to the funeral.

My problems were magnified by the fact that I was in Missouri and Kansas. All the living relatives from that side of the family, if in fact there were any, were located in New York, except for three first cousins and their widowed mother, all who live in Virginia. In a Christmas thank-you note to my aunt, I expressed my interest in finding out more about my grandfather. She responded back, about a month later, that she thought I knew he was buried in Antwerp, NY, and she thought he died in 1938 or 1939. While that got me closer than I had ever been, I was still more than 1200 miles away, with nothing more than the possibility of finding a headstone, if I could find the cemetery. Additionally, I had no known relatives much closer than I was and none of them has the interest level that I have. I don't even know anybody in Antwerp.

So there was the brickwall. What I thought was a last resort turned out to be so easy and so simple that I am convinced many people in that same situation might overlook the solution that worked for me. Working through the Internet, I contacted the public library in Antwerp and the young lady who took my call said that if I would call back at this same time the following Friday, she would tell me who managed the Antwerp Cemetery. She asked if I wanted the city cemetery, or the Catholic cemetery. I had no idea which so she got me both and the people who managed the cemeteries turned out to be brothers.

My grandfather is buried in the Catholic cemetery. The brother connected to the city cemetery even sent me a Polaroid picture of the headstone. He also connected me with a lady who had researched that cemetery and she provided me with the names of the parents of my grandfather. Now I have more names to chase. Her records also indicated that my grandfather was survived by two sons and my grandmother, who was referred to as his widow, thereby probably dispelling the divorce issue from many years back.

The gravestone for Nick Roach's grandfather.

The city library can be a great resource and, when you are 1,200 miles away and don't know anyone, it can be even better. Don't overlook the obvious. — Nick Roach, MO, buyboyroach@aol.com

*　　*　　*

An Unlikely Source To Knocking Down Brickwalls

A brickwall came tumbling down, but I can't lay claim to my knocking it down. A librarian in Dutchess county, NY, came upon the information and passed it along, not really realizing what a find it was for me.

For years we have been looking for my husband's third-great-grandfather's parents and his birth records. He shows up in the 1800 census in Orange county, NY. His death certificate stated he was born in Holland, but I've found death certificates aren't always correct. A fire in the local Orange county courthouse destroyed records that could have been helpful.

In the 1790 census, a man with the same surname was a reverend in Dutchess county. He had a son listed in the right age bracket, who could have been our ancestor, but no records of his birth or baptism were there, though only some of the reverend's children were listed.

What the librarian found was a book that had a country doctor's record of his daily visits to his patients. In 1790, he treated the reverend and his wife and family and one of the names listed was my husband's ancestor from Orange county.

This bit of information put his ancestor in Dutchess county, the right age for the 1790 census and is the only proof the Reverend could be my husband's fourth-great-grandfather. A very big brickwall was knocked down. — Agnes Rysdyk, NY

The Lost Brothers

I had been researching the Costianes/Costianis/Kostianes/Kostianis family tree since I was 15 years old. Our family was from a group that emigrated from near Sparta in Greece and began the first regional society at the turn of the century. This society, called the Tsintzinian Historical Society, still meets annually in Jamestown, NY.

One of the members was putting together a directory and had been to Greece and thoughtfully looked up some of the Costianes males on the village register. He also had made copies of the address list from some of the old Tsintzinian Society directories, which listed Costianes males (only men were full members then). I had pinned down most of them, but there were four brothers, listed as living in Philadelphia in 1923 and 1925, who eluded me. I could find no connection for them at all.

When I first went to the East Amherst FHC I played around with the SSDI. Several Costianeses came up, some I knew and some I didn't. Two men were listed as having their final benefits in Princeton, NJ. I looked at a map and found that this was quite close to Philadelphia. I had never written asking for copies of city directories or copies of obituaries from the library. So using the death dates, I forged ahead and got the obituaries from the *Princeton Packet* newspaper, courtesy of the Princeton Library. I had the names of the sons and daughters. I also received the death certificates from the state of New Jersey. Lucky for me that they released them after only 25 years instead of 50.

John A. Costianes, c. 1917.

I then went on the Internet White Pages, looking for last names of the daughters. Several were in Kansas, but there were some in the Philadelphia area. I called the first name on the list. I almost fell off my chair when the young lady on the telephone told me she was a granddaughter of one of the gentlemen whose death certificate and obituary I had obtained. She mentioned that the last living child of this man, her aunt, was still alive and actually had compiled her family genealogy.

I called the aunt who was delighted to have found another Costianes branch. I sent her the information I had compiled, along with copies of pictures and the story of the Tsintzinian emigration. She sent me the information she had taken from her father before his death and gave me telephone numbers and addresses. I was off and running to fill out that branch.

I finally got the chance to meet John A. Costianes' daughter Helen and his granddaughter Pamela and brother Louis' daughter Amanda recently in Doylestown, PA.

What delightful people! They shared some family pictures with me, further fleshing out the Costianes family tree. — Pauline Costianes, MI, pnc_52@hotmail.com

*   *   *

Digging For Clues In The Cemetery

My second-great-grandparents, Carl and Sophia Leibelt, immigrated to the US in 1852, from Saxony with their son Frederick. They settled in La-Crosse, WI but relocated to Schlei-singerville, WI prior to 1860. My great-grandfather Frederick married Wilhelmina Hager there in 1860.

Frederick entered the Army in 1861 and served in the Civil War. Meanwhile his father and mother returned to LaCrosse where Carl opened a shoe-making business and eventually purchased a farm.

About 20 years ago an aunt told me she had heard my great-grand-father Frederick had a brother who came over from Saxony. She also thought he settled in LaCrosse, but that he left there and went west and was never heard from again. I asked others but found nothing more. I decided to recheck the LaCrosse fed-eral census records again. I found nothing in the 1860 census so I began reading the 1870 census and sure enough I located an August and Margaret Leibelt and four children, two girls and two boys. I checked the 1875 Wisconsin state census and the family was still there, although only two children, females, were listed by number. I began reading the 1880 fed-eral census and located August and Margaret Leibelt and the two girls by their names, Wilhelmina and Louisa. The two boys were not listed. Anson would have been 16 years old and William 14. They had either left home or died. I checked the 1885 Wisconsin state census and only Margaret was in LaCrosse. August and the two girls were gone. Margaret either stayed behind or returned for some reason.

I went to LaCrosse once again and found nothing, not even in land records. There were several transac-tions but no evidence as to where they went. I checked church records and found nothing. The one bit of infor-mation I knew was that on the 1870 federal census the children were list-ed as Louisa, William, Wilhelmina and Anson. I suspected something was wrong since according to my knowledge Anson was not a German name. A mistake could have been made in recording the name.

My next stop that day was at the oldest cemetery in LaCrosse. I ex-plained I was looking for a cemetery plot for an August Leibelt family. The lady on duty informed me the old cemetery records had been destroyed in a fire. She said she would check a couple of old index files. She came out with an old index card and it indicat-ed there was a plot for six burials that was purchased by an August and Margaret Leibelt in 1871. Then she checked that plot card and it indicat-ed four of the burial places had been sold to two other families and that they did have grave markers, but there were still two of the burial spots evidently owned by August Leibelt and for which there were no grave markers. The card did indicate that an "Ernst" Leibelt was buried in one of those burial spots.

I only went about 100 feet and there was the plot. I found four mark-ers on the four places which had been sold. But on the end was an area, which had no markers, large enough for the other two burials. I noticed a very slight depression in the lawn covering that area with no markers. I took a steel rod and I began probing the grass every few inches to see if I would hit anything solid. I hit some-thing about two inches down. After a few more probes I pulled up the grass and found a grave marker, totally intact. I cleaned it off and read the inscriptions: "Ernst Leibelt, Son Of August and Margaret Leibelt, Geborn, 1 Feb 1864 and Gestorben, 9 August 1871." Checking the 1870 cen-sus ages of the children, as there are no birth certificates, Anson was defi-nitely Ernst.

My next task was to find the rest of the family. I only knew they went west. I began reading the German and English LaCrosse newspapers for Ernst's death. I found the correct obituary notice. Then knowing that the family, except for the two boys, were on the 1880 federal census for LaCrosse and that Margaret was listed alone on the 1885 state census, I decided they had to have moved between 1880 and the next few years.

The gravestone unearthed in the cemetery.

I began reading the LaCrosse papers beginning in 1880, starting with one of the two main English language papers. I began reading the *LaCrosse Republican And Leader* and in one issue I found a notice in the "All About Town" column, that: "August Leibelt, the shoemaker and musician, will leave this city to locate at Denver, Colorado." So, I finally broke through the brickwall. I then proceeded to track them down in Denver, CO which had a special federal 1885 census. I ordered that microfilm and found them in Denver. Only August, Margaret and one of their children, Wilhelmina, were there.

After numerous letters, I was successful with the Colorado State Archives. They sent me August's death certificate and Wilhelmina's marriage record. They also had a probate index, which gave the case file number for Margaret's probate in

1916. Wilhelmina (Minnie) was listed as the administrator. So I requested the complete probate file for Margaret.

Margaret's probate file was quite extensive. To my surprise, Louisa showed up in Denver for the probate proceedings. She had been living in Idaho and had been married three times. Wilhelmina indicated in the probate records that she thought her sister Louisa was deceased! This naturally created considerable revision of the probate proceedings as Louisa was also an heir to the estate. There was no mention of Ernst or William on any of the papers.

Knowing that Ernst had died in LaCrosse in 1871, I assume that William is probably buried next to him. So I will have to probe the burial site next to Ernst's grave for William's marker.

Why didn't I do that when I found Ernst's marker? I guess I wanted to make another trip to LaCrosse! — Don C. Leibelt, WI

Finding The Family Through Food

I was trying to locate the home town of my paternal grandfather, Henry Homburg. My still-living father was an only child but did not know where his father was born even though there had been correspondence from Germany in his early years. I had searched the records of several US censuses, the state censuses, his marriage, his arrival, his Declaration, Petition and Citizenship, his voting register, his property ownership and his death. He had no will. There was only one member of his family here in the US. I searched the same records for his sister but found nothing. Everything gave his home town or last residence as Germany or Hanover.

I remembered a conversation I had with him when I was 17. He told me he came from a large family and he was the youngest child. He was a shepherd. He came from a small town of 10 or so farm families, all named Homburg, but not related. For money he had dug peat and carted it to the canal. He carried a lump of peat in his pocket until he died. He spoke Plattdeutsch, the language of the lowland.

I also remembered the whole family going to the German Picnic Park. At these picnics, there was always smoked eel and pinkelwurst. I had read that pinkelwurst was a farmer's food and it was eaten with brunkohl. That is what grandpa called kale.

This was all I could find. In desperation I gave the problem to a researcher in Germany. He knew exactly where to look. Only one area in Germany ate smoked eel and had pinkelwurst. It was the area around the lake that is just west of Hanover City. Sure enough the family was there but not my grandpa. His grandfather had run away and hid from Napoleon's recruiters. He lived on the uninhabited moor 90 miles to the northeast. He dug a hole in the peat for shelter. And so I found my grandpa's home town.

The home town was not Homburg, but that was the name of the farm property. The townspeople were not all Homburgs, but 14 of the 16 families were related in one way or another.

Follow through on each and every clue, no matter how simple. — Edith Homburg Heinz, FL

Check Local Histories In The Library

After working on my family's genealogy for years I decided to begin on my husband's mother's family. Since both of his parents and anyone else of that generation were dead I had to go to Vital Statistics. On his parents' mar-

riage certificate his mother gave her age but there was no registration of her birth in the records. I knew she had Cree blood and was born in Alberta but no one seemed to know where. She gave her parents' names as James Whitford and Mary McDonnell.

After receiving the marriage certificate of James Whitford from Vital Statistics, I found her mother's name was Bella McDonnell, not Mary. I was certain it was the right James as I had his parents' names. It was not difficult to get the genealogy on the Whitford side but Bella was a brickwall. I had heard that she died during or following the birth of her only child, my husband's mother, but there was no death record.

James (Jimmy) McDonnell.

Going back to James and Bella's marriage certificate, I noticed Bella gave her parents' names as William McDonnell and Betsey, who was listed as squaw. The marriage took place in Wetaskiwin, AB. Bella gave her place of birthplace as Bear's Hill. Looking at a map of the area, I was unable to find Bear's Hill. Going to the town library in Wetaskiwin, AB where James and Bella were married, I began reading history books of the area. In one I saw Bear's Hill mentioned and it said, "now known as Hobbema". This is a Cree Indian Reserve near Wetaskiwin.

Though this all happened in the late 1800s, I took a chance and called the Hobbema Band Office asking if anyone there had ever heard of William McDonnell. After being passed to several different people, a man told me there was one old woman in the village who knew all about William. With much hesitation he gave me her name, with the promise that I wouldn't reveal who had told me.

My daughter and I called on this lady and she was very abrupt. She asked why I wanted to know about William McDonnell. When I told her he was my husband's great-grandfather and Bella was his grandmother she was shocked but ecstatic! I was welcomed with open arms and discovered that her father, Jimmy, was Bella's only brother. When their mother, Betsey, died they had been placed in a Native Indian Residential School and Bella left there when she was 15 years old. She must have married, given birth and died in only a few short years as she was 16 when she gave birth to my husband's mother. Jimmy got out of the school a few years later and located his other two sisters, Nancy and Anna, but could never find any trace of Bella. He died still trying to find her but now I had located my mother-in-law's first cousin and brought the living relatives back together.

My husband's mother, who was named Anna, must have been named after Bella's sister of that name. It is common knowledge that the spelling of people's names might have been changed but in my case the name of the town had changed. Now I that have finally located the village where they came from, it has opened up a vast amount of information.

If you have been unable to locate a town I would recommend history books from a local library. In history books of that era and area I was also able to find much about William McDonnell who is written about several times. They just may provide the missing key that you need to go further in your search. — Phyllis Shoop, AB, pshoop@telus.net

Connecting With Cousins

When I retired I decided to get serious about genealogy. At the time I was living in San Angelo, TX. I went to the Angelo State University Library and met a very nice librarian who was more than willing to help me get started. With the ideas she gave me I immediately went to work.

Over the years I have been able to go way back on some branches of my family tree. Unfortunately, I had only been able to trace back to my great-grandfather on my Kennedy family. I obtained his death certificate and learned his father was Thomas Kennedy, but his mother was not listed. My grandfather was the informant and evidently didn't know his grandmother's name.

For 10 years I searched, leaving no stone unturned, but could not find a Thomas Kennedy that tied into our family. I exhausted every source without success. Finally I decided to take a back door approach.

When I was 10 years old, I lived with a third cousin, who was in the oil business in Tulsa, OK. They had two grown children and several grandchildren. I figured his father was my great-grandfather's brother. If I could find his father then maybe I could find my family. After searching for sometime I finally located my cousin's daughter in Tulsa. She was able to give me a little information about her father's family.

Several years ago I bought a computer and immediately started looking through all the genealogy sites, but found nothing. I put out queries about a Thomas Kennedy, with no luck. Finally I decided to do it with my cousin Archibald Kennedy.

Several months went by and I got a telephone call. The person on the other end said he was my cousin. We started exchanging information and everything fell into place. At first I was a little leery because their records had my great-grandfather listed as Archibald Kennedy instead of Thomas Kennedy.

After careful checking I was able to determine my grandfather not only didn't know his grandmother's name but he didn't know his grandfather's name. From the information I was able to trace them back in the 1880, 1870, 1860 and 1850 censuses.

Additional information was obtained allowing me to trace back three more generations. — Hobart Kennedy, TX, silverfox1@ev1.net

My Search For The Schreiber Line

My grandmother passed away in 1984. Prior to her death I had often asked her about her roots. She always told the same story. She was born in 1902 in a town that was about 100 miles north of Vienna in Austria. When she was six years old, her older sister Marie, who had immigrated to the US with other family, came back to Austria to get her. They both returned to the US to live with an aunt. She did not remember anything about her parents.

I had been gathering family data off and on since the 1980s. But the time had come for me to get serious. My parents' 50th-wedding anniversary was a little over a year away and I wanted to complete a family tree for them. I really didn't know where to start. I went to my mother and asked

for any old documents she had. There were death records, Social Security numbers, obituaries, funeral books, cards and other items.

One item was my grandmother's old address book. People who had passed away were crossed out. I asked my mother about various names and she told me what she knew. I decided to write to every one in the book. What did I have to lose? Many letters were returned to me. But as luck had it, I received letters or telephone calls from three people. One promised to send me a copy of his mother's birth certificate, which was in German, with a translation attached. His mother was my grandmother's aunt. He also gave me a name of a distant relative who he said lived in California but he did not know the address. I did a search on the Internet, found a name and address and posted a letter to him as well.

Church in town of Raase (Razova) in the Czech Republic.

Nobody knew for sure where the town mentioned on the birth certificate was. The birth certificate said "Land: Mahren-Schlesien, Polit. Bezirk: Freudenthal, Erzdlozese: Olmutz, Dekanat: Freudenthal, and

Parish: Raase". I searched all the maps I could get my hands on to no avail. I soon found that the borders changed many times over the last century. I happened upon a German-Bohemia group on the Internet. I posted what information I had, asking for any help.

I got several replies. One was from a genealogist in the Czech Republic. He was able to tell me the location of the town was Raase. So I hired this gentleman to help me with my research. He was able to provide me with information through Olomouc Church records on my family into the 1700s. With that information I soon learned every birth was linked to a house number. He was not able to get me copies of my grandmother's and great-grandmother's birth certificates. He suggested I write to the Czech Republic Consulate in the US for assistance.

I sent an e-mail to the Consulate asking for assistance. They sent me forms that I filled, attached the fee and mailed it. Not long after I received copies of both birth certificates. I was excited but I wanted to know even more. What I really wanted to know was if there were any living relatives in this town. I sent another message to the to the Czech Consulate asking how I would address a letter to the postmaster who delivered the mail to Raase. I received a reply. The address was not in Raase itself but a town about 60 to 100 miles away. I figured I didn't have anything to lose so I sat down and wrote my letter.

About a month later I received a reply. The person writing the letter started off saying that the postmaster could not read English so she gave him my letter. He lived in the town but was sorry to tell me that no Schreibers lived there now. Two of the house numbers that I had written about (the ones connected with the births) were torn down after WWII but one of the houses was still stand-

Town of Rasse (Razova) in the Czech Republic.

ing. He also said he was willing to help me. We corresponded several times and he even went to the local graveyard and found my family's tombstone.

In September 2001, I traveled to Europe. I was able to visit Raase, the town in which my grandmother was born. An old church stood with the cemetery behind it. I located many family tombstones as well as houses, which were once owned by my family.

I am very lucky to have found out what I have. I couldn't have done this without the people mentioned above. I only wish my grandmother was alive to hear my stories. — Patricia Mensing, CA, plmensing@yahoo.com

Family Associations

I had been looking for information on one of my third-great-grandmothers, Amanda Royce. There was material on her early years. She was from Connecticut, married to Fitch Higgins, also from Connecticut. They moved with their five children to Kenosha, WI, before 1840. The move predated the 1840 federal census and Wisconsin was still a territory.

There were no vital records I could find but upon finding a later marriage for Fitch Higgins. I looked for a cemetery list; Amanda was buried in the

Kenosha area, but the portion of the cemetery where she was buried had eroded into Lake Michigan.

At this point, I was ready to try a séance, but the late Allen Royce saved me. He had just started a Royce Family Association. Allen's first input to the Association was to try to borrow the Helen Mears Royce collection: six rolls of microfilm, usually kept on reserve by the FHL. As soon as he was successful in borrowing the collection, he set to work to make the information easily available to members of the Royce Association.

One day, as he was turning microfilm, on his way to other information, something caught his eye. It was "Fitch Higgins, Kenosha, Wisconsin, 1830s". Allen looked again and found Fitch Higgins was married to a woman called "(Dan)" with the surname Royce. He checked further and it was the elusive Amanda.

I then got a letter from Allen and on the envelope was written in bright red ink, "Sit down before you read this." He had sent me family group sheets unto the emigrant ancestor, Robert Royce of Connecticut.

It may not be an unusual tactic but joining the brand-new Royce Family Association smashed a brickwall for me. — CH

Where Is Bennet Pond?

My father, Arthur Bennett, died when I was 11 years old. Years later when I became interested in genealogy, I realized how little I knew about the Bennetts. Using what I knew about his date and place of birth, I searched the census records. Using a funeral memorial of his sister's, I was led to yet another area. I established an approximate time of his father's death and sent for probate records. From the probate records I learned the date of death and turned to filmed newspaper records. The well-written obituary was complete with more information and sent me to search more census records. Grandfather William E. Bennett, his father Oliver E. Bennett and his mother, Abigail Bennett, were all born in New York. But where? Who were Oliver's parents?

Sometime later, I broke down and joined the Bennett Exchange newsletter. I didn't want to spend the money to get the information but now I know better. Since my research had turned up my grandfather Bennett's obituary, I sent it in because the editor always requests queries, just to keep the newsletter alive. I did not expect to hear from anyone.

A distant cousin sent me a pile of Bennett genealogy. From this I learned the Bennets were early Puritans and that I was a direct descendant of Elijah R. Bennet, a Revolutionary soldier. I even learned that Elijah's claim to fame was that he had a pond named after him. But where in New York was Bennet Pond?

In the fall of 1998 when I sent in my dues to the newsletter, I sat down reluctantly, looked at my information and sent in a query about Elijah R. Bennet, my second-great-grandfather, just to keep the editor happy.

My husband and I had been out of town for several days and had a pile of mail to sort through. At the bottom was a letter from New York. A historian for Lake Placid and North Elba answered my query. She had spent years researching Elijah R. Bennet because he was Lake Placid's first settler and she included a wonderful story of his life that she had written. That should be enough to make anyone happy, but it gets better.

The historian wrote: "In the year 2000, this great resort village of Lake Placid is going to have a huge celebration... its Centennial, and the bicentennial of the arrival of our first settlers in 1800, Elijah and Rebecca Bennet! How I wish that we could have one of their descendants here to join in the festivities.... Is there any chance you could be with us?"

How could we refuse? Next to Lake Placid is Mirror Lake, which had been known as Bennet Pond for 75 years. The address of beautiful Mirror Lake Inn is 5 Mirror Lake Road, right on the site of Elijah's cabin.

Bettie and Paul Kenck in September 2000. The village of Lake Placid posted a "Bennet Pond" sign for the week of the Centennial Celebration.

In September of 2000, my husband, our daughter and I had the privilege of attending Lake Placid's Centennial as honored guests. We spent three nights at the fabulous Mirror Lake Inn. We rode in a horse-drawn carriage in a parade, behind a fife and drum corps. We felt like visiting royalty, honored at two dinners and a special breakfast.

Best of all, we met the historian and the members of the Centennial Celebration Committee, whose influence changed me from an American to an American Yankee and proud of it! — Bettie Kenck, WA, benkenbp@crcwnet.com

Traveling Ancestors

Thomas Farmer Nairn and Janet Small Peddie, my maternal great-grandparents, sailed from Liverpool, England, aboard the ship *Emma*. They arrived in New Orleans on 1 December 1866. They then took a coastal schooner to the port of Matagorda, TX, and were married there on 22 April 1867. They then traveled up the Colorado River and settled in the little town of Manor, TX, not far from Austin. There they lived and raised their family of 10 children. My great-grandfather was manager of the cotton gin in Manor until just a few years before his death on 4 September 1920. My great-grandmother died 4 April 1921.

That all fits nicely together, but it took close to 20 years to find where they landed in the US and where and when they were married. Different family members gave different stories: They were married in Scotland before they left for the US. They ran away because their parents were against the marriage. They embarked in Liverpool and were married on board by the Ship's Master. They met on the ship and were married on the ship, or they met on the ship and were married when they arrived. No one had a guess as to which port they arrived at or when or where they were married.

The search had been going from about 1954 until 1972 when I was transferred to Fort Meade, MD. After we were settled in our quarters I went to the NARA in Washington, DC. I immediately sought the supervisor of the reading room and posed my problem to him. He told me to check the passenger ship lists for New Orleans because they were the only ones that were indexed.

In a few minutes I found my great-grandfather, noted as traveling unaccompanied. I rolled the film a bit more and found my great-grand-mother, also traveling unaccompanied.

I still needed to find the date and place of marriage. I tried to imagine how they would have traveled from New Orleans to Manor. It finally came to me that the best mode of travel was probably by water, so I made the assumption that they took a coastal schooner to some port in Texas and then either overland or on a river boat to their final destination.

I then sent a letter to the parish and county clerks of every parish and county, on the Gulf of Mexico, from New Orleans to Corpus Christi, TX. After several negative replies, a letter arrived from Matagorda county, TX, with the marriage information.

After almost 20 years of searching I had found the marriage date and place. With this information I was able to extend the Nairn line back four more generations. — Maurice T. Evans, AZ, m.evansjr@att.net

Networking On Message Boards

I solved my brickwall by posting information about the family who I was researching on the message boards of RootsWeb.com and Ancestry.com.

It is important in the heading to put the name of the person you are looking for, the state and county they are from and the year of their birth. Not everyone browsing will take time to open the message to find out this information. In the body of the message list every family member that you know, their dates of birth, who they married and so on. By listing all the family members that you know, chances are better that someone will recognize someone else in the family they are researching, or perhaps they will have all the family names. I have had such good luck in connecting siblings in this way. This is also how I

was able to solve my brickwall.

I posted all the information I knew about the family. Another researcher, who turned out to be a distant cousin I never met, was researching the same family and solved my brickwall. I will be meeting my cousins in Maryland and we have planned research trips to cemeteries, archives, historical societies and courthouses to search land records while I am there to solve more mysteries!

Clockwise from upper left; David Souder, Cherry Souder Kinnunen, David's father, Welling Barker Souder and David's mother, Mary Catherine Skonier Souder. Cherry had never met the family before receiving a call from David after he had seen a posting on RootsWeb.com from Cherry.

This was a great way to meet new people researching the same surnames. I have had such luck in helping others solve their problems and others have helped me solve brickwalls. — Cherry Souder Kinnunen, FL

*　　*　　*

Jurisdictional Approach

For the past 30 years, I have been doing genealogy. As I learned more and more — mostly from experience in making every mistake known to humanity in this interesting, intriguing, challenging field — it ultimately became my profession.

Early on, I learned that the key was to search in-depth any records in the area of residence. This method, which I learned later is called the Jurisdictional Approach, is accepted now by most authorities. For the research I did on my husband's family's surname, I am at the phase where instead of gathering and trying to connect all those folks with the same surname from anywhere in the world, I am tossing away most of this absolutely unrelated material. I had discovered there were at least four distinct Hicks families in the area of the Pee Dee, which became Florence county, SC. In order to determine which were ours, it was necessary to search all the Hicks surnames in order to sort the various lines.

The brickwall I ran into was not on my husband's family. I needed to solve a problem for a client whose ancestor, James Draffin, had immigrated to South Carolina from Ireland with his wife Margaret and their two-year-old daughter Mary on the *Admiral Hawk*. The Clerk of Council reported in 1768 that he had been on board the ship, which had arrived from Londonderry. James Draffin petitioned for 200 acres of land. The list of those arriving included James Dafter, age 28, Margaret Dafter, age 28 and Mary Dafter, age two. The warrant of survey on the bounty for 200 acres is listed as John Drafter. The problem was not in the misspelling of the name since the Plat, the Bounty Grant and the Memorial for this 200 acres on the west side of Catawba River is in the name of James Draffin.

The problem was that James Draffin never lived on this tract.

Having had so much success over the years in solving problems with the Jurisdictional Approach, I wondered how I could solve this one since I had not determined an area of residence for the immigrant. I had researched the records of Charleston county, SC which would have included the land records and the probate records prior to the establishment of the County Courts in 1785. I had also checked some Presbyterian Church records for the appropriate time period. The original grant of bounty land to James Draffin fell into the area which became Chester county, SC. A search of that county's deeds revealed that William Draffin and the heirs of Joseph Draffin signed this tract over to James H. Guy in 1827. We were able to trace a part of this land to a 1968 map near the area of Rowell in Chester county, SC.

Joseph, who had died by 1812, and William Draffin, sons of James and Margaret settled on the east side of Catawba River in what is now Lancaster county, SC. Lancaster county records revealed no trace of their father, James Draffin.

Where could I go from here without some clue? I did something I've never done before or since. I pulled out an old map and found the main road out of this area went to Monroe, NC. A cursory search of that area revealed the book *Union County And The History Of Pleasant Grove Camp Ground* by George T. Winchester. This led us to Providence Presbyterian Church organized in 1767 in Mecklenburg county, NC about 11 miles north of Waxhaw. There we found James, Margaret and Mary in the church records in Mecklenburg county. We found other records on James Draffin who was appointed an overseer of the road in 1778. He was deceased by 1779 when Margaret Draffin and William Haggans were the administrators of his estate. In

1781, the widow Draffin's home is mentioned as being on 12-Mile Creek.

The line between North Carolina (Bladen, Mecklenburg and Anson counties) and South Carolina in this area was begun in 1764 and not completed until 1813. A boundary dispute arose when it was determined that the Catawba Indians would be in North Carolina if the line were continued westward. In 1813, a compromise was reached with North Carolina and a cornerstone was placed to mark the spot.

That same year, a portion of York county was transferred to Lancaster county. At the time of Mills' *Atlas* in 1825, Lancaster county was bordered by North Carolina (present-day Mecklenburg and Union counties, NC), Chesterfield, Kershaw, Fairfield, Chester and York counties, SC. — Theresa M. Hicks, SC, genealogyguild@aol.com

Using Search Engines To Find Unusual Surnames

My great-grandfather, James Pfeifly, died in 1888. His marriage and death dates were between census years, so he was not listed on the 1880 or 1890 federal censuses in the locality where his wife was subsequently listed with her father. I had never asked about him when everyone who knew anything was still living. I paid a nominal fee for someone to check with no results, so this was a brickwall as far as I was concerned.

Recently I took a three-hour Internet course through the local junior college. While talking and demonstrating various sites, the instructor said that if anyone had an unusual family name that they were researching, they might try using the WhoWhere.com website and the general area to see if anyone was listed with that name. I did and there were

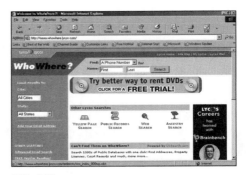

WhoWhere.com.

quite a few in the neighboring county. So I set about picking the five most likely and wrote letters to them, enclosing a self-addressed stamped envelope and my e-mail address. Within a very short time I had a reply, via e-mail from someone saying his father would be getting in touch with me.

I received a very nice letter and lots of information concerning my long-lost great-grandfather. Turns out my great-grandfather and his grandfather were brothers. Since receiving that information, I have been able to obtain much more and I will be eternally grateful to him for sharing with me. — Phyllis A. Jones, LA.

Inherited Occupations And Titles

While researching my mother's family in England I found there seemed to be at least three branches of the same family within the same town. There were many Georges and Johns within these families, which made matters difficult.

As a child, I heard my mother refer to the fact her father was a burgess of Newcastle Under Lyme in Staffordshire, England. I mentioned this to one of my co-researchers in England and he was able to locate these records at the Newcastle Under Lyme Museum. These records seem to be a part of the town's corporation meeting minutes. As a result I was able to connect male children to the correct father. These records gave the date of birth and occupation of the person who was a burgess as well as the date their father became a burgess and his occupation also. So far I have been able to confirm connections back to 1720.

Apparently a burgess-ship could be passed from a father to all his sons or it could be purchased. It could be earned by serving an apprenticeship but the recipient must live in the borough. If he left the borough for more than one year he lost the right to be a burgess. All burgesses shared in the income from the common lands within the borough. Generally two were elected to represent the borough within the governmental system. This information may help others as I am sure Newcastle Under Lyme is not the only town in England that had this system of burgesses. — Heather Hunter, ON, santee@sprint.ca

The Genealogy Of Littleton Goodman

It was early in my family genealogy career that I found myself facing probably the most frustrating brickwall I had or would ever have. While researching my Goodman ancestry, I found they were from Virginia and basically stayed in the area throughout most of the 1600s to 1800s.

I thought this would make researching easy. In a sense it did, but not in the way I thought. I had found my second-great-grandfather, Littleton B. Goodman, living in Powhatan county, VA. I had also found many Goodman families in the area and surrounding counties. In addition, someone had already connected these many Goodman families together, showing that they all were in the same line, all except my second-great-grandfather. I had talked to many researchers of this line and they all said the same thing, they had seen his name but did not know how he fit into the line.

Well, the obvious way to research would be to search the local courthouse and off I went. I found a lot of information on him and his family, his property dealings, chancery records, his children's marriages, etc. Everything I needed except the names of his parents. While scanning the land records I noticed many transactions between him and a man named Zachariah Goodman of Cumberland county, VA, which hinted to a connection.

While at the Powhatan courthouse, I noticed they did not have a birth or death register. So, I went to the Cumberland courthouse where I

The death register for Powhatan county, VA, showing the parents of Littleton Goodman to be Zachariah and Elizabeth Goodman (13th from top).

found much information on Zachariah and many other Goodman families. In all the deeds, registers and will books I looked in I did not find a single hint of connecting my second-great-grandfather to this Cumberland-county Goodman line.

Years went by with nothing from e-mails, letters or books. Then, while reading through rolls of microfilm, on a research trip to the Library of Virginia, I stumbled upon a roll labeled "Death Register of Powhatan County". Not too far into the roll, I came across the biggest breakthrough I had ever had in my family research.

I found the death register of my second-great-grandfather, which gave his age and occupation, but also gave the names of his parents. His father was indeed Zachariah Goodman of Cumberland county. His son provided the information, so it would have been first-hand. That thrill still lingers these many years later.

I have since learned that many courthouses send their old documents to an archives depository. — David M. Goodman, MD, dmg@bcpl.net

The Case Of The Missing Burial Plot

I decided to renew my search for the graves of my great-grandfather Samuel James Lynch and his parents, John Lynch and Mary "Sophia" McKeown. About 20 years earlier I had attempted to find their burial place by visiting the church they had attended, St. Agnes Catholic Church in Cohoes, NY. However after checking the church's records of supposedly everyone buried in St. Agnes Cemetery, also in my home town of Cohoes, I was told by a church official that none of my ancestors were found, which included searching under the McKeown/McEwen surname as well.

I was a bit surprised, but was then informed the Lynch lot might have been purchased by a relative with a different surname and thus filed under this name. Therefore I decided to put my efforts into thoroughly researching this side of my mother's family.

It was not until June 1997 that I felt I had finally obtained enough information to locate the resting place of my great-grandfather and his parents. Over the years I had also learned my great-grandfather's unmarried sister, Agnes Lynch had also been buried in St. Agnes Cemetery, almost certainly in the same plot. Upon calling St. Agnes Church I learned their records had been moved to the Albany Diocesan Cemetery Office in nearby Menands. I then called this office, which is in charge of 11 cemeteries throughout Albany county and spoke with the manager of St. Agnes Cemetery in Cohoes. He immediately told me how disorganized the records from the old St. Agnes Parish in Cohoes had been. He then checked the lot card file under Lynch and other surnames I gave him and found nothing.

At this point I was getting a little frustrated, blurting out that my great-grandfather was interred in 1941 not 1841 and so there should be a record of where he was buried. The manager then informed me that he had recently made individual interment cards for each person on every lot card and would gladly check these records as well. Once again no one was found. I then made an appointment with him to go through the lot and interment records myself.

In the meantime, the manager suggested I visit St. Agnes Cemetery, which has its own interment records. I found the cemetery's records were housed in several binders with the burial plots listed by owner's name in alphabetical order. Once again I checked under Lynch and also other surnames I knew of and found nothing. Then I stubbornly proceeded to check every name on every page, which took several hours. Once again I found nothing.

Finally I met with the manager of St. Agnes Cemetery and he allowed me to double check both the lot and interment card files, which again proved unsuccessful. After this I showed him my evidence consisting of obituaries, death certificates, etc. proving that my great-grandfather and some of his family were in fact buried in St. Agnes Cemetery. Before I left, he made a copy of my great-grandfather's death certificate, stating he would check in one last place and call me the next day.

ST. AGNES CEMETERY	
Lot Owner LYNCH, JOHN	Lot No. #73, 1 No.
Address	
Date of Purchase 12/1/1882	Date Paid
FOR SALE	Annual Care
(west side for sale)	
Frates and Ephemera - 2/20/05	

Lynch lot card from St. Agnes Cemetery in New York. Someone had later written incorrectly that the west side of the lot was for sale.

The following day he called back to tell me he had not only found my great-grandfather, his sister and their parents, but also a brother and a niece all buried together in the same plot as I had always thought. I was of course thrilled but had to ask him where he found this information. He then told me it was only because I had been so insistent and positive my ancestors were buried in St. Agnes Cemetery that he had checked as a last resort a file on lots where money was still owed.

This is where he found the Lynch lot card, which not only included its exact location but also the names and dates of interment for everyone in this family plot. He did not check this file earlier because he found nothing on my ancestors in either the lot or interment files, which meant they weren't

buried there. There was also a bill of sale disposing of six graves from the east side of the lot, sold to a party named Doody by my great-uncle Edward James Lynch after his dad and my great-grandfather passed away. Apparently the Doody family still owed money on the lot and as a result the Lynch lot card and bill of sale wound up together. Therefore my persistence paid off and was the reason why I was finally able to locate the resting place of my great-grandfather and his family. — Edward John Dudek, Jr., NY

Old Errors

All our sources for genealogical information may contain errors and lead to brickwalls. Parish records were not necessarily written at the time described events occurred and sometimes people used different names for personal reasons. Baptismal dates, particularly in very old records, may be incorrect by several years. Also the recorders of baptismal and other dates occasionally made errors in spelling or even entered incorrect names. I recently came across errors that presented a rather difficult problem and indicated a study of baptismal registers could lead to a barrier in tracing one's ancestry.

Several years ago, I learned from relatives that my grandmother, whose name was Mary Ann Smith was born in the village of Guist, Norfolk, UK, in 1854. Her certificate of marriage to my grandfather, Thomas Clipperton Pye, indicated her father's name to be Samuel Smith. A subsequent search of the baptismal registers by the Norfolk Record Office then showed two Ann Smiths were born in Guist in 1854. One was baptized on 29 April, the daughter of Samuel and Ellis Smith and the other, baptized on 29 June 1855, the daughter of Samuel and Alice Smith. To which of the two families did my grandmother belong?

I assumed there was only one

Samuel Smith and that Ellis and Alice were actually the same person. But the baptismal dates were a year apart. To further complicate matters, earlier records indicated there were two Samuel Smiths living in Guist in the early 1800s. One Samuel was born in 1827 and the son Robert and Sarah Smith and the other was born in 1833, the son of George and Elizabeth Smith. There seemed to be no answer to this rather perplexing problem in the parish registers and therefore little hope of tracing my grandmother's pedigree.

In 1997, I received a letter from my distant relative Joan Kenner. Joan is a descendant of Paul Pye, the brother of Martin Pye, my second-great-grandfather. Knowing from previous correspondence that my grandparents lived in Saham Toney, Norfolk, Joan kindly provided me with the results of a search of the Pye households listed in the 1891 census records. It was indeed a most pleasant surprise to learn that in 1891, Thomas Clipperton Pye's family included, not only his wife Mary Ann, but also a sister-in-law, Hannah Smith, who had been born in Guist, Norfolk, in 1866. Here might be the answer.

A subsequent investigation of the census records for 1871 showed there was only one Smith family living in Guist in 1870. This particular family did indeed include a daughter named Hannah. But there was no sign of my grandmother, Mary Ann Smith. However, by 1870, Mary Ann would have been 16 years of age and might have left home to earn a living. It was simple to conclude that by 1870, she had moved to Blofield, where she apprenticed as a hotel cook and, later in 1878, married my grandfather, Thomas Clipperton Pye.

The 1860-61 census records confirmed this to have been the case and she was indeed a member of the same Samuel Smith household as Hannah at that time. Further study of the census records indicated Mary Ann's father, Samuel Smith aged 37 in 1870, to have been born in Guist in 1833. After a lengthy investigation, it was finally concluded that my grandmother was born in Guist on 24 April 1854 and was baptized on 29 June 1855. Her mother's given name was in fact Alice, Ellis being an incorrect notation in the baptismal registers and that a mix-up in baptismal dates had been the unfortunate result of carelessness.

It is apparent that a single line of research may very easily lead to incorrect or inconclusive results, a so-called brickwall and every effort should be made to check one's research through more than a single approach. — E.G. Pye, ON

Sleuthing — Genealogy Style

I was searching for the birth record of my grandfather under the surname Gibbs because I was told that was his name! He lived in Great Yarmouth, Norfolk, England in the 1850s. My father, Cecil Arthur Gibbs was born in Great Yarmouth and his birth certificate named Arthur Augustus Gibbs as his father and Sarah Louisa Presland as his mother.

As a novice, I had no luck at all looking in the British Index of the General Register Office for Arthur Augustus Gibbs in Norfolk. I eventually found the local FHC and they assisted me in finding censuses. It was the census of Great Yarmouth 1891 that placed Arthur, as a boarder, in the home of Sarah Ann Presland, a widow, in Great Yarmouth. This confirms his use of the surname Gibbs, I thought. The 1891 census also showed

Marriage certificate of Arthur Gibbs and Sara Louisa Presland for 2 June 1891.

that Arthur was born in Hemsby, Norfolk.

I searched and found the marriage of Arthur and the widow Presland's daughter, Sarah Louisa Presland, on 2 June 1891 in the Parish of Great Yarmouth. His father is named as William Gibbs. Arthur's age in 1891 puts his birth at about 1861 or 1862.

The Hemsby census of 1861 was studied very carefully. I looked up and down each street and household for Arthur Augustus. At 38 Ormsby Road in Hemsby in the household of William Long there appeared a woman named Amelia age 24 and at the bottom of the household list, which named various sons and daughters, was grandson whose name was "Arthur A. — 1 yr." Also the notation "born in Hemsby" The window of time was about right, being 1861 or thereabouts. So his name is not Gibbs, but Long.

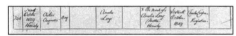

Arthur Augustus Gibbs as Long.

But where does the surname Gibbs come in? Continuing in the 1861 Hemsby census it also showed that the Gibbs family resided just down the street at 78 Ormsby. There appeared the name William Gibbs, age 24, born in Hemsby, which was the name on Arthur's marriage certificate! So Amelia Long and William Gibbs were both 24. So did Amelia Long and William Gibbs, both of Hemsby eventually marry?

Yes! Apparently their marriage was found on the British census index dated 1 September 1861, which regularized the use of the name Arthur Augustus Long into Gibbs, as the parents' names showed up as Amelia Long and William Gibbs.

The 1871 census for Hemsby showed: Amelia Gibbs (head of household, 29, widow) born Hemsby; Arthur Augustus Gibbs (son, 11, scholar) born Hemsby; William James Gibbs (son, seven, scholar) born Hemsby.

Arthur's Hemsby birth certificate of 9 October 1859 shows mother as Amelia Long of Hemsby, (no father is listed), county of Norfolk, England. Those censuses proved extremely useful in situations such as this.

The mystery was now fully explained, thanks to genealogical sleuthing! — Ken Gibbs, ON, ken.gibbs@sympatico.ca

Good Neighbors

I was trying to track down a distant cousin of mine who had moved out of town back in the late 1970s. The only contact we ever had with them was through my grandmother and after she died we lost contact. The only information I had about them was an old street address they had lived at before they moved. I used the city directory, which listed people alphabetically by surnames as well as by street name and number. I located their name for the last year that I knew they had been in the city. I then searched forward a few years and confirmed they no longer lived in the city. I then went to the street address listings. I searched for the address, but this time I went backwards and made note of neighbors living within a block of my cousin's address. This proved very successful.

At least one name, at a nearby address, had remained the same for several years prior to my relatives' move. I decided to call them. After I explained I was trying to locate a long-lost relative they happily agreed to help me. They were good friends with my cousin and told me the circumstances for their move.

It seemed my cousin had died in 1978 and his wife, who was also getting on in years, was having trouble taking care of herself and her house. In 1979, she sold the house and moved in with her daughter and her family.

The good neighbor supplied me with both the name of their new town as well as the daughter's married name. — Ed Robertson, ON, edrobertson_2000@yahoo.com

The Unconnected Baby

In looking through some old notes of an aunt, who had been our genealogy treasure house, I found a small note, "Aunt Ole had a baby that died."

I knew that Aunt Ole was Velva Powell Carroll, her cousin who had died in 1968. But I had only heard of one child and he lived to adulthood.

I wrote letters to ask all family members and no one had any additional information about this baby.

Most were unaware that Velva had had another child. Since I have a soft spot in my heart for unconnected babies, I began the hunt.

Knowing the family had lived in DeSoto, WI, I looked up the cemeteries in that town and found that there were four. I also guessed that the baby was born in 1925-26 as his parents were married in 1924.

Velva Powell Carroll.

I called each cemetery to no avail. However, one person did give me the name of the president of the DeSoto Village Association. I placed a phone call and he was helpful and willing, but in a few days I received an e-mail that he had not been able to find a baby with the 1925-26 date in any of the cemeteries.

I couldn't give up, so I went back to the stacks of paper scraps and old letters my aunt had kept. I found a 1992 letter naming other relatives, as well as Aunt Ole's baby, who were buried in DeSoto on a steep hillside. With this added bit of information of names and terrain, I contacted the DeSoto Village Association President again.

He was so generous with his time and, within a couple of days, he was able to locate baby Charles Carroll, son of Velva and William Carroll, who was born and died in 1925.

It reaffirmed to me the importance of reviewing again and again any scrap of information because, at a later date, it might be just the piece needed to fit someone into a family puzzle. — Jolayne Eastman, WA

Only Names To Me

For about 20 years I had been researching William and Ann Snider in Ontario. After everything I tried, absolutely nothing came up. I was convinced that Ann and William moved to another country and was ready to accept the fact that they would forever be only names to me.

I needed some information on our family in general, so I decided to go with an Internet query. About a week later, I got a reply telling me I had made a mistake, his name was William Quider. This came from one of their direct descendants and so it was a double blessing for me.

In talking to someone who was originally from Holland, she said that it was no surprise to her that I had misread the name. Apparently, in Holland the Q is written in such a way that it is often mistaken for an S. This certainly knocked down my brickwall. — Doreen Harvey, AB

The Challenges Of Genealogists

The positive thought that brickwalls are not obstacles but challenges that help to overcome the weaknesses in my searches is sometimes conquered by frustration. This frustration sends me to how-to books on genealogy research that would otherwise be ignored and improves my future research methods.

My grandmother's father was one of my brickwalls. I began collecting stories about John D. Maynard from other family members. This information led me to search unsuccessfully for his birth in Ontario. I soon learned to keep an open mind when it comes to information.

I have a large data file on each of the surnames I am researching. It is for people that do not appear on the family tree at the time the data is found. I call it my Unknown File.

Each file contains information I find at the county courthouses on that surname (including spelling variations) listing information for marriages, deaths and land records which can be sent for as needed, making a search easier and faster for the County Clerks Office because they have the book and page number.

I was looking for the Maynard family that adopted John D. since the family was not able to supply this information. I ordered his death certificate and it contained the couple's full name and that he was born in Michigan not Ontario. I assumed I would have to go to the courthouse in Sanilac again to find more information but first I looked in my Unknown File and there was a paper on three generations of Maynards back to the Parish of Northlew in England.

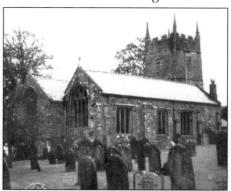

Parish of Northlew Church.

What a thrill to solve this mystery! Sharing information with other researchers is often helpful. One Internet researcher sent photos of the church and headstones of our mutual third-great-grandparents of Northlew after learning they were from the parish of Northlew. One giant leap over the wall! — Dorothy P. Heimnick, FL, djheim@nut-n-but.net

Genealogy Classes

If you're ever attending a genealogy class or conference, use the classroom effectively.

I saw this happen in 1999 when I attended the Brigham Young University Family History Conference in Provo, UT. There were people attending from all over Canada and the US.

I was attending a class on Loyalists when a woman from northern Utah made a comment and mentioned she was researching her cousin's Quaker ancestors in Uxbridge, ON. I was born and raised 15 miles from Uxbridge in Newmarket where I have lived all my life. Since some of the Quakers from the Newmarket area were the first settlers of Uxbridge, I could hardly wait to talk to her after class. She wrote down six surnames for me that she was researching. I recognized four of the names. I promised her I would go home and see what I could find.

When I returned home, I searched through all my notes and information. I found approximately 40 pages of information that I mailed to her. Some of the people she was researching had left the Quakers to join the Children of Peace, founded in 1812, when they broke away from the Quakers to start their own religion.

Since the Children of Peace were a local religion and generally unheard of outside of where I live, this woman probably would never have found any genealogical information about her cousin's Children of Peace ancestors. She wrote back to me and mentioned more information about her family. It turns out that we are related! — Ken Sisler, ON

Keep Looking

Five years ago, I learned that my great-grandfather, Isaac Willard Wykoff, had a first wife that gave him two daughters. Their names were Lucy and Ellen. My great-grandfather appeared in the census with a Sarah A. For the last few years I assumed that it was Sarah A. Haskins. Someone must have told me it was Haskins. Being new to genealogy I did not know where to find her.

Through FamilySearch.org I learned that Lucy married Charles Austin from Austin, PA. Then I got an Austin family tree from the Internet. I scrolled down to Wykoff and found Lucy and my great-grandfather although the last name was spelled differently. I realized I was successful when I saw that under Lucy's maiden name was the name of her mother.

Isaac W. Wykoff and Elizabeth Gibbs Wykoff.

Now I have to find Lucy's mother's ancestors. It will not take me so long. I know everything sounds easy but you just have to keep looking and look into other siblings or another person altogether. — Mary Jo Sibel, PA

*   *   *

Finding The Other Family

My second-great-grandfather William Jose lost his first wife, Mary Tippett Jose in Australia in March 1853 in a wagon accident. They went to Australia in 1847 as immigrants from Cornwall, England. Soon after Mary's death he joined the Mormon Church and left with them on *The Tarquena* for the US. As a group they went to Parawan, UT. His four young children, Grace and William, born in Cornwall, and Thomas and Mary Ann born in Australia, accompanied him on the long trip. In Parawan, he met Elizabeth Williamson, herself an immigrant from England, coming to Utah with her mother in the Martin Handcart Company.

He and Elizabeth were married and started their own family consisting of Elizabeth Ann, James W., Ellen, Mary Ann, Christian Jennie, Bessie Matilda, Margaret Alice, William Nicholas and John Henry. They lived in Parawan and Panguitch, UT; also in Reno and Pioche, NV. William died in Pioche on 17 February 1896. Elizabeth Ann went to Emmett, ID to be near several daughters although I did not know where they were at that time.

In beginning the research for my great-grandmother, Grace Jose, William's eldest daughter, I knew nothing of his second marriage. During my research in Australia I did find the death of Mary Tippett Jose and knew his first wife was dead along with a baby, James. As I began to follow William in the census, I found him with a new family.

I continued using the census and they eventually led me to Pioche. I went there to find William's grave and along with that information I located marriage certificates of several of his daughters. With that discovery I felt I had enough information to begin a book.

Soon correspondence with descen-dants of the first family members flew back and forth between Texas and several western states. I tried everything I could think of but could not locate a single member of William's second family. By this time they were no longer Mormons, so those records were of no use to me. I tried writing letters, using family names, to places in Idaho to no avail. My idea for a book was beginning to grow dim.

Then I remembered Elizabeth Ann was a Mormon when she came to the US as a child and I began to look in the Mormon records for people who might have submitted her name; I found one lady in Utah. Submissions are sometimes quite old, but I wrote her just the same and within a few days I received a telephone call from her and she told me she knew where these people were! She gave me the address of Laudine Allen who lived in Idaho. Again, I wrote a letter explaining I was descended from William Jose and what I wanted. And once again I received a telephone call. Mrs. Allen was the daughter-in-law of Christian Jennie Jose who married Russell Allen. She was so excited to hear from me that she called and wanted to know more.

At one time there was correspondence from cousins in Kansas, which was where Grace Jose Williams lived by then. Through the years the letter writing stopped and although Mrs. Allen knew names, she did not connect them with the right people. She was the last living daughter-in-law and her mother-in-law was my great-grandmother Grace's half-sister.

We were planning on being in Salt Lake City to research and I called Laudine to see if I could and come see her. She immediately said yes and anxiously waited for me to come with my husband, Henry. We talked for hours and she told me stories and showed me family pictures; I cannot express the thrill it was to meet her and share her excitement. She trusted me with her family pictures, which allowed me to have a picture of almost all 14 of William's children for my book.

But that did not end the story. We went to the central part of Idaho, as I knew another sister, Ellen, lived there and a brother Tom. I went to the courthouse and found their names in various records and tracked down people who might know something of the Jose family.

One gentleman told me he was a boyhood chum of Thomas and showed me where Tom lived as a boy, then he gave me his address in Washington. I could hardly believe my good fortune. Just as I was about to thank him and leave he said, "Oh, by the way there is another lady in town today researching the Jose family. I believe she is at the café having supper."

So off we ran and there she sat, Ardell Gardiol, almost a twin to two of my cousins, complete with the red hair and blue eyes. She was the second-great-granddaughter of Ellen, who married James Stevens and Richard Dick Bennetts. I told her who I was and it went from there.

To this day I marvel at what happened that allowed me to go forward with a book of all the families: *The Jose Family — Utah By Way Of Australia.* — Corlyn H. Adams, TX

The Missing Page

Searching for a missing page of my grandfather's family Bible led to a wealth of information about him. In researching my family history, I contacted all my cousins and asked if they had any information to share. I was excited to learn that one cousin had the Bible that belonged to my grandfather's parents. My excitement turned to disappointment when I found that there was no genealogical information. The page that probably contained such information had been ripped out.

I learned that sometimes an entry in the family Bible was used as proof of birth date. I knew my grandfather had retired on disability and later received a pension for his many years of work for the B&O Railroad, so I thought that he might have torn the page from the Bible with his birth date and sent it in when he applied for his pension. I contacted the B&O Museum in Baltimore, MD to get his Social Security number because it was not available in the SSDI. I then sent the Social Security number with the appropriate fee to the Railroad Retirement Board for his pension application. I received more than I expected. A copy of the missing page was included, which showed the birth dates of my grandfather as well as all his siblings. I also learned where my grandfather was born and where and when he was married.

Page from railroad pension application of S.H. Short showing work record and the cause for his termination due to a work related accident.

What was most moving for me, however, was the copy of my grandfather's work record. In 1900, when he was just 23 years old, he lost a leg after a train struck him while he was working. His work record vividly showed how his earning capacity was reduced as a result of the accident. Note that the Railroad Retirement Board only has records for persons who worked after 1936. Requests should be sent to Office of Public Affairs, Railroad Retirement Board, 844 North Rush Street, Chicago, Illinois 60611-2092. Enclose the Social Security number and the current fee. — Carolyn E. Fields, VA

Search For The Siblings

For 25 years my sister and I made five trips to Alsace-Lorraine. We spent hours in the libraries of Strasbourg and Metz and local small-town mayors' offices to find the birthplace of my grandfather with whom we lived as children.

We could get nothing more from him except that he came from Nancy, France. Countless other hours were spent in St. Louis gathering all the documents we could find about him. "Born in France" on a document is of no help.

Finally, in desperation we printed our genealogy with more than 300 years of data and stories with all the documentation to prove our findings. The very thing we started out to do was still incomplete.

Recently I resumed my search on the Internet with no results, so I finally listened to the professionals who say that when one comes to a brickwall turn to a collateral search. All the research had already been done on my grandfather's older brother to no avail. Now it was the final act to turn to his sister, about whom I had very little information. In an old document her name was mentioned as a minor in 1876 and in a second document she was living in Trier, Germany with citizenship in Nancy, France in 1882. Although her father had married her mother in Strasbourg in 1854 and they had one son, no other siblings could

be found there. Much later documents proved that the family of five had returned to Bliesbruck, France where the father died in 1872.

Could her sister have been married in Bliesbruck? Back to the Internet and the FHL. Suddenly, there she was, and attached to her church record of marriage was her birth certificate in Eschau, Bas Rhin, Alsace, which is nine miles south of Strasbourg. On the same reel was my grandfather's birth record for 15 October 1851. So much for Nancy, France and a sworn family record of birth for him in 1854!

Now we can understand the variation in his birth year. His mother had one son in the French Army and swore she would not give another to the Franco-Prussian War that was looming on the horizon. So, he left France as a "14-year-old" instead of a 17 year old in 1868 to live with his older cousins in St. Louis to avoid induction into the service.

Official French birth certificate, dated 1851, of Caroleen Hensgen's grandfather, Emile Charles Hensgen.

Motto: Listen to the professionals and never give up. — Caroleen Hensgen, TX

Newspaper Advertisements

I found the easiest way to expand my family tree was to find my living family in Norway and Sweden. This has served me very well and I am now in touch with many of my living family. They have supplied me with history on the family and pictures of my great-grandparents.

But there was one family that I had no success finding in Norway. This was my mother's maternal grandmother's family, the Evensens in Drammen, Norway. I found a member of the genealogy society in Drammen who agreed to help me.

He suggested as a last resort that we place an advertisement in the Drammen newspaper. So on 16 January 2001 I placed an advertisement in the paper and provided the little information I had about the family. Within a day the newspaper received a call from my family. The paper did a feature story about the family in Norway. The newspaper then sent me a copy and the names and addresses of my new-found cousins. — Burton R. Lundquist, AZ

Pizza With Aunt Alice

My wife's great-grandmother's sister is still living. We sent a letter to Aunt Alice and she replied with some information about her mother's family. She mentioned that she did not know her grandparents. We set up a time to visit with Aunt Alice. She took us to the pizza parlor and we listened. She talked about her father's brother and sister, Uncle Jim and Aunt Lucy, and how they would visit them in Oakland, IA.

Not being a native of Omaha, I did not realize that Oakland was just across the Missouri River in Pottawattamie county, IA. Our local library had cemetery inscriptions in a book and I found a James Thompson that turned out to be Uncle Jim. Paying a dollar for his uncertified death certificate, it told me his father was Jasper Thompson and that James was born in Valparaiso, Porter, IN.

Going back to the library I quickly found the Jasper and Elizabeth Thompson family in the 1860 US census at Porter Co., IN. The ages and birthplaces of the children indicated that this family would be enumerated in Virginia in 1850.

I checked the 1850 census for Virginia and found Jasper and Elizabeth with a one-year-old child. I called the Lewis County, West Virginia Courthouse and they found a marriage in 1849 between Jasper Thompson and Elizabeth Houghton. The letter had not asked about aunts and uncles so Aunt Alice skipped it. The friendly conversation with her at lunch got her talking about many things. Mentioning Uncle Jim and Aunt Lucy in passing led us across the country in a matter of days. — Kevin Cassidy, NE, kmct@earthlink.net

Spelling Imagination

Several incidents in my own research have highlighted the importance of using your spelling imagination when searching transcribed databases and even records that are not transcribed.

Let me share with you the following three examples in my own family: For years I have been trailing my second-great-grandfather, Hilus Harmon Starkweather. Supposedly Hilus was born in 1797 in Onondaga county, NY. Limited information had been found on Hilus and his parentage. Repeatedly I would find transcribed documents mentioning a Niles Starkweather. Eventually, I found a partially transcribed will for an Asa Starkweather (dated 1809) that mentioned his children and wife. One of his children was Niles. Knowing that there was an Asa as a head of household in that area, and believing Hilus' father to be Asa, I ordered the will. When I received it, I was delighted to see that it was actually Hilus and not

Niles. Looking at the will, it was easy to see that a stranger transcribing the unusual name Hilus, could mistake it for Niles. This mistake has been repeated again and again for the same person. Now when I see a reference to Niles, I take a look because it could inevitably lead to my Hilus.

The second example is again with the Starkweather family. I have learned to do broad searches with all conceivable misspellings: Starkwether, Starkwhether, Starkneather, etc. I always prefix my search with Stark* (* meaning wildcard). While pouring over census indexes, I discovered another variant I had overlooked. This name is Stackweather. On further investigation, there are no Stackweathers in the US or Canada. This is a frequent mistake made when transcribing this name.

There are many leads now that I can check using this new spelling. My advice is to take a careful look at the name you are researching written in old-fashioned penmanship from some old documents. Use your imagination as to how another person, unfamiliar with the name may erroneously transcribe it. Many documents may be just waiting for your perusal, if you can just experiment with creative spellings.

The third example of misspelling may have been a deliberate deception.

My great-uncle, Joseph Schlesinger was an American who fought in WWI, but signed up in Windsor, ON. Everyone in my family was determined that this was the case. I was told he sailed from Halifax the day my mom was born on 20 February 1918. When pursuing his records from the Canadian Expeditionary Force via the Internet, I could not find his name. I visited the National Archives in Ottawa and the staff there were perplexed. My mom told me Uncle Joe had been rejected from fighting for the US as he had only one eye. Supposedly, he had also been repeatedly rejected by the Canadians because he was too young and perhaps because of his eye. I was beginning to think that the whole episode was a cover-up.

The slight identity change by Joseph Schlessinger as indicated on this form may have been done to hide his German background or hiding his previously rejected application.

Then I decided to try different spellings. I tried doubling the S and removing the CH in Schlesinger. Up popped his record. Immediately I thought it was another transcription mistake. But when I received the records, it was evident that Uncle Joe had purposely changed the spelling, even signed it himself, incorrectly. When I got to the question on the application, "Have you ever applied before?" he had said "No". Perhaps, he did not want them to know that he was the same person, who had tried to join, but had been previously rejected or perhaps he was trying to hide the evidence of a German surname by removing the typical CH after the S! — Rena Sherring, ON

*   *   *

Finding My Birth Father

I started doing genealogy in 1997 by doing my stepfather's family. Then I started working on my mother's side of the family tree. After doing all I could do with her lines I realized that mine wasn't complete and wouldn't be until I found my birth father: Wendell George Drury of Rice county, KS.

I found in 1991, when my stepfather died, he had never got around to adopting me even though he gave me his surname. All I knew of my birth father was the three photos my mother gave me when my stepfather died and what was in my baby books and earlier years of what my aunt and grandmother had told me.

I began in earnest to find my birth father whom I don't remember, since I was one and a half years old when my mother divorced him. So I asked my cousin's husband, who is an insurance investigator, if he could help. He found an address in Colorado for my birth father. At the time I didn't think it was right, but have since found it was his last residence. The listing also gave a relative: Mark Drury of California.

After receiving this, I went to the SSDI on the Internet and found my grandfather Paul Drury. I sent for his

Wendell and Mary Drury in 1930.

application, which included his parents' names. I also sent for his death certificate in Oklahoma, which had my father as the informant in 1969. Then I went to the FHC in Santa Monica, CA and found the whole family in the 1900 and 1920 federal censuses of Rice county, KS. Finally with the use of the LDS web search, I found my second-great-grandfather and his ancestors back to 1616 England.

In September 2000, I found a person to do a cd look-up for Illinois. The person came back with my great-grandparents' marriage date. I posted it on the Drury Internet forum and got a quick response from a second cousin by marriage who had their wedding photo. She lived in Lompoc, CA and her sister-in-law had it in San Diego. Then she started sending me information from my grandfather Paul's brother's family.

I began thinking that since I found this, why can't I find my father whose last known address was Oxnard, CA. So I posted a message on the mailing lists. A researcher sent me the same information I already knew about Mark Drury.

This is when I started to drag my feet. What if our father didn't tell his family about me? I was scared of being rejected if I called Mark myself. Then my cousin in Lompoc called Mark and talked to him. Together they did some searching to see what the other knew about the family, so they would know they had the right person. Then Mark brought up my full name as his long-lost sister and everything fell into place. The cousin called me and told me about their talk.

Mark had a lot of information on my father and the best part was that he has been looking for me for 10 years! But he didn't know that I had changed my surname to match my stepfather's. I had also moved from the Los Angeles area in 1948 and grew up in Fresno. All he had were three photos from 1948. The photos were in a photo album that our father had carried with him all this time. Mark recovered it and the Drury family Bible when he went to Colorado to settle our father's affairs after his death in 1994.

I didn't know until 23 September 2000 that I had another brother. I have one that I grew up with who was a half-brother from my mother re-marrying in 1948. Mark B. Drury is my half brother. If his older brothers had lived I would have three half-brothers. I called Mark on a Saturday evening and we talked for an hour and a half. Then he called the next night and we talked for another three-and-a-half hours.

We have been sending each other photos and documents and sharing life stories. We met for the first time in late October 2000. — Pauline Drury, CA

Glossary Of Terms

FHC (Family History Center): local branches of the LDS Church's FHL. There are approximately 3,400 in operation worldwide (www.familysearch.org).

FHL (Family History Library): The LDS Church's main repository of genealogical information, located in Salt Lake City, UT (www.familysearch.org).

GEDCOM (GEnealogical Data COMmunication): A standardized form of computerized data exchange developed by the Family History Department of the LDS Church. GEDCOM files are a universal code allowing different genealogy programs to communicate with one another.

IGI (International Genealogical Index): A worldwide index of more than 200 million names created by the LDS Church. It is available at www.familysearch.org.

LDS (Latter-day Saints): The abbreviated form of the Church of Jesus Christ of Latter-day Saints, sometimes called the Mormons (www.mormon.org).

NARA (National Archives and Records Administration): A Washington, DC-based organization with facilities throughout the US, such as Research Centers, Records Centers and Presidential Libraries. (http://www.archives.gov).

SSDI (Social Security Death Index): An important research source that lists information about people who held Social Security Numbers (www.RootsWeb.com)

Soundex/Miracode: A code composed of a letter and three numbers, based on the way a surname sounds instead of how it is spelled. The letter represents the first letter of the surname and the numbers represent the remaining sounds of the name.

> 1 – B, F, P, V
> 2 – C, G, J, K, Q, S, X, Z
> 3 – D, T
> 4 – L
> 5 – M, N
> 6 – R

The letters A, E, H, I, O, U, W and Y are ignored. For example the name Lee is Soundexed as L 000. Surnames that sound the same but spelled differently like Smith and Smyth, have the same code (S 530) and are filed together.

Both Soundex and Miracode use the Soundex coding system, Soundex cards are handwritten, while Miracode cards are printed (http://www.archives.gov).

Index

A

address books — old 180, 301, 319, 372 *also see* ancestors' possessions

adoptions 193, 227, 298 *also see* orphans

adoption records 214 *also see* informants

advertisements 170, 327, 389 *also see* newspapers, queries

Åland Islands 128 *also see* Finland, Sweden

alms house records 361

aliases *see* names — aliases

Alsace-Lorraine 389

AltaVista's BabelFish 172, 307 *also see* Internet, Internet translation programs

American Congregational Association Library (Boston) 250

American Digest System 105

ancestors' possessions 3, 64, 67, 101, 125, 137, 187, 226, 241, 245, 245 *also see* address books — old, baby books, diaries, family Bibles, letters — old, military medals, newspaper clippings, photographs — old, scrapbooks

Ancestral File 357

Ancestry.com 21, 91, 97, 207, 219, 242, 376 *also see* Internet

apprenticeships 305 *also see* occupations — ancestors

archives 4, 16, 184, 201, 305, 380

archives — church 153

archives — county 153-154

archives — newspapers 157 *also see* newspapers — old

archives — regional 240

Australia 13

Australia — military records 341

Australia — Sands Directory 13-14

Azores Islands (Portuguese) 363

B

baby books 245 *also see* ancestors' possessions

band offices (Native North American) 371

baptismal certificates 29, 197

baptismal record books 55-56, 262

baptismal records 194, 227-228, 258, 324, 329, 363-364 *also see* birth records, church records, informants

Barnardo Homes (UK) 76-77 *also see* orphans

birth and death indexes (online) 233 *also see* Internet

birth certificates 197, 243, 299

birth certificates — delayed 137, 272

birth certificates — revised 261-262

birth indexes 53

birth records 228, 251, 305 *also see* baptismal records, informants

books — local history/history 9, 15, 45, 46, 49, 54, 70, 81, 99, 122, 145, 147, 171, 182, 193, 198, 204, 206, 217, 229, 234, 256, 260, 267, 290, 305, 314, 342, 346, 356, 366, 370 *also see* historical research

books/publications — family history/genealogy/biography 22, 24, 35, 47, 108, 123, 127, 152, 160, 182, 186, 187, 231, 251, 275, 309, 317, 344, 357, 374, 377

Britain *see* UK

Brides Index (US) 167, 247

burial records 61, 121, 311 *also see* cemetery records, death records, informants

C

Canada — attestation papers (Army) 277

D

Daughters of the American Revolution 313, 314
Daughters of the American Revolution Library (Washington, DC) 201
death books 223
death certificates 15, 45, 63, 73, 78, 93, 130, 171, 176, 178, 181, 193, 195, 213, 216, 219, 226, 253, 270, 286, 294, 304, 310, 311, 312-313, 318, 334, 357, 367, 392
death indexes 53, 71, 115, 285, 311
death indexes — states 115, 164, 176, 254
death notices 6, 54, 157 *also see* obituaries
death record searches 20
death records 12, 22, 39, 109, 112, 117, 144, 186, 212 *also see* burial records, cemetery records, funeral home records, informants, interment records, mortuary records
death registers 380
death registrations 49, 193
deed books 25
deed records 377 *also see* informants
deeds 97
diaries 78, 256 *also see* ancestors' possessions
divorce cases 163
divorce papers 160
divorce records 251, 333 *also see* informants
divorces 7, 107, 160

E

e-mails 11, 27, 41, 123-124, 147, 172, 185, 203, 233, 242, 274, 290, 352 *also see* Internet
England *see* UK
estate records 356 *also see* informants
estate settlements 211
estates 54, 91 *also see* probate, wills
Everton's Genealogical Helper 127

F

family associations 374,
family Bibles 21, 26-27, 94, 183, 185, 200, 388 *also see* ancestors' possessions
family history societies *see* societies — historical, genealogy, family history
family reunions 235
FamilyHistory.com 7 *also see* Internet
FamilySearch.org 91, 95, 240, 386 *also see* Internet
Family History Centers (FHC) 206, 305
Family History Library (FHL) 92, 96, 170, 254, 268
FHC *see* Family History Centers
FHL *see* Family History Library
Finland 128-129, 291
foreign language brickwalls 29, 88, 89, 101, 118, 141, 159, 170, 189, 192, 203, 279, 298, 307, 312, 329, 385 *also see* Internet translation programs, names — changes, names — misspellings, names — multiple spellings, names — variations, transcribing/typesetting errors
France 389
FreeBMD.RootsWeb.com 8 *also see* Internet
French Five Hundred 274
funeral home records 139, 144, 195, 223, 252, 286, 302, 314, 343 *also see* death records, informants
funeral homes 48, 93, 122, 173
funeral memorials 374 *also see* obituaries
funeral records 318, 355 *also see* informants
funeral sign-in books 20

G

GenConnect.com 7, 80-81 *also see* Internet
Genealogical Research Directory 153, 322

H

I

123, 246, 249, 337, 346, 361, 359, 382

orphans 213 *also see* adoptions, Barnardo Homes (UK), court records — orphans, informants

P

parish records 152, 302, 305, 353 *also see* church records, informants

passenger ship lists 27, 375

passenger ship lists — indexes 28

passenger ship records 132

patent records 33

pedigree files 225

Pennsylvania Dutchmen 25

photographs — old 16, 26, 34, 92, 98, 165, 166, 173, 203, 207-208, 213, 245, 253, 255, 294, 300, 314, 328 *also see* ancestors' possessions

plat maps 304

Poland 140

poorhouses 10-11, 361

Portugal 363

postal mailings — mass 6, 11, 24, 27, 29, 31, 40, 53, 57, 62, 63, 64, 96, 97, 138, 158, 162, 170, 172, 180, 187, 207, 209, 229, 256, 324, 342, 350, 352, 372, 375, 378 *also see* letters

probate *also see* estates, wills

probate files 369

probate index books 344

probate records 130, 144, 343, 357, 374 *also see* informants

probate research 90

professional genealogical researcher 109, 116, 133, 190, 226, 240, 340, 348, 370, 372

property records 78 *also see* informants

Q

Quaker records 168

Quakers 386 *also see* Children of Peace

queries (online, journals, newspapers) 49, 66-67, 91-92, 101, 103, 114, 132, 135-136, 144, 172-173, 203, 281, 282,

318, 322, 331, 339, 341, 374, 385, 392 *also see* advertisements, Internet message boards, networking

R

Railroad Retirement Board 334, 388

railway records (workers) 388, 389 *also see* occupations — ancestor, informants

research techniques 18, 19, 23, 25, 42, 45, 56, 80, 83, 95, 102, 125, 158, 163, 165, 168, 225, 237, 279, 287, 295, 300, 302, 319, 321, 325, 341, 343, 359, 361, 364, 376, 377, 386

Roman Catholic (entry into Puritan New England) 147

Roots Cellar (*Genealogical Helper* magazine) 79

RootsWeb.com 7, 10, 80-81, 227-228, 242, 253, 262, 376 *also see* FreeBMD.RootsWeb.com, Internet

RootsWeb.com list archives 146

RootsWeb.com mailing lists 263

RootsWeb.com surname lists 171

RootsWeb.com's WorldConnect 5, 24

Russia 128-129

Russian Mennonites 201

S

Salvation Army's Missing Persons Department 196

Scotland 322 *also see* UK

Scotland — Index to Births 358

Scotland — Kirk Session Minutes 322

Scottish old parish records index 322

scrapbooks 227 *also see* ancestors' possessions

ships' manifests 152, 238

societies — historical, genealogy, family history 17, 30, 35, 54, 69, 75, 79, 94, 111, 145, 146, 154-155, 160, 173, 180, 184, 188, 189, 197, 200, 213, 217, 222, 223, 234, 257-258, 260, 274, 282, 294, 308, 321, 328, 331, 353, 356, 367

363 *also see* informants

US — NARA — old military records section 234

US — NARA — pension records 362 *also see* informants

US — National Cemetery System (Washington, DC) 195

US — National Military Archives 34

US — National Soldiers Home records 320

US — naturalization papers 118, 219, 243, 304

US — pension files 199

US — pension records 261 *also see* informants

US — register books 180

US — service records — final statement 177 *also see* informants

US — Social Security applications 63, 301, 340

US — Social Security cards 7, 210

US — Social Security numbers 388

US — Soundex/Miracode 149, 152-153, 247, 287, 364 *also see* censuses

US — SS-5 records 115

US — SS-5s 286

US — Social Security Death Index (SSDI) 7, 114-115, 216, 302, 392

US — State Adjutant's books 8

US — Veterans Administration 43, 177, 216, 326

US — Veterans Administration claim number 177

US case law 105

USGenWeb.com 126 *also see* Internet

V

village association 384

vital records 63

W

Wales *see* UK

websites 19, 28, 48, 91, 123, 129, 140, 171, 199, 228, 230, 242 *also see* Internet

WhoWhere.com 378 *also see* Internet

widows 95

wills 4, 33, 36-37, 78, 88, 94, 97, 119, 183, 235, 270, 320 *also see* estates, probate, witnesses

wills — acquaintances 305 *also see* witnesses

witnesses 358 *also see* informants, contract witnesses

Notes

Notes

Notes

Notes

Notes

Notes

Notes

Notes

Notes